The African Tulip
Chic. Unique. Authentically African.

Each Room Features
- Wireless Internet access
- Air Conditioners
- Satellite and local Tv
- Direct Dial telephone
- Mini Safe
- Hair Dryers
- Large Bathrooms
- Mini Bar

Other amenities
- Laundry Service
- Spacious Lounge
- Fully stocked bars
- Business centre
- Conference room
- Swimming pool
- Gift Shops

Contacts
44/1 Serengeti Road
P. O. Box 15171, Arusha, Tanzania   Tel: +255-27-2543004/2543005
Email: info@theafricantulip.com   *www.theafricantulip.com*

"We go thru' every measure
to give you Wild pleasure"

Roysafaris@intafrica.com   www.roysafaris.com

Kenya–Tanzania shuttle services

Shuttle buses run daily between Kenya and Tanzania; Nairobi (city centre)–Nairobi Jomo Kenyatta International Airport–Arusha (via the Namanga border post)–Kilimanjaro International Airport–Moshi. There is an early morning and early afternoon departure, and expect to pay about US$30 for Nairobi to Arusha, US$40 for Nairobi to Moshi, and US$20 from Kilimanjaro International Airport to Arusha or Moshi. The journey time from Nairobi to Arusha is 6½ hours and it's another 1½ hours to Moshi via the airport. The company websites have booking facilities, timetables, prices and where to meet the buses. At the border drivers will assist passengers with formalities. **AA Shuttles**, www.aashuttles.com. **Bobby Tours**, www.bobbytours.com. **Impala Shuttles**, www.impalashuttle.com. **Riverside Shuttles**, www.riverside-shuttle.com.

with Ngala, where there is a clutch of basic board and lodgings if you need to stay overnight, which you may need to do if you are coming from the Kigali direction and have to wait for the buses on the following morning. From **Uganda** there is crossing at Mutukulu, northwest of Bukoba, but this is a rough road and the only option is to hitch, though minibuses do run from the Ugandan side of the border to Masaka. Unless you are in the extreme northwest of Tanzania anyway, the easiest way to get from Tanzania to Uganda is via Nairobi (Kenya). Scandinavia Express has buses from Dar via Arusha to Nairobi and on to Kampala. There are buses to the border with **Zambia** at Nakonde, see page 404. You have to walk between the border posts (or use a bicycle-taxi) to Tunduma where there are buses to Mbeya. Visas are available at the Ugandan and Zambian borders.

Overland trucks

Overland truck safaris are a popular way of exploring Tanzania by road. They demand a little more fortitude and adventurous spirit from the traveller, but the compensation is usually the camaraderie and life-long friendships that result from what is invariably a real adventure, going to places the more luxurious travellers will never visit. The standard overland route most commercial trucks take through East Africa (in either direction) is from Nairobi a two-week circuit into Uganda to see the mountain gorillas via some of the Kenya national parks, then crossing into Tanzania to Arusha for the Ngorongoro Crater and Serengeti, before heading south to Dar es Salaam, for Zanzibar. If you have more time, you can complete the full circuit that goes from Tanzania through Malawi and Zambia to Livingstone to see the Victoria Falls, and then another three weeks from there to Cape Town in South Africa via Botswana and Namibia. There are several overland companies with departures almost weekly from Nairobi, Dar es Salaam, Livingstone and Cape Town.

UK
Dragoman, T01728-861133, www.dragoman.co.uk.
Exodus Travels, T020-8675 5550, www.exodus.co.uk.
Explore, T0845-0131537, www.explore.co.uk.
Kumuka Expeditions,T0778-620 1144, www.kumuka.com.

Oasis Overland, T01963-363400, www.oasisoverland.co.uk.

South Africa
Africa Travel Co, T021-385 1530, www.africatravelco.com.
Wildlife Adventures, T021-385 1530, www.wildlifeadventures.co.za.

Sea

A US$5 port tax is applied to all ferry tickets departing from Tanzanian ports. From Burundi there is, in theory, a lake ferry to Kigoma from Bujumbura every Monday. However, at the time of writing this was currently suspended, though the service may resume at any time. From Mpulungu (Zambia) there is a weekly ferry on Friday that arrives in Kigoma on Sunday (see page 373 for further details). From Nkhata Bay (Malawi) there is a ferry to Mbamba Bay on Tuesday, though this is a very erratic service and should not be counted on.

Getting around

Air → *See also Transport in Dar es Salaam, page 94.*

Air Tanzania has a limited schedule of domestic flights between Dar, Zanzibar, Mwanza and Kilimanjaro. But the state-owned carrier has suffered from severe financial and operating difficulties recently, meaning that flights are cancelled and the schedules change all the time. The private airlines offer a much more extensive air coverage of the country and there are 62 airports and airstrips managed by the Tanzania Airports Authority (TAA). **Precision Air** has flights from Arusha, Kilimanjaro, Dar es Salaam, Tabora, Kigoma, Mwanza, Bukoba, Lindi, Mtwara, Grumeti and Seronera in the Serengeti National Park and Zanzibar and also connects with Nairobi. Sample one way fares are Dar-Zanzibar, from US$70; Pemba–Dar, from US$120: and Mwanza–Dar, from US$480. The smaller companies, **Air Excel, Regional Air, Zan Air** and **Coastal Air** run flights between Dar es Salaam, Zanzibar, Arusha and to the various smaller regional airports and national park airstrips such as Grumeti, Mafia, Lake Manyara, Pemba, Ruaha, Rubondo, Selous, Seronera, and Tanga. **Regional Air**, code shares with **Air Kenya**, so also has flights between Dar, Kilimanjaro and Zanzibar and Nairobi. **Air Excel**, code shares with **Safarilink**, in Kenya so also has a service between Kilimanjaro and Nairobi. These airlines use small six- or 12-seater planes and have frequent scheduled flights but will only fly with the required minimum of passengers, though sometimes this is only two people. Note that on the smaller aircraft, the baggage allowance is 15 kg so you may have to leave luggage at hotels in Dar or Arusha, which most will allow you to for a small fee. Specific schedules are detailed under each relevant chapter.

Airlines

Air Excel, Arusha, T027-254 8429, www.airexcelonline.com.
Air Tanzania, ATC Bldg, Ohio St, Dar, T022-211 7500, www.airtanzania.com.
Precision Air, Dar, T022-213 0800, www.precisionairtz.com.
Coastal Air, Dar, T022-211 7959, ww.coastal.cc.
Regional Air, Arusha, T027-250 4164, www.regionaltanzania.com.
Zan Air, Zanzibar, T024-223 3670, www.zanair.com.

Air charter

Several companies offer small planes for charter, especially between the parks and islands, and have flights most days of the week. These can work out to be economical for groups of 4-6 people, and some companies offer scenic flights.

Dar es Salaam: **Flightlink**, T022-284 2280, www.flightlinkaircharters.com, and **Zantas Air**, T022-213 7181, www.zantasair.com; Mwanza: **Renair**, T028-256 0403, www.renair.com; Kilimanjaro: **Kilimanjaro Air Safaris**, T027-275 0523, www.kiliair.com.

Rail *See also Transport in Dar es Salaam, page 97.*

There are two railway companies operating in Tanzania. **TAZARA** ① *T022-226 2191, www.tazara.co.tz*, is the name of the Tanzania-Zambia Railway Authority and the trains run from Dar es Salaam, southwest to Zambia (see Getting there, above). The other service is the **Tanzania Railway Corporation** ① *T022-211 7833, www.trctz.com*, which operates services between Dar es Salam and Kigoma with a branch line to Mwanza. The Northern line service to Tanga and Moshi has been discontinued. There are three classes of travel; first class compartment sleeping two, second class compartment sleeping six, and third class sitting. The latter gets very uncomfortable and crowded and you'll be sitting among piles of boxes and live chickens. All cabins on Tanzanian trains are sexually segregated unless you book the whole cabin. While the trains themselves are a little grubby, and more than a little infested by cockroaches, the bedding is very clean. It is essential to guard your possessions fiercely and keep cabin doors locked at all times. In fact you'll be given a piece of wood to wedge into the window to prevent anyone from opening it from the outside at night when the trains pull into stations. The trains have dining cars, which turn into rowdy bars late at night, and each first and second class carriage has a steward who can deliver a plate of adequate chicken and rice or *ugali* and beef or similar, which you can eat in your compartment. The better option really, so you don't have to leave your luggage. In the morning the steward comes round with tea and coffee and the trains stop for a while at a trackside village for breakfast, when the enterprising villagers set up a row of stalls of street food next to the train.

Road

Bus → *See also Transport in Dar es Salaam, page 96.*
There is now an efficient network of privately run buses across the country. On good sealed roads, buses cover 50-80 km per hour. On unsealed or poorly maintained roads they will average only 20 km per hour. Larger buses give a considerably more comfortable ride than minibuses and have more space for luggage, and are to be recommended on safety grounds as well. If you are taking a shorter journey (Dar–Morogoro or Mwanza–Musoma, say), the bus will leave when full. You can join an almost full bus and leave promptly on an uncomfortable journey, either standing or on a makeshift gangway seat. Or you can secure a comfortable seat and wait until the bus fills, which can take one or two hours on a less busy route. If you are making a long journey you can book a seat at kiosks run by the bus companies at the bus stations. On the larger and more travelled routes (Dar–Arusha, Dar–Mbeya, Dar–Mombasa in Kenya) there is now a choice of 'luxury', 'semi-luxury' and 'ordinary', and fares vary by a few dollars. The difference between them is that the 'luxury' and 'semi-luxury' buses often have air conditioning and only take the number of people the buses are designed to seat. On the 'ordinary' services, the buses are usually older, carry additional standing passengers and stop more frequently en route, making the journey considerably slower. Fares on all buses are very reasonable, for example on a 'luxury' bus the fare from Arusha to Dar es Salaam (a journey of 650 km or eight hours) is around US\$18, on a semi-luxury bus it's US\$11, and on an ordinary bus US\$9. On the main routes it is possible to book ahead at a kiosk at the bus stand and this is wise rather than turning up at the departure time on the off-chance. Consistently recommended is **Scandinavia Express**, which has its own terminal in Dar es Salaam, T022-218 4833, www.scandinaviagroup.com. They are very popular so book ahead when

Essentials Getting around ● 33

possible, the offices throughout the country issue computerized tickets, and you can choose your seat on screen. Buses are speed limited, luggage is securely locked up either under the bus or in overhead compartments, and complimentary video, drinks, sweets and biscuits are offered. On long journeys on the main highways, the buses stop at roadside restaurants for lunch.

Car

Driving is on the left side of the road. The key roads are in good condition, and there has been considerable road-building going on in Tanzania in recent years thanks to foreign aid. The best roads are the tarmac ones from Dar es Salaam to Zambia and Malawi, Dar es Salaam to Arusha and the new tarred road from Arusha to the Ngorongoro Crater. The road from Arusha to the Kenyan border at Namanga is presently being re-tarred. Away from the main highways, however, the majority of roads are bad and hazardous. Most of the minor roads are unmade gravel with potholes: there are many rough stretches and they deteriorate further in the rainy season. Road conditions in the reserves and national parks of Tanzania are extremely rough. During the rainy season, many roads are passable only with high clearance 4WD vehicles. Fuel is available along the main highways and towns, but if you're going way off the beaten track, consider taking a couple of jerry cans of extra fuel. Also ensure the vehicle has a jack and possibly take a shovel to dig it out of mud or sand. If you break down, it is common practice in Tanzania to place a bundle of leaves 50 m or so before and behind the vehicle to warn oncoming motorists.

Car hire Most people visit the national parks on an organized safari, but if you're confident driving in Tanzania, there is also the option to hire a car. Car hire is not as well organized in Tanzania as it is in Kenya. There are fewer companies (although this is changing) and they are more expensive. Also, many of the vehicles are poorly maintained and you may find it difficult to hire a car without a driver. In saying that however, by contrast to the rest of the country, hiring a Suzuki jeep on Zanzibar is a popular way to explore the island. To hire a car you generally need to be over 23, have an international driving licence, or pay a small fee to have your own country licence endorsed in Tanzania, and to leave a large deposit or sign a blank credit card voucher. Always take out the collision damage waiver premium as even the smallest accident can be very expensive, although you'll still be liable of an excess of around US$500-1000. Also consider taking out a theft protection waiver. Costs vary between the different car hire companies and are from around US$60-80 per day for a normal saloon car or a jeep on Zanzibar, rising to US$120-180 for a 4WD. Deals can be made for more than

seven days' car hire. Finally, Tanzania's rather hefty 20% VAT is added to all costs. It is essential to shop around and ask questions of the companies about what is and what is not included in the rates. On safari you will have to pay the park entrance fees for the car and the driver, if you have one, and although it will work out expensive this method does allow for greater flexibility than an organized safari. Most of the tour and travel agents listed in the book will be able to arrange vehicle hire.

Dala-dala

Called *dala-dala*, it is said, because they charged a dollar, although this seems a high sum, these are local private buses and passenger vehicles using Toyota (or other) minibuses. On Zanzibar they are also made from small trucks. They are by the far largest method of urban and rural transport and are cheap, US$0.30 for a short journey, rising to US$0.50 for a longer one. However they get very crowded and there is often a squeeze to get on. But fellow travellers will be very helpful in directing you to the correct *dala-dala* if you ask (most have a sign indicating their route and destination on the front), will advise on connections, fight on your behalf to try to get you a seat and tell you when to get off at your destination. Many *dala-dala*, have inspirational messages on the front and back windows like 'God is Great', 'Viva Manchester United', or (rather ominously) 'Still Alive'.

Hitchhiking

In the Western sense (standing beside the road and requesting a free ride) this is not an option. However, truck drivers and many private motorists will often carry you if you pay, and if you are stuck where there is no public transport you should not hesitate to approach likely vehicles like pickups on this basis.

Taxis

Hotels and town centre locations are well served by taxis, some good and some very run-down but serviceable. It is wise to sit in the back if there are no front seat belts. Hotel staff, even at the smallest locations, will rustle up a taxi even when there is not one waiting outside. If you visit an out-of-town centre location, it is wise to ask the taxi to wait – it will normally be happy to do so for benefit of the return fare. A short trip in the centre of Dar es Salaam should cost about US$3-4, while a longer trip to the outskirts of the city such as the university (13 km) would be about US$8-10. There is a bargaining element: none of the cabs have meters, and you should establish the fare (*bei gani?* – how much?) before you set off. Prices are generally fair as drivers simply won't take you if you offer a fare that's too low. A common practice is a driver will set off and *then* go and get petrol using part of your fare to pay for it, so often the first part of a journey is spent sitting in a petrol station. Also be aware that seemingly taxi drivers *never* have change, so try and accumulate some small notes for taxi rides.

Tuk-tuks

These motorized three-wheel buggies are starting to feature in many of African cities and are cheap and convenient. The driver sits in the front whilst two or three passengers can sit comfortably on the back seat. They offer a service that is at least half the price of regular taxis. They do not, however, go very fast so for longer journeys stick to taxis. In Tanzania they are known as *Bajajis*, after the Bajaj Auto Company that manufactures many of them.

Sea and lake

Ferries

Between Dar es Salaam and Zanzibar there are several sailings each day on modern hydrofoils and an older ferry (see page 96 for details). These are reliable and pleasant and on the newer ones movies are shown and refreshments are available. On **Lake Victoria**, the main sailings are between Mwanza and Bukoba (see pages 334 and 343), though small islands and some other lakeside towns are served. On **Lake Tanganyika** boats go from Kigoma to various small ports south (see page 373). Fares for non-residents greatly exceed those for residents, though they are not overly expensive. On **Lake Nyasa** (also known as Lake Malawi) there is a boat going from the northern port of Itungi to Mbamba Bay, the last Tanzanian port on the east shore (see page 399).

Maps

The best map and travel guide shop in the UK is **Stanfords**, 12-14 Long Acre, Covent Garden, London WC2 9LP, T020-7836 1321, www.stanfords.co.uk, with branches in Manchester and Bristol. The **Michelin Map of Africa**; Central and South, www.michelin-travel.com, covers Tanzania in detail. The **Map Studio**, T0860-105050, www.mapstudio.co.za, produces a wide range of maps covering much of Africa. In Tanzania you can pick up locally produced maps of the most popular parks like the Serengeti in book and gift shops and some of the lodges stock them.

Sleeping

There is a wide range of accommodation on offer from top-of-the-range lodges and tented camps that charge US$300-1000 per couple per day, to mid-range safari lodges and beach resorts with double rooms with air conditioning and bathroom for around US$150-250, standard and faded small town hotels used by local business people for around US$50-100 per room, and basic board and lodgings used by local travellers at under US$10 a day. At the top end of the market, Tanzania now boasts some accommodation options that would rival the luxurious camps in southern Africa – intimate safari camps with unrivalled degrees of comfort and service in stunning settings. The beach resorts too have improved considerably in recent years, and there are some highly luxurious and romantic beach lodges and hotels that again are in commanding positions

Generally, accommodation booked through a European agent will be more expensive than if you contact the hotel or lodge directly. Tanzania's hoteliers are embracing the age of the internet, and an ever-increasing number can take a reservation by email or through their websites. Low season in East Africa is generally around the long rainy season from the beginning of April to the end of June, when most room rates drop considerably. Some establishments even close during this period, though the resorts on Zanzibar remain open throughout the year.

For the more expensive hotels, the airlines, and game park entrance and camping fees, a system operates whereby tourists are charged approximately double the local rate and this must be paid in foreign currency and not TSh. In the cheaper hotels you should get away with paying in TSh but always ask before checking in.

Sleeping price codes

L over US$450	**A** US$300-450	**B** US$175-299
C US$100-174	**D** US$50-99	**E** US$20-49
F under US$20		

Unless otherwise stated, prices refer to the cost of a double room including tax, not including service charge or meals.

Hotels

Most town and city hotels tend to be bland with poor service, but increasingly, much nicer options are opening outside the major towns. For instance, many guesthouses have opened up on coffee farms around Arusha. In some areas, Stone Town on Zanzibar being the prime example, there is the opportunity to sleep in some historical and atmospheric hotels. Here, even the cheaper establishments are beautiful old houses decorated with fine antiques and Persian carpets, with traditional Zanzibar four-poster beds swathed in mosquito nets.

At the budget end there's a fairly wide choice of cheap accommodation. A room often comprises a simple bed, shared toilet and washing facilities, and may have an irregular water supply; it is always a good idea to look at a room before deciding, to ensure it's clean and everything works. Check that mosquito nets are provided. It is also imperative to ensure that your luggage will be locked away securely for protection against petty theft. At the very bottom of the budget scale are numerous basic lodgings in all the towns that cost under US$10. For this you get a bare room with a bed and a door that may or may not lock. Unless these are exceptionally secure or good value, they are generally not recommended and are often simply rooms attached to a bar that, more often than not, are rented by the hour.

Note that the word 'hotel' (or in Swahili, *hoteli*) means food and drink only, rather than lodging. It would be better to use the word 'guesthouse' (*guesti*).

Camping

Away from the campsites in the national parks and game reserves, camping in Tanzania is fairly limited to the road that runs from Kenya all the way to Malawi in the south. This is part of the great African overland route and each year thousands of independent overlanders travel in either direction. Campsites have sprung up along this route to accommodate the vehicles and campers and some are very good; indeed better than what is on offer in the national parks. The better ones have bars and restaurants, simple sleeping huts for those that don't want to camp, guards for tents and vehicles, and clean ablution blocks with plenty of hot water. In Dar es Salaam there are a few campsites that, for a small fee, will allow you to park your vehicle safely for a few days whilst you go to Zanzibar. If you are travelling overland in your own vehicle, we strongly advise you not to bush or free camp at the side of the road. We have heard too many stories of people being robbed in the middle of the night. Note camping on Zanzibar is illegal and sleeping on the beach is not permitted.

National park accommodation

All safari companies offer basically the same safari but at different prices, depending on what accommodation you want. For example, you can choose a three-day safari of the Ngorongoro Crater and Serengeti and the options would be camping (the companies provide the equipment) or a lodge safari, making it considerably more expensive. For those who want to spend more, there is the option of adding flights between destinations or staying at one of the luxury private tented camps. Either way, you are likely to have the same sort of game viewing experiences.

Park lodges vary and may be either typical hotels with rooms and facilities in one building, or individual *bandas* or *rondavels* (small huts) with a central dining area. Some of the larger lodges in the parks of the northern circuit are enormous impersonal affairs with little atmosphere that were built some decades ago, though comfort and service is good.

There are campsites in most national parks. They are extensively used by camping safari companies. Vehicles, guides, tents and equipment, as well as food and a cook, are all provided. Facilities are very basic though, and the Serengeti campsites, for example, have nothing more than a long drop loo, but sleeping here at night is really exciting: the campsites are unfenced and are frequent haunts of hyena and lion. Many of the camps advertise hot running water for showers. This is accurate when the sun is out, otherwise the water may be cold. Be careful about leaving items outside your tent. Many campsites have troupes of baboons nearby that can be a nuisance and a hyena can chew through something as solid as a saucepan. If you are camping on your own, you will almost always need to be totally self-sufficient, with all your own equipment. The campsites usually provide running water and firewood. Camping should always have minimal impact on the environment. All rubbish and waste matter should be buried, burnt, or taken away.

A luxury tented camp is really the best of both worlds; the comfort of extremely high facilities and service combined with sleeping closer to the animals. They are usually built with a central dining and bar area, are in stunning well designed locations, and each tent will have a thatched roof to keep it cool inside, proper beds and a veranda. They will often have a small bathroom at the back with solar-heated hot water. The added benefit is that they are usually fairly small with just a few tents, so the safari experience is intimate and professional.

Eating and drinking

Food

Cuisine on mainland Tanzania is not one of the country's main attractions. There is a legacy of uninspired British catering (soups, steaks, grilled chicken, chips, boiled vegetables, puddings, instant coffee). Tanzanians are largely big meat eaters and a standard meal is *nyama choma*, roasted beef or goat meat, usually served with a spicy relish, although some like it with a mixture of raw peppers, onions and tomato known as *kachumbari*. The main staple or starch in Tanzania is *ugali*, a mealie porridge eaten all over Africa. Small town hotels and restaurants tend to serve a limited amount of bland processed food, omelette or chicken and chips, and perhaps a meat stew but not much else. Asian eating places can be better, but are seldom of a high standard. There is a much greater variety in the cities and the tourist spots; both Dar es Salaam and Zanzibar in particular (with its exquisite coastal seafood) do a fine line in eateries. The Swahili style of cooking features aromatic curries using coconut milk, fragrant steamed rice, grilled fish and calamari,

Eating price codes

| ꛴꛴꛴ over US$30 | ꛴꛴ US$15-30 | ꛴ under US$15 |

Prices refer to the cost of a main course with either a soft drink, a glass of wine or a beer.

and delicious bisques made from lobster and crab. A speciality is *halau*, a sweet dessert made from almonds. Some of the larger beach resorts and safari lodges offer breakfast, lunch and dinner buffets for their all-inclusive guests, some of which can be excellent while others can be of a poor standard and there's no real way of knowing what you'll get. The most important thing is to avoid food sitting around for a long time on a buffet table, so ensure it's freshly prepared and served. Vegetarians are catered for, and fruit and vegetables are used frequently, though there is a limited choice of dishes specifically made for vegetarians on menus and you may have to make special requests. The service in Tanzanian restaurants can be somewhat slower than you are used to and it can take hours for something to materialize from a kitchen. Rather than complain just enjoy the laid-back pace and order another beer.

Various dishes can be bought at temporary roadside shelters from street vendors who prepare and cook over charcoal. It's pretty safe, despite hygiene being fairly basic, because most of the items are cooked or peeled. **Savouries** include: barbecued beef on skewers (*mishkaki*), roast maize (corn), samosas, kebabs, hard-boiled eggs and roast cassava (looks like white, peeled turnips) with red chilli-pepper garnish. **Fruits** include: oranges (peeled and halved), grapes, pineapples, bananas, mangoes (slices scored and turned inside-out), paw-paw (*papaya*) and watermelon.

Most food is bought in open air markets. In the larger towns and cities these are held daily, and as well as fresh fruit and vegetables sell eggs, bread and meat. In the smaller villages, markets are usually held on one day of the week. Markets are very colourful places to visit and as Tanzania is very fertile, just about any fruit or vegetable is available.

Drink

Local beers (lager) are decent and cheap, around US$1.40 for a 700 ml refundable bottle. Brands include Kilimanjaro and Safari lager, tasty Tusker imported from Kenya or Castle from South Africa. Imported **wines** are on the expensive side: US$10-12 in a supermarket and US$15-30 in a restaurant for a European or South African label. Tanzanian wines produced by the White Fathers at Dodoma, **Bowani Wine**, are reasonable. Wines made by the **National Milling Corporation** are undrinkable.

Spirits tend to be extremely expensive and imported brands can be found in the supermarkets and in bars. Local alternatives that are sold in both bottles and sachets of one tot include some rough vodkas and whiskies and the much more pleasant *Konyagi*, a type of scented gin, which is also produced as an alchopop, *Konyagi Ice*, with bitter lemon. Traditional Tanzanian drinks include **chang'aa**, a fierce spirit made from maize and sugar and then distilled. It is extremely powerful and has been known to kill so think twice before tasting any. Far more pleasant and more common is **pombe** (beer), brewed from sugar and millet or banana depending on the region. It tastes a bit like flat cider and is far more potent than it appears at first. **Palm wine** is drunk at the coast. **Soft drinks** are mainly limited to colas, orange, lemon, pineapple, ginger beer, tonic and club soda.

Like beer, you have to give the bottle back when you've finished. Fresh juices are common and quite delicious. **Bottled water** is widely available and safe. **Coffee**, when fresh ground, is the local Arabica variety with a distinctive, acidic flavour. In the evenings, particularly, but all day at markets, bus and railway stations there are traditional Swahili coffee vendors with large portable conical brass coffee pots with charcoal braziers underneath. The coffee is sold black in small porcelain cups, and is excellent. They also sell peanut crisp bars and sugary cakes made from molasses. These items are very cheap and are all worth trying. On the coast chai (**tea**) is drunk in small glasses; black with lots of sugar.

Festivals and events

If any holiday falls on a Saturday or Sunday, it is moved to the following Monday. **Good Friday**, **Easter Monday**, **Id-ul-Fitr** (end of Ramadan), **Id-ul-Haji** (Festival of Sacrifice), **Islamic New Year** and **Prophet Mohammad's Birthday** are holidays that vary from year to year. Muslim festivals are timed according to local sightings of the various stages of the moon. Christian holidays will not be observed by all Muslims and vice versa. **Note** During Ramadan and other Muslim holidays, it's considered very offensive to eat and drink in public.

There are a number of annual festivals held on Zanzibar each year including the Zanzibar Cultural Festival, the Zanzibar International Film Festival of the Dhow Countries, and the Sauti za Busara Swahili Music and Cultural Festival. For information on these see page 186, or visit www.ziff.or.tz.

January
1 Jan New Year's Day
1 Jan Nyerere Day
12 Jan Zanzibar Revolution Day (Zanzibar)

April
26 Apr Union Day

May
1 May Mayday Workers' Day

July
7 Jul Industrial Day

October
Oct Bagamoyo Arts Festival, www.sanaa bagamoyo.com. On the mainland, the Bagamoyo College of Arts (see page 107) organizes the annual 5-day festival, which features traditional performances of music and dance, acrobatics, exhibitions of art and sculpture, local hip hop and reggae bands and much more.
14 Oct Farmers' Day

December
Dec East African Safari Classic, T020-445 0030, www.eastafricansafarirally.com. Has been going since 1953 and was the first car rally run to celebrate the queen's coronation. It runs for 3 days over a course of about 3000 km of rough roads. **Note** This rally is normally held in Kenya but for the first time since 1972, the 2009 event will be run in Tanzania.
9 Dec Independence Day
25 Dec Christmas Day
26 Dec Boxing Day

Shopping

Tanzania has several interesting craft items for sale, including Makonde and ebony wood carvings, soapstone carvings, musical instruments, basketware and textiles. Masai crafts such as beaded jewellery, decorated gourds and spears are available to buy in northern Tanzania as well as the red checked Masai blankets. *Mkeka* are plain, straw-coloured mats woven from sisal by craftsmen in Karatu, near the Ngorongoro Crater. The women of Mafia Island make more colourful *mkeka* from dried and twisted palm fronds. In Zanzibar, you can find old tiles, antique bowls and the famous carved wooden Zanzibar chests. Brightly coloured sarongs called *kangas* are worn by women all over Tanzania. They're sold in pairs and emblazoned with a traditional proverb. Woven with vertical stripes, *kikois* are similar but are traditionally worn by the men. There are many other items made from these fabrics including trousers, tops and skirts, cushion covers and bags. You can pick up bags of Zanzibar spices direct from the market. Tanzania is the world's only source of tanzanite, a semi-precious stone found in the open mines around Arusha. The deep blue of Tanzanite is magnificent, ranging from ultramarine to a light purplish blue. Fakes abound, so if you're going to invest in one of Tanzania's largest exports, be sure to do it right. Don't buy from dealers on the street, most licensed curios shops and jewellers stock different grades, cuts, and colours. Also look out for Tingatinga paintings, which have a unique Tanzanian style (see box, page 78).

Prices in tourist shops are largely fixed, though in the depths of the quiet low season, can be negotiable. Prices at roadside stalls or markets are always negotiable. See page 46 for tips on bargaining.

Parks and safaris

National parks and reserves

Going on safari can be a most rewarding experience. However, it is something to be prepared for, as it will almost certainly involve a degree of discomfort and long journeys. Some of the roads in Tanzania can be very exhausting. The unsealed roads are bumpy and dusty, and it will be hot. It is also important to remember that despite the expert knowledge of the drivers, they cannot guarantee that you will see any animals. When they do spot one of the rarer animals, however, watching their pleasure is almost as enjoyable as seeing the animal itself. To get the best from your safari, approach it with humour, look after the driver as well as you are able (a disgruntled driver will quickly ruin your safari), and do your best to get on with, and be considerate to, your fellow travellers. Safaris to Serengeti National Park, Ngorongoro Conservation Area, Lake Manyara, Tarangire and Arusha National Parks are best arranged from Arusha (see page 278). For trips to Mikumi and Ruaha National Parks and Selous Game Reserve, arrangements are best made in Dar es Salaam (see page 93).

It is essential to tour the parks by vehicle and walking is prohibited in most of the parks. You will either have to join an organized tour by a safari company, or hire or have your own vehicle. Being with a guide is the best option as without one, you will miss a lot of game. There are a huge number of companies offering safaris which are listed in the relevant chapters. Safaris can be booked either at home or once in Tanzania. If you go for

Park fees

Park permit entry fees
(In any period of 24 hours, or part thereof. Children under 5, free entry)

Kilimanjaro

Adult	US$60
Child 5-16 years	US$5

Serengeti and Ngorongoro Conservation area

Adult	US$50
Child 5-16 years	US$10

Arusha, Tarangire and Lake Manyara

Adult	US$35
Child 5-16	US$10

Katavi, Mikumi, Ruaha, Rubondo and Udzungwa National Parks

Adult	US$20
Child 5-16 years	US$5

Gombe Stream

Adult	US$100
Child 5-16 years	US$20
Child under 5	Free

Mahale

Adult	US$80
Child 5-16	US$30

Vehicle entry to parks

Up to 2,000 kg	US$40 (foreign)
	TSh 10,000 (Tanzanian)
2,000-3000 kg	US$150 (foreign)
	TSh 25,000 (Tanzanian)

Note Only Tanzanian registered vehicles are allowed down into the crater itself, for which the additional Crater Service Fee is US$200 per vehicle.

Camping permit
(In any period of 24 hours, or part thereof. Fees as of May 2009)
Established campsites

Adult	US$30
Child 5-16	US$5

Special campsites

Adult	US$50
Child 5-16	US$10

Guide fees

Service of official guide	US$10
(outside his working hours)	US$15
Walking safaris guides	US$20

Special sport fishing fees
Applicable only to Gombe, Mahale and Rubondo Island National Parks (sport fishing allowed between 0700 and 1700 only)

Adult	US$50
Child 5-16	US$25
Child under 5 years	Free

Hut, hostel and rest house fees
(rates per head per night)

Kilimanjaro National Park: Mandara, Horombo and Kibo	US$50
Meru – Miriakamba and Saddle	US$20
Other huts – Manyara, Ruaha, Mikumi etc	US$20
Hostels – Marangu, Manyara, Serengeti, Mikumi, Ruaha and Gombe Stream (strictly for organized groups with permission of park wardens in charge)	US$10
Rest houses – Serengeti, Ruaha, Mikumi, Arusha, Katavi	US$30
Rest house – Gombe Stream	US$20

Rescue fees
Mounts Kilimanjaro and Meru: the park will be responsible for rescue between the point of incident to the gate on any route. The climber will take care of other expenses from gate to KCMC or other destination as he/she chooses.

The rates are payable per person for trip   US$20

Parks, reserves and heritage sites

National parks National parks are wildlife and botanical sanctuaries and form the mainstay of Tanzania's tourist industry. They are conservation points for educational and recreational enjoyment and are managed by Tanzania National Parks.

Game reserves Game reserves are similar to national parks but under certain conditions the land may be used for purposes other than nature conservation. Some controlled agriculture or grazing may be permitted. In marine reserves there may be monitored fishing permitted. Game reserves are often found adjoining national parks and have usually been created as a result of local pressure to return some of the seasonal grazing lands to pastoralists.

Biosphere reserves These are protected environments that contain unique landforms, landscapes and systems of land use. There are three in Tanzania: Serengeti-Ngorongoro, Lake Manyara and Usambara Mountains.

World Heritage Sites World Heritage Sites are even more strictly protected. Tanzania signed the convention with UNESCO (United Nations Educational, Scientific and Cultural Organization) in 1962; eight sites have been inscribed.

the latter it may be possible to obtain substantial discounts, but ensure that the company is properly licensed and is a member of the **Tanzania Association of Tour Operators (TATO)**, www.tatotz.org, which represents over 240 of Tanzania's tour operators and is a good place to start when looking for a safari. If you elect to book in Tanzania, avoid companies offering cheap deals on the street – they will almost always turn out to be a disaster and may appear cheap because they do not include national park entrance fees. At the tourist office in Arusha there is a blacklist of unlicensed operators and people with convictions for cheating tourists. Safaris do not run on every day of the week, and in the low season you may also find that they will be combined, meaning if you are on a six-day safari you could expect to be joined by another party say on a four-day safari.

Safaris vary in cost and duration, but on the whole you get what you pay for. The costs will also vary enormously depending on where you stay and how many of you there are in a group. For an all-inclusive safari staying in the large safari lodges that offer twice daily game drives and buffet meals, expect to pay around US$150-250 per person per day, more if you opt for air transfers. At the very top end of the scale, staying in the most **exclusive tented camps and lodges** and flying between destinations, expect to pay in excess of US$500 per person per day. At the lower end of the market, a **camping safari** using the basic national park campsites is about US$140-180 per person per day, which given that the park fees alone in some of the parks is US$50 per day, this is not unreasonable. These rates include park entrance fees, cost of vehicle and driver, and food. You'll need to take your own sleeping bag, and possibly a roll mat. Few companies provide drinking water and it is important to buy enough bottles to last your trip before you set off. It is surprising how much you get through and restocking is not easy. See page 38 for safari accommodation options and page 279 for 'How to organize a safari'.

Tipping

How much to tip the driver and guide on safari is tricky. It is best to enquire from the company at the time of booking what the going rate is. As a rough guide you should allow about 10% of your safari cost. Always try to come to an agreement with other members of the group and put the tip into a common kitty. Remember that wages are low and there can be long lay-offs during the low season. Despite this there is also the problem of excessive tipping, which can cause problems for future clients being asked to give more than they should.

Transport
It is worth emphasizing that most parks are some way from departure points, and obviously the longer you spend actually in the parks, rather than just driving to and from them, the better. If you go on a three-day safari by road, you will often find that at least one day is taken up with travelling to and from the park, often on bad bumpy and dusty roads – leaving you with a limited amount of time in the park itself. The easiest option, which is of course the most expensive, is to fly, and most parks and reserves have a good network of airstrips and there are daily flights. This gives you the optimum time game viewing in the parks themselves. On most safaris, vehicles will almost certainly be a Landrover, Land-cruiser or minibus accommodating six to eight people. They will have a viewing point through the roof (the really upmarket ones will also have a sun shade). In practice this means that only three to four people can view out through the roof at any one time – passengers usually take turns to stick their heads and cameras out of the top

What to take
There is very little room in the vehicles and you will be asked to limit the amount you bring with you. You'll have to leave excess luggage at a hotel or with the tour operator. There is very little point in taking too much clothing – expect to get dirty, particularly during the dry season when dust can be a problem. Try to have a clean set of clothes to change into at night when it can also get quite cold. Loose clothing and sensible footwear is best. The other important items are binoculars, a camera with a telephoto

National parks
Tanzania's 13 national parks and 1 conservation area together hold a population of over 4,000,000 wild animals.

Name	Area (sq km)
Arusha	137
Gombe Stream	52
Katavi	2253
Kilimanjaro	756
Lake Manyara	320
Mahale Mountains	1613
Mikumi	3230
Ngorongoro Crater	2288
Ruaha	12,950
Rubondo	457
Saadani	300
Serengeti	14,763
Tarangire	2600
Udzungwa Mountains	1000

Game reserves
In addition, there are 14 game reserves few of which have any tourist facilities.

Name	Area (sq km)
Biharamulo	1300
Burigi	2200
Ibanda	200
Kizigo	4000
Lukwika-Lumesule	600
Maswa	2200
Mkomazi	1000
Moyowosi	6000
Rumanyika-Orugundu	800
Rungwa	9000
Selous	55,000
Ugalla	5000
Umba River	1500
Uwanda	5000

See National Parks & Game Reserves in the colour map section.

Tanzania's UNESCO World Heritage Sites

Kilimanjaro National Park (page 244)
Kilimanjaro National Park encompasses 756 sq km and was declared a national park in 1993 and UNESCO site in 1987. At 5985 m, Mount Kilimanjaro is the highest point in Africa and one of the tallest free-standing dormant volcanoes in the world.

Stone Town, Zanzibar (page 171)
Awarded World Heritage status in 2000, Stone Town was inscribed for its rich cultural heritage of trading activity between Africa and Asia, illustrated today by the fine architecture and structure of the town that is still functioning today after more than a millennium. Its other criteria for inscription is the importance it played in the suppression of the slave trade. Once a slave port it was also the base for anti-slavery opponents such as David Livingstone.

Ngorongoro Conservation Area (page 303)
Located 180 km west of Arusha and covering an area of 8288 sq km, this is dominated by the spectacular collapsed caldera of the Ngorongoro Crater. The rich pasture and permanent water on the crater floor provides subsidence to large populations of animals. It was inscribed in 1979 for not only its ecological value, but for its geological value, and includes the Olduvai Gorge site where the remains of many early hominoids and early pre-historic creatures have been unearthed.

Selous Game Reserve (page 378)
The vast 54,600 sq km Selous became a World Heritage Site in 1982, for its undisturbed wilderness and diversity of wildlife, which has seen hardly any impact by humankind. It is believed that before the migration of early man and, much later, before the urbanization by relatively modern man, this is largely what the whole of East Africa looked like. It also gained protection for its exceptionally large populations of big game including herds of elephants hundreds strong.

Serengeti National Park (page 313)
Covering 14,763 sq km, and Tanzania's first national park, this is one of the world's greatest refuges for wildlife, and was designated a national park in 1952 and a World Heritage Site in 1981. The wildebeest migration between the Serengeti and the Masai Mara in neighbouring Kenya is perhaps one of the most impressive natural events on the globe.

Kondoa Rock Art Sites (page 352)
Tanzania's newest World Heritage Site, which was inscribed in 2006, the Kondoa cave system lies in the remote interior about 280 km south of Arusha bordering the Rift Valley. Here there are over 150 rocky walled shelters with hundreds of cave paintings of elongated figures, hunting scenes and animals. They are a testament to the early hunter-gatherers and the beliefs associated with different societies living in this region over a 2000 year period.

Ruins of Kilwa Kisiwani (page 137) and **Ruins of Songo Mnara** (page 139)
Designated World Heritage Sites in 1981, the ruins of these two ancient settlements lie on tiny islands on the remote south coast. From 2004, they have also been on the UNESCO's List of World Heritage in Danger, in a bid to call for more attention to safe-guarding and preserving them. From the 13th to 17th century they were wealthy East African ports dealing with the trade that crossed the Indian Ocean, and helped create the rich Swahili civilization still evident on the coast today.

lens (you will not get close enough to the animals without one). You may also wish to take a more detailed field guide. The Collins series is particularly recommended. The drivers are usually a mine of information. Take a notebook and pen – write down the number of species of animals and birds you spot (anything over 100 is pretty good).

Essentials A-Z

Accident and Emergency

Police, fire and ambulance T112.

Bargaining

Whilst most prices in the shops are set, the exception to this is shops selling typically tourist-related items such as curios, when a little good-natured bargaining is possible, especially if you are buying a number of things. Bargaining is very much expected in the street markets whether you are buying an apple or a Masai blanket. Generally traders will attempt to overcharge tourists who are unaware of local prices. Start lower than you would expect to pay, be polite and good humoured, and if the final price doesn't suit – walk away. You may be called back for more negotiation if your final price was too high, or the trader may let you go, in which case your price was too low. Ask about the prices of taxis, excursions, souvenirs and so on at your hotel. Once you have gained confidence, try bargaining with taxi drivers and at hotels when negotiating a room.

Begging

This is most common in Arusha, Moshi and poorer parts of Dar. Many Tanzanians give money to beggars who are clearly destitute and or disabled and, in a country with no social welfare, have few alternative means of livelihood. A fairly recent phenomenon has been the rise of street children in Arusha and Moshi, of which there is an estimated 1400 and many are glue-sniffing boys as

young as 8. Most find themselves on the streets as a result of abuse at home or are AIDS/HIV orphans. They can at times be fairly aggressive when it comes to begging, but it's best not to give money directly to them as this only encourages begging. It's much better to give a donation to a local school or project – ask your hotel or tour operator how best to go about this. It's recommended you make a donation to.the charity Mkombozi, www.mkombozi.org (the name means 'liberator' in Kiswahili), an organization which operates a residential home in Moshi for street children and raises money to educate them. Children for Children's Future, www.ccftz.org, also run a hostel for street children in Arusha.

Children

Tanzania has a great appeal for children: animals and safaris are very exciting, especially when they catch their first glimpse of an elephant or lion. However, small kids may get bored driving around a hot game park or national park all day if there is no animal activity. It's a good idea to get children enthused by providing them with checklists for animals and birds and perhaps giving them their own binoculars and cameras. At some game lodges children are not permitted at all, whereas others are completely child-friendly. If you travel in a group, think about the long hours inside the vehicle sharing cramped space with other people. Noisy and bickering children may annoy your travel mates and scare the animals away. But on a more positive note, there are usually young person's discounts for national park entry fees and some accommodation rates. Many travel agencies organize family safaris that are especially designed for couples travelling with children. There are also considerable discounts on accommodation at the beach for children, especially in the family orientated resorts of Zanzibar, when often under-12s get a sizeable reduction and under-6s go free. Many hotels have either specific family rooms or adjoining rooms suitable for families. This is always worth asking about when booking accommodation.

Disposable nappies, formula milk powders, and puréed foods are only available in major cities and they are expensive, so you may want consider bringing enough of these with you. It is important to remember that children have an increased risk of gastro-enteritis, malaria and sunburn and are more likely to develop complications, so care must be taken to minimize risks. See Health, page 48, for more details.

Conduct

Public displays of affection
Any public display of affection is ill advised, especially on the coast and islands where it offends the Muslim community. Police have arrested tourists canoodling on the beaches of Zanzibar in the past.

Taking photographs
Always ask before photographing local people. In some regions, the Masai are so used to tourists wanting to take pictures of them a fee is most definitely expected. Also, be careful where you point your camera when near government buildings or bridges.

Customs and duty free

There is now no requirement to change currency on entry. A litre of spirits or wine and 200 cigarettes can be taken in duty free. There is no duty on any equipment for your own use (eg laptop computers or cameras). Narcotics, pornography and firearms are prohibited. For more information contact the Tanzania Revenue Authority www.tra.go.tz. The CITES (Convention on International Trade in Endangered Species of Wild Fauna and Flora) Convention was established to prevent trade in endangered species. Attempts to smuggle controlled products can result in confiscation, fines and imprisonment. International trade in elephant ivory, sea turtle products and the skins of wild cats, such as leopard, is illegal. Casual vendors and small stalls can offer prohibited products – sea-shells can be a particular problem. Whilst you may legally buy curios made from animal products in Tanzania, you are unlikely to be permitted to take it out of the country or get it into your own country. If you were to buy such items, you should always consider the environmental and social impact of your purchase. Removal of coral, shells from turtles or any other kind of marine animal also causes a tremendous upset to the balance of marine life which is more often than not impossible to correct.

Disabled travellers

The towns have very uneven pavements, which are invariably blocked by parked cars, and wheelchairs are impossible to accommodate on public road transport, so you will probably need to come to Tanzania on an organized tour or in a rented vehicle. With the exception of the most upmarket hotels there are few designated facilities for disabled travellers. A few of the game park lodges have ground floor bedrooms, in contrast to most hotels where the bedrooms are upstairs and there are no lifts. Safaris should not pose too much of a problem given that most of the time is spent in the vehicle, and wheelchair-bound travellers may want to consider a camping or tented safari which provides easy access to a tent at ground level. Most operators are accommodating, and being disabled should not deter you from visiting Tanzania.

Based in Kenya, a safari company that deals with disabled travel to East Africa is **Go Africa Safaris**, T040-330 0102, www.go-africa-safaris.com, who have vehicles adapted for wheelchairs and can organize safaris for the visually or hearing impaired.

Dress

On Zanzibar, men and women should cover up and dress respectably when not on the beach.

Drugs

Importing or possession of drugs is prohibited and punished severely. Penalties for possession of any drugs will be extremely harsh.

Electricity

230 volts (50 cycles). The system is notorious for power surges. Computers are particularly vulnerable so take a surge protector plug (obtainable from computer stores) if you are using a laptop. New socket installations are square 3-pin but do not be surprised to encounter round 3-pin (large), round 3-pin (small) and 2-pin (small) sockets in old hotels – a multi-socket adaptor is essential. Some hotels and businesses have back-up generators in case of power cuts, which are more common at the end of the dry seasons.

Embassies and consulates

Australia, 23 Barrack St, Perth WA 6000, T08-9221 0033, www.tanzaniaconsul.com.
Canada, 50 Range Rd, Ottawa, Ontario KIN 8J4, T613-232 1509, www.tzrepottawa.ca.
France, 13 Av Raymond, Pointcare, 75116 Paris, T01-5370 6366, www.amb-tanzanie.fr.

Germany, Eschenallee 11, Berlin 14050 T030-303 0800, www.tanzania-gov.de.
Kenya, Continental House, Harambee Av/ Uhuru Highway, Nairobi, T020-331056, tanzania@users.africaonline.co.ke.
Malawi, Capital City, Lilongwe, T01-775038, wwwtzhighcomm@tz.lilongwe.mw.
Mozambique, Ujamaa House, Av Marites Da Machava 852, Maputo, T01-491165, safina@zebra.eum.mz.
South Africa, 822 George Av, Arcadia, 0007, Pretoria, T012-342 4371/93, www.tanzania.org.za.
Uganda, 6 Kagera Rd, Kampala, T041-256272, tzrepkla@imul.com.
UK, Tanzania House, 3 Stratford Pl, London W1C 1AS, T020-7569 1470, www.tanzania-online.gov.uk.
US, 2139 R Street NW Washington D.C. 20008, T202-939 6125, www.tanzania embassy-us.org.
Zambia, Ujamaa House, No 5200, United Nations Av, 10101 Lusaka, T01-227698, tzreplsk@zamnet.zm.
Zimbabwe, Ujamaa House, 23 Baines Av, Harare, 04-721870, tanrep@icon.co.zw.

Gay and lesbian travellers

Homosexuality is illegal in Tanzania and is considered a criminal offence, so extreme discretion is advised and there are no specific gay clubs or bars. Nevertheless, generally Tanzanians have the attitude that while being gay is considered 'un-African', they do accept that non-Africans may be gay, so you shouldn't suffer any discrimination.

Health

The health care in the region is varied and few medical facilities are available outside the big towns. There are many excellent private and government clinics/hospitals. As with all medical care, first impressions count. If a facility is grubby then be wary of the general standard of medicine and hygiene. It's worth contacting your embassy or consulate on arrival and asking where the recommended clinics are. If you do get ill, and you have the opportunity, you should also ask your medical insurer whether they are satisfied that the medical centre or hospital that you have been referred to is of a suitable standard.

The Flying Doctors, at Wilson Airport in Nairobi covers Tanzania. A 2-week tourist membership costs US$30, 2 months US$50. It offers free evacuation by air to a medical centre or hospital. You can contact them in advance for membership and information on T+254 (0)20 315454/5, www.amref.org.

Before you go
Ideally, you should see your GP or travel clinic at least 6 weeks before your departure for general advice on travel risks, antibiotics for travellers' bacterial diarrhoea, malaria and vaccinations. Make sure you have travel insurance, The Flying Doctors based at Wilson Airport in Nairobi cover Tanzania, see above and page 53); get a dental check (especially if you are going to be away for more than a month); know your own blood group; and if you suffer a long-term condition such as diabetes or epilepsy make sure someone knows or that you have a Medic Alert bracelet/necklace with this information on it.

Basic vaccinations recommended include polio, tetanus, diphtheria, typhoid and hepatitis A. If you are entering the country overland, you may well be asked for a yellow fever vaccination certificate.

A-Z of health risks
Altitude sickness
Acute mountain sickness can strike from about 3000 m upwards and in general is more likely to affect those who ascend rapidly (eg by plane) and those who over-exert themselves. Teenagers are particularly prone. On reaching heights above 3000 m, heart pounding and shortness of breath are almost universal and a normal response to the lack of oxygen in the air. Acute mountain sickness takes a few hours

or days to come on and presents with headache, lassitude, dizziness, loss of appetite, nausea and vomiting. Insomnia is common and often associated with a suffocating feeling when lying down. You may notice that your breathing tends to wax and wane at night and your face is puffy in the mornings – this is all part of the syndrome.

If the symptoms are mild, the treatment is rest, painkillers (preferably not aspirin-based) for the headaches and anti-sickness pills for vomiting. Should the symptoms be severe and prolonged it is best to descend to a lower altitude immediately and re-ascend, if necessary, slowly and in stages. Symptoms disappear very quickly with even a few 100 m of descent.

The best way of preventing acute mountain sickness is a relatively slow ascent. When trekking to high altitude, some time spent walking at medium altitude, getting fit and acclimatizing, is beneficial. On arrival at places over 3000 m a few hours' rest and the avoidance of alcohol, cigarettes and heavy food will prevent acute mountain sickness. Other problems experienced at high altitude include sunburn, cracked skin, sore eyes (it may be wise to leave your contact lenses out) and sore nostrils. Treat the latter with Vaseline. Do not ascend to high altitude if you are suffering from a bad cold or chest infection and certainly not within 24 hrs of scuba-diving.

Bites and stings
Mosquitoes and other insects such as tsetse flies can administer a wicked bite and can carry diseases such as malaria. It is essential to wear long sleeves and trousers in the evening when mosquitoes are at their most prevalent and use a mosquito repellent (see under Malaria, below). Rooms with a/c or fans also help ward off mosquitoes at night.

It is a very rare event for travellers but if you are unlucky enough to be bitten by a venomous snake, spider, scorpion or sea creature, try to identify the creature, without putting yourself in further danger (do not try to catch a live snake). Snake bites in particular are very frightening, but in fact rarely poisonous. Victims should be taken to a hospital or a doctor without delay. Commercial snake bite and scorpion kits are available but are usually only useful for specific types of snake or scorpion. Most serum has to be given intravenously so it is not much good equipping yourself with it unless you are used to making injections into veins. It is best to rely on local practice in these cases, because the particular creatures will be known about locally and appropriate treatment can be given.

Certain tropical sea fish when trodden upon inject venom into a bather's feet. This can be exceptionally painful. Wear plastic shoes if such creatures are reported. The pain can be relieved by immersing the foot in hot water (as hot as you can bear) for as long as the pain persists. The citric acid juice in fruits such as lemon can be useful.

Symptoms include swelling, pain and bruising around the bite and soreness of the regional lymph glands, perhaps nausea, vomiting and a fever. Symptoms of serious poisoning would be numbness and tingling of the face, muscular spasms, convulsions, shortness of breath or a failure of the blood to clot, causing generalized bleeding.

To treat a snake bite reassure and comfort the victim frequently. Immobilize the limb by a bandage or a splint and get the person to lie still. Do not slash the bite area and try to suck out the poison because this can do more harm than good, and the inexperienced should never apply a tourniquet.

Spiders and scorpions may be found in the more basic hotels. If stung, rest and take plenty of fluids and call a doctor. The best precaution is to keep beds away from the walls and look inside your shoes and under the toilet seat each morning.

Dengue fever
There is no vaccine against this and the mosquitoes that carry it bite during the day. You will feel like a mule has kicked you for

2-3 days, you will then get better for a few days and then feel that the mule has kicked you again. It should all be over in 7-10 days. Heed all the anti-mosquito measures that you can.

Diarrhoea and intestinal upset
It should be short lasting but persistence beyond 2 weeks, with blood or pain, requires specialist medical attention.

The key treatment with all diarrhoea is rehydration. Try to keep hydrated by taking the right mixture of salt and water. This is available as Oral Rehydration Salts (ORS) in ready-made sachets or can be made up by adding a teaspoon of sugar and a half teaspoon of salt to a litre of clean water. Drink at least 1 large cup of this for each loose stool. You can also use flat carbonated drinks as an alternative. Immodium and Pepto-Bismol provide symptomatic relief.

The standard advice to prevent problems is to be careful with water and ice for drinking. Ask yourself where the water came from. If you have any doubts then boil it or filter and treat it. Food can also transmit disease. Be wary of salads (what were they washed in, who handled them), re-heated foods or food that has been left out in the sun having been cooked earlier in the day. There is a simple adage that says wash it, peel it, boil it or forget it. Also be wary of unpasteurized dairy products as these can transmit a range of diseases.

Diving
If you go diving make sure that you are fit do so. The **British Sub-Aqua Club (BSAC)**, Telford's Quay, South Pier Road, Ellesmere Port, Cheshire CH65 4FL, UK, T0151-350 6200, www.bsac.com, can put you in touch with doctors who do medical examinations.

Protect your feet from cuts, beach dog parasites and sea urchins. The latter are almost impossible to remove but can be dissolved with lime or vinegar. Watch for secondary infection, which you'll need antibiotics for. Serious diving injuries may require time in a decompression chamber.

Check that the dive company knows what it is doing, has appropriate certification from BSAC or **Professional Association of Diving Instructors (PADI)**, Unit 7, St Philips Central, Albert Rd, St Philips, Bristol, BS2 OTD, T0117-300 7234, www.padi.com, and that the equipment is well maintained.

Hepatitis

Hepatitis means inflammation of the liver. Viral causes of the disease can be acquired anywhere in the world. The most obvious symptom is a yellowing of your skin or the whites of your eyes. However, prior to this all that you may notice is itching and tiredness. Pre-travel hepatitis A vaccine is the best bet. Hepatitis B (for which there is a vaccine) is spread through blood and unprotected sexual intercourse: both of these can be avoided. Unfortunately there is no vaccine for hepatitis C or the other hepatitis viruses.

Malaria

Malaria is present in almost all of Tanzania and can cause death within 24 hrs. It can start as something just resembling an attack of flu. You may feel tired, lethargic, headachy, feverish; or, more seriously, develop fits, followed by coma and then death. Have a low index of suspicion because it is very easy to write off vague symptoms, which may actually be malaria. If you have a temperature, go to a doctor as soon as you can and ask for a malaria test. On your return home if you suffer any of these symptoms, get tested as soon as possible, even if any previous test proved negative, the test could save your life. Remember ABCD: Awareness (of whether the disease is present in the area), Bite avoidance, Chemoprohylaxis, Diagnosis.

To prevent mosquito bites wear clothes that cover arms and legs and use effective insect repellents in areas with known risks of insect-spread disease. Use a mosquito net treated with insecticide as both a physical and chemical barrier at night in the same areas. Guard against the contraction of malaria with the correct anti-malarials. Note that the Royal Homeopathic Hospital in the UK does not advocate homeopathic options for malaria prevention or treatment.

Repellents containing DEET (Di-ethyltoluamide) are the gold standard. Apply the repellent every 4-6 hrs but more often if you are sweating heavily. If a non-DEET product is used check who tested it. Validated products (tested at the London School of Hygiene and Tropical Medicine) include Mosiguard, Non-DEET Jungle formula and non-DEET Autan. If you want to use citronella remember that it must be applied very frequently (ie hourly) to be effective. If you are a popular target for insect bites or develop lumps quite soon after being bitten, carry an Aspivenin kit. This syringe suction device is available from many chemists and draws out some of the allergic materials and provides quick relief.

Rabies

Avoid dogs and monkeys that are behaving strangely. If you are bitten by a domestic or wild animal, do not leave things to chance: scrub the wound with soap and water and/ or disinfectant, try to at least determine the animal's ownership, and seek medical assistance at once. The course of treatment depends on whether you have already been satisfactorily vaccinated against rabies. It is important to finish the course of treatment.

Schistosomiasis (bilharzia)

Bilharzia occurs in the freshwater lakes of Tanzania and can be contracted from a single swim. If you have swum or waded through snail infested water you may notice a local itch soon after, fever after a few weeks and much later diarrhoea, peeing blood, abdominal pain and spleen or liver enlargement. A single drug cures this disease but it can do damage to your liver, so get yourself checked out as soon as possible if you have any of these symptoms, or alternatively avoid swimming in any freshwater areas, there is no guarantee that they will not be contaminated, no matter what local advice you receive.

Sun

Long-term sun damage can lead to a loss of elasticity of skin and the development of pre-cancerous lesions. Years later a mild or a very malignant form of cancer may develop.

To prevent burning, use sunscreen. The higher the SPF the greater the protection. However, do not use higher factors just to stay out in the sun longer. 'Flash frying' (bursts of excessive exposure), as it is called, is known to increase the risks of skin cancer. Follow the Australians with their Slip, Slap, Slop campaign: Slip on a shirt, Slap on a hat, Slop on sun screen.

Ticks and fly larvae

Ticks usually attach themselves to the lower parts of the body often after walking in areas where cattle have grazed, and swell up as they suck blood. The important thing is to remove them gently, so that they do not leave their head in your skin because this can cause a nasty allergic reaction. Do not use petrol, Vaseline, lighted cigarettes, etc to remove the tick, but, with a pair of tweezers remove the beast gently by gripping it at the attached (head) end and rock it out in the same way that a tooth is extracted. Some tropical flies that lay their eggs under the skin of sheep and cattle also do the same thing to humans with the result that a maggot grows under the skin and pops up as a boil. The best way to remove these is to cover the boil with oil, Vaseline or nail varnish to stop the maggot breathing, then to squeeze it out gently the next day.

Water

There are a number of ways of purifying water. Dirty water should first be strained through a filter and then boiled or treated. Bringing water to a rolling boil at sea level is sufficient to make the water safe for drinking, but at higher altitudes you have to boil the water for a few minutes longer to ensure all microbes are killed. There are sterilizing methods that can be used and there are proprietary preparations containing chlorine or iodine compounds. Chlorine compounds generally do not kill protozoa (eg giardia). There are a number of water filters now on the market. Make sure you take the spare parts or spare chemicals with you and do not believe everything the manufacturers say.

Other diseases and risks

Fresh water can be a source of diseases such as bilharzia. Avoid infected waters, check the CDC, WHO websites and a travel clinic for up-to-date information. Lake Victoria and many smaller lakes are infected and it's always wise to ask locally about swimming.

Unprotected sex always carries a risk, with an awesome range of visible and invisible diseases including HIV, hepatitis B and C, gonorrhea, chlamydia, herpes, syphilis and warts, just to name a few. You can reduce the risk by using a condom, a femidom or avoiding sex altogether.

Further information

www.bloodcare.org.uk The Blood Care Foundation (UK) will dispatch certified non-infected blood of the right type to your hospital/clinic.
www.btha.org British Travel Health Association (UK). This is the official website of an organization of travel health professionals.
www.fitfortravel.scot.nhs.uk Fit for Travel (UK). A-Z of vaccine and travel health advice requirements for each country.
www.fco.gov.uk Foreign and Common- wealth Office (FCO). This is a key travel advice site, with useful information on the country, people and climate and lists of the UK embassies/consulates.
www.masta.org Medical Advisory Service for Travellers Abroad (MASTA). A-Z of vaccine and travel health advice and requirements.
www.medicalert.co.uk Medic Alert. Produces bracelets and necklaces for those with existing medical problems, where key

medical details are engraved, so that if you collapse, a medical person can identify you.

www.travelscreening.co.uk Travel Screening Services. A private clinic that gives vaccine and travel health advice.
www.who.int World Health Organization. The WHO site has links to the WHO Blue Book on travel advice.

Books

Lankester T, *Travellers' Good Health Guide* (2nd edition, Sheldon Press, 2006).

Insurance

Before departure, it is vital to take out comprehensive travel insurance. There are a wide variety of policies to choose from, so shop around. At the very least, the policy should cover medical expenses, including repatriation to your home country in the event of a medical emergency. If you are going to be active in Tanzania, ensure the policy covers whatever activity you will be doing (for example trekking or diving). If you do have something stolen whilst in Tanzania, report the incident to the nearest police station and ensure you get a police report and case number. You will need these to make any claim from your insurance company. Tanzania is covered by the **Flying Doctors' Society of Africa**, based at Wilson Airport in Nairobi. For an annual tourist fee of US$50, it offers free evacuation by air to a medical centre or hospital. This may be worth considering if you are visiting more remote regions, but is not necessary if visiting the more popular parks in the north as adequate provision is made in the case of an emergency. The profits go back into the service and the **African Medical Research Foundation (AMREF)** behind it; membership/information on T+254 (0)20-6903000, www.amref.org.

Internet

Internet cafés and email facilities offered in small business centres have mushroomed in all the major towns. The cost of access has fallen considerably to around US$0.50-1 per hr. Access is usually super-quick and band services are improving all the time. Most urban centres with their own server keep costs low but in more out-of-the-way places where a satellite connection is relied upon, the price per hour is 2 or 3 times higher. Many hotels and guesthouses also offer internet access to their guests.

Language

Greetings

Tanzania is a welcoming country and the first word that you will hear and come to know is the Kiswahili greeting 'Jambo' – 'hello', often followed by 'Hakuna matata' – 'no problem'! Lengthy greetings are important in Tanzania, and respect is accorded to elderly people, usually by the greeting *Shikamoo, mzee* to a man and *Shikamoo, mama* to a woman. In English, it is common for people to use the terms 'my sister' or 'my aunt', 'my brother' or 'my uncle' (depending on how old they think you are) as greetings. For anyone spending any length of time in East Africa, or returning over a period of a few years, it is a sad day indeed when you have reached the status of aunt or uncle – it means you are getting old!

Local languages

There are a number of local languages but most people in Tanzania, as in all East Africa, speak Kiswahili and some English. Kiswahili is the official language of Tanzania and is taught in primary schools. English is generally used in business and is taught in secondary schools. Only in the remote rural regions will you find people that only speak in their local tongues. A little Kiswahili goes a long way, and most Tanzanians will be thrilled to hear visitors attempt to use it. Although Kiswahili is a Bantu language in structure and origin, its vocabulary draws on a variety of sources including Arabic and English. The word for tea, *chai*, is the same in East Africa as it is in China and India for example. On the coast, Kiswahili is a little more grammatically developed. In other parts of the country, a more simplified version is spoken, known as 'kitchen swahili'. Since the language was originally written down by the British colonists, words are pronounced just as they are spelt.

Media

Newspapers and magazines
Tanzania has 2 English daily newspapers; the *Daily News* (www.dailynews.co.tz), and the *Guardian* (www.ippmedia.com), which both cover east and southern African news and syndicated international news and are available online, as well as several Swahili dailies. An excellent regional paper, *The East African*, (www.theeastafrican.co.ke) published in Nairobi, comes out weekly and has good Tanzanian coverage. The Kenyan daily, *The Nation*, is a high quality source of regional and international news. On a local level, the weekly *Arusha Times*, (www.arushatimes.co.tz) has good local news and sports. Copies of international newspapers from Europe and the US usually filter to the street vendors in Dar and Arusha a few days after publication along with well thumbed through magazines like *Time* and *Newsweek*.

Radio
Radio Tanzania broadcasts in Swahili, and news bulletins tend to contain a lot of local coverage. There are several popular FM stations that can be picked up in the cities such as Radio Free Africa, Clouds FM and Kiss FM, which mostly broadcast imported pop, rap and hip-hop music. *BBC World Service* is broadcast to Tanzania; check the website for frequencies (www.bbc.co.uk/worldservice).

Television
In 1994 *Television Tanzania* began to transmit with a mixture of locally produced Swahili items and international programmes, and it's widely believed that Tanzania was the last country in the world to get TV. There are now several local stations, and many hotels have satellite TV. This is usually DSTV (Digital Satellite Television), South African satellite TV, with scores of channels. The most popular with Tanzanians are the sports channels for coverage of European football.

Money

→ *US$1=TSh 1300, £1=TSh 1980, €1=TSh 1770 (May 2009)*

Currency
The Tanzanian currency is the Tanzanian Shilling (TSh), not to be confused with the Kenyan and Uganda Shilling which are different currencies. Notes currently in circulation are TSh 200, 500, 1,000, 5,000 and 10,000. Coins are TSh 50, 10 and 20 but these are hardly worth anything and are rarely used. As it is not a hard currency, it cannot be brought into or taken out of the country, however there are no restrictions on the amount of foreign currency that can be brought into Tanzania. There are banks with ATMs and bureaux de change at both Julius Nyerere International and Zanzibar International airports. The easiest currencies to exchange are US dollars, UK pounds and euros. If you are bringing US dollars in cash, try and bring newer notes – because of the prevalence of forgery, many banks and bureaux de change do not accept US dollar bills printed before 2000. Sometimes lower denomination bills attract a lower exchange rate than higher denominations. Travellers' cheques (TCs) are widely accepted, and many hotels, travel agencies, safari companies and restaurants accept credit cards. Most banks in Tanzania are equipped to advance cash on credit cards, and increasingly most now have

ATM machines that accept Visa and Master-Card. Departure taxes can be paid in local or foreign currency, but they are usually included in the price of an air ticket.

Exchange

Visitors to Tanzania should change foreign currency at banks, bureaux de change or authorized hotels, and under no circumstances change money on the black market which is highly illegal. All banks have a foreign exchange service, and bank hours are Mon-Fri 0830-1500, Sat 0830-1330. The government has authorized bureaux de change known as forex bureaux to set rates for buying foreign currency from the public. Forex bureaux are open longer hours and offer faster service than banks and, although the exchange rates are only nominally different, the bureaux usually offer a better rate on TCs. In the large private hotels, rates are calculated directly in US$, although they can be paid in foreign or local currency. Airline fares, game park entrance fees and other odd payments to the government (such as the airport international departure tax) are also quoted in dollars, though again these can be paid for in both foreign or local currency. Just ensure that you are getting a reasonable exchange rate when the hotel or airline, etc converts US$ to TSh.

Credit cards and travellers' cheques

These are now accepted by large hotels, upmarket shops, airlines, major tour operators and travel agencies, but of course will not be taken by small hotels, restaurants and so on. There may also be a 5% fee to use them. In any town of a reasonable size you will be able to use an ATM that allow you to withdraw cash from Visa, MasterCard, Plus and Cirrus cards. Diners Club and American Express are, however, limited. Your bank will probably charge a small fee for withdrawing cash from an ATM overseas. Most banks can also organize a cash advance off your credit card. Many banks refuse to exchange travellers' cheques without being shown the purchase agreement that is, the slip

issued at the point of sale that in theory you are supposed to keep separately from your travellers' cheques. Travellers' cheques are now accepted as payment for park entry fees by Tanzania National Parks, as well as cash.

Cost of travelling

In first-rate luxury lodges and tented camps expect to pay in excess of US$150 per person per night for a double rising to US$500 per night per person in the most exclusive establishments. There are half a dozen places aimed at the very top of the range tourist or honeymooner that charge nearer US$1000 per person per night. For this you will get impeccable service, cuisine and decor in fantastic locations either in the parks or on the coast. In 4- to 5-star hotels and lodges expect to spend US$200-300 a day. Careful tourists can live reasonably comfortably on US$100 a day staying in the mid-range places, though to stay in anything other than campsites on safaris, they will have to spend a little more for the cheapest accommodation in the national parks. Budget travellers can get by on US$20-30 per day using cheap guesthouses and public transport. However, with additional park entry fees and related costs, organized camping safari costs can exceed US$400 for a 3-day trip and climbing Mt Kilimanjaro is an expensive experience whatever your budget. Commodities such as chocolate and toiletries are on the expensive side, as they are imported but they are readily available. Restaurants vary widely from side-of-the-road local eateries where a simple meal of chicken and chips will cost no more than US$2-3, to the upmarket restaurants in the cities and tourists spots that can charge in excess of US$60 for 2 people with drinks.

Opening hours

Most offices will start at 0800, lunch between 1200-1300, finish business at 1700, Mon-Fri; 0900-1200 on Sat. Small shops and kiosks and markets in the bigger towns are open daily.

Banks are open Mon-Fri, 0830-1530, and Sat 0830-1330. Post offices are open Mon-Fri 0800-1630, Sat 0900-1200.

Police

Calling a policeman 'sir' is customary in Tanzania. If you get in trouble with the law or have to report to the police – for any reason – *always* be exceptionally polite, even if you are reporting a crime against yourself. Tanzania police generally enjoy their authoritative status and to rant and rave and demand attention will get you absolutely nowhere.

For petty offences (driving without lights switched on, for example) police will often try to solicit a bribe, masked as an 'on-the-spot' fine. Establish the amount being requested, and then offer to go to the police station to pay, at which point you will be released with a warning. For any serious charges, immediately contact your embassy or consulate.

Post

The postal system is fairly reliable. Airmail takes about 2 weeks to destinations in Europe and North America. Buy stamps at the hotel or at a postcard shop, as post offices are crowded and chaotic. If sending parcels, they must be no longer than 105 cm long and have to be wrapped in brown paper and string. There is no point doing this before getting to the post office as you will be asked to undo it to be checked for export duty. Items have been known to go missing, so post anything of personal value through the fast post service known as EMS; a registered postal service available at all post offices, or with a courier company. DHL has offices in the major cities, TNT and Fedex have offices in Dar es Salaam. Letters to Europe take 3 working days, to North America, 5 days.

If sending post to Tanzania, note there is no home delivery and addresses use post

office box numbers; known as 'private bag', and the location of the relevant post office.

Safety

The majority of the people you will meet are honest and ready to help you so there is no need to get paranoid about your safety. However, theft from tourists in Tanzania does occur and it will be assumed that foreigners in the country have relative wealth. Visitors on tours or who are staying in upmarket hotels are generally very safe. Otherwise, it is sensible to take reasonable precautions by not walking around at night, and by avoiding places of known risk during the day. Petty theft and snatch robberies can be a problem, particularly in the urban areas. Don't wear jewellery or carry cameras in busy public places. Bum-bags are also very vulnerable as the belt can be cut easily. Day packs have also been known to be slashed, their entire contents drifting out on to the street without the wearer knowing. Carry money and any valuables in a slim belt under clothing.

Always lock room doors at night as noisy fans and a/c can provide cover for sneak thieves. Be wary of a driver being distracted in a parked vehicle, whilst an accomplice gets in on the other side – always keep car doors locked and windows wound up. You also need to be vigilant of thieves on public transport and guard your possessions fiercely and be wary of pickpockets in busy places like the bus and train stations. Never accept food and drink from a stranger on public transport as it might be doped so they can rob you.

Armed robberies

Unfortunately there has been a spate of armed robberies on tourists since 2007 in the Arusha area. Possibly it's the same gang. These have included an attack on a group of tourists near Lake Duluti in 2007 when 2 tourists and a tour guide were shot, and 2 armed robberies on safari vehicles near the Ngorongoro Crater in the same year. In 2008 a large group of bandits carried out 2 separate attacks on tented camps near Tarangire, and in Jan 2009 a group of tourists were robbed at gunpoint while returning to Moshi after climbing Kilimanjaro. If you are attacked at gun point, *always* give over your valuables immediately. *Never resist*. This is alarming news, but nevertheless these appear to be isolated incidents, given the amount of safari vehicles that move around the region, and hopefully the culprits will be apprehended soon.

Night driving

Crime and hazardous road conditions make travel by night dangerous. Car-jacking has occurred in both rural and urban areas. The majority of these attacks have occurred on the main road from Dar es Salaam to Zambia, between Morogoro and Mikumi National Park. Travellers are advised not to stop between populated areas, and to travel in convoys whenever possible.

Game reserves and national parks

It's not only crime that may affect your personal safety; you must also take safety precautions when visiting the game reserves and national parks. If camping, it is not advisable to leave your tent or banda during the night. Wild animals wander around the camps freely in the hours of darkness, and a protruding leg may seem like a tasty take-away to a hungry hyena. This is especially true at organized campsites, where the local animals have got so used to humans that they have lost much of their inherent fear of man. Exercise care during daylight hours too – remember wild animals can be dangerous.

Telephone

→ *IDD 000. Country code 255.*
In most towns there is an efficient inter-national service from the Tanzania Telecoms (TTCL) offices (www.ttcl.co.tz) are usually within the post office or nearby. Connections are quick and about a third of the price of a call through hotels, which are expensive for phone calls and faxes. You pay in advance and the minimum time is 3 mins, but you get your money back if the call fails to connect. Fairly new card phone boxes are appearing in the cities and in theory you buy cards from the TTCL office, but they don't always have stock. You can also try shops and stalls near to the phones. In larger towns, private telecom-munication centres also offer international services. Telephone calls from Tanzania to Kenya and Uganda are charged at long-distance tariffs rather than international. If you have a mobile phone with a roaming connection, then you can make use of Tanzania's cellular networks, which cover most larger towns, the urban sections of the coast, Zanzibar and the tourist areas but not some of the parks and reserves or the south-west of Tanzania away from the towns and the main road. SIM and top-up cards for the pay-as-you-go mobile providers are available just about everywhere; in the towns and cities these often have their own shops, but you can buy cards from roadside vendors anywhere, even in the smallest of settlements. Indeed, mobile phones are now such a part of everyday life in Tanzania, many establish-ments have abandoned the less reliable local landline services and use the mobile network instead. You will see from listings such as hotels and restaurants in this book, mobile numbers are sometimes offered instead of landline numbers, they start T07. Indeed, if you find a taxi driver or tour guide you like, get their cell phone numbers as this is the best way to reach them. Quite remarkably, fishermen now use mobile phones to check the market prices of fish in the fish markets on Zanzibar and in Dar es Salaam before deciding to which they are going to sail to sell their catch. One of the cell phone providers Zain, have been operating a system called One Network since 2006, which is the world's first borderless network. It now covers 22 African countries from Zambia to Gabon and enables

callers to use their phones without roaming and all calls across this vast region are at local (not international) rates. The network now has a rather staggeringly 25 million subscribers. If you are travelling on, say to Kenya or Uganda, it's a good idea to opt for a Zain SIM card. The network was called Celtel before being rebranded under the Zain telecommunications umbrella so look out for both cards.

Time

GMT + 3. Malawi and Zambia are GMT+2 so when crossing from Tanzania, clocks go back 1 hr.

Tipping

It is customary to tip around 10% for good service and this is greatly appreciated by hotel and restaurant staff, most of whom receive very low pay. Some of the more upmarket establishments may add a service charge to the bill. It is also expected that you tip safari guides, and if climbing Kilimanjaro, porters too (see page 246). For information on tipping when on safari or visiting parks, see page 43.

Tour operators

If you plan to book an organized tour from your own country, the best bet is to locate a travel agent with a links to tour companies in Tanzania. Within Tanzania there is a bewildering array of tour operators offering safaris in Tanzania and East Africa, with most having offices in Dar es Salaam (see page 93) or Arusha (see page 278). There is no reason why you cannot deal with them directly and they may often be cheaper and better informed than travel agents in your home country. Many companies offer tailor-made guided trips for small groups to the more remote parts of the country, which can be economical for families or groups travelling together. See page 41 for parks and safaris, page 38 for safari accommodation options, and page 279 for 'How to organize a safari'.

Australia and New Zealand
African Wildlife Safaris, T(0)3-9249 3777, www.africanwildlifesafaris.com.au.
Classic Safari Company, T1300-130218, T(0)2-9327 0666, www.classicsafari company.com.au.
Peregrine Travel, T(0)3-8601 4444, www.peregrine.net.au.

Germany
Djoser Travel, T(0)21-920 1580, www.djoser.de.
A & E Reiseteam, T(0) 40-2787 8870, www.ae-reiseteam.de.
Iwanowski's Individuelles Reisen GmbH, T(0)21-3326030, www.afrika.de.

North America

Adventure Centre, T0800-228 8747, T151-0654 1879, www.adventure-centre.com.
Africa Adventure Company, T0800-882 9453, T954-491 8877, www.africa-adventure.com.
Bushtracks, T1707-433 4492, www.bushtracks.com.
Tanzania Odyssey, 1209 Meadowbrook Dr, Portland, Texas 78374, T186-6356 4691, www.tanzaniaodyssey.com.

South Africa

Africa Travel Co, T021-385 1390, www.africatravelco.com.
Pulse Africa, T011-325 2290, www.pulseafrica.com.
Wild Frontiers, T011-702 2035, www.wildfrontiers.com.

UK

Aardvark Safaris, T01980-849160, www.aardvarksafaris.com.
Abercrombie & Kent, T0800-554 7016, www.abercrombiekent.com.
Acacia Adventure Holidays, T020-7706 4700, www.acacia-africa.com.
Africa Travel Centre, 3rd floor, New Premier House, 150 Southampton Row, Bloomsbury, London WC1B 5AL, T0845-450 1520, www.africatravel.co.uk.
Africa Travel Resource, T01306-880770, www.africatravelresource.com.
Aim 4 Africa, 21-23 Chelsea Rd, Sheffield S11 9BQ, T0114-255 2533, www.aim4africa.com.
Audley Travel Ltd, T01993-838500, www.audleytravel.com.
Expert Africa, 9-10 Upper Sq, Old Isleworth, Middlesex TW7 7BJ, T020-8232 9777, www.expertafrica.com.
Footprint Adventures, T01522-804929, www.footprint-adventures.co.uk.
Global Village, 102 Islington High St, London N1 8EG, T0844-844 2541, www.globalvillage-travel.com.

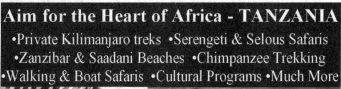

Odyssey World, T0845-370 7733,
www.odyssey-world.co.uk.
Rainbow Tours, T020-7226 1004,
www.rainbowtours.co.uk.
Safari Consultants, T01787-888590,
www.safari-consultants.co.uk.
Safari Drive, Windy Hollow, Sheepdrove,
Lambourn, Berkshire RH17 7XA, T01488-
71140, www.safaridrive.com.
Somak, T020-8423 3000, www.somak.co.uk.
Steppes Travel, T01285-880980,
www.steppestravel.co.uk.
Tanzania Odyssey, 1 Swan Mews, Fulham,
London SW6 4QT, T020-7471 8780,
www.tanzaniaodyssey.com. Tailor-made
safaris to Tanzania and beach extensions to
Zanzibar and other Indian Ocean islands.
Tim Best Travel, T020-7591 0300,
www.timbesttravel.com.
Wildlife Worldwide, T0845-130 6982,
www.wildlifeworldwide.com.

Tourist information

The **Tanzania Tourist Board**, has its offices
in the IPS Building, 3rd Floor, Samora Av/
Azikiwe St, Dar es Salaam, T022-2111 2244,
www.tanzaniatouristboard.com. Contact
them in advance and they will send you a
brochure. The **Tourist Information Office**
for drop in visitors is at the Matasalamat
Mansion, Samora Av, Dar, T022-213 1555.
Mon-Fri 0800-1630, and Sat 0830-1230. Staff
can make reservations at any of the larger
hotels in Tanzania and national park lodges
(payment in foreign currency only) but they
can't help you with budget accommodation.
It's better to book national park lodges
through a travel agency or tour operator, as
they may offer special deals. Brochures and
maps can also be picked up from the tourist
offices in Zanzibar and Arusha (see pages 162
and 259). **Tanzania National Parks (TANAPA)**

has an office in Arusha, T027-250 3471, www.tanzania parks.com (see page 259).

Useful websites

www.absolutetanzania.com Tourist information with interesting articles about the economy, government and conservation.
www.africaonline.com Comprehensive website covering news, sport and travel all over Africa.
www.marineparktz.com Website for Tanzania's Marine Parks and Reserves Authority who manage the Mafia Island Marine Park and smaller reserves off Dar es Salaam.
www.go2africa.com Full accommodation and safari booking service for East Africa, with useful practical information.
www.pemba.net One of the few online recourses of information on Pemba.
www.overlandafrica.com Sells a variety of overland tours throughout East Africa.
www.tfcg.org The website for the Tanzania Forest Conservation Group, with more information on the mountains and forests in the region.
www.zanzibar.net Good general information about Zanzibar including history and culture.
www.zanzibartourism.net Official site for tourist information for Zanzibar in English, German, French and Japanese.

Visas and immigration

Visas are required by all visitors except citizens of the Commonwealth (excluding citizens of the UK, Australia, New Zealand, South Africa, Canada, India and Nigeria who *do* require visas), Republic of Ireland and Iceland. Citizens of neighbouring countries do not normally require visas. For more information visit Tanzania's Ministry of Home Affairs website; www.moha.go.tz.

It is straightforward to get a visa at the point of entry (ie border crossing or airport) and many visitors find this more convenient

than going to an embassy. Visas are issued at the following entry points: The road borders of Namanga, Taveta, Isebbania and Lunga Lunga (all with Kenya), Tunduma (with Zambia), Mutakula (Uganda), Rusomu (Rwanda) Songwe (Malawi, and Kilambo (Mozambique), as well as Julius Nyerere International Airport, Kilimanjaro International Airport, Zanzibar International Airport, and the ports in Zanzibar and Kigoma. Visas are paid for in US dollars, Euros or UK pounds and have been set at US$50 or €50.

Visas obtained from Tanzanian Embassies require 2 passport photographs and are issued in 24 hrs. Visitors who do not need a visa are issued with a visitor's pass on arrival, valid for 1-3 months. Your passport must be valid for a minimum of 6 months after your planned departure date from Tanzania; required whether you need a visa or not.

It is worth remembering that there is an agreement between Tanzania, Kenya and Uganda that allows holders of single entry visas to move freely between all 3 countries without the need for re-entry permits. Also remember that although part of Tanzania, Zanzibar has its own immigration procedures and you are required to show your passport on entry and exit to the islands. You'll be stamped in and out but ensure your 3-month Tanzania doesn't expire when on Zanzibar.

Visas can be extended at the **Immigration Headquarters**, Ohio/Ghana Av, Dar es Salaam, T022-211 8637/40/43, www.moha. go.tz. Mon-Fri, 0730-1530. There are also immigration offices in Arusha and Mwanza (see pages 286 and 335). You will be asked to show proof of funds (an amount of US$1000 or a credit card should be sufficient) and your return or onward airline ticket. Occasionally, independent travellers not on a tour may be asked for these at point of entry.

Resident status for people permanently employed in Tanzania visas can be arranged after arrival. Your employer will need to vouch for you, and the process can take several weeks. Because of Tanzania's

2-tiered price system for residents and non-residents, resident status does give certain privileges (lower rates on air flights, in hotels, and game park entry fees).

Weights and measures

Metric.

Women travellers

Tanzania does not have a high record of sexual crime and tourists are unlikely to be targeted. It is a relatively safe country for women to travel in, but always keep vigilant, especially for petty theft, and follow the usual common sense about avoiding travelling alone after dark and avoiding quiet places. Women may experience unwanted attention from men, but this can usually be dealt with if you are assertive. Tanzanian women will generally be very supportive if they see you are being harassed and may well intervene if they think you need help. Older Tanzanian women are very much respected, so a few sharp words from them will diffuse any manner of situations. Women should be aware that the coast, and in particularly Zanzibar, is largely Islamic. It's fine to lie on the beaches in Zanzibar, as these are at tourist resorts (although see guidelines on page 170), but in local villages and in Stone Town, remember to cover up in loose fitting and non-revealing clothing so you don't cause offence. Many women travellers ignore this advice and seem to think because they're on an all-inclusive beach holiday, it entitles them to wear what they want. It doesn't. Non-Islamic women generally are not welcome around mosques.

Working in the country

Whilst there is a fairly large expatriate community in Dar es Salaam working in construction, telecommunications and the import/export industry, there are few opportunities for travellers to obtain casual paid employment in Tanzania and it is illegal for a foreigner to work there without an official work permit. A number of NGOs and Voluntary Organizations can arrange placements for volunteers, especially teachers and HIV/Aids educators, usually for periods ranging from 6 months to 2 years, see www.volunteerafrica.org, www.volunteerabroad.com/Tanzania or www.tanzaniavolunteer.org.

Contents

Footprint features

Dar es Salaam

At a glance

◎ **Getting around** Taxis are available on every street corner and plenty of *dala-dalas* and local buses. But traffic can be chaotic and the city is compact enough to walk around the main sites.

◉ **Time required** 1-2 days, an extra day if you want to explore the coastal suburbs.

☼ **Weather** Uncomfortably sticky and humid in Mar before the rains, with high temperatures. Pleasantly warm for the rest of the year and wet towards end Mar-May.

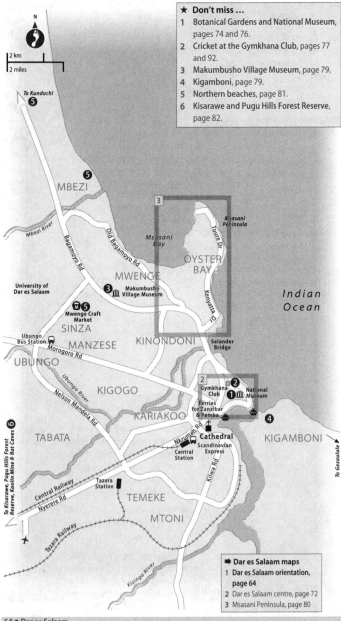

★ Don't miss ...

1 Botanical Gardens and National Museum, pages 74 and 76.

2 Cricket at the Gymkhana Club, pages 77 and 92.

3 Makumbusho Village Museum, page 79.

4 Kigamboni, page 79.

5 Northern beaches, page 81.

6 Kisarawe and Pugu Hills Forest Reserve, page 82.

N

2 km
2 miles

To Kunduchi

MBEZI

Mbezi River

Bagamoyo Rd

Old Bagamoyo Rd

University of
Dar es Salaam

Msasani
Peninsula

Msasani
Bay

Toure Dr

OYSTER
BAY

Kenyatta Dr

*Indian
Ocean*

MWENGE

Makumbusho
Village Museum

Mwenge Craft
Market

SINZA

MANZESE

Ubungo
Bus Station

Morogoro Rd

Ubungo River

Nelson Mandela Rd

UBUNGO

KIGOGO

KINONDONI

Selander
Bridge

Gymkhana
Club

National
Museum

Ferries
for Zanzibar
& Pemba

KARIAKOO

*To Kisarawe, Pugu Hills Forest
Reserve, Kaolin Mine & Bat Caves*

TABATA

Nkrumah Rd

Cathedral

Scandinavian
Express

Central
Station

KIGAMBONI

To Gezaulole

Kilwa Rd

Central Railway

Nyerere Rd

Tazara
Station

TEMEKE

MTONI

Tazara Railway

Kizinga River

➡ Dar es Salaam maps

1 Dar es Salaam orientation, page 64.

2 Dar es Salaam centre, page 72.

3 Msasani Peninsula, page 80.

Dar es Salaam, meaning 'haven of peace' in Arabic, is far from peaceful these days but, by African standards at least, is a relatively relaxed, unassuming yet atmospheric city. It's hardly a hive of activity for tourists – there are a handful of local museums, art galleries and craft markets to visit, and some interesting architecture of the 'faded colonial grandeur' category alongside mosques, an attractive Lutheran church and a Roman Catholic cathedral that dominate the harbour front. But, with a rapidly increasing population estimated at 4 million, it is a thriving port, business centre and administrative base for the country (even though its status of capital city was removed in 1973), and you could do far worse than spend a couple of days here simply watching urban Tanzanian life go by. People are relaxed and friendly, the main sights of the city centre are easily walkable and it's home to some excellent international-standard hotels and restaurants.

The city dates from 1857 and was successively under the control of Zanzibar, Germany and Britain before self-determination in 1961, with all these influences leaving their mark on its character. During German occupation in the early 20th century, it was the centre of colonial administration and the main contact point between the agricultural mainland and the world of trade and commerce in the Indian Ocean and the Swahili Coast. Today, the ocean provides a sparkling backdrop to the city, with everything from small fishing boats to cruise liners and tankers visiting the port. And should the urban bustle prove too much, nearby beaches to the north and south of town provide an easy escape. Further afield, Dar is the main springboard for ferries or flights to the islands of Zanzibar, Pemba and Mafia and to game parks across the country.

→ Phone code: 022. Population estimated at 4,000,000. Altitude: sea level.

Getting there

Air International and domestic flights depart from **Julius Nyerere International Airport** ① flight information T022-284 4212, www.jnia.aero, along Nyerere (formerly Pugu) Road, 13 km from the city centre. The airlines have desks at the airport and there are a range of facilities. For those international visitors requiring a visa for Tanzania, the visa desk is just before immigration at international arrivals. To get from the airport to the city, dala-dala and minibuses run regularly, are cheaper than regular taxis, but are crowded and there can be a problem with luggage, which will normally have to be accommodated on your knees. Taxis are the better option with fixed fares costing between US$25-35, depending on your destination. ▸▸ For airline office details, see page 94.

Bus The main bus station for up-country travel is on Morogoro Road in the Ubungo area, 6 km to the west of the centre. It is well organized and modern with cafés and shops and ticket offices on the main road outside. It is also reasonably secure as only ticket holders and registered taxi drivers are allowed inside; nevertheless watch out for pick pocketing. For a few shillings you can hire a porter with a trolley for luggage. A taxi into the city should cost around US$8-10. Outside on Morogoro Road, you can also catch a local bus or dala-dala to the centre, though again these are crowded and there is a problem if you are carrying a large amount of luggage. The best bus company recommended for foreigners, Scandinavia Express (see page 33), has an office at the Ubungo Bus Station where all their buses stop, though it also has a downtown terminal on Nyerere Road where all their services start and finish. ▸▸ For details, see page 96.

Ferry Ferries leave from the jetty on Sokoine Drive opposite St Joseph's Cathedral. Dhows and motorized boats leave from the wharf just to the south of the boat jetty, but it is now illegal for foreigners to take dhows along the coast and you would be ill-advised to arrange such a journey. The ferry companies request payment in US$ cash only and each company has a ticket office on or around the wharf. ▸▸ For details, see page 96.

Train Trains to the central regions of Tanzania (the Dar–Tabora–Kigoma/Mwanza line), run from the **Central Railway Station** ① Sokoine Dr, T022-211 0600. It is convenient for most hotels and is only a short walk to the ferry terminal. Trains for the southwest (the Dar–Mbeya–Zambia line) leave from **TAZARA Station** ① T022-286 5187, www.tazara.co.tz for online reservations, some 5 km from the centre. There are plenty of dala-dala and a taxi costs about US$7. ▸▸ For details, see page 97.

Getting around

Dala-dalas These are cheap at around US$0.40 for any journey (see page 35 for further information). The front of the vehicle usually has two destinations painted on the bonnet or a sign stating its destination, and sometimes another stating the fare. The main terminals in town are at the Central Railway Station (Stesheni) and the New Post Office (Posta) on Azikiwe Street. From both, if there are not enough passengers, the dala-dala will also make a detour to the Old Post Office on Sokoine Drive to pick up more people.

Taxis Taxis are readily available in the city centre and are parked on just about every street corner. They cost around US$2-3 per km. Any car can serve as a taxi, they are not painted in a specific colour, and they may be new or battered but serviceable. If you are visiting a non-central location and there is no taxi stand at the destination, you can always ask the driver to wait or come back and pick you up at an allotted time. These days most of Dar's taxi drivers have mobile phones, so it is easy enough to get the number and call the driver when you want to be picked up. Taxis do not have meters so always negotiate taxi fares before setting off on your journey.

Tuk-tuks (bajajis) These have increased in numbers over the past few years and are at least half the price of regular taxis. They don't go very fast, though, and are quite uncomfortable so for longer journeys stick to taxis. For more information on them, see page 35.

Tourist offices
If you contact the **Tanzania Tourist Board** ① *IPS Building, 3rd Fl, Samora Av/Azikiwe St, T022-211 1244, www.tanzaniatouristboard.com,* in advance they will post out brochures. The **Tourist Information Office** ① *Matasalamat Mansion, Samora Av, T022-213 1555, Mon-Fri 0800-1600, Sat 0830-1230,* for drop-in visitors has a limited range of glossy leaflets about the national parks and other places of interest, a noticeboard with transport timetables and fares, a (not too good) map of the city and, sometimes, a 1:2,000,000 scale map of Tanzania. Staff are very helpful, however and can also make reservations at any of the larger hotels in Tanzania and national park lodges (payment in foreign currency only) but they can't help you with budget accommodation. However, it's generally better to book the larger resort hotels and national park lodges through a travel agency or tour operator as they may offer special deals.

There are two free monthly publications available from some hotels and travel agencies; the *Dar es Salaam Guide,* which has transport timetables and good articles about destinations and sights in the city; and *What's Happening in Dar es Salaam.* The latter is better for information about upcoming events.

When to visit
The hottest months are December to the end of March, when the Indian Ocean is warm enough to swim in at night. The long rains are from March-May and the short rains November-December. The best season to visit is June-October, although there is sun all the year round, even during the rains, which are short and heavy and bring on intense humidity.

Background

Zanzibar period 1862-1886
The name Dar es Salaam means 'haven of peace' and was chosen by the founder of the city, Seyyid Majid, Sultan of Zanzibar. The harbour is sheltered, with a narrow inlet channel protecting the water from the Indian Ocean. An early British visitor in 1873, Frederic Elton, remarked that "it's healthy, the air clear – the site a beautiful one and the surrounding country green and well-wooded."

Despite the natural advantages it was not chosen as a harbour earlier, because of the difficulties of approaching through the narrow inlet during the monsoon season and there were other sites, protected by the coral reef, along the Indian Ocean coast that were used instead. However, Majid decided to construct the city in 1862 because he wanted to have a port and settlement on the mainland, which would act as a focus for trade and caravans operating to the south. Bagamoyo (see page 102) was already well established, but local interests there were inclined to oppose direction from Zanzibar, and the new city was a way of ensuring control from the outset.

Construction began in 1865 and the name was chosen in 1866. Streets were laid out, based around what is now Sokoine Drive running along the shoreline to the north of the inner harbour. Water was secured by the sinking of stone wells, and the largest building was the Sultan's palace. An engraving from 1869 shows the palace to have been a substantial two-storey stone building, the upper storey having sloping walls and a crenellated parapet, sited close to the shore on the present-day site of Malindi Wharf. In appearance it was similar in style to the fort that survives in Zanzibar (see page 174). To the southwest, along the shore, was a mosque and to the northwest a group of buildings, most of which were used in conjunction with trading activities. One building that survives is the double-storeyed structure now known as the Old Boma, on the corner of Morogoro Road and Sokoine Drive. The Sultan used it as an official residence for guests, and in 1867 a western-style banquet was given for the British, French, German and American consuls to launch the new city. Craftsmen and slaves were brought from Zanzibar for construction work. Coral for the masonry was cut from the reef and nearby islands. A steam tug was ordered from Germany to assist with the tricky harbour entrance and to speed up movements in the wind-sheltered inner waters. Economic life centred on agricultural cultivation (particularly coconut plantations) and traders who dealt with the local Zaramo people as well as with the long-distance caravan traffic.

Dar es Salaam suffered its first stroke of ill-luck when Majid died suddenly in 1870, after a fall in his new palace, and he was succeeded as Sultan by his half-brother, Seyyid Barghash. Barghash did not share Majid's enthusiasm for the new settlement, and indeed Majid's death was taken to indicate that carrying on with the project would bring ill-fortune. The court remained in Zanzibar. Bagamoyo and Kilwa predominated as mainland trading centres. The palace and other buildings were abandoned, and the fabric rapidly fell into decay. Nevertheless the foundation of a Zaramo settlement and Indian commercial involvement had been established.

Despite the neglect, Barghash maintained control over Dar es Salaam through an agent (*akida*) and later a governor (*wali*) and Arab and Baluchi troops. An Indian customs officer collected duties for use of the harbour and the Sultan's coconut plantations were maintained. Some commercial momentum had been established, and the Zaramo traded gum copal (a residue used in making varnishes), rubber, coconuts, rice and fish for cloth, ironware and beads. The population expanded to around 5000 by 1887, and comprised a cosmopolitan mixture of the Sultan's officials, soldiers, planters, traders, and shipowners, as well as Arabs, Swahilis and Zaramos, Indian Muslims, Hindus and a handful of Europeans.

German period 1887-1916

In 1887 the German East African Company under Hauptmann Leue took up residence in Dar es Salaam. They occupied the residence of the Sultan's governor whom they succeeded in getting recalled to Zanzibar, took over the collection of customs dues and, in return for a payment to the Zaramo, obtained a concession on the land. The Zaramo, Swahili and Arabs opposed this European takeover, culminating in the Arab revolt of 1888-1889, which involved most of the coastal region as well as Dar es Salaam. The city came under sporadic attack and the buildings of the Berlin Mission, a Lutheran denomination located on a site close to the present Kivokoni ferry, were destroyed. When the revolt was crushed, and the German government took over responsibility from the German East Africa Company in 1891, Dar es Salaam was selected as the main centre for administration and commercial activities.

The Germans laid out a grid street system, built the railway to Morogoro, connected the town to South Africa by overland telegraph, and laid underwater electricity cables to Zanzibar. Development in Dar es Salaam involved the construction of many substantial buildings, and most of these survive today. In the quarter of a century to 1916, several fine buildings were laid out on Wilhelms Ufer (now Kivukoni Front), and these included administrative offices as well as a club and a casino. Landing steps to warehouses, and a hospital, were constructed on the site of the present Malindi Wharf and behind them the railway station. Just to the south of Kurasini Creek was the dockyard where the present deep-water docks are situated. A second hospital was built at the eastern end of Unter den Akazien and Becker Strasse, now Samora Avenue. The post office is on what is now Sokoine Drive at the junction with Mkwepu Street. A governor's residence provided the basis for the current State House. The principal hotels were the Kaiserhof, which was demolished to build the New Africa Hotel, and the Burger Hotel, razed to make way for the present Telecoms building. The area behind the north harbour shore was laid out with fine acacia-lined streets and residential two-storey buildings with pitched corrugated-iron roofs and first-floor verandas, and most of these survive. Behind the east waterfront were shops and office buildings, many of which are still standing.

British period 1916-1961

In the 45 years that the British administered Tanganyika, public construction was kept to a minimum on economy grounds, and business was carried on in the old German buildings. The governor's residence was damaged by naval gunfire in 1915, and was remodelled to form the present State House. In the 1920s, the Gymkhana Club was laid out on its present site behind Ocean Road, and Mnazi Moja ('Coconut Grove') established as a park. The Selander Bridge causeway was constructed, and this opened up the Oyster Bay area to residential construction for the European community. The Yacht Club was built on the harbour shore (it is now the customs post) and behind it the Dar es Salaam Club (now the Hotel and Tourism Training Centre), both close to the Kilimanjaro Hotel Kempinski.

As was to be expected, road names were changed, as well as those of the most prominent buildings. Thus Wilhelms Ufer became Azania Front, Unter den Akazien became Acacia Avenue, Kaiser Strasse became City Drive. Other streets were named after explorers Speke and Burton, and there was a Windsor Street. One departure from the relentless Anglicization of the city was the change of Bismarck Strasse to Versailles Street – it was the Treaty of Versailles in 1918 that allocated the former German East Africa to the British.

The settling by the various groups living in the city into distinctive areas was consolidated during the British period. Europeans lived in Oyster Bay to the north of the city centre, in large Mediterranean-style houses with arches, verandas and gardens surrounded by solid security walls and fences. The Asians lived either in tenement-style blocks in the city centre or in the Upanga area in between the city and Oyster Bay, where they built houses and bungalows with small gardens. African families built Swahili-style houses, initially in the Kariakoo area to the west of the city. Others were accommodated in government bachelor quarters provided for railway, post office and other government employees. As population increased, settlement spread out to Mikocheni and along Morogoro Road and to Mteni to the south.

Independence 1961-present

For the early years of independence Dar es Salaam managed to sustain its enviable reputation of being a gloriously located city with a fine harbour, generous parklands with tree-lined avenues (particularly in the Botanical Gardens and Gymkhana area), and a tidy central area of shops and services. New developments saw the construction of high-rise government buildings, most notably the Telecoms building on the present Samora Avenue, the New Africa Hotel, the massive cream and brown Standard Bank Building (now National Bank of Commerce) on the corner of Sokoine Drive and Maktaba Street, and the Kilimanjaro Hotel on a site next to the Dar es Salaam Club on Kivukoni Front.

But with the Arusha Declaration of 1967 (see page 421), many buildings were nationalized and somewhat haphazardly occupied. The new tenants of the houses, shops and commercial buildings were thus inclined to undertake minimal repairs and maintenance. In many cases it was unclear who actually owned the buildings. The city went into steady decline, and it is a testament to the sturdy construction of the buildings from the German period that so many of them survive. Roads fell into disrepair and the harbour became littered with rusting hulks.

The new government changed the names of streets and buildings, to reflect a change away from the colonial period. Thus Acacia became Independence Avenue, the Prince of Wales Hotel became the Splendid. Later names were chosen to pay tribute to African leaders – Independence Avenue changed to Samora, and Pugu Road became Nkrumah Street. President Nyerere decided that no streets or public buildings could be named after living Tanzanians, and so it was only after his death that City Drive was named after Prime Minister Edward Sokoine.

Old Dar es Salaam was saved by two factors. First, the economic decline that began in the 1970s (see page 425) meant that there were limited resources for building new modern blocks for which some of old colonial buildings would have had to make way. Second, the government decided in 1973 to move the capital to Dodoma. This didn't stop new government construction entirely, but it undoubtedly saved many historic buildings.

In the early 1980s, Dar es Salaam reached a low point, not dissimilar from the one reached almost exactly a century earlier with the death of Sultan Majid. In 1992 things began to improve. Colonial buildings have now been classified as of historical interest and are to be preserved. Japanese aid has allowed a comprehensive restoration of the road system. Several historic buildings, most notably the Old Boma on Sokoine Drive, the Ministry of Health building on Luthuli Road and the British Council headquarters on Samora Avenue, have been restored or are undergoing restoration. Civic pride is returning. The Askari Monument has been cleaned up and the flower beds replanted, the Cenotaph Plaza relaid, pavements and walkways repaired and the Botanical Gardens restored. Very usefully, new signposts are a feature throughout the city, which not only clearly show the street names but places of interest, hotels, and major institutions such as banks or embassies. The main road into Dar es Salaam – the 109 km branch road off the Arusha–Mbeya road that neatly dissects the middle of the country – was for years a ribbon of potholed and broken tar. But this too has been upgraded into super-smooth highway thanks to foreign aid.

24 hours in the city

Dar es Salaam isn't brimming with life in the small hours but it is possible to spend a varied and active 24 hours here.

Start with a morning walk around the old town before it gets too hot and wander around the faded colonial architecture through to the **Botanical Gardens** and the **National Museum**. A guided walk will take you a good couple of hours. For a light lunch, call in at **L'Epi d'Or** patisserie on Samora Avenue and treat yourself to a freshly made sandwich and the best coffee in town. Then jump on a *dala-dala* to the **Makumbusho Village Museum** for a glimpse of tribal Tanzania's way of life, and take in one of their colourful dance displays in the afternoon. Make sure you spare some time for nearby **Mwenge Craft Market**, and watch expert carvers create wooden carvings and handicrafts – the best place for souvenir shopping in the city. Then head back to **Msasani Peninsula** in time for a sundowner on the terrace overlooking the bay at the **Peninsula Seaview Hotel**.

Dinner time could take you to the newest restaurant on the block – the **Oriental** at the trendy Kilimanjaro Hotel Kempinski or if you want to make the most of the seafood here, try the **Oyster Bay Grill**. **Q Bar** is the place for live music most evenings, then round off the night at **Club Bilicanos**, a world class nightclub that will keep you dancing till dawn. Just as the sun's rising, take a cab to the colourful **fish market** off Ocean Road and watch it come alive with fishermen bringing in their catch and stall-holders setting up for another busy day. Finally, wander over to the **Kigamboni** ferry port and join the locals heading south on the ferry for a brief 10-minute journey, before taking a cab a couple of kilometres to **Mikadi Beach** for a refreshing dip in the ocean or a plunge in their pool, and recover with an all-day breakfast …

Sights

The best way to discover the heart of Dar es Salaam is on foot and we have suggested two half-day walks that take in most of the historic buildings. An alternative is to join a guided **walking tour** ① *2½ hr morning walks through the old town cost around US$35 adult, US$15 child depending on the tour operator, with discounts for groups, and including tastings of Swahili, Arab and Indian foods.* Ask the tourist office to recommend a tour operator.

Walking tour of the old town

A walking tour (about half a day) of the historic parts of old Dar es Salaam might start at the **Askari Monument** at the junction of Samora Avenue and Azikwe Street. Originally on this site was a statue to Major Hermann von Wissmann, the German explorer and soldier, who suppressed the coastal Arab Revolt of 1888-1889 (see page 104) and went on to become governor of German East Africa in 1895-1896. This first statue erected in 1911 depicted a pith-helmeted Wissmann, one hand on hip, the other on his sword, gazing out over the harbour with an African soldier at the base of the plinth draping a German flag over a reclining lion. It was demolished in 1916 when the British occupied Dar es Salaam, as were statues to Bismarck and Carl Peters. The present bronze statue, in memory of all those who died in the First World War, but principally dedicated to the African troops and porters, was unveiled in 1927. The statue was cast by Morris Bronze Founders of Westminster, London, and the sculptor was James Alexander Stevenson (1881-1937), who signed himself 'Myrander'. There are two bronze bas-reliefs on the sides of the plinth by the same sculptor, and the inscription, in English and Swahili, is from Rudyard Kipling.

Proceeding towards the harbour, on the left is the **New Africa Hotel** on the site where the old **Kaiserhof Hotel** stood. This was once the finest building in Dar es Salaam, the venue for the expat community to meet for sundowners. The terrace outside overlooked the Lutheran church and the harbour, while a band played in the inner courtyard. Across Sokoine Drive, on the left is the **Lutheran cathedral** with its distinctive red-tiled spire and tiled canopies over the windows to provide shade. Construction began in 1898. Opposite is the **Cenotaph**, again commemorating the 1914-1918 war, which was unveiled in 1927 and restored in 1992.

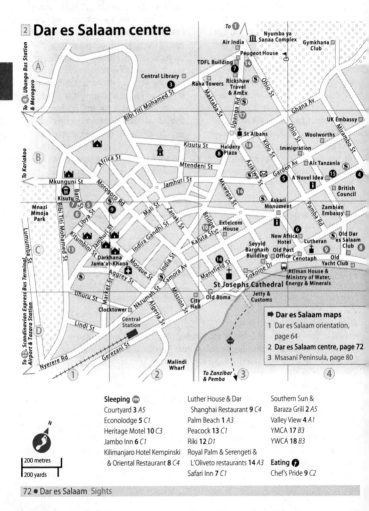

2 Dar es Salaam centre

➡ Dar es Salaam maps
1 Dar es Salaam orientation, page 64
2 Dar es Salaam centre, page 72
3 Msanani Peninsula, page 80

200 metres
200 yards

Sleeping
Courtyard 3 A5
Econolodge 5 C1
Heritage Motel 10 C3
Jambo Inn 6 C1
Kilimanjaro Hotel Kempinski
& Oriental Restaurant 8 C4

Luther House & Dar
Shanghai Restaurant 9 C4
Palm Beach 1 A3
Peacock 13 C1
Riki 12 D1
Royal Palm & Serengeti &
L'Oliveto restaurants 14 A3
Safari Inn 7 C1

Southern Sun &
Baraza Grill 2 A5
Valley View 4 A1
YMCA 17 B3
YWCA 18 B3

Eating
Chef's Pride 9 C2

Turning left along Kivukoni Front, there is a fine view through the palm trees across the harbour. Just past Ohio Street, on the shore side, is the **Old Yacht Club**. Prior to the removal of the club to its present site on the west side of Msasani Peninsula in 1967, small boats bobbing at anchor in the bay were a feature of the harbour. The Old Yacht Club buildings now house the harbour police headquarters.

Opposite the Old Yacht Club is the site of the German Club for civilians, which was expanded to form the Dar es Salaam (DSM) Club in the British period. It used to have a spacious terrace and a handsome bar. On the first floor are rooms that were used for accommodation, with verandas facing inward and outside stone staircases. Evelyn Waugh once stayed here. Today, after substantial renovation, this building is the smart new **Kilimanjaro Hotel Kempinski**, one of Dar's most luxurious hotels.

Further along Kivukoni Front is the first of an impressive series of German government buildings. The first two, one now the High Court, and the other the present Magistrates' Court on the corner of Luthuli Road, were for senior officials. In between is the old **Secretariat**, which housed the governor's offices. On the other corner of Luthuli Road is the German Officers' Mess, where some gambling evidently took place as it became known as the **Casino**. These buildings are exceptional, and it is a tribute to the high quality construction of the German period that they have survived, with virtually no maintenance for the past 30 years. Construction was completed in 1893. On the high ground further along Kivukoni Front is the site of the first European building in Dar, the **Berlin Mission**. It was built in 1887, extensively damaged in the 1888-1889 uprising and demolished in 1959 to make way for a hotel, which, in the event, was not constructed.

The eastern part of the city resembles an eagle's head (it is said the Msasani Peninsula is one of the eagle's wings). At the tip of the eagle's beak was a pier, just where the fish market (see page 77) stands today, constructed in the British period for the use of the governor. This was just a little further round the promontory from the present ramp for the ferry that goes over to Kigamboni. Past Magogoni Street is the **Swimming Club** (see page 93), constructed in the British period and now mostly used by the Asian community.

Following Ocean Road, on the left is the present **State House**, with a drive coming down to gates. This was the original German governor's residence. It had tall, Islamic-style arches on the ground floor rather similar to those in the building today, but the upper storey was a veranda with a parapet and the roof was supported on cast-iron columns. The building was bombarded by British warships in 1914 and extensively damaged. In 1922 it was rebuilt and the present scalloped upper-storey arches added, as well as the tower with the crenellated parapet.

The **German Hospital** is further along Ocean Road with its distinctive domed towers topped by a clusters of iron spikes. It is an uneasy mixture of the grand (the towers) and the utilitarian (the corrugated-iron roofing). It was completed in 1897 and was added to during the British period with single-storey, bungalow-style wards to the rear.

Turning left past the baobab tree down Chimera Road and taking the left fork, Luthuli Road leads to the junction with Samora Avenue. Here stood the statue of Bismarck, a replica of the celebrated Regas bust. The area either side of this boulevard, one of the glories of Dar es Salaam in the German era, was laid out as an extensive park. The flamboyant trees and *oreodoxa* (Royal Palms) still border it.

The first Director of Agriculture, Professor Stuhlmann, began laying out the **Botanical Gardens** in 1893. The building that houses the Agriculture Department as well as the Meteorological Station and the Government Geographer lies just to the southwest and was completed in 1903, by which time the gardens were well established, Stuhlmann using his position as Chief Secretary from 1900-1903 to channel resources to their development. The gardens became the home of the Dar es Salaam Horticultural Society, which still has a building on the site, and has undergone some rehabilitation with most of the exhibits labelled. Now, though, it's in need of some further care and attention, although it's a welcome escape from the city and the peacocks give it an air of exoticism. It is one of the few places in the world to see the coco-de-mer palm tree apart from the Seychelles.

To the left of the gardens is **Karimjee Hall**, built by the British and which served as the home of the Legislative Council prior to independence. It then became the home of the National Assembly, the Bunge. In the same area is the original **National Museum** (see page 76), a single-storey stone building with a red-tiled roof and arched windows constructed as the King George V Memorial Museum in 1940, changing its name in 1963. A larger, modern building was constructed later to house exhibits, and the old building was used as offices.

Turning left down Shaaban Robert Street, on the other side of Sokoine Drive, in a crescent behind the Speaker's Office is the first school built in Dar es Salaam (1899) by the German government. It was predominantly for Africans, but also had a few Indian pupils, all children of state-employed officials (*akidas*). Walking west down Sokoine Drive you return to the **New Africa Hotel**.

Walking tour of the City

A second half-day walking tour might begin at the **New Africa Hotel** and proceed west along Sokoine Street past the National Bank of Commerce building on the right. On the corner with Mkwepa Street is the German **Post Office** completed in 1893. Although the façade has been remodelled to give it a more modern appearance, the structure is basically unchanged. Just inside the entrance is a plaque to the memory of members of the Signals Corps who lost their lives in the First World War in East Africa. There are some 200 names listed with particularly heavy representation from South Africa and India whose loyalty to the British Empire drew them into the conflict.

On the opposite corner to the post office is the site of the old customs headquarters, the **Seyyid Barghash Building**, constructed around 1869. The building on the corner with Bridge Street is the modern multi-storey **Wizaraya Maji, Nishati na Madim** (Ministry of Water, Energy and Minerals), which is on the site of the old Customs House. Next door, sandwiched between the ministry building and Forodhani Secondary School, is the **White Fathers' House** – called **Atiman House**. It is named after a heroic and dedicated doctor, Adrian Atiman, who was redeemed from slavery in Niger by White Father missionaries, educated in North Africa and Europe, and who worked for decades as a doctor in Tanzania until his death, circa 1924. Atiman House was constructed in the 1860s in the Zanzibar period and is the oldest surviving house in the city, excluding administrative buildings. It was built as a residence for the Sultan of Zanzibar's Dar es Salaam wives, and sold by the Sultan to the White Fathers in 1922. In the visitors' parlour are two extremely interesting old photographs of the waterfront at Dar es Salaam as it was in German colonial times.

Continuing along Sokoine Drive to the west, the next building is **St Joseph's Roman Catholic Cathedral**. Construction began in 1897 and took five years to complete. St Joseph's remains one of the most striking buildings in Dar es Salaam, dominating the harbour front. It has an impressive vaulted interior, shingle spire and a fine arrangement of arches and gables. Next to the cathedral was Akida's Court.

On the corner of Morogoro Road is Dar's oldest surviving building, the **Old Boma** dating from 1867. It was built to accommodate the visitors of Sultan Majid and features a fine Zanzibar door and coral-rag walls. On the opposite corner is the **City Hall**, a very handsome building with an impressive façade and elaborate decoration.

On the corner of Uhuru Street is the **Railway Station**, a double-storey building with arches and a pitched-tile roof, the construction of which began in 1897. Between the station and the shore was the site of the palace of Sultan Majid and of the hospital for Africans constructed in 1895 by Sewa Haji, but which was demolished in 1959.

Turning right in front of the railway station leads to the **clock tower**, a post-war concrete construction erected to celebrate the elevation of Dar es Salaam to city status in 1961. A right turn at the clock tower leads along Samora Avenue and back to the Askari Monument.

There are other notable buildings in the City. On Mosque Street is the ornate **Darkhana Jama'at-Khana** of the Ismaili community, three storeys high with a six-storey tower on the corner topped by a clock, a pitched roof and a weathervane.

There are several other mosques, two (**Ibaddhi Mosque** and **Memon Mosque**) on Mosque Street itself (clearly signposted and stringed with coloured lights used for religious occasions), one on Kitumbini Street, one block to the southwest of Mosque Street, (a **Sunni mosque** with an impressive dome), and there are two mosques on Bibi Titi Mohamed Street, the **Ahmadiyya mosque** near the junction with Pugu Road and the other close by. On Kitsu Street, there are two Hindu temples, and on Upanga Road is a grand Ismaili building decorated with coloured lights during festivals.

St Alban's Church on the corner of Upanga Road and Maktaba Street was constructed in the interwar period. St Alban's is a grand building modelled on the Anglican church in Zanzibar. This is the Anglican Church of the Province of Tanzania, and was the Governor's church in colonial times. The **Greek Orthodox church**, further along Upanga Street, was constructed in the 1940s. **St Peter's Catholic Church**, off the Bagamoyo Road, was constructed in 1962, and is in modern style with delicate concrete columns and arches.

The Museum and House of Culture Dar es Salaam (formerly National Museum)

ⓘ *Shaaban Robert St next to the Botanical Gardens, between Sokoine Dr and Samora Av, T022-211 7508, www.houseofculture.or.tz. Daily 0930-1800. Entry US$5. Student US$2.*

The Museum opened in 1940 in the former King George V Memorial Museum building next to the Botanical Gardens. King George V's car can still be seen in the newer wing, which was built in front of the old museum in 1963. The museum is in a garden where a few peacocks stroll and where there is a sculpture in memory of victims of the 1989 American Embassy bombing. Created in 2004 by US artist Elyn Zimmerman, it comprises a group of six related geometric forms that surround a granite-rimmed pool. Their flatness and thinness, as well as their striking silhouettes and outlines, were inspired by shapes used in traditional African art, shields and other objects including Tanzanian stools, which Zimmerman said greatly influenced her work. Very interestingly, the very same artist designed the World Trade Centre Memorial in 1993, after a bomb set by terrorists exploded on the site of the World Trade Centre in New York. That sculpture was a cenotaph to an attack that predated both the 7 August 1998 bombings in Dar es Salaam and Nairobi, and the 11 September 2001 attacks in New York. Zimmerman's 1993 sculpture was destroyed in the 2001 attack at the World Trade centre.

The museum has excellent ethnographic, historical and archaeological collections. The old photographs are particularly interesting. Traditional craft items, headdresses, ornaments, musical instruments and witchcraft accoutrements are on display. Artefacts representing Tanzanian history date from the slave trade to the post-colonial period. Fossils from Olduvai Gorge kept there include those of Zinjanthropus – sometimes referred to as Zinj or 'nutcracker man' – the first of a new group of hominid remains collectively known as *Australopithecus boisei*, discovered by Mary Leakey. The coastal history is represented by glazed Chinese porcelain pottery and a range of copper coins from Kilwa. One of the more unusual exhibits is a bicycle in working order made entirely of wood. The museum also regularly stages exhibitions – see press for details.

West towards Kariakoo

The area to the northwest of India Street, on either side of Morogoro Road, was an Asian section of the city in the colonial period, and to a large extent still is. Buildings are typically several storeys high, the ground floor being given over to business with the upper storeys being used for residential accommodation. The façades are often ornate, with the name of the proprietor and the date of construction prominently displayed. Two superb examples on Morogoro Road, near Africa Street, are the premises of M Jessa. One was a cigarette and tobacco factory and the other a rice mill.

Further to the west is the open Mnazi Mmoja (coconut grove) with the **Uhuru Monument** dedicated to the freedom that came with independence, and celebrations take place here every year on 9 December to commemorate Independence Day. The original Uhuru monument is a white obelisk with a flame – the Freedom Torch. A second concrete monument, designed by R Ashdown, was erected to commemorate 10 years of independence. This was enlivened with panels by a local artist. On the far side of the space is **Kariakoo**, laid out in a grid pattern and predominantly an African area. It became known as Kariakoo during the latter part of the First World War when African porters (the carrier corps, from which the current name is derived) were billeted here after the British took over the city in 1916. The houses are Swahili style. The colourful **market** in the centre and the shark market on the junction of Msimbazi and Tandamuti streets are well worth a visit but watch out for pickpockets.

Casuarina cones

A particularly fine set of casuarina trees can be found along Ocean Road in Dar es Salaam. Strangely, they are also found in Australia. Quite unlike most other trees in East Africa, the theory is that the seed-bearing cones were carried by the cold tidal currents from the west coast of Australia into the equatorial waters flowing west across the Indian Ocean to the shore of Tanzania and then north along the East African coast in the Somalia current, eventually germinating after a journey of about 10,000 km.

Fish market and Banda Beach

At the point of the eagle's beak, where the ferry leaves for Kigamboni, is the **Integrated Fish Market Complex**. A fish market has been on this site since time immemorial, formerly part of an old fishing village called Mzizima, which was located between what is now State House and Ocean Road Hospital. The village met its demise when Seyyid Majid founded Dar es Salaam in 1862, although the fish market survived. In 2002, the Japanese government funded a substantial expansion programme and a new fish market was built. There are now zones for fish cleaning, fish frying, one for shellfish and vegetables, another for firewood and charcoal, an auction hall for wholesale vendors and buyers, and a maintenance area for the repair of boats, fishing nets and other tools of the trade. The complex is one of a kind and provides employment for 100 fishermen catering to thousands of daily shoppers. As you can imagine, this is an extremely smelly place. Fresh fish can be bought here and there is an astonishingly wide variety of seafood from blue fish, lobster, red snapper, to calamari and prawns. Be warned though, the vendors are quite aggressive and you'll need to haggle hard. You can also buy ice here to pack the fish.

Just north of the market is a stretch of sand known as **Banda Beach**, a well-known place for sittin' on the dock of the bay. Fishing boats, mostly lateen-sailed *ngalawas*, are beached on the shore.

Gymkhana Club

Further along Ocean Road, past State House and the hospital, are the grounds of the Gymkhana Club, which extend down to the shore. Amongst other sports practised here (see page 92) is golf, and there is an 18-hole course featuring what are called 'browns' as opposed to 'greens'. There were various cemeteries on the shore side of the golf course, a European cemetery between the hospital and Ghana Avenue, and a Hindu crematorium beyond.

Nyumba ya Sanaa Complex

① *Junction of Ohio St, Ali Mwinyi Rd and Bibi Titi Mohammed St, northwest of the Royal Palm Hotel, T022-213 1727. Open Mon-Fri 0800-2000, Sat-Sun 0800-1600.*

This art gallery has displays of paintings in various styles including oil, watercolour and chalk, as well as carvings and batiks. You can see the artists at work, and there is also a café on site. The centre was started by a nun and the present building was constructed with help from a Norwegian donation in the early 1980s. Traditional dances are held here on Friday evenings at 1930.

Tingatinga art

It is easy enough to recognize Tingatinga paintings for their powerful images and vivid colours. Canvasses are crowded with exaggerated figures of birds, fish and all manner of African creatures, with giant heads and eyes, that roam rainbow landscapes and brilliant seas. Detailed traditional village life or hospital and markets scenes take on an almost cartoon appearance. It's a style of pop art and is considered to be the only indigenous painted art of East Africa. The custom of painting on walls using natural pigments had been in existence in Africa for centuries, but it wasn't until the arrival of the Europeans that African painters were encouraged to produce canvasses.

Tingatinga art was created in the dusty back streets of Dar es Salaam by Edward Tingatinga in the late 1960s. Born in 1937 in the Tanga region of southern Tanzania, he went to Dar in 1959 in search of work. After attempting several jobs, he worked on building sites and began painting murals on the walls. He then progressed to boards and canvasses and used an enamel bicycle paint that is especially glossy. He sold his paintings underneath a baobab tree at the Morogoro Stores in Oyster Bay which attracted the rich Europeans. He took on several young apprentices and taught them his unique style. Tragically, in 1972, only four years into his discovery of art, he was shot dead by police who accidentally mistook his car for the getaway car in a local robbery. But his students continued to use the Tingatinga style and took on more apprentices. The Tingatinga Art Cooperative Society was established six years after his death, and is still going strong today in Oyster Bay. There are presently around 60-70 artists working here; most are illiterate and come from poor backgrounds, but have been accepted by the cooperative for their artistic skills. One of them is Daudi Tingatinga, Edward's son, who was only two when his father died. He continues to paint in memory of his father. In 1997, a Swedish customer introduced the art to a gallery in Stockholm and exhibitions appeared in other European cities. This instigated a TSh 60 million donation to build the gallery and workshop at Oyster Bay. After 25 years underneath a baobab tree, Tingatinga got its own home and Edward Tingatinga would no doubt have been impressed by the success of his legacy. Since then the art has also been exhibited in Japan where it has been reproduced on Japanese kimonos.

Further information

The Tingatinga Arts Cooperative is at the Morogoro Stores in Oyster Bay, off Haile Selassie Road, near Q Bar Guest House, T022-266 8075. There is a gallery of paintings for sale and more stalls outside on the street. Open daily 0900-1800.

Oyster Bay

At the intersection of Ocean Road and Ufukoni Road on the shore side is a rocky promontory which was the site of European residential dwellings constructed in the interwar period by the British. These are either side of Labon Drive (previously Seaview Road). Continuing along Ocean Road is Selander Bridge, a causeway over the Msimbazi Creek, a small river edged by marsh that circles back to the south behind the main part of the city. Beyond Selander Bridge, on the ocean side, is Oyster Bay, which became the main European residential area in the colonial era (Rita Hayworth had a house here), and today is the location of many diplomatic missions. There are many spacious dwellings, particularly along Kenyatta Drive, which looks across the bay. The area in front of the recently refurbished **Oysterbay Hotel** is a favourite place for parking and socializing in the evenings and at weekends, particularly by the Asian community. Ice cream sellers and barbecue kiosks have sprung up on the shore in the last few years.

Around Dar

Makumbusho Village Museum

① *Bagamoyo Rd, about 9 km from the city centre, on the right-hand side of the road just before the Peacock Hotel Millennium Towers, T022-270 0437, www.villagemuseum.home stead.com. Open daily 0930-1900, US$3, Tanzanians and children US$1, photos US$3, video cameras US$20. Taxis cost about US$10 from the city centre, or dala-dala from the New Post Office (Posta) heading towards Mwenge, which pass the entrance. Ask for Makumbusho bus stop or get off when you see the tall Millennium Towers Hotel and walk back a few metres.*
The museum gives a compact view of the main traditional dwelling styles of Tanzania, with examples of artists and craftsmen at work. There are constructions of tribal home-steads from 18 ethnic groups with examples of furnished dwelling huts, cattle pens, meeting huts and, in one case, an iron-smelting kiln. Traditional dances are performed daily from 1400 to 1800 with performers recruited from all over Tanzania. It's worthwhile having a guide to explain the origin of the dances, which end with a display of tumbling and acrobatics. There is a café, and an unusual compound, the Makumbusho Social Club, where the public is welcome. The small, corrugated-iron, partly open-sided huts are each named after one of Tanzania's game parks.

Kigamboni

The beaches on Kigamboni are the best close to the city and, like on the beaches to the north, the resorts here (see Sleeping page 85) are popular with day visitors especially at the weekends. The Kigamboni ferry (which takes cars) leaves from the harbour mouth close to the fish market, just before Kivukoni Front becomes Ocean Road, at regular intervals during the day. The ferry runs from 0600 to midnight and costs US$1 per vehicle and US$0.25 per person. Foot passengers can walk directly on to the ferry from the city side and at Kigamboni catch taxis and *dala-dala* that follow the beach road for several kilometres to where most of the more accessible resorts are. Hotels such as **Ras Kutani** and the **Amani Beach Hotel** are further down this road, around 30 km from the ferry, and you will need to contact these lodges to arrange transport if you are not driving yourself.

The small town of Kigamboni spreads up from where the ferry docks and is the site of Kivukoni College, which provided training for CCM party members (see page 422), but has now been turned into a school and a social science academy. Just before the college, which faces across the harbour to Kivukoni Front, is the Anglican church and a free-standing bell. The Anglican church was formerly a Lutheran church. The new Lutheran church, a fine modern building, lies 500 m into Kigamboni. On the Indian Ocean shore side there are several small enterprises making lime by burning cairns of coral.

Gezaulole

① *Part of the Cultural Tourism Programme operated from Arusha. Further details can be obtained from the Tanzanian tourist information centre in Arusha, T027-2503 8403, www.infojep.com/culturaltours. Brochures for each project can be downloaded from the website.*

3 Msasani Peninsula

➡ Dar es Salaam maps
1 Dar es Salaam orientation, page 64
2 Dar es Salaam centre, page 72
3 Msasani Peninsula, page 80

N

500 metres
500 yards

Msasani Bay

Yacht Club ☐

Masaki St

Halle-Selassie Rd

Toure Drive

Makunda St

Mwaya

Chole Rd

Msasani Slipway ☐

MSASANI PENINSULA

Chake Chake Rd

Chole Rd

Msasani Rd

Arcade Shopping Complex

Old Bagamoyo Rd

Kimweri Av

Shopper's Plaza

Tinga Tinga Arts Co-op & Morogoro Stores

Oyster Bay Shopping Centre

Ghuba Rd

Oyster Bay

REGENT ESTATE

Halle Selassie Rd

Guinea Rd

Uhuru St

US Embassy

Uganda Av

Albala Said

Karume Rd

Toure Drive

Bagamoyo Rd

Rashidi Trawawa Rd (Formerly Morocco Rd)

(Pol)

Catholic ✝

Bongoyo Rd

Little Theatre ☐

Mkwawa Rd

To Makumbusho Village Museum, Bagamoyo, Mwenge, North Coast Beaches, New World Cinema & Mlimani City

Baptist ✝
Lutheran ✝

KINONDONI

Tunisia Rd

Ali Hasan Mwimi Blvd

Kaunda Rd

Kenyatta Drive

Kinondoni Rd

Msimbazi Bay

HANNA NASIF

To Town Centre

Sleeping 🛏
Colosseum **2** D2
Coral Beach **5** A2
Golden Tulip **6** B3
Oyster Bay **3** C2
Peninsula Seaview **7** C2
Q Bar & Guest House **1** C2
Sea Cliff & Karambezi Restaurant **4** A3

Eating 🍴
Addis in Dar **1** D1
Azuma **2** B2
Coral Ridge Spur **7** A3
Fishmonger **7** A3
Hot (In Africa) **10** C2
Java Lounge **7** A3
L'Arca Di Noe' **12** D2
La Trattoria Jan **14** C2
L'Epi d'Or **7** A3
Mashua Grill **2** B2
Oyster Bay Grill **8** C2
Seacliff Village **7** A3
Shooter's Grill **3** D2
Sweet Eazy **8** C2
The Pub **2** B2
The Terrace **2** B2

The coastal village of Gezaulole lies 13 km or half an hour's drive southeast of the ferry at Kigamboni, reachable by *dala-dala*. This was chosen as one of the first Ujamaa villages, part of an ultimately unsuccessful settlement policy of the early 1970s, in which people from many areas of the country were relocated to form agricultural communes (see page 422). In earlier days it was a Zaramo settlement and they gave the village the name Gezaulole, which means 'Try and See' in the Kizaramo language. Today, the community has an active role in a cultural tourism programme that offers walks through the village and on the beach, short trips on a local dhow and visits to an old slave depot and a 400-year-old mosque. It is possible to stay with a local family, though it is easy enough to reach on a day trip. Inexpensive and tasty local meals are available and can be eaten with one of the families even if you are not staying for the night. Locally made handicrafts are also for sale. Profits from the programme go towards buying equipment for the local school.

Northern beaches

① *To get to either beach, a taxi from the city will cost in the region of US$15. To get to Kunduchi by public transport take a* dala-dala *from the New Post Office (Posta) in the city to Mwenge about 10 km along the Bagomoyo Rd, then change to one heading to Kunduchi (clearly signposted on the bonnet of the vehicle). Both rides will cost US$0.30. To get to Mbezi, take the same Kunduchi dala-dala from Mwenge, and at the sign for the White Sands Hotel on Bagamoyo Rd a couple of kilometres before the Kunduchi turn off, ask to get off (look out for the Kobil service station). At this junction you can catch a bicycle taxi for US$0.70 or a tuk-tuk for US$2, the couple of kilometres to the hotels. Do not walk along this road, as there have been muggings.*

The shore close to Dar es Salaam is not particularly good for swimming. The best beaches are at **Kunduchi**, some 25 km north of the city, and **Mbezi Beach,** 20 km north of the city. These beaches are separated by a lagoon but both are accessed along side roads off the Bagamoyo Road and are easily reached by good tarmac roads. Most of the hotels and resorts along this coast (see page 86) welcome day visitors who want to enjoy the facilities and beaches, including **Silver Sands Hotel, Kunduchi Beach Hotel, Bahari Beach Hotel, Jangwani Sea Breeze Resort** and the **White Sands Hotel**. Some charge a fee of US$5-10 for the day, and it's worth paying to use the hotels' private (and guarded) beaches – the stretches of beach between the hotels should not be visited unaccompanied, people have been mugged here. Some also charge an extra fee if you bring your own food and drink. This is because many Indian families bring full-on picnics for a day at the beach and the hotel benefits little from selling food and drink. Most have restaurants and bars with bands playing at weekends and public holidays, and some offer a variety of excursions to nearby islands and also windsurfing. Snorkelling is a bit hit and miss because the water is not always very clear, especially during the rainy seasons.

There is a good beach on the uninhabited **Bongoyo Island**, 2 km north of Msasani Peninsula. The island is a marine reserve popular for diving and snorkelling, and there are a few short walking trails, good beaches and simple seafood meals are available. A popular destination for a day trip from Dar es Salaam, boats take 30 minutes, cost US$14 return and leave from **The Slipway** on Msasani Peninsula at 0930,1130, 1330 and 1530, returning approximately one hour later. A similarly good beach can be found on **Mbudya Island**, 4 km north of Bongoyo Island, but there are no facilities here. Boat rides are available from **White Sands Hotel, Jangwani Sea Breeze Resort** and **Bahari Beach Hotel**.

Diving

On the mainland, local divers recommend the offshore islands around Dar es Salaam, though mainland reefs accessible from Tanga and Dar have been damaged through the illegal practice of dynamite fishing, which, through slack policing, is still a problem today. However, if you are not visiting Pemba or Zanzibar and need to get wet, there are a number of memorable dive sites around Dar worth a dip or two. Of particular note is Ferns Wall, which is on the seaward side of Fungu Yasin Reef, where you'll find large barrel sponges, gorgonian fans and 2-m long whip corals. Reef sharks are often spotted here. Because of its depth this site is for advanced divers only. Another favourite is Mwamba, a unique reef comprising large fields of pristine brain, rose and plate corals. Although slightly further out, Big T reef is a must dive for the experienced diver but only on a calm day. Latham Island, southwest of Dar, is an area surrounded by deep water where big game fish and elusive schools of hammerheads can be found. It can only be dived with a very experienced skipper who knows the area. ▸▸ *For further details, see Activities and tours, page 92.*

Kisarawe and Pugu Hills Forest Reserve

ⓘ *Follow the airport road to the south of the city. Buses to Kisarawe leave from Narungumbe St (next to the Tanzania Postal Bank on Msimbazi St in Kariakoo) about once an hour and cost US$2. To get to Pugu, turn left at the Agip petrol station in Kisarawe and the track into the reserve is a little further along on the right. It's 3 km from Kisarawe and if you're driving you'll need a 4WD.*

In the peaceful rural hill town of Kisarawe it is hard to believe that you are just 32 km southwest from the hustle and bustle of Dar es Salaam. During the colonial period Kisarawe was used by European residents of the capital as a kind of hill station to escape from the coastal heat. It receives a higher rainfall than Dar because of its slightly increased elevation. There is little to see in the town itself but the surrounding countryside is very attractive, in particular the nearby rainforest at Pugu Hills Forest Reserve about 3-4 km from the centre of Kisarawe town. It constitutes one of the few remaining parts of a coastal forest, which 10 million years ago extended from Mozambique to northern Kenya. It was gazetted as a reserve in 1954, at which time it stretched all the way to Dar's international airport and was home to many big game animals, including lions, hippos and elephants. Since then the natural growth of the metropolis, as well as the urban demand for charcoal (coupled with the lack of alternative sources of income), has seen a large reduction in the forested area. In the past few years a concerted effort has been made to counter this process and a nature trail has been established in order to encourage people to visit the area. Although Pugu contains flora and fauna which are unique to the forests of this district, you are unlikely to come across many animals in the forest; but it is a very beautiful spot and the perfect tonic for those in need of a break from Dar es Salaam. Most visitors spend the night in the new lodge here (**Pugu Hills**), though you can visit just for the day but still need to make a reservation for this with the lodge (see page 87).

Pugu Kaolin Mine and the Bat Caves

A further 3-4 km on from the Pugu Hills Reserve is Pugu Kaolin mine, which was established by the Germans in the early 1900s. Kaolin is a type of fine white clay that is used in the manufacture of porcelain, paper and textiles. The deposits here at Pugu are reputed to be the second largest in the world and should the market for it pick up, the mining of kaolin will clearly constitute a further threat to the survival of the remaining rainforest. If you continue through the mine compound you come to a disused railway tunnel, 100 m long and German built (the railway was re-routed after the discovery of kaolin). On the other side of this are a series of man-made caves housing a huge colony of bats. In the early evening at around 1800 or 1900 (depending on the time of year) the bats begin to fly out of the caves for feeding. It is a remarkable experience to stand in the mouth of the caves surrounded by the patter of wings as huge numbers of bats come streaming past you.

⊙ Dar es Salaam listings

For Sleeping and Eating price codes and other relevant information, see pages 36-40.

⊜ Sleeping

As far as top-grade accommodation is concerned, hotels in Dar es Salaam have improved in recent years and there is excellent international standard accommodation in the city centre, Msasani Peninsula and on the beaches to the north and south of the city. The lower end of the market is reasonable value, although it is always sensible to check the room and the bathroom facilities and enquire what is provided for breakfast. Also check on the security of any parked vehicle. Bear in mind that it is possible to negotiate lower rates, especially if you plan to stay a few days. Most upmarket hotels will ask visitors to pay in foreign currency – this really makes no difference but just check the rates in TSh and US$ against the current exchange rate, and make a fuss if you are charged more than the US$ equivalent of the TSh rate. Increasingly, more and more establishments are accepting credit cards, but this often incurs a commission of around 8-15%. In the middle and lower range it is usually possible to pay in TSh, and this is an advantage if money is changed at the favourable bureau rate. VAT at 20% was officially introduced in 1998 and is added to all service charges, though this is usually included in the bill.

Dar es Salaam *p66, maps p72 and p80*
The listings below are split between the city centre and the Msasani Peninsula. Msasani is the European side of town and is where most of the nice hotels can be found.

City centre

L-A Kilimanjaro Hotel Kempinski, Kivukoni Front, T022-213 1111, www.kempminski-dar essalaam.com. Occupying a commanding position in the centre of the city overlooking the harbour, this new hotel offers 5-star luxury with contemporary decor and excellent restaurants. A large 5-storey building enclosed in blue glass, it has 180 rooms with all the facilities you'd expect of a top class business hotel. Prices start at US$310 for a de luxe room. There's also a spa, a beautiful swimming pool on the 1st floor and a gym. The **Level 8** nightclub has live music and stunning views over the city. Despite all this, it's slightly lacking in character and service is efficient but impersonal.

A-B Southern Sun Hotel, Garden Av, T022-213 7575, www.southernsun.com. The former Holiday Inn, this is one of the nicest hotels in Dar town centre, conveniently located next to the Botanical Gardens (their peacocks regularly fly into the hotel's gardens) and close to the National Museum. 152 well-equipped rooms with Wi-Fi access, a business centre, gym, swimming pool and a popular restaurant and bar (see Eating, page 87). Recommended for its relaxing ambience and friendly and helpful staff.

B Royal Palm, Ohio St, T022-211 2416, www. moevenpick-daressalaam.com. Part of the Moevenpick chain, this hotel has conference and banqueting facilities, a shopping arcade and recreation centre, an outdoor swimming pool and lovely gardens. The 230 recently renovated rooms all have a/c and mod cons. The best rooms are at the rear. There's a British Airways office and several restaurants, a coffee shop and a bakery. Wi-Fi available.

B-C Peacock Hotel – Millenium Towers, 10 km north of the city on Ali Hassan Mwinyi Rd, (New Bagomoyo Rd), part of the Millennium Towers shopping centre, T022-277 3431, www.peacock-hotel.co.tz. In a glass tower block with ultra modern decor and facilities, all 60 rooms have a/c, satellite TV and internet access. The executive suites are twice the size of the standard rooms, and the junior suites have an extra spare bedroom, both for only US$20 more. Swimming pool, gym, 2 restaurants and bars. A smart business hotel near the **Makumbusho Village Museum** and **Mwenge Craft Market**.

C Heritage Motel, Kaluta/Bridge St, T022-211 7471, www.heritagemotel.co.tz. Easy to locate in the city centre, this new hotel in a tall, yellow building is conveniently located for the Zanzibar ferry terminal, and is excellent value for money. It has comfortable, spotless rooms (although single rooms are cramped). At the time of visiting, there was a noisy building site next door.

C Palm Beach, 305 Ali Hassan Mwinyi Rd, opposite the junction with Ocean Rd, T022-213 0985, www.pbhtz.com. Stylish art deco hotel, completely refurbished, a little away from the centre of town. Cool and modern decor, 32 rooms, Wi-Fi available, airy bar and restaurant. Popular beer garden with BBQ.

C Peacock Hotel, Bibi Titi Mohamed St, T022-212 0334, www.peacock-hotel.co.tz. Well run and centrally located modern hotel with 69 rooms, with a/c and TV, in a tower block. Great views of downtown Dar from the restaurant on the top floor, which serves good food with occasional theme nights. The unmistakable building was recently 'cocooned' in blue glass to make it cooler inside.

C Protea Hotel Courtyard, Ocean Rd, T022-213 0130, www.proteahotels.com/courtyard. A quality small hotel with good facilities, a bit more character than some of the larger hotels and with excellent food and service. Standard, superior and de luxe rooms, with a/c, TV and minibar. Wi-Fi, bar, restaurant and pool.

D Riki Hill Hotel, Kleist Sykes St, west of Mnazi Mmoja Park, T022-218 1820,

www.rikihotel.com. 40 rooms in a smart white block several storeys high, comfortable a/c rooms with bathrooms. Restaurant with very good à la carte food, bar and shops, 24-hr bureau de change. Will arrange a free pick up from the airport.

D Valley View Hotel, on the corner of Congo St and Matumba A St, T022-218 4556, www.valleyview-hotel.co.tz. A bit out of the way, off Morogoro Rd, a turning opposite United Nations Rd, about 1 km from the intersection with Bibi Titi Mohamed St. A friendly hotel in a neat white and stone building with 41 slightly dated rooms with a/c, TVs, fridge and 24 hr room service. Buffet breakfast.

D-E Luther House Hotel, on the corner of Sokoine Dr and Pamba Rd, T022-212 0734, luther@simbanet.com, behind the Lutheran church on the waterfront. Central and in considerable demand, so it's necessary to book. Simple freshly painted rooms with basic shower and toilet, TVs and a/c. The **Dar Shanghai** restaurant is on the ground floor (see Eating, page 88).

E Econolodge, corner of Libya St and Band St, T022-211 6048/50, econolodge@raha.com. A plain but functional place with sparsely furnished, clean self-contained rooms, the cheaper ones have fans, the more expensive have a/c. Small TV lounge. Price includes continental breakfast. Cheapest double US$21.

E Jambo Inn, Libya St, T022-211 4293, www.jamboinnhotel.com. Centrally located reasonable budget option popular with backpackers. With reliable hot water and working fans, the 28 rooms are self-contained. Rates are as low as US$20 for a double and for a little more you can get a/c. The affordable restaurant serves Indian food (no booze), fresh juice and ice cream; if you are staying in the hotel you get 10% off meals. Internet café downstairs.

E Safari Inn, Band St, T022-211 9104, safari-inn@lycos.com. Very central, similar to the nearby **Jambo Inn**, fairly simple but sound. 40 rooms, only 3 with a/c, in a square concrete block down an alleyway (there are security guards are at the entrance). Continental

breakfast is included but there's no restaurant. Doubles are US$20 and a single is US$15.
E-F YWCA, corner of Azikiwe St and Ghana Av, T022-213 5457, ywca.tanzania@africa online.co.tz, and the **YMCA**, T022-212 1196, are 1 block apart across Maktaba St. (The YWCA is above the Tanzania Post Bank on Azikiwe St). Both offer simple, clean and cheap accommodation with mosquito nets and fans. Men and women are accepted in both establishments.

Msasani Peninsula
L Oyster Bay Hotel, Toure Dr, T022-260 0530, www.theoysterbayhotel.com. This beautifully chic boutique hotel has recently opened, with 8 stylish bedrooms facing the Indian Ocean. Its British owners also own **Beho Beho** in Selous and place the same emphasis on luxury and relaxation. There's a quiet lawned garden with swimming pool and outdoor eating terrace and the interior is furnished with a mix of contemporary and antique African crafts. Rates are from US$300 per person full board.
L-B Hotel Sea Cliff, northern end of the peninsula, Toure Dr, T022-260 03807, www.hotelseacliff.com. Stylish hotel with whitewashed walls and thatched makuti roofing set in manicured grounds. 94 spacious and modern a/c rooms, most with ocean view, and 20 more units in garden cottages, all with satellite TV. **Coral Cliff** and **Ngalawa** bars, **Calabash Restaurant**, and the beautifully positioned **Karambezi** café bar over the bay. Also has a health club, gift shop, casino, bowling alley and shopping centre. One of the most luxurious hotels in Dar.
B Coral Beach Hotel, Coral La, T022-260 1928, www.coralbeach-tz.com. A new wing to this hotel opened in Jan 2009, with smart, boutique style rooms, far nicer than those in the old wing. The lobby is bright and breezy; a restaurant and bar overlook the pool set in slightly unkempt gardens, and there's a business centre, gym, sauna and jacuzzi.
B-C Colosseum Hotel, Haille Selassie Rd, T022-266 6655, www.colosseumtz.com.

42 rooms with a/c, plasma TVs and internet. Guests have free use of the sports facilities, which include a 20 m pool, a gym on 2 floors and 2 squash courts, and can then visit the exotic Cleopatra Spa to help soothe away the aches and pains afterwards. There's a pizzeria and a continental restaurant.
B-C Golden Tulip, Toure Dr, T022-260 0288, www.goldentulipdaressalaam.com. The best thing about this hotel is the huge infinity pool that faces the ocean, set in lovely gardens, which non-residents can use for US$7. The **Maasai Grill** serves good brunches at weekends. The hotel itself looks quite smart from the lobby, but the rooms are tired and shabby. All 91 rooms have TV, a/c and minibar. The Presidential Suite has an exercise bike.
C-D Peninsula Seaview Hotel, Chuibay Rd, T0787-330888 (mob), www.peninsulasea viewhotel.com. 12 modern en suite bedrooms with TV, Wi-Fi, fridge and fans (no mosquito nets). Food is available at **O'Willie's Irish Whiskey Tavern** on the ground floor with a restaurant terrace outside near the beach, although a sign warns not to walk on the shore without an *askari* (guard).
D-E Q Bar and Guest House, off Haile Selassie Rd, behind the Morogoro Stores, T0754-282474 (mob), www.qbardar.com. 20 comfortable, if a little noisy, rooms in a smart 4 storey block. All have a/c, fridge, bathroom, cool tiled floors and Tingatinga paintings on the walls. Also offer 6 dorm beds for US$12 each. A friendly and popular expat venue with live music and DJs. The bar and restaurant has 3 pool tables, a big screen for watching sport, and plenty of draught beer and cocktails (see Eating, page 89). Separate dining room for guests on the 2nd floor, breakfast included.

Around Dar *p79*
Southern beaches
L Amani Beach Hotel, 30 km south from the Kigamboni ferry, or air transfers can be arranged from Dar by the resort, T0754-410033 (mob), www.amanibeach.com for online information and reservations.

Quality hotel, with a/c, en suite rooms in 10 individual whitewashed cottages decorated with African art, and with garden terraces and hammocks where breakfast is delivered. Swimming pool, tennis courts, horse riding, restaurant, bar, conference facilities and TVs. Set in 30 ha of tropical woodland around a wide bay. Rates are from US$250 per person full board.

L Ras Kutani, T022-213 4802, www.ras kutani.com. 28 km further south of Kigamboni ferry, 2-hr road journey or a short charter flight from Dar es Salaam arranged by the resort. This resort is small and intimate with only 9 luxurious cottages, 4 suites and a family house beautifully decorated, in a superb location on a hill overlooking the ocean and the wide arch of white sandy isolated beach and freshwater lagoon. Windsurfing, swimming pool, watersports and snorkelling available but no diving. All rates are full board and are about US$400 per person, resident rates are considerably lower with specials on weekdays.

D South Beach Resort, 8 km south of the Kigamboni ferry, Mjimwema,T022-282 0666, www.southbeachresort-tz.com. A brash new resort with a large swimming pool and jacuzzi set in a huge paved area with an outdoor disco, pool tables, shisha lounge and **Whisky Shack** bar. 36 en suite rooms in a characterless block overlooking the pool. The camping ground is shadeless and a long walk from facilities. Day passes are available – Mon-Fri US$4, Sat-Sun US$6, with fines if you bring in your own food or fail to wear your wristband 'tag' which proves payment.

D Sunrise Beach Resort, Kipepeo Beach near Mjimwema, 7 km south of Kigamboni ferry, T022-550 7038, www.sunrisebeachresort. co.tz. Characterless 2-storey bandas with balconies and bathrooms, thatched restaurant and bar, Wi-Fi zones, sun loungers on the beach, watersports including jet skiing, quad bikes available for hire. Far better option for camping than the neighbouring **South Beach Resort**, tents are available for US$15 with decent ablutions blocks nearby.

D-F Kipepeo, Kipepeo Beach next to the **Sunrise Beach Resort** (above), near the village of Mjimwema, 7 km south of the Kigamboni ferry, T 0754-276178 (mob), www.kipepeovillage.com. 20 rustic beach huts built on stilts in a grove of coconut palms with en suite bathrooms. Plenty of space for vehicles and camping (separate hot showers). Overlanders can leave vehicles for a small daily fee while they go to Zanzibar. Very good food and drinks are served on the beach or at the beach bar. A relaxed and affordable option close to the city. Camping US$ 5 per person, basic beach bandas US$25, huts from US$65 including full English breakfast. Recommended.

F Mikadi Beach, 2 km from the Kigamboni ferry, T0754-370269 (mob), www.mikadi beach.com. Recently upgraded by new management, this popular campsite in a grove of coconut palms is right on the beach. Secure parking, clean ablutions, 12 simple double bandas, a swimming pool and a very good bar that gets busy at the weekends. Day rates US$4. For a small fee you can park vehicles here whilst you visit Zanzibar.

Northern beaches

Note It is unsafe to walk along the beach between the northern hotels. The hotels' private beaches are watched by security guards and at the end of the beaches are signs warning about the danger of mugging – take heed.

B-C Kunduchi Resort, Kunduchi, T0748-612231 (mob), www.kunduchiresort.com. Very elegantly decorated modern rooms with a/c, TV and minibar, a mixture of African and Islamic-style architecture and decor for main service areas. Bar, pool bar, excellent restaurants serving continental, seafood and Japanese food, swimming pool, tennis and squash courts, gym, beach with palms and flowers, live music at weekends, watersports facilities and trips to off-shore islands. The **Wet n Wild Water Park** is just next door.

B-C White Sands, Mbezi Beach, T022-264 7620/6, www.hotelwhitesands.com.

Offers 88 sea-facing rooms in thatched villas with TVs, a/c and minibar, and 28 apartments for short and long term lets. Swimming pool, gym, beauty centre and watersports including a PADI dive centre. Several restaurants, one off which (Indian) is superb, and bars. **Water World Waterpark** is adjacent to the hotel. Free shuttle service into the city.

C Beachcomber Hotel, Mbezi Beach, T022-264 7772/4, www.beachcomber.co.tz. Rather concrety development, a/c rooms with TV, minibar and phone. Swahili decor, health club with sauna, steambath and massage, watersports facilities and swimming pool. Offer a free shuttle between the hotel and the airport.

D Jangwani Sea Breeze Resort, Mbezi Beach, T022-264 7215, www.jangwani.org. 34 a/c rooms with flatscreen TVs and en suite bathrooms. Swimming pool set in pretty gardens with lots of flowering shrubs, right on the beach. 2 other pools (1 just for toddlers), watersports, gym, go-karting, 3 restaurants, pool bar, barbecues and live music at the weekends. Can organize excursions, free shuttle to town centre.

D-E Bahari Beach, Kunduchi, T022-265 0352, www.twiga.ch/tz/bahari.htm. With renovations planned at the time of writing, this hotel has self-contained accommodation in thatched rondavaals with a/c and TV. There's a large bar and restaurant area under the high thatched roofing (limited menu but good food). Swimming pool with bar, band at the weekends and public holidays, traditional dancing Wed night, sandy beach, garden surroundings, gift shop, tour agency and watersports centre. Reports welcome.

E-F Silver Sands, Kunduchi, T022-265 0567, www.silversands.netfirms.com. Pleasant old hotel with restaurant, bar and basic accommodation, some rooms have fans and are cheaper than those with a/c. The weekends attract a number of day visitors when a band plays on the terrace. The food is good and not badly priced. There is also a campsite with a well-maintained ablutions block and it is possible to pitch your tent

right on the beach. You can leave a vehicle here while you make a trip to Zanzibar.

Kisarawe and Pugu Hills Forest Reserve p82

D-F Pugu Hills, Pugu Hills Forest Reserve, 35 km south of Dar, T0754-56 5498 (mob), www.puguhills.com. 4 smart bamboo huts erected above the forest floor on poles, with hardwood floors and Swahili furnishings. Swimming pool, fabulously rustic restaurant offering snacks and 4 dishes a day including one vegetarian dish, and lovely nature trails through the forest (non-residents have to pay a US$30 fee for hiking in the reserve). The resort can also arrange visits to a local cattle market. Camping available, US$7 per person.

🍽 Eating

Most of the hotels, including those on the beach out of town, have restaurants and bars. While the city centre has a fair number of good places to eat, many of these are only open during the day, cater for office workers and do not serve alcohol. The best places for dinner and evening drinks are out of the centre on the Msasani Peninsula.

Dar es Salaam p66, maps p72 and p80
City centre
🍴 **Baraza Bar & Grill**, Southern Sun Hotel, see Sleeping, above. A deservedly popular restaurant serving a mix of Swahili and continental food, including pastas, curries, grills, seafood and vegetarian dishes. Outdoor terrace onto pool area and a relaxed bar.
🍴 **Istana**, Ali Hassan Mwinyi Rd, opposite Caltex petrol station, a few kilometres out of the city on the Bagamoyo Rd, T022-276 1348. Specializes in Malaysian cuisine. Theme nights throughout the week, Chinese on Tue, meat grill on Wed, satay buffet on Thu, etc. Specialities include *roti canai*, puffed bread filled with meat, chicken and apples and served with hot curries. Good value all you can eat buffets. Open kitchen, tables in

the garden, play area with staff to look after children.

¶¶¶ Oriental, Kilimanjaro Hotel Kempinski, see Sleeping, above. Open Tue-Sun. Smart, 1st floor restaurant serving a varied Southeast Asian menu with an excellent wine list and impeccable service. Bookings advised.

¶¶¶ Sawasdee, top floor of **New Africa Hotel**, Azikwe St, T022-211 7050. Exceptionally good and very authentic Thai food, wonderful harbour views, buffet on Tue and Fri.

¶¶¶ Serengeti and **L'Oliveto**, Royal Palm Hotel, see Sleeping, above. **Serengeti** open daily, **L'Oliveto** open Mon-Sat. Upmarket Italian restaurants, reservations recommended and you need to dress up. At the Serengeti there are themed nights every day of the week: Mediterranean on Mon, Italian on Tue, Oriental on Wed, seafood on Thu, popular fondue night on Fri, Tex-Mex on Sat and Indian on Sun. Serve good value buffet lunches with freshly made pasta or salads.

¶¶ Chef's Pride Restaurant, virtually opposite Jambo Inn Hotel, on road between Libya St and Jamhuri St. Closed evenings. Good food at excellent prices, fast service. Italian, Chinese, Indian and local dishes available.

¶¶ Mediterraneo, Kawe Beach off Old Bagomoyo Rd, midway between the city and the northern beaches, T022-261 8359. Italian pastas, salads and Chinese, occasional live music and Swahili-style buffets. On Sat afternoon there is a barbecue from 1200-2000. Overlooks the ocean, a good place for kids.

¶¶ Sichuan Restaurant, Bibi Titi Mohamed St, T022-215 0548. Excellent and authentic Chinese restaurant. Most main course dishes are around US$5, and there is a large range to choose from. Plenty of vegetarian options.

¶ Chinese Restaurant, basement of NIC, Samora Av. Good, inexpensive Chinese cuisine, also African and some continental dishes. Has been going some 30 years.

¶ City Garden Restaurant, corner of Garden Av and Pamba St, T022-213 4211. African, Indian and Western meals, buffets at lunchtime, excellent juices, tables are set in garden, good service and consistently popular,

especially at lunchtime. A new branch has opened on Bridge St. Highly recommended.

¶ Cynics' Café and Wine Bar, in the TDFL building opposite the **Royal Palm Hotel**. Open Mon-Thu until 1800, Fri until 2100. Fresh pastries, salads, sandwiches, wine by the glass, beer and coffee.

¶ Dar Shanghai, behind the Swiss Air office in Luther House Hotel, Sokoine Dr, T022-213 4397. Chinese and Tanzanian menus, canteen-style atmosphere. The food's not brilliant but it's quick and filling. No booze but soft drinks.

¶ Debonair's and **Steer's**, corner of Ohio St and Samora Av, T022-212 2855. Quality South African chains. **Debonair's** serves pizza and salads, while **Steer's** offers burgers, ribs and chips. Also in the Steer's Complex is **Hurry Curry**, an Indian takeaway, **Chop Chop**, **Chinese**, and a coffee shop. Eat at plastic tables in a/c surroundings.

¶ Garden Food Court, on the 2nd floor of the Haidery Plaza, Kisutu St. Daily 1100-2300. Here you'll find the **Red Onion**, a fairly formal Indian and Pakistani restaurant serving good value lunchtime buffets for US$8; **Natasha Spiced Chicken** for barbecued fast food; and the **Coffee Bud** for snacks and drinks. Food can be taken out of each restaurant and eaten on the outside terrace.

¶ Jambo Inn, Libya St, T022-211 0711. Excellent cheap Indian menu, huge inflated chapattis like air-cushions, also Chinese and European dishes. Outside and inside dining .

Ice cream parlours ¶ Sno-cream, Mansfield St. An old-fashioned ice cream parlour serving excellent ice cream. Incredibly elaborate sundaes with all the trimmings.

Msasani Peninsula

¶¶¶ Addis in Dar, 35 Ursino St, off Migombani St/Old Bagomoyo Rd in the Oyster Bay area, near the site of the new US Embassy, T0713-266299 (mob). Open Mon-Sat 1200-1430, 1800-2300. Small and charming Ethiopian restaurant with an outside terrace. Plenty of choice for vegetarians. It is wise to drop in and book ahead.

¶¶¶ **Azuma**, 1st floor at **The Slipway**, T022-260 0893. Open Tue-Fri for dinner, Sat-Sun for lunch and dinner. Japanese and Indonesian restaurant, authentic cuisine with good views over the bay. Very good sushi. If you book ahead, the chef will come out from the kitchen and prepare food at your table.

¶¶¶ **Fishmonger**, upstairs, Sea Cliff Village Food Court, T0754-30 4733 (mob). Excellent fish and seafood from US$12-20, nice outdoor terrace. Non-fishy options are limited.

¶¶¶ **Hot (in Africa)**, off Haile Selassie Rd, T0784-839607 (mob). Afro-European food, some of the most inventive cuisine in Dar, traditional roast lunches on a Sun, very trendy decor and a good atmosphere.

¶¶¶ **Karambezi**, Hotel Sea Cliff, see Sleeping, above, T0787-044555 (mob). Beautiful setting on wooden decking overlooking the ocean. Good selection of wines and a varied menu with pizzas, pastas, seafood and grills. Treat yourself to the seafood platter for 2, for US$46.

¶¶¶ **Oyster Bay Grill**, Oyster Bay Shopping Centre, T022-260 0133. Daily 1800-2300. Very elegant and some of the best food in Dar, specializing in steak, seafood and fondue. Average price with wine US$30 per head, much more if you go for the lobster thermidor. Huge range of international wines, whisky and cigar bar, jazz music, outside terrace and more formal fancy tables inside. Accepts credit cards.

¶¶ **Coral Ridge Spur**, Sea Cliff Village Food Court, T0752-201745 (mob). South African steak and ribs chain, geared up for families with a play area, Wild West themed decor, big portions and help-yourself salad bar. The meat is good but if you have eaten at a **Spur** elsewhere in Africa there are no surprises.

¶¶ **L'Arca di Noe'**, Kimweri Av, T0713-601 282 (mob). Open Wed-Mon. Italian pastas, seafood, pizzas from US$5, range of desserts, wide selection of wines, pleasant atmosphere. Wed night is an all you can eat buffet with 26 different pastas and sauces, and on Thu you get a free glass of wine with every pizza.

¶¶ **La Trattoria Jan**, Kimweri Av, T0754-282969 (mob). Excellent Italian cuisine, ice creams, open air seating at the rear, pleasant atmosphere and good value. The pizzas are some of the best in town, takeaway available.

¶¶ **Mashua Bar and Grill**, at The Slipway, T022-260 0893. Open evenings only. Grills, burgers, salads and pizza. Offers ocean views and live music and dancing on Thu.

¶¶ **Q Bar and Guest House**, see Sleeping, above. Open daily 1700 until late, happy hour 1700-1900. The bar has 3 pool tables, a big screen for watching sport, pub grub and plenty of draft beer and cocktails. Live music on Fri and Sat is 1970s soul night.

¶¶ **Shooter's Grill**, 86 Kimweri Av, Namanga, T0754-304733 (mob). Very good steaks, ladies get a free glass of wine on Wed and men get a free beer with every T-bone steak sold on a Thu. Live music on Sun, good atmosphere.

¶¶ **Sweet Eazy**, Oyster Bay Shopping Centre, Toure Dr, T0755-754074 (mob). Open daily until midnight, happy hour 1700-1900 and all night on Fri. Cocktail bar and restaurant, African and Thai cuisine. Jazz band on Sat.

¶¶ **The Pub**, at **The Slipway**, T022-260 0893. International food, mainly French and Italian in an English-style pub setting, also serves burgers, sandwiches and grills, draft beer and there are good Sun roast lunch specials.

¶¶ **The Terrace**, at **The Slipway**, T022-260 0893. Open Mon-Sat. Italian cuisine and barbecued grills and seafood. Moorish painted arches and outside dining area.

¶ **Java Lounge**, Sea Cliff Village Food Court, T0748-467149 (mob). Very good service, outdoor deck, range of cocktails and 20 different coffees. Good breakfasts, light meals.

¶ **L'Epi d'Or**, Samora Av and Sea Cliff Village, T022-213 6006. Mon-Sat 0700-1900. Coffee shop and bakery serving very good sandwiches with imaginative fillings, cappuccino and fresh juice, croissants, pastries and salads.

Around Dar p79
Southern beaches

¶ **Mikadi Beach**, see Sleeping, above. A great spot on the beach for weekend lunch or all-day breakfasts if you want to escape the city. Speciality alcoholic slushies and a varied menu including fish and chips, home-made burgers, steak sandwiches, vegetarian crêpes and a seafood platter. Day rate of US$4 covers use of the swimming pool next to the shore.

🎵 Bars and clubs

Dar es Salaam *p66, maps p72 and p80*
There are few nightclubs as such in Dar, though many of the hotels and restaurants mentioned above crank it up late in the evening with live music or a DJ, especially at weekends when tables are cleared away for dancing. Some discos are in attractive outdoor settings. Those hotels and restaurants that have regular discos and/or live music are notably **Jangwani Sea Breeze Resort**, and **White Sands Hotel** on the northern beaches; **South Beach Resort** on the southern beaches; **O'Willie's Irish Whisky Tavern** at the Peninsula Sea View Hotel; and the **Q bar** on the Msasani Peninsula. In the city centre, **Level 8** cocktail bar on the 8th floor of the Kilimanjaro Hotel Kempinski, Kivukoni, T022-213 1111, provides mesmerizing views of downtown Dar at night and occasional live jazz **Club Bilicanas**, Mkwepu St, T 0788-904169 (mob). Open every night until around 0400. Entry at weekends is US$23 per person (half of this is redeemable against food and drink). Reopened in Jan 2009 after an extensive 2 year renovation programme, this is far and away the most popular club in Dar. It has been imaginatively designed, with a VIP lounge, 7 bars and glass decor, and has all the effects you'd expect from a world-class night club. Drink prices are reasonable and the place is fully a/c.

🎭 Entertainment

Dar es Salaam *p66, maps p72 and p80*
Casinos
Las Vegas Casino, corner of Upanga Rd and Ufukoni Rd, T022-211 6512. Roulette, poker, blackjack, vingt-et-un and slot machines.

There are also casinos at the **Kilimanjaro Hotel Kempinski**, T022-213 1111 (open until 0400) and **Hotel Sea Cliff**, T022-260 0380.

Cinema
Visitors seldom go to the cinema, which is a pity as the audience reaction makes for an exciting experience. Programmes are in the newspapers or monthly guides such as *Dar Life* and *Dar es Salaam Guide*. The cinemas show mostly Indian, martial arts or adventure films. Entrance is about US$4.
British Council, Ohio St, T022-211 6574. Shows films fairly regular film on a Wed.
Century Cinemax, in the Mlimani City Shopping Mall near the university, T022-277 3053. New complex, discounts on Thu.
New World Cinemas, New Bagamoyo Rd, T022-277 1409. Discounts on Tue.

Live music
Concerts of classical music by touring artists are presented by the **British Council**, the **Alliance Française** and occasionally other embassies. African bands and artists and Indian groups play regularly at the hotels and restaurants especially at weekends. Look for announcements in the *Dar es Salaam Guide*, and *What's Happening in Dar es Salaam*.

Theatre
British Council, Ohio St. Occasionally presents productions, check the papers.
Little Theatre, Haile Selassie Rd, off Ali Hassan Mwinyi Rd, next door to the Protea Apartments, T0784-277388 (mob), daressalaamplayers@raha.com. Presents productions on an occasional basis, perhaps half a dozen a year, usually drama and comedy and 1 musical a year. Very popular, particularly the Christmas pantomime.

🛍 Shopping

Dar es Salaam *p66, maps p72 and p80*
There are shops along Samora Av (electrical goods, clothing, footwear) and on Libya St

(clothing and footwear). Supermarkets, with a wide variety of imported foods and wines, are on Samora Av between Pamba Av and Azikawe St; on the corner of Kaluta St and Bridge St; opposite Woolworth's on Garden Av; in Shopper's Plaza; and in the Oyster Bay Hotel Shopping Mall. The new Mlimani City Shopping Mall, Sam Nujoma Rd near Dar University is also home to a huge **Shoprite** supermarket. A popular location for buying fruit and vegetables is the market on Kinondoni Rd, just north of Msimbuzi Creek.

The Namanga shops are at the corner of Old and New Bagamoyo Rd, and are basically stalls selling household supplies and food; there's a good butcher's towards the back. **Manzese Mitumba Stalls**, Morogoro Rd, Manzese, has great bargains for second-hand clothing and Uhuru St has several *kanga* shops (the traditional wrap-arounds worn by women) usually for little more than US$3. **Ilala Market**, on Uhuru St, sells vegetables, fresh and dried fish and second-hand clothing. Fresh fish and seafood can be bought at the **Fish Market** on Ocean Rd, just past the Kigamboni ferry.

Shopping centres and department stores

Haidery Plaza, at the corner of Upanga Rd and Kisutu St in the city centre. A small shopping centre that as well as shops has an internet café and a popular food court.
Mayfair Plaza, opposite TMJ Hospital, Old Bagomoyo Rd, Oyster Bay, www.mayfairplaza.co.za. This centre has a number of quality shops, including upmarket clothes and shoe shops, jewellers, dry cleaners, banks, pharmacies and a branch of **Shoprite**, plus coffee shops and a food court.
Mlimani City Shopping Mall, San Nujoma Rd, near the university. Dar's latest shopping centre with a huge cinema complex, one of the biggest **Shoprite** supermarkets in Tanzania, and a plethora of smaller shops covering everything from clothes to electronics.
Oyster Bay Hotel Shopping Centre, see Sleeping, page 85. Supermarket, internet

café, and gift and art shops. There are plans to renovate this centre.
Sea Cliff Village, Hotel Sea Cliff, see Sleeping, page 85. Has a branch of the excellent bookshop **A Novel Idea** (see below), a French bakery, and a good shop upstairs called **Mswumbi** that sells fresh coffee beans. There are 'day rooms' for rent here – bedrooms that are only let out during the day for people who have returned to Dar from safari and are not flying out until the evening (contact the hotel). There's also a vastly overpriced supermarket catering for expats.
Shoppers' Plaza, Old Bagomoyo Rd, on the Msasani Peninsula. Has a good variety of shops, including a large supermarket. The Arcade nearby, has a travel agency, boutiques, hairdresser, nail technician, glass and framing shop, and restaurants.
The Slipway complex, on the Msasani Peninsula, facing Msasani Bay. Expensive, high quality goods can be found here. Another branch of **Shoprite**, an internet café, a craft market, a hair and beauty salon, several restaurants and a branch of Barclay's Bank with an ATM. There are also a few 'day rooms'. To book these contact Coastal Air, T022-260 0893, www.slipway.net.
Woolworths, in the New PPF Towers building on Ohio St. The only department store in Dar, this is a South African clothing store very similar to the UK's Marks & Spencer.

Bookshops

Second-hand books can be found at the stalls on Samora Av, on Pamba St (off Samora), on Maktaba St and outside Tancot House, opposite Luther House. Most of these also sell international news magazines such as *Time, Newsweek, New African*, etc.
A Novel Idea, branches at **The Slipway**, Msasani Peninsula, at the **Hotel Sea Cliff**, and on the corner of Ohio St and Samora Av, T022-260 1088, www.anovelidea-africa.com. The best bookshop in Dar by far, this is perhaps the most comprehensive bookshop in East Africa with a full range of new novels, coffee table books, maps and guide books.

Other bookshops are the **Tanzanian Bookshop**, Indira Gandhi St, leading from the Askari Monument; and **Tanzania Publishing House**, Samora Av. Both have only limited selections.

Curios and crafts

Traditional crafts, particularly wooden carvings, are sold along Samora Av to the south of the Askari Monument. Good value crafts can be purchased from stalls along Ali Hassan Mwinyi Rd near the intersection with Haile Selassie Rd and, in particular, at **Mwenge**, along Sam Njoma Rd, close to the intersection with Ali Hassan Mwinyi Rd. This is the best place for handicrafts in Dar, and for ethnographia from all over Tanzania and further afield (notably the Congo). There are a large number of shops and stalls offering goods at very reasonable prices and you can watch the carvers at work. The market is 10 km or about 30 mins from the town centre towards the northern beaches, easily reached by *dala-dala*. It is just around the corner from the *dala-dala* stand.

More expensive, quality modern wood products can be obtained from **Domus**, in The Slipway complex, which also houses **The Gallery**, selling wood products as well as paintings by local artists. There is a craft market here selling tablecloths, cushions and beadwork, and a Tingatinga workshop.

▲ Activities and tours

Dar es Salaam *p66, maps p72 and p80*
Athletics
Meetings at the National Stadium, Mandela Rd to the south of the city.

Cricket
Almost entirely a pursuit of the Asian community. There are regular games at weekends at: **Annadil Burhani Cricket Ground**, off Aly Khan Rd; **Gymkhana Club**, off Ghana Av; **Jangwani Playing Fields**, off Morogoro Rd, in the valley of Msimbazi Creek; and **Leaders Club**, Dahomey Rd, off Ali Hassan Mwinyi Rd.

Diving
Sea Breeze Marine Ltd, White Sands Hotel, T022-264 7620, www.seabreezemarine.org.

Fishing
Marine fishing can be arranged through many of the hotels on the beaches.

Fitness and running
The **Hash House Harriers** meet at 1730 on Mon afternoons, details are available from the British Council, Ohio St, T022-211 6574. **Colosseum Hotel & Fitness Club**, Haille Selassie Rd, T022-266 6655. Has a state-of-the-art gym spread over 2 floors, a range of fitness classes, 2 squash courts, a swimming pool and spa. A day pass is US$15 with discounts for multiple days.
The Fitness Centre, off Chole Rd on Msasani Peninsula, T022-260 0786. A gym with weights and also aerobics and yoga classes. **Millenium Health Club**, Mahando St, at the north end of Msasani Peninsula, T022-260 2609. Has a gym, aerobics, sauna and beauty parlour.

There are also gyms at the **Hotel Sea Cliff** and **White Sands Hotel**.

Golf
Gymkhana Club, Ghana Av, T022-212 0519. Only guests are permitted to play golf at the club. Costs are around US$28 for 18 holes, you can hire very good quality clubs and shoes . Here, because of a shortage of water, you will be playing on browns not greens.

Sailing
Yacht Club, Chole Rd, Msasani Peninsula, T022-260 0132. Visitors can obtain temporary membership here. The club organizes East Africa's premier sailing event, the Dar to Tanga (and back) Yacht Race every Dec.

Soccer
The main African pursuit, followed by everyone from the President and the Cabinet down. Matches are exciting occasions, with radios throughout the city tuned to the commentary.

Terrace entrance is around US$2 (more for important matches). It is worth paying extra to sit in the stand. There are 2 divisions of the National league, and Dar es Salaam has 2 representatives – Simba and Young Africans (often called Yanga) – and there is intense rivalry between them. Simba, the best-known Tanzanian club, have their origins in Kariakoo and are sometimes referred to as the 'Msimbazi Street Boys' – they have a club bar in Msimbazi St. Initially formed in the 1920s as 'Eagles of the Night', they changed their name to 'Sunderland FC' in the 1950s. After independence all teams had to choose African names and they became Simba. See www.simbasportsclub.com, for more information.

The 2 main venues for watching soccer:
Karume Stadium, just beyond the Kariakoo area, off Uhuru St.
National Stadium, Mandela Rd to the south of the city. This has recently been renovated. The national team **Taifa Stars** play regularly here, mostly against other African teams.

Swimming

Many of the larger hotels have swimming pools that charge a small fee for non-guests.
Swimming Club, Ocean Rd near Magogoni St. This is the best place to swim in the sea. Otherwise, the best sea beaches are some distance to the north and south of the city.
Water World, next to White Sands Hotel, Mbezi Beach. Tue-Sun. US$5 adults, US$4 children. Has several different water slides and games for children.
Wet 'n' Wild, Kunduchi Beach, T022-265 0326. This is an enormous complex largely, though not exclusively, for children. There are 7 swimming pools with 22 water slides, 2 are very high and 1 twists and turns for 250 m. There is an area for younger children, tennis and squash courts, go-karting, an internet café, hair and beauty parlour, fast food outlets and a main restaurant, and also facilities for watersports on the open ocean, including windsurfing and fishing trips; there is even a qualified diving instructor.

Tour operators

A variety of companies offer tours to the game parks, the islands (Zanzibar, Pemba, Mafia) and to places of historical interest (Kilwa, Bagamoyo). It is well worth shopping around as prices (and degrees of luxury) vary. It is important to find an operator that you like, offers good service, and does not pressure you into booking something.
Bon Voyage Travel, Ohio St, T022-211 8198, www.bonvoyagetz.com.
Cordial Tours, Sokoine Rd T 027-250 6495, www.cordialtours.com.
Easy Travel & Tours, Raha Towers, Bibi Titi Mohamed St, T022-212 3526, T022-212 3842, www.easytravel.co.tz.
Ebony Tours & Safaris, T0773-011153 (mob), www.ebony-safaris.com.
Emslies Travel Ltd, NIC Investment House, 3rd Flr, Samora Av, opposite Royal Palm Hotel, T022-211 4065, www.emsliestravel.biz.
Fortune Travels & Tours Ltd, Jamhuri St, T022-213 8288, www.fortunetz.com.
Hakuna Matata, The Arcade, Old Bagamoyo Rd, T022-270 0231.
Hima Tours & Travel, Simu St, T022-211 1083, www.himatours.com.
Hippo Tours & Safaris, Mwalimu Nyerere Cultural Centre (Nyumba ya Sanaa), T022-212 8662, www.hippotours.com.
Hit Holidays, Bibi Titi Mohamed St (near Rickshaw Travel), T022-211 9024, www.hitholidays.com.
Holiday Africa Tours & Safaris, TDFL Bldg, Ohio St, T022-212 7746.
Interline Travel & Tours, NIC Life House, Sokoine Dr/Ohio St, T022-213 7433.
Kearsley Travel and Tours, Kearsley House, Indira Gandhi St, T022-211 5026/30, www.kearsley.net.
Leopard Tours, Movenpick Royal Palm Hotel, Ohio St, T022-211 9754/6, www.leopard-tours.com.
Lions of Tanzania Safari & Tours, Peugeot House, Bibi Titi Mohamed Rd, T022-212 8161, www.lions.co.tz.
Luft Travel & Cargo Ltd, GAK Patel Bldg, Maktaba St, T022-213 8843.

Planet Safaris, Ohio St, T022-213 7456, www.planetsafaris.com.
Reza Travel & Tours, Jamhuri St, opposite Caltex Station, T022-213 4458, reza@rezatravel.com.
Rickshaw Travel (American Express Agents), Royal Palm Hotel, Ohio St, T022-211 4094, www.rickshawtravels.com.
Skylink Travel & Tours, TDFL Bldg, Ohio St, opposite Royal Palm Hotel, T022-211 5381; airport, T022-284 2738; Mayfair Plaza, T022-277 3983, www.skylinktanzania.com.
Sykes, Indira Ghandi St, T022-211 5542, www.sykestours.co.uk.
Takims Holidays Tours and Safaris, Mtendeni St, T022-211 0346/8, www.takimsholidays.com.
A Tent with a View Safaris, Zahara Towers, Zanaki St, T022-211 0507, www.saadani.com, www.selouslodge.com, www.safariscene.com.
Walji's Travel Bureau, Zanaki St/Indira Ghandi St corner, T022-211 0321, www.waljistravel.com.
Wild Thing Safaris, corner of Makunganya St and Simu St, www.wildthingsafaris.com.

⊖ Transport

Dar es Salaam *p66, maps p72 and p80*
Air
For air charter operators see page 32. Domestic flight schedules change regularly and it's always best to check with the airlines before making plans. It's also necessary to reconfirm your bookings a day or so before flying since timings often change. **Precision Air** depart from the International Terminal at Dar airport, the other airlines all depart from the domestic terminal. Most domestic flights have a baggage limit of 15 kg per person.
Air Tanzania, T022-211 8411, www.air tanzania.com, has 2 daily flights from Dar to **Zanzibar** at 0900 and 1600 (25 mins); a daily flight to **Kilimanjaro** at either 0910 or 2000 (55 mins) depending on the day of the week; and 2 daily flights to **Mwanza** at 0700 and 1600 (1 hr 30 mins).

Coastal Air, T022-284 2700/1, www. coastal.cc, has a scheduled service from Dar to **Arusha** (2 hrs) via **Zanzibar** daily at 0900. This service continues on to the **Serengeti**. To **Kilwa** (1 hr) via **Mafia Island** (30 mins) at 1500. To **Pemba** at 1400 (1 hr). Flights to **Ruaha** (3 hrs) via **Selous** (30 mins) depart at 0830. There's another daily flight to the Selous at 1430 which stops at all the camps. **Tanga** (1 hr 30 mins) daily via Zanzibar and Pemba at 1400. Flights to **Zanzibar** daily every 1½ hrs from 0730-1530, and 1645 and 1745 (20 mins, US$75).
Precision Air, T022-213 0800, T022-212 1718, www.precisionairtz.com, flies to **Mwanza** Wed, Fri and Sun at 0810, Mon, Tue, Thu and Sat at 1055 (2 hrs). To **Tabora** (2 hrs) and **Kigoma** (3 hrs 15 mins) Fri-Wed at 1100. To **Zanzibar** daily 0650 and 1320 (20 mins). There are additional flights to Zanzibar on Thu and Fri at 0830, and on Mon, Tue, Wed, Sat and Sun 1100. To **Arusha** daily 0820 and 1320 (1 hr 15 mins). To **Shinyanga** on Mon, Wed, Fri and Sun at 1330 (2 hrs).
Zanair, T024-223 3768, www.zanair.com, have daily flights from Dar to **Zanzibar** at 0900, 1215, 1645 and 1815; direct to **Pemba** at 1345; and to the **Selous** at 0840.
Airline offices Air India, Bibi Titi Mohamed St, opposite Peugeot House, T022-215 2642, www.airindia.com. **Air Malawi**, JM Mall, Samora Av, T022-212 4280, www.airmalawi.com. **Air Tanzania**, ATC Bldg, Ohio St, T022-211 8411, www.airtanzania.com. **British Airways**, based at the Royal Palm Hotel, Ohio St, T022-2113 8202, www.britishairways.com. **Emirates**, Haidery Plaza, Kisutu St, T022-2116 1003, www.emirates.com. **Ethiopian Airlines**, TDFL Bldg, Ohio St, T022-2117 0635, www.flyethiopia.com. **Gulf Air**, Raha Towers, Bibi Titi Mohamed St/Maktaba St, T022-2137 8526, www.gulfairco.com. **Kenya Airways**, Peugeot House, Bibi Titi Mohammed/Ali Hassan Mwinyi Rd, T022-211 9376, www.kenya-airways.com. **KLM**, Peugeot House as above T022-211 3336,

The dala-dalas of Dar es Salaam

Ownership of one or more minibuses, or *dala-dalas*, remains a favourite *mradi* (income-generating project) for Dar es Salaam's middle class and, judging by the numbers squeezed into their interiors and the speed at which they travel between destinations, those returns are handsome. Realizing that they can't monitor the number of passengers using their buses, the *dala-dala* owners stipulate how much they expect to receive at the end of the day from the 'crew' they hire to operate the vehicle; anything left over constitutes the crew's wages. It is a system that appears to work to everyone's advantage other than that of the passenger, who suffers the consequent overcrowding and the suicidal driving as *dala-dala* competes with *dala-dala* to arrive first and leave fullest.

In a forlorn attempt to reduce the number of accidents, the Tanzanian government passed a law in early 1997 requiring all public service vehicles to install governors restricting speeds to under 80 kph. However, *dala-dala* and coach operators soon worked out ways to override them, or simply disconnected them completely, and within weeks the drivers were proceeding with their old reckless abandon.

The basic crew of each *dala-dala* is made up of two people: the driver (clearly picked for the ability to drive fast rather than well) and the turnboy (in Dar slang *Mgiga debe* – literally 'he who forces things into a tin can'), whose job it is to collect money and issue tickets, harangue passengers who fail to make room for one more, as well as to entertain the remainder of the bus with hair-raising acrobatic stunts hanging from the door of the bus (there is at least one *Mpiga debe* currently working in Dar who has just one leg – it's not hard to imagine how he lost the other one). Supplementing this basic crew at either end of the journey is a tout, who bawls out the intended destination and route, attempting to attract or, if necessary, intimidate people (at times this stretches to actual manhandling of passengers) into entering his *dala-dala*. He is paid a fixed amount for each bus that he touts for. In addition, when business is slow, there are people who are paid a small amount to sit on the bus pretending to be passengers in order to give the impression that it is fuller than it actually is to the potential passenger, who will then enter the *dala-dala*, assuming it will be leaving sooner than the next one along.

The *dala-dala* network radiates from three main termini in the town centre, Posta at Minazi Mirefu ('Tall palm trees') on the Kivukoni Front opposite the Old Post Office; Stesheni, close to the Central Railway Station; and Kariakoo, around the Uhuru/Msimbazi Street roundabout for destinations south and at the central market for those in the north. From each of these you can catch *dala-dalas* to destinations throughout Dar es Salaam, although the four main routes are along Ali Hassan Mwinyi to Mwenge (for the Makumbusho Village Museum, Mwenge handicrafts market and the university); along the Kilwa Road to Temeke, Mtoni and Mbagala (these take you to the Salvation Army); to Vingunguti via Kariakoo and Ilala (for the TAZARA Railway Station); and along the Morogoro Road to Magomeni, Manzese and Ubongo. For a *dala-dala* going to the airport ask for Uwanja wa Ndege at Minazi Miretu.

www.klm.com. **Oman Air,** airport, T022-213 5660, www.oman-air.com. **Qatar Airways,** Barclays House, Ohio St, T022-211 8870, www.qatarairways.com. **South Africa Airways,** Raha Tower, Bibi Titi Mohammed St, T022-2117 0447, www.flysaa.com. **Swiss Air,** Luther House, Sokoine Dr, T022-211 8 8703, www.swiss.com.

Bus

The main bus station is **Ubungo Bus Station** on Morogoro Rd, 6 km from the city centre, which can be reached by bus, *dala-dala* or taxi. Outside on the road is a long line of booking offices. Recommended for safety and reliability is **Scandinavia Express,** which has its own terminal on Nyerere Rd at the corner of Msimbazi St (taxi from the city centre approximately US$2), though all buses also stop at the Ubungo bus station, T022-285 0847, www.scandinaviagroup.com. There is a small airport-style arrival and departure lounge at the terminal with its own restaurant. Buses are speed limited, luggage is securely locked up either under the bus or in overhead compartments, and complimentary video, drinks, sweets and biscuits are offered. Buses depart daily for **Arusha** at 0745, 0830 and 0915 (9 hrs, US$30 luxury service, US$20 standard); **Mbeya** at 0645 and 0745 (12 hrs, US$20); **Tanga** at 0800 (6 hrs, US$8.50), and **Dodoma** at 0915 and 1100 (4 hrs, US$10). **International destinations** Mombasa and **Nairobi** in Kenya, **Kampala** in Uganda and **Lusaka** in Zambia.

Other bus companies include **Dar Express** T0754-373415 (mob) and **Royal Coaches** T022-212 4073.

Car hire

Car hire can be arranged through most of the tour operators. Alternatively try: **Avis,** in the TDFL building, opposite the Royal Palm Hotel, Ohio St, run by Skylink Travel & Tours, T022-211 5381, www.avis.com; **Business Rent a Car,** 16 Kisitu St, T022-212 2852, www.businessrentacar.com; **Green Car Rentals,** Nukrumah St, along Nyerere Rd,

T022-218 3718, T0713-227788 (mob), www.greencarstz.com; **Hertz,** airport, T022-211 2967, www.hertz.com; or **Tanzania Rent-A-Car,** airport, T022-212 8062.

Ferry

All ticket offices of the ferry companies with services to **Zanzibar** and **Pemba** are on Sokoine Dr adjacent to the jetty. Ignore the touts who may follow you to the offices to claim credit and take commission. The companies themselves advise travellers to completely ignore them and it is easy enough to book a ticket on your own.

Most ferries are fast and comfortable hydrofoils or catamarans that take on average 90 mins to reach Zanzibar, and the tourist fare is fixed at US$45 one way (including port tax) for all companies. The slow overnight boat back from Zanzibar with **Flying Horse** is US$25. Payment for tickets is in US$ cash. Companies no longer accept TCs.

Services to **Zanzibar and Pemba:**
Azam Marine, T022-213 4013, www.azam-marine.com. Australian-built Seabus catamarans that take 1 hr 40 mins to Zanzibar. They depart daily at 0800, 1115, 1330, 1400 and 1600. From Zanzibar to Dar, ferries depart at 0700, 0930, 1330 and 1630. On Tue and Fri they also operate a service from Dar es Salaam to Pemba via Zanzibar at 0730 which arrives in Zanzibar at 0855, departs again at 1000 and arrives in Pemba at 1205. The return boat on Tue and Fri departs Pemba at 1230, arrives in Zanzibar at 1435, departs again at 1630 and arrives in Dar at 1755.
Flying Horse (Africa Shipping Corporation), T022-212 4507. Outward journey to Zanzibar departs at 1200 and takes 2 hrs, the overnight return from Zanzibar departs 2200. For some this return journey is inconvenient as passengers are not let off at Dar until 0600, when Customs open. However, tourists are accommodated in comfortable, a/c compartments, and provided with mattresses to sleep on until 0600. A good option for budget travellers as the fare is only US$20 each way and you save on accommodation for 1 night.

Sea Express, T022-213 7049, www.sea-express.net. Daily ferry from Dar at 0715 which arrives in Zanzibar at 0915, leaving Zanzibar for the return at 1600. On Mon, Wed, Fri and Sun the ferry continues from Zanzibar (departing at 1000) to Pemba where it arrives at 1200, leaving Pemba at 1300 to return. Dar es Salaam to Pemba US$70.
Sea Star, T022-212 4988. Fast service to Zanzibar that takes 1 hr 30 mins, departs Dar at 1030. The return leaves Zanzibar at 0700.
Sepideh, T0713-282365 (mob). Departs Dar at 0700, continuing on to Pemba at 0930 on Sat, Mon and Thu, arriving there at 1300.

Train
The **Central Railway Station** is off Sokoine Dr at the wharf end of the city at the corner of Railway St and Gerezani St, T022-211 7833, www.trctz.com. This station serves the passenger line that runs through the central zone to **Kigoma** on Lake Tanganyika and **Mwanza** on Lake Victoria.

TAZARA Railway Station is at the junction of Mandela Rd and Nyerere Rd, about 5 km from the city centre, T022-286 5187, www.tazara.co.tz. You can book train tickets online. It is well served by *dala-dala* and a taxi from the centre costs about US$5. This line runs southwest to **Iringa** and **Mbeya** and on to **Tunduma** at the Zambia border (24 hrs). It is a broader gauge than the Central and Northern Line.
To Zambia Express trains go all the way to **New Kapiri Mposhi** and this journey takes 40-50 hrs. The local trains, which stop at the Zambian border, are a little slower, and take approximately 23 hrs to get to **Mbeya**. First class cabins on both trains contain 4 berths and second class 6.

❶ Directory

Dar es Salaam *p66, maps p72 and p80*
Banks
All banks listed have ATMs, though some may only accept Visa cards. **Standard Chartered**,

in the Plaza on Sokoine Dr near Askari Monument, and at International House on corner of Garden Av and Shaaban Robert St. **Barclay's**, TDFL Building, Ohio St, and at The Slipway. **CitiBank**, Peugeot House, Bibi Titi Mohammed Rd. **National Bank of Commerce**, Samora Av and corner of Sokoine Dr and Azikiwe St. Bank hours are Mon-Fri 0830-1500, Sat 0830-1130.

Currency exchange Foreign exchange bureaux are to be found in almost every street, and are especially common in the area between Samora Av and Jamhuri St. They are usually open Mon-Fri 0900-1700 and Sat 0900-1300. Some are also open Sun morning. Rates vary and it is worth shopping around. Tanzania's sole agent for American Express is **Rickshaw Travel**, at the Royal Palm Hotel, T022-211 4094, www.rickshaw travels.com, open Mon-Fri all day, Sat-Sun mornings only, will issue TCs to card-holders.

Money transfers Western Union money transfer is available at the Tanzanian Postal Bank, on Samora Av, and at the General Post Office on Azikiwe St.

Embassies and consulates
You can usually be sure that diplomatic missions will be open between 0900 and 1200. Some have afternoon opening, and some do not open every day. Even when a mission is officially closed, the staff will usually be helpful if something has to be done in an emergency. **Austria**, Samora Av, T022-260 1492. **Belgium**, 5 Ocean Rd, T022-211 2688. **Burundi**, 1007 Lugalo Rd, T022-211 7615. **Canada**, 38 Mirambo St, Garden Av, T022-216 3300, dslam@ dfait-maeci.gc.ca. **Denmark**, Ghana Av, T022-2113 8878. **Egypt**, 24 Garden Av, T022-211 3591. **Finland**, Mirambo St and Garden Av, T022-219 6565. **France**, 34 Ali Hassan Mwinyi Rd, T022-2666 0213. **Germany**, Umoja House, Garden Av and Mirambo St, T022-211 7409, www.dares salam.diplo.de. **Ireland**, 353 Toure Dr, T022-260 2355. **Italy**, 316 Lugalo Rd, T022-211 5935/6. **Japan**, 299 Ali Hassan Mwinyi Rd, T022-211 5827/9. **Kenya**, 127 Mafinga St,

Kinondoni T022-266 8285. **Malawi,** 38 Ali Hassan Mwinyi Rd, T022-266 6248. **Mozambique,** 25 Garden Av, T022-211 6502. **Netherlands,** Umoja House 4th floor, Mirambo St T022-211 0000. **Norway,** 160 Mirambo St, T022-213 8852. **Rwanda,** 32 Ali Hassan Mwinyi Rd, T022-211 5889. **South Africa,** 1338 Mwaya Rd, Oyster Bay, T022-260 1800. **Spain,** 99B Kinondoni Rd, T022-266 6936. **Sudan,** 64 Ali Hassan Mwinyi Rd, T022-211 7641. **Sweden,** Extelcoms Bldg, Samora Av, T022-219 6500. **Switzerland,** 79 Kinondoni Rd, T022-266 6008/9. **Uganda,** Extelcom Bldg, Samora Av, T022-266 7391, daily 0830-1600. **UK,** Umoja House, Garden Av, T022-211 0101. **USA,** 686 Old Bagamayo Rd, Msasani, T022-266 8001. **Zambia,** Ohio St and Sokoine Dr, T022-2118 4812. **Zimbabwe,** Off Ali Hassan Mwinyi Rd, T022-211 6789.

Immigration
The immigration office is on the corner of Ohio St and Garden Av, T022-211 2174, open Mon-Fri 0730-1530.

Internet
There are hundreds of internet cafés all over the city centre and you will not have a problem accessing your email. The cost of internet access has fallen considerably over the last few years, and is available for less than US$0.50 per hour, although it is usually quite slow. Some places offer additional services such as printing or scanning.

Libraries
Alliance Française, behind Las Vegas Casino, T022-213 1406, offers library facilities, French TV news, occasional concerts and recitals, open Mon-Fri 1000-1800. **British Council,** on the corner of Ohio St and Samora Av, T022-2116 5746, has an excellent library, with reference, lending, newspapers and magazines. **National Central Library,** Bibi Titi Mohamed Rd, near the Maktaba St intersection, T022-215 0048/9.

Medical services
Hospitals The main hospital is **Muhimbili Hospital,** off United Nations Rd, northwest of the centre towards Msimbazi Creek, T022-215 1298. **Oyster Bay Medical Clinic,** follow the signs along Haile Selassie Rd, T022-266 7932, is an efficient and accessible small private medical centre. **Aga Khan Hospital,** Ocean Rd at the junction with Ufukoni Rd, T022-2115 1513. All these hospitals are well equipped and staffed. See also **Flying Doctors Society of Africa,** page 53. **Pharmacies** In all shopping centres, and small dispensaries are also found in the main residential areas.

Police
The **main police station** is on Gerazani St near the railway station, T022-211 5507. There are also stations on Upanga Rd on the city side of Selander Bridge, T022-212 0818; on Ali Hassan Mwinyi Rd at the junction with Old Bagamoyo Rd (Oyster Bay), T022-266 7322/3; and at the port T022-211 6287.
Emergencies For police, ambulance and fire brigade, T112.

Post office
The **main post office** is on Azikiwe St, and it's here that you will find the poste restante. There's a small charge for letters collected. Other offices are on Sokoine Dr, behind the bus stand on Morogoro Rd; and Libya St. Post offices are generally crowded.
Courier services Several branches of the major courier companies around town which will collect. **DHL** at DHL House, 12B Nyerere Rd, T022-286 1000/4, www.africa.dhl.com. **Fedex,** T022-270 1647. **TNT,** T022-212 4585.

Telephone
International calls and faxes can be made from the telecoms office near the main post office on Simu St. There are also many private telephone offices all over town. Hotels will usually charge up to 3 times the actual cost. There are mobile phone shops all over Dar and international calls may well be cheaper if you buy a local phone or pay-as-you-go SIM card.

Contents

Footprint features

Border crossings

Coastal Tanzania

At a glance

◉ Getting around Self-drive or public buses are really the only options.

◉ Time required 1 week to explore the north coast and spend a day or 2 on the beaches around Pangani; 4-5 days to get down to Kilwa; 1-2 nights on Mafia Island.

☀ Weather Tropical and balmy most of the year.

✕ When not to go There are heavy showers in the afternoons from Mar-May.

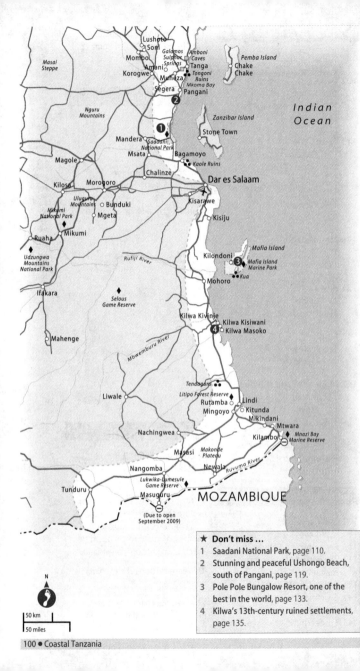

Masai
Steppe

Lushoto
Soni
Mombo
Galamos Amboni
Sulphur Caves
Springs
Amani
Korogwe
Tanga
Muheza
Segera

Pemba Island
Chake
Chake

Nguru
Mountains

Mandera
Saadani
National Park
Msata

Zanzibar Island

Indian
Ocean

Stone Town

Magole
Chalinze
Bagamoyo
Kaole Ruins

Kilosa
Morogoro

Dar es Salaam

Uluguru
Mountains
Bunduki

Kisarawe

Mikumi
National Park
Mgeta

Kisiju

Ruaha
Mikumi

Udzungwa
Mountains
National Park

Rufiji River

Kilondoni

Mafia Island

Mafia Island
Marine Park
Kua

Ifakara

Mohoro

Selous
Game Reserve

Mahenge

Kilwa Kivinje
Kilwa Kisiwani
Kilwa Masoko

Mbwemburu River

Liwale

Tendaguru
Litipo Forest Reserve
Rutamba
Mingoyo

Lindi
Kitunda
Mikindani
Mtwara

Nachingwea

Kilambo
Mnazi Bay
Marine Reserve

Masasi
Makonde
Plateau
Newala
Ruvuma River

Nangomba

Tunduru
Lukwika-Lumesule
Game Reserve
Masuguru

MOZAMBIQUE

(Due to open
September 2009)

N

50 km
50 miles

★ **Don't miss ...**

1   Saadani National Park, page 110.
2   Stunning and peaceful Ushongo Beach,
    south of Pangani, page 119.
3   Pole Pole Bungalow Resort, one of the
    best in the world, page 133.
4   Kilwa's 13th-century ruined settlements,
    page 135.

The 800 km of the Tanzanian mainland coast has blindingly white beaches, coconut groves and mangrove swamps, but much of it is virtually undiscovered by modern tourism. Generally overlooked in favour of Zanzibar, the coast (away from Dar es Salaam) is rarely visited. With little development of any kind (tourist or otherwise), the coast has just a few farming and fishing villages dotted along its shoreline with nearby coral reefs and natural lagoons. Yet there are vivid reminders of the Swahili past to be found and the coast has a bloody and fascinating history. Palatial remnants of Persian and Omani kingdoms still remain and ancient mosques dating from the 12th century testify to the far-reaching roots of Islam. Bagamoyo was the last point reached by slave caravans before shipment and fortified houses still stand, as does the tree under which they were brought to be sold. There is also the fading grandeur of Tanga in the north, and the relatively undiscovered island of Mafia, location of the newly gazetted marine park and a wonderful place for scuba-diving. Towards the Mozambique border there is the historic ruined city of Kilwa.

Things are beginning to change, however, and there is now a clutch of upmarket beach resorts, and a new road from Dar es Salaam to Bagamoyo has recently been completed thanks to an EU grant. Also the beaches around Pangani have recently seen some tourist development and now offer some excellent rustic beach resorts, which you should enjoy while tourism there is still in its infancy. In the future this part of Tanzania could attract many more visitors.

Roads south are improving too, and slowly but surely the 21st century is arriving here, with oil and bio fuel developments creeping in. They've not changed the beauty of the areas yet, and they may not, but if you want to visit them in their most pristine state, don't leave it too late.

Ins and outs

Getting there

North coast Although there is a new tar road from Dar es Salaam to Bagamoyo, north of here the road deteriorates into a sandy track, and there is no access to Saadani and the coastal towns of Tanga and Pangani further in the north, as there is presently no crossing over the Wami River. Instead, these are reached from the inland road. From Dar this stretches the 109 km to the junction at Chalinze before heading north to Moshi and Arusha, off which are roads that go back towards the coast. The Tanga road continues on to the border with Kenya and there is good access along this route from Dar to Mombasa (Kenya) and the journey can easily be made in a day by bus.

South coast Off the coast is the island of Mafia, which now is partially protected as the Mafia Island Marine Park. It's an idyllic setting and a paradise for scuba-divers and snorkellers and, with its stunning lodges, a haven for those at the luxury end of the market. Flights connect Dar es Salaam and Mafia Island, as well as Kilwa and Mafia Island and Dar es Salaam and Mtwara. The main coastal road south from Dar es Salaam to Lindi and then on to the new Unity Bridge over the Ruvuma River into Mozambique has recently been tarred. It passes the town of Kilwa, with the small island of Kilwa Kisiwani just off the mainland. This is the location of the intriguing Kilwa ruins and although very remote, worth the trouble to get to. Outside the towns, there are few facilities along this road. Buses make the journey from Dar es Salaam to Lindi and on to Mtwara, and it remains to be seen if services will extend to the new border with Mozambique once it is operational later in 2009.

Bagamoyo

→ *Colour map 1, B5. 6°20'S 38°30'E. Phone code: 023. Altitude: sea level. www.bagamoyo.com.*
Bagamoyo, whose name means 'lay down my heart' in Kiswahili, has a host of historical associations and as the oldest town in Tanzania, Bagamoyo is currently being considered as Tanzania's 8th World Heritage Site (for a list of the others, see page 45). The town has seen Arab and Indian traders, German colonial government and Christian missionaries, and although Bagamoyo is no longer the busy port city that it once was, it does have dozens of ruins. Unfortunately, however, most are fairly dilapidated and the town hasn't seen the attention to restoration on a scale anyway near the likes of Zanzibar's Stone Town. Hopefully it will if it's awarded World Heritage status. In recent years many of the buildings have lost their intricate carved doors and window frames, as they have either been stolen or sold. About a decade ago a clutch of large holiday resorts were built on the beach to the north of town but, with a couple of exceptions, they haven't proved popular and today they are mostly empty or cater for local conferences. These days the resorts to the north of Dar or lovely Ushongo Beach south of Pangani appear to be far more popular with foreign visitors.

Bagamoyo makes a very interesting day trip from Dar es Salaam and the journey only takes about 90 minutes. Be aware though that the public beaches are not that great and there's a fair amount of debris along them. There is also the issue of not wandering around public places in swimwear or shorts (this will offend the local Muslim community) and the possibly of petty theft and muggings on the beaches. If you do want swim and sunbathe, go to one of the resorts. ➙ *For listings, see pages 110-112.*

Ins and outs

Getting there About 70 km north of Dar es Salaam by road, there are several *dala-dala* a day between Dar es Salaam and Bagamoyo and some of the Bagomoyo hotels offer a shuttle service to their guests. From Dar get a *dala-dala* to the bus stand at Mwenge and swap to another to Bagamoyo. The journey shouldn't cost more than US$1.80.

Getting around There are a number of taxis at the bus stand but all destinations in Bagamoyo are within walking distance. It is a good idea to hire a guide, and being with a local person provides security to get to places on isolated roads. Any of the hotels can organize guides if you're staying overnight or you can pick up a guide at either the Holy Ghost Mission or Livingstone's Church, or go to the **tourist office** ① *Boma St, T023-244 0155.* Expect to pay around US$10 for a three-four hour walking tour. Alternatively, you may be able to negotiate with local people to hire a bike for an hour or two.

Background

The coastal area opposite Zanzibar was first settled by fishermen and cultivators. Towards the end of the 18th century, 12 or so Muslim diwans arrived to settle, build dwellings and establish their families and retinues of slaves. These diwans were all related to Shomvi la Magimba from Oman. They prospered through levying taxes whenever a cow was slaughtered, or a shark or other large fish caught, as well as on all salt produced at Nunge, about 3 km north of Bagamoyo.

Bagamoyo's location as a mainland port close to Zanzibar led to its development as a centre for caravans and an expansion of commerce in slaves and ivory soon followed. Although the slave trade officially ended in 1873, slaves continued to be sold and traded in Bagamoyo until the end of the 19th century. During this time, it was not uncommon to see hundreds of slaves walking through the streets of Bagamoyo chained together by the neck. There was also growing trade in sun-dried fish, gum copal and the salt from Nunge. Copra (from coconuts) was also important, and was used to make soap. A boat-building centre was established, which supplied craft to other coastal settlements.

In 1880 the population of the town was around 5000 but this was augmented by a substantial transient population in residence after completing a caravan or undertaking preparations prior to departure. The numbers of those temporarily in town could be considerable. In 1889, after the slave trade had been suppressed, significantly reducing the numbers passing, it was still recorded that 1305 caravans, involving 41,144 people, left for the interior.

The social composition of the town was varied. There were the initial Muslim Shomvi and the local Zaramo and Doe. Among the earliest arrivals were Hindus from India, involving themselves in administration, coconut plantations and boat-building. Muslim Baluchis, a people based in Mombasa and Zanzibar, and for the most part mercenary soldiers, also settled and were involved in trade, financing caravans and land-owning. Other Muslim sects were represented, among them the Ismailis who settled in 1840 and by 1870 numbered 137. A handful of Sunni Muslims from Zanzibar established shops in Bagamoyo, some Parsees set up as merchants, and a small group of Catholic Goans was engaged in tailoring and retailing.

In 1888 the German East Africa Company signed a treaty with the Sultan of Zanzibar, Seyyid Khalifa, which allowed the company to collect customs duties along the coast. The Germans rapidly made their presence felt by ordering the Sultan's representative (the Liwali) to lower the Sultan's flag and, on being refused, they axed down the flag-pole.

Mangroves

Up and down the coast of East Africa you come across stretches of mangrove forest. Ecologically these can be described as evergreen saline swamp forests and their main constituents are the mangroves Rhizophora, Ceriops and Bruguiera. These are all described as viviparous, that is the seeds germinate or sprout when the fruits are still attached to the parent plant. Mangrove forests support a wide range of other plants and animals including a huge range of birds, insects and fish.

Economically mangrove forests are an important source of building poles, known on the coast as *boriti*, which were once exported in large quantities to the Arabian Gulf. Their main property is that they are resistant to termite attack. Mangrove bark is also used as a tanning material and charcoal can be obtained from mangrove wood. As with so many natural resources in East Africa, care needs to be taken in the use of mangrove forests. Their over-exploitation could lead to the delicate balance that is found in the forests being upset, with serious consequences for these coastal regions.

Later in the year a dispute between a member of the company and a townsman culminated in the latter being shot. The Usagara trading house of the company was besieged by irate townspeople, 200 troops landed from the *SS Moewe*, and over 100 local people were killed.

Further resentment was incurred when the Germans set about registering land and property, demanding proof of ownership. As this was impossible for most residents there was widespread fear that property would be confiscated.

One of the diwans, Bomboma, organized local support. They enlisted the help of Bushiri bin Salim al-Harthi who had earlier led Arabs against the Germans in Tabora. Bushiri had initial success. Sections of Bagamoyo were burned and Bushiri formed up in Nzole about 6 km southwest of the town ready for an assault. The German government now felt compelled to help the company and Hermann von Wissmann was appointed to lead an infantry force comprising Sudanese and Zulu troops. Admiral Denhardt, commanding the German naval forces, played for time by initiating negotiations with Bushiri whose demands included being made governor of the region from Dar es Salaam up to Pangani, payment of 4000 rupees a month (about US$10,000 in present-day values), and the right to keep troops.

By May 1889 Wissmann had consolidated his forces and built a series of fortified block houses. He attacked Nzole and Bushiri fled. The alliance of the diwans and Bushiri weakened, and in June the Germans retook Saadani and in July, Pangani. Bushiri was captured and executed at Pangani in December. Bomboma, and another of the diwans leading the resistance, Marera, were also both executed, and other diwans were deposed and replaced by collaborators who had assisted the Germans.

It was now clear that the German government intended to extend their presence and, in October 1890, rights to the coast were formally purchased from the Sultan of Zanzibar for 4 million German marks.

In early 1891 German East Africa became a formal colony, but in April it was decided to establish Dar es Salaam as the capital. Commercial activity in Bagamoyo revived, and in the last decade of the century rebuilding began with the construction of new stone buildings including a customs house and the boma, which served as an administrative centre.

The caravan trade resumed and there was a further influx of Indians together with the arrival of Greeks who established a European hotel. William O'Swald, the Hamburg trading company, arrived and the company Hansing established vanilla plantations at Kitopeni and Hurgira. An important Koran school was established in the town. Yet, despite these developments Bagamoyo was destined for steady decline: its harbour was unsuitable for deep draught steamships and no branch of the railway was built to serve the port. The ending of the German rule further reduced commercial presence in the town, and the last century saw Bagamoyo decline steadily, lacking even a sealed road to link it to Dar es Salaam. These days, thanks to the new tar road from Dar es Salaam trade has improved considerably and it's now easily reachable by tourists.

Bagamoyo

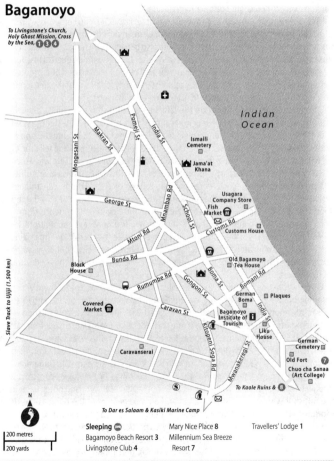

Sleeping
Bagamoyo Beach Resort 3
Livingstone Club 4

Mary Nice Place 8
Millennium Sea Breeze
Resort 7

Travellers' Lodge 1

Old Bagamoyo

On the south approach to the town, on the road from Kaole, is the fully restored **Old Fort** (sometimes referred to as the Old Prison). It is the oldest surviving building in Bagamoyo having been started by Abdallah Marhabi around 1860, and extended and strengthened by Sultan Baghash after 1870, and then by the German colonialists. It was used as a police post until 1992. Initially one of its functions was to hold slaves until they could be shipped to Zanzibar. It is said there is an underground passage through which the slaves were herded to dhows on the shore, although this passage is not apparent today. Since its restoration in 1992, it's a particularly handsome building, whitewashed, three storeys high, and with buttresses and battlements and an enclosed courtyard. For a small fee and if anyone's there you should be able to go inside.

Off to the right on the path to Badeco Beach Hotel is the **German cemetery** with some 20 graves dating from 1889/1890, and most are Germans killed during the uprising led by Bushiri in those years (see page 103). There are also graves of two females – one a German nurse and one a German child who died six days after birth. A German deed of freedom for a slave is reproduced on a tree. The cemetery is well tended, surrounded by a coral wall. In the grounds of the Badeco Beach Hotel (currently closed), is the site of the tree reputedly used by the German administration for executions, it is marked by a plaque.

Continuing along India Street on the left is an old two-storey building, **Liku House**, with an awning supported by slender iron columns and a central double door. This served as the first administrative headquarters for the Germans from 1888 until the boma was completed in 1897. German explorer Emin Pasha stayed there in 1889 and fell drunk from the balcony, which resulted in a fractured skull and six weeks in hospital. He was a member of Henry Morton Stanley's party. Today it's used as the District Commissioner's office.

The **German Boma** is a two-storey building topped by crenellations, constructed in a U-shape. There are pointed arches on the first floor and rounded arches on the ground floor. This was the German administrative centre and governor's residence from 1897. Unfortunately it's now no more than a ruin and needs urgent restoration. Until 1997 it served as the local District Commissioner's office but after heavy rain during El Niño the office had to be relocated as the balcony caved in under the weight of heavy water and this was after a long period of poor maintenance. Since then the roof has been stripped off by vandals.

On the shore side is a semi-circular levelled area on which was a monument with brass commemorative plaques erected by the Germans. With the fall of Bagamoyo to the British, the monument was razed and replaced with the present construction which commemorates the departure of Burton and Speke to Lake Tanganyika from nearby Kaole in 1857. The old German plaques have been reset in the walls which support the levelled area, on the shore side. To the left is an Arabic two-storey building fronted by six columns, a fretted veranda and curved arch windows, said to be the **Old Bagamoyo Tea House**, and thought to be one of the oldest buildings in the town, constructed by Abdallah Marhabi in 1860 who ran it as a tea house, general store and hotel. Later under the British it was used as both a school and a bank. In front of the boma is the **Uhuru Monument**, celebrating Tanzania's independence in 1961, and a derelict bandstand.

Continuing north along India Street there is a particularly fine residential house on the right with columns and arched windows just before Customs Road. This leads down to the **Customs House**, built in 1895 by Sewa Haji and rented to the Germans. It is a

Bagamoyo Art College

The Bagamoyo Art College, also known as the Chuo cha Sanaa is a school for the arts where music, drama, dance and painting are taught. The college, established in 1981, is the most famous art institute in Tanzania and one of very few training institutions in Africa offering practical training in the arts. Most of the 40 or so students are Tanzanian, but several artists from Europe, America and the Far East attend seminars and events throughout the year. Students learn traditional drumming, sculpture, carving and painting, as well as acting and stage management. Other courses cover instrument manufacture, music improvization and dance. The main buildings are located along the road to Kaole to the south of Bagamoyo.

There's not much to see for most of the year, but you may see the students practising around the buildings. The main thatched theatre built with Swiss funding unfortunately burnt down in 2003, but the annual Bagamoyo Arts Festival is still held on the soccer pitch in the last week of September. It includes performances, exhibitions and workshops.

For more information, contact Bagamoyo College of Arts, T023-244 0032.

double-storey lime-washed building with an open veranda on the first floor, buttresses and arched windows. It looks on to a walled courtyard and the beach but many of the stone pillars on the beach side have collapsed. Opposite the Customs House are the ruins of the **Usagara Company Store** built in 1888 with the arrival of the German commercial presence. The unusual construction had stone plinths on which were mounted cast-iron supports for the timber floor, raised to keep the stores dry. The cast-iron supports have cups surrounding them in which kerosene was poured to prevent rats climbing up to eat the stored grain.

Halfway down Customs Road is the covered **Fish Market** with stone tables for gutting fish. When not used for this purpose they are marked out with chalk so informal games like checkers can be played with bottle-tops. At the top of Customs Road, just before the intersection with India Street is the **Post Office**, with a fine carved door and a blue-painted upstairs veranda. Further north along India Street is a series of Arabic buildings in various states of repair.

Continuing north, on the right, is the **Jama'at Khana**, the Ismaili mosque, which dates from 1880, double-storeyed with a veranda and carved doors. Behind the mosque on the beach side are some 150 tombs in the Ismaili Cemetery. On the right beyond the mosque is the Bagamoyo District Hospital, now part of Muhimbili Teaching Hospital in Dar es Salaam, which is based on the original Sewa Haji Hospital, constructed in 1895. On the death of Sewa Haji in 1896, the hospital was run by the Holy Ghost Mission, and then from 1912 by the Germans. The present hospital, where goats loll about in the covered walkways between the wards, has some handsome old buildings and some more modern blocks. In 2006 the roof of the original building was renovated.

At the northern end of the town on the right is a substantial **mosque** and Muslim school with curved steps up to the carved door over which is a delicate fretted grill.

Close to the intersection of Sunda Road and Mongesani Street at the western approach to the town is the white **Block House**, constructed in 1889 by Hermann Wissman during the Bushiri uprising (see page 103). There is a mangrove pole and coral stone roof and an outside ladder, which enabled troops to man the roof behind the battlements. The walls have loopholes through which troops could fire, standing on low internal walls, which doubled as seating, to give them the height to fire down on their adversaries. Behind the Block House is a disused well.

The **slave track** to the interior departed from this point, a 1500 km trail that terminated at Ujiji on Lake Tanganyika. Off Caravan Street is the **Caravanserai**, a courtyard with single-storey buildings at the front and a square, two-storey building with a veranda at the centre (the corner of which is collapsing). This latter building was used for storing ivory and other precious commodities. It was here that preparations were made to fit out caravans to the interior and it was believed to be surrounded by a large fenced area to hold livestock and temporary shelters for porters. The great explorers – Burton, Speke, Grant, Livingstone, etc – passed through here at various times in the latter half of the 1800s. Today it is headquarters for the Bagamoyo Department of Antiquities.

Livingstone's Church
This is a simple construction with a tin roof, curved arch windows and wooden benches. Its formal name is the Anglican Church of the Holy Cross. Above the entrance is the sign 'Through this door Dr David Livingstone passed', referring to the fact that his body was kept in the church prior to it being returned to England and buried in Westminster Cathedral.

Cross by the Sea
There's a monument in green marble surmounted by a cross on the path leading to the sea from Livingstone's Church. It marks the spot where, in 1868, Father Antoine Horner of the French Holy Ghost Fathers crossed from Zanzibar (where they had operated a mission since 1860) and stepped ashore to establish the first Christian church on the mainland.

Holy Ghost Mission
Opposite the path to the Cross by the Sea is **Mango Tree Drive**, which was established in 1871 as the approach to the Mission. A statue of the Sacred Heart, erected in 1887, stands in front of the **Fathers' House** which was begun in 1873 – the third storey finally added in 1903. In 1969 the building was taken over by MANTEP as a training centre for educational management.

Behind the Fathers' House is the **First Church**, construction of which started in 1872. It comprises a stone tower topped with arches with a cross at the centre and crosses on the pediments at each corner. The main building is a simple rectangular structure with a tin roof, unusually behind and to the side of the tower so that the tower sits at one corner.

It was here on 24 February 1874 that the body of David Livingstone was brought by the missionary's African followers, Sisi and Chuma, who had carried their master 1500 km from Ujiji. Speke, Burton, Grant, Stanley, Peters, Emin Pasha and Wissmann all visited the church at one time or another.

Following the path to the right of the First Church is a cemetery where the early missionaries are buried. Further down this path is a small shrine built by freed slaves in 1876 with the sign 'Salamnus Maria' picked out in flowers. A great baobab tree, planted in 1868, stands to the side of the First Church. At the base can be seen the links of the chain where Mme de Chevalier, a mission nurse, tethered her donkey.

The **New Church**, constructed of coral blocks, begun in 1910 and completed in 1914, stands in front of the First Church. A small iron cross commemorates the centenary, in 1968, of the Holy Ghost Mission in Bagamoyo.

The **Mission Museum** is housed in the **Sisters' Building**. The displays present a history of Bagamoyo and there are relics and photographs from the slave period. One intriguing exhibit is the uniform, presented by HA Schmit in 1965, that he wore during the East African Campaign under von Lettow (see page 418). Adjacent to the museum is a **craft workshop** with *Ufundi* ('craftsmen') picked out in flowers.

One of the main activities of the Holy Ghost Mission was to purchase slaves and present them with their freedom. A certificate of freedom was provided by the German authorities. These freed slaves had originally been captured hundreds of kilometres away in the hinterland, and the Mission undertook to rehabilitate them in **Freedom Village** just to the north of the main Mission buildings.

Kaole Ruins → *Colour map 1, B5.*

ⓘ *It is possible to walk around the ruins, but it's a good idea to take a guide for security.*

The Kaole Ruins are 5 km south of Bagamoyo, along the road past Chuo Cha Sanaa (Bagamoyo Art College), on the coastal plane of the present-day village of Kaole. The site consists of the ruins of two mosques and a series of about 30 tombs, set among palm trees. Some of the tombs have stone pillars up to 5 m high. The older of the two mosques ('A' on the site plan) dates from some time between the third and fourth centuries AD and is thought to mark one of the earliest contacts of Islam with Africa, before the main settlement took place. The remains of a vaulted roof constructed from coral with lime mortar can be seen, which formed the *mbirika* at the entrance. Here ceremonial ablutions took place, taking water from the nearby well. There is some buttressing with steps that allowed the muezzin access to the roof to call the faithful to prayer. The recess (*kibula*) on the east side, nearest to Mecca, has faint traces of an inscription on the vaulting.

The stone pillars that mark some of the tombs were each surmounted by a stone 'turban' and the remains of some of these can be seen on the ground. Delicate porcelain bowls with light green glaze were set in the side of the pillars and the indentations can be seen. The bowls, identified as celadon made in China in the 14th century and the main indication of the likely age of the structure, have been removed for safekeeping to the National Museum in Dar es Salaam. Some of the tombs have frames of dressed coral and weathered obituary inscriptions. Bodies would have been laid on the right side, with the face toward Mecca.

Mosque 'B' is of later construction and has been partially restored. It is similar to the triple-domed mosque at Kilwa Kisiwani (see page 137) in style, and it is thought that the builder may well have been the same person.

The community that gave rise to these ruins would have been founded during the Muslim period AD 622-1400. The first Muslim colonies were established from AD 740 by sea-borne migrations from the Persian Gulf down the East African coast as far as Sofala, the area round the Zambezi River. The settlement at Koale would have traded mangrove poles (see page 104), sandalwood, ebony and ivory. It is suggested that Koale might have had several hundred inhabitants. The dwellings would have used timber in their construction and would therefore have been less durable than the all-stone mosques and tombs. As they were on more fertile soil inland, they rapidly became overgrown when the dwellings collapsed. The settlement went into gradual decline as the shore became more densely packed with mangroves, making its use by dhows difficult, and commercial activity shifted to Bagamoyo.

Saadani National Park ◉ ➤ pp110-112. Colour map 1, B5.

ⓘ *The entrance fee to the reserve is US$20 adults, US$5 children (5-16), vehicle US$40 per day; www.tanzaniaparks.com; www.saadinipark.org.*

About 70 km north of Bagamoyo, Saadani was gazetted as a National Park in 2003 and it is the only national park in East Africa with ocean frontage. Some of the animals come down to the beach, especially in the early morning, and you may see elephants frolicking in the sand and sometimes even venturing into the crashing surf. This makes Saadani one of the more special and unique parks to visit in Tanzania. Its boundaries have been expanded to include land north of the Mligaji, which contains the only permanent elephant population in the area, as well as sable antelope. It also incorporates the Zaraninge forest, noted for its variety of indigenous vegetation and animal and birdlife, and land south of the Wami river. The total protected area now covers over 1100 sq km and the park headquarters are based at Mkwaja Ranch. It has plentiful game including giraffe, hartebeest, waterbuck, wildebeest, eland, buffalo, hippo, crocodile, reedbuck, black and white colobus monkey and warthog. Also present but harder to see are lion, leopard, elephant, sable antelope, greater kudu and the Beisa oryx. To the north of the reserve is a green turtle breeding beach and here, **A Tent With a View Safari Lodge** (see page 112) has started its own turtle hatchery to help conserve this endangered species. A particular highlight is the thousands of flamingos found in the salt marshes in the Wami River estuary. There is also an extensive range of bush, river and sea birds.

Ins and outs

Generally the park is accessible all year round, but the access roads are sometimes impassable during April and May. The best game viewing is in January-February and from June-August. Charter flights can be arranged through the lodges from Zanzibar (US$65) or Dar es Salaam (US$125). Although its only 60 km north of Bagamoyo you can't get from there by road as there is no crossing over the Wami River. Instead you have to drive on the inland road from Dar via Chalinze and Msata and turn right at Mandera which is 60 km from the village of Saadani. From the north, Saadani is 35 km south of the ferry at Pangani but a 4WD is needed for the sandy track. The lodges operate shuttles from Dar for about US$75 each way, they take about 3½ hours.

◉ Bagamoyo listings

For Sleeping and Eating price codes and other relevant information, see pages 36-40.

◉ Sleeping

Bagamoyo *p102, map p105*
Bagamoyo has a splendid, curved, palm-fringed beach, though often the sea is too rough for swimming. There are a few beach hotel resorts around town but some are becoming rather faded and thus overpriced. It seems a lot was expected of Bagamoyo's tourism when these huge resorts were built

a few years ago but they rarely have more than a handful of guests and as such, service and standards have slipped considerably. Some offer full board package rates. 2 of the biggest resorts, the **Paradise Holiday Resort** and neighbouring **Oceanic Bay Hotel**, were completely destroyed by fire in Mar 2009. It remains to be seen whether they'll be rebuilt.

There are a couple of good smaller places offering accommodation. For restaurants and bars, the hotels are your best bet but there are some snack bars near the covered market on Caravan St.

B Lazy Lagoon Island, private luxury island off the coast, a 20-min boat ride across the water from a jetty close to Mbegani Fisheries (a private airstrip is nearby), 8 km east of Bagamoyo. Bookings through Foxes of Africa, www.tanzaniasafaris.info. A beautiful thatch and wood construction on a perfect swathe of beach, 12 bandas with en suite bathrooms, swimming pool, spacious lounge and restaurant area linked to the rooms by a nature trail through the indigenous forest. Price includes all meals, seafood is a speciality, and dining is outside with an exceptional view of the lights of Bagamoyo in the distance. Snorkelling, kayaking, windsurfing and sailing, fishing and boat trips cost extra. Recommended.

C Livingstone Club, 2 km to the north of town, T023-244 0059/80, www.livingstone. ws. Fairly new complex with 40 a/c rooms with fridge and minibar in 10 brick cottages with thatched roofs in lovely gardens. The restaurant has an international menu. Facilities include a swimming pool, tennis courts, watersports and it is possible to arrange local excursions. Rates for a double are bed and breakfast US$114, half board US$144, full board US$168. However, the level of luxury has dropped in recent years and some readers have complained it's now overpriced.

C Millennium Sea Breeze Resort, adjacent to **Bagamoyo Art College**, T023-244 0201/3, www.millennium.co.tz. Accommodation in attractive double storey thatched rondavaals with wrought iron staircases, satellite TV and minibar, but decor is starting to look rather faded. Set in pleasant grounds though, with a swimming pool, extensive buffets for lunch and dinner, and 2 bars. Dhow trips available. Full- and half-board rates available.

D Kasiki Marine Camp, approximately 7 km east of Bagamoyo along the road to Dar es Salaam, T0744-278590 (mob), www.bagamoyo.org/kasiki.htm. Quiet resort with 6 simple bungalows, the price includes breakfast (US$56), or full board accommodation at twice the cost (US$108).

The restaurant specializes in Italian cuisine and you can buy items such as home-made pesto from the Italian chef. Can organize boat trips, and there are massages on offer.

D Travellers' Lodge, at north end of town on India St, T023-244 0077, www.travellers-lodge.com. The best mid-range option with friendly German management and good value small bungalows with shared facilities, or pleasant, traditional thatched-style self-contained rooms with a/c or fans, all built out of local materials. Excellent bar, restaurant serving plenty of seafood and watersports. Camping is available in the grounds (US$4). Recommended.

D-F Bagamoyo Beach Resort (sometimes called **Gogo**), at the north end of town, continue along India St, T023-244 0083, www.bagamoyo.org/bagbeach.htm. Another good option with French management, a/c and traditional-style rooms with thatched roofs, a/c and hot water, set in pretty gardens facing the ocean. Given the French influence, the food is exceptional, plus there's a pleasant open-air bar with thatched roof overlooking the beach. Sports facilities include wind-surfing, snorkelling, mini-golf and volleyball and there's a pool. Doubles are US$52 or you can camp for US$4.

E-F Mary Nice Place, about 200 m from **Bagamoyo College of Arts**, near the police station, T0754-024015 (mob), www.mary niceplacehotel.com. Recently renovated with several neat, spotless self-contained rooms in a smart white house with pillared balcony and veranda. Good value budget accommodation but no beach view. The owner, Mary Chibwana, is a teacher at the college and a member of the Bagamoyo Players.

Saadani National Park *p110*
L Saadani Safari Lodge, 1 km north of Saadani Village, reservations, Dar T022-277 3294, www.saadanilodge.com. Nestled among palms and spread across the beach, the 9 attractive cottages here have makuti thatch roofs, wooden floors and sailcloth

walls, and the spacious bathrooms have solar-heated hot water. Behind is a hide overlooking a waterhole where you can be served tea and cake, and a fire is lit on the beach for drinks before dinner. Activities include game drives, fishing and boat rides on the Wami River, and snorkelling in the ocean.

L-A A Tent with a View, about 30 km north of Saadani Village, reservations Dar, T022-211 0507, www.saadani.com. This has 8 tented bandas with en suite bathrooms, elegantly perched on stilts individually spaced out along the beach, and large balconies with hammocks, decorated in bright colours. There are another 2 units at beach level. Activities include walking safaris through the bush and on the beach, birdwatching by canoe on the Mafue River, and game drives and a boat safari on the Wami River. A cultural tour offers an opportunity to meet the local fishing community in Saadani Village. There are 2 rates: US$195 per person per night sharing full board, with the option of paying for activities separately depending on what you want to do, or US$295 per person per night sharing including all safari activities and park entry fees.

A Kisampa, just on the edge of the south eastern boundary of the park on the banks of the Wami River, access is usually be charter flight, reservations www.sanctuary-tz.com. A small eco-friendly camp with compost toilets and bush 'bladder' showers hanging from trees with 7 spacious tents or cottages with furnishings made from natural materials, and good set meals – they make their own bread and produce their own honey. Activities include game drives into Saadani, bush walks, village visits, fishing and canoeing on the river.

○ Shopping

Bagamoyo *p102, map p105*
There are some small general and pharmacy stores on School St. The covered market on Caravan St is excellent for fruit, vegetables, meat and dried fish. Fresh fish can be found at the fish market on Customs Rd. Some of the larger resorts have (tacky) curio shops.

⊖ Transport

Bagamoyo *p102, map p105*
Dala-dala
Several *dala-dala* a day leave from the bus stand opposite the covered market on Caravan St. A journey to **Dar** costs US$1.80 and takes 1-2 hrs, swap vehicles in Mwenge.

⊙ Directory

Bagamoyo *p102, map p105*
Banks At present there are no foreign exchange bureaux in Bagamoyo. The National Microfinance Bank, Dar es Salaam Rd, opposite the post office, will change money as will the resorts, though these tend to offer poor exchange rates. Increasingly, many of the resorts are accepting credit cards but check first. **Medical services** Bagamoyo District Hospital, India St, T023-244 0008. **Police** Intersection of Caravan St and Boma St at south end of town, T023-244 0026. **Post office** Customs Rd.

Tanga and around

→ Colour map 1, B5. Phone code: 027.
Tanga is Tanzania's second biggest seaport and third largest town. It is an attractive place with a sleepy ambiance and many fine German and Asian buildings in its centre. It has a natural deep water harbour and was briefly the German colonial capital following the treaty between the Sultan of Zanzibar and the German East Africa Company. Much of its wealth came from the sisal plantations in the hinterland but with the advent of alternative rope-making fibres this industry has fallen into decline, adversely affecting the region. Nearby places of interest include the enormous Amboni limestone caves, the Shirazi ruins at Tongoni, dating from the 10th century, and offshore coral gardens, consisting of three reefs, Mwamba Wamba, Mwamba Shundo and Fungu Nyama. The Usambara Mountains are worth a detour; Lushoto and Amani can be visited either on the way to Tanga, or when travelling to Kilimanjaro and Arusha; and Pangani, on the coast south of Tanga, makes for a decent beach holiday destination. ▸▸ *For listings, see pages 122-127.*

Tanga ⊖❼▲❸❻ ▸▸ *pp122-127. 5°5'S 39°2'E.*

→ Altitude: sea level.
The centre of Tanga (meaning 'sail' in Kiswahili) is a congested grid of roads centred around the bustling market. The buildings along Market Street are old and traffic stained, but the street is a hive of activity of small traders, food kiosks and women carrying bunches of vegetables. There are a number of interesting colonial buildings around Market Street and Independence Avenue. Most are in a poor state of repair, but it's a relaxing and easy walk around the tree lined streets, and easy to imagine that Tanga was very grand in its heyday. It's a very friendly place and lots of men on bicycles bumping in and out of the potholes will take the time to say *jambo*. Further out of town on Hospital Road towards the Yacht Club, are the quieter and sedate leafy suburbs of the more upmarket residential area, where the large houses look out into the bay from a hill. There are good views to uninhabited Toten Island out in the bay, especially when the tide is low and the yellow sandstone cliffs of the island are exposed.

Ins and outs

Getting there There are scheduled air services between Tanga and Dar es Salaam, Pemba and Zanzibar. Now that passenger rail services between Dar es Salaam and Tanga have been terminated, the only land route to Tanga is by road. Bus services take four to six hours to cover the 460 km from Dar es Salaam via Chalinze and Segera (the junction on the Dar–Moshi road from where the branch road to Tanga veers off to the right). There are also services from Moshi to Tanga, 360 km. *Dala-dala* take one to three hours between Tanga and the Kenyan border and there is also the option of getting the Scandinavia Express bus from Mombasa to Tanga, which then goes on to Dar. There is presently not the option of driving between Dar and Tanga on the coast road as there is no crossing on the Wami River, but in a 4WD it is possible to drive from Saadini National Park up to Tanga via Pangani, having got to Saadini from Dar via Mandera first (see page 110). There is now a weekly ferry linking Tanga with Zanzibar and Pemba, though historically this service has always been somewhat unpredictable. ▸▸ *For further details, see Transport, page 126.*

Getting around Taxis, buses and *dala-dala* can be found in Uhuru Park. However, most of Tanga is within walking distance. Taxis are advisable after dark. Bikes can be hired at several places. Try around the bus stand or wherever there is a row of bikes lined up on the side of the street. You can organize tours through the **Tanga Youth Development Association (TAYODEA)**, an organization that is well worth supporting as it employs disadvantaged young local people as guides and 30% of fees taken from tourists go into community projects. For more information on the tours they offer, see Activities and tours, page 125.

Background

Carl Peters and the German East Africa Company arrived in 1885 and in 1888 leased a 16-km wide strip from the Sultan of Zanzibar along the entire coast of what is now Tanzania, between the Ruvuma and the Umba rivers. The Germans appointed agents (calling them *akidas*), though they were often not of the same tribe as the people they administered, to collect taxes and enforce law and order.

With the advent of European settlement and trade, Somalis arrived, trading in cattle but seldom intermarrying. Islanders from the Comoros also settled here.

Agriculture in the Usambara area expanded and, with the construction of the railway to Moshi, Tanga became a flourishing port. Tanga was the site of a substantial reversal for the British during the First World War. Allied troops, including 8000 Indian soldiers, found it difficult to disembark through the mangrove swamps and were repulsed by the well-organized German defence and some hostile swarms of bees that spread panic among the attackers. Over 800 were killed and 500 wounded, and the British abandoned substantial quantities of arms and supplies on their withdrawal.

After the eventual German withdrawal from Tanga, the German population was steadily replaced by Greek plantation owners. Tanga's prosperity declined with the collapse in sisal prices in the late 1950s and the large estates were nationalized in 1967. Some have now been privatized, and sisal has made a modest recovery.

The African groups in the Tanga area, excluding those in the coastal belt, number six. The **Pare** who now live in the Pare Hills came originally from the Taveta area of Kenya in the 18th century. The **Zigua** inhabited the area south of Tanga and have a reputation for aggression: Bwana Heri attacked and defeated the force of the sultan of Zanzibar in 1882. The **Nguu** clan to the west occupy the Nguu Hills and the **Ruvu** clan inhabit the Pangani islands. The **Shambaa** are around the Lushoto area and are closely allied with the **Bondei** who occupy the area between Tanga and Pangani.

Sights

The open space in the centre of town is **Uhuru Park**, originally named Selous Square after the celebrated naturalist and hunter (see box, page 380). At the junction of the square with Eukenforde Street are the German buildings of **Tanga School**, the first educational establishment for Africans in Tanzania.

On Market Street to the east of Uhuru Park is **Planters Hotel**. This once grand wooden building is now virtually derelict, but is reputed to have seen wild times as Greek sisal plantation owners came into town for marathon gambling sessions at which whole estates sometimes changed hands. It was an ornate building with arches, columns and plinths. The ground floor had a bar with a huge antique corner cabinet full of miniatures.

Proceeding north across Independence Avenue leads to the **Tanga Library**, originally the King George VI Library. The west wing was opened in 1956 and the east wing in 1958 by the then governor, Sir Edward Twining. There is a courtyard behind with cloisters and Moorish arches. To the west is the **Old Boma**, a substantial structure in typical style. Opposite the boma is a building from the German period with keyhole-style balustrades. Further to the west down Mombasa Road leading down to the shore is **St Anthony's Cathedral**, a modern 1960s octagonal building with a free-standing bell tower, a school and various mission buildings. On Boma Road there is a small, white **Greek Orthodox church**.

Following Independence Avenue back east you reach the **clock tower** and the **post office**. To the west of the Clock tower is the German Monument in marble, decorated with an eagle and oak leaves, dedicated to the 18 who died in 1889 during the Arab Revolt led by Bushiri (see page 103) and listing the five German naval vessels, under the command of Admiral Denhart, supporting Major Hermann Wissmann on the ground.

Just to the east of the Clock tower are some ruins thought to be part of the fortifications built during the First World War. On the corner of Independence Avenue and Usambara Street is the **Old Court House**, dating from the German period. Today it has been fully restored and serves as the Tanga Medical Hospital. It is a fine, double-fronted building with a Mangalore tiled roof, offices on the mezzanine level, a fluted façade and fretwork over the windows.

Opposite the Court House is **Tanga Ropeworks** where you can see examples of the ropes and twine made from sisal, known as 'white gold' in the 1950s. The **German Cemetery** is on Swahili Street and contains the graves of 16 Germans and 48 Askaris killed in the action of 4-5 November 1914. One of the Askaris is listed as *sakarini* ('crazy drunk'). Also buried here is Mathilde Margarethe Scheel (1902-1987), known as 'Mama Askari',

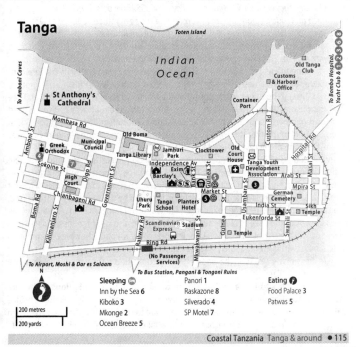

Tanga

Toten Island

Indian Ocean

To Amboni Caves →

← To Bombo Hospital, Yacht Club & ① ② ③ ⑥ ⑧

Old Tanga Club

Customs & Harbour Office

Container Port

+ St Anthony's Cathedral

Mombasa Rd

Greek Orthodox

Municipal Council

Old Boma

Tanga Library

Jamhuri Park

Clocktower

Old Court House

Tanga Youth Development Association

Arab St

Sokoine St

Independence Av

Exim

Barclay's

Bank

Guinea St

Market St

German Cemetery

Mpira St

Masai St

Custom Rd

Hospital Rd

High Court

Chianbageni Rd

Uhuru Park

Tanga School

Planters Hotel

India St

Sikh Temple

Government St

Digo Rd

Kilimanjaro Rd

Boma Rd

Eukenforde St

Temple

Scandinavian Express

Stadium

Railway Rd

Ring Rd
(No Passenger Services)

Mkwakwani

Guinea

Usambara St

Swahili St

↙ To Airport, Moshi & Dar es Salaam

↓ To Bus Station, Pangani & Tongoni Ruins

N

200 metres
200 yards

Sleeping 🛏
Inn by the Sea 6
Kiboko 3
Mkonge 2
Ocean Breeze 5

Panori 1
Raskazone 8
Silverado 4
SP Motel 7

Eating 🍴
Food Palace 3
Patwas 5

who looked after the welfare interests of the African soldiers of the *Schutztruppe* (see box, page 419) after Tanganyika became a British protectorate. Crossing over the railway line along Hospital Road to Ocean Drive is the old Tanga Club of the British period. Further east of the centre, the **Bombo Hospital** is a handsome German building, with a three-storey central block, a first-floor veranda overlooking the ocean, a Mangalore tile roof and a gatehouse.

Around Tanga

Toten Island
You can arrange a boat trip out to Toten Island, which faces the town in the bay about 1 km offshore. It's very overgrown though and surrounded by mangroves, so it's best to go at low tide when access to the beach is easier. Though they are difficult to find, there are ruins of two 15th century mosques and some German graves; hence it's name – Toten – meaning 'dead bodies' in German. TAYODEA (see page 125) can organize a motorboat to get you there and back for US$28 per person and the full guided tour lasts about four hours.

Amboni Caves → *Colour map 1, B5.*
① *Open 0900-1600, US$2. The caves are 8 km to the north of Tanga on the road to Horo Horo at the Kenyan border. They are badly signposted. The best way to get there is to cycle. It's a good way to meet the local people, the birds are numerous and you might spot a dikdik. Bikes can be hired in town for about US$1 per hr. Tours can be arranged through TAYODEA (see page 125), and they will cycle with you to the caves for US$25 per person including bikes, entry fees, lunch and sodas. Before entering the mouth of the cave you are required to write your name in the official record book, which is kept in the tour guide's office. All visitors entering the caves are recorded in the event of someone becoming lost. Take a powerful torch and go in pairs with a guide. There have been fatalities when people have explored the caves alone.*
Formed during the Jurassic Age some 150 million years ago, when reptiles were dominant on land, these natural limestone caves extend over a wide area, lying mostly underground, accessed through openings in the gorges of the Mkilumizi River and the Sisi River. They form the most extensive cave system in East Africa (estimated at over 230 sq km) and there are chambers up to 13 m high with stalactites and stalagmites. A German-Turkish survey in 1994 found that there are 10 separate cave systems, and the longest cave was 900 m. Only one of the caves is used for guided tours.

The location is of great religious significance to local people, and offerings to ensure fertility are made in one of the shrines. There are many legends associated with the caves, including beliefs that they form a 400-km underground passage to the foothills of Mount Kilimanjaro. The main cave, known as *Mabavu*, is said to be the home of the Snake God. The Digo people were reputed to dispose of unwanted albino babies in a section of the caves known as the Lake of No Return. The caves were also used by the Mau Mau as a refuge during the troubles in Kenya. A guide will escort you round the caves, illuminating the chamber with a burning torch. The caves are home to many thousands of bats (called *popo* in Kiswahili) – watching the '*popo flight*', when the bats fly out of the cave entrance at sunset, is popular.

On the way back to Tanga you can stop at the **Galamos Sulphur Springs**, 3 km from the caves off the Tanga–Mombasa road. Discovered by a local Greek sisal planter, Christos Galamos, the springs are hot and sulphurous and are said to relieve arthritis and cure skin ailments. A small spa was erected, but it has now fallen into disrepair. It is still possible to

The legend of the Shirazi migration

Ali ben Sultan Hasan of Shiraz in Persia (now Iran) had a dream in AD 975 in which a rat with jaws of iron devoured the foundations of his house. He took this as a sign that his community was to be destroyed. The court in Shiraz ridiculed the notion but his immediate family and some other followers resolved to migrate. They set out in seven dhows from the nearby port of Bushehr and sailed through the mouth of the Persian Gulf, into the Indian Ocean. There they were caught in a great storm and separated, making landfalls at seven different points on the East African coast where they settled. Among these were Zanzibar, Tongoni and Kilwa.

bathe in the springs, however but they are very smelly and muddy underfoot. From Amboni Village, the guide will take you to the Ziggi River. Here, children will look after your bicycles and you can pay a small fee to cross the river by canoe. The springs are on the other side.

Tongoni Ruins → *Colour map 1, B5.*

ⓘ *20 km south of Tanga on the road to Pangani, about 1 km off the road. Buses or dala-dala from Tanga cost about US$1 and will take up to 1 hr. A return taxi will cost about US$20; ask the driver to wait for you. Entry is US$2 if the caretaker is there to collect the fee, open daily 0900-1600.*

The Tongoni Ruins date from the Shirazi period (see box above) and the settlement was started at the end of the 10th century. The community would have been similar to that at Kaole (see page 106), but it was almost certainly larger. There are 40 tombs, some with pillars, and the remains of a substantial mosque. The mosque is of the type found along the north part of the East African coast. There is a central *musalla* (prayer room) with arches leading to aisles (*ribati*) at each side. The mosque is constructed of particularly finely dressed, close-grained coral, especially on the lintel of the *kibula,* the side of the building that faces towards Mecca. The roofs were coral on mangrove rafters. There are depressions in the pillars where there were porcelain bowls, all apparently removed during the German period. It is said that Tongoni was founded by Ali ben Sultan Hasan at much the same time as he established the settlement at Kilwa (see page 135). There are Persian inscriptions at Tongoni that would seem to establish a link with Shiraz. Vasco de Gamma visited the settlement in 1498. Again TAYODEA (see page 125) runs four-hour guided tours out here by car for US$30 per person.

Muheza ⍆ *Colour map 1, B5.*

→ *Phone code: 027.*

A sprawling, bustling town, 35 km west of Tanga along a good road, Muheza provides a link between the coastal beaches and the lush, cool Usambara Mountains. Access to the Amani Nature Reserve is from here (see below) and although part of the Usambara Mountains, which are dealt with in the North to Moshi chapter (see page 226), Amani is in the eastern mountains and accessed from the Tanga side. The town is being improved under a government urban renewal programme that has already produced a new bus stand and market (market days Thursday and Sunday). There is a post office and bank, but there are no money-changing facilities. Scandinavia Express buses stop here en route between Dar and Tanga and Mombasa, but accommodation is very primitive and there are better options in either Tanga, Korogwe to the west, or Amani.

Amani ● ⟫ pp122-127.

① To get there, you will need to make a connection at Muheza on the road linking Tanga to the Dar es Salaam to Moshi highway. There is a bus that leaves Muheza at around 1400 daily for the 25-km trip to Amani, which takes about an hour and costs US$1. In the mornings the bus leaves Amani when full, usually around 0800. The reserve charges a one-off fee of US$30 per adult, US$5 children (under 16), and a US$10 fee for photography.

The Amani Nature Reserve, part of the Eastern Usambara Mountains, is 25 km from Muheza on a dirt road that most of the year requires a 4WD vehicle, as it is steep and winding in places. In 1898, the Germans established an agricultural research institute here that was the envy of Africa. With the twin benefits of the north railway from Tanga to Moshi and the Amani Institute, the Usambara area flourished under settler farming. By 1914, 40,000 ha were under sisal, 80,000 ha under rubber and 14,000 ha under cotton, as well as extensive areas of tobacco, sugar, wheat and maize. One of the great lessons of farming in Africa is that crops have to be carefully adapted to local conditions. Amani tested soils, experimented with insecticides and developed new varieties. After 1914, Amani turned its hand to the war effort, developing a local quinine for use against malaria from cinchona bark and manufacturing chocolate, tooth-powder, soap and castor oil.

In 1997 the Nature Reserve was established to protect the biodiversity of the flora and fauna of the sub-montane rainforests of the East Usambara Mountains. This joint venture of the Tanzanian and Finnish governments seeks to protect an area whose biological significance in terms of plant and animal diversity has been compared to the Galapagos Islands. There are, for instance, three endemic bird species, the Usambara alethe, Naduk eagle owl and the Usambara weaver. The rainforests also provide the water supply for 220,000 people in Tanga.

The total area of the Amani Nature Reserve is 8380 ha, which includes 1065 ha of forests owned by private tea companies under the management of the East Usambara Tea Company. It also includes the Amani Botanical Garden, established in 1902, which has over 460 plant species and is one of the largest botanical gardens in Africa. Amani also has a medical research centre run by the Tanzanian government. Birdlife and small animals such as monkeys abound. It is excellent hiking country.

The reserve's information centre is housed in the recently rehabilitated old German Station Master's house (there was a short railway line here built in 1911 but abandoned in 1924) in the small settlement of Sigi which is also the entrance gate to the reserve. A small resthouse has also been constructed nearby. The East Usambara Catchment Forest Project has made efforts to strengthen the villagers' rights to manage their own forests, and pilot farm forestry activities have been set up in a number of villages in an effort to improve local land husbandry. A dozen forest trails have been established, including three driving routes. The East Usambara Conservation Area Management Programme created and maintains the nature trails, as well as training guides in an effort to encourage village collaboration and conservation efforts. Short or long walks can be arranged, and the guides are very knowledgeable about local species, bird and insect life and uses for traditional plants.

➤ Phone code: 027.

Pangani Village, 52 km south of Tanga, is located at the point where the Pangani River empties itself into the Indian Ocean. The river passes through the north side of the village, separating the old buildings and the present-day market from the farms and small houses on the south side. The river itself has a car and passenger ferry that runs from early morning to 1800. There are some handsome old Arab houses in town, though these are in poor repair. Around Pangani there are some excellent beaches. There has recently been a mushrooming of resorts similar to those on the north coast of Zanzibar with thatched cottages, laid back rustic bars and restaurants serving fragrant Swahili seafood, and increasingly a good choice of watersports. None of them are in the super luxury category but instead are friendly and informal retreats for mid-range and budget travellers. When choosing where to stay, bear in mind that while the resorts to the north of town are more than adequate, most are on cliff tops where there is a short walk to the beach and much of the surrounding landscape is made up of sisal plantations. **Ushongo Beach** to the south of town however, is glorious – a long swath of white sand backed by towering coconut palms. It's possible to swim even in low tide in water that averages around 25°C, and when the tide does go out, it's possible to cycle along the smooth sand on the edge of the surf. In the afternoons you will be greeted by the delightful sight of school children walking home along the beach. This is one of Tanzania's best kept secrets and makes a fine and more peaceful alternative from Zanzibar or the Kenyan coast for a beach holiday and is a long way from mass tourism. Another great advantage of visiting Pangani is the unbelievably friendly and helpful **Pangani Coast Cultural & Eco Tourism Programme** (PCCT) who can organize a vast range of tours and activities in the region, most of which involve interaction with the local community.

Ins and outs

The approach to Pangani is along the unpaved road from Tanga. The road is fine in the dry season but becomes slippery in the wet. Much of it passes through a vast sisal plantation. There are regular buses from Tanga until about 1400, which take about two hours (depending on the season) and costs US$1.50. It is only 52 km but the road is very bumpy. The bus will drop off outside the beach resorts between Tanga and Pangani. None of them are more than 1 km off the road. Once in Pangani, an option for budget travellers is to stay in cheap accommodation in town and hire a bike from places at the bus stand, take the ferry across the river and cycle to one of the beach resorts south of town for lunch and to enjoy the beach. If you get back too late for the ferry, which stops at 1800, you can try and negotiate with a local boatman to take you across. Bring cash with you from Tanga; while there is a bank in Pangani it doesn't change money and has no ATM. This has caused problems for travellers before who have had to return to Tanga and back to Pangani to pay for hotels. Be aware, as in other places in Tanzania, it's fine to wear bikinis and shorts on the beach, but in town it's important to cover up so as not to offend the Muslim community.

Background

Swahili for 'distribute' or 'arrange', it comes as no surprise that Pangani was one of the earliest ports established by the Arab settlers. A prosperous port during the 19th century, the community was ruled by an Arab Liwali, five Shirazi Jumbes and a network of *akidas*. Indian traders financed parties under Akidas to collect ivory and rhinoceros horn in the interior, and there was some trading in slaves. The town prospered as the trade in ivory and slaves flourished. It was at Pangani that Bushiri, leader of the Arab revolt of 1888-1889, was finally captured and executed (see page 103).

The mouth of the Pangani River is crossed by a sand bar. This provided shelter for dhows, and prevented them from being pursued by steam vessels when the slave trade was being suppressed after 1873. However, it also meant that vessels of deeper draught could not use the port. Traffic drifted steadily to the newer facilities at Tanga, subsequently accelerated by the railway linking Tanga to Dar es Salaam and Moshi.

In 1930 the population was around 1500 but the substantial houses on the north side of the river, built largely by slave labour, have fallen into disrepair. The economy of the town shifted to reliance on the sisal plantations, Pangani being served by shallow-draught steamers, but sisal declined drastically in price with the advent of synthetic fibres in the mid-1960s (see box opposite). There are still many coco-palms and some fishing.

Sights

The old **Customs House**, originally built in 1916 as the post office, and the old **CCM Building** are both fine structures, unfortunately in poor repair. Next to the Customs

Pangani

Sleeping	Peponi Resort 8	Tides Lodge 5
Beach Crab Resort 12	River View Inn 3	Tinga-Tinga 6
Emayani Beach Resort 1	Safari Lodge 4	Tulia Beach Lodge 11
Mashado Beach Resort 2	Seaside Community	Ushongo Beach Cottages 13
Mkoma Bay Tented Camp 7	Hostel 10	YMCA 9

Tanzania's 'White Gold'

Sisal (*Agave sisalana*) is a stiff spiky plant that looks a bit like a yucca and is used to make rope, twine and sacks (and an exceptionally little known fact – dartboards). It's strong enough to make ropes big enough to moor large ships. It is grown in many places in Tanzania and is an important export crop. It was introduced in 1882 on estates around Pangani by Dr Richard Hindroph who imported 1000 plants from Florida. However, only 62 survived the voyage via Hamburg but from such a small nucleus the plant flourished in Tanzania's favourable climate. By 1913, Tanzania was the biggest producer of sisal in the world and it became known as the 'white gold' of Tanzania. Much of it went to the German Navy during the First World War, as heavy duty rope to secure battleships. The industry flourished until the 1960s when nationalization of the economy and the replacement of natural fibres by synthetic fibres sent the industry into decline. Nevertheless, it's recovered significantly since the 1990s, as the worldwide use of natural fibres is becoming popular again and investment has meant that there has been some exploration into new uses for sisal, including making cloth, paper, bricks and roof tiles from it.

House is the old slave depot, built around 1850 and still largely intact, with some characteristic carved doors and remnants of whipping posts. It is also thought that there are underground tunnels and pits that lead to the river, along which weak slaves were taken to be washed out to sea. Just by the ferry is a plaque recording the capture of Pangani by the British on 23 July 1916, and the **Uhuru** or **Jamhuri Monument**, celebrating independence. The **Boma** is also a handsome building. Built in 1810, it is said that slaves were buried alive to strengthen the foundations. The distinctive roof was added in the German period. It is now the District Commissioner's Office and some of the original carved doors remain.

Across the river by ferry (US$0.15, US$4 cars) is the village of **Bweni**. From the hill behind the village are fine views of Pangani and of the Indian Ocean. It is possible to hire a boat, through the Pangani Coast Cultural & Eco Tourism Programme (PCCT) (see Activities and tours, page 126), to travel up the river for around two hours (around US$25-35 for a boat taking up to eight people). There are many birds, best seen at dusk, and crocodiles further upstream. You will also see local fishermen in dugout canoes and vast coconut plantations beside the river. Men climb the trees to collect coconuts or the sap from cut branches – used to make *mnazi*, an alcoholic drink.

Mkoma Bay

This is a tranquil area about 3 km north of Pangani on the road to Tanga. There are several places to stay, all set in attractive, well-kept gardens with good sea views at the edge of a small cliff. Steps lead down to the beach, which is quiet but a little rocky in places and does not have the brilliant white sands found elsewhere. Along the coral shoreline in the area known as Mkomo and Mwanaunguja, the fossilized remains of dinosaurs have been found, estimated to be 200-300 million years old.

Maziwe Marine Park

About 10 km off the coast of Pangani, Maziwe Island is incorporated in the Maziwe Marine Park. It used to be an important site for nesting turtles, and harboured mangrove forests and causarina trees, but it was partly submerged in 1978-1979 due to erosion resulting mainly from clearance of the island's vegetation cover. Today, the highlight is snorkelling and diving off the offshore reefs, although the quality can be disappointing in the rainy seasons when the water is not clear. Over 200 species of fish, 35 genera of coral (soft and hard) and a number of sea-grasses, algae and sponges are found in and around the reserve. Boats can be arranged through the resorts.

◉ Tanga and around listings

For Sleeping and Eating price codes and other relevant information, see pages 36-40.

● Sleeping

Tanga *p113, map p115*
D Mkonge Hotel (sometimes known as the Sisal Mkonge Hotel), is about 1 km east from the centre along Hospital Rd, which leads into Ocean Dr, T027-264 3440, mkongehotel@ kaributanga.com. Set in grounds by the sea, in what was designed as Amboni Park, there are lovely views over the bay and vervet monkeys play in the gardens. Completely refurbished to very high standards in 2004, the staff are excellent, credit cards are accepted, and this is easily the best place to stay in town. The 48 rooms have a/c, are a very reasonable US$80, and there's a good bar and restaurant and a swimming pool. It's worth coming here just to eat in the lovely surroundings (see Eating, page 125).
E Panori Hotel, east of the centre, south of Hospital Rd, in a quiet area beyond the Yacht Club and the other hotels, T027-264 6044, panori@africaonline.co.tz. Colonial-style building with new wing added in 1997 (though there is nothing new about any of the furnishings), with 22 rooms, some have a/c and TV. Indian and international food in an attractive open banda restaurant, and bar built around a mango tree. Well run and comfortable with secure parking.
E Silverado Hotel, Boma Rd, T027-264 6054. Reasonably new hotel with 9 modern rooms, en suite bathrooms, cable TV, fridge

and phone. Rates include breakfast and there's a small terrace restaurant and bar. Only street parking available.
E-F Raskazone Hotel, Fertilizer Rd, east of centre off Hospital Rd, T027-264 2897. Rooms with a/c and minibar are on offer, or slightly cheaper rooms without a/c. It also has a restaurant and a garden bar and the old colonial building is covered in established creepers. Breakfast is included. You can camp here for US$5 per person.
F Inn by the Sea, close to Mkonge on Ocean Dr, T027-264 4614. The 24 rooms have a/c or fans, and mosquito nets. Price includes breakfast but there is no restaurant or bar (Muslim owned). A good location on cliffs overlooking the harbour. Rather neglected in recent years but clean and at US$12 a room, cheap and has secure parking.
F Kiboko, Bombo St, in the residential area to the north of Ocean Dr, T0784-469292 (mob), jda-kiboko@bluemail.ch. Run by a very nice Swiss man who is a fantastic chef, this is better known as a great place to eat (see Eating, page 125), but you also camp here in the beautiful garden and rent a tent. The camping rate of US$4 includes breakfast, and there's an immaculate ablution block.
F Ocean Breeze, just off Independence Av, T027-264 4545. Superb value, this is easily the best budget option in town. Neat and fairly modern block, with 55 rooms but fills up quickly and is deservedly popular. Self-contained rooms with mosquito nets and cool tiled floors cost US$8. Restaurant with curries, grilled chicken and fish.

F SP Motel, Kilimanjaro St, T027-264 4435. Not much character, but 10 modern and clean en suite rooms, with fans, pay US$4 extra for a/c, rates include breakfast and there's a bar.

Amani *p118*

E Emau Hill Forest Camp, to get here go through Amani Nature Reserve and out the other side and follow the road for a few kilometres, turn right at the sign for Emau Hill (4WD only), email ahead to get directions, T0782-656526 (mob), emauhill@gmail.com. This is a mission post and school that offers some accommodation in rooms or in 3 tented bandas for US$45 per person full board or you can pitch a tent for US$7.50 per person. There's a dining banda and bar, and the menu makes good use of local produce. Lovely forested spot, along the border of the plot is a winding creek, lots of bushbabies and birds in the trees. They can provide bird lists and printed guides for local walks.
F Sigi Resthouse, near to the **Amani Forest Information Centre**, T027-264 6907, usambara@twiga.com. Very comfortable triple rooms with mosquito nets and en suite showers, and toilets in a new smart white wooden block. Serves fresh produce and can make arrangements for guided forest walks. Also camping for US$5.

Pangani *p119, map p120*

The better accommodation options are on the beaches to the north and south of town. There are, however, a couple of budget places in town itself – useful if arriving late.
B Mashado Beach Resort, on the hill south of the river ferry, T0784-659898 (mob). A luxury hotel with 40 a/c rooms, en suite bathrooms, a swimming pool, lovely gardens, nice restaurant and its own private airstrip, which the lodges south of Pangani use. In fact nothing faults it but there are no guests! Despite its plushness the hotel has become a bit of a folly since it was built in the mid-1990s and has twice gone bust and closed. The reason is that it is not a beach resort at all

and is built on the top of the cliff. On our visit it was remarkably still open and well maintained but was completely empty. Nevertheless, if you want to stay here give them at least 4 days notice and the only contact is the mobile number. Rates are a (very negotiable) US$100 per person full board.
E Seaside Community Hostel, right by the beach about 1 km to the east of town, T027-263 0318. Offers 8 simple but good quality rooms set in a large garden with restaurant and bar under thatch selling beer, soft drinks, local dishes and some seafood.
F River View Inn, Jamhuri St, just east of the old slave depot (no phone). Very basic, shared bathrooms with cold water, rooms have fans and mosquito nets, food available, nice river view as the name suggests.
F Safari Lodge, Tanga Rd, straight up the road from the ferry, T027-263 0013. Reasonable budget option in town, the 9 rooms are US$7-10 depending on size, breakfast of eggs and bread is available but not included in the rate. Tatty but clean, simple local meals and cold beers are available on the thatched terrace outside, friendly service and a good place to meet the locals. There are another 10 rooms in the annex building.

Beaches

To get to the resorts on beautiful Ushongo Beach south of Pangani you will need to take the ferry. All the lodges seem to use the same taxi guy so expect to pay about US$40 for a transfer. As you drive south from the ferry and follow the signs to the beach hotels there is a fork in the road. Turn left to **The Tides Lodge**, **Ushongo Beach Cottages** and **Beach Crab Resort** (reached in that order). Turn right to **Tulia Beach Resort** and **Emayani Beach Resort**. All the resorts to the north of Pangani are off the Tanga road.
B The Tides Lodge, 16 km south of Pangani, T027-264 0844, www.thetideslodge.com. Intimate lodge with 7 comfortable thatched and brightly painted bandas with en suite

bathrooms and verandas, romantic bar and restaurant lit by lamplight, and a swimming pool. Seafood is a speciality. Arranges snorkelling trips to the marine park and sunset cruises on the Pangani River. Can arrange air transfers. Accepts all credit cards. This is the most upmarket lodge on Ushongo Beach and gets consistently good reports. Recommended.

C Emayani Beach Resort, 17 km south of Pangani, reservations, Arusha T027-264 0755, www.emayanilodge.com. Thatched resort on the beach. The 12 bungalows with en suite bathrooms have verandas with ocean views surrounded by coconut trees. Rates are half board, considerable discounts for children, friendly cocktail bar, swimming pool, watersports, lots of boats for fishing and snorkelling, and it has its own airstrip. Accepts Visa. **Kasa Divers** (page 125) are based here.

C Mkoma Bay Tented Camp, 4 km north of Pangani at Mkoma Bay, T027-263 0000, www.mkomabay.com. Whitewashed buildings decorated with antiques, beautifully furnished tents or cheaper bandas, all have en suite bathrooms with hot water and flush toilets and mosquito nets. They also have a self-catering family house. There's a safety deposit box, swimming pool, well-stocked bar, restaurant offering excellent but quite expensive Western food (US$5-15) and they accept credit cards. Can organize boat trips on the Pangani River for US$25 and a walking tour of Pangani for US$15. Run by a friendly Danish/American couple.

D Tulia Beach Resort, 10 km south of Pangani, T027-264 0680, www.tuliabeach lodge.com. Neat set-up with 7 makuti thatched cottages with white stone walls, facing the ocean, plus a pleasant bar and restaurant. Activities include sundowner trips on a dhow and fishing rods can be hired for US$5 per hr/US$25 per day, though you need to leave a hefty US$100 deposit.

D Ushongo Beach Cottages 16 km south of the ferry, T0784-214412 (mob), www. ushongobeach.com. A bit different from the other resorts in that the 1 or 2 bedroom cottages have kitchenettes for self-catering. Fruit and veg are available locally and you can buy fresh seafood directly from the fishermen. Alternatively there's a higher full board rate which includes food and your own cook, or you can eat out at the other lodges along the beach. All drinks are available and there's a good range of watersports.

D-F The Beach Crab Resort, 17 km south of Pangani, T0784-543700 (mob), www.the beachcrab.com. Highly rated by travellers, this is run by friendly Sonja and Alex who were part of a German TV series that followed their progress in setting it up; hence its popularity with Germans. Accommodation is in en suite thatch and reed bungalows or cheaper permanent tents, again under thatch, or you can camp for US$3. There's a sociable bar with pool table, good food and they rent out bikes, snorkelling gear and windsurfs. They also organize boat transfers to Zanzibar (see page 127). Recommended.

D-F Peponi Resort, further north from Mkoma Bay, 15 km north of Pangani at Kigombe Village, T0748-202962 (mob), www.peponiresort.com. Thatched bandas with 2-5 beds, en suite bathrooms; for a group of 4 or more accommodation can work out about US$15 per person. Includes continental breakfast. Advisable to book in advance, rates are negotiable for longer stays. Good restaurant and pleasant bar that can get especially lively if there is a crowd. Camping US$4. Game fishing in the Pemba Channel on the resort's own dhow, snorkelling trips can also be arranged, wild pigs have been known to come into the resort at night.

E Tinga-Tinga, perched on the cliff 2 km north of Pangani, T027-263 0022, www.tinga tingalodge.com. Set in a grove of coconut palms, 10 neat makuti thatch cottages with fans, minibar and tea and coffee stations, TV, stone showers and locally made furniture. The partially open restaurant and bar specializes in seafood and Cajun food and has good ocean views. Rates are very good value and service is of high standard – think welcome drink and damp face towel on arrival.

F YMCA, on the same road towards the beach as **Mkoma Bay Tented Camp**, T027-263 0044. The building itself is dilapidated, but you can still camp here for US$4 per person and it's in a fine setting overlooking Mkoma Bay's beach. You can cook for yourself or walk to Mkoma Bay Tented Camp to eat.

● Eating and drinking

Tanga p113, map p115

♥♥ **Kiboko**, Bombo St, T027-264 4929. With a good local reputation, the kitchens here are immaculate and very modern, and the tables are surrounded by a flowering garden. Inventive dishes of red snapper, prawns and calamari. Open daily for lunch and dinner but call ahead first to discuss menus with the friendly Swiss Chef.

♥♥ **Mkonge Hotel**, on Ocean Dr, T027-264 3440. Fantastic setting overlooking the town and bay and set in lovely gardens. Dine inside in a dark wood dining room or outside on the terrace. Serves up very good grills and salads, or try the excellent prawn curry, and there's a full bar and some wines.

♥♥ **Ocean Breeze Hotel**, just off Independence Av, T027-264 4545. Terrace restaurant serves excellent curries, grilled chicken and fish, and cold beer. Popular and busy and the outside area is lively for a few drinks in the evening.

♥♥ **Yacht Club**, Ocean Dr. Day membership US$2, for which you can use the bar and restaurant. While you pay cash for food you need to buy a book of tickets to pay for drinks. Very large menu, good seafood, well stocked bar. A real expat hangout, but entertaining nonetheless, and the service is excellent. Dining tables are spread out on lovely stone terraces overlooking the bay.

♥ **Food Palace**, Market St, look for the red corrugated roof. Serves grills, curries, ice

cream and fruit juices. The Indian food is cheap and superb for around US$5 a plate, plus extra for rice and naan bread. It's cooked from scratch so expect to wait about 30-45 mins. Takeaway also available. There's no alcohol and the restaurant is closed during Ramadan. Good value and highly recommended.

♥ **Patwas Restaurant**, off Market St just south of market. Well run, with snacks of egg-chop (Scotch egg), meat chop, kebabs, burgers, curries and samosas. Excellent ice-cold drinks: lemon, mango, pineapple, papaya, lassi and milkshakes. Recommended for cheap eats.

Pangani p119, map p120

There are many small food stalls along the river front, where you can get items such as chapatti, omelette and rice very cheaply. Otherwise, look to the hotels which have excellent restaurants, mostly under thatch on the beach and serve superb Swahili seafood.

▲ Activities and tours

Tanga p113, map p115

Tanga Youth Development Association (TAYODEA), Independence Av, T027-264 4350, www.tayodea.org. An organization that is well worth supporting, as it employs disadvantaged young local people as guides and 30% of fees taken from tourists go into community projects. They can take you on a walking tour around town to see the historical buildings; to Amboni Caves; Tongani Ruins; arrange a boat ride to Toten Island; or a visit to a working sisal plantation. Costs are in the region of US$20 per person for a walking tour and other prices are in the listings. Guides will rightly expect a tip and bike/boat hire is extra.

Pangani p119, map p120

Kasa Divers, between Emayani and Tulia lodges on the south coast, T0786-427645 (mob), www.kasa-divers.com. A new set up with 2 experienced instructors and 8 sets of dive equipment for trips to Maziwe Marine

Border essentials: Tanzania–Kenya

Horo Horo (Tanzania)–Lunga Lunga (Kenya)

The border is at Horo Horo, 61 km north of Tanga and 5 km south of the Kenyan formalities at Lunga Lunga, which is 94 km south of Mombasa. While unpaved in places, the road is reasonable. Formalities at the border are fairly efficient, and visas for Tanzania and Kenya can be purchased. Remember you can go into Kenya and return to Tanzania on your same visa if it's still valid without paying for a new one. You'll also need to produce a yellow fever vaccination certificate to enter Kenya from Tanzania.

Transport There are through buses from Tanga to Mombasa with Scandinavia Express that leave daily at 1315, take four hours and cost US$8. In the opposite direction, buses leave Mombasa at 0800 and arrive in Tanga at 1200. Very usefully, these drop off at Ukunda, which is the village where the turn off is to Diani Beach 25 km to the south of Mombasa. There are taxis and tuk-tuks at this junction to take you on to the beach resorts.

Banks After the border on the Kenyan side the next banks are in Mombasa and Diani Beach, and on the Tanzanian side in Tanga.

Park, US$65 single dive or US$95 for 2 dives, and offers 4-day PADI Open Water courses for US$395. Can also arrange windsurfing, snorkelling, kayaking and fishing.

Pangani Coast Cultural & Eco Tourism Programme (PCCT), Jamhuri St (or Harbour Rd), next to the post office, T0748-489129 (mob), www.panganitourism.com. This programme is co-ordinated by Mr Sekibaha who has been the district cultural officer for 20 years. Drop into the office (open Mon-Sat 0800-1600) and discuss what you want to do. On offer are walks through the town; excursions to local farms, coconut and sisal plantations; visits to homes for a traditional meal and perhaps to have your hair plaited or hands and feet decorated with henna; river cruises to the mangrove swamps; and fishing with local fishermen. Can also arrange bicycle hire, snorkelling and other excursions. Emmanuel 'Hot Hot' Petro is a well recommended guide and appears to know everyone in town. All the guides carry ID so ensure you go to the office and pick up an official one as part of the fees goes towards local community development projects and this is an excellent initiative to support.

● Transport

Tanga *p113, map p115*
Air
Coastal Air, T0713-566485 (mob), Tanga airport, reservations, Dar, T022-2117959/960, www.coastal.cc. Daily flight at 1600, arrives in **Pemba** at 1630, **Zanzibar** 1710, and **Dar** at 1735.

Bus and dala-dala
Buses and *dala-dala* leave from the bus station south of the town on the other side of the railway track. Buses for **Dar** run 0800-1600 about every 30 mins, 5-6 hrs, a regular bus costs US$9 and a luxury one US$11. To **Moshi**, 4-6 hrs, US$11; to **Pangani**, regularly until about 1400, 2 hrs, US$1.50. Although it is only 52 km, the road is very bumpy and buses may take over 2 hrs depending on the season. The bus will drop off outside the beach resorts between Tanga and Pangani. None of them are more than 1 km off the road. There are also several departures a day to **Lushoto**, 3-4 hrs, US$3.

The **Scandinavia Express** office is on Ring Rd between the railway station and

stadium, T027-264 4337, www.scandin
aviagroup.com. Daily buses to **Dar** at
0730 and 1300 (4-6 hrs, US$11).

Ferry
There is a ferry to **Pemba** and then **Zanzibar**
called the *Spice Islander*. It leaves Tue at 0800,
US$20 to Pemba and US$30 to Zanzibar.
There is a 5 hr wait at Pemba before
continuing on to Zanzibar. It makes
its return journey on Sun.

Note Ferry services have been hopelessly erratic from Tanga in the past, so this
is not to be relied on. The better option is
to go from Pangani (below) to catch a
boat to Zanzibar. Remember it is illegal
for foreigners to go from the mainland to
the islands by dhow.

Pangani *p119, map p120*
Bus
The bus stand in Pangani is on Jamhuri St
opposite the ferry. There are no buses to
Bweni on the other side of the river. The only
regular service is to **Tanga** (2 hrs, US$1.50).
It is only 52 km but the road is very bumpy
and the journey time varies depending on
the s eason.

Motorboat
To the south of Pangani the string of new
lodges around Ushongo Beach can now
organize motorboat transfers to **Kendwa
Beach** on Zanzibar that take 8-10 people
(3½ hrs, US$130-150). This is a very useful
service and the best place to enquire is at
the **Beach Crab Resort**, where you may be
able to tag along with another group.

Alternatively, arrange for a boat to come
and pick you up again after a few days on
the island.

Note There was concern that people
arriving at Kendwa (where there is no
immigration) and then leaving Zanzibar
through the port at Stone Town might get
into trouble as they wouldn't have an entry
stamp for Zanzibar. However, travellers have
reported that the immigration people in
Stone Town are fully aware that people
arrive and depart in Kendwa from Ushongo
Beach and have reported no problems.

⊙ Directory

Tanga *p113, map p115*
Banks Exim Bank, and Barclay's are on
Market St, near Planters Hotel. **Internet**
Globe Net Works on Market St; Impala
Internet, Market St; or there are plenty
of other places around town. **Medical
services** Bombo Regional Hospital on
Ocean Dr to east of town centre, T027-264
4390. **Police** off Independence Av, near
Tanga library. **Post office** Independence Av
near Msambara St.

Pangani *p119, map p120*
Banks The only bank in Pangani does
not change money. It's essential to bring
cash with you. **Telephone** Telephone
calls may be made from the TTCL shop
just west of the Jamhuri Monument.

Mafia Island

→ *Colour map 1, B6. 7°45'S 39°50'E. Phone code: 023.*

Mafia, the southernmost of the islands along the coast, is a wonderful little island at the centre of the largest marine park in East Africa. At around 20 km long and 8 km wide, it's a real sleepy backwater, a remnant of the old Swahili coast and a place to visit now if you want to see how Zanzibar was 30 years ago. Unlike Zanzibar and Pemba which, along with a number of smaller islands, form the semi-autonomous state of Zanzibar, Mafia is politically an integral part of mainland Tanzania. The inhabitants are mainly fishermen but other industries involve the coconut palms and cashew nut tree plantations. Geographically, as well as politically, the island, with its central areas covered with bush, light woodland and plantations, is much more like the mainland in character than the other islands. The coast is generally lined with palm trees, but there are no sweeping sandy beaches like those on Zanzibar. Here the shoreline is narrow and mangrove forests are widespread, so it's not primarily a beach destination. It is, however, an excellent diving destination. The recent gazetting of Mafia Island Marine Park – the largest protected area in the Indian Ocean – which includes surrounding villages in its conservation efforts means that the millions of fish and coral species that thrive in the warm waters around Mafia are fully protected.
▶▶ *For listings, see pages 132-134.*

Ins and outs

Getting there Flights from Dar es Salaam take 30-40 minutes. There are now several operators offering daily flights, including **Coastal Air**, T022-284 2700, T023-240 2426 (Mafia), www.coastal.cc, whose scheduled service departs Dar at 1500 (US$110). **Coastal Air** also operates daily flights from Zanzibar at 1400 (1½ hours; US$145). By sea, there are irregular services out of Dar. ▶▶ *For further details, see Transport, page 134.*

Getting around The airport is about 12 km from the lodges at the southern tip of the island around Chole Bay. The lodges will collect you in their vehicles. There are few taxis on the island; indeed there are very few vehicles of any sort. Mafia has no public transport system. The upmarket lodges and hotels ferry their guests around the island, and budget travellers have the option of walking, hitchhiking – which can involve lengthy waits – or hiring a bicycle. Enquire at New Lizu Hotel in Kilindoni.

Background

There is evidence of foreign, probably Shirazi, settlers on Mafia from as early as the 8th or 9th century. From the 12th to the 14th century it was an important settlement and the remains of a 13th-century mosque have been found at Ras Kismani, at the southwestern point of the island. By the 16th century, when the Portuguese arrived, it had lost much of its importance and was part of the territory ruled by the king of Kilwa. There is little left of the site of the settlement of the 12th to 14th century, although old coins and pieces of pottery are still found occasionally, particularly to the south of Kilindoni where the sea is eating away at the ruins. On the nearby island of Juani can be found extensive ruins of the town of Kua. The town dates back to the 18th century and the five mosques go back even further to the 14th century. In 1829 the town was sacked by Sakalava cannibals from Madagascar who invaded, destroyed the town and dined on the inhabitants.

From the beginning of the 19th century traders from all over the world had been plying these coastal waters. 'Americani' cloth proved itself to be perhaps the most popular of all the traded goods among the resident population. The trading of goods and of slaves was soon to be followed by the interest of European politics but it was not until the end of the century that this affected territorial rights. Under the treaty of 1890, Mafia, along with Zanzibar and Pemba, were initially allotted to the British sphere. However, it was later agreed that Mafia should go to Germany in exchange for some territory on the southern border, which was allocated to the British Territory of Nyasaland (now Malawi). The island was therefore included in the purchase of the coastal strip from Sultan Seyyid Ali and the German flag was raised in 1890.

The Germans established a headquarters at Chole and in 1892 a resident officer was posted here together with a detachment of Sudanese troops. A large two-storey boma was constructed with various other buildings such as a gaol. The site seemed ideal with good anchorage for dhows, but with the opening of a regular coastal steamship service a deeper harbour was needed and the headquarters were moved to Kilindoni in 1913.

During the First World War it became clear that Mafia represented an extremely useful base from which attacks could be launched. In particular the British needed a base from which to attack the SS *Königsberg*, which was wreaking havoc up and down the East African coast. In January 1915 a British expeditionary force under Colonel Ward landed on the island at Kisimani and the islands were captured with little resistance. A garrison of about 200 troops remained on the island. The *Königsberg* had been damaged and gone into the mouth of the River Rufiji for repairs. The delta, with its many creeks and maze of streams, proved the perfect hiding place. It was important that the British should find and destroy the ship before any further damage could be done. In 1915 a British warplane was assembled on Mafia, took off from there, spotted the ship and boats then went into the delta to destroy it. This was the first use of aerial reconnaissance in warfare. The wrecked remains of the crippled boat could be seen until 1979 when it finally sank out of sight into the mud.

For a short period the islands were under military rule, and were later administered by Zanzibar. In 1922 the islands were handed over by the government of Zanzibar to become part of the Tanganyika Territory under the United Nations Mandate.

These days, the coconut industry is particularly important and Mafia has the largest coconut factory in East Africa at Ngombeni Plantation. It produces copra

Mafia Island

Ras Mkundi

Barakuni Island

Kirongwe

Kilondoni

Ras Kismani

Chole Bay

Chole Island

Juani Island

Kua

Mafia Island Marine Park

Jibondo Island

N

2 km
2 miles

Sleeping
Big Blue **5**
Blue House **7**

Chole Mjini Lodge **1**
Harbour View **8**
Kijiju Guest House **9**
Kinasi Lodge **6**
Mafia Island Lodge **2**
New Luzi **4**
Pole Pole **3**
Ras Mbisi Lodge **11**
Whale Shark Lodge **10**

(dried kernels), oil, coir yarn and cattle cake. More recently, geological surveys have shown that the Mafia Deep Offshore Basin, an area of 75,000 sq km, contains deposits of oil and gas. Exploration has already started and, given the extreme poverty of many of the people on the island, the onset of employment opportunities has given a renewed sense of optimism to Mafia's inhabitants – ecological concerns notwithstanding.

Sights

Kilondoni → *Colour map 1, B6*

Kilondoni is the main town and a refreshingly simple place. The only road is flanked on either side for a kilometre or so by classic Swahili buildings with carved doors and in the centre of town there is a small market. Whilst dhows remain commonplace to this day all along the East Coast of Africa, the huge ocean-going *jahasi* are increasingly rare. Here, on the beach at Kilondoni, there are usually three or four of these giant boats, which are still in service providing an essential means of trade with the mainland. This working beach-front at Kilondoni is one of the highlights of a visit to Mafia. On the shore you can watch the construction of boats 20-25 m in length and weighing up to 100 tonnes. Timbers are prepared by hand and the frame of the boat is made from naturally V-shaped forked branches of trees.

Ruins at Kua

① *Local fishermen will take you to Kua for US$3-4.*

The largely 18-century ruins of the town of Kua are on Juani Island to the south of Mafia Island. The remains are tucked away inconspicuously on the western side of the island covering a large area of about 14 ha. In 1955, when the site was cleared of bush, one observer stated that he believed that these ruins were 'potentially the Pompeii of East Africa'. However, the remains still require a lot of work on them to bring them up to anything like that standard. There are several houses, one of which was clearly double-storeyed. Beneath the stairs leading to the upper level is a small room in which slaves could be confined for punishment. Under the building is the *haman* (bathroom), with a vaulted ceiling of curved coral blocks. A soil pipe runs from the remains of an upper room to a pit below. Two mosques and a series of tombs, some with pillars, are nearby. The evidence suggests that the town did not have a protective wall and that the inhabitants were mainly involved in agricultural pursuits on the island rather than in sea-trading.

There is also a cave on the island formed by the action of the sea. The water streaming out of the cave as the tide turns is reputed to cure *baridi yabis* ('cold stiffness' – rheumatism) and other ailments. The cure is not effective, however, unless the hereditary custodian of the cave is paid a fee and the spirits of the cave appeased by an offering of honey, dates or sugar.

Nororo Island

Nororo is a small island 12 km off the north coast of Mafia with a fishing community of about 50 local boats. There are two small *hotelis* selling rice, *ugali* and fish and it's possible to camp on the beach in a thatched shelter.

Baracuni Island

This is a beautiful small island with fine beaches about 12 km off the northwest coast of Mafia and an hour's sailing from Nororo. It's used as a base for fishing dhows. You need to have your own food, water and tent if you want to stay.

Swimming with whale sharks

Measuring up to 12 m in length and weighing around 13 tonnes, the whale shark is the largest fish in the world. Known as 'Papa Shillingi' along the Swahili coast, from the story that its spots derived from God throwing shillings at it, this solitary beast swims off the coast of Mafia and its lagoons during feeding times from October to March. Its mouth alone can measure up to 1.5 m, which can be filled with as many as 350 rows of teeth. And yet, it's perfectly safe to swim with …

Whale sharks are the gentle giants of the Indian Ocean and eat only plankton, so there's no danger of a repeat of a grisly scene from *Jaws*. No special skills are required if you want to try swimming with them – as long as you can snorkel, you can have a go. However, because the whale shark can cover huge distances, as with any wild animal, there's no guarantee you'll find one.

The main hotels on the island all offer snorkelling trips, especially to see whale sharks during the season and it's an unforgettable experience – even seasoned divers have been silenced by the awkward beauty of these enormous beasts gliding beneath them. As with any wildlife encounter, always respect their space and you may just be rewarded: there have been several reports of whale sharks playing with swimmers, even allowing them to tickle their tummies and scratch away their parasites.

Whale sharks are vulnerable and relatively little is known about their behaviour and biology. To find out more, and to share your experiences, go to www.whalesharkproject.org, and contribute towards their survival.

Mafia Island Marine Park → Colour map 1, B6

① *Park fee of US$10 per day, payable whether or not you go diving. All the lodges (see Sleeping below) have dive schools and rent out equipment. Note that during Apr-Sep the monsoon winds blow too hard, making it impossible to dive outside the lagoon and leading to a deterioration in visibility.*

To protect an internationally significant ecosystem, the Mafia Island Marine Park (the first in Tanzania) was opened in July 1995. The project is backed by the World Wildlife Fund, which contributes human and financial resources for its development and maintenance. Here you can experience some of the best deep-sea diving in Tanzania. There is something here for everyone, from the most experienced diver to those who want to snorkel in the shallower pools. The coral gardens off Mafia are marvellous – wonderfully vivid fish, shells, sponges, sea cucumber and spectacular coral reefs. Two of the most beautiful reefs are the Okuto and Tutia reefs around Juani and Jibondo Islands, a short distance from Chole Bay. About 1 km off Mafia's coastline there is a 200-m deep contour along the seabed of the Indian Ocean. The depth contributes to the wide variety of sea life. Due to its position alongside the barrier, the island is the meeting place of large oceanic fish and the vast variety of fish common to the Indian Ocean coral reefs. There are over 400 species of fish in the park. Mafia Island and some of the uninhabited islands around are also traditional breeding sites for the green turtle. Sadly, you would be very lucky to see these as the local population is now close to being wiped out – they are killed both as adults for their meat and as eggs. Another threatened species is the dugong, which lives in sea grass such as that found between Mafia and the Rufiji delta. Because of their strange shape, early sailors thought they had breasts (giving rise to the legend of the mermaid).

The legend of Ras Kismani

The town of Ras Kismani was originally settled by the Sakalava from Madagascar. The townspeople built a large ship, and when it was completed they invited the local people of Kua to a feast. During the celebrations, the Sakalava seized several children and laid them on the sand in the path of the ship as it was launched.

The Kua people planned revenge at their leisure. Seven or eight years later they invited the Sakalava of Ras Kismani to attend a wedding at Kua. The celebrations were in a special room beneath a house. Gradually the hosts left, one by one, until only an old man was left to entertain the guests. As he did so, the door was quietly bricked up, and the bodies remain to this day. A message was sent to the headman at Ras Kismani that the account was now squared. Within a month, Ras Kismani was engulfed by the sea.

This strange beast is protected by law, but hunting continues. It's also possible to swim and snorkel with whale sharks at certain times of the year, particularly between October and March, and most local hotels offer this through their diving schools (for more information, see box, page 131).

Diving The diving around Mafia can be described as a 'shallow Pemba with more fish' – beautiful reefs and spectacular fish life. Jino Pass and Dindini Wall are two sites to the northeast of Chole Bay. Both reefs have flat tops at 8 m dropping vertically in a spectacular wall to 25 m with a sandy bottom. Whip corals 2-3 m long grow out from the walls. There are a couple of interesting (if tight) swim-throughs and a long tunnel cave at 20 m on 'Dindini Wall'. Impressive sightings include huge malabar, potato and honeycomb groupers, giant reef rays, green turtles, great barracuda, kingfish, bonito, shoals of bluefin trevalley and snappers in their thousands.

On the eastern entrance to Chole Bay lies Kinasi Pass. There is a recommended drift dive in the Pass but it must be dived on an incoming tide and is for experienced divers only if diving on a spring tide. The Pinnacle in the centre of the mouth of the Pass is a good opportunity to see large rays, groupers, eagle rays and jacks. Best dived on slack or gentle incoming tide and you will need an experienced guide to find the site.

Tanzanian authorities are now waking up to need to protect the marine environment and several areas have been set aside for marine conservation, funded through conservation agencies and tourism, including the whole of Mafia Island.

⊙ Mafia Island listings

For Sleeping and Eating price codes and other relevant information, see pages 36-40.

⊜ Sleeping

Mafia Island *p128, map p129*
There are few places to stay on the island, but this is changing as more varied accommodation is opening up. People running the low-budget guesthouses may not be able to speak English and they are more likely to quote rates and want payment in TSh rather than in dollars. **Pole Pole, Kinasi** and **Chole Mjini** close during rainy season from the beginning of Apr to the end of May.
L-A Chole Mjini Lodge, on the 1 sq km Chole Island, UK reservations, T+ 44 (0)1306-880770, www.africatravelresource.com.

The lodge has been developed by Jean and Ann de Villiers with the prime intention of using the money earned to help local people on the island. The lodge is truly eco-sensitive, built by local people using local materials, and revenues have helped to establish a school and medical centre on the island. Chole is part of the Mafia Island Marine Park, so there is an additional park fee of US$10 per day. The 7 rooms are actually treehouses, built partially on stilts, most with private bathrooms with long-drop toilets, solar heated water for the showers and balconies. There is a restaurant and bar area, the meals being primarily seafood, and snorkelling and diving are on offer. Rates vary seasonally from US$200-340.

A Kinasi Lodge, 100 m up the beach from **Mafia Island Lodge**, T024-223 8220, www.mafiaisland.com. Set up on a hillside above the bay, on the site of an old cashew plantation, the lodge has a dozen rooms arranged around a stylish central dining and lounge area. Its beach is not quite as nice as its rivals but it has a beautiful main complex with old coastal traditional decor, and a small library, bar, patio and dining room. It accommodates 20 people, the rooms are beautifully decorated with en suite bathrooms (some with corner baths) and mosquito nets, but there's no a/c. The swimming pool over-looks its beach and there's a new – very opulent – spa here that even has a honey-moon spa room for 'his and her massages'. The lodge can arrange diving and other watersports. Satellite TV and internet is available for guests at a charge of US$5 for the duration of your stay.

A Pole Pole Bungalow Resort, between **Kinasi Lodge** and **Mafia Island Lodge**, Chole Bay, reservations Dar, T022-260 1530, www.polepole.com. 7 spacious bungalows on stilts with wide verandas facing the Mafia Island Marine Park and the islands of Chole, Juani and Jibondo. Built using natural materials, the decor is stunning with hard wood floors and mahogany furniture, and linen imported from Italy. This is a beautiful, peaceful spot and the emphasis is on relaxtion, with a massage parlour that overlooks the sea. You're requested not to use mobile phones in the public areas. The lodge shares a dive school with the nearby **Mafia Island Lodge**. US$220 per person sharing but the rates are full board and include boat trips to the nearby coves and islands.

A Ras Mbisi Lodge, on the west coast, about 15 km north of the airport, T0754-663739 (mob), www.mafiaislandtz.com. Mafia's newest lodge has 9 tented bandas, all en suite and with private balconies, set in lovely grounds by the beach and made from sustainable coco-wood. At the time of writing, there were no other lodges in the area so it currently has an air of seclusion about it. They grow their own vegetables here and, as much as possible, source food from nearby villages for their restaurant overlooking the beach. They can arrange visits around the island to local villages and to Chole Bay and the marine park.

B Mafia Island Lodge, Chole Bay, reservations Dar, T022-211 6609, www.mafia lodge.com. Well-managed by Gabriel, an Italian American, this lodge is in a lovely setting overlooking Chole Bay, with friendly and efficient staff. The are 35 comfortable and colourful rooms here, all have a/c. The relaxing thatched bar and restaurant are the main hub of the lodge and the food is excellent. The lodge has its own beach, where there's a dive centre, windsurfs and Hobicats for rent. Great value at US$90 half board per person in a superior room.

D Big Blu Diving College, just down the beach from **Mafia Island Lodge**, T0784-918 069 (mob), www.bigblumafia.org. Described by Mario, the Italian owner, as a diving college with accommodation, this place offers diving courses, dives and snorkelling. Has 3 simple but comfortable bandas on the beach, with private bathrooms. US$45 per person including breakfast. There's also a small restaurant here with lunch for US$16 and dinner for US$20, with meals organized by a local cooperative as part of the Mafia

Island Self Sustaining Programme. Single dives US$40, double dives US$70 and snorkelling US$15. Internet access available.

F Blue House, Utende Village by Chole Bay, signposted on the left if driving towards the bay, T0755-828825 (mob), nyundo91@yahoo.co.uk. This new guesthouse, run by the enterprising Mohammed who speaks excellent English, is the only budget accommodation in Chole Bay. The rooms are basic with fans and shared squat toilets with showers over them. US$15 for a double, although disounts are available for students and volunteers. Mohammed's mother will cook meals with advance notice. Internet access available for guests. There are plans for another small bungalow and camping facilities for next summer.

F Harbour View, on the harbour in Kilindoni, T0755-560314 (mob). The location is fun – there's a lot of local life here, with food stalls and boat building. But the lodge itself is fairly gloomy. Rooms have mosquito nets, fans and their own bathrooms. Price includes breakfast but lunch and dinner need to be pre-ordered. The bar is in an enormous thatched building towards the harbour, lots of space but not much atmosphere.

F Kijuju Guest House, Kilindoni, on the left of the main road to Chole Bay, T0757-077065 (mob). A very simple budget option. No en suite bathrooms, but the 8 rooms do have nets and fans and they are clean and secure.

F The New Lizu Hotel, in the centre of Kilondoni, T023-240 2683. A basic guesthouse in a good location with simple rooms offering nets and fans for about US$8-9, not including breakfast. It is aimed at the resident market, so don't expect anywhere near a Western level of comfort or facilities, but the place is friendly and there is a restaurant here serving fish, rice, etc but you need to pre-order dinner. Internet facilities available.

F Whale Shark Lodge, about 2 km from the aiport in the opposite direction from Kilidoni, T0755-696067 (mob). There are 4 bungalows here, quite basic with squat toilet, shower and fan. The price includes breakfast. Camping is

US$6 per tent and an additional US$6 for breakfast. The restaurant and bar overlook the bay where whale sharks come to bathe at sunset, and there's access to the beach. Serves fish, octopus, calamari, samosas and chapati.

▲ Activities and tours

Mafia Island *p128, map p129*
Diving
For more information on diving on Mafia Island, see page 132.

Mafia Island Lodge and Big Blu Diving College (see page 133) both offer diving excursions.

Fishing
Fishing is at its best from Sep-Mar when the currents and the northeast monsoon (*kaskazi*) give rise to an enormous variety of fish. When the south monsoon (*kusi*) blows during the rest of the year fishing can be rather sparse. 'Big game' fish that can be caught in the area include marlin, shark, kingfish, barracuda and red snapper.

Game fishing, diving and other boat excursions can be arranged at **Chole Mjini Lodge**, **Pole Pole** and **Kinasi Lodge**. Guests are taken out by an experienced skipper. **Kinasi Lodge** is a member of the International Game Fishing Association and has weighing facilities. It also holds a fishing competition every Feb.

⊙ Transport

Mafia Island *p128, map p129*
Air
Coastal Air, T022-284 2700, T023-240 2426 (Mafia), www.coastal.cc, has a daily service to **Dar** that departs at 1700 (30 mins, US$110). They will also run a daily service between Mafia and **Kilwa**, if there are enough takers, leaving Mafia at 1540 (35 mins, US$110) and Kilwa at 1650 on the return to Mafia.

Kilwa

→ *Colour map 1, C6. 9°0'S 39°0'E.*

Of exceptional historical interest, Kilwa is a group of three settlements magnificently situated on a mangrove-fringed bay dotted with numerous small islands. It grew up as a gold trade terminus and when its fortunes faded some magnificent ruins were left behind. These are said to be some of the most spectacular on the East African coast but are today giving themselves slowly to the encroaching jungle and the relentless cycles of the tide. Once an important centre of Swahili culture and civilization, the baked limestone, coral blocks, the fig tree roots growing through the windows and a few shattered tiles give witness to many years' habitation here. If Kilwa was in Kenya the place would be full of tourists – it is an extraordinarily rewarding place to visit. As it is, it gets just a handful of visitors each week. The town itself is pleasant and quiet, with a few local bars and restaurants and a busy market. The area is, however, beginning to see changes due to potential industrial developments involving oil and biofuels: there's talk of extending the harbour for freight ships, the road to Dar has improved, there are better bus facilities and even a couple of new internet cafés in town (although the electricity supply is still fairly erratic). In the future, as the infrastructure improves, it is unlikely that Kilwa will remain as unspoilt and inaccessible as it is at present.
▶▶ *For listings, see pages 139-140.*

Kilwa area

Ins and outs

Getting there The road from Dar es Salaam to Kilwa is part tar, part dirt. There is now a new bridge over the Rufiji river so there is no more hassle catching ferries or buses waiting overnight at the crossing. The road from Dar has improved too but there is a 60 km stretch about 180 km north of Kilwa, which is still very rough and takes three hours. The journey takes about eight to ten hours, depending on the weather. Buses go direct from the Ubungo Bus Station in Dar at 0500 and cost US$15. Confirm exact departure time and book a ticket the day before you travel. Alternatively, take one of the numerous buses heading for destinations south of Kilwa, such as Mtwara, Lindi or Nachingwea. These leave Dar between 0700 and 0900. Again it is advisable to book at least a day in advance. Seats closer to the front are recommended as the going is rough. This bus will drop you off at Nangurukuru, a village 12 km from Kilwa Masoko, from where you have to transfer to a minibus or pickup to complete the journey (US$1).

Coastal Air flies to Kilwa from Dar at 1500 (two hours) if there are enough passengers needing the service. It's always best to check with Coastal before making firm plans. A charter is a possibility, particularly for groups. ▸▸ *For further details, see Transport, page 140.*

Getting around The town is split between Kilwa Kisiwani (Kilwa on the Island), 2 km offshore; Kilwa Kivinje (Kilwa of the Casuarina Trees) on the mainland; and Kilwa Masoko (Kilwa of the Market), which was built as an administrative centre on a peninsula and is the site of the main present-day town. There is a superb beach a stone's throw from Kilwa Masoko centre and another, even better, one a few miles north of the town (ask for *Masoko pwani*). There are frequent minibuses or pickups between Kilwa Kivinje and Kilwa Masoko.

Background
Kilwa Kisiwani contains the ruins of a 13th-century city of the Shirazi civilization, which is well preserved and documented. The town was founded at the end of the 10th century by Shirazis (see box, page 117), and flourished with the core of commercial activity based on the trade of gold from Sofala (in present-day Mozambique). It grew to be the largest town on the south coast and prospered to the extent that Kilwa could maintain an independent status with its own sultan and coinage.

The large stone town that grew up thrived and the architecture was striking. The largest pre-European building in equatorial Africa was located here – the Husuni Kubwa. However, Kilwa's fortunes were reversed in the 14th century. Vasco da Gama was said to have been impressed by the buildings of Kilwa and in 1505 a large Portuguese fleet arrived and took the town by force. Their aim was to take control of the Sofala gold trade and they did this by erecting a garrison and establishing a trading post in the town from where they set up a gold trade link with the interior. Without the gold trade the Shirazi merchants were left with little to keep the wealth growing and the town quickly went into decline. Having taken over the gold trade, and thus triggering the decline of the town, the Portuguese decided there was little point in staying in Kilwa, now an out-post that was expensive to maintain. So they withdrew and continued the gold trade from further afield.

Deprived of the main source of income, the town continued to decline. In 1589 disaster struck when a nearby tribe, the Zimba, attacked the town, killing and eating many of the inhabitants. In the 17th century, with the arrival of the Oman Arabs, Kilwa began to revive and many of the buildings

Kilwa Masoko

N

200 metres
200 yards

Sleeping 🛏
Hilton Guest House
  & Restaurant **1**

Kilwa Dreams **5**
Kilwa Guest House **2**
Kilwa Ruins Lodge **4**
Kilwa Seaview Resort **6**
Kimbilio **8**
Masasi Guest House **9**
New Mjaka Guest Houses **3**

were taken over by the sultans as palaces. The slave trade (see page 415) made a significant impact on this area and Kilwa Kivinje on the mainland flourished from the caravan route from the interior, which terminated at the port.

Sights

Kilwa Kisiwani

ⓘ *Small dhows in the harbour at Kilwa Masoko will take you across the 2 km channel for US$8 (with a motor), or it's possible to get there in a passenger boat for US$0.30, which usually leaves early in the mornings when full. However, it is first necessary to get a permit to visit the site (approximately US$2) from the Cultural Centre at the district headquarters, which is on the road leading to the harbour. Alternatively, Kilwa Seaview Resort (see Sleeping, page 139), are able to arrange the whole trip including boat, permit and guide for US$30 per person, plus an additional US$10 per person if using their car to get to the harbour. Jamilla, who works at Kilwa Seaview, is an extremely knowledgeable guide and will take you through the ruins, giving some background information on the buildings and their former inhabitants. Allow at least half a day for your visit and note that the ruins are spread around the island so some walking is inavoidable. You'll need to bring water and sun protection.*

Gereza Fort The original Gereza was built in the 14th century. The one standing there today was built by the Omani Arabs in the 19th century on the site of the original on the orders of the Imam of Muscat. It is a large square building built of coral set in lime. The walls, with circular towers at the northeast and southwest corners, are very thick and it has an impressive entrance of fine wood carving.

Great Mosque (Friday Mosque) This mosque is said to have been built in the 12th century and is probably the largest of this period on the east coast. It was excavated between 1958 and 1960 and parts of it have been reconstructed. The oldest parts that remain are outer sections of the side walls and the north wall. The façade of the *mihrab* (the aspect that points towards Mecca) is dated from around 1300. The domed chamber was supposed to have been the sultan's prayer room. The water tanks and the slabs of stone were for rubbing clean the soles of the feet before entering the mosque.

Great House The large single-storey building is said to have been the residence of the sultan, and the remains of one of the sultans are said to reside in one of the four graves found within its walls. The building is an illustration of the highly developed state of building and architectural skills in this period with examples of courtyards, reception rooms, an amphitheatre that is unique to this part of the world, latrines, kitchens and cylindrical clay ovens.

Small Domed Mosque About 150 m southwest of the Great House, this is without doubt the best preserved of all the buildings in Kilwa. It is an ornamental building with beautiful domes. The long narrow room on its east side is thought once to have been a Koran school.

House of Portico Little remains of this once large building. There are portico steps on three of its sides from where it gets its name and its doorway has a decorated stone frame.

Makutini Palace (Palace of Great Walls) This large, fortified building is believed to date from the 15th century. It is to the west of the Small Domed Mosque and is roughly triangular in shape. Its longest wall, which ran along the coast, is in ruins. Within the complex is the grave of one of the sultans.

Jangwani Mosque The ruins of this stone building are concealed under a series of mounds to the southeast of the Makutini Palace. This mosque was unique for having ablution water jars set into the walls just inside the main entrance.

Malindi Mosque This mosque to the east of the Gereza Fort was said to have been built and used by immigrants from Malindi on the Kenya coast.

Husuni Kubwa This building is thought to be the largest pre-European building in equatorial Africa. It is between 1-2 km to the east of the main collection of ruins on top of a steep cliff. It is certainly an exceptional construction with over 100 rooms and a large conical dome that reaches about 30 m above the ground. The mosque has 18 domes on octagonal piers, separated by high barrel vaults. The piers are decorated with bowls of white porcelain set in the plaster.

Husuni Ndogo This is a smaller version of Husuni Kubwa separated from it by a small gully. It is said to have been built in the 15th century with walls 1 m thick and towers in the corners.

Kilwa Kivinje → *Colour map 1, C6*

About 29 km north of Kilwa Masoko, Kilwa Kivinje is an attractive historical trading centre whose heyday was during the slave trading times of the 18th and 19th centuries, but which remained the district headquarters up until 1949. It retains many interesting old buildings dating back to the 19th century as well as the colonial period and is somewhat reminiscent of Bagamoyo. A handsome old boma on the shore dates from the German period, as does the covered market. Several fine, though rather dilapidated, houses stand

Kilwa Kivinje

along the main street. There is an old mosque in the centre, and to the east of the town is a cemetery with tombs and pillars. The town can be reached by *dala-dala*, heading for Manguruturu, costing about US$1. There are half a dozen or so each day.

Songo Mnara and offshore islands

Songo Songo is an island about 25 km northeast of Kilwa Kivinje, protected by a reef, lying close to the site of a large natural gas field in a Lower Cretaceous sandstone reservoir. The Songo Songo gas field contains unusually dry petrogenic gas, which is 97% methane. From 2003 the Songas Project has been operational and the gas is being extracted from the gas field and piped to Dar es Salaam to fuel a power station that was until recently fuelled by more expensive oil. Songo Songo, **Jewe Island** and the surrounding smaller islands are an important marine bird breeding site. Access is by dhow, and there is usually at least one service each day transporting the gas employees, which takes around three hours each way, arranged in Kilwa Kivinje.

About 10 km south of Kilwa Kiswani there is another group of islands. To get there you can hire a motorized dhow from **Kilwa Seaview** (US$100 for up to five people), or it's possible to catch a local boat from Kilwa Masoko through the district headquarters office. The ruined buildings at Songo Mnara are exceptional. The settlement is surrounded by the remains of a wall and the main mosque is distinguished by herringbone stonework and it has a double row of unusually high arches at one end. The Sultan's Palace, with its high walls, is extensive and was evidently at least two storeys high. The doorways, faced with slender stonework, are particularly fine. The building to the east of the palace has a room with a vaulted roof and porcelain bowls are set into the stonework. There are three other smaller mosques, two of which abut the surrounding wall. Fragments of porcelain and earthenware abound, and some relics have been identified as Egyptian, dating from the 14th and 15th centuries.

About 3 km southwest of Songo Mnara is an area known as **Sanje Majoma**, which also contains the ruins of a number of once-beautiful houses, complete with courtyards and stone arches. **Sanje ya Kati** is a nearby uninhabited island, which was once settled by the Shanga people who are now extinct. In the 13th century they were considered a force to be reckoned with and strongly resisted foreign control. There are ruins of oblong-shaped houses estimated to date from the 14th to 15th century.

⊙ Kilwa listings

For Sleeping and Eating price codes and other relevant information, see pages 36-40.

🍽 Sleeping

Kilwa *p135, maps p135, p136 and p138*
Kilwa Masoko
B-C Kilwa Seaview Resort, set on a cliff overlooking Jimbiza Beach, reservations T022-265 0250, lodge T0784-613335 (mob), www.kilwa.net. The atmospheric restaurant and bar has a palm thatched roof, built around an old baobab tree, and serves tasty 3 course

dinners and good seafood dishes. Staff are very friendly and helpful. Spotless rooms with bathrooms are in stone bandas, and many have views over Kilwa Kisiwani. There's access to Jimbiza Beach as well as a swimming pool overlooking the coast. Activities include day trips to Kilwa Kivinje; birding, magrove and hippo trips; and there are several fishing boats and dhows to be rented out with all fishing equipment.
B-C Kilwa Ruins Lodge, Jimbiza Beach, T0785-972960 (mob), www.kilwaruins lodge.com. Extensive changes were in

the pipeline when we visited, as the Kilwa Ruins Lodge had just come under new management. Currently it has 14 rooms of varying standards, some large and spacious overlooking the beach and others much smaller in wooden bungalows up on the hill. All have a/c, en suites, fans and mosquito nets. This is a popular fishing lodge, including for big game fishing, and all the rooms are named after different fish. There's a pleasant bar area off the beach and a restaurant with a pool table, darts board and TV lounge. There's a small swimming pool in the well-kept grounds. Prices vary depending on the room, but are around US$80-120 per person half board.

D Kimbilio, Jimbiza Beach, next to the Kilwa Ruins, T0787-034621 (mob), www.kimbilio lodges.com. This new lodge is Italian-run but had recently changed hands at the time of our visit. The popular Italian restaurant (with Italian chef) is likely to remain, it's well known for its pasta and pizza and for its daily fresh fish. There are 5 en suite bandas near the beach, US$90 including breakfast. This is predominantly a diving and scuba resort and has its own boat and diving equipment. It also offers PADI courses.

D-E Kilwa Dreams, in a very pretty location on Masoko Bay, 3 km out of town, T0784-585330 (mob). This small, pleasant but isolated lodge is run by a Danish man. There are 7 bungalows, all en suite and clean with mosquito nets and terraces. There's a bar, restaurant and gift shop. Rates are US$60 including breakfast for a double room and are overpriced for what you get. There's also camping for US$15 per person per night.

E Masasi Guest House, opposite National Microfinance Bank (NMB), Mapinduzi St. A new guesthouse with only 2 rooms at present but more being built. Double rooms with en suite, mosquito net and fan. There's a simple restaurant and bar area with views over the coast and mangrove beach.

F Hilton Guest House, Mapinduzi St, T0777-547588 (mob). Simple rooms with fan, with

or without bathroom, a bit run down and dingy but all less than US$5. There is a restaurant adjoining the guesthouse offering local dishes and breakfast, the fish here is good.

F Kilwa Guest House, Mapinduzi St. Similar to the **Hilton Guest House**, simple but basic rooms with fans cost US$3. There's no restaurant here.

F New Mjaka Guest House/Majaka Enterprises, there are 2 of these, both with the same name, T023-201 3071. One is on the main road to the harbour in the centre of town near **NMB**; the other is 500 m down the road near the harbour. They're both similar, serve local food and offer clean rooms with en suite, mosquito net and fan. The choice depends mainly on how close you want to be to town.

○ Transport

Kilwa p135, maps p135, p136 and p138
Air
Coastal Air, T022-284 2700, T023-201 3004 (Kilwa), www.coastal.cc, flies between Kilwa and **Dar** (2 hrs) via **Mafia** (45 mins). The flight leaves Kilwa at 1630. **Note** The plane will only call at Kilwa if there are enough passengers needing the service, so it's always best to check with Coastal before making firm plans. A charter is a possibility, particularly for groups.

Bus
Buses go direct from **Kilwa** to the Ubungo bus station in **Dar**, at 0500 (8-10 hrs, US$15). Confirm exact departure time and book a ticket the day before you travel. There are some direct buses south to **Lindi**, **Mtwara** and **Masasi**, although they're few and far between and you may have to catch buses coming from Dar at **Nangurukuru**. They start arriving from about 1400 onwards. The journey takes 5 hrs minimum as the road is poor. You'll be lucky to get a seat.

Lindi

→ *Colour map 1, C6. 9°58'S 39°38'E. Phone code: 023. Population: 40,000.*
Despite the fact that Lindi translates from Ki Mwera (a local language) as 'a pit latrine', the place still has a great deal of charm, albeit faded. It was an important port for early traders and travellers, and the Arab influence is visible. The centre has many attractive colonial buildings, but poor communications and the collapse of the Groundnut Scheme (see page 421), one site for which was at nearby Nachingwea, have hampered development. Since the opening of the deep-water harbour at Mtwara in 1954, Lindi's harbour, too shallow for modern ships, is only used by local fishing boats, and the quay is slowly crumbling away. Around Lindi Bay there are several attractive beaches fringed with palm trees. ►► *For listings, see pages 145-146.*

Ins and outs

Getting there The airstrip is at Kikwetu about 25 km north of town but at present there are no commercial flights. The only way to get there is by road, perhaps breaking your journey at Kilwa as the daily bus journey from Dar takes up to 12 hours or more if it's the rainy season. The road both south and north of Kilwa has seen extensive improvements over recent years but repairs are ongoing and there are still stretches which can be impassable in heavy rains. The drive between Kilwa and Lindi can take up to five hours depending on the road condition, but would normally take about three. Seek advice on road conditions before travelling. ►► *For further details, see Transport, page 146.*

Getting around Lindi itself is a very compact town and most of the places of interest are within walking distance. *Dala-dalas* can be caught at the market, the bus stand or along the main streets (Kawawa, Market and Mchinga roads).

Background

Initial settlement was by Shirazi migrants (see box, page 117). Being the main seaport for Lake Nyasa (now Lake Malawi), it was a destination for slave caravans from the interior in the 19th century. The only remnant of this Omani Arab period is the massive round tower on the beach side of the stadium.

The colonial German powers chose Lindi as the administrative headquarters of the Southern Province, a huge administrative area, which encompassed the whole of the south of Tanganyika right across to Lake Nyasa at the end of the 19th century. A Custom House and store for the German East African Company were constructed close to the remains of the fort. These, and other buildings of the colonial period, are now very dilapidated. One German building, the police station, is still in use, it's easily identifiable by its solid build and ornamental finishes. The German Boma is disappearing behind the trees growing out of it.

Lindi has a long history as a trading port for ivory, beeswax and mangrove poles. Rock salt is extensively mined nearby. Its advantages were the comparatively easy approach along the Lukuledi River valley and the relative proximity of Mozambique, source of much of the produce.

There are fine examples of Asian-inspired architecture along Market and Kawawa roads, dating from when the town used to support an Asian community trading in grain, sisal and cashew nuts.

There are ornamental decorative finishes on some of the buildings, especially the mosques, such as those on Makongoro Street facing the stadium. The modest mosque next to the bus station possesses a wonderful elaborately carved and colourful door. Lindi is now essentially a Muslim town and the Muslim Brotherhoods or *tariqa* are quite active. You are likely to hear, if not see, noisy celebrations at night on feasts such as *maulid*, the commemoration of the Prophet's birth. It involves Quran school teachers and their students singing in turn, drumming, lots of incense, and possibly deep-breathing exercises known to Muslim mystics as *dhikr*. If you want to see a *maulid*, dress modestly and exercise discretion. Other rather high-pitched drums heard at night are for girls' initiation ceremonies or spirit possession dances – no contradiction for the local brand of Islam.

Sights

The present centre of town around the bus stand dates from the British period. The historic centre of the town between Kawawa Road and the beach is now a poor area with a reputation for rampant witchcraft. Here the last descendant of the once-dominant Jamalidini family, of Mombasa origins, lives in a mud hut on a waterlogged compound. Several of the newer houses resemble pillboxes made of cement or breeze-blocks or occasionally mud and wattle.

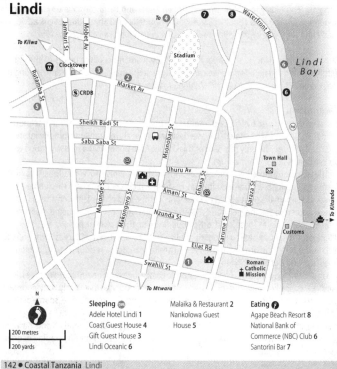

Lindi

Sleeping
Adele Hotel Lindi **1**
Coast Guest House **4**
Gift Guest House **3**
Lindi Oceanic **6**

Malaika & Restaurant **2**
Nankolowa Guest
House **5**

Eating
Agape Beach Resort **8**
National Bank of
Commerce (NBC) Club **6**
Santorini Bar **7**

Cashew nuts

Cashew nuts are the main export product in the Lindi, Mtwara and Kilwa regions of Tanzania. They grow on massive trees, rarely more than 10 m tall, but with sprawling, shady crowns, which line many of the streets in these districts. They supply elephant repellent, poison, furniture varnish, high-voltage liquor and, of course, nuts. Two properties combine to make the fruit so versatile. First, cashew nuts come attached to cashew apples, a tasty, brightly coloured fruit which is easily fermented. Second, between the shell and the kernel, cashew nuts contain a noxious oil strong enough to cause serious wounds. Hence the use of cashew nuts to drive off elephants: the animals detest the smell of the burning oil.

The oil makes the shelling difficult and the shelled nuts expensive. The trick is to burn the shells and the oil of the nuts, but not the kernels, by roasting them quickly and then as quickly extinguishing the fire. If people do this in their back yards in old gasoline drums, the kernels end up spotty, half raw, half charred. Nuts like these are sold cheaply in the countryside and some-times in Dar. Better quality ones, shelled in factories, are much more expensive, and a andful might cost more than a meal.

Tanzania's cashew shelling industry has not fared well. Most of the nuts are exported raw and shelled in India. In Tanzania, the state-owned cashew marketing board tried to introduce industrial processing of the nuts. Factories have been opened and closed at various times in Mtwara, Nachingwea and Dar es Salaam. At present, only the one in Dar is working efficiently.

Cashew trees are not indigenous to Africa. They entered Tanzania from Mozambique, where they had arrived from Brazil, a fringe benefit of Portuguese colonialism. For a long time, Mozambique was the only African cashew nut exporter, the nuts being sent to Goa, Portugal's colonial possession in India, for processing. In Tanzania, efforts to build up production only started in the late 1940s, British reluctance to support cashew production being partly due to colonial officials' fear of drunkenness among Africans – cashew apples make a good raw material for distilling illicit spirits.

In the 1940-1960s, cashew nuts helped improve the economic situation of one of the poorest parts of Tanzania where, until then, grain had been the main export crop. But from the early 1970s, the spread of a tree disease, low producer prices, and the effects of the 'villagization' policy combined to almost destroy cashew production. Villagization separated cultivators from their plots and occasionally even involved cutting down trees to build the villages, while disease caused yields to dwindle.

Production was revived only at the end of the 1990s, when people were again free to live where they chose, and it was discovered that if sulphur was sprayed on the leaves, it protected the trees against disease. It has been rising since. In the 1999/2000 season, prices to farmers for Tanzanian cashew nuts hit an all-time high because of a poor harvest in India, the world's largest cashew supplier. The southern regions had a bumper harvest, and in 2000 cashews became Tanzania's top foreign-currency earning cash crop.

The beach doubles as a boulevard and soccer pitch in the evenings, and you sometimes see fishermen unloading their catch, including octopus, kingfish and sharks (caught outside the bay). The catch of the day is for sale after dark at the bus stand, freshly cooked. The beach by the town is good for swimming, but you are likely to be observed by the locals.

Mitema

There are several excellent beaches around Lindi Bay, the best probably at Mitema, 4 km north of the town, just a 10-minute drive from the centre. This is where Lindi's few expatriates go swimming. The long beach, often deserted, is sheltered by palms and closed off at each end by rocks and enormous baobab trees. Occasionally you may meet a herd boy with his goats or a couple of Lindi's Asian traders in their 4WD vehicles. The ground is a bit rocky at low tide and the waves are high in the evening but it makes an enjoyable excursion – if you don't have your own transport make arrangements with *dala-dala* operators at the bus stand.

Kitunda and 'ngambo'

Many of Lindi's residents come from 'ngambo', which means 'the other shore', and in Lindi it refers to the peninsula across the bay, Kitunda being the beachside village. For a negligible fare, and at approximately half-hour intervals from Lindi harbour until 1800, you can take a wooden motorboat ferry to Kitunda. Here the water is clearer than at Lindi though mangroves make swimming difficult at low tide. You can hire a dugout very cheaply from a local fisherman to paddle along the shore or across the bay. Take the owner along for safety. Locals can show you around the hill behind the village. You will be shown many edible plants and odd animals such as *ndandanda*, a small wedge-shaped fish with large eyes at the top of its head that uses its fins for crawling and jumping in shallow water. The sisal and coconut estates here are in terminal decline and there are the remains of a railway and jetty jutting out over the water, a good vantage point for swims at high tide. Across the hill to the south lie the villages of **Mwitingi**, once the home of Arab plantation owners, and **Shuka**, where locals catch sharks.

Kikwetu

Kikwetu is a breezy promontory 25 km north of Lindi, the location of the town's **airfield** and also of the last sisal estate to close in the area. It closed in 1999 after 100 years of production because sisal, used as coarse fibre for sackcloth and ropes, was no longer profitable. Hidden among the large fields is the manager's mansion, from where there are excellent views. There is regular transport to the airport – to see the mansion, a 20-minute walk away from the roadside village, ask for *kambi* and the locals will show you.

Kisiwa cha popo

This small island in Lindi Bay is famed for its large bat population. Chiroptera fanciers can take a boat trip to the island where the trees are heavy with sleeping bats hanging from the branches during the day. You may also see crocodiles if you take a boat ride south across the Lukuledi River estuary to the other side of Lindi Bay.

Litipo Forest Reserve → *Colour map 1, C6*

① *Litipo is 30 km west of Lindi, just north of Rutamba. To get here you really need your own vehicle as there are no buses. Although only 30 km or so, the journey takes at least 3 hrs. To get into the reserve, go along the road leading to Tandangogoro Village and take one of the paths leading north that go into the reserve. To get more information about Litipo it may be worth asking the forest reserve officer who is usually stationed at Rutamba.*

There are numerous little-known forest reserves dotted throughout Tanzania, including many that exist to help preserve some of the remaining patches of coastal rainforest that millions of years ago covered the whole coastal area. Several of these reserves are in Lindi

East African wildlife

Introduction

A large proportion of people who visit East Africa do so to see its spectacular wildlife. This colour section is a quick photographic guide to some of the more fascinating mammals you may encounter. We give you pictures and information about habitat, habits and characteristic appearance to help you when you are on safari. It is by no means a comprehensive survey and some of the animals listed may not be found throughout the whole region. For further information about East Africa's mammals, birds, reptiles and other wildlife, see the Land and environment section of the Background chapter, page 429.

The Big Nine

It is fortunate that many of the large and spectacular animals of Africa are also, on the whole, fairly common. They are often known as the 'Big Five'. This term was originally coined by hunters who wanted to take home trophies of their safari. Thus it was, that, in hunting parlance, the Big Five were elephant, black rhino, buffalo, lion and leopard. Nowadays the hippopotamus is usually considered one of the Big Five for those who shoot with their cameras, whereas the buffalo is far less of a 'trophy'. Equally photogenic and worthy of being included are the zebra, giraffe and cheetah. But whether they are the Big Five or the Big Nine, these are the animals that most people come to Africa to see and, with the possible exception of the leopard and the black rhino, you have an excellent chance of seeing them all.

■ **Hippopotamus** *Hippopotamus amphibius*. Prefers shallow water, grazes on land over a wide area at night, so can be found quite a distance from water, and has a strong sense of territory, which it protects aggressively. Lives in large family groups known as 'schools'.

■ **Black rhinoceros** *Diceros bicornis*. Long, hooked upper lip distinguishes it from white rhino rather than colour. Prefers dry bush and thorn scrub habitat and in the past was found in mountain uplands. Males usually solitary. Females seen in small groups with their calves (very rarely more than four), sometimes with two generations. Mother always walks in front of offspring, unlike the white rhino, where the mother walks behind, guiding calf with her horn. Their distribution was massively reduced by poaching in the late 20th century, and now there are conservation efforts in place to protect black and white rhino and numbers are increasing. You might be lucky and see the black rhino in Ngorongoro Crater and in the Selous.

■ **White rhinoceros** *Diceros simus*. Square muzzle and bulkier than the black rhino, it is a grazer rather than a browser, hence the different lip. Found in open grassland, it is more sociable and can be seen in groups of five or more. Probably extinct in much of its former range in East Africa, it still flourishes in some places.

Opposite page:
Leopard with a kill.
Above left:
Black rhinoceros.
Above right:
White rhinoceros.
Right:
Hippopotamus.

■ **Common/Masai giraffe** *Giraffa camel-opardis*. Yellowish-buff with patchwork of brownish marks and jagged edges, usually two different horns, sometimes three. Found throughout Africa, several differing subspecies.

■ **Common/Burchell's zebra** *Equus burchelli*. Generally has broad stripes (some with lighter shadow stripes next to the dark ones) that cross the top of the hind leg in unbroken lines. The true species is probably extinct but there are many varying subspecies found in different locations across Africa.

■ **Leopard** *Panthera pardus*. Found in varied habitats ranging from forest to open savannah. It is generally nocturnal, hunting at night or before the sun comes up to avoid the heat. Sometimes seen resting during the day in the lower branches of trees.

■ **Cheetah** *Acinonyx jubatus*. Often seen in family groups walking across plains or resting in the shade. The black 'tear' mark is usually obvious through binoculars. Can reach speeds of 90 kph over short distances. Found in open, semi-arid savannah, never in forested country. Endangered in some parts of Africa. More commonly seen than the leopard.

■ **Elephant** *Loxodonta africana*. Commonly seen, even on short safaris, elephants have suffered from the activities of ivory poachers in East Africa. Tarangire is famous for its elephant population, with as many as 4000 at certain times of the year. Elephants are also prevalent in all other parks in Tanzania.

■ **Buffalo** *Syncerus caffer*. Were considered by hunters to be the most dangerous of the big game and the most difficult to track and, therefore, the biggest trophy. Generally found on open plains but also at home in dense forest, they are fairly common in most African national parks. They need a large area to roam in, so are not usually found in the smaller parks.

■ **Lion** *Panthera leo* (see page i). The largest of the big cats in Africa and also the most common, they are found on open savannah. They are often not disturbed at all by the presence of humans and so it possible to get quite close to them. They are sociable animals living in prides or permanent family groups of up to around 30 animals and are the only felid to do so. The females do most of the hunting.

Left: Common giraffe.
Above: Common zebra.
Opposite page top: Elephant.
Opposite page middle: Cheetah.
Opposite page bottom: Buffalo.

Top: Chimpanzee. **Left:** Spotted hyena. **Bottom:** Chacma baboon.

■ **Vervet monkey** *Chlorocebus pygerythrus*, 39-43 cm. A smallish primate and one of the most recognized monkeys in Africa. Brown bodies with a white underbelly and black face ringed by white fur, and males have blue abdominal regions. Spends the day foraging on the ground and sleeps at night in trees.

■ **Chimpanzee** *Pan troglodytes*, 0.6-1.2 m tall. A primate that is the closest living relative to a human being, with black/brown fur, and human-like fingers and toes. Uses tools, has a complex structure of communicating and displays emotions, including laughing out loud.

■ **Chacma baboon** *Papio ursinus*. An adult male baboon is slender and weighs about 40 kg. Their general colour is a brownish grey, with lighter undersides. Usually seen in trees, but rocks can also provide sufficient protection, they occur in large family troops and have a reputation for being aggressive where they have become used to the presence of humans.

Larger antelopes

◼ **Beisa oryx** *Oryx beisa*, 122 cm. Also known as the East African oryx, there are two sub-species; the **common Beisa oryx** is found in semi-desert areas north of the Tana River, while the **fringe-eared oryx** is found south of the Tana River and in Tanzania. Both look similar with grey coats, white underbellies, short chestnut-coloured mane, and both sexes have long straight ringed horns. They gather in herds of up to 40.

◼ **Common waterbuck** *Kobus ellipsiprymnus* and **Defassa waterbuck** *Kobus defassa*, 122-137 cm. Very similar with shaggy coats and white markings on buttocks: on the common variety, this is a clear half ring on the rump and around the tail; on the Defassa, the ring is a filled-in solid area. Both species occur in small herds in grassy areas, often near water.

Top: Beisa oryx. **Bottom left**: Defassa waterbuck. **Bottom right**: Common waterbuck.

■ **Sable antelope** *Hippotragus niger*,
140-145 cm, and **Roan antelope**
Hippotragus equinus 127-137 cm. Both are
similar in shape, with ringed horns curving
backwards (both sexes), longer in the sable.
Female sables are reddish brown and can
be mistaken for the roan. Males are very
dark with a white underbelly. The roan
has distinct tufts of hair at the tips of its
long ears. The sable prefers wooded areas
and the roan is generally only seen near
water. Both species live in herds.

■ **Greater kudu** *Tragelaphus strepsiceros*,
140-153 cm. Colour varies from greyish to
fawn with several vertical white stripes
down the sides of the body. Horns long and
spreading, with two or three twists (male only).
Distinctive thick fringe of hair running from the
chin down the neck. Found in fairly thick bush,
sometimes in quite dry areas. Usually lives in
family groups of up to six, but occasionally in
larger herds of up to about 30.

■ **Topi** *Damaliscus korrigum*, 122-127 cm.
Very rich dark rufous, with dark patches on
the tops of the legs and more ordinary looking,
lyre-shaped horns.

Top: Greater kudu. **Middle:** Sable antelope. **Bottom:** Topi.

■ **Hartebeest** The horns arise from a bony protuberance on the top of the head and curve outwards and backwards. There are two sub-species: **Coke's hartebeest** *Alcephalus buselaphus*, 122 cm, is a drab pale brown with a paler rump; **Lichtenstein's hartebeest** *Alcephalus lichtensteinii*, 127-132 cm, is also fawn in colour, with a rufous wash over the back and dark marks on the front of the legs and often a dark patch near the shoulder. All are found in herds, sometimes they mix with other plains dwellers such as zebra.

■ **White-bearded wildebeest** *Connochaetes taurinus*, 132 cm. Distinguished by its white beard and smooth cow-like horns, often seen grazing with zebra. Gathers in large herds, following the rains.

■ **Eland** *Taurotragus oryx*, 175-183 cm. The largest of the antelope, it has a noticeable dewlap and shortish spiral horns (both sexes). Greyish to fawn, sometimes with rufous tinge and narrow white stripes down side of body. Occurs in groups of up to 30 in grassy habitats.

Top: White-bearded wildebeest. **Middle**: Coke's hartebeest. **Bottom**: Eland.

Smaller antelope

■ **Bushbuck** *Tragelaphus scriptus*, 76-92 cm. Shaggy coat with white spots and stripes on the side and back and two white, crescent-shaped marks on neck. Short horns (male only), slightly spiral. High rump gives characteristic crouch. White underside of tail is noticeable when running. Occurs in thick bush, often near water, in pairs or singly.

■ **Kirk's dikdik** *Rhynchotragus kirkii*, 36-41 cm. So small it cannot be mistaken, it is greyish brown, often washed with rufous. Legs are thin and stick-like. Slightly elongated snout and a conspicuous tuft of hair on the top of the head. Straight, small horns (male only). Found in bush country, singly or in pairs.

■ **Steenbok** *Raphicerus campestris*, 58 cm. An even, rufous brown with clean white underside and white ring around eye. Small dark patch at the tip of the nose and long broad ears. The horns (male only) are slightly longer than the ears: they are sharp, smooth and curve slightly forward. Generally seen alone, prefers open plains and more arid regions. A slight creature that usually runs off very quickly on being spotted.

■ **Bohor reedbuck** *Redunca redunca*, 71-76 cm. Horns (males only) sharply hooked forwards at the tip, distinguishing them from the oribi (see page xiii). It is reddish fawn with white underparts and has a short bushy tail. It usually lives in pairs or in small family groups. Often seen with oribi, in bushed grassland and always near water.

■ **Grant's gazelle** *Gazella granti*, 81-99 cm, and **Thomson's gazelle** *Gazella thomsonii*, 64-69 cm (see page xii). Colour varies from a bright rufous to a sandy rufous. Grant's is the larger of the two and has longer horns. In both species the curved horns are carried by both sexes.

■ **Common (Grimm's) duiker** *Sylvicapra grimmia*, 58 cm (see page xii). Grey-fawn colour with darker rump and pale colour on the underside. Its dark muzzle and prominent ears are divided by straight, upright, narrow pointed horns. This particular species is the only duiker found in open grasslands. Usually the duiker is associated with a forested environment. It is difficult to see because it is shy and will quickly disappear into the bush.

■ **Oribi** *Ourebia ourebi*, 61 cm (see page xiii). Slender and delicate looking with a longish neck and a sandy to brownish-fawn coat. It has oval-shaped ears and short, straight horns with a few rings at their base (male only). Like the reedbuck, it has a patch of bare skin just below each ear. Lives in small groups or as a pair and is never far from water.

Above: Bushbuck.

■ **Suni** *Nesotragus moschatus*, 37 cm (see page xiii). Dark chestnut to grey-fawn in colour with slight speckles along the back, its head and neck are slightly paler and the throat is white. It has a distinctive bushy tail with a white tip. Its longish horns (male only) are thick, ribbed and slope backwards. They live alone and prefer dense bush cover and reed beds.

Top: Kirk's dikdik. **Bottom left**: Steenbok. **Bottom right**: Bohor reedbuck.

■ **Impala** *Aepyceros melampus*, 92-107 cm. One of the largest of the smaller antelope, the impala is a bright rufous colour on its back and has a white abdomen, a white 'eyebrow' and chin and white hair inside its ears. From behind, the white rump with black stripes on each side is characteristic and makes it easy to identify. It has long lyre-shaped horns (male only). Above the heels of the hind legs is a tuft of thick black bristles (unique to impala), which are easy to see when the animal runs. There is also a black mark on the side of abdomen, just in front of the back leg. Found in herds of 15 to 20, it likes open grassland or sometimes the cover of partially wooded areas and is usually close to water.

Top: Thomson's gazelle. Bottom: Common duiker.

Top left: Oribi. **Top right:** Suni. **Bottom:** Impala.

Other mammals

There are many other fascinating mammals worth keeping an eye out for. This is a selection of some of the more interesting or particularly common ones.

■ **African wild dog** or **hunting dog** *Lycacon pictus*. Easy to identify since they have all the features of a large mongrel dog: a large head and slender body. Their coat is a mixed pattern of dark shapes and white and yellow patches and no two dogs are quite alike. They are very rarely seen and are seriously threatened with extinction (there may be as few as 6000 left). Found on the open plains around dead animals, they are not in fact scavengers but effective pack hunters.

■ **Spotted hyena** *Crocuta crocuta*. High shoulders and low back give the hyena its characteristic appearance and reputedly it has the strongest jaws in the animal kingdom. The spotted variety, larger and brownish with dark spots, has a large head and rounded ears. The **striped hyena**, slightly smaller, has pointed ears and several distinctive black vertical stripes around its torso and is more solitary. Although sometimes shy animals, they have been known to wander around campsites stealing food from humans.

Top: African wild dog.
Middle: Spotted hyena.
Bottom: Black-backed jackal.

■ **Black-backed jackal** *Canis mesomelas*, 30-40 cm tall. Also known as the silver-back jackal, a carnivore with dog-like features, a long muzzle, bushy tail and pointed ears. So-called for the strip of black hair that runs from the back of the neck to the tail.

■ **Warthog** *Phacochoerus aethiopicus*. The warthog is almost hairless and grey with a very large head, tusks and wart-like growths on its face. It frequently occurs in family parties and when startled will run away at speed with its tail held straight up in the air. They are often seen near water caking themselves in thick mud, which helps to keep them both cool and free of ticks and flies.

■ **Rock hyrax** *Procavia capensis*. The nocturnal rock hyrax lives in colonies amongst boulders and on rocky hillsides, protecting themselves from predators like eagles, caracals and leopards by darting into rock crevices.

■ **Caracal** *Felis caracal*. Also known as the African lynx, it is twice the weight of a domestic cat, with reddish sandy-coloured fur and paler underparts. Distinctive black stripe from eye to nose and tufts on ears. Generally nocturnal and with similar habits to the leopard. They are not commonly seen, but are found in hilly country.

Top: Warthog. **Middle:** Rock hyrax. **Bottom:** Caracal.

district, the most accessible of which is west of Litipo. The reserve here consists of a patch of rainforest lying between two small lakes. Litipo Forest Reserve covers an area of 999 ha. It is a beautiful spot and although you are unlikely to see many animals, the area is rich in visible birdlife, including the red-tailed ant thrush, African pitta and Livingstone's flycatcher. On the nearby Rondo Plateau the spotted ground thrush, the green-headed oriole and green barbet are also found.

Tendaguru → *Colour map 1, C6*

ⓘ *The natural resources administration of Lindi (Mali Asili) will be able to help to arrange a visit, something only possible in the dry season. This geological site is quite remote, so a fossil enthusiast will need at least 3 days for getting there, looking around and getting back. As elephants may be present you'll need to be accompanied by a game warden. You should also be self-sufficient as there are no facilities, although you may be able to arrange accommodation with local villagers.*

The richest African deposit of the Late Jurassic strata is found in Tendaguru. The Natural History museums in London and Berlin both boast complete dinosaur skeletons from Tendaguru, among the largest ever discovered. Bernhard Sattler, a German mining engineer who was prospecting in the region for minerals and semi-precious stones, first uncovered fossil remains in 1907. Between 1909 and 1913, W Janensch and E Hennig of the Natural History Museum of Berlin uncovered about 225,000 kg of bones and, using porters, transported them along footpaths – there were no roads – for 70 km to the coast at Lindi and shipped them to Europe. British palaeontologists later continued the research, undertaking excavations from 1925-1929. Post-independence, smaller research investigations have been carried out with the permission of the Tanzanian authorities. Many bones remain under the ground and fragments can be seen at the sites of previous digs. The beds consist of three strata of terrestrial marls alternating with marine sandstone interbeds. Remains of the giant vegetarian, long-necked sauropod, *Brachiosaurus brancai*, named after the museum's director at the time and measuring 22 m long by 12 m high, and the spiny-plated stegosaurus, *Kentrurosaurus aethiopicus*, 4.8 m long by 1.7 m high, both of which were found here, are now on display in Berlin.

◉ Lindi listings

For Sleeping and Eating price codes and other relevant information, see pages 36-40.

◎ Sleeping

Lindi *p141, map p142*
There is 1 decent hotel in Lindi, but beyond this there's little choice. Most options are cheap guesthouses with very basic amenities, although a couple of better quality ones are opening. Prices are quoted in TSh and little English is spoken by guesthouse owners.
D Lindi Oceanic Hotel, Waterfront Rd towards the ferry, T023-220 2829, www. lindioceanichotel.com. Opened in Aug 2008,

this is the top hotel in town with a swimming pool, 2 restaurants (1 indoor and 1 outdoor) serving either buffet food or an à la carte menu, a bar and access to the beach. The smart rooms all have a/c, en suite facilities, mosquito nets, fans, minibars, TVs, safes and balconies. The suite has a separate sitting room and an additional bathroom. The only international standard hotel in town.
E-F Adele Hotel Lindi, Ghana St, T023-220 2310, T0784-703332 (mob). This guesthouse has been open for some years, but has recently added 7 spacious, en suite rooms in a new block, all with a/c, TV, mosquito net and fridge. In the old block there are 15 cheaper

self-contained rooms with mosquito nets and TVs. There is an outside restaurant and dinners need to be ordered in advance. Unusually for a guesthouse in Lindi, there's a bar that sells beer. Good value and well run. The owner also runs 2 other guesthouses in town: the **Adele Guest House (F)**, Ghana St, T023-220 2571, not far from the hotel; and the **Veronica Adela (F)**, Swahili St, T023-220 2570. Both are low budget with en suite or shared facilities.

F Coast Guest House, about 500 m north of the ferry, T023-2202496. Fans and mosquito nets in single rooms. Run down but in a good location amongst palm trees on the beach.

F Gift Guest House, near Malaika Hotel on Market Av, T023-2202462. Clean, decent sized rooms with fans and mosquito nets. A good location for the bus station.

F Malaika Hotel, Market Av, T0713-263335 (mob). Rather grubby self-contained rooms, with TVs, fans and mosquito nets. Also has a restaurant with limited, if any, choice – despite what's on the menu. US$12 for a double room and breakfast. If you want to stay near the bus station, this is a good option.

F Nankolowa Guest House, Rutamba St, signposted from the clock tower, T023-220 2727. Good value, self-contained double rooms, single rooms have shared toilet. Price includes large breakfast, and they serve other good meals on request, after a long wait.

❷ Eating

Lindi p141, map p142
All hotels have restaurants, although many expect food to be pre-ordered, and there are snack bars around the bus station that serve sweet, milky tea, well as *maandazi*, chapattis and other snacks. Fresh fruit and simple fare can be purchased at the market on Jamhuri St. The fishermen's catch of the day is for sale, freshly cooked, at the bus stand after dark.

A couple of bars on Waterfront Rd serve food. **Santorini Bar** is a friendly place which does good chicken and chips and **Agape Beach Resort**, next door, has a few

thatched gazebos around the rather tired gardens. Both serve beer, as do some of the small bars on Makongoro St down towards the stadium, which also serve local food.

National Bank of Commerce (NBC) Club, also called the **Lindi Club**, on the beach, further down from Market Av. Good choice for a beer. A bit dilapidated, but the sea view makes it one of the most pleasant locations. With plenty of notice they can cook something basic.

❸ Transport

Lindi p141, map p142
Bus
The bus to **Dar** leaves at 0500 from the bus stand on Makongoro Rd (12-20 hrs, US$20), it stops at **Kilwa** along the way (US$10). There are also a few direct buses to Kilwa leaving at 0900 and 1300 for the same price. To **Mtwara** buses run fairly frequently (about 4 hrs, US$3). To **Nachingwea** and **Newela** there are daily buses (5-6 hrs, both about US$5); the road rising up to the Makonde plateau is pretty grim.

❹ Directory

Lindi p141, map p142
Banks There is now only one bank in town, the **CRDB** near the clock tower, where there's an ATM and TCs can be cashed. **Internet** There are a couple of internet cafés: **Malaga Café**, near the junction with Makongoro St and Uhuru Av; and **TCCIA Lindi**, near the junction of Armani St and Ghana St. Both suffer from low speed connections and an erratic electricity supply. **Medical services** Sokoine Hospital, T023-220 2027/8. There is a medical clinic at the corner of Amani St and Msonobar St. **Police** Police station, housed in an old German building beside the waterfront, towards the NBC Club, T023-220 2505. **Post office** Uhuru Av not far from the ferry.

Mikindani and Mtwara

Mikindani is, for now at least, a sleepy fishing village with an interesting history reflected in crumbling old Arab-style buildings with carved doors and elaborate balconies. However, changes are likely in the near future as oil and gas companies move in following successful discoveries by propsectors. At the time of our visit, some areas of pristine palm forest beyond the village were already being cleared to make space for workers' camps and this peaceful way of life will inevitably be altered. This really is a 'go now, before it's too late' destination.

The two best places to stay in the region are here, the Old Boma and 10° South, which both offer good value accommodation, excellent food and trips to the region's local attractions including the Mnazi Bay Marine Reserve. Mtwara, 10 km to the south, is more modern and the administrative town of the south coast region. There is little to see here, though it offers facilities such as a bank and post office and the immigration office is here if you are planning to cross the border into Mozambique. ▸▸ *For listings, see pages 151-153.*

Mikindani ⊜❼▲⊜▸▸ *pp151-153. Colour map 1, C6.*

→ *Phone code: 023.*

The small town of Mikindani is 11 km to the northwest of Mtwara on the Mtwara to Lindi road. Unlike most towns in this region, Mikindani has managed to retain much of its traditional Arab charm. A very Muslim town, you should dress and act appropriately. It is located beside a sheltered circular lagoon, itself an inlet from the larger Mikindani Bay, fringed with palm forests and mangroves. The lagoon has made an excellent harbour for the dugout canoes and dhows of local fishermen for centuries and there has been a settlement here for almost 1000 years. When the Arabs arrived, Mikindani grew in prosperity, its importance as a trading centre being greatest in the 15th century. Later, with the arrival of the first Europeans, notably the explorer Dr Livingstone, and with the subsequent ban on slave trade, Mikindani began to decline. There was a revival when the German colonial government briefly made the town the district headquarters in 1890. However, by the 1950s production of groundnuts and oil seed demanded larger ships, for which the port was unsuitable, and Mikindani declined once more.

Ins and outs
Getting there If you fly in to Mtwara, you'll need to get a *dala-dala* or a taxi to Mikindani. The Old Boma (see Sleeping, page 151) can arrange a pick up if you're staying there.

Sights
Much of the town's traditional character remains. There is an interesting mix of thatched mud houses and Arab-style buildings, including several fine two-storey townhouses with elaborate fretwork balconies. Arabs, Portuguese, Germans and British have all occupied the town at different times. The 500-year-old Portuguese fort was used as a slave prison and later bombarded by the British in the First World War. There is an old slave market, now a collection of small art shops, and a fort, dating from the German period and built in 1895, which has been renovated to become a hotel. Most of the other old colonial buildings are in a poor state of repair. Mikindani was the port from which Livingstone departed on his final journey to the interior in 1867 (see page 360) and a house with a fine carved door bears a plaque to mark the site where the explorer is said to have camped.

Trade Aid UK, Livingstone House and the Old Boma

Since 1996 a British charity called Trade Aid UK has been working in Mikindani helping local people build and develop sustainable ecotourism businesses, and thus help to alleviate poverty. They started by rehabilitating and converting the old German Boma and turning it into the best hotel in the area, in the process training local people in all kinds of skills from masonry and gardening to hotel management. Profits from the hotel are ploughed back into the local community and are used to fund projects involving education, conservation and sustainable employment. The Old Boma is the base for the charity, which actively encourages small businesses within the village by providing micro-credit loans and business advice. So far, some 150 loans have been given, involving around 450 local people who act as business partners, in enterprises as diverse as beekeeping, fishing, furniture making, hair-dressing, shop keeping and catering.

Aside from their local employment, Trade Aid are also keen to preserve the village of Mikindani, where many of the buildings, all with stories to tell, are slowly crumbling. Livingstone House, for example, claims to have been the great explorer's base while he was in the area and probably has even greater historical significance, as Trade Aid recently discovered ornately carved Zanzibari doors, 200 years old or more, inside. Other than a few add-ons by Indian traders in the late 19th century, the structure has remained relatively untouched compared to other examples of Arab buildings of this time. They're now hoping to assist in restoring the building to its former glory as they did so successfully with the Boma.

Trade Aid takes on UK volunteers and to find out more, or to offer financial or practical help, contact Trade Aid, 11 Glasshouse Studios, Fryern Court Rd, Burgate, Fordingbridge, Hants SP6 1QX, T01425-657774, www.tradeaiduk.org.

A walk up the hill behind the Old Boma will bring you to a very large hole. A witchdoctor saw his lucky chicken scratching in this spot several years ago and ever since has been digging for German gold that he firmly believes is buried there.

Mtwara ⊖🏠⊖❶ ⇨pp151-153. Colour map 1, C6. 10°20'S 40°20'E.

→ Phone code: 023. Population: 80,000.

Mtwara is a sizeable town that came to prominence during the British period. It has been a centre for agricultural processing, and there is a factory for shelling and canning the cashew nuts that are grown extensively in the southeast (see box, page 143). Although the town itself is set a little way from the shore, Mtwara boasts a magnificent sheltered harbour. However the port, built in 1948-1954, has never been used to capacity as there is relatively little traffic generated in this economically depressed region. The second deepest port in Africa, it was built as part of the ill-fated scheme to grow and export groundnuts from southern Tanzania, a project that included the construction of a railway from Mtwara to Nachingwea – now dismantled. The scheme was implemented after the Second World War, when the British had taken control of what was then Tanganyika from the Germans, and the groundnuts were expected to make up for post-war food shortages in the United Kingdom and for export to the rest of Europe. There are current plans to dredge and widen the port's entrance channel to facilitate the handling of larger modern vessels.

Ins and outs

Getting there There are flights from Dar with Air Tanzania, Wednesday-Monday at 1030 and flights every day except Mondays and Wednesdays with Precision Air at 0815. Buses leave from Dar early in the morning (roughly 12 hours, US$25). It's about 640 km along a mostly tarred but occasionally rough, unsurfaced road and you are advised to break the journey in either Lindi or Kilwa.

There is a passenger ferry service between Dar and Mtwara on the *MV Safari*, though this service is constantly disrupted and may not run at all during certain times of the year.

Mtwara

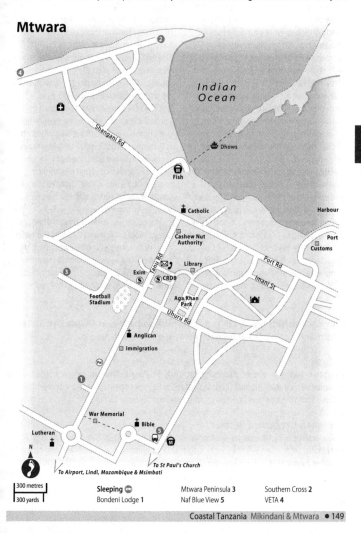

Sleeping		
Bondeni Lodge 1	Mtwara Peninsula 3	Southern Cross 2
	Naf Blue View 5	VETA 4

Lip plugs

The origin of the lip plug is not clear, but about 40 years ago it was fairly common to see elderly women in south Tanzania wearing them. One suggestion is that they were introduced to stop the women being taken away as slaves in the slave-raiding days. Others suggest that they were in use long before the slave trade and they were originally purely ornamental. No special rights were associated with the wearing of a plug and there was no religious significance attached to them. They were worn by a variety of ethnic groups and principally among tribes that had originated from what is now Mozambique. The tribes that wore the lip plug most commonly included the Makonde, Mwera, Mukua, Mawiha and Metu.

The procedure that was necessary for the wearing of a lip plug began when a girl was just five or six. One of the older women in the tribe would pierce the girl's upper lip using a thorn and would then thread a blade of grass into it. Three days later another blade of grass would be inserted, this time a little larger. This would be repeated about three times until a millet stalk about the thickness of the little finger would be inserted. A week later a second, thicker stalk would be inserted and would be left in place for about a month. By this time the lip would have healed and from then on a series of lip plugs would be inserted each just a little wider in diameter than the last so that the upper lip would gradually be stretched. The first three plugs usually have a circumference of about 50 mm. The first plug was worn for about two months and the second for about four months. When the third plug was inserted a number of markings would be cut into the girl's face – usually about three vertical lines each side of the eyes. When the girl reached puberty a plug of about 125 mm in circumference would be used and kept in place until the birth of her second child when it would be replaced by a larger one. In Makonde plugs of about 100 mm in diameter were fairly common.

The plugs were mostly made of ebony. They would be hollowed out by the older men of the tribe and often were highly polished. The wearer could not remove it at any time in public – in fact it would only have been taken out to be washed.

In theory it departs Dar at 1200 on Wednesday and arrives at Mtwara 24 hours later. Enquire at the port in Dar. ➤➤ *For further details, see Transport, page 152.*

Sights

The town has one site of particular interest, **St Paul's Church**, which houses some remarkable murals of Biblical scenes painted by German priests. There are some **beaches** about 2 km from the town centre good for swimming and diving.

The Mnazi Bay Marine Reserve

① *The reserve is 22 km along a dirt track off the main road, which is in a good state of repair and accessible to all vehicles because of a gas drilling operation on the peninsula. The road is, however, frequented by fairly heavy traffic and is liable to flooding during the wet season. The charge for entering the reserve is US$10 per person for a 24-hr period. There is at present no charge for vehicles. Currently there is only one (not very good) place to stay in the reserve, the Ruvula Sea Safari Lodge. 10° South and its dive centre Eco2 Diving do, however,* *offer tailor-made diving safaris to the reserve, with night beach camps and dives in the afternoon and morning. Prices depend on the duration of the safari and the number of people involved. The Old Boma in Mikindani can also arrange excursions here.*

Mnazi Bay Marine Reserve was gazetted in 1999 and is similar in status to the Mafia Marine Reserve further up to the coast to the north. It offers superb snorkelling and scuba-diving and, as the reef along the coast is not tidal, it is good for swimming at all times of the day. It is 30 km south of Mtwara. The **Msimbati Beach** is a pristine, white sandy beach that shelves steeply. There is a fabulous coral reef lying offshore and turtles are common.

The self-proclaimed 'Sultan of Msimbati', a British eccentric named Leslie Latham Moore, came to these parts after the First World War. He attempted to declare independence from Tanganyika – a situation that was briefly tolerated before he was arrested. The remains of his dilapidated house can still be seen. Geological surveys on **Msimbati Island** in the Ruvuma Basin have shown several oil seeps, some with characteristics of true degraded crude oil. There is also a gas seep on the island, believed to be of biogenic origin. This basin lies at the southern end of the large East African Karoo Rift System that extends from Somalia. Exploration licences have been granted to the oil companies, and there is a new gas installation offshore.

◉ Mikindani and Mtwara listings

For Sleeping and Eating price codes and other relevant information, see pages 36-40.

● Sleeping

Mikindani *p147*

There are 2 excellent places to stay and eat in Mkindani, catering for all budgets.
B-C The Old Boma, off the main Mikindani Bay Rd, overlooking the bay, T023-233 3875, www.mikindani.com. A charismatic 100-year-old converted fort run by the British charity, Trade Aid UK. It has 9 standard and superior rooms, the latter with balconies overlooking the coast. All have fans, en suite bathrooms, tremendous views and are individually furnished with beautiful local-style beds and handicrafts. A quirky new room is being created within the tower of the fort, with its own bathroom above. Rates are US$100-200 depending on the room, and include breakfast. Even if not staying, come and eat here as the food is superb, made using their own organically grown vegetables. They also stock a good range of wines. There is a swimming pool for use by guests or diners, and email for guests only. The hotel can arrange excursions to local attractions such as Mnazi Marine

Reserve for US$75 and town tours for US$15. Free Swahili language and cookery lessons. Run as a training centre for local people, profits are ploughed back into the community (see box, page 148). Highly recommended.
D-E 10° South (Ten Degrees), just off of the bay road, T084-855833, www.tendegrees south.com. Managed by Lucasz from Poland and Martin, an English Marine Biologist. Has a new block with 4 rooms looking out to sea. All are en suite and spotlessly clean, with fans inside the nets and a small terrace outside. Price includes breakfast. Also offer 5 cheaper, simple but very clean rooms with shared bathrooms for US$20. The bar, with friendly staff, is probably the most atmospheric place for a drink. The dining area has comfortable chairs and excellent food, including local fish, calamari and a variety of other good Western dishes. There's usually a barbecue on Sat evenings. **Eco2 Diving**, is attached to the guesthouse, see Activities and tours, below.

Mtwara *p148, map p149*
D Naf Blue View Hotel, Sinani St, in the town centre, T023-233 4466, T0776-467066 (mob), nafblueviewhotel@yahoo.com. Don't be put off by the name, it's the best accommodation

option in Mtwara town (N, A and F are the initials of the owner's 3 children). Smart building with a/c throughout. There are 9 rooms at present but more are planned. All have nets, flat screen TV, fridge and are en suite. Some even have their own PC (you pay more for this). There's a gym, 4 pieces of equipment in a small room, and a small, spotless restaurant that serves Chinese, Indian and local food. Price includes breakfast.

D Southern Cross Hotel (Msemo Hotel), on the Shangani Peninsula overlooking the bay, T023-233 3206, www.msemo.com. The best place to stay if you want to be out of town. Swedish-owned but locally run. The food is OK, with seafood and curry dishes from US$6. The rooms, which are all doubles, are in terraced bungalows, many overlooking the sea. They're exceptionally clean and spacious with their own bathroom and fridge. There is also a TV lounge. They can provide dhow trips around the bay on request. Camping is available here for US$10. Service can be slow.

E VETA, on the Shangani Peninsula, T023-233 4094. A local conference and training centre, this place is new and rather character-less. It offers 20 clean, single rooms that are bland, typical conference bedrooms. Staff are friendly and efficient. There's a large restaurant.

E-F Mtwara Peninsula Hotel, west of town near the soccer stadium, T023-233 3638. Run down but adequate, executive rooms have TV and minibar, all have a/c and en suite bathrooms. Room prices vary. Good restaurant with an extensive menu of seafood, curries and some vegetarian dishes.

F Bondeni Lodge, Tanu Rd, south of police station, T023-233 3769. Plain but spacious rooms with fans, nets and en suite bathrooms with squat toilets. The garden bar has satellite TV and is a popular place for a few beers.

⊕ Eating

Mikindani p147
There are 2 excellent guesthouses which serve food, see Sleeping, above.

Mtwara p148, map p149
The hotels (see Sleeping, above) offer a limited selection of inexpensive simple meals, with little variety – usually rice with chicken or fish. The best cheap street food is at the fish market, beside the beach, where fresh fish and cassava chips are sold.

▲ Activities and tours

Mikindani p147
Diving
Eco2 Diving, 10° South, see Sleeping, above, T0783-279446 (mob), www.eco2tz.com. Run by Isobel, offers PADI dive courses up to divemaster level. PADI open water costs US$400, advanced US$350 and recreational dives US$75 with discounts for multiple dives and own equipment. Dives go to 12 local reefs, and also to the Mnazi Marine Reserve as either day trips or over-nighters. They are planning to start marine conservation volunteering courses on special observation and on coral bleaching in the summer of 2009, with tuition on the issues and identification of different types of coral and bleaching examples, followed by 2 days monitoring the reefs and a final day diving.

⊖ Transport

Mikindani p147
Bus and dala-dala
All buses stop at Mikindani en route to **Mtwara**. Dala-dala to **Mtwara** (US$0.40).

Mtwara p148, map p149
Air
Air Tanzania flies to **Dar** Wed-Mon, 1215. **Precision Air** flies to Dar Mon, Tue, Thu, Fri, Sat and Sun at 0940 (US$200). Check times with the airlines, as they change frequently.

Bus and dala-dala
Buses leave for **Dar** at 0500 from the bus stand on Market St. Book a ticket the day

Border essentials: Tanzania–Mozambique

Mtwara is close to Mozambique but it's not the easiest border crossing if you have a vehicle. There used to be a car ferry that crossed the Ruvuma River but this sank in 2008 and has not been replaced. There are reports of people with vehicles crossing the river with the help of local boatmen using two *mokoro* with a raft between them to transport the car. This isn't officially approved and rumours suggest it can cost as much as US$500.

Mtambaswala–Negomano

A new bridge is under construction here, due to open in September 2009. This border connects southern Tanzania at Masuguru Village with northern Mozambique at Negonane Village in the Cabo Delgado Province, which is about 200 km from the coast and is accessed by road (currently being tarred) from Lindi.
Visas Visas for Mozambique are not available at the border and must be arranged in Dar es Salaam beforehand.

Kilambo–Namuiranga

If you don't have a vehicle, you can cross the Ruvuma River at Kilambo, which is an hour's *dala-dala* ride south of Mtwara, by passenger ferry or *mokoro*. If water levels are low you may have to wade to get to and from the boat on the Tanzanian side. The crossing shouldn't cost more than US$8.
From Mozambique Daily pickups connect Moçimboa da Praia with Namiranga, the border post on the Mozambique side. The driver will generally wait for you to have your passport stamped at the immigration office and then drive you to the banks of the Ruvuma.
Visas It is essentials to have a visa for Mozambique, which can be obtained from the embassy in Dar es Salaam.

For up-to-date information on crossing to Mozambique, see www.mozguide.com.

---

before and confirm departure time. Buses to **Masasi** leave fairly frequently (US$6). Regular buses and *dala-dala* to **Lindi** (US$2). *Dala-dala* to **Mnazi Mmoja** (US$3), **Mikindani** (US$0.40). All buses stop at **Mikindani** en route to **Dar**.

Ferry

This stretch of ocean can be rough – travel sickness tablets are recommended. There is a passenger ferry to **Dar**, the *MV Safari*, though this service is constantly disrupted and may not run at all during certain times of the year. In theory it leaves **Mtwara** on Fri (24 hrs). 1st class US$25, 2nd class US$15, plus US$5 port tax. Enquire at the ferry office near

the market. 1st class includes a bed of sorts, and you can buy meals but it's still a good idea to take your own food and drink.

Directory

Mtwara *p148, map p149*
Banks Cash TCs at **Exim Bank** on Tanu Rd, and CRDB. The latter now also has an ATM. **Immigration** The immigration office is to the south of the NBC Club, Tanu Rd. **Police** The police station is across the road from the immigration office. **Post office and telephone** Tanu Rd.

Tunduru via Makonde Plateau

Travel to the extreme southern district of Tanzania is not for the faint-hearted, as the roads that run from the coast to Tunduru are little more than tracks and can become completely impassable in the wet. Accommodation is limited and it is a gruelling bus journey but you will be rewarded by meeting the remote communities on the Makonde Plateau and get good views of the scenic granite Masasi Hills. ▸▸ *For listings, see pages 155-156.*

Newala → *Colour map 1, C6.*
This area is occupied by the Makonde people who have three claims to distinction. The first is their exceptional ebony carvings, groups of exaggerated figures, the traditional work related to fertility and good fortune. The second is their spectacular *sindimba* dancing with the participants on stilts and wearing masks. The third is that Makonde women are celebrated throughout Tanzania for their sexual expertise. The best place to experience the atmosphere of the Makonde is to visit Newala, 150 km southwest of Mtwara. The road passes through dense woodland as it climbs up to the plateau from the coast.

The livelihood of the wood carvers is under threat from excessive sawmill logging of the *Mpingo* trees in the region. The carvers now have to cycle distances of 20 km or more to obtain supplies of wood. This tree plays both an economic and socio-cultural role in the lives of the villagers. It is used for its medicinal qualities and, traditionally, new-born babies must be bathed in water containing the leaves to ensure they grow up to be strong.

Masasi → *Colour map 1, C5. Phone code: 023. Altitude: 440 m.*
The other main Makonde town is Masasi, surrounded by granite hills, some 140 km southwest of Lindi and 190 km west of Mtwara. In 1875 Masasi was selected by Bishop Steere of the Universities Mission to Central Africa as a place to settle freed slaves and it has been an important mission centre since then. Nowadays it is a pretty undistinguished town, although it is strikingly situated between a series of large *gneiss kopjes* (hills). It acts as an important junction for Nachingwea, Tunduru/Songea, Lindi, Mtwara and Newala and the Makonde Plateau. There are some pleasant walks around town (head towards the *kopjes*) and there is a cave that contains rock paintings nearby.

Lukwika-Lumesule Game Reserve → *Colour map 1, C5*
① *To get to the reserve, follow the Tunduru road out of Masasi, and at the village of Michiga, there is a left turn to Lukwika-Lumesule. Driving time from Masasi is about 4 hrs and a 4WD is essential.*
The Lukwika-Lumesule Game Reserve is one of the least visited wilderness areas in Africa. About 100 km south of Masasi on the Ruvuvi River, which marks the border with Mozambique, the reserve covers an area of approximately 600 sq km and it adjoins the Niassa Reserve in northern Mozambique though there are no bridges or border crossings, or any facilities for visitors. Herds of elephant migrate across the Ruvuma River on the southern edge of the reserve in September. The reserve is also home to lion, leopard, crocodile, hippo, antelope and numerous bird species. Less well known is the fact that this is one of the reserves in which a Spanish tour company arranges safaris where professional game hunters bring clients for trophy shooting holidays, and it is closed to visitors during the hunting season (July to December).

Man-eating lions

The sparsely populated district of 20,000 sq km surrounding Tunduru has achieved a certain notoriety for man-eating lions. There are extensive forests and savannah that offer the big cats good cover. In 1986-1987 lions, believed to have come into the region from Mozambique, were reported to have killed 30 people in Tunduru District within one year. Because all the victims were male, women were sent out to work in the fields.

The attacks may have resulted from the shortage of natural prey due to over-hunting, which has decimated most of the larger wild mammals in the area. People have been reported to be killing game to eat as they have so few remaining cattle or domestic animals. There has also been macabre speculation that lions acquired the taste for human flesh from eating the victims of the war in nearby Mozambique. Among the victims was a game warden sent to deal with the problem. However, it is also thought that some of the human deaths were in fact paid killings carried out by 'lion men'.

Tunduru → *Colour map 1, C5. 11°5'S 37°22'E. Altitude: 701 m.*
From Masasi to Tunduru you pass through mile after mile of miombo scrub, where monotony is only broken by some impressive *gneiss kopjes* scattered about the countryside for the first few hours after leaving Masasi.

After the journey from Masasi or Songea – over 340 km distance – you'll be pleased to reach Tunduru. Be prepared to pay more for your drinks here. The state of the road you came in on today (along with the state of the one you'll probably be leaving on tomorrow) means that sodas are around twice the normal price. It's a pleasant enough town in its own modest way, attractively situated with fine views over the surrounding undulating countryside, but there's little to keep you here for more than one night – unless you are a gem dealer, for the surrounding area is rich in gemstones, including amethyst, diamonds and sapphires. The population is poor, mostly subsistence farmers growing maize and cashew nuts. Extensive damage is frequently done to crops by wild animals, especially boars, monkeys and elephants.

◉ Tunduru via Makonde Plateau listings

For Sleeping and Eating price codes and other relevant information, see pages 36-40.

⬤ Sleeping

Tunduru via Makonde Plateau *p154*
There are several very basic guesthouses in Newala (near the bus stand), Masasi and Tunduru, none of which stand out and all rooms are very similar. For little more than US$2 you will get a bare room with a bed, bucket of water and shared WC. Some serve food and beer.

◒ Transport

Newala *p154*
Road
Newala is 150 km from **Mtwara** but you need to stay at least 1 night in Newala as the bus journey takes 3-4 hrs. There are a few buses a day to Mtwara that leave in the morning (US$4). There is a daily bus to **Masasi** that leaves Newala at 0500, arrives in Masasi around 1100 and returns again to Newala in the afternoon.

Masasi *p154*

Be prepared for breakdowns or punctures on all the journeys. The buses are in a sorry state and the roads are atrocious (impassable without a 4WD during the rainy season). For those travelling across the south it is worth knowing that the average speeds of the buses plying the awful roads are around 25 kph or less.

Bus

Masasi is 200 km from Mtwara and there are several buses from Masasi to **Lindi** (about 4 hrs, US$4) and to **Mtwara** daily (5-6 hrs, US$5). There is a daily bus from **Newala** that leaves at 0500, arrives in Masasi around 1100 and returns again to Newala in the afternoon. There is usually 1 bus per day going to **Tunduru** (7-8 hrs, US$8). Travelling along this route by bus from Mtwara to **Songea** via Masasi will take a minimum of 3 days on very unpleasant roads. There are no direct buses to Songea from Mtwara, you have to first go to Masasi and overnight there and then to Tunduru and overnight there, before the final leg to Songea.

Tunduru *p155*
Bus and Land Rover

There are daily buses to **Masasi** (7-8 hrs, US$8). There is at least 1 bus leaving for **Songea** early every morning at about 0500 (10-12 hrs, US$9). Try to book a seat in front of the back axle, as this can make a big difference considering the state of the road.

There are also Land Rovers (ask for *ëgari ndogo*) that do this trip carrying passengers though the cost is slightly more and they are very overcrowded. They are quicker although more uncomfortable than a bus – unless you happen to get a front seat – but they may be the only thing going on a particular day. There are also lorries which take passengers in the back.

Contents

Footprint features

Zanzibar & Pemba

At a glance

⊜ **Getting around** Buses, *dala-dala* and taxis go almost everywhere on Zanzibar, but Pemba is much more limited. Cars, motorbikes and bikes can be hired, and local boatmen will take you in their dhows.

◉ **Time required** 3 days for a beach break after a safari or trek, 1-2 weeks to explore the islands and still have time to chill. At least 1 day in Stone Town.

☼ **Weather** Hot and sticky between Nov-Dec and Apr-May. Jun-Oct has a cooler, balmier climate and is the best time to visit.

✘ **When not to go** Many places close in the rainy season (Apr-Jun). During Ramadan local cafés and bars will be shut, although tourist restaurants and hotels stay open.

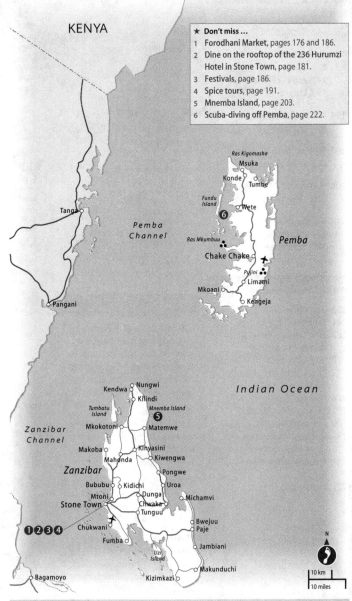

KENYA

★ Don't miss ...
1 Forodhani Market, pages 176 and 186.
2 Dine on the rooftop of the 236 Hurumzi Hotel in Stone Town, page 181.
3 Festivals, page 186.
4 Spice tours, page 191.
5 Mnemba Island, page 203.
6 Scuba-diving off Pemba, page 222.

Ras Kigomasha
Msuka
Konde
Tumbe
Fundu Island 6 Wete
Pemba Channel
Ras Mkumbuu
Chake Chake
Pujini
Limani
Tanga
Mkoani
Kengeja

Pemba

Pangani

Indian Ocean

Kendwa Nungwi
Kilindi
Tumbatu Island *Mnemba Island* 5
Mkokotoni Matemwe
Zanzibar Channel
Makoba Kihyasini
Mahonda Kiwengwa
Zanzibar Pongwe
Bububu Kidichi Uroa
Mtoni Dunga
Stone Town Chwaka Michamvi
1 2 3 4 Tunguu
Chukwani Bwejuu
Paje
Fumba
Uzi Island Jambiani

Bagamoyo Makunduchi
Kizimkazi

N

10 km
10 miles

The very name Zanzibar conjures up exotic and romantic images. The main town on Zanzibar Island, Stone Town, with its intriguing, winding alleyways, old Arabian townhouses and heaving port, is steeped in history, full of atmosphere and immensely attractive. Zanzibar's coastlines offer some of the best beaches in the world, but sand and surf vary depending on what side of the island you're on. On the east coast, waves break over coral reefs and sand bars offshore, and low tide reveals small pools of starfish. Up north, ocean swimming is much less susceptible to the tides, and smooth beaches and white sand make for dazzling days in the sun. Roads to the southeast coast take visitors through the Jozani Forest, home to Zanzibar's rare red colobus monkeys and a number of other primate and small antelope species. But Zanzibar attracts hundreds of thousands of visitors a year, and to some extent the island has suffered from the consequences of over-zealous mass tourism. In recent years its popularity as a European charter destination has seen the growth of all-inclusive resorts housing tourists on sun, sea and sand holidays, from where visitors experience little of the island outside the compound of their resort.

Quite by contrast, Pemba is hardly visited at all and is infinitely more difficult to get around. The sea around Pemba is dotted with desert islands and is the location of some of the best scuba-diving in the Indian Ocean. The Pemba Channel drops off steeply just off the west coast and the diverse species of marine life and coral are exceptional. Unlike Zanzibar, tourism is still in its early stages and a visit here is truly a Robinson Crusoe experience.

→ *Phone code: 024.*

Getting there

Immigration The islands that make up the Zanzibar Archipelago – Unguja (usually known as Zanzibar Island), Pemba and numerous smaller islands – lie roughly 35 km off the coast of mainland Tanzania. Whilst still part of Tanzania they are administered autonomously and have their own immigration procedures. Therefore, you will be asked to show your passport to an immigration official on entry and exit and have it stamped in and out. Likewise, your passport is stamped on arrival once back on mainland Tanzania. Note that the agreement between Tanzania, Kenya and Uganda, that allows holders of single entry visas to move freely between all three countries without the need for re-entry permits, also covers travel to Zanzibar. You also require a vaccination certificate for yellow fever to get onto the islands, and this is asked for on arrival at the port or airport.

Travel There are frequent ferries between Dar es Salaam and Stone Town on Zanzibar, from big old slow overnight boats to 90-minute hydrofoils, and how much you pay depends on the level of comfort and how quickly you want to get there (see Dar es Salaam, page 96, for further information). There are less frequent ferry services between Dar and Mkoani on Pemba, of which almost all stop at Zanzibar en route. It is also possible to cross by motorboat from Pangani on the north coast to Kendwa, see page 127. **Zanzibar's International Airport** ① *T024-223 0213*, is 6 km outside of Stone Town and is equipped to receive small planes from the mainland, larger jets from Nairobi and further afield, as well as European charter flights. Visitors arriving on Zanzibar from outside Tanzania will be able to obtain a visa on entry. The small airport at Pemba is near Chake Chake and the smaller airlines link Pemba with Dar es Salaam and Zanzibar. There is an international airport departure tax of US$25, and a domestic departure tax of US$5, although these are sometimes included in the price of your flights so check with your airline (the latter is payable in local currency). ➻ *For further details, see Transport, page 192.*

Getting around

Public transport on Zanzibar in the way of buses and *dala-dala* is cheap, with regular services, and the main roads around the island are now all tarmac. The other option is to use reasonably priced transfers in minibuses organized by the tour operators. If you want to drive yourself cars, jeeps and motorbikes can be hired, and for a group of four people, hiring a car can sometimes work out cheaper than paying for individual transfers. There is a vehicle rental office in the Old Post Office in Stone Town or you can go through one of the tour operators (see page 191). You will need an international driver's licence, and recently it has also been necessary to have a Zanzibar Driver's Permit. These are issued by the car hire company or tour operator when you arrange your vehicle and cost US$10-20. Without this permit you may get harassed at the police road blocks on the island, of which there are several, so discuss this with your tour operator. Some of the more exclusive lodges are on the smaller islands. To get to these the lodge will organize a boat transfer. On Pemba, *dala-dala* and the odd bus run up and down the main roads from early morning to early afternoon and their regularity rather depends on how many people want to use them.

Climate

The climate is generally tropical, but the heat is tempered by a sea breeze throughout the year. The average temperature fluctuates between 25-30°C. There are long rains from March to mid-June and short rains in November and December. The hottest time is after

Zanzibar Island

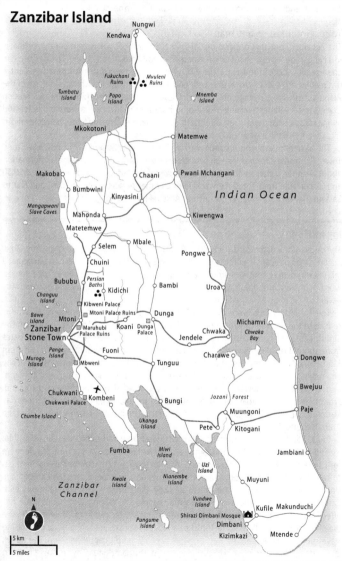

the short rains from December-February, with temperatures up to 34°C at midday. The most comfortable time of year is June-October, with lower temperatures, little rain and plenty of sun, made bearable by the cooling winds from the southeast, known as the *Kusi* or the Southeast Monsoons. From October-March the winds change, blowing from the northeast, and they are known as the *Kaskazi* or the Northeast Monsoons.

Tourist information and maps

The **Zanzibar Tourism Cooperation (ZTC)** ① *T024-223 8630, www.zanzibartourism.net*, is in Livingstone House about 1 km along the road to Bububu, Stone Town. They can arrange all tours of the island. The ZTC also has another **Tourist Information Centre** ① *Creek Rd, T024-223 3430*, at the north end in the Kikoni district, which sells maps of the island but otherwise is not terribly helpful. *The Swahili Coast* is a free bi-monthly publication from Coastal Airlines available from some hotels, tour agencies, a few embassies and airline offices. It lists hotels, restaurants, transport services, etc, and features articles about local events on the islands and along the mainland coast.

The best maps available are produced by **The Zanzibar Gallery** ① *Gizenga St*, in Stone Town; *Illustrated Zanzibar Map* and *Illustrated Pemba Map*, both have extra information about weather, distances and very usefully, *dala-dala* routes. Each costs around US$0.50 and is available from The Gallery and various other outlets in Stone Town and Dar es Salaam. Try the bookshops in Dar such as **A Novel Idea**, see page 91.

Background

The origin of the name Zanzibar is disputed. The Omani Arabs believe it came from *Zayn Zal Barr*, which means 'Fair is the Island'. The alternative origin is in two parts – the early inhabitants of the island were from the mainland and were given the name *Zenj*, a Persian word that is a corruption of *Zangh* meaning negro. The word *bar* meaning 'coast' was added to this to give 'Negro Coast'.

The earliest visitors were Arab traders who brought with them Islam, which has remained the dominant religion on the island. They are believed to have arrived in the eighth century. The earliest remaining building is the mosque at Kizimkazi that dates from about 1100. For centuries the Arabs had sailed with the monsoons down from Muscat and Oman in the Gulf to trade in ivory, slaves, spices, hides and wrought-iron. The two main islands, both of roughly similar size, Unguja (usually known as Zanzibar Island) and Pemba, provided an ideal base, being relatively small islands and thus easy to defend. From here it was possible to control 1500 km of the mainland coast from present day Mozambique up to Somalia. A consequence of their being the first arrivals was that the Arabs became the main landowners.

In 1832 Sultan Seyyid Said, of the Al Busaid dynasty that had emerged in Oman in 1744, moved his palace from Muscat to Zanzibar. Said and his descendants were to rule there for 134 years. In 1822, the Omanis signed the Moresby Treaty that made it illegal for them to sell slaves to Christian powers in their dominions. To monitor this agreement, the United States in 1836 and the British in 1840 established diplomatic relations with Zanzibar, and sent resident consuls to the islands. The slaving restrictions were not effective and the trade continued to flourish. Caravans set out from Bagamoyo on the mainland coast, travelling up to 1500 km on foot as far as Lake Tanganyika, purchasing slaves from local rulers on the way, or, more cheaply, simply capturing them. The slaves, chained together, carried ivory back to Bagamoyo. The name Bagamoyo means 'lay down your heart' for it was here that the slaves would abandon hope of ever seeing their homeland again. They were shipped to the slave market in Zanzibar Town, bought by intermediary traders, who in turn sold them on without any restrictions.

All the main racial groups were involved in the slave trade. Europeans used slaves in the plantations in the Indian Ocean islands, Arabs were the main capturers and traders, and African rulers sold the prisoners taken in battle to the traders. Alas, being sold into slavery was not the worst fate that could befall a captive. If a prolonged conflict led to a glut, the Doe tribe from just north of Bagamoyo would run down excess stocks of prisoners by the simple expedient of eating them. Nevertheless, it is the perception of the African population that the Arabs were mainly responsible.

Cloves had been introduced from Southeast Asia, probably Indonesia, prior to the advent of Sultan Seyyid Said. They flourished in the tropical climate on the fertile and well-watered soils on the western areas of both Zanzibar and Pemba islands. Slaves did the cultivation and harvesting and the Sultan owned the plots: by his death in 1856 he had 45 plantations. Other plantations were acquired by his many children, as well as by numerous concubines and eunuchs from the royal harem. In due course cinnamon, nutmeg, black pepper, cumin, ginger and cardamom were all established, their fragrance was everywhere and Zanzibar became known as the 'Spice Islands'. Slaves, spices and ivory provided the basis of considerable prosperity, mostly in the hands of the Arab community, who were the main landowners, and who kept themselves to themselves and did not intermarry with the Africans.

This was not true of a second group that came from the Middle East to settle on the East African coast, the Shirazis (see box, page 117). Intermarriage between Shirazis and Africans gave rise to a coastal community with distinctive features, and a language derived in part from Arabic. This became known as Swahili. In Zanzibar the descendants of this group were known as the Afro-Shirazis. They were not greatly involved in the lucrative slave, spice and ivory trades. They cultivated coconuts, fished and became agricultural labourers. Those Shirazis who did not intermarry retained their identity as a separate group.

Two smaller communities were also established. Indian traders arrived in connection with the spice and ivory trade, and, as elsewhere, settled as shopkeepers, traders, skilled artisans, money-lenders, lawyers, doctors and accountants. The British became involved in missionary and trading activities in East Africa while attempting to suppress the slave trade. And when Germans began trading on the mainland opposite Zanzibar, things needed to be sorted out with the Sultan of Zanzibar, who controlled the 10-mile coastal strip that ran for 1500 km from Mozambique to Somalia. The Germans bought their strip of the coast from the Sultan for £200,000. The British East African Company had been paying the Sultan £11,000 a year for operating in the Kenyan portion. In 1890, Germany allowed Britain to establish a protectorate over Zanzibar in return for Heligoland, a tiny barren island occupied by the British, but strategically placed opposite the mouth of the River Elbe, 50 km from the German coast. In 1895 Britain took over responsibility for its section of the mainland from the British East African Company and agreed to continue to pay the £11,000 a year to the Sultan. The British mainland territory (later Kenya), was administered by a Governor, to whom the British representative in Zanzibar, the Resident, was accountable.

The distinctive feature of Zanzibar as a protectorate (Kenya had become a colony in 1920) was recognized in 1926 when the British Resident was made directly responsible to the Colonial Secretary in London. Germany had by this stage lost control of its section of the mainland when, as a result of its defeat in the First World War, the territory was transferred to British control and became Tanganyika.

Zanzibar of the Sultans

Salme Said was the daughter of one of the concubines of Sultan Said, who ruled from 1804 to 1856. Later known as Emily Ruete, she described her life in *Memoirs of an Arabian Princess from Zanzibar* (Princeton: Markus Wiener), from which the following extracts were distilled:

On life at Mtoni Palace

The Palace buildings were arranged round a large courtyard in which roamed a variety of exotic wildlife – peacocks, gazelles, geese, flamingos and ostriches. One side of the courtyard contained 12 bathhouses, each with two baths 15 ft by 12 ft by 4 ft deep. Platforms, either side of the baths, covered with mats served for rest and prayer areas. The baths were in continual use during waking hours. The older children had riding lessons, twice a day, in the morning and evening. When they were sufficiently competent, each boy was given a horse, and each girl a white donkey. A regular diversion for these children was a ride in the country.

The Sultan's wife occupied the rooms overlooking the sea. The Sultan only spent four nights a week at Mtoni, the rest at the Palace by the promenade in Stone Town. Other palace rooms were occupied by concubines and their children, while the outbuildings housed slaves and eunuchs. In all there were estimated to be about 1000 people living in and around the palace.

On the shore side was a tower with a vaulted roof and balcony that caught the breeze. Coffee was taken and a telescope offered sightings of approaching vessels and a view of Stone Town to the south. A flagpole on the shore was used to run up messages for the Sultan's ships at anchor in the bay.

A typical day at the palace in Stone Town

The first set of prayers would begin some time between 0400 and 0530. After these prayers sleep would be resumed until around 0800 when there would be a massage from a slave followed by a bath. At 0900, the children all went to greet their father after which the Sultan would preside over breakfast attended by his wife, relatives and children, but not the concubines. After breakfast small children would play, older children attend lessons, the women engage in conversation or embroidery. The slaves were dispatched to arrange evening visits.

The Sultan would repair to the audience chamber on the first floor. A rather grand entrance was made with an African guard followed by a detail of eunuchs then the Sultan, followed by his sons. All senior notables were expected to attend and the company rose as the Sultan's party entered. Disputes, requests and complaints were dealt with, the Sultan delegating minor matters to his ministers, judges or the senior eunuchs. The business was all transacted verbally and the senior eunuchs recorded the decisions.

At 1300, the second prayers took place, followed by siestas, perhaps a visit to the bathhouse, while fruit and cake were partaken.

Third prayers were at 1600 and were followed by the evening meal, with much the same food being served as for breakfast. During the meal there would usually be organ music or some Taraab.

Fingers were used for eating, and rinsed in bowls of scented water. Sherbet water and coffee were available after the meal. The assembly sat on the floor and ate in silence around a long, low table with the Sultan at the head. A variety of rice dishes, meat and fresh breads and sweetmeats were served onto small dishes.

The fourth prayers were said at 1900 after which the Sultan would conduct a second audience session at which coffee would be served. This was also the time for womenfolk to visit each other, and for men to do likewise, proceeding through the narrow streets of Stone Town accompanied by slaves carrying lanterns. The day concluded with the fifth prayers before bed at around 2200.

On the education of women
School (*madresse*) for the children of the affluent began at the age of six and continued to 12 or so. Usually all the children of the household would be taught privately by a female teacher in a room in the house, sitting on the floor, on matting. There were a few schools for the children of poorer parents. Children often brought their personal slaves to class with them, and they sat at the back.

The only book would be the Koran, open on a folding wooden book holder. As a result, the Koran would more-or-less all be learnt by heart, but there would be no discussion of the text or its interpretation, which was regarded as irreverent. The girls would be taught the Arabic alphabet first and then reading from sections of the Koran. Except in a few cases, only the boys learned to write. Quill pens and washable ink were used to copy sections of the Koran onto smooth tablets made from a camel's scapula (shoulder-blade). After use the tablets could be scrubbed clean and used again. A little arithmetic was taught, mostly simple addition and subtraction. Classes started at 0700, breakfast was at 0900 and school finished at noon. Discipline was strict, and the teacher used a bamboo cane to punish pupils. Girls learned sewing, embroidery and lace-making from their mothers.

On the role of women
Women in society, as long as they were not concubines or slaves, had equal rights with men. Dress conventions demanded that a woman must be completely veiled except for the eyes when meeting with any male who was not a relative or a slave. Furthermore, a woman was forbidden to speak with a male stranger. This made life very difficult for single women, particularly as this restriction prevented discussions with employees or officials.

Although Islamic law allowed four formal wives, in Zanzibar it was unusual for a man to have more than one wife. There was no restriction on the number of concubines or slaves, which were purchased. Children born to concubines were free, and in the event of the master's death, the concubines, too, became free.

Marriages were arranged. The girl was not allowed to meet with her intended husband, but endeavoured to find out as much as possible about him from relatives. Normally the girl was required to agree to the match, although occasionally the match went ahead against her wishes. Brides tended to be youthful, sometimes as young as nine.

Prior to the wedding, the bride-to-be was required to spend eight days in a darkened room. The marriage ceremony took place in the bride's house. The bride would not be present but represented by a male relative.

The colonial period

Further legislation in 1873 had made the slave trade illegal, the slave market in Zanzibar was closed and the Protestant cathedral erected on the site. But slavery lingered on. The trade was illegal, but the institution of slavery existed openly until Britain took over the mainland from the Germans in 1918, and covertly, it is argued, for many years thereafter. Many former slaves found that their conditions had changed little. They were now employed as labourers at low wage rates in the clove plantations. Zanzibar continued to prosper with the expansion of trade in cloves and other spices. The fine buildings that make Zanzibar Stone Town such a glorious place were constructed by wealthy Arab slavers and clove traders, British administrators and prosperous Indian businessmen and professionals. These structures were so soundly built that they have survived for the most part without repairs, maintenance and redecoration from 1964 to the present.

The wealth of the successive Sultans was considerable. They built palaces in the Stone Town and around Zanzibar Island. Islamic law allowed them to have up to four wives, and their wealth enabled them to exercise this privilege and raise numerous children. Until 1911 it was the practice of the Sultan to maintain a harem of around 100 concubines, with attendant eunuchs. The routine was established whereby the Sultan slept with five concubines a night, in strict rotation. The concubines had children, and these were supported by the Sultan.

Social practices changed with the succession of Khalifa bin Harab, at the age of 32, as Sultan in 1911. He was to reign until his death, in 1960, at the age of 81. The harem and concubines were discontinued – apart from anything else, this proved a sensible economy measure. Gradual political reforms were introduced and the practice of Islam was tolerant and relaxed. Social pressures on non-Muslims were minimal. But the office of the Sultan was held in considerable awe. As the Sultan drove each day to spend the afternoon a few kilometres away at his palace on the shore, his subjects would prostrate themselves as he passed. In 1959, when it was suggested that there should be elected members of the Legislative Councils, and Ministers appointed to deal with day-to-day matters of state, the Sultan received numerous delegations saying change was unnecessary and the Sultan should retain absolute power. The present Sultan is still addressed as 'Your Highness' when Zanzibaris visit him.

David Reed, writing for *Readers' Digest* in 1962, described Zanzibar as the "laziest place on earth – once a Zanzibari has caught a couple of fish, he quits for the day, to retire to his bed, or the heavenly chatter of the coffee house". He developed his theme – "Once a clove has been planted, its lethargic owner has only to sit in the shade and watch as its tiny green buds grow into handsome pounds sterling. Even when the market is in the doldrums, a good tree may produce as much as £6 worth of cloves a year for its owner. In better times, it simply rains money on those who sleep below."

Despite these impressions of tropical torpor under a benevolent ruler, however, there were significant tensions. Several small Arab Associations combined to form the Zanzibar National Party (ZNP) in 1955. The leader was Sheikh Ali Muhsin, educated at Makerere University in Uganda with a degree in agriculture. The leadership of the party was Arab, and their main objective was to press for independence from the British without delay. Two African associations, active with small landless farmers and agricultural labourers, formed the Afro-Shirazi Party (ASP) in 1957. The leader was Sheikh Abeid Karume, at one time a school teacher, a popular and charismatic personality, with great humorous skills that he exercised to the full at public meetings.

John Okello – drifter who destroyed a dynasty

John Okello was born in Uganda in 1937. There is no record of him having had any early schooling. He left home at the age of 15 and did a variety of jobs while travelling, including work as a domestic servant, a tailor and as a building labourer. Eventually he worked as a mason in Nairobi and went to evening classes where he learnt to read and write. In 1957 he was given a two-year prison sentence for a sexual offence. On his release he travelled to Mombasa, and did some casual building jobs. In 1959 he crossed illegally, at night, in a dhow, to Pemba. While doing odd jobs he attended some ZNP political meetings. Later he began a stone-quarrying business, and joined ASP, campaigning for them in the three elections in the run-up to Independence.

After the third election, Okello moved to Zanzibar Island. The Shamte administration was anxious about the police force containing many African recruits from the mainland, and began to replace them with inexperienced Zanzibaris. It was in this context that John Okello began to form plans to overthrow the government, recruiting mainly from Africans who were not Zanzibaris (including some disaffected former policemen) and who feared that they might be expelled by a pro-Arab government. Okello warned his followers that after Independence all male African babies would be killed, Africans would be ruled as slaves, and 3000 Africans would

be slaughtered in reprisal for the 64 Arabs killed in the 1961 disturbances. By November Okello was having visionary dreams and commanding his men to abstain from sex until after the revolution and not to wear other people's clothes, in order to keep strong. He designed a Field-Marshal's uniform and pennant for himself. Final battle instructions indicated who should be killed (males aged between 18 and 55) and who could be raped (no wives of men killed or detained, and no virgins). The Sultan and three specified politicians were to be killed and the remainder captured. Some of his followers thought that Independence Day, 10 December 1963, would be an appropriate day for the revolution, but Okello thought it would be a pity to spoil the celebrations for the many overseas visitors.

On 12 January 1964, Okello led the crucial attack on Ziwani Police Station which overthrew the government and resulted in the flight of the Sultan into exile. Following this coup Okello pronounced himself Field-Marshal, and for a while assumed the title of Leader of the Revolutionary Government. As a semblance of order was restored, it was clear that Okello was an embarrassment to the ASP Government, and by 11 March he was expelled, resuming his former career of wandering the mainland, taking casual employment, and languishing for spells in prison.

Although the ZNP tried to embrace all races, the fact was that they were seen as an Arab party, while the ASP represented African interests. Arabs comprised 20% of the population, Africans over 75%. Elections to the Legislative Council in 1955 were organized on the basis of communal rolls – that is, so many seats were allocated to Arabs, so many to Africans, and so on. This infuriated the ZNP who wanted a common electoral roll so that they could contest all seats. They boycotted the Legislative Council. When a ZNP member broke ranks, he was assassinated, and an Arab was executed for his murder. The next elections, in 1957, were held on the basis of a common roll, and the ZNP did not win a single one of the six seats that were contested. ASP took five and the Muslim League one. More damaging, Ali Muhsin insisted on a head-to-head with Karume in the Ngambo constituency, and was soundly beaten, polling less than 25% of the votes cast. ZNP's belief that they could draw broad-based support was very badly dented. In the next four years, the ZNP greatly increased its efforts with youth and women's organizations, and published five daily papers. It was also felt that wealthy Arab landowners and employers flexed their economic muscles to encourage support for ZNP among Africans. ZNP was greatly assisted in 1959 by a split in the ASP. Sheikh Muhammed Shamte, a Shirazi veterinary surgeon with a large clove plantation in Pemba, formed the Zanzibar and Pemba People's Party (ZPPP). Two other ASP members of the Legislative Council joined Shamte, and the ASP was left in a minority with just two seats.

In the run-up to Independence, there were three more elections. In the first, in January 1961, ASP won 10 seats, ZNP took nine and ZPPP was successful in three. A farce ensued in which both ASP and ZNP wooed the three ZPPP members. One supported ASP and the remaining two supported ZNP, creating a deadlock with 11 apiece. In the event, ZNP and ASP formed a coalition caretaker government on the understanding that new elections be held as soon as possible.

For the June 1961 elections a new constituency was created, to make a total of 23 seats. ASP and ZNP won 10 each, and ZPPP three. However, ZPPP had committed itself to support ZNP, and this coalition duly formed a government. However, ASP had gained a majority of the popular vote (albeit narrowly at 50.6%) and this caused resentment. The improved performance of ZNP in the two elections after the debacle of 1957 was bewildering to ASP. There were serious outbreaks of violence, and these were clearly along racial lines and directed against Arabs. There were 68 deaths of which 64 were Arab.

In 1962 a Constitutional Conference was held at Lancaster House in London, attended by the main figures of the three political parties. A framework was duly thrashed out and agreed, with the Sultan as the constitutional Head of State. The number of seats was increased to 31 and women were given the vote. Elections in 1963 saw ASP gain 13 seats, ZNP 12 and ZPPP six. A ZNP/ZPPP coalition government was formed under the leadership of Muhammed Shamte of ZPPP. Once again ASP had the majority of the popular vote with 54%. Independence was set for later that year, on 10 December.

The old Sultan had died in 1960 and was succeeded by his son Abdullah bin Khalifa, who was to reign for less than three years, dying of cancer in July 1963. His son, Jamshid Bin Abdullah, became Sultan at the age of 34.

The revolution

It has been described as 'the most unnecessary revolution in history'. At 0300 on the night of 12 January 1964, a motley group of Africans, armed with clubs, pangas (long implements with bent, curved blades, swished from side to side to cut grass), car springs, bows and arrows, converged on the Police Headquarters at Ziwani on the edge of Zanzibar Stone Town. There were two sentries on duty. John Okello (see box, page 167) was the leader of the attacking force. He rushed forward, grappled with one of the sentries, seized his rifle and bayonetted him. The other sentry was hit by an iron-tipped arrow. Encouraged, the attackers stormed the building. In a matter of moments the police had fled, and the mob broke into the armoury. Thus armed, they moved on to support other attacks that had been planned to take place simultaneously at other key installations – the radio station, the army barracks, and the gaol. By midday, most of the town was in the hands of Okello's forces.

As the skirmishes raged through the narrow cobbled streets of the historic Stone Town, the Sultan, his family and entourage (about 50 in all) were advised to flee by the Prime Minister and his Cabinet. Two government boats were at anchor off-shore. The Sultan's party was ferried to one of these, and it set off to the northwest to Mombasa, in nearby Kenya. The government there, having gained Independence itself only a month earlier, had no desire to get involved by acting in a way that might be interpreted as hostile by whatever body eventually took control on the island. The Sultan was refused permission to land, and the boat returned southwards down the coast to Dar es Salaam in Tanganyika. From there the party was flown to Manchester and exile in Britain.

Okello began the business of government by proclaiming himself Field-Marshal, Leader of the Revolutionary Government, and Minister of Defence and Broadcasting. Members of the ASP were allocated other ministries, with Abeid Karume as Prime Minister. Meanwhile there was considerable mayhem throughout the islands, as old scores were settled and the African and Arab communities took revenge upon one another. Initial figures suggest that 12,000 Arabs and 1000 Africans were killed before the violence ran its course.

A trickle of countries, mostly newly independent African states and Soviet regimes recognized the Karume regime fairly promptly. In February 1964 Karume expelled the British High Commissioner and the Acting US Chargé d'Affaires as their countries had not recognized his government.

Army mutinies in Kenya, Tanganyika and Uganda earlier in the year, the presence of British troops in the region and some ominous remarks by the US Ambassador in Nairobi about Communist threats to the mainland from Zanzibar all served to make Karume anxious. He felt vulnerable with no army he could count on, and what he saw as hostile developments all around. He needed some support to secure his position.

On 23 April, Karume and Julius Nyerere signed an Act of Union between Zanzibar and Tanganyika to form Tanzania. Later the mainland political party merged with ASP to form Chama Cha Mapinduzi (CCM), the only legal political party in Tanzania.

The union

The relationship between Zanzibar and the mainland is a mess. It is neither a proper federation nor a unitary state. Zanzibar retains its own President (up to 1995, *ex officio* one of the Vice-Presidents of the Union). It has a full set of ministries, its own Assembly, and keeps its own foreign exchange earnings. Mainlanders need a passport to go to Zanzibar, and cannot own property there. No such restrictions apply to Zanzibaris on the mainland. Despite comprising less than 5% of Tanzania's total population, Zanzibar has 30% of the aseats in the Union Assembly. The practice of rotating the Union Presidency between Zanzibar and the mainland meant that from 1985-1995 two of the occupants of the top three posts (the President and one of the two Vice-Presidents) come from Zanzibar. Zanzibar has not paid for electricity supplied by the mainland for over 15 years.

Despite all these privileges (which annoy the daylights out of many mainlanders) the Zanzibaris feel they have had a rough time since 1964. The socialist development strategy pursued by Tanzania after 1967 has seen living standards fall in Zanzibar. Where once the inhabitants of Zanzibar Town were noticeably better off than the urban dwellers in mainland Dar es Salaam, they now feel themselves decidedly poorer. They consider that if they had been able to utilize their historical and cultural links with oil-rich Oman they would have benefited from substantial investment and development assistance.

The legitimacy of the Act of Union has been called into question – it was a deal between two leaders (one of whom had come to power unconstitutionally) without any of

Sensitivity to Zanzibar culture

Zanzibar has a relaxed and sympathetic attitude to visitors. However, the islands are predominantly Muslim and as such Zanzibaris feel uncomfortable with some Western dress styles. In the towns and villages it is courteous for women to dress modestly, covering the upper arms and body, with dress or skirt hemlines below the knee. Wearing bikinis, cropped tops, vests that reveal bra straps, or shorts causes offence. For men there is no restriction beyond what is considered decent in the West, but walking around the towns bare-chested or with no shoes is considered offensive. Zanzibaris are either very vocal in expressing their offence, or by contrast are too polite to say anything. It is because of the latter that many tourists continue to take this advice unheeded. When on the beach it is acceptable to wear swimwear, but if a fisherman or harvester wanders by, it is polite to cover up. Some tourists sunbathe topless on the beaches – this is hugely insensitive and completely inappropriate. It is worthwhile remembering that whilst you may see other tourists wandering around in inappropriate dress, this doesn't mean that you should do the same. Behave like a responsible tourist and cover up. Other sensitivities to consider are during the holy month of Ramadan when most Muslims fast during daylight hours. It is considered the height of bad manners to eat, drink or smoke in the street or public places at this time. Although alcohol is freely available, drunken behaviour is not regarded with tolerance and is considered offensive by most non-drinking Muslims. Finally, public displays of affection are also considered to be inappropriate.

the democratic consultation such a radical step might reasonably require. Separatist movements have emerged, pamphleting sporadically from exile in Oman and Scandinavia, and suppressed by the Tanzanian government. A Chief Minister in Zanzibar, Seif Sharrif Hamad, was dismissed when it was thought he harboured separatist sympathies. Later he was detained for over two years on a charge of retaining confidential government documents at his home.

Sharrif Hamad was the candidate for the Zanzibar Presidency of the Civic United Front (CUF), an already registered party. Support for CUF in the islands prior to the election was very strong but, victorious by a only narrow margin in both the Presidential and Assembly elections, a recount was called, and the incumbent Salim Amour was declared President with 50.2% of the vote (Hamad had 49.8%). CUF and Hamad were incensed at the outcome, and CUF briefly boycotted the Zanzibar Assembly. Political turmoil and outbreaks of violence followed, but CCM kept its position as poll winner. The CCM won further elections in 2000, and again violence flared amid accusations of fraud. Many CUF supporters fled to Kenya after deadly clashes with police. Both parties signed a reconciliation agreement in 2001. Under the ruling pro-union CCM, Zanzibar is set to remain part of Tanzania. But the CUF, which enjoys strong support on Pemba, has called for greater autonomy; some CUF members have called for independence. In 2005, the political status quo was maintained with CCM winning the elections with a majority, but there was anger, particularly on Pemba – a stronghold of the CUF party – caused by the belief that the results had been rigged. The next elections will be held in December 2010. Because of the possibility of violence on Zanzibar and Pemba during elections, you are ill advised to visit during these times.

Stone Town

It may not have a particularly romantic name, but Stone Town is the old city and cultural heart of Zanzibar, where little has changed for hundreds of years. It's a delightfully romantic place of narrow alleys, crumbling mosques, and grand Arab houses with giant brass-studded wooden doors. Most of the buildings were built by the Omani sultans in the 19th century when Zanzibar was one of the most important trading centres in the Indian Ocean. European influences such as balconies and verandas were added some years later. The walls of the houses are made from coralline rock, which is a good building material, but erodes easily. Many of Stone Town's 1900 historical houses have crumbled beyond repair, whilst others have been beautifully renovated. Since Stone Town was deservedly declared a World Heritage Site by UNESCO in 2000, the Stone Town Conservation Authority is working towards restoring the ancient town before these buildings are lost for ever. Most hotel accommodation is in the restored old houses and rooms are decorated with antiques, Persian rugs and the delightful four poster Zanzibarian beds. At least two nights is warranted in Stone Town to soak up the atmosphere, take one or more of the interesting half or full day tours on offer to sights in and around the city, and to learn a little about its fascinating history. ▸▸ *For listings, see pages 180-193.*

Ins and outs → *See also Ins and outs, page 160.*

Getting there If arriving at the airport, which is 6 km from town, you will be badgered by the many taxi drivers. Ask inside the airport what you should pay for a taxi to take you the short distance into town, which will help with bargaining once outside. A taxi should cost in the region of US$10-15, or alternatively there are buses and *dala-dala* to town for less than US$1. There is a bureau de change in the airport. Some of the more upmarket hotels and resorts offer free airport pick ups, so it always worthwhile asking.

The ferry terminal is in the Malindi area of Stone Town. Many of the hotels are within walking distance of the ferry terminal, or alternatively you can take a taxi directly from the port. The booking offices for the ferries are clustered around the jetty where you will need to reconfirm the date of your return ticket to Dar if you have not already done so when booking the ticket. The dhow harbour is next to the port, but remember it is illegal for foreigners to travel between the mainland and the islands by dhow. ▸▸ *For further details, see Transport, page 192.*

Safety

Safety is becoming an increasing concern on Zanzibar. There have been violent robberies, at knifepoint, of tourists even during daylight hours in Stone Town and its environs. There is speculation that the perpetrators are mainland Tanzanians, as Zanzibaris are usually noted for their honesty. Be careful walking after dark, especially in poorly lit areas. Avoid alleyways at night, particularly by the Big Tree on Mizingani Road and the Malindi area near the port. Valuables can usually be left in your hotel safe as an extra precaution. At night use taxis to get back to the hotel, which can be found easily around the major restaurants and nightclubs. Exert caution on quiet beaches. Ignore anyone that might offer you drugs on the street. Drug use is illegal and the police may be watching the drug pushers – you will get into all sorts of serious trouble if caught negotiating with them. Quite surprisingly, there is a growing problem of heroin use amongst some young Zanzibaris and there is a concern about how and by whom the drug made its way on to

Stone Town

100 metres
100 yards

Sleeping
236 Hurumzi & Tower Top
  Restaurant 10 C4
Abuso Inn 2 D2
Africa House 1 D2
Al Johari 16 D2
Beit-al-Amaan 3 E3
Beyt al Chai 21 D1
Chavda 6 D3
Clove 7 C4
Coco de Mer 8 D3
Dhow Palace 9 D2
Flamingo Guest
  House 11 E4

Florida Guest House 12 E4
Garden Lodge 13 E3
Haven Guest House 14 E3
Karibu Inn 17 D2
Karibu Zanzibar 29 D2
Kiponda 18 C4
Malindi Guest House 20 A6
Marine 22 A5
Mazson's 23 D2
Pyramid Guesthouse 26 B5
Shangani 30 D2
St Monica's Hostel 27 D5
Tembo House 31 D2
Zanzibar House 33 D3
Zanzibar Palace 37 C4
Zanzibar Serena Inn 36 D1
Zenji 38 A5

Eating
Archipelago 9 C2

Baobab Tree 2 D4
Dolphin 7 D2
Forodhani Gardens 6 C2
Kidude Café 19 C4
La Fenice 5 D2
Le Spices
  Rendez-vous 10 E2
Livingstone's 4 C2
Luis Yoghurt Parlour 11 D3
Mercury's 1 B4
Monsoon 3 C2
Old Fort 18 C3
Pagoda 13 D2
Sea View Indian 17 B4

Bars & clubs
Dharma Lounge 8 E4
Starehe 12 D1

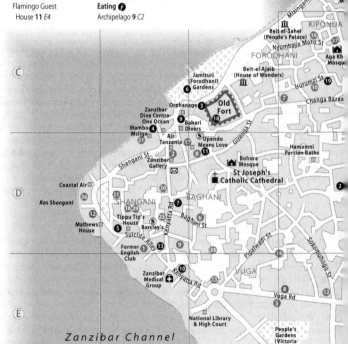

the island. It is not uncommon for travellers in hire cars or motorcycles to be stopped by the police while driving to one of the beaches. The police may try to claim that your papers are not in order – basically they are looking for a small bribe. If you ask for a receipt or suggest that you want to go to the actual police station to pay the fine, they will wave you through.

Sights

The area west of Creek Road is the original Stone Town and a tour of it will take at least a day. But it is such a fascinating place that you could easily spend a week wandering the narrow streets and still find charming and interesting new places.

Creek Road

A good place to start a walking tour is from the **Central Darajani Market** on Creek Road. This was opened in 1904 and remains a bustling, colourful and aromatic place. Here you will see Zanzibarian life carrying on as it has done for so many years – lively, busy and noisy. Outside are long, neat rows of bicycles carefully locked and guarded by their minder while people are buying and selling inside the market. Fruit, vegetables, meat and fish are all for sale here as well as household implements, many of them locally made, clothing and footwear. On Wednesday and Saturday there is also a flea market selling antiques and bric-a-brac. Note that the chicken, fish and meat areas are not for the squeamish – the smell and flies can be somewhat overwhelming.

Returning to Creek Road, after a further 200 m there is a large crossroads. To the left, a dual carriageway leads up to the 1960s developments of Michenzani – ugly concrete flats built by the East Germans during Tanzania's socialist period. To the right is New Mkunazini Road, and after about 50 m another right leads into the cathedral courtyard. The building to the left of the entrance to the courtyard is the

Anglican Missionary Hospital, which is constructed on top of the old slave chambers. The **Anglican Cathedral**, was built in 1887 on the site of the old slave market to commemorate the end of the slave trade. You can pick up guides here who will for a small fee give you a short tour of the slave chambers and cathedral (daily 0800-1800). The altar is on the actual site of the slave market's whipping post. The marble columns at the west end were put in upside down, while the bishop was on leave in the UK. Other points of interest are the stained-glass window dedicated to David Livingstone who was instrumental in the abolition of the slave trade, and the small wooden crucifix said to have been made from the wood of the tree under which Livingstone died in Chitambo in Zambia. If you can, try to go up the staircase of the cathedral to the top of the tower from where you will get an excellent view of the town. There are services in Swahili every Sunday, and in English once a month. Also on Creek Road is the **City Hall**, a wonderfully ornate building that has recently been restored.

Western tip

The People's Gardens on Kaunda Road, also known as the Victoria Gardens, were originally laid out by Sultan Barghash for the use of his extensive harem. The grand pavilion was renovated in 1996 by German aid agencies. Many of the plants in the garden were added in the 1880s by naturalist and British Resident Sir John Kirk. Opposite the gardens and behind a white wall is the **State House**. Originally built as the British Residency, it was designed to complement the earlier Arabic buildings such as the People's Palace. Since independence the building has housed the President's Office. Note that photography is not permitted around the State House.

Mathews House is close to Africa House Hotel, just to the south of Ras Shangani at the western tip of the town. Before the First World War it was the residence, with characteristic overhanging balconies, of Lloyd Mathews (1850-1901). Mathews was a naval officer who was put in charge of the Sultan's army in 1877 (he was a mere Lieutenant of 27 at the time). Later he became Chief Minister and was known as the 'Strong Man of Zanzibar'. The **Africa House Hotel** is on Suicide Alley and was once the English Club, opened in 1888 (the oldest such club in East Africa), see box, page 175. One of the great events at the English Club used to be the New Year's Eve fancy dress ball, when great crowds of dumfounded Zanzibaris would gather to stare at the crazy *wazungu* (whites) in their costumes. It has been beautifully restored to its former glory and the upstairs terrace bar is one of the best places in Zanzibar for a drink at sunset (see also Sleeping, page 181). A little further down Suicide Alley is **Tippu Tip's House**, named after the wealthy 19th-century slave-trader, which has a splendid carved wooden door and black and white marble steps. Tippu Tip was the most notorious of all slavers and Livingstone's arch-enemy – the latter's report of the massacre at Nyangwe, in the Congo, where Tippu Tip had commercial hegemony, led ultimately to the abolition of the slave trade.

Also at the western tip of the town is the building known now as **Mambo Msiige**, which was built in 1847 and was once owned by a slave trader. It is said that he used to bury slaves alive within the walls of the building and added many thousands of eggs to the mortar to enhance the colour. Since then the building has been used as the head-quarters of the Universities Mission to Central Africa and later as the British Consulate.

Old Fort

The Old Fort (also known as the Arab Fort or *Ngome Kongwe*) is in the west of the town next to the House of Wonders (see below). This huge structure was built in 1700 on the

Zanzibar under the British – the English Club

The British in Zanzibar (as everywhere) were profoundly insular, and in general reluctant to establish social relations with other communities. This was expressed in the formation of the English Club, which subsequently provoked every other significant community to establish its own club, thereby underscoring the religious and racial divisions in the society.

Although the English Club was formed some time before the turn of the 20th century, it was only in 1907 that it began to look seriously for substantial premises. A suitable building was located in Shangani just back from the shore, which is now the Africa House Hotel and, backed by a government loan, the club opened in 1908 on its new site with a restaurant, a committee room that doubled as a library, a bar and a billiards room.

In 1911 the club proposed taking over two rooms in an adjoining building to provide accommodation for out of town members. The government was approached to provide the capital to buy a lease and to refit the rooms. It agreed on condition that the rooms would be made available to the government for officials and their wives, and other visitors needing accommodation in Stone Town.

The Secretary, EWP Thurston, reported that the constitution of the club did not allow Americans or Europeans, and that it was a 'Man's Club', and there were the "strongest social and sanitary reasons against ladies occupying rooms". The government reacted vigorously to the proposed exclusions.

Women were allowed in to use the library in the mornings and between 1800-2000 in the evenings. They were also admitted to take lunch and dinner in the restaurant. As for the Committee's sanitary objections to women using the accommodation, these were dismissed by the government as the "merest bogies of their perfervid imaginations". In April 1912 the club gave way, and the two rooms were added. Later some garages were built on the shore site of the building, and more rooms for women were added above them.

In 1916 the club had plans to demolish a warehouse on the shore and build a swimming pool and squash courts. But the war interfered with these plans and they never went ahead. The space was cleared, however, and became known as 'German Forodhani' (Forodhani means 'customs house' – the German Consulate was nearby) or 'Shagani Steps'. Coloured lights were strung from cast-iron telegraph poles (two can still be seen on the site), and on Tuesday evenings the Sultan's band played a selection of classical and popular music, for the benefit of locals who sat around on the grass and those taking sundowners in the club's veranda bar.

site of a Portuguese church, the remains of which can be seen incorporated into the fabric of the internal walls. Its tall walls are topped by castellated battlements. The fort was built by Omani Arabs to defend attacks from the Portuguese, who had occupied Zanzibar for almost two centuries. During the 19th century the fort was used as a prison and in the early 20th century it was used as a depot of the railway that ran from Stone Town to Bububu. It is possible to reach the top of the battlements on the west side and look at the towers. The central area is now used as an open air theatre, with a traditional music and dance show on Tuesdays, Thursdays and Saturdays at 1930. The fort also houses an art gallery, several small shops selling crafts and spices, plus a tourist information desk. There is also a charming café, with tables in the shade of a couple of large trees.

On the south side of the fort you can take a walk down Gizenga Street (used to be Portuguese Street) with its busy bazaars. This will lead you to **St Joseph's Catholic Cathedral**, designed by Henri Espérandieu, who designed the Basilica in Marseille and loosely based this work on it. The cathedral is well used and holds regular Mass. When not in use, the doors may be closed, in which case entrance can be gained by the back door, through the adjoining convent. On the opposite side of the road is the **Bohora Mosque**.

Beit-el-Ajaib (House of Wonders)

Close to the fort and opposite the Jamituri Gardens, this is Zanzibar's tallest building. It has four storeys surrounded by verandas and was built in 1883 by a British marine engineer for Sultan Barghash and served as his palace. The name 'House of Wonders' came about because it was the first building on the island to have electricity and even a lift. It has fine examples of door carving. At the entrance are two Portuguese cannons, which date from about the 16th century. In 1896 in an attempt to persuade the Sultan to abdicate, the palace was subjected to a bombardment by the British navy. Inside, the floors are of marble and there are various decorations that were imported from Europe; there are also exhibits from the struggle for independence. The building once served as the local headquarters of Tanzania's political party CCM, but was fully restored in 2002 as the **Museum of History and Culture** ① *Mon-Sat 0900-1800, US$3*, with several permanent exhibitions on the history of the Swahili Coast.

Jamituri (or Forodhani) Gardens

The formal gardens are in front of the House of Wonders and the Old Fort and were once the location for the port's customs sheds before the port was moved in 1936 to the deepwater anchorage. Complete with a bandstand, the gardens are a pleasant place to stroll and watch the young boys diving off the sea wall but since 2008, the gardens have been closed for renovation and their re-opening has been postponed several times. In the meantime, the food stalls of the **Forodhani Market** have been moved to the streets near the Old Fort and sheets of corrugated steel surround the site. The market sells an extraordinary variety of snacks and seafood cooked on charcoal burners under paraffin lamps. Kebabs, freshly squeezed sugar-cane milkshakes, grilled calamari and prawns, omelettes, chips, pieces of fried fish, mussels, crab claws – everything is quite delicious and very cheap. At the time of writing, it remains to be seen whether the renovated gardens will retain their original charm or whether the area might be somewhat 'sanitized'.

Adjacent to the Jamituri Gardens is Zanzibar's **Orphanage**, which has previously been an English Club and an Indian School. The road here passes through a tunnel and if you follow it, the second building on the right has a plaque on the wall that reads: "This building was the British Consulate from 1841 to 1874. Here at different times lived Burton, Speke, Grant and Kirk. David Livingstone lived here and in this house his body rested on its long journey home." If the tide is low enough it is possible to pass down the side of the British Consulate and onto the beach, from where the magnificent houses can be viewed to their best advantage. Today, this building houses **Livingstone's Bar and Restaurant**, another good sundowner location with tables on the beach.

Beit al-Sahel (People's Palace)

① *Tue-Sat 1000-1800. US$3.*

The palace on Mizingani Road, north of the House of Wonders, is where the sultans and their families lived from the 1880s until their rule was finally overturned by the revolution of 1964. It was built in the late 1890s for members of the Sultan's family and for his harem. Following the revolution in 1964 it was renamed the People's Palace and was used by various political factions until it was turned into a museum in 1994. There are three floors of exhibits and it is well worth a visit. There is a wide variety of furniture including the Sultan's huge bed. Look out for the formica wardrobe with handles missing – obviously very fashionable at the time. There are good views from the top floor. The palace has grounds that can sometimes be viewed, containing the tombs of Sultan Seyyid Said and his two sons Khaled and Barghash. Heading north from the People's Palace is the **Big Tree**, which was planted in 1911 by Sultan Khalifa. Today it shelters local dhow builders.

Na Sur Nurmohamed Dispensary
Often called the 'Old Dispensary', this very ornate building is on Mizingani Road, north of the Big Tree. It was built in 1887 by Thaira Thopen, Zanzibar's richest man at the time, to commemorate Queen Victoria's Silver Jubilee. It's one of the most imposing of Stone Town's buildings, with four grand storeys and wrap-around decorative balconies. It served as a dispensary in colonial times and was one of the first buildings to be successfully restored to its former glory and today is the **Stone Town Conservation and Development Corporation**. Inside is a small tourist development known as the Zanzibar Cultural Centre with fixed priced shops, including a jeweller, curio and clothes boutique and a small, very pleasant cheap restaurant with a shady courtyard.

Port and dhow harbour
Further up Mizingani Road is the main port and the dhow harbour, which is a lively and bustling part of the Malindi quarter. The deepwater harbour has wharfs piled high with containers, and the landing is most frequently used by boats and hydrofoils from Dar es Salaam and Pemba. Built in 1925, the port remains essentially the 'industrial' end of town, with docks, cargo sheds and a clove distillery. The dhow harbour is at its busiest in the morning when the dhows arrive and unload their catches, and buyers bargain and haggle over the prices. These days very few dhows cross the Indian Ocean, unlike times gone by when fleets would arrive carrying goods from Arabia and the Orient, returning loaded with slaves, ivory and the produce of the islands' plantations. The best time to see one of these large ocean-going dhows is between December and March, before they return on the south-westerly monsoon. There is still plenty of smaller dhow traffic all year round between Zanzibar and the mainland, most bringing building materials and flour to Zanzibar.

Livingstone House
On Malawi Road, Livingstone's House was built around 1860 for Sultan Majid. It was also used by many missionaries and explorers as a starting point for expeditions into deepest, darkest Africa. Most notably, David Livingstone lived here before beginning his last journey to the mainland in 1866. Since then, it's been a laboratory (among other things) for research into clove production. It is now home to the Zanzibar Tourism Corporation.

Hammani Persian Baths
In the centre of Stone Town on Hammani Street, these baths were built by Sultan Barghash in 1888 for use as public baths and have been declared a protected monument. The building of the baths was overseen by a specialist team from Persia. If you want to look inside, ask for the caretaker who will show you around for a small fee (US$0.50). There is no water any more, so you have to use your imagination to imagine it in its heyday.

Zanzibar doors

At last count, there were 560 original carved doors in Zanzibar. When a house was built the door was traditionally the first part to be erected, and the rest of the house built around it. The tradition itself originates from the countries around the Persian Gulf and spread through Afghanistan to Punjab in India where they were reported in the first half of the 12th century. They started to feature in Zanzibar houses in the 15th century, but most of those surviving today were built in the 18-19th centuries. The greater the wealth and social position of the owner of the house, the larger and more elaborately carved his front door. The door was the badge of rank and a matter of great honour amongst merchant society. British explorer Richard Burton remarked in 1872: "the higher the tenement, the bigger the gateway, the heavier the padlock and the huger the iron studs which nail the door of heavy timber, the greater the owner's dignity".

Set in a square frame, the door is a double door opening inwards that can be bolted from the inside and locked from the outside by a chain and padlock. Popular motifs in the carvings on the doors include the frankincense tree that denotes wealth, and the date palm denoting abundance. Some of them feature brass knockers, and many are studded with brass spikes. This may be a modification of the Indian practice of studding doors with sharp spikes of iron to prevent them being battered in by war elephants. In AD 915, an Arab traveller recorded that Zanzibar island abounded in elephants, and in 1295 Marco Polo wrote that it had 'elephants in plenty'. These days there are no elephants, and the studs are there merely for decoration. The doors are maintained by the Stone Town Conservation and Development Corporation who keep a photographic record, and a watchful eye that they are not removed and exported.

National Museum

① *Creek Rd, south end of town. Mon-Sat 0900-1800. US$3 for both buildings.*

The museum is in two buildings and although fairly run down and shabby has some interesting exhibits relating to Zanzibar's history. It was built in 1925 and has relics and exhibits from the sultans, the slave traders and European explorers and missionaries. Livingstone's medicine chest is here and the story of the German battleship the *Königsberg*, sunk during the First World War in the Rufiji Delta (see page 129), is documented. There are also displays of local arts and crafts. If you are 'out of season' for the Spice Tour, it has an interesting exhibition on clove production. There is a giant tortoise in the grounds of the natural history museum and library next door and a door here, near the junction of Creek Road with Nyerere and Kuanda Roads, is reputedly one of the oldest doors on the island.

Around Stone Town 🚍🏔 ▶▶ *pp180-193.*

Changuu Island

① *You can get there through one of the tour agencies on a half day tour for about US$30, but it is just as easy – and cheaper – to find a boat yourself. Many boats will take you across to the island, and come back at a prearranged time to pick you up for about US$10 per person. Ask around on the beaches in front of the Sea View Indian Restaurant or Tembo Hotel. Just ensure that you only pay when you have been safely deposited back on the mainland. There is also a US$4 landing fee on the island.*

Also known as **Prison Island**, Changuu Island is almost 5 km northwest of Stone Town. It was once owned by an Arab who used it for 'rebellious' slaves. Some years later in 1893 it was sold to General Mathews, a Briton who converted it into a prison. However, it has never actually been used as such and was later converted to serve as a quarantine station in colonial times. The prison is still relatively intact and a few remains of the hospital can be seen including the rusting boilers of the laundry. There is good snorkelling, windsurfing and sailing from the beautiful little beach, though jellyfish can sometimes be a problem. The island is also home to giant tortoises, which are supposed to have been brought over from Aldabra (an atoll off the Seychelles) around the turn of the 20th century. They stand up to a rather staggering 1 m high and could feasibly be hundreds of years old. The tortoises are no longer roaming freely over the island because many were stolen. Now they are kept in a large fenced area. You can buy leaves to feed the tortoises. The **Changuu Island Resort** is a simple and reasonable café serving cold beers and basic meals like grilled fish and salad and also rents out snorkelling gear.

Chapwani Island

Also known as **Grave Island**, Chapwani Island is a nearby private island with one exclusive lodge on it (see page 184). There is an interesting cemetery with headstones of British sailors and marines who lost their lives in the fight against slavery and in the First World War. The island itself is 1 km long and 100 m wide with a perfect swath of beach on the northern edge. The forested section is home to a number of birds, duikers and a population of colobus monkeys (how they got here is a bit of a mystery).

Kiungani, Mbweni and Chukwani

① *To the south of town off the airport road near the Mbweni Ruins Hotel.*

The route south of Stone Town will take you past Kiungani where there was once a hostel built in 1864 by Bishop Tozer for released slave boys. A little further on are the ruins of the **Mbweni Settlement**, which was also established for rescued slaves. This was built in 1871 by the Universities Mission to Central Africa. In 1882 St John's Church was built in the same place for the use of the released slaves. There is a fine carved door and a tower. Also at Mbweni is **Kirk House**, which was built by Seyyid Barghash in 1872. Kirk came to Zanzibar as the Medical Officer as part of Livingstone's expedition to the Zambezi. He played an important role in the fight to end the slave trade and in 1873 was appointed His Majesty's Agent and Consul General in Zanzibar. He was also a botanist, introducing to the island a number of plants said to have originated from Kew Gardens, including cinnamon, vanilla, mahogany and eucalyptus. Further south at Chukwani are the **Mbweni Palace Ruins**. This was once a holiday resort of Sultan Seyyid Barghash and it had a wonderful position overlooking the sea. However, it has been totally neglected and as a result is slowly crumbling away. The main palace has completely disappeared, although some of the other buildings do remain and may be toured.

Chumbe Island

① *The island is a private conservation project and has an all-inclusive resort of the same name (see page 184). A day trip can be booked directly with the park, T024-223 1040, www.chumbeisland.com, or through Mbweni Ruins Hotel, US$80 per person including transport, snorkelling equipment, nature trail guides and a buffet lunch. Note that they only take day guests if they're not fully booked with overnight visitors – it's best to make enquiries in advance.*

Approximately 4 km offshore southwest from the Mbweni Palace ruins lies the **Chumbe Island Coral Park**. This is an important marine park with a wonderful reef of coral gardens that can be viewed from glass-bottomed boats. The reef remains in a pristine state and is shallow (between 1-3 m according to tides). If you swim up to the reef ridge it's possible to spot shoals of barracuda or dolphins.

There are nearly 400 species of fish here: groupers, angelfish, butterfly fish, triggerfish, boxfish, sweetlips, unicornfish, trumpetfish, lionfish, moorish idols, to name but a few. The snorkelling opportunities are excellent but scuba-diving is not permitted in the park. There are nature trails through the forest on the island, the home of the rare roseate tern and coconut crab, the largest land crab in the world that can weigh up to 4 kg, and it is now a refuge for the shy Ader's duiker, introduced to the island with the assistance of the World Wide Fund for Nature. There is also an old mosque, and a lighthouse built in 1904.

◉ Stone Town listings

For Sleeping and Eating price codes and other relevant information, see pages 36-40.

● Sleeping

Accommodation on Zanzibar ranges from town hotels to beach resorts, and from local-style, budget accommodation to 5-star luxury. The decor and furnishings in most are traditional Zanzibar, with antiques and ornate Zanzibari 4-poster beds. Bookings can be made directly through the hotel, or through tour operators. Check that the VAT is included in the quoted prices on the hotel tariff. Reservations for the peak seasons (Jul-Sep and Nov-Jan) should be made well in advance. Note that there is often a surcharge over the Christmas and New Year period. At most places children under 18 years get substantial discounts. Most beach resorts offer bungalow-type accommodation and watersports like diving and snorkelling. Some of these are all inclusive, while others offer the option of B&B, half board or full board rates. Note that camping is not permitted on Zanzibar. As with elsewhere in Tanzania, room rates are quoted in US$, though the smaller budget hotels will often accept TSh. Credit cards are now accepted by all the larger hotels and resorts. If you have not pre-booked accommodation in Stone Town, you need to walk around and find a hotel that suits. Young men will tout for business, offering hotels, taxis, spice or other tours.

They will usually pounce on you as soon as you get off the ferry. Some can be very aggressive and persistent. A polite 'no thank you' is rarely a successful method to rid yourself of their services. If you have just arrived you could tell the touts that you have already booked hotel accommodation from Dar es Salaam, and if you make your own way to a hotel insist that the management give no commission to any touts who may be following. Other strategies for tout evasion include saying you have been on all the tours, and that you are leaving tomorrow and have already bought the ferry ticket. It is better to deal directly with one of the many tour companies for excursions and organize everything in the confines of their office.

Stone Town *p171, map p172*
L Zanzibar Serena Inn, Shangani St, Shangani Sq, direct lodge number T024-223 3587, www.serenahotels.com. One of the best hotels in East Africa and a member of Small Luxury Hotels of the World. Stunning restoration of 2 historic buildings in Stone Town funded by the Aga Khan Fund for Culture. A seafront hotel with 51 luxury rooms and 10 suites and a swimming pool. Beautifully decorated with antique clocks, Persian rugs, carved staircases, chandeliers and brass-studded doors. The several restaurants have excellent but pricey menus. Wonderful location with first-class service.

A-C Beyt al Chai, Kelele Square, opposite Serena Inn, T0774-444111 (mob), www.stonetowninn.com. Closed during May. This beautiful hotel takes its name from its previous occupation as a tea house and has just 6 exotically and individually decorated rooms with 4-poster Zanzibari beds, silks and organza fabrics in an opulent Arabian style. Breakfast is served in the pretty courtyard and the restaurant is highly recommended (see Eating, page 185). Doubles start at US$155 with breakfast.

A-C Zanzibar Palace Hotel, Kiponda, T024-223 2230, www.zanzibarpalacehotel.com. Another beautiful boutique hotel with all 9 rooms individually furnished in stunning Arabian styles. The rooms even have DVD players and there's a DVD library in the lobby. Tea and coffee is served in the bedrooms before breakfast and some of the rooms have huge stone baths as their centre-piece. It's worth checking the website to choose a room before booking because they are all so different. The restaurant has a daily and à la carte menu and pre-ordering is preferred. Set menu of 5 courses US$37, 3 courses US$28.

B Africa House Hotel, just off Kenyatta Rd, on Suicide Alley, T0774-432340 (mob), www.theafricahouse-zanzibar.com. This used to be the English Club in the pre-independence days and in 2001 was completely restored to its former glory. The hotel is now under new management.The building has many archways, studded wooden doors, cool stone floors, 2 restaurants and a wide rooftop terrace with a bar which is *the* place on Zanzibar to sit and watch the sunset, sundowner in hand (although there have been reports of slow service). There are 15 elegantly decorated rooms with a/c, TV and Wi-Fi. Tastefully furnished throughout with antiques, original photographs and paintings by local artists, and the library houses a rare collection of many first editions and antiquarian books. Considerable discounts on room rates during low season (Apr-Jun).

B Al Johari, 116 Shangani, T024-223 6779, www.al-johari.com. A brand new boutique

hotel, which opened in Jan 2009. A lovely wooden turning staircase leads to the 15 rooms on 3 floors, all decorated in a very contemporary style with flat-screen TVs, minibars, a/c, and some with jacuzzi baths and double sinks in the bathrooms. The rooftop lounge and bar have great dual-aspect views of Stone Town and the ocean, and a waterfall feature that runs all the way down to the ground floor. Good reports of the food here at their Zanzibar Fusion restaurant, live Taarab music on Sat. Reports welcome.

B-D 236 Hurumzi, behind the House of Wonders, T0777-423266 (mob), www.236 hurumzi.com. 236 Hurumzi is the new name for the **Emerson and Green Hotel**, now that Emerson has moved on to other ventures. (His new hotel, **Emerson Spice** in the Kiponda area is completed but remains closed at the time of writing, with no indication of an opening date). Beautiful, individually themed rooms in restored 19th-century house with old Zanzibari furniture and fittings, original stucco decor, ornate carved doors and stone baths, lower rooms have a/c. All rooms have a bottle of water and fresh jasmine flowers are scattered on the pillows at bedtime. 2006 saw the opening of a new block of 6 rooms, following the same individual styles as the original ones but larger and slightly more expensive. There is also an apartment next door at 240 Hurumzi where the 6 bedrooms are let out individually and are particularly good value. The highlight here is the spectacular open-sided rooftop restaurant **Tower Top** – no shoes, sit on cushions, not cheap but worthwhile – a really magical experience. This is the second tallest building in Stone Town so the views over the rooftops are quite spectacular.

C Tembo House Hotel, Forodhani St, T024-223 3005, www.tembohotel.com. This is a beautifully restored historic building that was the American Consulate in the 19th century. Rooms are decorated with antique furniture and have a/c, satellite TV, and balconies overlooking either the ocean or swimming pool courtyard. Great location on the beach, the food is good, and the staff are very friendly and willing to negotiate over rates. Excellent value. Recommended.

C Chavda, in the heart of Stone Town, off Kenyatta Rd, T024-223 2115, www.chavda hotel.co.tz. A good mid-range establishment in a large restored Arab mansion with 40 large rooms, comfortable and well decorated, if slightly inauthentic. Reasonable restaurant serving international and Chinese food and a good rooftop bar, both open to non-guests.

C Dhow Palace Hotel, just off Kenyatta Rd, T024-223 0304, www.dhowpalace-hotel.com/ dhowpalace.html. Substantially extended 4 years ago, there's an attractive pool in a lovely interior courtyard between the old and new wings, with a bar selling snacks and soft drinks. Large rooms with high beamed ceilings, lovely bathrooms, a/c variable effect, fans, fridge, phone and antique furniture. Central courtyard and a very good rooftop restaurant that is rarely busy.

C Zanzibar House Hotel, at the back of the **Dhow Palace Hotel**, off Kenyatta Rd, T0774-432340 (mob), www.zanzibarhotel.co.tz. 15 rooms along similar lines to those in **Africa House Hotel**, its sister hotel and the place guests here go to for their restaurant and bar – it's a 5 min walk – since there are no facilities. There is a spa here though, and a huge lawned garden for guests to relax in. Doubles US$160.

D Abuso Inn, Shangani, opposite **Tembo House Hotel**, T0777-425565 (mob), abusoinn@gmail.com. The 22 en suite rooms here are spacious and spotless, with lovely wood flooring and furniture, a/c, mosquito nets and fans. Reception is on the first floor. Rates US$75 for a double including breakfast.

D Beit-al-Amaan, Vuga Rd, opposite Victoria Gardens, T024-223 9366. As an alternative to staying in a hotel, this private apartment with a large salon and 6 rooms can be booked for a group or each individual room can be let out, suitable for groups of 2-11 people. Very nicely furnished, each of the rooms have private bathrooms, and there's also shared kitchen with fridge and microwave and large living room. Breakfast is included in the room rate and is served to all the guests in the salon. Friendly and excellent value from US$79 for a double.

D Clove, Hurumzi St, behind the House of Wonders, T0777-484567 (mob), www.zanz ibarhotel.nl. A good mid-range option, run by Lisette, a Dutch lady. It's in a nice quiet square with an excellent roof bar and restaurant with free Wi-Fi access for residents and a great sea view. The building itself is quite modern by Stone Town standards, but the interiors have been remodelled to include elements of the more traditional Zanzibari style. Rooms have fridge, fan and en suite bathrooms with hot water. Don't take bookings for single nights.

D Hotel Marine, Malawi Rd, Malindi, diagonally across from port entrance, T024-223 2088, hotelmarine@africaonline.co.tz. 3-star establishment near the gates of the main harbour. Comfortable rooms have a/c, satellite TV and en suite bathrooms and are decorated with traditional Zanzibari furniture. The restaurant serves local, Indian and Chinese dishes and there's room service. Note that this is a busy area and the street noise can be obtrusive. Be wary around the port area at night.

D Mazson's Hotel, Kenyatta Rd, Shangani, T024-223 3694, www.mazsonshotel.net. 35 rooms with a/c, fridge, TV, rooftop restaurant, in a whitewashed 19th-century building with wraparound balconies and gardens with a fountain. Being renovated at the time of our visit – reports welcome.

D Shangani Hotel, Kenyatta Rd, across from the Old Post Office, T024-223 3688, www.shanganihotel.com. Clean and straightforward rooms with a/c, TV, fridge, fans, mosquito nets, own bathrooms and balconies overlooking the old town. There are nicer places to stay in this price range – with more polite managers – but the location is central and convenient and they have an internet café next door. Double bed and breakfast is US$75.

D Zenji Hotel, Malindi, opposite Cine Afrique building, T0776-705592 (mob), www.zenji hotel.com. Owned by a Zanzibari/Dutch couple, this small hotel near the port is very community focused, with all local furniture and crafts, locally sourced food and Zanzibari staff. It has 9 individual rooms very reasonably priced from US$50 including breakfast, served in the rooftop restaurant. Very good reports and helpful, friendly staff.

E Coco de Mer Hotel, between Shangani St and Gizenga St, 1 block east of Kenyatta Rd, T024-223 0852, cocodemer_znz@yahoo.com. This is a popular backpackers' choice with 13 basic rooms with bathrooms, fans and mosquito nets and some have TVs. Has a good restaurant (See Eating, page 186) and bar and it's in a central location. Clean and friendly, double rooms are about US$50.

E Garden Lodge, Kaunda Rd, in Vuga opposite the National Library/High Court, T024-223 3298, gardenlodge@zanlink.com. Lovely gardens, peaceful and quiet with friendly staff. The rooms are basic and a bit tired but cheap. There is a combination of twins, triples and a 5-bed dorm, with bathrooms. Rates US$40 for a double.

E The Haven Guest House, off Vuga Rd, T024-223 5677/8, thehavenguest@ hotmail.com. Secure budget place to stay. Rooms with or without bathrooms, plenty of hot water, mosquito nets and fans. Breakfast included in the price, self-catering kitchen, spotlessly clean and very friendly, owned by Mr Hamed.

E Hotel Kiponda, Nyumba ya Moto St, behind the People's Palace, T024-223 3052, www.kiponda.com. Another nicely restored building with simple clean rooms, mosquito nets, some rooms are self-contained, others have spotless shared bathrooms. Central location with sea views, fans. Good value but look at the rooms before deciding as they vary in size. Breakfast is served in the rooftop restaurant but no other meals are available.

E Karibu Zanzibar, Shangani, next door to **Al Johari**, not to be confused with **Karibu Inn**

next to **Coco de Mer Hotel**, T024-223 0932, magoma.52@hotmail.com. This is a straight-forward guesthouse with 9 small but spotless rooms, all gleaming new and with their own bathrooms, nets, fan, a/c and TV. US$50 for a double with breakfast.

E Malindi Guest House, Funguni Bazaar, Malindi St, T024-223 0165, www.zanzibar hotels.net/malindi. Excellent value place with a wonderful atmosphere. Central courtyard with plants, plenty of space to relax, clean, prices include breakfast. There's a rooftop coffee shop and bar with views of the harbour and the fisherman landing their catch every morning. Some of the rooms have bathrooms whilst others are dormitories with shared facilities. The only downside is that Malindi is not the safest part of Stone Town after dark – exercise caution if coming home late at night.

E Pyramid Guesthouse, Kokoni St, behind the Ijumaa Mosque near the seafront, T024-223 3000, pyramidhotel@yahoo.com. Charming staff, modest accommodation, a mixture of self-contained rooms and dorms for as little as US$10 per person. The rooms vary in size so ask to see a few, simple but recommended. Breakfast is served on the roof and they offer free pick up from the port or airport.

E St Monica's Hostel, New Mkunazini St, T024-223 0773, secactznz@zanlink.com. An old building next to the Anglican Cathedral with very clean and comfortable but simple rooms with or without bathrooms, mosquito nets and balconies. Price includes breakfast. Has a restaurant next door.

E-F Karibu Inn, next to Coco de Mer Hotel, T024-2233058, karibuinnhotel@zanzinet.com. Very popular and deservedly so, one of the best locations in Stone Town, tucked away behind the Old Fort. 25 rooms all with bathrooms, a/c is US$10 extra, fans, double rooms have fridges, also dorms for about US$15 per person, pre-booking is advised as it is frequently used by large overland groups. Excellent management who are very helpful and can organize all activities.

F Flamingo Guest House, Mkunazini St, just north of junction with Sokomuhogo St, not far from Vuga Rd, T024-223 2850, flamingo guesthouse@hotmail.com. Very good value at around US$10-15 per person. Simple, most rooms with shared showers, a small book exchange and satellite TV in the lobby.

E Florida Guest House, off Vuga Rd, T024-223 3136, floridaznz@yahoo.com. Has been recommended by some readers, another simple budget guesthouse but in a noisy location, communal showers, twin rooms, the ones upstairs are quieter and nicer, and 1 room has 4 beds with a/c and TV, that is ideal for a group of friends travelling together.

Around Stone Town p178

L Chapwani Private Island, reservations, Italy, T+39 (0)51-234974, www.chapwani island.com. This is an exclusive private island about 10 mins from Stone Town by speed boat, offering super-luxury and privacy in only 10 rooms in 5 bandas right on the beach in reed chalets with 4-poster beds. At night there are fantastic views of Stone Town. Seafood is the main feature on the restaurant menu, activities include volley ball, canoeing, and snorkelling. Prices are in the region of US$160 per person half board.

L Chumbe Island Coral Park, T024-223 1040, www.chumbeisland.com. This is a special place to stay. The utmost care has been taken to minimize the environmental impact of this resort; sustainably harvested local materials were used in the construction of the 7 luxury cottages and dining area, there is solar power and composting toilets, and rainwater is collected as the source of fresh water. Recognition of these efforts has been given through various awards and nominations over recent years. The emphasis is very much on the wildlife, coral reefs and ecology of the island and a stay here makes for an interesting alternative to the other beach resorts. Excellent food. Rates from US$250 per person, including all meals and soft drinks, boat transfers, snorkelling trip and forest trail.

B Mbweni Ruins Hotel, south of Stone Town, T024-223 5478/9, www.adventure camps.co.tz. Built in the spacious grounds of the ruins of the first Anglican Christian missionary settlement in East Africa. Private beach, pool, garden setting, open-air restaurant under thatch, art gallery, 13 suites with a/c and fans, 4-poster beds, mosquito nets, balconies, free shuttles to Stone Town 5 times a day. Organizes various tours around the island.

D Zanzibar Ocean View, 10-min walk from Stone Town along Nyerere Rd, close to the beach, T024-223 3882, www.amaan bungalows.com. This newly refurbished hotel on the beachfront at Kilimani is the closest beach resort to Stone Town. Rooms are comfortable and clean with nets, own bathrooms and sea view. Restaurant and bar, and they can arrange all the usual tours and transfers.

❼ Eating

Stone Town p171, map p172

There are a few moderate standard eating places in Zanzibar, many of them serving good, fresh seafood, and you will not usually need to reserve a table. Since this is a Muslim society, not all of the restaurants serve alcohol and if a bottle of wine is an essential part of your dining pleasure, it's advisable to check whether this is available beforehand. Most of the hotels have good restaurants and bars, many of which are on rooftops, that are also open to non-guests. During Ramadan it is difficult to get meals in the day time, other than in tourist hotels. It is not easy to find shops that sell spirits, although there is one on Kenyatta Rd in the Shangani area, opposite the Old Post Office.

♈♈♈ Africa House Hotel, see Sleeping, above. As well as a bar on the terrace that's perfect for sundowners, there are 2 restaurants here. **Tradewinds** is the more formal of the 2 with very good gourmet cuisine as well as Swahili dishes and seafood, whilst the **Sunset Grill**

has an outside terrace, fresh fish dishes and BBQ meat grills. The atmosphere is great although there have been reports of slow service.

Baharia, Zanzibar Serena Inn, see Sleeping, above. An expensive à la carte restaurant with fantastic food and attentive service in one of the most beautiful of the restored buildings on Zanzibar. It's worth eating here for a treat even if you are not staying. It's very romantic and you need to dress up.

Beyt al Chai, see Sleeping, above. Popular up-market restaurant with a Zanzibari theme, carved wooden ceiling beams and brightly coloured cushions. Lunch menu includes avocado salad with smoked sailfish for US$7 and various baguettes for US$6, and there are local specialties like green banana soup and fresh seafood on the dinner menu.

Tower Top Restaurant, 236 Hurumzi, see Sleeping, above. Here you can eat in wonderful surroundings on the rooftop; if you are not staying here you need to book a day ahead as space on the roof is limited. Semi-fixed dinner menus with the emphasis on seafood, with one seating starting at 1900, then take all evening to enjoy the excellent food and the sumptuous setting.

Archipelago, Kenyatta Rd, opposite the National Bank of Commerce, T024-223 5668. Open daily for breakfast, lunch and dinner, traditional Swahili dishes, salads, burgers and daily specials. Good coffee and cakes. Outdoor terrace with modern furniture overlooking the harbour. No alcohol.

Kidude Café, 236 Hurumzi, on the ground floor, see Sleeping, above, T024-2232784. Named after the famous Taarab singer Bi Kidude, this is a good place for lunch with a selection of sandwiches and wraps, as well as more exotic choices like creole fishcakes for US$7 and delicious shrimps with passion fruit dressing for US$8. Dinner is also excellent and there's a good wine list, albeit expensive.

La Fenice, on seafront just around the corner from **Serena**, T0777-411868 (mob).

Good lunch as well as a dinner, authentic continental and Swahili seafood dishes.

Le Spices Rendez-vous, Kenyatta Rd, near the High Court, T0777-410707 (mob). Tue-Sun. Formerly the **Maharaja Restaurant**, it still serves up excellent Indian meals, snacks and seafood. Recommended.

Livingstone's Restaurant, in the old British Consulate Building, on the seafront just down from Kenyatta Rd, T0773-271042 (mob). In a great location on the beach, with a varied menu of continental and Swahili dishes, salads and pastas. Lively and popular, with occasional bands and artwork on the walls that's for sale. If you want a table on the beach in the evenings, it's best to book ahead. Wi-Fi available.

Mercury's, Malindi, T024-223 3076. Named after Freddie, with an atmospheric wooden outdoor terrace overlooking the harbour, serves pizzas, pasta, seafood BBQ, Thai, Indian and Zanzibari food and cocktails with good service. Great place to watch soccer games on the beach but food is a little overpriced. Live bands occasionally.

Monsoon, between Forodhani Gardens and the Old Fort, T0777-410410 (mob). Deservedly popular restaurant full of Zanzibari atmosphere, cushions on the floor indoors and a lovely garden terrace outside. Great food and friendly service, with traditional Swahili cuisine including dishes like king fish in coconut sauce and ginger-marinated beef salad. Taarab music in the evenings.

The Old Fort Restaurant, inside the fort, T0754-278737 (mob). Nothing special but the only place to eat in the fort now that **Sweet Eazy** has closed. Burgers for US$6, pizzas for US$6-9, Swahili dishes and BBQs too. Expensive for what you get – you're probably paying for the location. Traditional music and dance show on Tue, Thu and Sat.

Pagoda, has relocated from Funguni to the Shangani area, and is now only a few paces away from **Africa House Hotel**, T024-223 4688. Has really excellent spicy Chinese cuisine, generous portions. Go for a beer at the hotel first to watch the sunset.

¶¶ **Sea View Indian Restaurant**, Mizingani Rd, T024-223 7381. A splendid location overlooking the harbour. You can eat inside or out and there is a wide range of food on the menu including delicious and good value curries, freshly cooked to order, but nevertheless service can be slow, and if you want to sit on the balcony, book ahead.

¶ **Baobab Tree**, New Mkunazini Rd, near the UMCA cathedral. Large thatched roof built around the trunk of a baobab tree, open-sided seating area beneath, some meals, snacks, juices, bar.

¶ **Coco de Mer**, see Sleeping, above. A popular place with good quality food at low prices including chicken Kiev, pili pili crab, octopus in coconut sauce, chicken tikka and sandwiches all for around US$4.

¶ **Dolphin Restaurant**, Kenyatta St, T024-223 1987. Popular place selling mainly seafood. Nothing special but one of the cheapest places where you can sit down. A sandwich will cost you about US$2.

¶ **Forodhani Gardens** (also known as Jamituri), between the fort and the sea. At the time of writing, the gardens were closed and the stalls were on the streets around the Old Fort, so the market's lacking its true charm. Vendors were hopeful of returning by the summer but the re-opening of the gardens has been postponed twice so far. When up and running, this is a lively, atmospheric place to eat and shouldn't be missed. Here you can get excellent meat or prawn kebabs, lobster, grilled calamari and fish, corn on the cob, cassava and curries all very cheaply. It is very popular with tourists who return night after night, and fun to wander around even if you don't feel hungry. If you're thirsty, try some fresh coconut milk or freshly squeezed sugar cane juice. The 'African Pizza' (mantabali) is also well worth a try. You may need to haggle over some of the prices, but you will still come away very full and with change from US$10. Just ensure everything is cooked well and inspect it carefully in the dim light. If it's not ask the vendor to throw it back on the coals for a little longer Try to keep a tab of what you have, or pay as you go along – some of the vendors have been known to bump up the bill when it comes to settling up.

Cafés

¶ **Luis Yoghurt Parlour**, Gizenga St, not far from **Africa House Hotel**, T0765-759579 (mob). Mon-Sat 1000-1400, 1800-2200. Closes for long periods in low season while the owner goes away.Very small place serving excellent local dishes including lassi, yoghurt drinks, milk shakes, fresh fruit juices, spice tea, and fabulous Italian ice cream.

⑪ Bars and clubs

Stone Town p171, map p172
Africa House Hotel, see Sleeping, page 181. The most popular bar in the town on a wide marble upstairs terrace which looks out across the ocean. The beers are cold and plentiful although rather expensive, and it is a good place to meet people. Get there early if you want to watch the sun set.

Dharma Lounge, Vuga Rd, T024-223 3626. A popular nightclub, open 2000 until the early hours. Modern hi-tec club with a large dance floor and good selection of music.

Livingstone's and **Mercury's** (see Eating, page 185) are slightly cheaper places than Africa House (see above) to watch the sun set, both with a wide range of cocktails, Savannah cider, beers and wines. They both have live bands playing occasionally and Mercury's is a great spot to watch the locals playing soccer on the beach – they have some very skilled players.

Starehe, next to the Serena Inn. Good reggae music especially on Sat nights. Very popular.

⊛ Festivals and events

Stone Town p171, map p172
Feb Sauti za Busara Swahili Music and Cultural Festival. Held annually during the

second weekend in Feb, the 4-day festival attracts talent from all over East Africa with performances in music, theatre and dance. See Dhow Countries Musical Academy, www.zanzibarmusic.org, or www.busara music.org, T024-223 2423, for more information. Sauti za Busara means 'songs of wisdom' in Kiswahili, and this annual festival of Swahili music attracts the best musicians and performers in the region. Held in Stone Town, there are concerts (mostly in the Old Fort) of traditional music, from Swahili taarab and *ngoma* to more contemporary genres that mix African, Arab and Asian music.

Feb Eid al-Haj (also called Eid al-Adha or Eid al-Kebir). The Islamic festival of the annual pilgrimage, or haj, to Mecca. It is the second major holiday of Islam and a 3-day festival of feasting and celebration in all Muslim communities in Tanzania. For Muslims, this holiday is about sacrifice, faith, and honouring the prophet Ibrahim. Along the Swahili Coast, and the islands of Zanzibar, each family sacrifices a goat or sheep; a third of the meat is given to the poor, another third to family and friends, and the final third is kept by the family to be served in a lavish meal. Any family members or friends who made the pilgrimage to Mecca that year are welcomed home with much rejoicing. During the night there is live Swahili taraab music and much rejoicing.

Jul Zanzibar International Film Festival of the Dhow Countries, held every year during the first 2 weeks of Jul, www.ziff.or.tz. Celebrates and promotes the unique culture that grew as a result of Indian Ocean trade and the wooden sailing dhow. All nations around the Indian Ocean known as the dhow countries are included in the celebration. Contemporary artists, musicians, cultural troupes, photographers and film makers are showcased and their work promoted, discussed, awarded, and explored. The highlight is the Zanzibar International Film Festival; film screenings take place around Stone Town in various historic landmarks. During the festival, workshops, seminars, conferences and a variety of cultural and arts-related programmes are open to the public, with specific forums to attract and creatively empower women and children.

Jul Zanzibar Cultural Festival, held annually, directly after the Zanzibar International Festival of the Dhow Countries, www.ziff.or.tzis. Held throughout the archipelago, many performers from around Africa perform at the annual Zanzibar Cultural Festival but the Swahili culture is mostly represented. Zanzibari taarab music and traditional dances are performed by a rich ensemble of cultural troupes and there are exhibits of arts and crafts. Street carnivals in Stone Town, small fairs, and canoe races also take place.

Nov/Dec Eid al-Fitr (in Kiswahili also called 'Idi' or 'Sikuku,' which means 'celebration'). The Muslim holiday that signifies the end of the holy month of Ramadan. It is without a doubt the central holiday of Islam, and a major event throughout Tanzania, but especially observed on the coast and Zanzibar. Throughout Ramadan, Muslim men and women fast from sunrise to sunset, only taking meagre food and drink after dark. The dates for Eid al-Fitr vary according to the sighting of the new moon, but as soon as it is observed the fasting ends and 4 days of feasting and festivities begin. Stone Town is the best place to witness this celebration when the whole of the town takes to the streets.

⊙ Shopping

Stone Town *p171, map p172*
Central Darajani Market on Creek Rd, sells mainly fresh fruit and vegetables and meat. However, the shops nearby sell *kikois* and *kangas* (sarongs), wooden chests and other souvenirs. Also try the small shops in the Old Fort, one shop sells only locally hand-crafted wooden boxes, many made of fragrant rosewood.
Abeid Curio Shop, Cathedral St, opposite St Joseph's Cathedral, T024-223 3832. Sells old Zanzibari furniture, clocks, copper and brass.

Capital Art Studios, Kenyatta St. Sells wonderful black and white photographs of old Zanzibar as well as prints of the Masai and other Tanzanian people. These make great souvenirs and look particularly good when framed in heavy wood.

Masomo Bookshop near the Old Empire Cinema just behind the Central Market, T024-223 2652. Has a good range of books and also sells Tanzanian and Kenyan newspapers.

Memories of Zanzibar, opposite Shangani post office, T024-223 9377, www.memories-zanzibar.com. Another upmarket shop with quality souvenirs, jewellery, handbags, cloth, cushions and books.

Upendo means love, just off Gizenga St, near Karibu Inn, T0784-300812 (mob), www.upendomeanslove.com. A new shop which sells great clothes for women and children made from *kangas* and *kikoi*. It's all about empowering local women and all the proceeds go to running a sewing school and workshop where women are trained and employed.

The Zanzibar Gallery, Mercury House, Shangani, T024-223 2721, gallery@swahili coast.com. Reputedly the former home of Freddie Mercury, this beautifully decorated shop boasts the most comprehensive range of books in Zanzibar; guidebooks, wildlife guides, coffee table books and the best of contemporary and historical fiction from the whole of Africa. The CD collection focuses on the best of Swahili music traditions such as taarab. Authentic artworks, antiques, fabrics and textiles from Zanzibar and mainland Africa, and clothes. It also sells excellent postcards taken by the owner's son. Accepts credit cards.

▲ Activities and tours

Stone Town *p171, map p172*
In order to maximize your time in Zanzibar it is worth considering going on a tour. All the tour companies listed under Tour operators offer the following range of tours:

City tour
This includes most of the major sites of Stone Town, such as the market, national museum, cathedral, Beit al-Sahel and Hammani baths. If you are interested in the architecture, this is a good opportunity to learn more about the buildings. Half day, US$20-25.

Cruises
Sabran Jamiil is a traditional 36 ft *jahazi* (ocean going dhow) that has been fully restored and is decorated with Persian cushions, flowing cloth and storm lanterns. Each evening between 1700-1900 she sails along the coast of Stone Town and you can get on at either the Tembo Hotel or the Forodhani Gardens. The views of the city from the water at sunset are gorgeous. The price of US$40 includes drinks and snacks.
Safari Blue, T0777-423162 (mob), www. safariblue.net This daily cruise departs from Fumba to the southwest of Stone Town several kilometres beyond the airport; transfers can be arranged. A full day trip around sandbanks, small islands and coral reefs, includes use of top quality snorkelling equipment with guides and instructors, sodas, mineral water and beer, and a seafood lunch of grilled fish and lobster, fruit and coffee. Dolphins can be seen most of the time. US$80 per person.

Diving → *See also box, page 190.*
Zanzibar is a great place to go diving. There are 2 recommended diving schools in Stone Town that both offer good value. It is worth noting that the best time for diving in Zanzibar is Feb-Apr and Aug-Nov.
Bahari Divers, next to the National Bank of Commerce on the corner of Shangani and Kenyatta road, T0777-484873 (mob), www.zanzibar-diving.com. Offer all PADI courses to instructor level and snorkelling using a motorized dhow, German owned. If you book on line there is a 10% discount. PADI Open Water course US$400, single dives US$70, discounts for multiple dives, snorkelling trips with lunch US$30.

Being dolphin friendly

Dolphin trips are big business on Zanzibar and provide an essential livelihood for the people of Kizimkazi, where fishing and tourism are the only sources of income. In the height of the season, as many as 100 people a day will go out to swim with dolphins and there's growing concern about the sustainability of this activity. If you do go on a trip, bear in mind that, as cute as they seem, they are still wild animals and that they live in a fragile ecosystem. A few simple guidelines can make for a more dolphin – and environmentally – friendly experience:

→ Stay quiet – loud noises or splashy water entries will scare the dolphins.

→ If you see a school, ensure that your boatman doesn't try to chase them or get too close, as this will only scare them off or possibly distress them.

→ If you're lucky enough to get close to them, ask the boatman to turn off the engine, and then slide gently into the water.

→ Swim with your arms along your body and duck/dive/spiral – do interesting things to attract their attention. Dolphins are curious mammals but they are wild. Again, if you're lucky they will surround you and nudge you.

→ Try not to touch them and don't feed them. Note also that dolphins are usually found in the open sea, which frequently has a marked swell – getting into the water with them isn't recommended if you're not a strong swimmer.

In view of their increasing popularity, an NGO called KIDOTOA (Kizimkazi Dolphin Tourism Operators Association) is working to ensure that dolphin tours are conducted in a more sustainable way, economically, socially and environmentally, by educating both tour operators and tourists about the marine environment and its ecosystem.

They've recently teamed up with a 'Responsible Tourism' award-winning gap volunteer company called Camps International to offer a four-day course on cetacean (dolphin and whale) conservation in Kizimkazi. (This forms part of a varied month-long gap break in the village, which also includes community work in the local school.) The course covers marine mammal biology, ecology and conservation, explains dolphin behaviour and teaches about dolphin identification. After the theory, you get to go out on trips to monitor and identify the dolphins in the bay, contributing to ongoing research. If your interest in dolphins goes beyond a quick swim with them, take a look at www.campsinternational.com and click on Camp Zanzibar – at the time of writing, this was only available to gap year students but they are considering opening it up to other clients soon

Zanzibar Dive Centre-One Ocean, bottom of Kenyatta Rd, on the seafront, T024-223 8374, www.zanzibaroneocean.com. Motorized dhows and custom-built dive boats go to several coral reefs. PADI certificate course US$450 for open-water diving, including PADI materials. If you have a scuba certificate, 1 dive including boat trip to the reef costs US$75 and 2 dives US$100, including all equipment hire and lunch. The inexperienced are offered 'fun dives' for US$125, which include 30 mins' instruction of the basics, plus a 12-m deep dive on a coral reef, snorkelling is US$30 a trip, safety highest priority, with fully trained dive masters/ instructors. Recommended.

Dolphin tour

Humpback and bottlenose dolphins swim in pods off Kizimkazi Beach on the southwest of

Zanzibar dive sites

Pange Reef The first sandbank west of Stone Town with a maximum depth of 14 m. There is an enormous variety of coral and lots of tropical reef fish such as clown fish, parrot fish, moorish idol and many others. Pange reef is ideal for Open Water Diver courses, as it offers calm and shallow waters. This is also a good spot for night dives, where you may see cuttle fish, squid, crab and other nocturnal life.

Bawe Island Bawe has a reef stretching around it with a maximum depth of 18 m. Here you will find beautiful corals like acropora, staghorn, brain corals and a large variety of reef fish.

Wrecks Wreck diving for all levels: At 12 m *The Great Northern* (built 1870), a British steel cable-laying ship, which sank on New Year's Eve 1902. She has become a magnificent artificial reef and is home to a number of leaf fish, lionfish and morays. Parts of the ship can still be identified and some relics may still be found (though not taken). *The Great Northern* is an ideal wreck for the beginner diver as she is only 12 m below the surface and is also great for snorkelling. The 30 m wreck of the *Royal Navy Lighter*, is home to large schools of rainbow runners, trevally, sweepers, and sometimes reef sharks, best suited for experienced advanced divers. At 40 m a steam sand dredger, *The Penguin*, is only suitable for very experienced deep water divers. Here you can find huge numbers of barracuda, big stingrays and morays.

Murogo Reef Maximum depth 24 m, 25 mins from Stone Town by boat. Sloping reef wall with a huge variety of coral and fish. Turtle are often seen here and this is usually the preferred dive site for the Open Water Diver course.

Nyange Reef The largest of all reefs on the west coast of Zanzibar and containing several dive sites, all of which are unique. A new species of coral has recently been identified here and marine biologists believe it to be endemic to Nyange.

Boribu Reef One of the best dive sites off Zanzibar and huge barrel sponges, large moray eels, pelagic fish and large lobsters are all features of this dive. In season whale sharks pass through. The maximum depth is 30 m.

Leven Banks On the north coast, this site is popular with advanced divers as it lies near the deep water of the Pemba Channel and is home to big shoals of jacks and trevally. Famous for remote 'holiday brochure style' beaches and colourful reefs, the east coast diving is the most talked about on Zanzibar.

Mnemba Island Reached from Nungwi or Matemwe also on the north coast, has a wide range of sites varying in depth with exciting marine life. Great for snorkelling too. Pungu Wall, East Mnemba, is a recommended dive for experienced divers looking for sharks, rays and groupers. This site can only be dived in calm conditions.

Thanks to **Zanzibar Dive Centre-One Ocean**, www.zanzibaroneocean.com.

---

the island, and are not always easy to spot. A dolphin tour includes transport by minibus to Kizimkazi, and transfer to a boat at the beach, a route that easily allows for a visit of Jozani Forest (see page 206). Prices and the quality of the boats vary, and many of the small

boats do not run to a timetable but wait to fill up, usually accommodating 6-8 tourists. Book this excursion through a tour operator rather than with the touts on the beachfront in Stone Town. From Stone Town, a half day trip is around US$50-60. Full day including the dolphins in the morning and Jozani Forest in the afternoon is about US$60-70, depending on how many are on the tour, whether you want a private tour, etc.

North and east coast tour

All operators offer transport to the north and east coast beaches, which can be combined with tours. For example, you can be picked up in Stone Town and taken to the east coast via the Jozani Forest (US$35, US$25 if you only go to Jozani and return to Stone Town, see page 206) where the rare red colobus monkey is found. On the way to the north coast, you have the option of combining a morning Spice Tour and perhaps a visit to the Mangapwani slave caves, and ending the tour by being transferred to the hotels in Nungwi.

Spice tour

For centuries Zanzibar's cloves, nutmeg, cinnamon, pepper and many other spices attracted traders across the Indian Ocean. The exotic spices and fruits are grown in the plantations around Stone Town and there's ample opportunity to dazzle the senses as you taste and smell them and guess what they are. This tour is highly recommended in during season, out of season you may get weary of looking at leaves that look very similar. Most tours are by *dala-dala*, the longer ones also include lunch. Guides give detailed descriptions of the various plants. The henna tree produces a dye from its crushed leaves used by women to elaborately decorate their hands and feet in delicate patterns. On the tour you'll have the opportunity to have a body part painted, but with quick-drying Indian ink instead (henna takes all day to dry). The tours last 4 hrs and are offered by various tour operators, Half day, around US$25; full day with additional visits to the slave caves and beach at Mangapwani, around US$30.

Tour operators

All these operators offer the tours listed above and others including: historical ruins and slave relics, Prison Island. Some are also able to arrange dhow sailing trips to the smaller islands, visits to Pemba, domestic flights, and car and motorbike hire. This is certainly not a comprehensive list, there are so many tour operators to choose from. Alternatively, you may be able to book all excursions through your hotel.

Classic Travels & Tours, Shangani, T024-223 8127, kassimabdalla@hotmail.com.

Discover Zanzibar, Chukwani Rd, T024-223 3889, www.discover-zanzibar.com.

Easy Travel & Tours, Malawi Rd, opposite Hotel Marine, T024-223 5372, www.easy travel.co.tz.

Eco Culture Tours, Hurumzi St, T024-223 0366, www.ecoculture-zanzibar.org.

Equator Tours and Safaris, Sokomohogo St, T024-233 3722, eqt@zanlink.com.

Exotic Tours and Safaris, 1st floor, Bombay Bazaar Building, Mlandenge, T024-223 63923, www.zanzibarexotictours.com.

Fisherman Tours and Travel, Vuga Rd, T024-223 8791/2, www.fishermantours.com.

Forodhani Car Hire, near Forodhani Gardens near the Old Fort, T0747-410186 (mob).

Furaha Tours, opposite La Fenice Restaurant, T024-223 2973, www.furahatours.com.

Links Tours and Travel, at the port, T024-223 1081, linktours@yahoo.com.

Marzouk Tours & Travel, opposite 236 Hurumzi, T024-223 8225, www.mtt-znz.com.

Mitu, T024-223 4636. Mr Mitu is one of Stone Town's most famous and formidable residents and has been running excellent Spice Tours in numerous languages for decades. He's now retired but guides he has trained run the show. They will take you on a tour visiting the Marahubi Palace, 2 spice plantations, the Kidichi Baths and a 1-hr trip to relax on the beach. They are good value. However, they have become very popular and you may find yourself in a large group of 30 or more. US$15 per person, including vegetarian lunch. Bookings are taken the evening before or from 0800 on the day, get there by 0900, depart 0930, return 1300-1600 (depending on whether or not you go to the beach).

Ocean Tours, opposite Zanzibar Serena Inn, T024-223 8280, www.oceantourszanzibar.com.
Sama Tours, Changa Bazaar St, T024-223 3543, www.samatours.com .
Simba Tours, T024-223 0687, www.simba tours.com.
Tanzania Adventure, Diplomat House, Mianzini, T024-223 2119, www.tanzania-adventure.com.
Tima Tours and Safaris, Mizingani Rd, T024-223 1298, tima@zitec.org.
Tropical Tours and Safaris, Kenyatta Rd, Shangani, T0777-413454 (mob), tropicalts@ hotmail.com.
Zan Tours, Malindi St, T024-223 3116, www.zantours.com.

Around Stone Town p178
Zanzibar Heritage Conservation Park
An alternative to going on a Spice Tour is to visit this park in Jumbi, 12 km southeast of Stone Town. The park is a private enterprise, operated by the very knowledgeable Omar Suleiman, who will show you around the large garden of herbs, fruits and other plants, and also the small museum and aviary. A small entrance fee is charged, to get there ask a taxi driver to take you to Jumbi as the park is not widely known. There is a small sign on the left of the road as you approach the village.

⊙ Transport

Stone Town p171, map p172
You can arrange transfers by minivan through most tour agencies to get around the island. It will cost about US$10 per person to get to the beaches in the north or east. You can hire cars for about US$-50-60 per day, motorbikes for US$25-30 per day, and bicycles for US$5-10, from many of the tour operators. Sometimes they also charge a refundable deposit. Ensure all your paperwork is in order if driving.

Air
Several airlines have scheduled services to and from the mainland and Zanzibar airport.

Expect to pay in the region of US$81 one way. Some also operate a service between Zanzibar and **Pemba** which is around US$100 one way. The airline industry is highly changeable, so check times before travelling. **Air Tanzania** has flights to **Dar** daily at 0950 and 1700 (25 mins). These services connect with onward flights.

Precision Air has flights to **Dar** at 0830, 1150 and 1700 (20 mins) and there are connections to other domestic destinations from Dar. There are also daily direct flights between Zanzibar and **Nairobi** at 0730 (1 hr 45 mins); to **Arusha** at 1410, (1 hr 10 mins); and to **Mombasa**, Tue and Sat 1140, Thu and Fri 0915 (40 mins).

Coastal Air have daily flights to **Dar** at 0645, 0800, 0930, 1100,1300, 1400, 1430, 1600 and 1715. The 1400 from Zanzibar continues to **Selous** and costs a further US$160 from Dar. There are also daily return flights to **Arusha**, which depart Zanzibar at 0930 and Arusha at 1215, take approximately 2 hrs and cost US$220 one way. There's a daily flight from Zanzibar to **Pemba** at 1430 (30 mins) that costs US$101.

Zan Air has scheduled daily flights to **Dar** at 0650, 1130, 1300, 1600 and 1730. To **Pemba**, 0945 and 1600. There is also 1 daily direct flight to **Arusha** at 1030.

Airline offices International airlines that serve Zanzibar are: **Emirates**, T024-223 4950, www.emirates.com. **Ethiopian Airlines**, T024-2231526, www.flyethiopian.com. **Gulf Air**, just off Malindi Rd towards the port, T024-223 2824. **Kenya Airways**, Kiponda, T024-223 2041, www.kenya-airways.com.

The domestic airlines that serve Zanzibar are: **Air Tanzania**, Shangani St, T024-223 0213, www.airtanzania.com. **Precision Air**, Dar, T022-213 0800, T022-212 1718, Zanzibar, Kiponda T024-223 4520, www.precisionair tz.com. **Coastal Air**, reservations, Dar, T022-284 2700, Zanzibar Airport office T0713-670 815 (mob), www.coastal.cc. **Zan Air**, to the west of Malawi Rd, Malindi area, T024-223 3670, www.zanair.com.

Bus and dala-dala

Dala-dala, which are usually converted pickup vans with wooden benches in the back, and regular buses are the cheapest way of getting around the island. It will cost about US$2 to the east or north coasts, but they are hot, dusty and not very comfortable. Most go from the bus station on Creek Rd opposite the market. Buses with lettered codes serve routes in and around Stone Town. A to **Amani**, B to **Bububu**, and U to the **airport**, amongst others. Numbered vehicles go further afield, and tend to leave once a day around noon, returning early the next morning. Bus No 9 goes to **Paje**, **Jambiani** (3 hrs) and **Bwejuu** (4½ hrs), costing about US$4. Other buses from Creek Rd go to **Pwani Mchangani** and **Matemwe** (bus No 1), **Mangapwani** (bus No 2), **Fumba** (bus No 7), **Makunduchi** and **Kizimkazi** (bus No 10), **Nungwi** (bus No 16), and **Kiwengwa** (bus No 17). There is another bus station, Mwembe Ladu, 1 block north of the New Post Office about 1.5 km east of Stone Town. Bus No 6 from here goes to **Chakwa** (1½ hrs), **Uroa** and **Pongwe**.

Ferry

The booking offices of the ferry companies are on the approach road to the harbour. **Azam Marine**, T024-223 1655. **Flying Horse**, T0784-472497 (mob). **Sea Express**, T024-223 4690. **Sea Star**, T0707-223 3857 (mob). **Zanzibar Port's Corporation**, for general enquiries, T024-223 2857.

ⓘ Directory

Stone Town *p171, map p172*
Banks There are ATM facilities at many of the banks in Zanzibar, including Barclay's near Maszon's Hotel, Shangani; **People's Bank of Zanzibar**, T024-221 31118/9, behind the fort on Gizenga St, also has a branch at the

Airport Terminal, T024-221 1189. **Barclay's**, ZSTC Building, Malawi Rd, Gulioni, T024-223 5796; **National Bank of Commerce (NBC)**, Shangani St, T024-223 31541. **Currency exchange** Banks often give an inferior rate compared with the foreign exchange (forex) bureaux, which are also open for longer hours. There are plenty of these all over Stone Town, just ensure you go into an office and do not deal with money changers on the street. **Immigration** Director of Immigration, T024-223 9148. If you lose your passport whilst on Zanzibar contact the immigration department who will arrange for an emergency travel document to get you back to Dar where the international embassies and high consulates are located. **Internet** There are many internet cafés all over Stone Town. Services are particularly good, with fast connections and reasonable prices. Expect to pay around US$1 for 1 hr. **Lost and stolen cards** Visa and MasterCard Assistance Point, next to Serena Inn, Mon-Sat 0830-1730. You can withdraw cash against your credit card. **Medical services** Mkunazini Hospital, near the market, T024-223 0076, British trained doctor, pay fee to register, wait to see doctor then pay for any prescription necessary, pay again when you go to collect medicine: this may be at the clinic or in a nearby drug-store; Zanzibar Medical & Diagnostic Centre, near Majestic Cinema, off Vuga Rd, T024-223 3113; Zanzibar Medical Group, off Kenyatta Rd, T024-223 3134, 24 hr emergency number T0777-410954 (mob). **Money transfers** Western Union money transfer is available from the Tanzanian Postal Bank on Malawi Rd, Malindi area, T024-223 1798, open Mon-Sat 0830-1800. **Police** T024-223 0772. **Post office** The New Post Office is outside Stone Town, in Kijangwani, just over 1 km east of the Karume Monument, T024-223 1260. Bus A or M from the market will take you there. Poste restante are held there. **Old Post Office**, Kenyatta Rd, Shangani area, has a fax and they should be able to help with poste restante. DHL, opposite Serena Inn.

North to Nungwi

The stretch of coastline immediately to the north of Stone Town was once an area of villas, recreational beaches, and Sultans' out-of-town palaces. This is also the route that was once followed by the Bububu light railway and an iron pipeline that carried domestic water supplies to the town during the reign of Sultan Barghash. Today many of the ruined palaces can be visited, though little of their previous opulence remains and they are fairly overgrown. Nevertheless they offer an interesting excursion off the road to Nungwi. At the northern end of the island are the villages of Nungwi and Kendwa. Until recently these were sleepy fishing villages hosting a couple of backpacker's lodges, but today the two settlements are almost joined together by a ribbon of hotel development and this is one of the most popular spots on the island for a beach holiday. The party atmosphere along the Nungwi Strip may not appeal to everyone, but there is no denying that this is a wonderful stretch of palm lined beach. Days are warm and sunny, the Indian Ocean is a brilliant blue and the snorkelling and diving are excellent. ▸▸ *For listings, see pages 197-200.*

Maruhubi Palace ruins

The Maruhubi Palace ruins are about 3 km to the north of the town. They were built in 1882 by Sultan Barghash for his harem of what is said to be one wife and 99 concubines. The Palace was once one of the most impressive residences on the island. Built in the Arabic style, the main house had balustrade balconies, the great supporting columns for which can still be seen. From here you can imagine him looking out over his beautiful walled gardens, which are believed to have been inspired by the Sultan's 1875 visit to Richmond Park in London. An overhead aqueduct and lily-covered cisterns (or 'pleasure ponds') can also be seen on the site and are evidence of the extensive Persian Baths. On the beach are the remains of a fortified *seble* or reception area, where visiting dignitaries would have been welcomed. The palace was almost completely destroyed by a fire in 1899, the site is now very overgrown, and marble from the baths has long since been stolen.

Mtoni Palace ruins

Shortly after the Marahubi Palace, just before the small BP oil terminus, are the ruins of the earlier Mtoni Palace. Shortly before he relocated his court from Muscat to Zanzibar in 1840, Sultan Seyyid constructed the Royal Palace at Mtoni as his primary residence. The palace was abandoned by 1885, in favour of more modern residences built by Sultan Barghash (see Maruhubi Palace, above) and quickly fell into disrepair. Use as a storage depot in World War I caused further damage and now only the walls and part of the roof remain. The site, sadly, is sandwiched between commercial premises and the BP oil refinery.

Around 3 km North of Mtoni, to the left hand side of the road is **Kibweni Palace**. This fine whitewashed building is the only Sultan's Palace on the island to remain in public use, accommodating both the President and state visitors.

Persian Baths at Kidichi

ⓘ *1 km north of Kibwenii. Take a right hand turn opposite a small filling station, along a rough dirt road. Follow the track for 4 km out through the clove and coconut plantations.*

Built on the highest point of Zanzibar Island by Sultan Seyyid Said in 1850, they were for his wife who was the grand-daughter of the Shah of Persia, Fatah Ali, and are decorated in ornamental Persian stucco work. The remarkably preserved baths have a series of domed

Maviko ya Makumbi

As you walk along the beach you will see mounds of what look like stones, known locally as 'Heaps of Stones', but which are in fact deposits of coconut husks. Each Heap of Stones belongs to a family or sometimes an individual, and some are 60 years old, passed down from one generation to the next. They are made into coir and then used to make ropes, matting and decorations. The coconuts are buried in the mud for three to six months, which accelerates the decay of unwanted parts of the coconut, leaving the coir (the sea water helps to prevent insect infestation). The coir is then hammered to separate it out from the vegetable matter.

If you see a group of women working on the Maviko ya Makumbi, request permission before taking a photograph.

bathhouses with deep stone baths and massive seats. This is quite a contrast to the plain baths nearby at **Kizimbani**, which were built within Said's clove tree and coconut plantation. Persian poetry inscribed inside the baths at Kidichi has been translated (approximately) as "Pleasant is a flower-shaped wine/With mutton chops from game/Given from the hands of a flower-faced server/At the bank of a flowering stream of water". The beaches to the west of here are good and are the location of several resorts. **Fuji Beach** can be easily reached from Bububu Village, and is a great place to take a relaxing swim if you've been exploring the area. There is a disco on the beach every Friday. Any *dala-dala* with the letter B from the main road will get you to Fuji beach.

Mangapwani slave caves

ⓘ *If you want to get there independently, the caves can be reached by taking bus No 2 from Creek Rd opposite the market. It's best to take a torch.*

About 20 km north of Stone Town, these were used to hide slaves in the times when the slave trade was illegal but still carried on unofficially. One particular trader, Mohammed bin Nasser, built an underground chamber at Alwi that was used as well as the naturally formed cave. The cave itself is said to have been discovered when a young slave boy lost a goat that he was looking after. He followed its bleats, which led to the cave containing a freshwater stream (a blessing for the illegally confined slaves). You may well see women carrying water from this very same stream today.

Tumbatu Island

ⓘ *The White Sands Hotel in Kendwa organizes trips here.*

Northwest of Zanzibar, the island of Tumbatu is the third largest island in the archipelago and despite being only 8 km long by 3 km wide, it has a very individual history. The island contains Shirazi ruins of a large ancient town dating from the 12th century and about 40 of the stone houses remain. The Mvuleni ruins are in the north of the island and are the remnants of the Portuguese attempt to colonize Zanzibar. The island's people, the Watumbatu, are distinct from the people of Unguja. They speak their own dialect of Kiswahili and are fiercely independent, renowned for their aloofness and pride rather than their hospitality. They are strictly Muslim and generally do not welcome visitors to the island. They also have the reputation of being the best sailors on the East Coast of Africa.

Kendwa

South of Nungwi (see below), about 20 minutes walk (3 km) along the beach, is the small resort of Kendwa. It is reached by the same minibuses that transport visitors to Nungwi or by boat from Nungwi. The beach is especially known as a good place to swim (as is Nungwi) because the tide only retreats about 6 m at low tide, so swimming is possible at any time of day. A band of coral lies about 20 m off shore which offers interesting snorkelling, and trips can be organized by the hotels.

Nungwi

① *Tourist minibuses go from Stone Town throughout the day, take approximately 1 hr, and cost about US$10 each way, ask from any hotel or tour operator. There are also local dala-dala and the No 16 bus from Creek Rd also goes to Nungwi. These take about 2 hrs and cost about US$1 each way.*

At the north tip of the island is Nungwi, about 56 km from Zanzibar town. It's a pleasant fishing village surrounded by banana palms, mangroves and coconut trees, with a local population of around 5000. However, don't come to Nungwi expecting a quiet beach holiday – over recent years tourism has rapidly expanded in this area, large new resorts are going up at the time of writing, and Nungwi and nearby Kendwa Rocks have firmly established themselves as the party destination of the island. As well as resorts, there are a number of good beach-side bungalows, a short line of lively outdoor bars and restaurants known as the 'Nungwi Strip', and a few dive

schools. The accommodation is of a good standard and most of Nungwi's cottages are built in a traditional African style with makuti thatched roofs to blend in with the natural surroundings. The bars are fantastically rustic and you'll find beautifully carved Zanzibari furniture sitting on the beach.

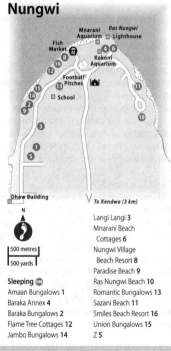

Down on the beach, you'll often see local men working in groups to build dhows or dhow fleets heading out to fish in the mid-afternoon. Boat building here has been a traditional skill for generations using historic tools and a 12-m boat takes approximately six months to build. Goats are slaughtered when certain milestones are reached (eg raising the mast) and verses and prayers are read from the Koran. Upon completion a big ceremony is organized and all the villagers are invited. Before the launch the boat builder hammers the boat three times in a naming ceremony.

The name of the village is derived from the Swahili word *mnara*, referring to the 70-ft lighthouse built here 1886 by Chance and Brothers. Currently it's in a restricted area, with access permitted only by special request and photography is prohibited.

Sleeping 🛏
Amaan Bungalows 1
Baraka Annex 4
Baraka Bungalows 2
Flame Tree Cottages 12
Jambo Bungalows 14

Langi Langi 3
Mnarani Beach
  Cottages 6
Nungwi Village
  Beach Resort 8
Paradise Beach 9
Ras Nungwi Beach 10
Romantic Bungalows 13
Sazani Beach 11
Smiles Beach Resort 16
Union Bungalows 15
Z 5

Nearby, there are two natural aquariums. **Mnarani Aquarium** ① *US$2.50,* was established in 1993 by a local resident in an attempt to help restore the local turtle population. Four varieties of turtle are endemic to Zanzibar; the hawksbill (*Ng'amba*); the green turtle (*Kasakasa*); the leatherback turtle (*Msumeno*) and the loggerhead turtle (*Mtumbi*). The aquarium has green turtles, which have a light grey/yellowish shell and hawksbill turtles, which have a yellowish/red shell. Their diet is seaweed and the hawksbill also eats fish. Any turtles hatched at the aquarium are released into the sea. Wild vervet monkeys live in the trees surrounding the rockpool.

You can buy basics at the small shops along the beachfront but it is much cheaper to go into the village where water, bread and other items are available. Remember to respect local custom if you go into the village. Women should cover their arms, shoulders and thighs. There are several places to check email in Nungwi at the resorts or at the small shopping centre on the Nungwi strip. However, the best place to get online is at the school; it's US$1 per hour but the proceeds go back into the school.

◉ North to Nungwi listings

For Sleeping and Eating price codes and other relevant information, see pages 36-40.

● Sleeping

North to Nungwi *p194*
C Imani Beach Villa, Bububu Beach, T024-225 0050, www.imani.it. Only 7 clean, comfortable rooms with a/c, own bathrooms and traditional-style furniture. Breakfast is served in pleasant gardens that run down to the beach, other meals are a fusion of Mediterranean and African influences, with organic vegetables from their gardens. The quality and presentation of food is very high and you eat Swahili-style, seated on cushions around low tables. Restaurant open to non-residents. US$110 double B&B or US$700 for private use of the whole house for up to 14 people half board. Recommended.
C Mtoni Marine Centre, between the ruined palace of Maruhubi and the Mtoni ruins to the north, 8 km from Stone Town, T024-225 0140, www.mtoni.com. Set in a large palm tree garden, the centre has a range of accommodation from shared bungalows to club rooms and suites. The Palm Garden apartments have private verandas, are traditionally furnished and have views of the beach. The bungalows have 1-3 bedrooms and are ideal for families. The restaurant is

open air and has barbecue buffets and themed nights with live jazz or taarab music. There's also a beach cocktail and snack bar, a sports café, a spa and a sushi restaurant.
C Salome's Garden, Fuji Beach, reservations through British agent, T+44 (0) 130 688 0770 www.africatravelresource.com. Lovely early 19th-century restored royal house surrounded by 7 ha of walled private orchards and tropical gardens running down to the beach full of bougainvillaea. Refurbished in 1997 as a luxury guesthouse or you can rent the whole house. There are 4 bedrooms sleeping a maximum of 10, with traditional Zanzibari 4-poster beds with mosquito nets, fans and beautiful antique decor.
E Bububu Beach Guest House, Bububu Beach, T0777-422747 (mob), www.bububu-zanzibar.com. Rooms with en suite bathrooms, hot water, mosquito nets and fans. Laundry, fax and email available. Free shuttles to and from Stone Town on request. There's also a whole house that can be let out to a group of up to 8. The owner Omar Kilupi is a former chess master of Zanzibar and is always up for a game. Arranges transfers and tours.
E Kibweni Beach Villa, 4 km north of Stone Town, T024-223 3496, www.geocities.com/kibwenibeach. Simple and friendly. Singles, doubles or triples (US$20/35/45), in a double story whitewashed building with tiled roof.

Some rooms have sea views, all have a/c and en suite bathrooms. Restaurant serves local and oriental food. Can organize all tours.

Kendwa p196

D Kendwa Amaan Bungalows, T0777-411 141 (mob), www.kendwa.tanzania-adventure. com. 39 rooms in bungalows with mosquito nets, balconies, en suite bathrooms. Some set back on the hill and others on the beach. The restaurant is on the beach with tables in the sand and a cocktail bar. Lots of hammocks to lounge around in. Can arrange tours and offers free transfers to Nungwi.

D White Sands Hotel, T0777-417412 (mob), www.ajvtours.co.tz/whitesands. En suite bandas or bungalows on the hillside near the beach. A reasonably good restaurant specializing in seafood but lacking ambience. Can arrange diving and snorkelling.

D-E Kendwa Sunset Bungalows, T0777-413 818 (mob), www.sunsetkendwa.com. One of the better places to stay in Kendwa, with a choice of accommodation ranging from new apartment blocks to beach bandas – all are reasonably priced for what you get, perched on top of a small cliff above the beach. There is a very good bar and restaurant which does great fresh fish and pizzas. It has a slightly more organized feel to it, at least most of the time, with friendly staff. Dive centre on site.

E-F Kendwa Rocks Hotel, T0774-415474 (mob), www.kendwarocks.com. This was the original backpackers' lodge at Kendwa and will appeal to people laid back enough not to worry about the variable levels of service and surly staff. Basic thatched bandas on the beach US$15 per person, or better quality bungalows for US$45 for a double. Fish, veggie and Indian food is available. Sometimes music pumps out late into the night, which may or may not be your thing – it's a popular place for 'full moon' parties. 24 hr Mermaid bar, Wi-Fi access available.

Nungwi p196, map p196

The price of a hotel room in Nungwi varies from US$20-500, so the resort appeals to all budgets. In recent years, new hotels, including large, soulless package resorts, have been built here and they effectively join up Nungwi with Kendwa to the south. If you want to avoid the crowds, the northwest of the peninsula is generally quieter and has some smaller, more intimate places to stay. The beach party crowds tend to hang out around the southern part of the village.

L-A Ras Nungwi Beach Hotel, T024-223 3767, www.rasnungwi.com. 32 rooms, some in the lodge, some beach chalets and 1 suite that is a huge detatched house with a plunge pool and total privacy from the rest of the hotel, costing US$900 a night. All rooms have ocean views, 4-poster beds, carved doors, en suite bathrooms, fans and balconies. The more expensive rooms have CD players and minibars. Restaurants and bars, pool, TV room and lounge areas under thatched roofs. There's a full range of watersports on offer, mountain bikes can be hired, excellent dive centre with good diving on the reef and deep-sea fishing. The hotel supports the local Nungwi Village community through the Labayka Development Fund, assisting with health and hygiene projects and schooling.

A-B The Z Hotel, on the west coast near **Amaan Bungalows**, T0732-940303 (mob), www.theZhotel.com. Opened in Jun 2008, Nungwi's newest hotel looks set to compete with Ras Nungwi as the best in the area. A boutique hotel with 35 elegant sea-view rooms boasting plasma TVs, Wi-Fi access and Phillip Starke furniture, it's a classy mix of Zanzibari and contemporary style. There's a relaxing infinity pool overlooking the beach and an open-air restaurant, serving African-continental fusion food, built up on stilts over the sea for more great views. The Cinnamon bar is also the perfect spot for sundowners. US$260 double room B&B.

B-C Langi Langi, T0773-911000 (mob), www.langilangizanzibar.com. 34 rooms in bungalows just across the track from the beach; singles, doubles and triples, all with en suite bathrooms, hot water, a/c, fan, mosquito nets, veranda and hair dryer.

The lounge area has satellite TV, telephone and fax, and there's a rooftop restaurant with reasonably priced food. Swimming pool, internet café, pleasant garden.

C Flame Tree Cottages, on the northwest side of Nungwi peninsula, T0777-479429 (mob), www.flametreecottages.com. Set in colourful gardens with coconut palms, frangipane and bougainvillea just off the beach, the 16 immaculate cottages are all named after trees or plants that are common to Zanzibar. All are en suite, with a/c, TV, fridge, net and fan, and are beautifully appointed with private verandas where guests are served breakfast. Some also have kitchenettes and self-catering can be arranged for a small surcharge. There's a candle-lit restaurant specializing in seafood and the whole place has an air of tranquillity about it. Rates are negotiable for longer stays.

C Mnarani Beach Cottages, near the lighthouse, a 20-min walk from the main strip, T024-224 0494, www.lighthousezanzibar. com. Ranges from simple cottages, to rooms in the main building, to family cottages, all with en suite bathrooms and Zanzibari beds. Friendly management, clean, comfortable and well maintained, great service and a good atmosphere. Discounts in low season. Near enough to Nungwi to enable you to visit the bars and restaurants, but far enough away to let you get a decent night's sleep afterwards. Breakfast included, full- and half-board available. Great seafront bar with hammocks, restaurant that focuses on seafood and international cuisine, laundry facilities, hot water, snorkelling, fishing and diving trips. Accepts major credit cards. Recommended.

C Nungwi Village Beach Resort, www.nungwivillage.com. Beach cottages with thatched roofs, furnished with traditional-style Zanzibari wooden decor, en suite bathrooms, premium rooms have a/c. Bar, restaurant specializing in seafood, facilities for watersports including diving. Internet access, henna painting and massages also available.

C Sazani Beach Hotel, near to **Ras Nungwi Beach Hotel**, T024-224 0014, www.sazani beach.com. 10 en suite rooms, double or twin beds, veranda, electricity and fans, sea views. Tropical garden setting, quiet and well away from the 'strip'. The Pweza Juma bar and restaurant serves original dishes with local flavour, specializing in seafood and barbecues, morning tea brought to your room and buffet breakfasts are included in the price. There is a dive school on site offering PADI courses or snorkelling trips, and kitesurfing can be arranged.

C Smiles Beach Resort, just south of **Nungwi Village Beach Resort**, T0774-444334 (mob), www.smilesbeachresort.com. The 16 en suite rooms are in 2-storey houses with wide spiral staircases to the upper floors. Each has nets, a/c and a TV, and their own terraces or balconies. There's a restaurant just off the beach (it doesn't serve alcohol).

C-D Amaan Bungalows, T024-224 0026, www.amaanbungalows.com. Clean, self-contained rooms – the best are those with balconies right over the beach, although you pay more for this. 3 bars and a restaurant on site serve good quality food, and there's an internet café. Amaan is really the centre of the whole Nungwi strip and Fat Fish bar, with its thumping music is hugely popular, which means there is often a bit of a party scene. **Nungwi Travel**, who can organize tours, transfers and bicycle hire is based here.

D Paradise Beach Hotel, T0777-416308 (mob), shaabani_makame@hotmail.com. 18 rooms in a rather ugly, tired-looking block facing the sea, all with bathrooms and fans. The beach restaurant is popular with good quality food and a lively beach bar. **Zanzibar Watersports**, who are also based at Ras Nungwi, have recently opened here and offer PADI courses and snorkelling.

E Baraka Bungalows, behind Paradise Beach, T0777-415569 (mob), http//barak bungalow.atspace.com. Has no direct sea frontage yet it is a beautiful little garden oasis with some of the best bungalows in this price range in Nungwi, simply furnished, all have own bathrooms and terraces, fans and nets, and some have a/c. US$45 for a double, includes breakfast, and there is a cheap restaurant with generous portions. There's also a sister guesthouse, **Baraka Annex** (same contact details), which is just opposite the entrance to Mnarani Beach Cottages on the northeastern side of the peninsula, and so about a 20-min walk from the main Nungwi drag. The 4 rooms here are more basic but cheaper at US$30 for a double with fans and nets and include breakfast. They also have a natural aquarium here, a massive rock pool with several turtles, the oldest and largest of which is 28 years – they plan to put him back into the sea to breed when he matures at 30.

E Jambo Brothers Beach Bungalows, behind **East Africa Dive Centre** on the west side, T0777-492355 (mob), jambobungalows @yahoo.com. This is a bigger concern than its neighbours, **Union** and **Baraka Bungalows**, with 19 rooms set just back from the beach, 2 of which have a/c that bumps up the cost to US$80 – a lot for what you get. Otherwise, prices range from US$35-50 for a double for simple rooms with nets and fans, bathrooms and a small terrace outside. They have a restaurant and café selling soft drinks, and a beauty centre should you fancy a massage.

E Romantic Bungalows, 2 mins' walk from the beach, set back behind **Flame Tree Cottages** and **Smiles**, T0732-940330 (mob), www.romanticbungalowszanzibar.com. Owned by the affable Eddy, this laid-back, friendly place is a good option for lower budgets, with 8 rooms in 4 bungalows set in secluded gardens. All rooms have their own bathroom, nets, fans and terraces, some have fridges. The gardens have hammocks and sunbeds scattered around, and there's a restaurant, satellite TV, internet and safe parking for vehicles. Dinner needs to be pre-ordered and it's soft drinks only, but there's a supermarket nearby where you can buy beer. Good value at US$40 for a double with breakfast, reductions in low season.

E Union Beach Bungalows, on the west side of the peninsula, just north of **Baraka Bungalows**, T0777-876345 (mob), mrpoudi@ live.com. Low budget with 10 bungalows on the beach, each with their own bathrooms,

nets and fans. Rates from US$35-60 for a double including breakfast.

☯ Festivals and events

See page 186 for information on festivals which are held throughout the archipelago.

▲ Activities and tours

North to Nungwi p194
The beaches around Ras Nungwi are one of the few areas without a coral reef and you can swim at all tides here without walking out for miles to reach the sea, as is the case on the east coast.

A number of places organize 'sunset cruises' on dhows for US$15 per person.

Fishing
FishingZanzibar.com, Nungwi, T0773-387 5231 (mob), www.fishingzanzibar.com. Offers full- or half-day big game fishing trips to Levan Bank or Mnemba Island or longer live-aboard trips to Pemba Island. Rates start from US$500 for a half day for 6 fishermen.
Zanzibar Big Game Fishing, Ras Nungwi Beach Hotel, T0777-415660 (mob), www.zanzibarfishing.com. This is a similar operator to FishingZanzibar.com, and rates for a boat start from US$400 for a 5 hr trip.

Diving
Diving is good around Nungwi and Kendwa and several dive schools operate here. The recommended ones are: **Zanzibar Dive Centre-One Ocean Divers**, www.zanzibar oneocean.com, see page 189. They provide all equipment. Sorkelling equipment can also be hired from local shops.
Zanzibar Watersports, at Paradise Beach Hotel, www.zanzibarwatersports.com.

Kitesurfing
Nungwi has also become popular for kitesurfing, www.kitezanzibar.com.

To the northeast coast

The very northeast part of the island seems miles away from the party scene of the Nungwi area and has a more remote, 'get away from it all' feel. Villages like Matemwe stretch right up the coast, fringed with shady palms. The local people live a peaceful existence making a living from farming seaweed or octopus fishing. An extensive coral reef runs down the whole east coast of the island, protecting a long, idyllic white sandy beach that runs for miles and is one of Africa's most beautiful beaches. The only problem here is that the ocean is tidal, and during some parts of the day it's a very long walk over the tidal flats to reach the sea. Further south, particularly around Kiwengwa and Pongwe, there has been a mushrooming of fully inclusive resort properties along the coast, which are quite characterless and could quite frankly be anywhere in the world, many of them frequented by European package holiday makers. For the most part, it is necessary to book these through a tour operator in Stone Town, Dar es Salaam or Europe (many are Italian or Swiss owned) – or take a chance on getting a room when you arrive, although several do not take 'walk-in' guests. This is particularly risky in high season from June to September and over the Christmas and New Year period. There is very little choice of budget accommodation along the stretch of coast around Pongwe or Kiwengwa, although Matemwe has more options. ▸▸ *For listings, see pages 202-205.*

Ins and outs
Getting there Minibus transfers can be arranged in Stone Town and cost around US$15. Bus No 6 from the Mwembe Ladu station in Stone Town goes to Chwaka (1½ hours), and then continues north to Uroa and Pongwe. The No 17 bus from the Creek Road station in Stone Town also goes along the better part of the beach road as far north as Kiwengwa. Both cost approximately US$1.50.

Dunga Palace
Just over 20 km down the road from Stone Town are the ruins of the Dunga Palace, which was built by Chief Mwinyi Mkuu Ahmed bin Mohamed Hassan. Legend has it that during the palace's construction slaves were killed in order that their blood could be mixed with the mortar to bring strength and good fortune to the building. During the 1920s a nearby well was found to be 'half full of human bones'. King Muhammad died in 1865 and was succeeded by his son Ahmed, who died without an heir in 1873, ending forever the line of the Mwinyi Mkuu. Unfortunately, there is little left of the palace today beside bits of wall and arches, and the area has been taken over by a plantation.

Chwaka Bay
At the end of this road, 32 km from Stone Town via Dunga you will reach Chwaka Bay. On the way you will pass the small **Ufufuma Forest**, a home for Zanzibar red colobus monkey, Ader's duiker, impala and many bird species, and also the site of several caves. The forest has been actively conserved since 1995, and although not a very well-known attraction, tourists are welcome, with guided walks costing around US$5. Chwaka is a quiet fishing village overlooking a broad bay of shallow water and mangrove swamps. Its history is evident from a line of fine but decayed villas, standing above the shoreline on the coral ridge, and it was once popular as a holiday resort with slave traders and their families in the 19th century. There is a lively open-air fish market but little accommodation and most visitors head north along the coast to the hotels.

North of Chwaka

The road from Chwaka heads north through the coastal fishing villages where there are several accommodation options and watersports centres on what is a fantastic beach. **Uroa** is a lovely fishing village 10 km to the north of Chwaka, and is close to the Dongwe Channel, which offers suitable diving for novices. **Pongwe** is 5 km north of Uroa, and **Kiwengwa** another 10 km north of Pongwe, followed by **Pwani Mchangani**. From the main road between Kiwengwa and Pongwe, which is all tarmac now, there are sections where there seems to be one gated tourist package hotel after another but these diminish as you head further up the coast road to **Matemwe**, a small village 45 km from Stone Town and 15 km north of Kiwengwa. Inland from Matemwe, is some of the most fertile land on the island, a centre for rice, sugar and cassava production. Matemwe beach itself makes few concessions to tourists in that it's a centre for gathering seaweed and fishing. Depending on the position of the tide, you'll either see scores of women wading fully dressed into the sea to collect their daily crop or fleets of dhows sailing away to fish. It's one of the most interesting stretches of coast on the island and beautiful in the way that its very much a locals' place carrying on their traditional way of life. About 1 km off the coast of Matemwe lies the small island of **Mnemba**. About 500 m in diameter, the island, surrounded by a circular coral reef, is renowned for its diving and game fishing. It is privately leased and to visit it is necessary to stay in the exclusive lodge (see below).

⊙ To the northeast coast listings

For Sleeping and Eating price codes and other relevant information, see pages 36-40.

⊜ Sleeping

North of Chwaka *p202*
Uroa

B Zanzibar Safari Club, T0777-844482 (mob), sales@hotelsandlodges-tanzania.com. Recently acquired by the Hotels and Lodges Tanzania group, there are 50 rooms in bandas in the gardens here. The resort has very brightly painted decor throughout, there's a dive school, tennis courts, 3 bars, 1 of which is at the end of a wooden pier out to sea where they have a disco, 2 restaurants, internet café and tours desk.

D Tamarind Beach Hotel, T0777-411191 (mob), www.tamarind.nu. This lodge has a relaxed and informal atmosphere, with 18 simple bungalows near the beach with own bathrooms, nets and ceiling fans. European-run, with a pleasant restaurant that has an exensive menu and open-air bar. They can arrange diving at Mnemba Atoll, snorkelling, game fishing, bike hire for US$10,

and massages. Free internet. Their new pool should be ready for summer 2009 and they offer good reductions for low season

Pongwe

C Pongwe Beach Hotel, T0773-662579 (mob), www.pongwe.com. Nice stone and thatch beach bungalows with en suite bathrooms, Zanzibari beds with mosquito nets, and fans, set in lovely relaxing gardens. Attractive swimming pool area with decking overlooking the beach. They allow day visitors to use the pool, but limit this to 4 a day with a minimum spend of US$25 per person.The English consultant chef used to work at the Dorchester Hotel in London. Internet available. Can arrange all the usual tours, snorkelling and game fishing.

Kiwengwa

L-A Bluebay Beach Resort, T024-224 0240 /4, www.bluebayzanzibar.com. Completely refurbished in 2008, this all round quality family resort on a lovely stretch of beach has 112 rooms ranging from ultra-luxurious Sultan's Suites to pretty garden rooms with en suite bathrooms and sea views, 4-poster beds, a/c, mosquito nets, satellite TV and minibar. There are several restaurants and bars, disco, swimming pool, fitness centre, tennis court, children's club, watersports. **One Ocean Diving** have a base here.

L-A Zamani Zanzibar Kempinski, just off the main road from Pongwe to Kiwengwa, T024-224 0066, www.kempinski-zanzibar. com. Set in 12 ha of gardens, this is one of the newer – and more expensive – of Zanzibar's hotels, with 110 rooms and 7 private suites. The hotel has all the luxury facilities you'd expect of a Kempinski, with a 60 m infinity pool, a lap pool in the fitness suite, and private pools for each of the 7 villas. There's a private beach about 1 km away from the main hotel at the Zamani Beach Club (beyond the **Shooting Star Inn**), and there are several bars, including a very attractive bar on a jetty over the ocean, and restaurants serving top of the range international cuisine. Double rooms from US$330, suites from US$670-$6700. See website for special offers.

L-B Shooting Star Inn, on headland at the north end of the beach, a 15-min walk along the road or beach from the village, T0787-195029 (mob), www.shootingstarlodge.com. Still owned by the charismatic Ali who opened this lodge 13 years ago as the first in Kiwengwa, it is now surrounded by land belonging to the luxury **Zamani Zanzibar Kempinski**. Thankfully, he's declined to sell his property to his new neighbour because it's a beautiful, intimate place to stay with 16 rooms ranging from pretty garden lodge rooms to top-class luxury suites with private pools. All are furnished in Zanzibari style and the suites, spread out over 3 floors with a rooftop sunbathing area, are stunning. Open-air bar and restaurant on sand and with makuti roof is very atmospheric and serves seafood, grills and traditional Zanzibari cuisine – some of the best food to be had on the east coast. Meals are included in the room rates. Bicycles for hire and there is a lovely salt water infinity pool 10 m above the beach. Recommended.

Pwani Mchangani

A Mapenzi Beach Resort, 2 km south of Pwani Mchangani Village, roughly half way between Matemwe and Kiwengwa, T0774-414268 (mob), www.planhotel.ch. All-inclusive resort with watersports centre, good food, 87 a/c rooms, Swahili decor, set in 4 ha of gardens, swimming pool, shops, internet café and tennis courts. Rates include all meals and alcoholic drinks and activities such as windsurfing and canoeing, but diving and fishing are extra. Popular with Italians and Swiss. Most people book through tour operators but they will take 'walk-in' guests on a fully inclusive basis only.

B Mchanga Beach Lodge, just outside the village, signposted on the right heading towards Matemwe, T0773-569821 (mob), www.mchangabeachlodge.com. A small, intimate lodge, with 6 sea view lodge rooms and 2 garden suites, all set in pretty gardens opening on to the beach. A quiet, low-key place with a pool right by the beach and nearby an open-air restaurant specializing in Swahili cuisine and seafood. Internet available, tours and diving can be arranged.

Mnemba Island

L Mnemba Island Lodge, central reservations, South Africa, T+27-11-809 4300, www.andbeyond.com. Mnemba Island lies 4.5 km or 15 mins by boat from northeast Zanzibar. This beautiful little private island has a reputation as one of the world's finest beach retreats and is impossibly romantic. Very stylish, very discreet and very expensive. The coral reef that circles the island is the finest in Zanzibar. 10 self-contained cottages, full board accommodation, includes most watersports and big game fishing. The US magazine, *Travel & Leisure* said of it, "It's the closest two people can get to being shipwrecked, with no need for rescue." If you can afford it, enjoy. Rates are over US$1200 per person in high season, fully inclusive of meals with house wines, and all watersports including 2 dives a day providing you have a PADI certificate.

Matemwe

L Matemwe Bungalows/Matemwe Retreat, at the far north of the beach, www.asilialodges.com. A luxury lodge with adjacent private villas, impeccable service and beautiful accommodation, opposite Mnemba Atoll. The lodge has 12 bungalows all with private verandas, and hammocks that overlook the sea (as does the infinity pool). The 3 private villas at Matemwe Retreat have their own pools on their roof terraces and guests here can choose whether to have dinner in their private gardens or go to the restaurant at Matemwe Bungalows, which specializes in seafood. Privacy comes at a price – US$525 per person for the villas, while the bungalows are US$310 per person.

L-A Azanzi Beach Village, turn right along main road in village, signposted on the right, just north of Matemwe Beach Village, T0772-284346 (mob), www.azanzibeachhotel.com. Opened in Dec 2008, this classy boutique hotel has 35 well-appointed rooms furnished in a contemporary style with lovely Zanzibari touches, including locally carved wood furniture and doors. The bathrooms have huge showers (some have outdoor showers too) and free-standing baths. Rooms are accessed by wooden walkways through lush gardens and the Mnemba View bar and Bridge restaurant on the 1st floor of the main building have great views. There's also a bar by the swimming pool just back from the beach, a games room, TV lounge, internet access and spa. Check out their glass-bottomed kayaks for a different perspective on exploring the sea and coral. Room rates flexible depending on season.

L-A Fairmont Zanzibar, about 1 km to the south of the village, T024-224 0391, www.fairmont.com/zanzibar. A very stylish, new hotel with 99 rooms and 10 suites, this is one of the more attractive of the larger hotels in the region. The rooms are spread out in beautiful gardens, some with direct access to the beach, with colourful decor, a/c, satellite TV, nets and private verandas. There are 2 beachside pools here, 2 restaurants (the intimate Zama Grill restaurant up on the first floor has great views over the ocean), a spa and a fabulous cocktail bar just above the beach. It also has its own dive centre (complete with decompression chamber), and offers a whole range of water sports from kitesurfing to deep-sea fishing. Check website for early booking discounts.

B Zanzibar Retreat, signposted to the right as you enter Matemwe, T0776-108379 (mob) www.zanzibarretreat.com. With a very hospitable Finnish manager, this small but beautifully appointed hotel has just 7 rooms around the edge of the main house and feels like a home-from-home. There's a good sized pool near the beach and a relaxing bar, and the place is very much a 'foodie' delight. The rooms are elegant with sleek hardwood furniture and floorings. Staff can arrange all the usual tours but the hotel also has an interesting Community Programme of village walkabouts, coral reef and seaweed safaris, and visits to a local women's group working on alternative energy projects – with money from the proceeds supporting the village.

B-C Matemwe Beach Village, to the north of the village, signposted as you enter, on the right heading north, T024-223 8374, www.matemwebeach.com. One of the nicest places to stay in Matemwe, with friendly staff, 16 pretty rooms, 5 suites and great food. Its strongest point is its chilled atmosphere. The swimming pool cascades into another pool below, conveniently close to the bar and BBQ area where dinner is served twice a week. The main restaurant is near the beach, as are some of the rooms, with others located further back in the gardens. There are some lovely touches here, like the sunrise tea and coffee on the beach if you make the effort to get up early, the Dhow Lounge above the pool furnished with old dhows, the honeymoon suite with its own private chef and beach area, and the free dhow trip that takes residents up to the reef at full tide. **One Ocean Diving** operate from here and offer PADI courses and diving trips to Mnemba Atoll, see www.zanzibaroneocean.com. Good value. Recommended.

C Matemwe Baharini Villas, north of the village, T0777-417768 (mob), www.matemwe villas.com. 15 stone bungalows with makuti roofs. Don't be too put off by the untidy screens on the outside of the windows – inside the rooms are fine, with a/c, fans, mosquito nets and TV. There's a decent sized swimming pool overlooking the beach and a cavernous open-air restaurant.

D Nyota Beach Bungalows, on the beach to the south of Matemwe Village, T0777-439059 (mob), www.nyotabeachbungalows.com. A relaxing place with 10 rooms in 4 bungalows mostly in gardens set back from the beach, although one overlooks the sea. All rooms have fans, mosquito nets and bathrooms, and are simply furnished and clean. There's a nice bar under a makuti roof and a restaurant that serves reasonable food. Friendly staff.

E Keys Bungalows, on beach further north from **Mohammed's Bungalows**, T0777-411797 (mob), allykeys786@yahoo.com. A low-budget option with plenty of character, there are 6 rustic bungalows here, simply but nicely furnished with sturdy padlocks on cupboards made from old dhows for security. US$50 for a double with breakfast. There's a cool seating area outside with hammocks and loungers, and the bar right on the beach plays reggae music, serves fresh fish, and uses more old dhows for furniture. Very chilled atmosphere.

E Mohammed's Bungalows, just north of **Azanzi Beach Village**, on the beach, T0777-431881 (mob). A decent low-budget option with just 4 bungalows right on the beach. Each has its own bathroom and is clean but basic with mosquito nets and fans for US$20 per person including breakfast. There's also a small restaurant here that serves straightforward meals like chicken and fresh fish.

⊛ Festivals and events

To the northeast coast *p201*
See page 186 for information on festivals which are held throughout the archipelago.

Southeast Zanzibar

→ www.zanzibareastcoast.com.

To get to the southeast of the island leave Stone Town's Creek Road at the junction that leads out through the Michenzani housing estate. Eventually the houses begin to peter out and are replaced by small fields of cassava, maize, banana and papaya. The road continues via Tunguu and Bungi to the Jozani Forest near Pete, before joining the coastal road linking the resorts of Jambiani, Paje and Bwejuu, about 50 km from Stone Town. There is a magnificent beach here that runs for nearly 20 km from Bwejuu to Jambiani, with white sand backed for its whole length by palm trees, laced with incredibly picturesque lagoons. You will see the fishermen go out in their dhows, while the women sit in the shade and plait coconut fibre, which they then make into everything from fishing nets to beds. ►► *For listings, see pages 208-213.*

Ins and outs

Getting there There's a good tarmac road that leads from Stone Town to Paje. The trip there by minibus takes just over an hour and costs around US$10. Bus No 9 from the Creek Road in Stone Town serves Paje and continues to Jambiani and Bwejuu. Bus No 10 from Creek Road goes to Kizimkazi via Jambiani and Makunduchi.

Jozani Forest

ⓘ *Most people visit the reserve as part of a tour, usually combined with a dolphin tour, but you can get here independently by* dala-dala *and either bus No 9 or 10 from Creek Road in Stone Town. Going there by taxi will cost around US$40 (for 4 people in 1 car), which is competitive with the price of an organized tour.*

Most of Zanzibar's indigenous forests have been lost to agriculture or construction, but the Jozani Forest in the centre of Zanzibar has been declared a protected reserve. It covers 44 sq km, roughly 3% of the whole island. It is 24 km southeast of Stone Town, an easy stop-off en route to the southeast coast beaches. It is home to roughly one third of the remaining endemic Zanzibar red colobus monkeys, one of Africa's rarest primates. Only 1500 are believed to have survived. In Zanzibar the Kiswahili name for the red colobus monkey is *Kima Punju* – 'Poison Monkey'. It has associations with the kind of poisons used by evil doers. Local people believe that when the monkeys have fed in an area, the trees and crops die, and dogs will lose their hair if they eat the colobus. Although legally protected the colobus remain highly endangered. Their choice of food brings them into conflict with the farmers, and their habitat is being destroyed due to demands for farmland, fuel, wood and charcoal. The monkeys appear oblivious to tourists, swinging above the trees in troups of about 40, babies to adults. They are endearing, naughty and totally absorbing. There is a **visitor centre** on the main road to the south where you pay US$10 per person for a guide for the 45 minute nature trail through the forest. The reserve is completely managed by the local people who operate tree nurseries and act as rangers and guides. Stout shoes are recommended as there are some venomous snakes. Lizards, civets, mongooses and Ader's duiker are plentiful and easy to see, and there are also Sykes' monkey, bush babies, hyraxes, and over 50 species of butterfly and 40 species of birds. Unless you state otherwise you are unlikely to be taken into the reserve at all as the best place to get close to the monkeys is an area adjacent to farmland to the south of the road.

On the way to Jozani Forest from Stone Town, you can visit the **Zanzibar Butterfly Centre** ⓘ *T0773-999897 (mob), www.zanzibarbutterflies.com, daily 0900-1700, entry US$5,* *the butterflies are most active between 1030-1530.* This is a great new centre where the funds generated help local communities and conservation. They have a colourful collection of Tanzanian butterflies, often in their hundreds, farmed sustainably in the nearby villages and provide tours lasting around half an hour to explain the project and the butterfly's life cycle.

About 1 km south of the Jozani Forest Visitor Centre there is the **Pete-Jozani Mangrove Boardwalk**. From the visitor centre the walk takes you through coral forest to an old tamarind tree, which marks the beginning of the boardwalk. The transition from coral forest to mangroves is abrupt. The boardwalk, which is horseshoe shaped, takes you through the mangrove swamp. Mangroves anchor the shifting mud and sands of the shore and help prevent coastal erosion. There are 18,000 ha of mangrove forests along the muddy coasts and inlets of Zanzibar. When the tide is out the stilt-like roots of the trees are visible. Crabs and fish are plentiful and easily seen from the boardwalk. The construction costs of the boardwalk were paid for by the government of The Netherlands, with local communities providing labour. Part of the profits made from tourists is returned directly to the local villagers.

ZALA Park

The road continues south to the village of Kitogani, and just south is **ZALA Park** ① *US$5*, which is primarily a small educational facility set up in conjunction with the University of Dar es Salaam for Zanzibari children to help them learn about and conserve the island's fauna. ZALA stands for Zanzibar Land Animals. Entry is free to local children if they are unable to pay, subsidized by the tourists' donations. The aim is to make it a self-funding enterprise in time. There is a small classroom where the children are taught. The adjacent **zoo** has a number of reptiles, including lizards, chameleons and indolent rock pythons weighing up to 40 kg, Eastern tree hyrax, as well as Suni antelopes, an endemic Zanzabari subspecies. Donations to support this worthwhile enterprise are appreciated.

Paje

Paje is the first village on the coast you are likely to get to as it lies on the junction with the direct road from Stone Town. It has its share of guesthouses and there is an old mausoleum, a long, low rectangular building with castellations and old plates and dishes set into the walls. This design, along with other reliefs and designs used in the villages are of typical Shirazi origin and indicate that this area was settled very early in Zanzibar's history. There's a convenient little supermarket in Paje on the main road as you enter the village which has a post office, a small café, does takeaway cooked food and can even provide car and bike hire.

Bwejuu

Bwejuu is best known for its proximity to 'the lagoon' and the Chwaka Bay mangrove swamps. The mangrove swamp at Chwaka Bay can be reached by a small road leading inland from the back of Bwejuu Village. It is possible to find a guide locally, who can navigate the way through the maze of channels and rivers in the swamps. Here you can stroll through the shallow rivers looking at this uniquely adapted plant and its ecosystem, there is also a good chance of seeing a wide variety of crabs that live in the mud-banks amongst the tangle of roots. The best snorkelling in the area is to be found at 'the lagoon', about 3 km to the north of Bwejuu, just past the pier at Dongwe. Bicycles and snorkels can usually be hired from any of the children on the beach.

Michamvi

Michamvi is a small village right at the tip of the eastern peninsula, another 5 km north of Dongwe and about 68 km from Stone Town. A handful of mid-range hotels and lodges have opened here recently and the area still has an 'off the beaten track' feel to it. A couple of new developments are being built on the western side of the peninsula, one of which is rumoured to be a five-star resort owned by the President's daughter. Local transport only goes as far as Bwejuu, so you'd need to arrange a taxi or car through your hotel.

Jambiani

The name Jambiani comes from an Arabic word for dagger, and legend has it that early settlers found a dagger here in the sand – evidence of previous visitors. These days the village spreads for several kilometres along the coast road and there are a number of resorts (see Sleeping below).

Kizimkazi

This small fishing village was once the site of a town built by King Kizi and his mason Kazi from whom the name Kizimkazi originates. Most people visit here as part of a tour to swim with the dolphins and there is a growing industry springing up around the large resident pods of humpbacked and bottlenose dolphins.

> ◑ *Marine biologists assess these dolphins as being very stressed by the uncontrolled jostling and chasing of boat operators. They advise that if you snorkel with these dolphins you exercise respect, restraint and common sense. Splashy water entries and boat drivers in hot pursuit will only drive them away.*

The beach is attractive and there is a restaurant where those on dolphin tours from Stone Town are often taken to have a meal. A few hotels have opened here in recent years as people realize this is a pretty location in its own right, aside from being the centre of the dolphin-swimming industry on the island. The village is split into two parts, Kizimkazi Dimbani in the north and Kizimkazi Mkunguni in the south. Other than when the dolphin-trippers come in the mornings, it's a fairly quiet area, so if you're after a lively night scene, this wouldn't be your best option, apart from between Boxing Day and New Year's Day when the new Kizimkazi Cultural Music Festival takes place (see Promised Land, page 213, and Festivals and events, page 213). The **Shirazi Dimbani Mosque ruins** are near Kizimkazi and contain the oldest inscription found in East Africa – from AD 1107. The mosque has been given a tin roof and is still used. However, its significance should not be under-estimated for it may well mark the beginnings of the Muslim religion in East Africa. It was built by Sheikh Abu bin Mussa Lon Mohammed and archaeologists believe that it stands on the site of an even older mosque.

◉ Southeast Zanzibar listings

For Sleeping and Eating price codes and other relevant information, see pages 36-40.

◉ Sleeping

Paje *p207*
B Hakuna Majiwe, on the borders of Paje and Jambiani, signposted off the main road,

T0777-515371 (mob), www.hakunamajiwe. net. A boutique lodge set on the beach with 20 individual and very attractively decorated rooms in stone bandas, surrounded by palms and shrubs and sand. The swimming pool's set back from the beach and there's a huge, open dining area with big sofas at the bar. Wi-Fi available. Snorkelling and diving centre.

C Arabian Nights, on the beach near **Paje by Night**, T024-224 0190, www.zanzibararabiannights.com. Rooms are in stone cottages either facing the beach or around the garden or pool and are well-equipped with spacious bathrooms, private terraces, TVs, mosquito nets, fans and a/c. There's also a nearby block with rooms for gap year groups which are let out to individual travellers when there are vacancies. These are really good value at US$40-65 for a double and this block has its own pool. The owner, Mohammed, also owns the new **Buccaneer Diving Centre** which is about to open here, just down the beach from the hotel. It promises to be the biggest diving centre in Tanzania with 2 restaurants and a training pool and will offer a whole range of PADI courses and water sports including kitesurfing.

C Kinazi Upepo and **Cristal Resort**, at the end of the group of lodges on the beach, T0777-875515 (mob), www.cristalresort.net. These 2 properties more or less merge into 1 and share facilities in a pretty location surrounded by palm trees and pines. They have 25 single and 40 double rooms either in de luxe bungalows or in attractively rustic 'eco' bungalows which are cheaper but nicer, all with fans, mosquito nets and bathrooms. **Cristal** has a swimming pool near the beach and there's a very chilled bar at **Kinezi**.

C-D Paje by Night, on the beach in the village centre, T0777-460710 (mob), www.pajebynight.net. Very rustic verging on ethnic, run by an Italian. Self-contained thatched bungalows with ceiling fans and mosquito nets, including a useful family bungalow with 2 double en suite rooms. Bar and restaurant with local and international food including good pizzas. An unashamed party place, bar stays open all night, hence the name.

D Paradise Beach Bungalows, 1 km north of the village, T024-223 1387, www.geocities.jp/paradisebeachbungalows. Run by a nice (but scatty) Japanese lady, Saori. There are 10 en suite double rooms and 3 bandas sharing bathrooms a small restaurant and bar

serving expensive Japanese meals that must be ordered in advance. Rates are between US$28-50 per person including breakfast.

Bwejuu *p207*

L The Palms, a few kilometres north of Bwejuu towards Pingwe, reservations, Nairobi, T+254-20-272 9333, www.palms-zanzibar.com. Stunning resort, super-luxurious with attentive service. At US$650 per person you'd expect nothing less, but rates are inclusive of meals, soft drinks, house wine, and return airport transfers. For your money you get a villa with satellite TV, DVD player, private terrace with plunge pool, living room and bar. Facilities in sumptuous surroundings include tiered swimming pool, beauty spa, fitness centre, tennis court, elegant dining room, bars and lounge areas. The beach here is magnificent and there's a watersports centre and dive school.

L-A Breezes Beach Club, 3.5 km north of the village, T024-224 0102 www.breezes-zanzibar.com. This well-appointed resort is an established favourite on Zanzibar. All 70 rooms have a/c, fans and en suite bathrooms. There are standard, de luxe and superior de luxe rooms, the latter have sea views, with either balconies or terraces. Shopping arcade, beauty spa, conference facilities, restaurants, bars, large swimming pool, fitness centre, watersports centre, tennis courts and disco. The **Rising Sun Dive Centre** is based here. Rates vary depending on the season.

A Karafuu Hotel Beach Resort, 3 km north of the village before Michamvi, in Karafuu Village, T0777-413647-8 (mob), www.karafuu zanzibar.com. The name means 'cloves' in Swahili. Winner of 4 awards, including 'The Best Resort in Tanzania 2008', this is a large but quiet and professionally run resort, with almost 100 a/c rooms with thatched roofs in spacious gardens. 3 restaurants, numerous bars, watersports, excellent food, swimming pool, tennis courts, nightclub and diving. The beach is good although watch out for the very sharp coral close offshore.

B Echo Beach, signposted off the main road to Paje, just south of Breezes T0773-593260 (mob), www.echobeachhotel.com. Owned by a British couple, one a French-trained chef and the other an interior designer, this place is as you might expect very stylish with an excellent restaurant menu. All 12 rooms in local stone and makuti bungalows, are individually designed with African antiques, silk fabrics and locally crafted wooden furniture, with spacious verandas. The swimming pool and jacuzzi are near the beach and the lodge has its own dive centre.

C Sunrise Guest House, 2 km north of the village, T0777-415240 (mob), www.sunrise-zanzibar.com. All bungalow rooms are self-contained with fans and mosquito nets, and face towards the sea. Very good food, especially the chocolate mousse, courtesy of the Belgian chef/owner. Bikes can be hired and there's a swimming pool.

D-E Evergreen Bungalows, 3 km north of Bwejuu Village, T024-224 0273, www.ever green-bungalows.com. 9 bungalows in a palm grove directly on the beach with 14 rooms, each with a different touch and very nicely decorated using local materials, with mosquito nets, solar power supply and balcony with chairs and a table. Some rooms are self-contained while others, including some dorm rooms, have shared bathrooms. Bar and restaurant offers a meat, fish and vegetarian dish each night for dinner. **Africa Blue Divers** offer single dives from US$50 and a PADI Open Water Course for US$400.

D-E Mustapha's Place (although the sign outside says **Mustapha's Nest**), in the village, the No 9 bus will drop you outside, T024-224 0069, www.mustaphasplace.com. A chilled out, low budget hotel run by Mustapha, a friendly Rastafarian. Lovely gardens with hammocks, reggae music, bar where you can play drums, good seafood. The rooms are fun and bright, with paintings on the walls and 1 called Treetops is on huge stilts. Prices range from US$35 for a double room with shared bathroom, to US$55 for a double room with bathroom, although some rooms

can sleep up to 8 people with floor space in the loft and can then work out a lot cheaper. Very relaxing, it's across the road from the beach and a pretty pathway leads you to it.

E Robinson's Place, 2 km north of Bwejuu, take the road signposted to Evergreen, go past **Evergreen** and Robinson's is on the right when you reach some palm raffia fencing and gates on both sides, T0777-413479 (mob), www.robinsonsplace.net. In a similar vein to **Mustapha's**, but smaller with a maximum of 10 guests, and run by the charming Rastafarian Eddy and his wife Ann. It's essential to book here because it fills up very quickly. All rooms have nets and some have bathrooms. There's no electricity here, just solar power and a generator, and they serve local Zanzibari food (with floor seating) for a very reasonable US$6.

Michamvi *p208*

B-C Kichanga Lodge, signposted off main road to Michamvi, then 1 km along dirt road, T0773-175124 (mob), www.kichanga.com. British owned and Italian managed, this sleepy place is in a secluded beach location with 23 pretty bungalows spread out in gardens. The Ocean Villas have a mezzanine floor with extra beds which overlook the ground floor bedroom and share their bathroom, so if you want privacy, that may not be the best set-up. But they're nice rooms, with fans, mosquito nets and private terraces. The bar and dining area is in a breezy makuti-roofed building with a mezzanine lounge that has great views over the ocean. For a more unusual souvenir, their gift shop makes up dresses to order in contemporary styles out of traditional *kangas* in 24 hrs. Massage centre, mountain bikes and canoes for hire. They also have their own dhow for snorkelling excursions and can arrange all the usual tours.

C Michamvi Water Sports Resort, Michamvi Village, there's a faded sign on the right which leads along a dirt road, then turn left at a better signpost, T0777-878136 (mob), www.michamvi.com. This is not the easiest place to find but the manager has promised better signage. As the name suggests, the activities at this new hotel are very much water based – they offer waterskiing, parasailing, windsurfing, kitesurfing, paddle skis, kayaking, wakeboarding, etc, and arrange diving and deep-sea fishing through a Paje outfit. Their 20 attractive rooms are in 4 blocks facing the sea and the swimming pool, all with a balcony or terrace, a/c, fans and mosquito nets, and old dhows are used as furniture. The bar and restaurant serves international cuisine.

C Ras Michamvi Beach Resort, signposted with **Kichanga Lodge** off the main road to Michamvi, then 1 km down a dirt road and follow the signs. T024-223 1081, www.ras michamvi.com. This is a discreet and very pretty new lodge right at the tip of the peninsula. The 15 en suite rooms are in 4 stone bungalows with cool tiled flooring, a/c, fans, mosquito nets and big Zanzibari beds. There are 3 small beaches here, 1 of which – Coconut Beach – has resident red colobus monkeys and fossils have been found amid the coral. It's also a great spot for sundowners. Nice swimming pool above the beach and an outdoor gym. The restaurant is open to non-residents and in the season they have Swahili entertainment – Bi Kidude, the queen of Taarab music has played here. Good value at US$140 for a double half board.

Jambiani *p208*

B-C Kikadini Villas, next door to **Hotel Casa del Mar** on the beach, T0777-707888 (mob), www.kikadinivillas.com. 5 villas beautifully decorated in understated Zanzibari style right on the beach that can be booked for exclusive use or as individual rooms. They sleep from 2-6 people if booked exclusively, and Villa Maroc is particularly suitable for loved-up couples, having a private roof terrace and bath to soak in under the stars. If booked exclusively, you get full butler service and meals are served in your villa or there's a candlelit restaurant for dinner.

C-D Sau Inn, T024-224 0169, www.sauinn zanzibar.com. A pleasant, friendly hotel with 39 en suite rooms set in thatched cottages with fans and mosquito nets. The upstairs bar has a nice terrace overlooking the beach and the restaurant serves good seafood and generous portions, with buffets on Fri evenings. There's a swimming pool just back from the beach and snorkelling and diving are available from the hotel's own dive centre. B&B, half- or full-board rates. Good value.
D Hotel Casa del Mar, next to the internet café in Jambiani Village, on the beach, T024-224 0400, www.casa-delmar-zanzibar. com. This hotel has an excellent restaurant and bar and although the service is sometimes slow, it's worth the wait for the generous portions and the fresh non-alcoholic cocktails (highly recommended). 12 rustic rooms in 2 buildings on 2 floors, all en suite with sea views. US$80 for a double on the ground floor and US$100 on the 1st floor where rooms are bigger with a sleeping gallery on the mezzanine. Rates include breakfast.
D-E Blue Oyster Hotel, T024-224 0163, www.zanzibar.de. Very congenial, Tanzanian owned, hotel. The 13 rooms have beautiful carved beds, mosquito nets, and are arranged around a serene ornamental pool and garden. Good food in the rooftop restaurant. Bike rental, watersports, their own dhow for fishing and snorkelling trips. An en suite double is US$80 and doubles without bathrooms are US$42, including breakfast.
D Coco Beach, on the beach in Jambiani Village, T0773-492670 (mob), cocobeach@ zitec.org. Self-contained rooms with hot water, fan and mosquito nets. Good restaurant serving reasonably priced seafood, and bar. US$50 for a double including breakfast. Can arrange tours and activities.
D Coral Rocks, just south of Jambiani Village on a coral rock above the sea, T024-224 0154, www.coralrockhotelzanzibar.com. Rooms here are slightly tired but have nice Zanzibari beds, nets, a/c, fans and bathrooms. There's a pleasant swimming pool on the edge of the beach and a popular bar nearby.

D Visitor's Inn, T024-224 0150, www.visitors
inn-zanzibar.com. 39 basic but good value
rooms either in the guesthouse or bungalows
set in flowering gardens, each has a fridge,
hot water, a fan, mosquito net and a porch.
TV room, restaurant and bar with fish, noodle
and vegetarian dishes, internet.

E Red Monkey Lodge, Jambiani Village, on
the beach, T024-224 0207, www.zanzibar-
jambiani.com. This is a fun place, rooms are
in white-washed stone cottages with makuti
roofs and have their own bathrooms, fans
and mosquito nets. They're a bit scruffy but
in a lovely location on a gentle slope above
the beach and cost US$50 for a double,
including breakfast and light snacks which
are served from lunchtime until 1700.
Evening meals are charged separately.
There's a happy, lively atmosphere here and
the place is named after a red monkey that
lives in the gardens.

Kizimkazi *p208*

A Unguja Resort, in Kizimkazi Mikunga,
T0774-855868 (mob), www.unguja
resort.com. A very atmospheric, discreet
resort set in tropical gardens with huge
baobab trees and palms, it's an expensive
but beautiful place. Accommodation is in
10 stunningly designed cottages with makuti
roofs and curved walls, semi-outdoor living
rooms and bathing areas, and a spacious
bedroom indoors, with another bed on
the mezzanine level. Most cottages have
sea views with private terraces but the
3 that don't have their own jacuzzis as
compensation. If you can tear yourself away
from your cottage, there's a large swimming
pool and a coral beach, and the owner's son
acts as guide on coral reef walks. One Ocean
looks after all their diving requirements.

C Dolphin Beach Hotel, to the south
of Kizimkazi Dimbani, T024-224 0348,
www.dolphinbeach-resort.com. There are
33 en suite rooms here in rondavaals with
makuti roofs, most with a sea view and all
with a small garden and beachy terrace
outside. Simply furnished with Zanzibari

beds, fans and mosquito nets. Unusually
there is a huge natural cave here where
wooden decking and electricity have been
installed, making an atmospheric venue
for Swahili dance and food evenings or for
private parties. There are 2 swimming pools,
(1 shallow for families) and they can arrange
all the usual trips and deep-sea fishing.

C Karamba, Kizimkazi Dimbani beach, at
the northern end, T0773-166406 (mob),
www.karambaresort.com. This lovely, laid-
back lodge has its own yoga teacher and
offers various yoga classes, Ayurvedic
massage and even Vedic options on its
extensive restaurant menu (over 100 dishes),
which also includes sushi and sashimi, Indian,
Italian and tapas. The 14 en suite rooms are
on a small cliff above the sea, all have fans
and mosquito nets and are pleasantly
decorated. There's a natural swimming pool
here in the sea at high tide, with steps down
the cliff straight into the water, although they
are also planning a 'normal' pool for Aug
2009. They support the local school and
guests are able to visit and work there for a
day if they wish.

C Swahili Beach Resort, Kizimkazi
Mkunguni, T024-224 04913, www.swahili
beachresort.com. A sister hotel to **Arabian
Nights** in Paje (see page 209) and almost
identical in appearance and facilities, they
have 19 rooms in stone bungalows, as well
as guesthouse rooms for gap year groups,
which again represent good value for
independent travellers if they're available.
Swimming pool, PADI diving centre, internet
and the usual tours and excursions. There are
more charismatic places to stay perhaps, but
good value.

D Kizimkazi Coral Reef Bungalows, in
Kizimkazi Mkunguni, near **Swahili Beach
Resort**, T0777-479615 (mob), www.coral
reefzanzibar.com. 6 simple but clean rooms
in pretty palm gardens with own bathrooms,
Zanzibari beds and mosquito nets. The
restaurant is very reasonably priced and
overlooks the bay. Chilled atmosphere and
good value.

E-F Promised Land, about 20 mins walk (1 km) from Kizimkazi Mkunguni Village, past Swahili Beach turn left after 0.5 km, then right after another 0.5 km, signposted, T0783-576036 (mob), shaaban1976@ hotmail.com.This is a very chilled place, owned and run by a Rastafarian called Shaaban. Offers 4 double rooms with own bathrooms, fans and mosquito nets in the main house for US$40, and a dorm-style mezzanine floor above the dining/living room, accessed by steep wooden steps, which has 5 single beds for (a rather pricey) US$20 a person. There's also a huge field where 6 tents have been set up under raffia shelters (US$15 per person) and plenty of space for people to bring their own tents. All rates include breakfast and there's a beach bar, restaurant and hammocks for hanging out. If you're into music festivals, then you should come between Boxing Day and New Year's Day when Shaaban hosts the **Kizimkazi Cultural Music Festival**, see below.

⊛ Festivals and events

Southeast Zanzibar *p206*
See also page 186 for more information on festivals held throughout the archipelago.
Jul Mwaka Kogwa, held in the 3rd week of Jul. The traditional Shirazi New Year on Zanzibar and celebrated with traditional Swahili food, taraab music, drumming and dancing on the beach all night. Although the festival is celebrated around the island, the village of Makunduchi is the heart of the celebration. The men of the village have a play fight and beat each other with banana fronds to vent their aggressions from the past year. Then, the *mganga*, or traditional healer, sets fire to a ritual hut and reads which way the smoke is burning to determine the village's prosperity in the coming year.
Dec Kizimkazi Cultural Music Festival, starts on Boxing Day and concludes in a great finale on New Year's Eve/Day. Attracts musicians, taarab bands, drummers, dancers and acrobats from mainland Tanzania and Kenya as well as local Zanzibaris. It's held at the Promised Land (see Sleeping, above). The first festival in 2008 was a success, despite a few teething problems like the generator blowing, and they're now planning to make this an annual event. Reports welcome.

▲ Activities and tours

Kizimkazi *p208*
Diving
One Ocean, various bases all over the island, T024-223 8374, www.zanzibaroneocean.com.

Pemba Island

→ *Colour map 1, B6. 5°0'S 39°45'E. Population: 300,000.*

Unlike Unguja, which is flat and sandy, Pemba's terrain is hilly, fertile and heavily vegetated. The early Arab sailors called it 'Al Huthera', meaning 'The Green Island'. Today more cloves are grown on Pemba than on Zanzibar Island. Pemba has a wealth of natural resources ranging from beaches to mangrove ecosystems to natural forests. The coral reefs surrounding the island protect a multitude of marine species and offer some of the best scuba-diving in the world. Zanzibar Island is connected to the African continent by a shallow submerged shelf. Pemba, however, is separated from the mainland by depths of over 1000 m. During September and March the visibility around Pemba has been known to extend to a depth of 50 m and there are great game fish such as sharks, tuna, marlin and barracuda. While much of the coast is lined with mangroves, there are a few good stretches of shoreline and attractive offshore islands with pure, clean beaches and interesting birdlife. There are also some important ruins and charming Swahili villages. The tourism industry here is still in its infancy and the infrastructure is still quite basic, but is slowly beginning to develop, with new lodges opening up and a few more foreigners visiting than before, although nothing on the scale of visitors to Zanzibar. ⬩⬩ *For listings, see pages 219-222.*

Ins and outs

Getting there
Pemba Airport is 7 km to the southeast of Chake Chake. The island can be reached by air either from Zanzibar Island or from Dar es Salaam, though most flights from Dar go via Zanzibar. Coastal Air also fly direct between Tanga and Pemba. The airport tax for flights out of Pemba is US$2.50 but this is payable in Tanzanian Shillings and may be included in your ticket price. Public transport from the airport only operates when there is a flight due.

Ferries to Pemba can be unreliable, often cancelled at the last minute, uncomfortable and often with very bumpy crossings. Nearly all ferries coming into Pemba arrive at the town of Mkoani, on the southwestern end of Pemba Island. Very few ships or dhows actually use Chake Chake anymore, as the old harbour is silted up and only canoes can actually gain entrance. The journey between Zanzibar and Pemba can take between three and six hours depending on the company and boats used, and prices are about US$40 excluding Zanzibar's port tax of US$5. Dar es Salaam to Pemba via Zanzibar US$65. ⬩⬩ *For further details, see Transport, page 222.*

Getting around
The island of Pemba is about 70 km long and 22 km wide. There is one bumpy main road in Pemba running from Msuka in the north to Mkoani in the south, which is served by public transport. There are buses or *dala-dala* along the main roads but these tend to operate in the mornings and early afternoons only and there are very few vehicles after 1500. *Dala-dala* No 606 runs between Chake Chake and Wete and the No 603 between Chake Chake and Mkoani. Each journey takes about one hour and costs US$0.50. Other less frequently run routes include the No 24 between Wete and Konde (for the Ngezi Forest). Besides this, it is very difficult to get around on public transport and budget travellers will need to walk to get to the more out of the way places. It is possible to hire cars at around US$80 for a day, motorcycles for around US$30 and bicycles for around

US$10 – ask at the hotels and remember that negotiation is necessary, as ever. The motorcycle is the most comfortable form of transport on the island, more so than cars, as potholes are more readily avoided, and it's a little too hilly in most places for cycling.

Background

There is nothing on Pemba that holds as much historical or cultural significance as Stone Town on Zanzibar Island, but it is the site of many historical ruins that bear testament to its role in the spice trade and early commerce with the other Indian Ocean dynasties. The major income for islanders is from cloves and the island actually produces about 75-80% of the archipelago's total crop. It is the mainstay of the island's economy. Also, unlike Zanzibar, production is largely by individual small-scale farmers who own anything from 10 to 50 trees each. Most of the trees have been in the family for generations and clove production is very much a family affair, especially during the harvest when everyone joins in the picking. Harvest occurs about every five months and everything is worked around it – even the schools close. The cloves are then laid out in the sun to dry and their distinctive fragrance fills the air.

The island is overwhelmingly Muslim, with more than 95% of the population following Islam. But the island is tolerant of other cultures, and alcohol is available at hotels, some guesthouses and in the police messes (where visitors are welcome). Local inhabitants do, however, like to observe modest dress and behaviour.

Pemba Island

Ras Kigomasha
Panga ya Wataro Beach
Vumawinbi Beach
Verani
Ngezi Forest Reserve
Msuka
Taponi
Konde
Tumbe
Njao Island
Kin Yasini
Maputo
Fundu Island
Wete
Chapaka
Nyali
Idya
Uvinje Island
Kivumori
Kokota Island
Ras Mkumbuu
Ziwani
Kangagni
Mesali Island
Ole
Tundaua
Chake Chake
Limami
Chonga
Pujini
Mkoani
Chuaka
Makongwe Island
Mtangari
Kendeja
Fufuni
Matumbini Island
Yombi Island
Ras Kiuyu
Ras Kiuyu Forest
Kiuyu
Wingwi
Msitu Kuu Forest
Kajani Island
To Dar es Salaam & Zanzibar
Indian Ocean

N
5 km
5 miles

Sleeping
Fundu Lagoon 2

Jondeni Guest House 3
Kervan Saray Beach 4
Manta Resort 1
Pemba Crown 5
Pemba Paradise Beach 6
Sharook Guest House 7
Sharook 2 8

Diving

Known as the Emerald Isle for its lush vegetation and idyllic setting, Pemba is most definitely the jewel in East Africa's dive-site portfolio. On the more chartered west coast the deep waters of the Pemba Channel have conspired to create dramatic walls and drop-offs, where glimpses of sharks and encounters with eagle rays, manta rays, Napoleon wrasse, great barracuda, tuna and kingfish are the norm. Visibility can range from 6 m in a plankton bloom to 60 m, though 20 m is classed as a bad day and 40 m is average. Some of the coral has been affected by El Niño, but Pemba remains a world-class diving destination.

It would be impossible to single out the best dive sites; they are all breathtaking.

Clove production

It has been estimated that there are about 6 million clove trees on the islands of Zanzibar and Pemba and they cover about one-tenth of the land area. The plantations are found mainly in the west and northwest of the islands where the soil is deeper and the landscape hillier. To the east the soil is less deep and fertile and is known as 'coral landscape'.

Cloves were at one time only grown in the Far East and they were greatly prized. On his first trip back from the East, Vasco da Gama took a cargo back to Portugal and they were later introduced by the French to Mauritius and then to Zanzibar by Sayyid Said who was the first Arab Sultan. At this time all the work was done by slaves who enabled the plantations to be established and clove production to become so important to the economy of the islands. When the slaves were released and labour was no longer free, some of the plantations found it impossible to

survive although production did continue and Zanzibar remained at the head of the world's clove production.

Cloves are actually the unopened buds of the clove tree. They grow in clusters and must be picked when the buds are full but before they actually open. They are collected in sprays and the buds are then picked off before being spread on the ground to dry out. They are spread out on mats made from woven coconut palm fronds for about five days, turned over regularly so that they dry evenly – the quicker they dry the better the product.

There may be many clove trees on Zanzibar now – but there were even more in the past. In 1872 a great hurricane destroyed many of the trees and it was after this that Pemba took over from Zanzibar as the largest producer. Zanzibar, however, has retained the role of chief seller and exporter of cloves so the Pemba cloves go to Zanzibar before being sold on.

On Mesali Island and the surrounding reefs, the West Coast is a protected marine park and entrance of US$5 must be paid to dive or snorkel there. ▶ *For more information on dive operators, see page 221. For information on Pemba's dive sites, see page 222.*

Around the island 🖃🚗 ▶ *pp219-222.*

Pemba Channel Marine Conservation Area

Since 2006, the whole of the west coast of Pemba, from the island's northernmost tip at Ras Kigomasha to the southern tip in Panza Island, has been protected as part of a new marine conservation area known as PECCA. In all, it covers some 1000 sq km. The ultimate aim for PECCA is to have the area declared a UNESCO World Heritage Site to further protect both its marine habitats and its rich cultural heritage. All visitors to the area pay a US$5 fee, regardless of whether they dive or not.

Mkoani → *Colour map 1, B6*

Mkoani is Pemba's third largest town and the port of entry for ferries from Zanzibar and Dar es Salaam. The town is set on a hill overlooking a wide bay and comprises a mix of palm-thatch huts and rundown multi-storey apartment buildings. The landing stage is a modern jetty which projects out from the shallow beach on either side, where fishermen load their daily catch into ox-carts for the short trip to market. The main road runs directly from the port up the hill and most of this distance is rather surprisingly covered by a dual carriageway, complete with tall street lights on the central reservation. This, along with the ugly apartment blocks around town is evidence of the East German influence in Tanzania during the 1970s, which is also present at Chake Chake and Wete, and in the concrete estates on the edge of Stone Town on Zanzibar Island. Following the winding road up the hill from the port, the old colonial District Commissioners Office is on the right, where there is a bandstand in front of the compound. On the left is Ibazi Mosque, with a fine carved door. South of the dock there are steep steps down to the market by the shore.

Chake Chake → *Colour map 1, B6. 5°15'S 39°45'E. Phone code: 024.*

This is Pemba's main town, about halfway up the west coast of the island. The town sits on a hill overlooking a creek and is fairly small. The oldest surviving building in the town is the **Nanzim Fort,** which is thought to date back at least to the 18th century and possibly as far back as the Portuguese occupation (1499-1698). Records dating back to the early 19th century describe the fortress as being rectangular, with two square and two round towers at the corners, topped by thatched roofs. Round towers are typical of the Arab and Swahili architecture of the time, but the square towers are unusual and indicate possible Portuguese influence. Construction of the old hospital destroyed all but the eastern corner and tower which now houses the Ministry of Women and Children. A battery, dating from the same period, overlooked the bay to the west, but only two cannons remain to mark the site. There are some handsome Moorish-style administrative buildings near the fort with verandas, and a **clock tower**. On the outskirts of town is a new hospital, built by the European Community overseas aid programme and a few kilometres past the old centre a huge new sports stadium, which is home to the local football team. The market and bus stand are both in the centre close to the mosque. There have been some strikes and riots during elections in recent years, as Pemba is the stronghold of the CUF opposition party.

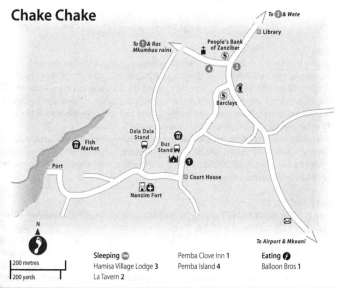

Chake Chake

To ③ & Wete

☐ Library

To ① & Ras Mkumbuu ruins

People's Bank of Zanzibar
✝ (S)

④   ②

(S) ⓘ
Barclays

Dala Dala Stand
🚐

Fish Market
🅜

Bus Stand
🚐

Port

🏠 ❶

☐ Court House

🅷➕
Nanzim Fort

✉

To Airport & Mkoani

N
🧭

| 200 metres |
| 200 yards |

Sleeping 🛏
Hamisa Village Lodge **3**
La Tavern **2**

Pemba Clove Inn **1**
Pemba Island **4**

Eating 🍴
Balloon Bros **1**

Ruins at Pujini

About 10 km southeast of Chake Chake, this settlement is thought to date back to the 15th century. There was a fortified enclosure and rampart surrounded by a moat, the only known early fortification on the East Africa coast. It is believed to have been built by a particularly unpleasant character, nicknamed Mkame Ndume, which means 'a milker of men', because he worked his subjects so hard. He was known to order his servants to carry the large stones used to build the fortress whilst shuffling along on their buttocks. The memory remains and local people believe that the ruins are haunted. The settlement and the palace of Mkame Ndume were destroyed by the Portuguese when they arrived on the island in about 1520. Today the site is largely overgrown and there is little left of the fortications except for a crumbling staircase and some remains of 1 m thick walls. There are also the remnants of a two-chambered well that reputedly was used by the two wives of Ndume who lived in separate parts of the palace and never met. It is best to visit by hiring a bicycle (ask in Chake Chake).

Ruins at Ras Mkumbuu and Mesali Island

About 20 km west of Chake Chake, Ras Mkumbuu is probably Pemba's most important ruins, believed to date back about 1200 years, the oldest settlement south of Lamu Island in Kenya. It is the site of a settlement originating in the Shirazi period (see page 117). The ruins include stone houses and pillar tombs and the remains of a 14th-century mosque. Of interest are the tombs decorated with pieces of porcelain that suggest an early connection with the Chinese. Most people visit by boat on the way to Mesali Island where the marine life on the reef make it excellent for diving and snorkelling and there is a fine beach. There are pleasant trails through the forest in the middle of the island which is rich in birdlife, and is also home to vervet monkeys and the Pemba flying fox (a large bat). Legend has it that the notorious 17th-century pirate Captain Kidd once had a hideout here and perhaps even buried some treasure during his stay. Dive schools regularly visit here on dives, and most of the lodges and guesthouses can arrange boat trips here.

Wete

This town is on the northwest coast of Pemba and serves as a port for the clove trade. It is a laid-back place on a hill overlooking the port with houses and small shops lining the main road down to the dhow harbour. Clustered close to the dock area is a pleasant group of colonial buildings. On the north side of the market a craftsman makes very fine carved doors. The town has a post office and police station and the *dala-dala* station is about halfway up the hill, *dala-dalas* to Chake Chake cost US$1.

The small island of **Mtabmwe Mkuu** opposite Wete, which means 'great arm of the sea', is linked to Pemba at low tide. It was once home to an 11th-century town and a number of silver coins have been discovered at the site, though there is nothing to see today and a small fishing village stands on the spot.

Tumbe and Konde

Tumbe is at the north end of Pemba and is a busy fishing village with a market where people from all around buy their fish in the mornings. Local fishermen contract to provide catches for firms, which chill the fish and export it to the mainland. At the end of the cool season in October, there is a boat race. Teams of men compete, paddling dug-out canoes and the day is completed with a feast provided for contestants and onlookers. Konde is to the northeast of the island and is at the end of the tarmac road and the furthest most point of the *dala-dala* network. Access to Ngezi Forest is from here. There is no accommodation in Tumbe or Konde but both can be reached by *dala-dala* from Chake Chake.

Ngezi Forest Reserve

① *www.ngeziforest.or.tz, entrance fee US$3.*

The reserve covers 1440 ha and compromises ancient coastal forest that once covered all of Pemba. The area was declared a reserve in the 1950s after much of the island had been cleared for clove production. This is a thick blanket of forest with vines and creepers and a dense undergrowth that supports a variety of plants and wildlife. It has its own plant species and sub-species that are unique to this area. Most of the 27 species of bird recorded on Pemba have been spotted in the forest, some endemic to Pemba including hadada, the African goshawk, the palm-nut vulture, Scops owl, the malachite kingfisher and the Pemba white eye. Much of the ground is ancient coral rag, often sharp edged, containing pockets of soil. Mangrove forests grow on the tidal coastal creeks and the incoming tide sees seawater running deep upstream, forming brackish swampy areas. The central area contains heather dominated heathland where the soil is leached sand. The heather, *Philippia mafiensis*, is only found on Pemba and Mafia Islands.

Pemba's flying fox, a large fruit-eating bat, is found in Ngezi. Tree mammals include the Pemba vervet monkey and the Zanzibar red colobus monkey. Indolent-looking hyrax can also be seen climbing in the trees eating leaves. The Pemba blue duiker, an antelope about the size of a hare, is also here though it is very shy and is rarely spotted. Feral pigs, introduced long ago by the Portuguese, can be found along with the Javan civet cat, which was probably brought to the island by southeast Asian traders for the production of musk for perfume. The only endemic carnivore in Ngezi is the marsh mongoose, which normally lives by ponds and streams. There is a 2-km walking trail from the entrance that takes about an hour.

To the north of here is the secluded **Panga ya Watoro beach** on a peninsula that juts out from the island. At the end is the lighthouse at Ras Kigomasha, the far northwestern tip of the island; authorities are very sensitive so photography is not advised.

⊛ Pemba Island listings

For Sleeping and Eating price codes and other relevant information, see pages 36-40.

⊜ Sleeping

Mkoani *p216*

L Fundu Lagoon, north of Mkoani across the bay near the village of Wambaa and reached by boat organized by the resort (US$40), T0777-438668 (mob), www.fundulagoon. com. This luxury British-owned development is the top place to stay on Pemba. Very stylish, with 18 tented rooms on stilts, overlooking a beautiful mangrove-fringed beach, and furnished with locally crafted hardwood furniture. 4 suites have private plunge pools and decks and are perfect for honeymooners.

There's an infinity pool and spa, and all variety of watersports are available, including diving, sailing and windsurfing. 2 restaurants and 3 bars. Supports local communities through its Village Fund and has built a school for 500 children, installed several water wells and is planning a medical clinic. Bteween US$305 and US$610 per person, depending on the room and season, this includes all meals and drinks. Recommended.

E-F Jondeni Guest House, Mkoani overlooking the bay, T024-245 6042, T0777-460680 (mob), jondeniguest@hotmail.com. Rooms are simple but spotless with fans, nets and Zanzibari beds, some are en suite. Doubles from US$25-35, dorm beds US$10, including breakfast. The extremely friendly and helpful owner, Ali, serves good value meals and arranges local excursions including snorkelling at Mesali Bay, sailing, Wambaa village trips, sunset dhow cruises and canoeing. He can also arrange bike, motorbike and car hire. Internet available for guests. The garden has views of the bay and hammocks and loungers. Ali is planning to open 5 villas in Wambaa on the opposite side of the lagoon in Sep 2009.

Chake Chake *p217, map p217*
B Pemba Paradise Beach and Resort, 7 km from Chake Chake near Vitongoji, T0763-444 666 (mob) seif@pajebeachbungalows.com. This new lodge set in theMakoba Bay on the east coast is due to open in Jul 2009. There are 20 en suite rooms in bungalows, some overlooking the sea and each with their own small sunbathing area. Swimming pool and pool bar. Full board only for US$100 per person, which includes soft drinks but no alcohol. They can arrange transfers from the airport, diving and snorkelling, and excursions.
D Hamisa Village and Lodge, signposted on the left of the main road into Chake Chake if approaching from the north, T0754-015 148 (mob), hamisahotel@yahoo.com. About 500 m out of town, with 4 clean double rooms in bungalows. More are being built although work has currently stopped. There's a VIP room which is the same price as the doubles, even though it has a kitchen (not yet completed), a TV and a/c. The restaurant serves fresh fish and local food. Friendly staff.
D Pemba Clove Inn, Wesha Rd, Tibirinzi, about 500 m from town centre, T024-245 2795, pembacloveinn@zanzinet.com. By far the nicest place to stay in Chake Chake. 13 spotless rooms, with coconut wood beds, a/c, TVs, minibars and nets. Swimming pool and outdoor restaurant are planned for next year. Decent indoor restaurant. The friendly staff can arrange the usual island tours.
D Pemba Island Hotel, Wesha Rd, T0777-478464 (mob), www.pembaislandhotel.co.tz. There's nothing special about this hotel, rooms are fine and offer a/c, fans, nets and fridges, and there's a restaurant on the roof.

Reception staff are unhelpful and there's a notice saying that guests must be indoors by 2200, with silence in the rooms until 0600.
E Hotel La Tavern, opposite the People's Bank of Zanzibar, T024-245 2660. 4 spotlessly clean rooms, nets and towels are provided, some rooms with own bathrooms. Evening meals are available if pre-ordered.

Wete *p218*
E Pemba Crown Hotel, Wete Main Rd, T0777-429208 (mob), T0777-493667 (mob), sales@pembacrown.com. All 13 rooms have a/c, fans, mosquito nets, TVs and en suite bathrooms. They're clean and in a handy location for the market and bus stand. Dinner must be pre-ordered. Doubles US$35, singles US$25 including breakfast.
E Sharook Guest House, near the market and bus stand, down the track that leads to the harbour, T024-245 4386, sharookguest house@yahoo.com. Run by a friendly guy called Suleiman, it's very simple but clean, and has a restaurant with the best food in town, though it has to be pre-ordered. Own generator. Can arrange excursions, snorkelling trips to local islands and bicycle hire.
E Sharook 2, on the road to the port, take the road opposite the **Pemba Crown Hotel**, and it's on the left about 10 m up a small track. Also owned by Suleiman and with the same contact details as above. There are 8 rooms here, all gleaming new and clean, all en suite. Zanzibari beds, fans and nets. Suleiman is planning a rooftop restaurant (partially) overlooking Fundu Island and an internet café on the ground floor. Reports welcome.

Ngezi Forest Reserve *p219*
B-D Kervan Saray Beach, near Makangale Village, T0773-176737 (mob), www.kervan saraybeach.com. The new home of **Swahili Divers** (see Activities and tours, below), and primarily a diving centre with accommodation, although there's plenty here for non-divers too. A very chilled lodge in lovely gardens, with an open restaurant and bar/lounge area, and a new swimming pool opening in

An underwater resort for Pemba?

At the time this book was going to print, there was much speculation on the island about the development of an underwater resort off the coast of Pemba. The new owners of **The Manta Resort**, Monsoon Empires, were in the process of applying for permission from the authorities to build this resort, some environmental impact studies have apparently already been conducted and there are suggestions that the company expects the resort to be completed by 2010. Not surprisingly, this is causing some concern, since much of the islands' coast and marine habitats are protected by the Pemba Channel Marine Conservation Area (PECCA).

Although there's little information online at present, watch for the latest news at www.pembaunderwaterresort.com or www.monsoonempires.com.

autumn 2009. The 11 clean and spacious rooms are in 6 bungalows, have traditional *barazza* beds, mosquito nets with fans inside, and private bathrooms. US$140 per person full board, and there's a dorm room with 3 bunk beds for US$45 per person. Also offer some excellent packages such as 6 nights' full board with 5 days diving for US$1250 per person sharing or US$850 with dorm accommodation. Excursions, including forest walks into the nearby Ngezi Reserve, sea kayaking, fishing, and airport transfers.

Panga ya Watoro Beach
L-B The Manta Resort (formerly Manta Reef Lodge), in the extreme northwest of the island, T0777-511293 (mob), www.themanta resort.com. Quiet and wonderfully remote location on a cliff overlooking a private beach, the lodge has a large central area with terrace, veranda, lounge, restaurant and snooker room. 20 en suite double rooms in individual cottages, some with sea view, all attractively decorated. New swimming pool and beach bar, and snorkelling, kayaking, game fishing can be arranged. Also has a dive centre.

🍴 Eating

Many of the places listed under Sleeping have restaurants, see above.

Chake Chake *p217, map p217*
🍴 **Balloon Bros**, just south of the market and bus stand and opposite the mosque on main street. Charcoal grill, cold drinks, pleasant patio with thatched bandas to sit under.

▲ Activities and tours

Pemba Island *p214, map p215*
Diving
To appreciate Pemba's magical diversity fully, take the liveaboard option and dive the east coast, for this is the territory of the schooling hammerheads. For more information on diving Pemba, see page 222.
Dive 7/10, Fundu Lagoon, T024-223 2926, www.fundulagoon.com. Luxury outfit.
The Manta Resort, see Sleeping. Luxury.
Swahili Divers, Kervan Saray Beach, T0773-176738 (mob), www.swahilidivers.com. 5-star PADI Gold Palm Resort dive centre. Dive on the east and west coast of Pemba and during Feb-May, head for the southern coast for the migrating whale sharks. Single dives cost US$80, doubles US$130 and 3 dives US$180, plus US$30 for equipment hire. Have very reasonable diving packages for residents at their lodge, see Sleeping, page 220). Day guests can be picked up at Konde if they arrive by *dala-dala* by 0800. PADI courses available, including Discover Scuba, Open Water, Advanced, Rescue Diver, Dive Master. Highly recommended for budget travellers.

Dive Pemba

Pemba has some of the most spectacular diving in the world. The Pemba channel separates Shimoni in Kenya from Pemba Island. The channel runs deep until it approaches the Pemba coastline and then begins a dramatic rise creating a sheer wall off the coast. Diving is characterized by crystal clear, blue water drop-offs along with pristine shallow reefs. Hard and soft coral gardens abound with schools of coral fish, pelagic marine life, mantas and turtles. Here are a few of the more famous dive sites with their descriptions, although there are many more spectacular sites around Pemba's smaller offshore islands.

Fundu Reef The visibility ranges from 20-40 m and there is a large sheer wall with overhangs and caverns. The coral is remarkable, especially the large rose coral and red and yellow sea fans. You can see many types of fish here including kingfish, triggerfish and wrasse. The reef is relatively shallow and therefore Fundu is a good spot for a first dive.

Kokota Reef Ideal for night diving, the waters are shallow and generally calmer, ranging from between 8-20 m. Of all the creatures that come out after dark, the Spanish dancer is a particular attraction.

Manta Point Visibility averages from between 20-40 m. Manta Point is one of the best sites in the world for close encounters with the giant manta rays that inhabit this area. The rays can be seen in groups of up to 15 and rise to depths as shallow as 9 m. The enormous variety of coral, fish and other marine life is so concentrated here you should try and include at least 2 dives. This is truly one of the finest dive sites in the region.

Mesali Island Visibility averages between 40-50 m. This is a wall dotted with small caves and ridges. Large rivers of sand run off the top of the reef to form wide canyons that enter the wall at approximately 25 m. Gorgonian fans are in abundance below 20 m and on a turning tide the marine life is exceptional and the currents strong. Giant grouper drift lazily through the reef and hundreds of surgeonfish cruise below divers.

Njao Gap Njao Gap is well known for its amazing wall diving. Mantas can be seen here in season and the coral is spectacular, but what distinguishes this particular location is the profusion of titan trigger-fish. Visibility varies from day to day, but is usually good to 30 m.

Tour operators

Most hotels and guesthouses can arrange excursions. Ali at **Jondeni Guesthouse** (see Sleeping, page 219) is keen to show travellers that Pemba has lots to offer, and is very helpful. **Faizin Tours**, near the bank, Mkoani, T024-223 0705. Ferry tickets and tours of the island.

⊖ Transport

Pemba Island *p214, map p215*
Air
Coastal Air, T024-2452162, Pemba Airport, flies to **Dar** daily at 1635 (50 mins, US$121).

To **Zanzibar** at 1640 (30 mins, US$101).
To **Tanga** at 1515 (25 mins, US$75).
    Zanair fly daily to **Zanzibar** at 1045, 1500, 1645 (US$101).

Ferry
The quickest ferry is **Sepiddeh**, T0713-282 365, which departs Pemba to **Zanzibar** and **Dar**, Wed-Mon at 1300. 1st class costs US$60, economy US$55. To Zanzibar 1st class costs US$40 and economy US$35.
    Sea Express, T024-211 0217, operates a ferry to **Dar** on Mon and Thu, and runs between Pemba and **Zanzibar** at 1300. See also Dar es Salaam transport, page 96.

Contents

Footprint features

At a glance

⊖ **Getting around** Buses regularly ply the Dar to Moshi road and there are connecting buses and *dala-dala* into the Usambara Mountains. Climbing operators include transfers to the ascent points of Kilimanjaro.

◉ **Time required** 2-3 days from Dar to Moshi with a night or 2 in Lushoto. A week to climb Kili, which includes a night on either side in Moshi or Marangu.

☼ **Weather** Temperate all year around the bottom of the mountain; icy conditions at the top.

✖ **When not to go** Avoid climbing in the long rainy season, late Mar to mid-May.

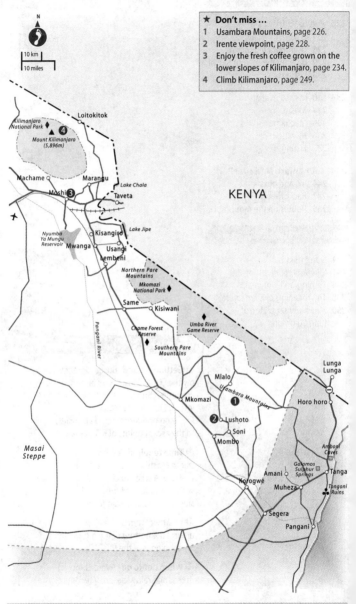

★ Don't miss ...
1 Usambara Mountains, page 226.
2 Irente viewpoint, page 228.
3 Enjoy the fresh coffee grown on the
   lower slopes of Kilimanjaro, page 234.
4 Climb Kilimanjaro, page 249.

N

10 km
10 miles

Loitokitok

Kilimanjaro
National Park ◆ 4
Mount Kilimanjaro
(5,896m)

Machame ○   Marangu
   Moshi 3   Lake Chala
                           Taveta

KENYA

Nyumba
Ya Mungu
Reservoir   Kisangiro   Lake Jipe
   Mwanga   Usangi
                  Lembeni

Northern Pare
Mountains
                  Mkomazi
                  National Park ◆

Same ○ Kisiwani

Chome Forest
Reserve ◆   Umba River
                          Game Reserve
Pangani River
              Southern Pare
              Mountains

                                              Lunga
                                              Lunga

                  Mlalo
                          Usambara Mountains
   Mkomazi   Horo horo ○

   2 ○ Lushoto
        ○ Soni   Amboni
     Mombo   Caves

Masai   Galanos
Steppe   Sulphur
                           Amani ○   Springs □   Tanga
                    Korogwe ○   Muheza ○
                                              Tongoni
                                              Ruins

                              Segera ○
                                   Pangani ○

The main road out of Dar es Salaam travels inland and joins the highway that runs the length of Tanzania and effectively links Kenya to the north with Malawi to the south. Travelling north from Dar to Arusha is a scenic drive of some 650 km, through extensive farmland and sisal plantations with the ever-present backdrop of the Pare and Usambara mountain ranges to the east. The main road is very busy, with a steady stream of buses linking Dar with Arusha, and the small regional towns offer petrol stations and services for bus passengers and drivers wishing to take a break from their journey. Away from the main road is the small mountain town of Lushoto, which is very attractive and a recommended spot for some good hiking in the hills. The forests and mountain scenery of the Usambara are not what is normally expected by visitors to Tanzania. Moshi is the town at the foot of Kilimanjaro and climbs start just a few kilometres away at the entrance of the Kilimanjaro National Park. On the approach to Moshi you may well be rewarded with a glimpse of the snow-capped top of Kili when the mists lift off the summit in the late afternoon. Climbing Mount Kilimanjaro is an adventurous break from game viewing and reaching the 'Roof of Africa' is one of the continent's greatest challenges. It is the highest mountain in the world that can simply be walked up.

The road from Dar to Moshi

From Dar es Salaam, the main road goes 109 km to the west to Chalinzi and the junction with the main north-south road. North from Chalinzi it passes through the regional centres such as Korogwe, Mombo and Same before reaching Moshi at the foothills of Kilimanjaro. This is where climbers begin their ascent of the mountain. The road will not hold your attention long: the small towns that you pass through are fairly nondescript, but they do provide facilities such as petrol stations and shops and access to the Usambara Mountains to the east, which are worth a detour for the good hiking opportunities and country lodges, and the attractive town of Lushoto. Further north closer to Moshi are the Pare Mountains and Mkomazi National Park. ▸▸ *For listings, see pages 230-233.*

Ins and outs
The driving time between Dar and Moshi is roughly seven to eight hours and there are scores of buses each day that ply this route. From Moshi it is a further 80 km to Arusha. There are daily flights between Dar es Salaam and Zanzibar and **Kilimanjaro airport**, which lies roughly midway between Moshi and Arusha. ▸▸ *For further details, see Transport, page 233.*

Korogwe → *Colour map 1, B5. 5°0'S 38°20'E. Phone code: 022.*
Korogwe is a small town that you pass through on the way from Tanga or Dar es Salaam north to Moshi. It lies at 52 m, on the north bank of Pangani/Ruvu Rivers, whose fertile valley, with its many settlements, stretches to the west. The local people are of the Zigua and Wasambaa tribes but call themselves Waluvu. It is a local administrative centre due to its position near the local sisal estates, the Dar es Salaam–Nairobi road and railway and its proximity to the Usambara and Pare Mountains. There are a few shops, a market, a hospital and a Christian mission. Most buses stop here at one of the many petrol stations in and around town, which also feature restaurants and shops catering for the bus passengers. There are a couple of reasonable places to stay and eat if you want to break the journey between Dar and Moshi but there's little reason to.

Mombo → *Colour map 1, B5.*
Mombo is a small town on the Dar es Salaam to Moshi highway. There's little of interest here, its main activity is the provision of services for travellers and again lots of buses stop here at either the oddly named **Liverpool Hill Breeze**, 1.5 km north of Mombo, or the **Manchester Executive Inn** in town, which have petrol stations and serve fast food. It is worth a mention, however, as this is the junction with the road to Soni and Lushoto in the Usambara Mountains (see below). You can jump off the bus here and switch to one of the many *dala-dala* that climb the mountain road the 33 km from Mombo to Lushoto.

Usambara Mountains ☺🄵🄴🄲 ▸▸ *pp230-233. Colour map 1, A5.*
The Usambara Mountains are approximately 110 km long, range 30-60 km in width and at their highest point at Mount Mgamba are 2440 m above sea level. They are accessible from Lushoto in the west and Amani (see page 118) in the east. The Usambaras are fairly unique in that they support tropical forests of the kind normally only found in West Africa forest and are home to euphorbias, acacias, giant ferns, palms, lobelias, camphors

(Japanese and Usumbaru) eucalyptus and fig trees. Wildlife to be seen includes the elegant Colobus monkey, blue monkeys and a wide variety of birds. Several bird species are endemic, including the Usambara Eagle-owl and Usambara weaver. The views on the southern and western sides of the mountains are of spectacular vistas of the Masai plains below. Kilimanjaro can be seen on a clear day and at the end of the day the sun turns the land an unforgettable colour.

Lushoto is about 1½ hours or 33 km off the main Korogwe–Moshi road where the turn-off is at Mombo. The road up to Lushoto via the small town of **Soni** is spectacular as it twists and turns through the mountains, with glimpses of small waterfalls in Mlalo River. The tiny market town is reminiscent of an Indian hill station and the country lodges in the region have a charming colonial atmosphere. The climate changes quickly as you rise up into the mountains. Sunny days are warm, but cloudy and windy days get very cool and it is comfortable to sit around a fire in the evening throughout the year. The big pull here is exploring the Usambara Mountains, dotted with streams and waterfalls and rural villages.

There is plenty of opportunity for hiking or mountain biking through the deep forests and green hillsides, and this part of Tanzania is a long way from the scorched plains of the game parks. From the hotels you can hire a guide for walks into the forest and up the peak of Kwa Mongo, a hike of three to four hours.

Lushoto → *Colour map 1, B5. 4°4'S 38°20'E.*
Phone code: 027. Altitude: 1500 m.

Lushoto, at an elevation of around 1500 m, was the town chosen by early German settlers to escape from the heat and dust of the plains for the holidays. Back then it was called Wilhemstal and the cool, fresh air and lush, green surroundings were greatly appealing. It was even once thought that it might develop into the capital of the colonial administration. It can get quite cold from June-September so take warm clothes.

Many of the surrounding farms and government buildings are originally German. There is a very fine Dutch-style **Governor's House**, just out of town on the road going north. Other reminders of the colonial connection are the horse riding arenas and the red tiles on some of the roofs of the buildings. There is a group of **German Alpine-style buildings** with flat red, rounded end tiles, chimney stacks and shutters on the east side of the main road near the Mission Hospital. The British changed the town very little. Their main

Lushoto

Old Cricket Ground
Pavilion

Catholic
Parade Ground
Mission Hospital
Council Offices
Lutheran
NHB
Village Hall
Adventista

Forestry Office

To Governor's House, Herbarium, District Offices, Mlalo &

To Soni, Mombo & Dar es Salaam

300 metres
300 yards

Sleeping
Grant's Lodge 1
Irente Farm 7
Irente View Cliff Lodge 9

To Irente Viewpoint
Karibuni Lodge 8
Lawns 2
Lushoto Executive Lodge 3
Mandarin Grand 6
Muller's Mountain Lodge 4
Shooting Star Inn 10
St Eugene's Guesthouse 5
Sun 11
White House Annex 12

contribution was to lay out a **cricket ground** just to the west of the town centre. Although football is played here now and not cricket, it is still possible to see the old weather-boarded cricket pavilion with a veranda, albeit in poor repair. East of the main road, near the Catholic church, is the **Parade Ground**. Horse riding was a favourite recreation of the Germans, and this was where the mounted officials were paraded, in front of the timber review stand. The **Lutheran church**, just west of the centre, is an attractive building, with blue window frames, black and white walls, Mangalore tile roof, a front stone arch and a free-standing bell in a wooden tower.

The **Tafori Arboretum** on the slope 1 km to the north of the town dates from the German colonial period and has thousands of pressed plants from all over Tanzania – ask for Mr Msangi or Mr Mabula if you would like to see the collection. The town also holds a fine **market** (close to the bus station) that is very colourful and lively with several small, inexpensive eating places, hair salons, tailors and a maize mill making *posho* (maize flour). Among the many products on sale is the locally produced pottery, with a variety of pots for cooking, storage or serving. One of the ancient beliefs of the Shambaa people is that Sheuta, their God or Supreme Being, made people from a handful of soil in the manner of a potter. In the Usambaras, potters are traditionally women, with the skills passed on from mother to daughter. Men are discouraged from participating in any stage of the potting process, as it is believed that to do so brings great misfortune including sterility. There is good fishing in the mountain streams, one of which runs through the centre of the town, but you'll need to be fully equipped.

This area is a place to enjoy the views and countryside. It is fertile and verdant and there are plenty of tracks to walk along. One such walk takes about 45 minutes from Lushoto to reach **Irente viewpoint** 5 km away, from where the view of the hills and the Masai Plain 1000 m below really is breathtaking. Take the road out of town towards Irente and head for the children's home. Ask around and you'll be shown the track. On the way is **Irente Farm**, where fresh fruit, vegetables, preserves, bread and cheese are sold – the large garden is an excellent picnic spot. There's now a hotel very near to the view point, aptly named **Irente View Cliff Lodge** (see page 231), with fantastic views from all the rooms.

Western Usambara Mountains Cultural Tourism Programme

① *Guides are available from the information centre just off the road opposite the bus station, open daily 0800-1800, which is run by the Friends of Usambara Society, T027-264 0132. Here there are details and photographs of each tour offered and you can discuss with the staff exactly what you would like to do. Further details from the Tanzanian Tourist Information Centre in Arusha, see page 259.*

This is a local tourism initiative advised and supported by the Dutch Development Organisation (SNV) and the Tanzanian Tourism Board. This has been one of the most successful of Tanzania's cultural tourism programmes and these days runs largely self-sufficiently. Local development projects benefiting from the scheme include maintaining traditional irrigation systems and soil erosion control for small farmers. It aims to involve and ultimately benefit the small local communities who organize tourist projects off the usual circuits. These include several one-day walking trips from Lushoto to the Irente viewpoint overlooking Mazinde village 1000 m below (see above), a walking tour of Usambara farms and flora, the increasingly popular rock tour from Soni and the Bangala River tour, which includes wading through the water. You can also visit and stay in **Carters Camp** at **Ndekia**. This is a hut precariously perched on a rocky outcrop, built by an

American writer as his launch pad for hang-gliding. There are also longer three- to five-day excursions walking into the Western Usambara Mountains via the villages of **Lukozi**, **Manolo** and **Simga** to reach the former German settlement of **Mtae**, a small village perched high up on the western rim of the escarpment, and the tour to the **Masumbae Forest Reserve**. Another hike is to **Mlalo** and **Mount Seguruma** (2218 m) about 25 km north of Lushoto. One of the more ambitious tours offered is a seven-day bike ride from Lushoto to Moshi through the mountains. On overnight hikes and rides, you stay in local guesthouses and in some cases local homes, or the tourist office will supply tents and sleeping bags. The costs for all these trips varies greatly but expect to pay in the region of US$10-15 per day per group and US$3 per day per person for a guide. There are additional costs for accommodation and food. Most of the guides are former students of the Shambalai secondary school in Lushoto, speak fair to good English, and can give you information on the history of, and daily life in, the Usambara Mountains.

Back on the road to Moshi ● ›› *pp 230-233.*

Same → *Colour map 1, A5.*
A small town 126 km north of Korogwe and 103 km south of Moshi, Same is a base for a visit to Mkomazi National Park (see below). The market has covered and open sections, with a good selection of earthenware pots and bowls, baskets and mats. The bus station is particularly well organized with bus shelters clearly displaying the destinations and routes of the various buses. A feature of the area is the hollowed-out honey-logs hanging from the trees. Every Friday there's a cattle market at Mgagau about 15 minutes drive away. Ask at the **Elephant Motel** (see page 232) for directions.

Mkomazi National Park → *Colour map 1, A5. 4° S, 38° E.*
ⓘ *www.tanzaniaparks.com. Open daily sunrise to sunset. Entry into the park is US$20 per day per adult and US$5 per child (5-16). Access to the park is through the Zange Gate, 7 km east from Same. There is very little tourist development in the park, it is well off the normal safari circuit and there is only one camp (see page 232). The reason for this is it's primarily being kept as a conservation area (see below). There are 3 small airstrips inside the reserve used by chartered planes.*

This national park of 3600 sq km lies about 100 km north of Tanga and is contiguous with Kenya's Tsavo National Park. In the rainy season herds of elephant, zebra and oryx migrate between the parks. The name means 'where the water comes from' in the local Pare language and refers to the Umba River on the south eastern border. Mkomazi Game Reserve was established in 1951, but by 1988 heavy poaching had destroyed its rhino and elephant populations, and overgrazing by pastorals who brought their cattle into the reserve had taken its toll. In 1989 the government gave Tony Fitzjohn, a conservationist with The George Adamson Trust a mandate to rehabilitate the wilderness. He set about building an infrastructure of roads, airfields, water pumps and dams, and recruited anti-poaching rangers. These efforts have proved successful and now Mkomazi is so well protected that the government upgraded it from a game reserve to a national park in 2005. In the 1980s, there were only 11 individual elephants; today there are over 1000.

The landscape is wide savannah dotted with baobab trees, which is an ideal environment for rhino. The **Mkomazi Rhinos Resettlement Project**, coordinated by the Tanzania Wildlife Protection fund, has taken a lead role in relocating black rhino from South Africa to Mkomazi Reserve and Ngorongoro. The eight released rhino here are kept in intensive protection zones and it is hoped that they will breed, after which they will be relocated within Tanzania to other traditional natural habitats. It is an expensive programme. The cost of transferring 10 rhinos is put at over US$1 million.

African hunting dogs, the endangered wild dog and other big mammals such as zebra, giraffes and gazelles have also been reintroduced. The reserve is home to about 400 bird species including falcons, eagles, hawks, hornbills, barbets, starlings, weavers and shrikes.

◉ The road from Dar to Moshi listings

For Sleeping and Eating price codes and other relevant information, see pages 36-40.

● Sleeping

Korogwe *p226*

E Motel White Parrot, from the bus stand turn left for 400m, T022-264 1068, motelwhiteparrot@yahoo.com. By far the best place to stay in Korogwe, and fairly new. The white double-storey building has 22 small but smart a/c rooms with hot showers, satellite TV and phones. You can also camp at the back for US$4 per person and there's a toilet and shower. There is a separate thatched restaurant and bar.

E-F Segera Highway Motel, at Segera, the junction with the turn-off for Tanga, 17 km south of Korogwe, T022-264 0815. For motorists this is a useful stop en route to Tanga or Moshi, either overnight or just for a cup of tea at the Engen petrol station on this busy junction. The thatched roadside restaurant has a surprisingly large menu of steaks, salads, breakfasts, pizza and pastas, plus shakes and juices. Out back you can camp for US$5 or there are 23 very smart new motel-style chalets for US$25 a double.

F Korogwe Transit Hotel, on the main road, T022-264 0640. Mosquito nets, private bath with hot water most of the time, some rooms have a/c, overpriced for what you get, front rooms have a balcony but are very noisy because of the traffic. With the number of people around security could be an issue.

F Korogwe Travellers' Inn, main road opposite the bus station, T022-264 0564. Bar, restaurant, fans, very basic, only baths

with cold water, no showers or toilet seats. Only stay if other places are full.

F Sunrise Guest House and Bar, Main Rd, 400 m from post office, T022-264 0967. Best of the budget options, clean with toilet and shower, fan and mosquito net, basic food available.

Usambara Mountains *p227*

D-E Maweni Farm, 2 km from Soni up a good dirt road, at the foot of a large rockface, T027-264 0427, www.maweni.com. This guesthouse on a farm has 1 single and 7 double rooms, 4 with en suite bathrooms. Lovely restaurant with veranda, organic locally grown food and home-made bread, bar serving local wine, lounge with fire place, established gardens, sauna and swimming pool, internet access. A very pretty setting next to a small lake, lots of nature trails through the forest, and they run 1-3 day guided hikes. En suite rooms are US$50, those with a shared bathroom are US$36. Rates are B&B, lunch is US$5 and dinner US$10. Pick ups can be arranged from the bus in Mombo.

E Soni Falls Hotel, about 1 km from Soni, a 5-min walk from the bus stand, T0787-765 378 (mob). Originally built in the 1930s and recently refurbished, there are 10 double rooms with nets and en suite bath, shower and flush toilet facilities and hot water. Restaurant has a mixed local and European menu (meals US$2-5), and the well-stocked bar offers wine made by the local Benedictine monks. From the veranda there are good views of the river and falls and the peak of Kwa Mongo. Space for parking. Excellent value, price includes breakfast. Camping in the grounds, from where you can hear the waterfall, US$3.50.

F Hotel Kimalube, on the hill coming up into Soni before reaching the bus stand, T0787-755385 (mob). There are 6 rooms with mosquito nets and warm bucket showers, very basic, warm beers and sporadic electricity, but cheap at US$4.

Lushoto *p227, map p227*

There are a number of basic guesthouses around the market in Lushoto itself, but by far the best places to stay to enjoy the mountain scenery are the country lodges on the outskirts.

C Grant's Lodge, Mizambo, Lushoto, T027-264 2491, www.grantslodge.com. 15 km from Lushoto along a road that is rough in places; signposted from Lushoto, start by heading north on the road that passes the post office and district offices. Lovely brick house, 5 rooms, a welcoming atmosphere, open fireplace, games are organized on the lawn, lots of classic movies to watch. Generous helpings of tasty home-cooked food – soups are excellent as is the hot chocolate. Can organize short or long walking safaris with photocopied instructions. Car safaris can also be arranged. Range of bird reference books in the library. Highly recommended. Payment can be made in US$ or TSh.

C Irente View Cliff Lodge, Irente Viewpoint, 5 km from Lushoto, T027-264 0026, www.itenteview.com. The newest and best positioned mid-range lodge in the region on a stunning cliff top location with 18 comfortable rooms with balconies, TV, phone, tea and coffee trays, hot water, spacious grounds with amazing views, restaurant and bar. Can organize guides for hikes. A single is US$50, a double US$65 and a triple US$95. Recommended. Adjacent to it is a campsite (US$3 per person) with hot showers and its own bar serving cheap meals.

C-D Lushoto Executive Lodge, 1.5 km from town T027-264 0076, www.lushotoexecutive lodge.co.tz. With comfortable self-contained

rooms in single-storey brick buildings with TV and 4-poster beds, some have self-catering kitchens and thatched roofs, set in manicured gardens, restaurant and bar, meals are prepared from local farm produce. There's also a gym and sauna.

D Muller's Mountain Lodge, 13 km from town on the road to Migambo, on the same road as **Grant's Lodge**, so follow their signs, T027-264 0204, www.mullersmountain lodge.co.tz. Built in 1930 in the style of an English country home, it has brick gables, attractive gardens and orchards, and lovely views. 7 bedrooms, shared dining and living rooms with outsized fireplaces, large camping area on the hill above the house, plus very good food and service; they offer guided walks. Pick ups can be arranged from town.

D-E Lawns Hotel, 1 km before town on Soni Rd, T027-264 0005, www.lawnshotel.com. Old colonial-style hotel, has wonderful views with fireplaces in the rooms plus a veranda, restaurant and lively bar. Rates include a very good breakfast. Some rooms are self-contained, the cheaper ones have shared facilities. Given that the building is over 100 years old, the quality of the rooms varies so look at a few. Run by a football-loving Cypriot who is quite a character and a good source of information about Tanzania. Camping possible, US$5 per person, with fairly new ablutions block with hot water.

D-F Irente Farm, 5 km from town southwest towards Irente viewpoint, T027-264 0000, murless@elect.org. Run by the Evangelical Lutheran Church. Has a wonderful cheese factory. You can buy a picnic lunch from the farm to take with you to climb to the viewpoint, including rich brown bread, several types of jam, fresh butter, cheese and fruit juice. Accommodation on offer is in a simply furnished self-catering house, sleeping up to 6 (US$83); doubles (US$16); or there's a campsite with an ablution block and watchman (US$4).

E St Eugene's Guesthouse, 2 km before Lushoto on the Soni Rd, T027-264 0055. Run by the Usambara Sisters, plain but comfortable, 14 self-contained rooms in a double-storey building decked with vines, hot water and phones. Check out the white starched bed linen and hand embroidered bed covers. Serves food, including delicious home-made ice cream, and in the farm shop you can buy home-made jam and marmalade made from various fruits such as passionfruit and grapefruit, herbed cheeses and rather potent banana wine. This is a convent and a Montessori teacher training centre with modern buildings in gardens well tended by the sisters.

E-F Mandarin Grand Hotel, 1 km on the hillside to the west of town, T027-264 0014. Best of the simple board and lodgings and cheap – from US$10 – and safe with good views over Lushoto. With 21 rooms there's a choice of singles with shared bathrooms or en suite spacious doubles with bath tubs and hot water, or you can negotiate to camp in the garden. There's also a restaurant and bar but service can be slow. The charismatic owner, Mr. Mandari is very helpful and has a 1951 Mercedes-Benz parked outside that he's owned that long.

F Karibuni Lodge, 1 km south of town on a hill to the left of the road, T027-264 0104. A stone house with a wide veranda, set in a lush tract of vegetation with a lounge and bar, self-catering kitchen or meals can be organized. Accommodation is in a 6-bed dorm, in rooms with or without bathrooms or you can pitch a tent in the garden. Can organize local guided walks.

F Lushoto Sun Hotel, Boma Rd near the police station, T027-264 0082. Popular, has a good restaurant and 10 large, but a little gloomy, double rooms with nets and hot water for US$12. Safe parking.

F Shooting Star Inn, Chakechake Rd to the south of town, T027-264 0192. Neat and modern with en suite bathrooms with showers and long drop toilets, in a bright white block with concrete patio and small restaurant serving basic meals. They plan to put TVs in the rooms, meaning the price of US$8 for a double will go up.

F White House Annex, in town near the market, T0784-427471 (mob), whitehouse@ raha.com. Self-contained singles and doubles in a tidy 1-storey white house near the tourist office and bus stand, TV room, bar and small restaurant, local food but good and big portions, sitting room. There is also an adjoining internet café here.

Same *p229*
E Elephant Motel, T027-275 8193, www. elephantmotel.com. Simple but more than adequate, 16 double rooms with mosquito nets, bathroom with hot water, and TV with limited DSTV (BBC and CNN). Staff are helpful. Also has a good restaurant and bar serving Western and Oriental dishes. Set in well maintained gardens, you can also camp for US$5 per person and there's toilets and showers. You can organize a guide here to take you to some of the local farms or a cattle market.

Mkomazi National Park *p229*
L Babu's Camp, 11 km from the entrance gate of Zange, T027-254 8840, www.babus camp.com. Not as luxurious as the usual tented camps, but simple and comfortable, and the only accommodation within the park. The 6 tents are spacious and have attached bathrooms with shower and toilet. Activities include day and night game drives, game walks, and they can ask permission to take guests to see the rhino. Transport into the reserve is usually organized when you make a reservation.

Eating

Refer to Sleeping, above.

Lushoto *p227, map p227*
All guesthouses and lodges have restaurants and bars, and in town itself there are a number of cheap food stalls and local bars, again around the bus stand and market.

☉ Transport

Lushoto *p227, map p227*
Bus, dala-dala and 4WD
The roads to Lushoto are excellent, all
sealed, even the 33-km gradual climb up
from Mombo, which was resurfaced by
the Germans in 1989 and is still in fairly
good repair. Public transport is frequent and
hitching is possible as there are plenty of
4WDs who will give lifts in this area. Buses
and *dala-dala* from **Mombo** take about
1½ hrs and cost US$2. You can also get a
direct bus from **Tanga**, but it is slow, 6 hrs,
and there are also slow buses between
Lushoto and **Arusha** (6 hrs) and **Moshi**

(5½ hrs). Direct buses from **Dar** leave the
stand on Mafia St in the Kariakoo area
throughout the morning and take 7 hrs.

☉ Directory

Lushoto *p227, map p227*
Banks National Microfinance Bank (NMB),
on the main road opposite the bus station,
changes money but at poor exchange rates
and although it has an ATM it doesn't take
foreign cards. **Internet** There is internet
access at White House Annex and some
of the hotels offer access. **Post office** At
the northern end of main street.

Moshi and Marangu

→ *Colour map 1, A5.*

Moshi is the first staging post on the way to climbing Mount Kilimanjaro and a pleasant place to spend a few days organizing your trip. It's an unusual African town in that it has very few European or Asian residents, unlike Arusha. Climbing expeditions depart from the town into Kilimanjaro National Park early each morning. The two peaks of this shimmering snow-capped mountain can be seen from all over the town and it dominates the skyline except when the cloud descends and hides it from view. Moshi means 'smoke' – perhaps either a reference to the giant volcano that once smoked or the regular smoke-like cloud. Marangu is 23 km from Moshi and is the closest village to Kilimanjaro National Park, the entrance to which is 5 km away. Accommodation here is more expensive than Moshi, and if you're on a tight budget you should plan your assault on the mountain from Moshi. ▶▶ *For listings, see pages 237-243.*

Background

The area around Moshi is particularly fertile due to the volcanic soils and there are lots of melt-water streams fed by the snow. This is where Arabica coffee, the premium quality of the two coffee varieties, is grown by the Chagga people, helping them to become one of the wealthiest of the Tanzanian groups. All around the town, and on the lower slopes of Kilimanjaro, vast plantations of coffee blanket the area. Notice that the low coffee bushes are grown with taller banana palms for shade. The first coffee grown in Tanzania was planted at the nearby Kilema Roman Catholic Mission in 1898. Growth was steady and, by 1925, 100 tons were being produced each year. The Chagga people are particularly enterprising and formed the Kilimanjaro Native Cooperative Union (KNCH) to collect and market the crop themselves.

Moshi is the centre of Tanzania's coffee industry; the Coffee Board is located here and coffee from all over Tanzania is sold at auction to international buyers. However, apart from the coffee produced in the immediate locality, the crop does not pass through Moshi, it is auctioned on the basis of certified type, quality and grade, and then shipped directly from the growing area to the buyer. Not all of the wealth generated by the sale of coffee makes its way back to the growing community. Local small farmers have been known to receive only half the Moshi export price. By the time the coffee is sold in London their purchase price amounts to only one-tenth of the London price. Interestingly, only 1-2% of the coffee grown in Tanzania is consumed in the country; simply because Tanzanians are traditionally chai (tea) drinkers. Moshi was the site of the signing of the Moshi Declaration after the war with Uganda in February 1979, which created the Uganda National Liberation Front (UNLF) government to replace Idi Amin.

Moshi ⊖🕐▲⊖🕓 ▶▶ *pp237-243.*

Moshi is a pleasant town with the former European and administrative areas clustered around the clock tower, and the main commercial area southwest of the market. Despite being an attractive town, there are few places worth visiting in Moshi itself, and many visitors stay here just long enough to arrange their trek up the mountain and to enjoy a hot shower when they get back. The limited sights include the (non-operating) **Railway Station** southeast of the clock tower, a two-storey structure from the German period,

Moshi

with pleasing low arches, a gabled roof with Mangalore tiles and arched windows on the first floor. On the corner of Station Road and Ghalla Road is a fine **Indian shop building** dating from the colonial period, with wide curved steps leading up to the veranda, tapering fluted stone columns and a cupola adorning the roof. To the north of town on the roundabout marking the junction with the Dar–Arusha road, the **Askari Monument** is a soldier with a rifle and commemorates African members of the British Carrier Corps who lost their lives in the two World Wars. **Shah Industries Ltd** ① *T027-275 2414*, employ many disabled workers producing high-quality crafts like wood carvings, leatherwork, batiks and furniture. Their shop is on Karakana Street in the industrial area to the west of town.

Around Moshi

West Kilimanjaro The road running in a northerly direction from Boma ya Ngombe on the Moshi–Arusha road passes through Sanya Juu and Engare Nairobi to reach Olmolog. This was the main area for European farming in northern Tanzania prior to independence. After independence most estates were nationalized. These days while pockets of farmland still exist, most of the plains in this region are used by wildlife on a migratory route between Arusha National Park and Kenya's Amboseli

Sleeping
AMEG Lodge Kilimanjaro **11**
Bristol Cottages **7**
Buffalo Inn **10**
Horombo Lodge **18**
Keys **14**
Kilemakyaro Mountain Lodge **15**
Kilimanjaro Backpacker's **9**
Kilimanjaro Crane **2**
Kindoroko **8**
Leopard **6**
Mountain Inn **16**
Mt Kilimanjaro View Lodge **4**
Newcastle **5**

Parkview Inn **1**
Springlands **3**
YMCA **13**
Zebra **12**

Eating
Aroma Coffee House **3**
Chrisburger **1**
Coffee Shop **7**
Deli Chez **6**
El Rancho **5**
Golden Shower **2**
Indoitaliano **9**
Milan's **8**
Panda **4**
Tanzania Coffee Lounge **10**

National Park. In the dry season up to 600 elephant use this corridor and it's an important calving area for zebra, wildebeest, and Grant's and Thompson's gazelles. In addition to its diverse habitats and wildlife communities, West Kilimanjaro is also home to 12 Masai communities that depend on cattle grazing. Unfortunately, poaching for elephant ivory and bushmeat has been a problem in recent years, as this region is not protected by national park status. The Hifadhi Network is an African Wildlife Foundation (www.awf.org) initiative that has recruited local game scouts from the Masai communities who, with the rangers from Arusha and Kilimanjaro national parks, are involved in reporting and apprehending poachers. Since 2003, the Hifadhi Network has caught more than 50 poachers and this is an excellent example of how simple measures that involve local communities can be an effective conservation tool. There is a very good lodge in this region hosted by Hoopoe Safaris.

Machame ● ⤞ *pp237-243*.

Machame is the village 30 km northwest of Moshi and the road turns off the Arusha-Dar road 12 km from Moshi. This is the start of the second most popular route up Kilimanjaro, the Machame Trail (see page 252), which is tougher than the Marangu Trail but is considered one of the most beautiful routes up. Machame itself lies in a fertile valley of farmland on the lower slopes of the mountain and the park gate is 4 km beyond the village. Accommodation is presently limited to the **Protea Hotel Aishi** (see page 239), but climb operators will transport you to the park gate from Moshi.

Marangu ● ⤞ *p237-243*.

Most people visit Marangu only to attempt the climb to the summit of Mount Kilimanjaro. However, Marangu is an excellent base for hiking, birdwatching and observing rural Africa. Marangu is 11 km north of Himo, a village 27 km east of Moshi on the road to the Kenya border.

The Ordnance Survey map of Kilimanjaro (1:100,000) is an essential guide for walks. The main tracks in the region radiate from the forest boundary, through the cultivated belt of coffee and bananas, to the road that rings the mountain. Other maps are less accurate but widely available at about US$10. For full details of climbing Kilimanjaro, see page 249.

Foothill walks

The **Marangu/Mamba Cultural Tourism Programme** ① *further details from the Tanzanian tourist information in Arusha, see page 259, www.infojep.com/culturaltours*, supported by the Dutch Development Organisation SNV, arranges guided walks through the attractive scenery of the valleys near Marangu and Mamba. **Mamba** is a small village 3 km from Marangu. From here you can also visit caves where women and children hid during ancient Masai-Chagga wars or see a blacksmith at work, using traditional methods to make Masai spears and tools. From Marangu there is an easy walk up Ngangu hill, a visit to a traditional Chagga home, or a visit to the home and memorial of the late Yohano Lawro, a local man who accompanied Dr Hans Meyer and Ludwig Purtscheller on the first recorded climb of Mount Kilimanjaro in 1889. He is reputed to have guided Kilimanjaro climbs until he was 70 and lived to the age of 115. Profits from the programme are used to improve local primary schools. Any of the Marangu hotels can organize guides from the programme.

● Moshi and Marangu listings

For Sleeping and Eating price codes and other relevant information, see pages 36-40.

● Sleeping

Most of the hotels offer arrangements to climb Kili, or at the least will recommend a tour operator. Without exception they all offer a base from which to begin your climb. Ensure that the hotel will store your luggage safely whilst you are on the mountain. Facilities to consider include hot water and a comfortable bed, and of course cold beer and a good hot meal on your return from the climb. Some establishments also offer saunas and massages. The Marangu hotels are better located on the lower slopes of Kilimanjaro but are considerably more expensive. Almost all hotels have restaurants.

Moshi *p234, map p235*

C Kilemakyaro Mountain Lodge, 7 km from Moshi, take the Sokoine road out of town, T027-2754925, www.kilimanjaro safari.com. Perched on a hill above Moshi, set in a 240-ha coffee plantation at an altitude of 1450 m, a stay here will very much help climbers with acclimatization. The reception, bar and dining room are in the main house, a restored 1920s farmhouse, while rooms are in chalets dotted throughout the garden. Can organize climbs of Kilimanjaro and also Meru, and quite uniquely organize weddings at Uhuru Peak at the top of Kili.

C Mt Kilimanjaro View Lodge, 16 km from Moshi, follow the unpaved road out of town north of the **YMCA** or arrange a pick up, bookings through the website, www.mtkilimanjaroviewlodge.com. A country retreat in the Kilimanjaro foothills with great views and accommodation in colourful stone and thatch Chagga huts with bathrooms and home-made chunky wooden furniture. There's a restaurant and bar serving authentic African food, jacuzzi, lots of local walks to nearby waterfalls and in the evenings traditional dancing

and storytelling. An excellent opportunity to interact with the local Chagga people. They'll pick up 1-3 people from Moshi for US$40, and from Kilimanjaro International Airport for US$90.

D AMEG Lodge Kilimanjaro, off Lema Rd, near the Moshi International School, Shanty-town, T027-275 0175, www.ameglodge.com. Very new, set in 1.5-ha garden, 20 rooms with en suite bathrooms and lovely modern, bright furniture, satellite TV, phone and fan. The more expensive suites have a/c and internet access for laptops. Good value in this price range with the cheapest double only US$55. Swimming pool and pool bar, good restaurant, gym and business centre.

D Bristol Cottages, Rindi Lane, T027-275 0175, www.bristolcottages.com. Within walking distance from the bus stand, this is set in a pretty garden compound with parking. The 8 cottages, including 3 family ones, are spacious and have TV, hot water and Wi-Fi. The pleasant restaurant and bar serves continental and Indian food, and rates include an English breakfast.

D Mountain Inn, 6 km from Moshi on the road to Marangu, T027-275 2370, www.kilimanjaro-shah.com. 35 basic but comfortable rooms, a dining room with a veranda, set meals and an à la carte menu, Indian food at the pool bar, lush gardens, swimming pool, sauna. This is the base for **Shah Tours**, see page 242, a quality operator for Kilimanjaro climbs.

D Parkview Inn, Aga Khan Rd, T027-275 0711, www.pvim.com. Local business hotel with little character but nevertheless spacious rooms with modern bathrooms, TV, a/c, internet, secure parking in a compound, spotless swimming pool and a restaurant serving continental and Indian food and can make up lunch boxes to takeaway.

D Springlands Hotel, Tembo Rd, Pasua area towards the industrial area, T027-275 3581, www.springlandshotel.com. Set in large, attractive gardens, this place offers all sorts of treats that are ideal to recover from a Kili climb. 37 rooms with bathrooms. Restaurant, bar, swimming pool, TV room, massages, sauna, manicures and pedicures, bicycle hire, internet. Double room is US$60 with breakfast. Base for **Zara Travel**, see page 242, a recommended operator for climbs.

D Zebra Hotel, New St, T027-275 0611, www.zebrahotelstz.com. A 7-storey block with 70 neat rooms with TV and fridge (and rather garish flowery bedspreads), plus fans or pay a little more for a/c. Spacious lobby, internet café, restaurant, lounge and bar. A good buffet breakfast is included in the rates. Increasingly becoming popular with overseas visitors.

D-E Keys, Uru Rd, just north of the town centre, T027-275 2250, www.keys-hotels.com. This hotel functions primarily as a base for budget climb operations. Accommodation is in the main building or simple round huts and there is a restaurant and bar. The location itself is not particularly interesting and probably not as pleasant as basing yourself out in the more rural locations, but nevertheless a firm favourite. Special rates for residents, food and rooms OK, but some rooms over the rear entrance can be noisy at night because of late returners or early starters for climbing. Single/double/triple are US$30/40/50, with breakfast, and camping is available in the grounds for US$5 per person.

D-E Kilimanjaro Crane, Kaunda St, T027-275 1114, www.kilimanjarocranehotels.com. 30 simple but neat rooms with mosquito nets and TV, en suite bathrooms. Facilities include swimming pool, sauna, fitness centre, gardens, good views, pizza kitchen, several bars including one on the roof with fantastic views of the mountain. There is a very good bookshop in the lobby. A good mid-range option; single/double/triple US$40/50/60. Can organize transfers from Kilimanjaro International Airport.

E Horombo Lodge, Old Moshi Rd, above the Tanzania Postal Bank, T027-275 0134, www.eliamensontours.com/horombo_lodge. This has 33 rooms with en suite bathroom,

TV and phone, a small restaurant downstairs serving drinks and affordable meals for guests only. It's reasonably new so still fairly smart but with garish furnishings, hot water all day, doubles from US$25.

E Kindoroko, Mawenzi Rd, close to market, T027-275 4054, www.kindorokohotels.com. One of the best mid-range options in the middle of town, very organized and friendly, and fantastically decorated. 46 rooms which are on the small side but have satellite TV, some also have fridges and bathrooms have plenty of hot water. Rates include a hot breakfast. Downstairs is a restaurant and bar, internet café and tour booking office, upstairs is the rooftop restaurant and bar with excellent views of Kili. The menu's very good and includes authentic Indian dishes and 3-course set meals. A great place to meet other travellers even if you are not staying here. They operate their own Kili climbs on all routes, prices include a night before and after the climb in the hotel. Recommended.

E Leopard Hotel, Market St, T027-275 0884, www.leopardhotel.com. This small centrally located hotel claims to have received an award for good service from Bill Clinton when he visited Tanzania … a fact which makes the mind boggle. 16 clean but cramped rooms, with balconies, a/c, satellite TV and en suite bathrooms, half of which have a view of Kilimanjaro. Reasonable bar and restaurant downstairs, and a bar with nice views on the roof.

F Buffalo Inn, 2 blocks south and east of the bus station, T027-275 0270. Clean budget hotel, very friendly, hot water with/without bathroom. Good restaurant and bar. Will store your luggage if you are going on safari. Rates include breakfast.

F Kilimanjaro Backpacker's Hotel, Mawenzi Rd, T027-275 5159, www.kilimanjaro backpackers.com. Here there are 10 rooms, which are small but comfortable with fans and shared bathrooms. There's a small restaurant and bar with TV showing sports, or guests can also use the facilities at the

Kindoroko next door, which has the same owner. You can't argue with the price here; just US$4 for a single and US$6 for a double.

F Newcastle, close to the market on Mawenzi St, T027-275 0853. Offers 51 rooms on 5 floors, 36 with bathrooms, the rest with shared bathrooms, good views from the top, hot water, rooms are well kept though all the dark wood makes the place a little gloomy. Rooftop bar.

F YMCA, Uhuru Highway, to the north of the clock tower, T027-275 1734. Facilities include gym, shop, several tour desks, bar, restaurant and swimming pool (non-guests can use the pool for US$2). Mostly used by local people, this has 60 bare rooms with communal showers with hot water. Nevertheless, it's secure and clean with spotless sheets and mosquito nets and has recently been repainted. A double is US$15.

Camping There is camping at the **Golden Shower Restaurant**, 2 km from Moshi on the road to Marangu (see Eating). It is also possible to camp at the **Keys Hotel**.

West Kilimanjaro

L West Kilimanjaro Tented Camp, reservations, Hoopoe Safaris, Arusha T027-250 7011, T027-250 7541, www.kiru rumu.com. The 5 tents are spacious with en suite bathrooms and fully and tastefully furnished, set under the spreading branches of an acacia tree. Views of Kilimanjaro are superb and there is game in this region. Game drives, night drives, walks with the Masai and fly camping away from camp are possible. High season rates are US$540 per person full board and there's a conservancy fee of US$30 per day and minimum stay is 2 nights.

Machame *p236*

C Protea Hotel Aishi, 30 km from Moshi in Machame Village, T027-275 6941, www.proteahotels.com. This is one of the most luxurious hotels in the region run by South African chain Protea, and is an ideal base to conquer Kili on the Machame Trail (see page 252). The hotel arranges mountain climbing, safaris and also nature trails in the area. The 30 rooms, with private facilities, have recently been completely refurbished to the highest standard. Set in well-kept gardens, there's also a restaurant, bar and gym.

Marangu *p236*

C Marangu Hotel, 5 km back from Marangu towards Moshi, T027-275 6594, www.maranguhotel.com. Long-established, family-owned and run country-style hotel, warm and friendly atmosphere, self-contained cottages with private baths and showers, hot water, set in 5 ha of gardens offering stunning views of Kilimanjaro, swimming pool, croquet lawn, one of the original operators of Kilimanjaro climbs with over 60 years' experience. Can arrange treks on all the routes. Also has a pretty campsite and will safely look after vehicles for overlanders doing the climb. Partnered with the Kilimanjaro Porters Assistance Project.

D Ashanti Lodge, close to the Marangu Gate, T027-275 6443, www.ashanti-lodge.com. Old-style country hotel. Spacious but rather plain rooms with en suite bathrooms, in thatched bungalows in the garden. Bar, restaurant, can organize local cultural tours and safaris. There is ample parking so if in your own vehicle, and climbing Kili, you could negotiate to leave your car here.

D Babylon Lodge, 500 m from the post office on the Jarakea Rd, T027-275 6355, www.babylonlodge.com. Clean and comfortable, sited in well kept gardens, built into the hillside, all 30 slightly small rooms have private facilities, and there's a bar and restaurant with a set 4-course meal each evening and a swimming pool with sun deck.

D Kibo Hotel, about 1 km from Marangu Village towards the park gate, T027-275 1308, www.kibohotel.com. Old German building with 45 old fashioned but adequate rooms, restaurant, bar, swimming pool and fine gardens. Evelyn Waugh stayed here in 1959 and found it "so comfortable" with its "cool verandah". You can also camp here for US$5 and 3 course dinners cost US$16. Climbs can be organized.

F Coffee Tree Campsite, 2 km before the park gate, T027-275 6604, www.coffeetree campsite.com. Grassy lawns for camping (US$8 per person), you can hire 2-man tents for US$8 and they sell beers, soft drinks, firewood and charcoal. Cook for yourself in the kitchen hut or they can provide basic meals with notice. There's also a cabin that sleeps 5 for US$12 per bed with a toilet and guests can use the camper's hot showers and wooden sauna – a godsend after the Kili climb.

❷ Eating

Moshi p234, map p235

¶¶ **El Rancho**, off Lema Rd, Shanty Town, T027-275 5115. Tue-Sun 1230-2300. Northern Indian food, good choice for vegetarians, very authentic and full range of curries, each dish is prepared from scratch so it can take a while. However, there are plenty of diversions in the garden to keep you occupied, including table football, a crazy golf course and a pool table. There's a full bar with 16 brands of whisky.

¶¶ **Golden Shower**, 2 km from Moshi on the road to Dar, T027-275 1990. Daily 1200-1500, 1700-2300. The owner, John Bennet, is the son of the legendary character 'Chagga' Bennet, ex-First World War Royal Flying Corps ace, and economic adviser to the former Kilimanjaro Native Co-operative Union. He is a wonderful source of local information. Excellent restaurant serving continental food and friendly bar. Disco at weekends that goes on until the early hours. You can also camp here.

¶¶ **Indoitaliano**, New St, T027-275 2195. Daily 1200-2230. A wide selection of Indian and Italian food with main dishes for around US$6, the outside veranda is popular and

serves a good choice of wine, including a bottle of Moet for US$80 a pop.

¶¶ **Panda**, off Lema Rd, Shanty Town, just south of the Impala Hotel, T0744-838193 (mob). Daily 1200-1500, 1800-2200. Good Chinese food served by ladies in Chinese clothes, tables set up in a house, very good seafood, including king size prawns and sizzling dishes.

¶ **Aroma Coffee House**, Boma Rd, T027-275 134. Daily 0800-2100. Pleasant café selling a good range of coffee from the region, including creamy cappuccinos and lattes and iced coffee, plus snacks and ice cream.

¶ **Chrisburger**, Kibo Rd, close to the clock tower, T027-275 0419. Mon-Sat 0830-1630, Sat 0830-1400. Has a small veranda at the front and sells cold drinks and snacks, including burgers and very good fruit juice and sometimes home-made soup, closes mid-afternoon though.

¶ **Coffee Shop**, Hill St, near the bus station, T027-275 2707. Mon-Fri 0800-2000, Sat 0800-1630. Lovely food using fresh produce from Irente Farm in Lushoto – cakes, home-made jam, cheese and tea. Healthy breakfasts, and light meals include omelettes, carrot and lentil soup and quiche. Try the cheese platter with apple, pickle and brown bread. Garden to sit in at the back. Outlet of St Margaret's Anglican Church. It also sells Tanzanian coffee beans.

¶ **Deli Chez**, Hill St, T027-275 1144. Daily 1000-2200. Popular white tiled restaurant with a/c and decorated with mirrors and plants. Comprehensive menu of good Indian and Chinese food, plus lighter meals and shakes and ice cream desserts. No alcohol though.

¶ **Milan's**, Double Rd, T027-275 1841. Daily 0830-2300. With bright pink walls, clean plastic tables and a TV in the corner, this serves a large range of vegetarian Indian dishes and snacks like bhajis and samosas from the takeaway counter.

¶ **Tanzania Coffee Lounge**, Chagga St, opposite the fruit and vegetable market, T027-275 1006. Mon-Sat 0800-2000,

Kilimanjaro Marathon

Now in its fifth year, a fairly new event in Moshi is the Kilimanjaro Marathon, held in March and run on a 42.2 km route around the town and in the foothills of the mountain. The route is at an altitude of 800 to 1100 m and passes along a stretch of the Moshi-Dar road before crossing a countryside of banana plantations and smallholder farms, with Africa's highest mountain as a backdrop. It's open to professionals, many of which are famed Tanzanian, Kenyan and Ethiopian long-distance runners, as well as amateurs. In 2009 it attracted some 1500 for the full- and half-marathon and 5 km fun run.

A new event started in 2009 is the Kili(man)jaro Adventure Challenge, which is a seven-day climb to the top of Kili, a two-day mountain bike race around the mountain, followed by the marathon. Visit www.kilimanjaromarathon.com.

Sun 0800-1800. A Western-style café serving good coffees, milkshakes, juices, muffins, bagels, waffles and cakes. Also has 8 terminals for high speed internet and is consistently popular with travellers.

▲ Activities and tours

Moshi *p234, map p235*
Tour operators

It is cheaper to book tours for Kilimanjaro from Moshi than it is from either Arusha or Marangu. Like booking an organized safari in Arusha for the game parks (see box, page 279) give yourself a day or 2 in Moshi to talk to a couple of the tour operators that arrange Kilimanjaro climbs. Find one that you like, does not pressure you too much, and accepts the method of payment of your choice. Ignore the touts on the street. You may find if it is quiet that the tour companies will get together and put clients on the same tour to make up numbers. All tour operators below offer Kili climbs on most of the routes, some offer additional tours. This is a far from comprehensive list. A good place to start looking for a registered tour operator is on the Kilimanjaro Association of Tour Operator's website (www.kiato.or.tz). Some of the hotels also organize climbs and packages usually include a night's accommodation before and after the climb. The **Keys** (see page 238)

and **Marangu Hotel** (see page 239) have long established reputations. Also consider **Hoopoe Safaris** (see page 281, and **Tropical Trails** (see page 283) in Arusha.

Akaro Tours Co Ltd, ground floor of NSSF House on Old Moshi Rd, T027-275 2986, www.akarotours.com. Kilimanjaro climbs and northern circuit tours.

Kilimanjaro Crown Birds Agency, based in the **Kindoroka**, see page 238, T027-275 1162, www.kilicrown.com. Offers a good, friendly service, and offers Kili climbs, Mt Meru climbs and road safaris to the parks.

Kilimanjaro Serengeti Tours & Travel Ltd, Old CCM Building, Mawenzi Rd, T027-275 1287, www.kilimanjaroserengeti.com. All Kili routes plus a day trip to Mandara Hut and back.

Kilimanjaro Travel Services Ltd, THB Building, Boma Rd, T027-275 2124, www.kilimanjarotravels-tz.com. Meru and Kilimanjaro climbs, budget camping safaris to Ngorongoro, Serengeti and Manyara.

Mauly Tours & Safaris, Mawenzi Rd, opposite Moshi post office, T027-275 0730, www.mauly-tours.com. Well established operator.

MJ Safaris International, CCM Building, Taifa Rd, T027-275 2017, www.mjsafarisafrica. com. Climbing and trekking and tailor-made safaris to the northern and southern circuit parks.

Moshi Expedition & Mountaineering (MEM), Kaunda St, T027-275 4234, www.memtours.com. A professional company with experience of the lesser used routes.

Shah Tours and Travel, Mawenzi Rd, T027-275 2998, www.kilimanjaro-shah.com. There is also an office at the **Mountain Inn Hotel** (see Sleeping, page 237), where all tours start. A recommended operator with lots of experience.

Snow Cap, CCM Building, Taifa Rd, T027-275 4826, www.snowcap.co.tz. Also has French speaking guides.

Summit Expeditions and Nomadic Experiences, based in Marangu, T027-275 3233, www.nomadicexperience.com. Well regarded company owned by Simon Mtuy who currently holds the fastest ascent-descent record for climbing Kili – 8 hrs 27 mins – and he's been to the top of the mountain more than 300 times. Trekkers stay in cottages on his family farm before and after the climb.

Trans-Kibo Travels Ltd, YMCA Building, T027-275 1754/275 2017, www.transkibo. com. All Kilimanjaro routes, one of the oldest operators in existence, also Meru and Mt Kenya.

Zara Tanzania Adventure, at Springlands Hotel, see page 237, T027-2753581, www. zara.co.tz, www.kilimanjaro.co.tz. Kilimanjaro climb US$1172 for 5-day 'Coca-Cola route' or Marangu route, US$1447 for Machame and the Umbwe route, the safari charges are from US$240 per person per day for a tour of Serengeti/Ngorongoro but these drop considerably for 4 or more people, as does the Kili climb. Recommended for groups as prices are very good. There are also discounts of up to US$50 per day in low season (Apr-Jun). Zara takes thousands of people up the mountain each year, recommended as one of Tanzania's best budget operators.

◎ Transport

Moshi *p234, map p235*
Air
Kilimanjaro International Airport
is halfway between Moshi and Arusha, for flight details, see **Arusha** page 284. A taxi between Moshi and the airport should cost around US$40-50 or arrange for one of the tour operators or your hotel to organize a shuttle. **Kilimanjaro Aero Club**, based at Moshi Airport, T027-275 0555, www.kiliman jaroaeroclub.com, can arrange charter flights, sightseeing flights and flying lessons.

Bus and dala-dala
Moshi is 580 km from Dar, 79 km from Arusha and 349 km from Nairobi. Local buses and *dala-dala* to nearby destinations like **Marangu** and **Arusha** cost little more than US$1 and go from the stand just to the south of the main bus stand, which are both on Market St. There are daily buses to and from

MOUNT
KILIMANJARO
Climb to the rooftop of Africa

WWW.KILIMANJARO-SHAH.COM
kilimanjaro@kilinet.co.tz

Dar, US$18 'luxury', US$12 'semi-luxury' and US$9 'ordinary' which take about 7 hrs and stop for 20 mins at one of the roadside restaurants en route. The road has improved considerably. For **Tanga** the bus takes 4-6 hrs and costs US$10. It is possible to get a direct bus to **Mombasa**, cost approximately US$13, 7-8 hrs. These go through the Taveta border, on to **Voi** in Kenya where they join the main road from Nairobi to Mombasa. Take lots of care at the bus stands as pick pocketing is rife and you need to protect your belongings. On arrival its best just to jump straight in a taxi as soon as you get off the bus. The hustlers, who try to get people on to their buses can be particularly annoying too.

Regular *dala-dala* to **Marangu**, 45 mins, US$3. A taxi will cost in the region of US$25, whilst those who organize a climb in Moshi will be transferred to the park gate by their tour operator.

To Kenya There are private shuttle services to **Nairobi** via Arusha and the Namanga border. **Impala Shuttle**, Kibo Rd, T027-275 1786, departs daily for Nairobi at 0630 and 1130, US$40. **Riverside Shuttle**, THB House, T027-275 0093, www.riverside-shuttle.com, departs daily at 0630 and 1100, US$40. **AA Shuttles**, www.aashuttles.com, picks up and drops off at the hotels and leaves Moshi at 1100, US$40, and on request it will pick up/drop off at the Marangu Hotel at 0800, US$70.

Taxi
A taxi to **Marangu** will cost in the region of US$25, whilst those who organize a climb in Moshi will be transferred to the park gate by their tour operator.

❶ Directory

Moshi *p234, map p235*
Banks Standard Chartered Bank on Rindi Lane and opposite the Kindoroko Hotel on Mawenzi Rd, and the **National Bank of Commerce** on the clock tower roundabout both have ATM facilities and will advance money on Visa and MasterCard. **Internet** There are several places around Moshi to check email. These include **Dot Café**, Rengua Rd; **Duma** and **Fahari**, both on Hill St, next door to the Coffee Shop; and **Tanzania Coffee Lounge** near the market (page 240). **Medical services** Moshi is home to what is said to be the best hospital in Tanzania, the **Kilimanjaro Christian Medical Centre (KCMC)**, which is 6 km out of town beyond Shantytown, T027-275 4377, www.kcmc.ac.tz. **Mawenzi Moshi District Hospital**, in town. **Police** Market St, T027-275 5055. **Post office** In the centre of town near the clock tower. **Courier services**, DHL, Kahawa House on the clock tower roundabout, T027-275 4030, www.dhl.com. **Telephone** International calls can be made from the post office.

Kilimanjaro National Park

→ *Colour map 1, A5.*
In The Snows of Kilimanjaro, *Ernest Hemingway described the mountain: "as wide as all the world, great, high, and unbelievably white in the sun, was the square top of Kilimanjaro". It is one of the most impressive sights in Africa, visible from as far away as Tsavo National Park in Kenya. Just 80 km east of the eastern branch of the Rift Valley, it is Africa's highest mountain with snow-capped peaks rising from a relatively flat plain, the largest freestanding mountain worldwide, measuring 80 x 40 km and one of earth's highest dormant volcanoes. At lower altitudes, the mountain is covered in lush rainforest, which gives way to scrub – there is no bamboo zone on Kilimanjaro – followed by alpine moorland until you get to the icefields. Try to see it in the early morning before the clouds mask it. Despite its altitude even inexperienced climbers can climb it, provided they are reasonably fit and allow themselves sufficient time to acclimatize to the elevation.*

Ins and outs

Getting there
There are a number of ways of getting to Mount Kilimanjaro. The easiest is to fly to **Kilimanjaro International Airport** – during your approach you will get a magnificent view of the mountain if it is not covered by cloud. The park entrance is about 90 km from the airport, which takes about 1½ hours by road. Alternatively by road go to Moshi and from there to Marangu, the village at the park entrance at the base of the mountain. Many *dala-dala* go from Moshi to Marangu each day; they take 45 minutes and cost US$2. It is also cheap and easy to get to Kilimanjaro from Kenya by taking a shuttle. Alternatively, for the Machame Trail, there are regular *dala-dala* from the bus stand in Moshi the 30 km to the village of Machame taking about an hour and again cost around US$2.

Climate
Kilimanjaro can be climbed throughout the year but it is worth avoiding the two rainy seasons (late Mar to mid-May and October to the beginning of December) when the routes become slippery. The best time to visit is January-February and September-October when there is usually no cloud.

Information
Anyone planning to climb Mount Kilimanjaro is advised to buy the *Trekking Guide to Africa's Highest Mountain* by Henry Steadman (Trailblazer Guides), which is full of practical information and covers preparing and equipping for the climb, much of the book's information is available on Henry's website, www.climbmountkilimanjaro.com; *Kilimanjaro & East Africa; a Climbing and Trekking Guide* by Cameron M Burns (Mountaineers Books) is also a useful guidebook. There are plenty of maps on the market, many of which now list GPS coordinates, and other locally produced maps and coffee-table books are available in both Moshi and Arusha. The tour operators that offer climbs have comprehensive information about the climbs on their websites and visit Tanzania National Parks, www.tanzaniaparks.com.

Altitude sickness

Altitude sickness is often a problem while climbing Kilimanjaro. If you know you are susceptible to it you are advised not to attempt the climb. Symptoms include bad headache, nausea, vomiting and severe fatigue. It can be avoided by ascending slowly – if at all possible, spend an extra day half-way up to help your body acclimatize. Mountain sickness symptoms can often be alleviated by descending to a lower altitude. The drug Diamox helps if taken before the ascent. Other more serious conditions include acute pulmonary oedema and/or cerebral oedema. In the former, the sufferer becomes breathless, turns blue in the face and coughs up froth. The latter is even more serious – symptoms are intense headache, hallucinations, confusion and disorientation and staggering gait. It is caused by the accumulation of fluid on the brain and can cause death or serious brain damage. If either of these conditions are suspected the sufferer should immediately be taken down to a lower altitude to receive medical care. It is, however, normal to feel breathless and fatigued at high altitudes and these are not always precursors to the more serious conditions.

Kilimanjaro National Park

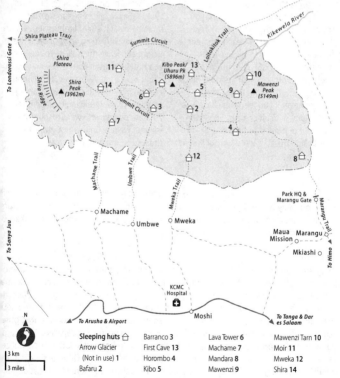

Sleeping huts ⌂	Barranco 3	Lava Tower 6	Mawenzi Tarn 10
Arrow Glacier	First Cave 13	Machame 7	Moir 11
(Not in use) 1	Horombo 4	Mandara 8	Mweka 12
Bafaru 2	Kibo 5	Mawenzi 9	Shira 14

Tipping on Kilimanjaro

On the last day of the tour your guide will request a tip for himself and his cook and porters. Tipping is more or less mandatory, as a way of supplementing the low incomes of people who essentially have a remarkably physically demanding job. Porters in particular are very poorly paid (as little as US$8 a day) and cannot always afford the right equipment/clothes needed on the mountain. A good tour operator will have a fair tipping procedure in place or at least will be able to give advice. Generally, advice is that one method that is popular with groups is for everybody to contribute 10% of the total cost of their trek towards tips. So if you paid US$1200 for your trek, you should pay US$120 into the tip kitty. Another approach is for each member of the trekking staff to receive a set amount; roughly US$5 per porter per day, US$7 for the cook or assistant guide per day, and US$10 for the guide per day. However if you feel your climb was particularly difficult or a certain person went out of his way to help you, or, on the flipside the staff were surly or weren't as helpful as they should have been, then this should reflect in the tipping. If at all possible, give tips out to the trekking team individually, and don't give a lump sum to the guide as the money may not always go to who it's intended for. You may want to have the right denomination US$/TSh notes to be able to do this. For more information about tipping on Kilimanjaro (and why you should do it) visit the website for the Kilimanjaro Porters Assistance Project; www.kili porters.org. Something else to consider, is that you won't need much 'stuff' on the mountain – you'll be wearing most of it anyway – and porters are limited to 15 kg of trekkers' packs and 5 kg of their own things. Kili is a hard slog for anyone – imagine what it's like climbing it over and over again with 20 kg on your back? Keep it light and leave the bulk of your luggage at a hotel. Finally, if you're never going to climb a big mountain again, think about making gifts of your specialist clothing and gear to your trekking team; it is after all these people who were responsible for your welfare on the mountain and (hopefully) got you to the top.

Guides

A guide is compulsory on all routes and it essential to go with a tour operator who wi supply not only guides but porters and relevant equipment (see Moshi tour operators page 241). Marangu is the usual route for tourists and only fit and experienced hikers o climbers should use the other routes.

Equipment

Being well equipped will increase your chances of reaching the summit. In particular b sure you have a warm sleeping bag, insulating mat, warm rainproof jacket, therma underwear, gloves, wool hat, sunglasses or snow goggles, sun cream, large water bottl and first-aid kit. Some of these are available to buy or hire in Moshi from the tou operators; at the park gate for example is a shop that sells thick socks amongst othe items. However, the quality is variable and it is best to come fully prepared. As regard clothing, it is important to wear layers as they provide better insulation than bulkie items, and sturdy waterproof hiking boots should be well worn-in. Other essential item include a small daypack for things you'll need during the day – porters carry your mai pack but tend to go on ahead by some distance – a head torch and spare batteries (essential for the final midnight ascent), toilet roll, and you may want to consider a light weight trekking pole. Energy snacks are also a good idea.

Costs

Climbing Mount Kilimanjaro is an expensive business, though everyone who makes it to the summit agrees that it is well worth it. The costs are much higher than those in the Alps or the Andes. Park fees alone, charged by Tanzania National Parks, are US$60 per person per 24 hours, camping or hut fees US$50 per person per day (whether you use the huts or not), a rescue fee insurance of US$20 per person, and guides at US$20 per day, cooks US$15 per day and porters US$10 per day per 15 kg of luggage. These are the set fees that the tour operator must pay on your behalf to Tanzania National Parks and can amount to over US$900 for a six-day trip, though while everyone needs a porter, costs come down if a group are sharing a guide and cook. On top of this, other costs for the tour operators include the salaries of the guides and porters, the additional 20% VAT on the total invoice, 10% commission if booking through a third party travel agent, transport to the start of the trail, food and the costs of equipment. The absolute cheapest you will probably manage to do it for will be around US$1175 for the five-day Marangu Route. An extra day on this route (recommended) is about US$200 per person. The other more technical or longer climbs are US$1400 or more.

Background

Formation

Kilimanjaro was formed about 1 million years ago by a series of volcanic movements along the Great Rift Valley. Until this point, the area was a flat plain at about 600-900 m above sea level. About 750,000 years ago volcanic activity forced three points above 4800 m – Shira, Kibo and Mawenzi. Some 250,000 years later Shira became inactive and collapsed into itself forming the crater. Kibo and Mawenzi continued their volcanic activity and it was their lava flow that forms the 11-km saddle between the two peaks. When Mawenzi died out, its northeast wall collapsed in a huge explosion creating a massive gorge. The last major eruptions occurred about 200 years ago and Kibo now lies dormant but not extinct. Although Kibo appears to be a snow-clad dome, it contains a caldera 2.5 km across and 180 m deep at the deepest point in the south. Within the depression is an inner ash cone that rises to within 60 m of the summit height and is evidence of former volcanic activity. On the southern slopes the glaciers reach down to about 4200 m, while on the north slopes they only descend a little below the summit.

Vegetation and wildlife

Kilimanjaro has well-defined altitudinal vegetation zones. From the base to the summit these are: plateau, semi-arid scrub; cultivated, well-watered southern slopes; dense cloud forest; open moorland; alpine desert; moss and lichen. The lower slopes are home to elephant, rhino, buffalo, leopard, monkey and eland. Birdlife includes the enormous lammergeyer, the scarlet-tufted malachite sunbird as well as various species of starlings, sunbirds, the silvery-cheeked hornbill and the rufous-breasted sparrowhawk.

The meaning of Kilimanjaro

Since the earliest explorers visited East Africa, people have been intrigued by the name Kilimanjaro and its meaning. The Chagga people do not have a name for the whole mountain, just the two peaks: *Kibo* (or kipoo) means 'spotted' and refers to the rock that can be seen standing out against the snow on this peak; *Mawenzi* (or Kimawenze) means 'having a broken top' and again describes its appearance.

Most theories as to the origin of the name Kilimanjaro for the whole mountain break the word down into two elements: *kilima* and *njaro*. In Swahili the word for mountain is *mlima* while *kilima* means hill – so it is possible that an early European visitor incorrectly used *kilima* because of the analogy to the two Chagga words Kibo and Kimawenzi.

The explorer Krapf said that the Swahili of the coast knew it as Kilimanjaro 'mountain of greatness', but he does not explain why. He also suggests it could mean 'mountain of caravans' (*kilima* = mountain, *jaro* = caravans), but while *kilima* is a Swahili word, *jaro* is a Chagga word. Other observers have suggested that *njaro* once meant 'whiteness' and therefore this was the 'mountain of whiteness'. Alternatively, *njaro* could be the name of an evil spirit, or a demon. The first-known European to climb Mount Kilimanjaro mentions 'Njaro, the guardian spirit of the mountain' and there are many stories in Chagga folklore about spirits living here – though there is no evidence of a spirit called Njaro, either from the Chagga or from the coastal peoples.

Another explanation suggests that the mountain was known as 'mountain of water', because of the Masai word *njore* for springs or water and because all the rivers in the area rose from here. However, this theory does not explain the use of the Swahili word for 'hill' rather than 'mountain', and also assumes that a Swahili word and a Masai word have been put together.

The final explanation is from a Kichagga term *kilelema* meaning that 'which has become difficult or impossible' or 'which has defeated'. Njaro can be derived from the Kichagga words *njaare*, a bird, or else *jyaro*, a caravan. Thus the mountain became *kilemanjaare*, *kilemajyaro* or *kilelemanjaare*, meaning that which defeats or is impossible for the bird or the caravan. This theory has the advantage of being composed entirely of Chagga elements.

It seems possible either that this was the name given to the mountain by the Chagga themselves, or by people passing through the area, who heard the Chagga say *kilemanjaare* or *kile-majyaro*, meaning that the mountain was impossible to climb. Over time the name was standardized to Kilimanjaro.

History

When, in 1848, the first reports by the German missionary Johannes Rebmann of a snow-capped mountain on the equator arrived in Europe, the idea was ridiculed by the Royal Geographical Society of Britain. In 1889 the report was confirmed by the German geographer Hans Meyer and the Austrian alpine mountaineer Ludwig Purtscheller, who climbed Kibo and managed to reach the snows on Kilimanjaro's summit. At the centenary of this climb in 1989, the Tanzanian guide was still alive and 115 years old. Mawenzi was first climbed by the German Fritz Klute in 1912.

The mountain was originally in a part of British East Africa (now Kenya). However, the mountain was 'given' by Queen Victoria as a gift to her cousin, and so the border was moved and the mountain included within German Tanganyika. This is why if you look at a map of the border between Tanzania and Kenya, Tanzania juts into Kenya to include Kilimanjaro on the otherwise dead straight border drawn up by the colonialists. The national park was established in 1973 and covers an area of 756 sq km.

Routes up the mountain

About 22,000 climbers attempt to get to the top of Kilimanjaro each year. The altitude at Marangu Gate is 1829 m and at Kibo Peak 5895 m – that's a long way up. Officially anyone aged over 12 may attempt the climb. The youngest person to climb the mountain was a 10 year old, while the oldest was 79. However, it is not that easy and estimates of the number of people who attempt the climb and do not make it to the top vary from 20-50%. The important things to remember are to come prepared and to take it slowly – if you have the chance, spend an extra day half-way up to give you the chance to acclimatize.

There are a number of different trails. The most popular is the Marangu trail, which is the recommended route for older persons or younger people who are not in peak physical condition. The climbing tends to be much more strenuous than anticipated, which when combined with lower oxygen levels accounts for the 20-50% failure rate to reach the summit.

The Marangu trail is the only one that uses hutted dorm accommodation. On the other routes, even though the campsites are called huts this actually refers to the green shacks. Some of these have fallen into disuse or are usually inhabited by the park rangers on the lower slopes, they are also sometimes used by the guides and porters. Trekkers are accommodated in tents carried and set up by the porters.

Marangu trail

This is probably the least scenic of the routes but by being the gentlest climb and by having a crop of hotels at the beginning in Marangu and hutted accommodation on the way up, this is the most popular.

Day 1 The national park gate (1830 m) is about 8 km from the **Kibo Hotel**. This is as far as vehicles are allowed. From here to the first night's stop at **Mandara Hut** (2700 m) is a walk of three to four hours. It is through *shambas* – small farms growing coffee – as well as some lush rainforest, and is an enjoyable walk although it can be quite muddy. On the walk you can admire the moss and lichens and the vines and flowers, including orchids. There is an alternative forest trail, which branches left from the main track a few minutes after the gate and follows the side of a stream. It is a little slower than the main track, which it rejoins after about three hours. The Mandara Hut, near the Maundi Crater, is actually a group of A-frame huts that can sleep about 60 people. Mattresses, solar lighting and stoves are provided but nothing else. The complex was built by the Norwegians as part of an aid programme. There is piped water, flushing toilets and firewood available, and a dining area in the main cabin.

Day 2 The second day will start off as a steep walk through the last of the rainforest and out into tussock grassland, giant heather and then on to the moorlands, crossing several ravines on the way. There are occasional clearings through which you will get wonderful views of Mawenzi and Moshi far below. You can also enjoy the views by making a short detour up to the rim of Maundi Crater. You will also probably see some of the exceptional vegetation that is found on Kilimanjaro, including the giant lobelia, Kilimanjaro's

The snow sepulchre of King Solomon

Legend has it that the last military adventure of King Solomon was an expedition down the eastern side of Africa. Exhausted by his battles the aged king was trekking home with his army when they passed the snow-covered Mount Kilimanjaro. Solomon decided this was to be his resting place. The next day he was carried by bearers until they reached the snows. As they steadily trudged up to the summit they saw a cave glittering in the sunlight, frost sparkling in the interior, icicles hanging down to close off the entrance. As they watched, two icicles, warmed by the sun, crashed to the ground. They carried the old king inside and placed him on his throne, wrapped in his robes, facing out down the mountain. Solomon raised a frail hand to bid farewell. The bearers left with heavy hearts. The weather began to change and there was a gentle fall of snow. As they looked back they saw that icicles had reformed over the entrance.

'everlasting flowers' and other uncommon alpine plants. The walk to **Horombo Hut** (3720 m) is about 14 km with an altitude gain of about 1000 m and will take you five to seven hours. This hut is again a collection of huts that can accommodate up to 120 people. There are flushing toilets and plenty of water but firewood is scarce. Some people spend an extra day here to help get acclimatized and if you are doing this there are a number of short walks in the area but remember to move slowly, drink plenty of water and get lots of sleep. It is a very good idea to spend the extra day here – but there is the extra cost to be considered.

Day 3/4 On the next day of walking you will climb to the **Kibo Hut** (4703 m), which is 13 km from Horombo. As you climb, the vegetation thins to grass and heather and eventually to bare scree. You will feel the air thinning and it is at this altitude that altitude sickness may kick in. The most direct route is the right fork from Horombo Hut. It is stony and eroded, a climb of six-seven hours up the valley behind the huts, past **Last Water** and on to the **saddle**. This is the wide, fairly flat, U-shaped desert between the two peaks of Mawenzi and Kibo and from here you will get some awe-inspiring views of the mountain. After **Zebra Rocks** and at the beginning of the saddle, the track forks. To the right, about three hours from Horombo Hut, is Mawenzi Hut and to the left across the saddle is Kibo Hut. The left fork from Horombo Hut is gentler, and comes out on to the saddle 1 km from Kibo Hut. Kibo Hut is where the porters stay and from here on you should just take the absolute bare essentials with you. It is a good idea to bring some biscuits or chocolate for the final ascent to the peak, as a lunch pack is not always provided. Mawenzi Hut sleeps about 60 people. There is a stone-built main block with a small dining room and several dormitory rooms with bunks and mattresses. There is no vegetation in the area and no water unless there has been snow recently, so it has to be carried up from Last Water. However, the camp does sell bottled water and soft drinks but they are understandably expensive. Some people decide to try and get as much sleep as possible before the early start, while others decide not to sleep at all. You are unlikely to sleep very well because of the altitude and the temperatures anyway.

Day 4/5 On the final day of the climb, in order to be at the summit at sunrise, and before the cloud comes down, you will have to get up at about midnight. One advantage of beginning at this time is that if you saw what you were about to attempt you would probably give up before you had even begun. You can expect to feel pretty awful during this final five-hour ascent and many climbers are physically sick. You may find that this climb is extremely slippery and hard going. The first part of the climb is over an uneven trail to **Hans Meyer Cave**. As the sun rises you will reach **Gillman's Point** (5680 m) – it is a wonderful sight. From here you have to decide whether you want to keep going another couple of hours to get to **Kibo Peak** (5896 m). The walk around the crater rim to Kibo Peak is only an extra 200 m but at this altitude it is a strenuous 200 m. At the peak there is a fair amount of litter left by previous climbers. You will return to **Horombo Hut** the same day and the next day (**Day 5/6**) return to Marangu where you will be presented with a certificate.

Umbwe trail

Note This route is presently closed because of four fatalities in 2005 after a serious rock fall but check locally. The climb is hard, short and steep but is a wonderfully scenic route to take to reach **Uhuru Peak**. However, it is not recommended for inexperienced climbers. Many climbers descend this way after climbing up by a different route. To get to the start of the trail take the turning off the Arusha road about 2 km down on the right. From there it's 14 km down the Lyamungu Road, right at the T-junction towards Mango and soon after crossing the Sere River you get to **Umbwe** Village (1400 m).

Day 1 ① *Umbwe to Bivouac I, 4-6 hrs' walk.* From the mission the former forestry track continues through rainforest for about 3 km up to **Kifuni Village**. From there it's another 6 km before you get to the start of the trail proper. There is a sign here and the trail branches to the left and climbs quite steeply through the forest along the ridge between the Lonzo River to the west and Umbwe River to the east. In several places it is necessary to use branches to pull yourself up. You will reach the first shelter, a cave, about six to eight hours' walk from Umbwe. This is **Bivouac I** (2940 m), an all-weather rock shelter formed from the rock overhangs. It will shelter about six or seven people. There is firewood nearby and a spring about 15 m below under a rock face.

If you made an early start and are fit and keen you can continue on to Bivouac II on the same day. However, most climbers take an overnight break here, camping in the forest caves.

Day 2 ① *Bivouac I to Barranco Hut, 5 km, 4-5 hrs' walk.* From the caves, continue up, past the moorland and along the ridge. It is a steep walk with deep valleys on each side of the ridge and this walk is magnificent with the strange 'Old Man's Beard' – a type of moss – covering most of the vegetation. The second set of caves is **Bivouac II** (3800 m), three to four hours from Bivouac I. There are two caves – one about five minutes further down the track – and this is where you will camp. There is a spring down the ravine about 15 minutes to the west.

From the second set of caves the path continues less steeply up the ridge beyond the tree line before reaching **Barranco** or **Umbwe Hut** (3900 m). Barranco Hut is about five hours away from the first caves or two hours from Bivouac II. The path is well marked. About 200 m beyond the hut is a rock overhang, which can be used for camping. There is one pit latrine, water is available about 250 m to the east and firewood is available in the area. Some people may choose to spend an extra day at Barranco Hut to acclimatize to the altitude.

Day 3/4 ① *Barranco Hut to Lava Tower Hut, 3-4 hrs' walk.* Just before reaching Barranco Hut the path splits in two. To the left, the path goes west towards Shira Hut (five to six hours) and the northern circuit, or you can climb the west lateral ridge to the **Arrow Glacier Hut** (now defunct after it was buried in an avalanche) towards the **Lava Tower Hut** (4600 m) about three to four hours away. Up this path the vegetation thins before disappearing completely on reaching the scree slopes. The campsite at Lava Tower Hut is very barren and there is no shelter so you need to be prepared for the extreme cold. There are no toilets, but water is available in a nearby stream.

Day 4/5 ① *Lava Tower Hut to Uhuru Peak, 4-6 hrs' walk.* Having spent the night at Lava Tower Hut you will want to leave very early for the final ascent. Head torches are imperative and if there is no moonlight the walk can be quite difficult. Climb up between **Arrow Glacier** (which may have disappeared completely if you are there towards the end of the dry season) and **Little Breach Glacier** until you get to a few small cliffs. At this stage the course follows the Western Breach summit route and turns to the right heading for the lowest part of the crater rim that you can see. This part of the walk is really steep on scree and snow, and parts of it are quite a scramble. From December to February, crampons and ice axes are recommended. Having reached the crater floor, cross the **Furtwangler Glacier** snout to a steep gully that reaches the summit plateau about another 500 m west of **Uhuru Peak** (5895 m), returning to **Mweka Hut**, among the giant heathers, for an overnight stop.

Day 5/6 ① *Descent from Mweka Hut to Mweka Gate, 14 km, 5-7 hrs' walk.* The return journey can be achieved in approximately half the ascending time.

Umbwe trail – alternative route
Day 3/4 ① *Barranco Hut to Bafaru Hut, 5 km, 4-5 hrs' walk.* The route is well marked at lower levels but not at higher altitudes. If you take the path to the right from **Barranco Hut** (eastwards on the southern circuit) you will cross one small stream and then another larger one as you contour the mountain to join the **Mweka trail**. The path then climbs steeply through a gap in the **West Breach**. From here you can turn left to join the routes over the south glaciers. Alternatively, continue along the marked path across screes, ridges and a valley until you reach the **Karangu Campsite**, which is a further two to three hours on from the top of the Breach. A further couple of hours up the **Karangu valley** (4000 m) will come out at the **Mweka-Barafu Hut** path. If you go left down along this you will get to the **Barafu Hut** after 1-1½ hours. If you go straight on for about three hours you will join the Marangu trail just above the **Horombo Hut**.

Day 4/5 ① *Barafu Hut to Uhuru Peak to Mweka Hut, 5-6 hrs' walk to crater rim plus another hour to Uhuru Peak.* Parties heading for the summit set off around midnight to 0100, reaching the crater at Stella Point. If the weather conditions are favourable, **Uhuru Peak** (5895 m) is normally reached by first light. From here it is often possible to see the summit of Mount Meru to the west. Descend to **Mweka Hut** for an overnight stop.

Day 5/6 ① *Descent from Mweka Hut to Mweka Gate, 14 km, 5-7 hrs' walk.*

Machame trail
This trail is considered by some to be the most attractive of the routes up Kilimanjaro. It is between Umbwe trail and Shira trail and joins the latter route at Shira Hut. The turn-off to the trail and the village of Machame is to the west of Umbwe off the main Arusha–Moshi road.

Day 1 From the village to the first huts takes about nine hours so be sure to start early. Take the track through the *shambas* and the forest to the park entrance (about 4 km), from where you will see a clear track that climbs gently through the forest and along a ridge that is between the Weru Weru and Makoa streams. It is about 7 km to the edge of the forest, and then four to five hours up to the **Machame Huts** (3000 m), where you camp. There are pit latrines and plenty of water down in the valley below the huts and firewood available close by.

Day 2 From the Machame Huts go across the valley, over a stream, then up a steep ridge for three to four hours. The path then goes west and drops into the river gorge before climbing more gradually up the other side and on to the moorland of the Shira Plateau to join the Shira Plateau trail near the **Shira Hut** (3800 m). This takes about five hours. From the Shira Plateau you will get some magnificent views of Kibo Peak and the Western Breach. The area is home to a variety of game including buffalo. The campsite at the Shira Hut is used by people on the Shira Plateau trail as well as those on the Machame trail. There is plenty of water available 50 m to the north and firewood nearby, but no toilets.

Day 3 onwards From here there are a number of choices. You can go on to the **Barranco Hut** (five to six hours, 3900 m) or the **Lava Tower Hut** (four hours, 4600 m). The path to **Arrow Glacier Hut** is well marked. The ascent includes scrambling over scree, rocks and snow fields – tough at times and probably only suited to experienced hikers. It goes east from Shira Hut until it reaches a junction where the North Circuit route leads off to the left. The path continues east, crossing a wide valley before turning southeast towards the Lava Tower. Shortly before the tower a route goes off to the right to Barranco Hut and the South Circuit route. To the left the path goes to Arrow Glacier Hut and the Western Breach.

Shira Plateau trail

This route needs a 4WD vehicle and so for this reason is little used. The road can be impassible during wet periods. However, if you do have access to such a vehicle and are acclimatized you can get to the **Arrow Glacier Hut** in one day.

The drive is a complex one and you may need to stop and ask the way frequently. Pass through West Kilimanjaro, drive for 5 km and turn right. At 13 km you will pass a small trading centre on the left. At 16 km you will cross a stream followed by a hard left. At 21 km you will enter a coniferous forest which soon becomes a natural forest. The plateau rim is reached at 39 km. Here the track continues upwards gently and crosses the plateau to the roadhead at 55 km. Just before the roadhead, about 19 km from **Londorossi Gate**, is a rock shelter. This site is suitable for camping and there is a stream nearby. From the roadhead you will have to walk. It is about 1½ hours to **Shira Hut** (3800 m). From here you continue east to join the Umbwe trail to the **Lava Tower Hut**. The walk is fairly gentle and has magnificent views.

Mweka trail

This trail is the most direct route up the mountain. It is the steepest and the fastest. It begins at Mweka Village, 13 km north of Moshi.

Day 1 The first day's walk takes six to eight hours. The trail follows an old logging road, which you can drive up in good weather, through the *shambas* and the forest, for about 5 km. It is a slippery track that deteriorates into a rough path after a couple of hours.

From here it is about 6 km up a ridge to the **Mweka Huts** (3100 m) where you camp, which are some 500 m beyond the tree line in the giant heather zone. Water is available nearby from a stream in a small valley below the huts five minutes to the southeast and there is plenty of firewood. There are no toilets.

Day 2 From the Mweka Huts follow the ridge east of the Msoo River through heathland, open tussock grassland and then on through alpine desert to the **Barafu Huts** (4400 m), a walk of six to eight hours. There are no toilets, and no water or firewood available – you will need to bring it up from Mweka Huts.

Day 3 From the Barafu Huts the final ascent on a ridge between **Rebmann** and **Ratzel** glaciers takes about six hours up to the rim of the crater between **Stella** and **Hans Meyer Points**. From here it is a further hour to **Uhuru Peak**. At the lower levels the path is clearly marked, but it becomes obscured further up. It is steep, being the most direct non-technical route. Although specialized climbing equipment is not needed, be prepared for a scramble. To catch the sunrise you will have to set off no later than 0200 from Barafu Huts. You return to the huts the same day, and (**Day 4**) make the final descent the next day.

Loitokitok trail

This, and the Shira Plateau trail, both come in from the north unlike the other trails. It used to start on the Kenya border and was known as the Rongai trail (and is still today confusingly referred to as that) but the start has been shifted eastward to start in Tanzania from the village of Loitokitok and has been renamed. You register at the Marangu Gate and then operators transfer you to the village and the trail head which takes about 2½ hours.

The first part of the trail crosses maize fields and then a pine plantation and is not very steep. Beyond is heather and moorlands until you reach First Cave (2600 m) where you camp. It is a total of approximately five to six hours or 8 km to the caves from the trail head.

From these caves follow the path that heads towards a point just to the right of the lowest point on the saddle. You will pass **Bread Rock** after about 1½ hours. The track then divides. To the right is the **Outward Bound Hut** that you will almost certainly find locked. The path continues upwards to the saddle towards the **Kibo Huts** – a climb of three to four hours. To the left another path crosses towards the **Mawenzi Hut**.

The Summit Circuit

A route around the base of Kibo, the Summit Circuit links Horombo, Barranco, Shira and Moir Huts. The southern section of the circuit is most spectacular, as it cuts across moorland, in and out of valleys and under the southern glaciers.

Contents

Footprint features

At a glance

◉ **Getting around** The centre's easily walkable (but not at night), and *dala-dalas*, buses and taxis are all over the town. Tour operators can help you trek Mt Meru or explore Arusha National Park.

◉ **Time required** 1-2 days to sort out safari arrangements and see the town, another day for a trip around the National Park, 3 days to climb Mt Meru and 1 day to recover.

☀ **Weather** Mostly warm and sunny, but Mt Meru can be tough in the rainy season from end of Mar-May and the summit, at over 4000 m, can be cold at any time of year.

✗ **When not to go** The city is accessible all year. You may want to avoid Mt Meru in rainy season, when the climb can hard-going, slippery and sometimes dangerous.

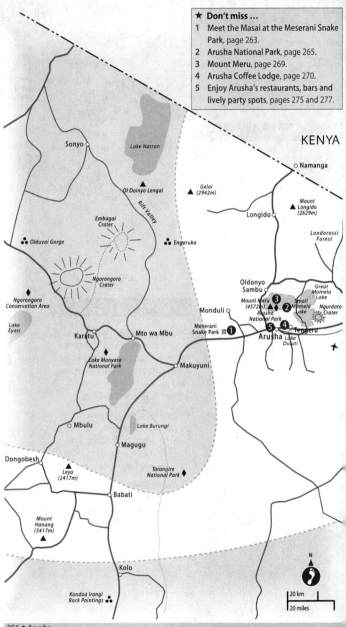

★ **Don't miss ...**
1 Meet the Masai at the Meserani Snake Park, page 263.
2 Arusha National Park, page 265.
3 Mount Meru, page 269.
4 Arusha Coffee Lodge, page 270.
5 Enjoy Arusha's restaurants, bars and lively party spots, pages 275 and 277.

KENYA

Sonyo

Namanga

Lake Natron

Ol Doinyo Lengai

Gelai (2942m)

Mount Longido (2629m)

Longido

Rift Valley

Embagai Crater

Londorossi Forest

Engaruka

Olduvai Gorge

Ngorongoro Crater

Oldonyo Sambu

Great Momela Lake

Ngorongoro Conservation Area

Mount Meru (4572m)

Small Momela Lake

Ngurdoto Crater

Monduli

Arusha National Park

Lake Eyasi

Karatu

Mto wa Mbu

Meserani Snake Park

1

5 4 Tengeru

Arusha Lake Duluti

Lake Manyara National Park

Makuyuni

Mbulu

Lake Burungi

Magugu

Dongobesh

Leya (2417m)

Tarangire National Park

Babati

Mount Hanang (3417m)

Kolo

Kondoa Irangi Rock Paintings

N

20 km
20 miles

In the northern highlands of Tanzania, beneath the twin peaks of Mount Meru and Mount Kilimanjaro, Arusha is the safari capital of the country. It is a pleasant town set at an altitude of 1380 m above sea level, and is the halfway point between Cairo and Cape Town (the actual point is in a field 20 km or so to the south of town). The drive up from Dar es Salaam to Arusha passes through the semi-arid grass plains, gradually becoming greener, more cultivated and more heavily populated; Mount Meru, in the Arusha National Park appears on the right with its fertile, cultivated slopes. Built by the Germans as a centre of colonial administration in the early 20th century, Arusha was a sleepy town with a garrison stationed at the old boma and a few shops around a grassy roundabout. But from its backwater status amidst the farmlands and plantations of northern Tanzania, Arusha has today been transformed into one of the busiest Tanzanian towns after Dar es Salaam. Its prominence has particularly increased in recent years since becoming the headquarters of the East African Community and being the host town for the Rwandan War Crimes Tribunals. The International Conference Centre has witnessed the signing of some of the most important peace treaties and international agreements in modern African history. Arusha is also the starting point for safaris in the north of Tanzania – the Serengeti, Ngorongoro, Lake Manyara, Tarangire, Olduvai Gorge and Arusha national parks. It can be very busy with tourists, mostly either in transit to, or returning from, these attractions. The dusty streets are filled with 4WD game-viewing vehicles negotiating potholed roads, and Masai warriors in full regalia mingling with tourists clad in crisp khaki. There are lots of good hotels and restaurants, and tourism has made Arusha a very prosperous town.

Ins and outs ▶ Colour map 1, A4. 3°20'S 36°40'E.

→ Phone code: 027. Population: 400,000. Altitude: 1380 m.

Getting there

Arusha is 50 km from Kilimanjaro International Airport, which is well served by international flights, 79 km from Moshi, and 650 km from Dar es Salaam. If you fly into Kilimanjaro International Airport with Air Tanzania or Precision Air, shuttle buses will meet the incoming flights. Passengers travelling with other airlines will have to get a taxi for about US$40, or can arrange to be picked up by one of the hotels, lodges or safari companies. Closer to town is Arusha Airport, 10 km west along the road to Dodoma. This is mostly used for charter flights and scheduled services operated by Coastal Air.

The road between Dar es Salaam and Arusha has recently been upgraded and is now smooth tar all the way. The journey by bus takes eight to nine hours. It is also only 273 km south of Nairobi, with the Namanga border with Kenya being roughly halfway. The two cities are linked by regular shuttle buses and the journey normally takes around four hours. At the time of writing, however, extensive road repairs were being carried out on this road, almost doubling journey times. ▶ For further details, see Transport, page 284.

Getting around

The town is in two parts, separated by a small valley through which the Naura River runs. The upper part, to the east, contains the government buildings, post office, immigration, most of the top-range hotels, safari companies, airline offices, curio and craft shops, and the huge Arusha International Conference Center (AICC), which is on East Africa Community Road (Barabara ya Afrika Mashariki). This road used to be called Simeon Road and the name Simeon Road has now been given to the road further east that links Old Moshi Road and the Nairobi–Moshi Road, near the Impala Hotel (formerly Nyerere Road). This can be quite confusing when reading local maps. Further down the hill and across the valley to the east are the commercial and industrial areas, the market, small shops, many of the budget hotels and the bus stations. In the middle of the centre is the clock tower and roundabout. From here, Sokoine Road neatly bisects the town to the west and continues further out of town to become the main road that goes to both Dodoma and the parks of the northern circuit. To the southeast of the clock tower is Old Moshi Road, along which some of the better hotels are located. *Dala-dala* run frequently up and down the main throroughfares, costing US$0.30, taxis are everywhere and should cost little more than US$3-4 for a short journey around town.

Safety

Alas safety is becoming an increasing concern in Arusha. Muggings have become more common, and in 2004 there was a serious attack just outside Arusha when a group of 32 tourists were ambushed and robbed. Sokoine Road and Moshi Road towards the Impala Hotel are unsafe at night, unless you are in a big group, and the area around the bridge crossing River Themi on Old Moshi Road has seen increasingly higher numbers of muggings recently – if you have to carry a laptop make sure it's not in an obvious laptop bag and be discreet with cameras, valuables, etc. Taxis are advised at night, and extra caution should be taken around the market and bus station where pickpockets (especially street children) are common. If you are in a vehicle, ensure that it is securely locked.

Tourist information

Information for tourists in Arusha, with displays on the surrounding attractions, can be obtained from the following places. The **Tanzanian Tourist Board** ① *Information Centre, 47E Boma Rd, T027-250 38402/3, www.tanzaniatouristboard.com, Mon-Fri 0800-1600, Sat 0830-1330, this office does not arrange bookings or hotel reservations*, a useful source of local information, including details of the excellent Cultural Tourism Programmes that were set up in conjunction with SNV, the Netherlands Development Agency. In the office are all the leaflets outlining these tours, which directly involve and benefit the local people. It is best to make reservations and arrangements here before going out to the individual locations. To date, this initative has involved 32 villages around Arusha, Kilimanjaro, Iringa, Pangani, Mbeya and other regions. These programmes are an excellent way to experience traditional customs, music and dance, and modern ways of life in rural areas. They tend to be off the beaten track, giving a very different tourist experience. An example is the Usambara Mountains Cultural Tourism Programme (see page 228). The tours offered by each programme have been described by one traveller as relatively expensive but worth the cost. More information can be found at www.tanzaniacultural tourism.com, from which you can download each of the programme's brochures. See Around Arusha, below, for the ones in the immediate region. The Tanzanian Tourist Board office also holds a list of registered tour companies as well as a 'blacklist' of rogue travel agencies (see page 284). They also provide copies of "The official Arusha City Map" which has the latest street names (see above).

Ngorongoro Information Office ① *Boma Rd, T027-254 4625*, is a couple of doors along from the tourist information office. There's not much to pick up here in the way of leaflets, but it does sell some books and maps of the national parks, and there is an interesting painting on the wall that shows all the parks in the northern circuit, which gives a good idea where they all are in relation to each other. There is also a model showing the topography of the Ngorongoro Crater. **Tanzania National Parks (TANAPA) head office** ① *Dodoma Rd, T027-250 3471, www.tanzaniaparks.com*, stocks booklets on the national parks at much more competitive prices than elsewhere, and is a useful resource if you require specialist information. It also provides information about the accommodation options in the more remote national parks.

There are also a couple of noticeboards with feedback bulletins from travellers at **Dolly's Patisserie** on Sokoine Road (see page 276) and the **Jambo Makuti Garden** on Boma Road (see page 275). There is a superb colour map of Arusha and the Road to Moshi by Giovanni Tombazzi, which can be obtained from bookshops (see page 277) or **Hoopoe Safaris** on India Street (see page 281).

Sights

Centre

The centre of town is the **clock tower**, which was donated in 1945 by a Greek resident, Christos Galanos, to commemorate the Allied victory in the Second World War. The German Boma now houses the **National Natural History Museum** ① *north end of Boma Rd, www. houseofculture.or.tz/natural_history_museum, daily 0900-1700, entry US$5*, opened in 1987. The building was built by the Germans in 1886 and it has an outer wall, with block towers at each corner. Inside the fortifications are a central administrative building, a captain's mess, a soldiers' mess, a guard house and a large armoury. A laboratory has been established for paleoanthropological research (study of man's evolution through the record of fossils).

Arusha

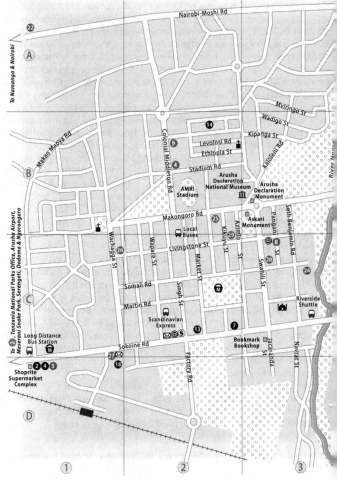

To Namanga & Nairobi

Nairobi-Moshi Rd

Mviringo St

Wadigo St

Kipanga St

Makao Mapya Rd

Colonial Middleton Rd

Levolosi Rd

Ethiopia St

Stadium Rd

AMRI Stadium

Arusha Declaration National Museum

Arusha Declaration Monument

River Naura

Makongoro Rd

Askari Monument

Pangani St

Seth Benjamin Rd

Karofani Rd

Wachagga St

Local Buses

Wapare St

Livingstone St

Kikuyu St

Azimio St

Swahili St

To Tanzania National Parks Office, Arusha Airport, Meserani Snake Park, Serengeti, Dodoma & Ngorongoro

Somali Rd

Singh St

Market St

Riverside Shuttle

Martin Rd

Scandinavian Express

Bookmark Bookshop

Jacaranda St

Naval St

Long Distance Bus Station

Sokoine Rd

Factory Rd

Shoprite Supermarket Complex

N

200 metres

(1)   (2)   (3)

Sleeping

Africa Tulip **13** *D5*	Arusha View	L'Oasis Lodge **14** *A*
Arusha **19** *C4*	Campsite **28** *B5*	Masai Camp **3** *D6*
Arusha Backpackers **27** *C1*	Chinese Everest Inn **1** *D5*	Naura Springs **31** *A*
Arusha by Night Annexe **4** *B2*	Flamingo **29** *C2*	New Safari **21** *C4*
Arusha Coffee Lodge **2** *C1*	Golden Rose **9** *B2*	Outpost **23** *D5*
Arusha Crown **25** *B2*	Ilboru Safari Lodge **7** *A6*	Pamoje Expedition
Arusha Naaz **18** *C4*	Impala **11** *D6*	Palm Court **26** *C1*
Arusha Tourist Centre	Karama Lodge **5** *D6*	Pepe One & Pepe's
	Klub Afriko **16** *A6*	Restaurant **32** *C5*

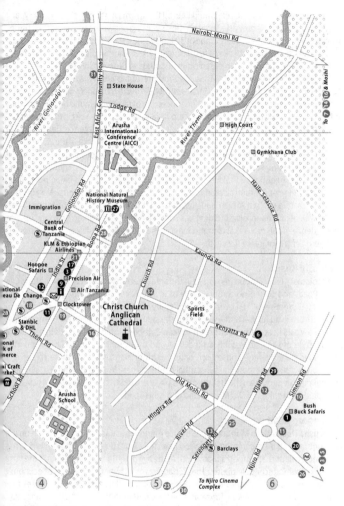

Spices & Herbs & Ethiopian
Restaurant **10** *D6*

Eating 🍴
Albero's **6** *C6*
Bayleaf **29** *C6*
Café Bamboo **3** *C4*
Chopstix **2** *D1*
Cio Gelati **4** *D1*
Dolly's Patisserie **7** *C2*

Dragon Pearl **20** *D6*
Jambo Coffee House **17** *C4*
Jambo Makuti Garden **9** *C4*
McMoody's **13** *C2*
Patisserie **11** *C4*
Picasso Café **1** *D6*
PizzArusha **14** *B2*
Shanghai Chinese **18** *D1*
Steers **12** *C4*
Via Via **27** *B5*

Bars & clubs 🍸
Chrystal Club & Disco **24** *C3*
Colobus **26** *D6*
Empire Sports Bar **5** *D1*
Greek Club **25** *D6*
Maringu City Centre **28** *C4*
Matongee **16** *C4*
Triple A **22** *A1*

The museum contains the celebrated **Laetoli Footprints**, dating back 3,500,000 years, set in solidified volcanic grey ash. Three hominids walking on two legs have left their tracks. The discovery was made at Laetoli, about 30 km southwest of Olduvai Gorge, by Andrew Hill, who was visiting Mary Leakey's fossil camp in 1978. Another display of interest is the tracing of the evolution of man based on the findings at Olduvai Gorge (see page 307).

The new **Tanzanite Museum** ① *on the 3rd floor of the Blue Plaza Building, India St, T027-250 5101, www.tanzaniteexperience.com, Mon-Fri 0900-1600, Sat 0900-1300*, is nearby and explains about the history, mining and processing of tanzanite, found only in Tanzania, on the foothills of Kilimanjaro. There's a shop here where you can buy certified gems.

North of the museum, the huge **Arusha International Conference Centre (AICC)** ① *T027-250 3161, www.aicc.co.tz*, is made up of three main blocks – the Kilimanjaro, Ngorongoro and Serengeti wings. It has been an important centre for international deliberations, with recent events such as the Rwandan War Crimes Tribunal and the Burundi peace negotiations taking place here. The centre also has a bank, post office, foreign exchange bureau and cafeteria, as well as various tour operators and travel agents.

On the east side of East Africa Raod, just north of the AICC complex, is the former **State House**, a small but handsome building with double gables and a green tin roof. This was the residence of the provincial commissioner in the colonial period. Nowadays it houses the Nyere Centre for Peace Research.

Old Moshi Road
In the colonial period Europeans settled in the area adjacent to the River Themi, along Old Moshi Road, and to the north and south of it. The Asian community lived near their commercial premises, often over them, in the area between Boma Road and Goliondoi Road. Africans lived further to the west on the far side of the Naura River. On the north side of the Old Moshi Road is **Christ Church Anglican Cathedral**, built in the 1930s in traditional English style of grey stone with a tiled roof and a pleasant interior. The cathedral is surrounded by a vicarage and church offices. Further along the road there are several bungalows with red tile roofs and substantial gardens. These housed government servants. One building in particular, the **Hellenic Club** (or Greek Club), stands out with its classical porticos, on the corner of Old Moshi Road and Njiro Road.

Makongoro Road
The **Arusha Declaration Monument** is set on a roundabout past the police station on the Makongoro Road. Also commonly referred to as the Uhuru (Freedom) Monument, it has four concrete legs that support a brass torch at the top of a 10-m column. Around the base are seven uplifting scenes in plaster. The Declaration of 1967 outlined a socialist economic and political strategy for Tanzania. The nearby **Arusha Declaration National Museum** is dedicated to this landmark in Tanzania's history, outlining the evolution of Tanzania's political and economic development. It also has historic photographs of the German period and a display of traditional weapons including clubs, spears and swords. South of the museum is a small park containing the **Askari Monument**, dedicated to African soldiers who died in the Second World War. On the east side of Azimio Street is an interesting **temple** with a portico, fretworked masonry and a moulded coping.

Arusha School
Arusha School dominates the area on the left bank of the Themi River. It is sited on sloping ground, has huge eucalyptus trees and is surrounded by a large swathe of playing fields.

Nyerere's two sons were taught there. It also hosted the meeting of the Organization of African Unity (OAU) Heads of State in 1966, which included Nyerere, Obote, Kaunda, Moi (as vice president), Haile Selassie and Nasser. Sadly, the school and grounds are now very neglected. On the opposite side of School Road near Arusha School is the recently relocated **Masai and Crafts Market**, which has a good selection of crafts and souvenirs.

Around Arusha ⊜🏛️⚠️ » pp270-286.

Meserani Snake Park
① 25 km from Arusha on road to the Ngorongoro Crater and Serengeti, T027-253 8282, www.meseranisnakepark.com. US$1. See also Camping, page 274.
Meserani houses mostly local snake species with the non-venomous snakes housed in open pits, though the spitting cobras, green and black mambas and boomslangs are kept behind glass. There are other reptiles including monitor lizards, chameleons, tortoises and crocodiles, and also a few species of birds that are orphaned or injured for whom a temporary home is provided at the park. There are gardens, a campsite, a restaurant and a bar. Run by Barry and Lynn Bale from South Africa, this project works very well with the local community and the local Masai village. Some of the snakes in the park were brought in by the local Masai who instead of killing snakes that may harm livestock, captured and took them to the park. The Bales also provide antidote treatment for snake-bites and other basic health services for the Masai and other local communities free of charge, as well as providing antivenom for most of Tanzania. Barry has recently established an excellent museum of the local Masai culture, which has mock-ups of Masai huts and models wearing various clothing and jewellery, and a Masai guide will explain the day-to-day life of the Masai. Local craftspeople sell their goods, and camel rides and treks can be arranged to meet the people in the Masai village.

Lake Duluti
Just south of **Mountain Village Hotel**, about 15 km from Arusha along the Moshi road, this small crater lake, fringed by forest, provides a sanctuary for approximately 130 species of birds, including pied and pygmy kingfishers, anhinga, osprey, and several species of buzzards, eagles, sandpipers, doves, herons, cormorants, storks, kingfishers and barbets. Reptiles including snakes and lizards are plentiful too. The pathway around the lake starts off broad and level, but later on it narrows and becomes more difficult to negotiate. There are wonderful views of Mount Meru and occasionally the cloud breaks to reveal Mount Kilimanjaro. 'Ethno-botanical' walks are available, starting from the hotel through the coffee plantation and circumnavigating the lake. The walks are accompanied by guides who are knowledgeable about the flora and birds.

Cultural tourism programmes
Several villages on the lower slopes of Mount Meru, north of Arusha, have started cultural tourism programmes with help from the Dutch development organization, SNV, and the Tanzanian Tourist Board. Profits from each are used to improve the local primary schools. Further details of the programmes described below can be obtained from the Tanzanian tourist information centre in Arusha (see page 259), www.tanzaniaculturaltourism.com.

Ng'iresi Village *① 7 km from Arusha north of the Moshi Rd, transportation by pickup truck can be arranged at the Arusha tourist centre.* Offers half-day guided tours of farms and local development projects such as irrigation, soil terracing, cross breeding, bio gas and fish nurseries. Longer tours can involve camping at a farm and a climb of **Kivesi**, a small volcano with forests where baboons and gazelle live. The Wa-arusha women will prepare traditional meals or a limited choice of Western food. Profits go towards enlarging the local school.

Ilkiding'a Village ① *7 km north of Arusha along the road signposted to Ilboru Safari Lodge from Moshi Rd.* You will be welcomed in a traditional boma, be able to visit craftsmen and a traditional healer, and walk through farms to one of several viewpoints or into **Njeche canyon**. A three-day hike is also available, stopping at various villages and culminating in a visit to a Masai market. The guides of both this and the Ng'iresi programme are knowledgeable and have a reasonable standard of English. Funds go towards improving the local primary school.

Mulala Village ① *1450 m above sea level on the slopes of Mt Meru about 30 km from Arusha, the turn-off is just before Usa River, follow signs for the Dik Dik Hotel, after the hotel the road climbs for about 10 km.* This programme is organized by the Agape women's group. There are walks through the coffee and banana farms to Marisha River, or to the top of Lemeka hill for views of mounts Meru and Kilimanjaro, and on to the home of the village's traditional healer. You can visit farms where cheese- and bread-making and flower-growing activities have been initiated. The women speak only a little English but interpreters can be arranged.

Mkuru camel safari ① *North side of Mt Meru, the camp is 5 km from Ngarenanyuki Village, which is 5 km beyond the Momela gate of Arusha National Park.* The Masai of this area began keeping camels in the early 1990s and there are now over 100 animals. Camel safaris of half a day or up to one week, towards Kilimanjaro, to Mount Longido, or even further to Lake Natron can be arranged. Alternatively, there are walks through the acacia woodland looking for birds, or up the pyramid-shaped peak of Ol Doinyo Landaree. In the camel camp itself, it is possible to see the Masai carry the new-born camels to their overnight shelters and watch them milk the camels. The guides are local Masai who have limited knowledge of English, communicating largely by hand signals – another guide to act as translator can be arranged with advance notice. There are three cottages at the camel camp, meals can be prepared if notice is given. Profits are used to support the village kindergarten, which was established because the nearest schools are too far for young children to walk to.

Mount Longido → *Colour map 1, A4. Altitude: 2629 m.*
① *100 km north of Arusha on the road to Namanga on the border with Kenya. The town of Longido lies on the main road, at the foot of the mountain. To get here by public transport from Arusha take one of the shuttle buses or dala-dala that go to Namanga or on to Nairobi; the journey to Longido should take about 1½ hrs. The tours are co-ordinated locally by Mzee Mollel, a local Masai who studied in Zambia and Australia. Mzee is happy to answer any enquiries about the Masai way of life.*
Mount Longido rises up steeply from the plains 100 km north of Arusha on the border with Kenya and forms an important point of orientation over a wide area. To climb Mount Longido is useful preparation for Mount Meru or Mount Kilimanjaro. The **Longido Cultural Tourism programme** is an excellent way of supporting the local Masai people and learning about their lifestyle and culture. There are several walking tours of the environs, including a half-day 'bird walk' from the town of Longido across the Masai plains to the bomas of Ol Tepesi, the Masai word for acacia tree. On your return to Longido you can enjoy a meal

cooked by the FARAJA women's group. The one-day walking tour extends from Ol Tepesi to Kimokonwa along a narrow Masai cattle trail that winds over the slopes of Mount Longido. On clear days there are views of Kilimanjaro and Mount Meru and from the north side there are extensive views of the plains into Kenya. The tour includes a visit to a historic German grave. There is also a more strenuous two-day tour climbing to the top of the steep Longido peak, following buffalo trails guarded by Masai warriors armed with knives and spears to protect you. Accommodation is in local guesthouses or at campsites. Part of the money generated by this cultural tourism project goes to the upkeep of the cattle dip in Longido. The Masai lose about 1500 head of cattle per annum, mainly because of tick-borne disease. Since Masai life is centred around their livestock this creates serious problems as reduced herd size means less work, income and food. Regular cattle dipping eradicates tick-borne diseases.

Babati and Mount Hanang → *Colour map 1, A4.*

① *There are regular bus services from Arusha to Babati (172 km) starting from 0730. Once there ask for Kahembe's Guest House, a 5-min walk from the main bus stand.*

Mount Hanang is the ninth-highest peak in East Africa and the fourth highest in Tanzania, with an altitude of 3417 m, and a challenge for more adventurous trekkers. It lies to the southwest of Babati, a small town approximately 170 km southwest of Arusha on the road to Dodoma. Here, ethnic commercial and farming groups co-exist with conservative cattle herders and provide a distinguished cultural contrast. Amongst these people the Barbaig's traditional culture is still unchanged and unspoiled. The women wear traditional goatskin dresses and the men walk around with spears. English-speaking guides who know the area will help you around, and a Barbaig-born guide will tell you about Barbaig culture. **Kahembe's Trekking and Cultural Safaris** (see page 284) offers a two-day trek up Mount Hanang along the Katesh route for US$128 per person. The Katesh route can be completed in one day with the ascent and descent taking up to 12 hours in total. They also have a number of imaginative local tours for US$45 per person per day (US$40 each for three or more people). Independent exploration of the area is possible but not common.

Arusha National Park ☺ ↠ *Colour map 1, A4. 4°0'S 36°30'E.*

The compact Arusha National Park is remarkable for its range of habitats. It encompasses three varied zones: the highland montane forest of Mount Meru to the west, where black and white colobus and blue monkeys can be spotted; Ngurdoto Crater, a small volcanic crater inhabited by a variety of mammals in the southeast of the park; and, to the northeast, Momela Lakes, a series of seven alkaline crater lakes, home to a large number of water birds. On a clear day it is possible to see the summits of both Mount Kilimanjaro and Mount Meru from Ngurdoto Crater rim. There are numerous hides and picnic sites throughout the park, giving travellers an opportunity to leave their vehicles and this is one of the few of the country's parks where walking is permitted. Climbing Mount Meru or enjoying the smaller trails that criss-cross its lower slopes is a popular activity for visitors to the park. Although only taking three days to reach the crater's summit, it's something of a short, sharp shock – a quieter, but some say more challenging, alternative to the famous peak of nearby Mount Kilimanjaro. Along the lower slopes, paths through ancient fig tree forests, and crystal clear cascading rivers and waterfalls make a relaxing day's hike for visitors who don't want to attempt the longer and more arduous climb. Canoeing on Small Momella Lake, where there are several hippos and interesting birdlife, is also an option for the active and allows you the chance to see wildlife from a slower, quieter perspective. Green Footprint Adventures operate these canoeing safaris (see page 281). Park fees for canoeing are US$20 per person for a half day and US$40 for a full day. ▸▸ *For more information on national parks and safaris, see page 41.*

Ins and outs

Getting there Arusha National Park is about 25 km east of Arusha and 58 km from Moshi. The road is a good one and the turning off the main road between Arusha and Moshi, about 35 km from Kilimanjaro International Airport, is at Usa River and is clearly signposted. From the airport the landscape changes from the flat dry and dusty Sanya Plain, gradually becoming greener, more fertile and more cultivated. Take the turning (on the right if you

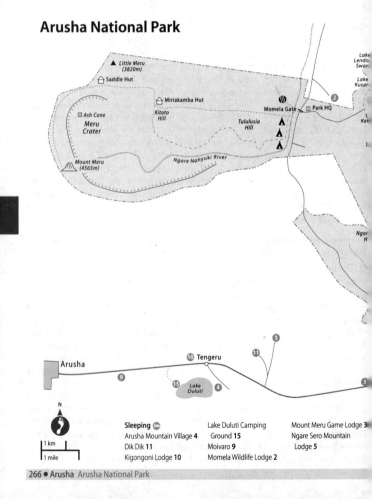

Arusha National Park

▲ Little Meru (3820m)
⌂ Saddle Hut
⌂ Miriakamba Hut
Lake Lendo Swar
Lake Kusar
〽 Momela Gate
▢ Park HQ
Kitoto Hill
☐ Ash Cone
Meru Crater
Tululusia Hill
Mount Meru (4565m)
Ngare Nanyuki River
Ngor H

N

1 km
1 mile

Sleeping
Arusha Mountain Village **4**
Dik Dik **11**
Kigongoni Lodge **10**

Lake Duluti Camping
Ground **15**
Moivaro **9**
Momela Wildlife Lodge **2**

Mount Meru Game Lodge **3**
Ngare Sero Mountain
Lodge **5**

Arusha
⑨
⑮ Lake Duluti
④
⑩ Tengeru
⑪
⑤
③

are heading towards Arusha) and follow the gravel road for about 10 km until you reach the **Ngurdoto Gate**. This is coffee country and you will see the farms on each side of the road. On reaching the park entrance this changes to dense forest.

There's a second gate, **Momela Gate**, from which you access Mount Meru, to the north of the park. There are two routes leading to Momela Gate, starting near the village of Usa River, close by the Arusha/Moshi road. From here it is 8 km to Ngurdoto Gate. A single road enters the park, dividing near Serengeti Ndogo. The road to the northwest is known as the Outer Road (25 km) and National Park fees are not payable if in transit. The only available transport are pickup trucks, which take a few passengers and go the village of Ngare Nanyuki, beyond the Momela Gate. It is permissible to walk this route too. The right fork takes you to the road that runs northeast towards Ngurdoto Crater, before turning north

(18 km) beside the Momela Crater Lakes, and this route attracts the National Park fee. These roads through the park meet up again at the Momela Gate. If you don't have your own vehicle many safari companies offer day trips to Arusha National Park.

The best time to visit is October-February. There are several excellent lodges around Usa River and on the lower slopes of Meru. Entry to the park is US$35.

Park information

At the main entrance a small museum provides information for the visitor on the bird, animal and plant life of the park. Park accommodation can be booked in advance through Tanzania National Parks (TANAPA) head office, see page 259.

Background

The Arusha National Park, which contains Mount Meru, was established in 1960. The Howard Hawks film *Hatari* was made here in 1962, starring John Wayne, Elsa Martinelli, Red Buttons and Hardy Kruger. The park has changed its name a number of times from Ngurdoto Crater National Park to Mount Meru National Park and finally to Arusha National Park. It covers an area of 137 sq km and rises from 1524 m at the Momela Lakes (also spelt Momella) to 4565 m at the peak of Mount Meru. Although it is only small, because of this gradation there is a variety of landscapes, a variety of eco-systems and therefore a wide variety of flora and fauna. Within the park are the Ngurdoto Crater and the Momela Lakes.

Ngurdoto Mountain
Lodge **14**
Rivertrees Country Inn **13**
Tanzanite **8**

Mount Meru is believed to have been formed at around the time of the great earth movements that created the Rift Valley, about 20 million years ago. The crater was formed about 250,000 years ago when a massive explosion blew away the eastern side of the volcano. A subsidiary vent produced the volcano of Ngurdoto, which built up over thousands of years. In a way similar to Ngorongoro, when the cone collapsed the caldera was left as it is today. Ngurdoto is now extinct, while Meru is only dormant, having last erupted about 100 years ago. The lava flow from this eruption can be seen on the northwest side of the mountain. It was at around this time in 1872 that the first European, Count Teleki, a Hungarian, saw the mountain.

Arusha National Park contains many animals including giraffe, elephant, hippo, buffalo, rhino (if you're lucky), colobus monkey, bush buck, red forest duiker, reed buck, waterbuck and warthog and reportedly the highest density of giraffes in the world. There are no lions but you may see leopard. Birds include cormorants, pelicans, ibis, flamingos and grebes.

Ngurdoto Crater

Within the park there are over 50 km of tracks but no roads have been built into the Ngurdoto Crater in order to protect and preserve it. From the Ngurdoto Gate a road leads off towards the Ngurdoto Crater. This area is known as the 'connoisseur's park' – rightly so. The road climbs up through the forest until it reaches the rim. At the top you can go left or right, either going around the crater clockwise or anti-clockwise. The track does not go all the way round the rim of the crater so you will have to turn round and retrace your tracks back to the main road. You will be able to look down on to the animals in the crater below but will not be able to drive down. The crater is about 3 km in diameter and there are a number of viewing points around the rim from which you can view the crater floor, known as the 'park within the park'. These include Leitong Point (the highest at 1850 m), Glades Point, Rock Point, Leopard Hill, Rhino Crest and Mikindani Point. From this latter point you will be able to see Mount Kilimanjaro in the distance.

Momela Lakes route

From Ngurdoto Gate, if you take the left track you will reach the Momela Lakes. This track goes past the Ngongongare Springs, Lokie Swamp, the Senato Pools and the two lakes, Jembamba and Longil. At the peak of the dry season they may dry up but otherwise they are a good place to watch the animals and in particular the birdlife. At various spots there are observation hides. At **Lake Longil** there is a camping and picnic site in a lovely setting.

From here the track continues through the forest, which gradually thins out and through the more open vegetation you will be able to see Mount Meru. The Hyena Camp (Kambi ya Fisi) is reached at the point where you will probably see a pack of spotted hyenas. Beyond this there is a small track leading off the main track to **Bomo la Mengi** – a lovely place from which to view the lakes. Unless the cloud is down you will also be able to see Kilimanjaro from here. The main track continues past two more lakes – **Lake El Kekhotoito** and **Lake Kusare** – before reaching the Momela Lakes.

The **Momela Lakes** are shallow alkaline lakes fed by underground streams. Because they have different mineral contents and different algae their colours are also different. They contain few fish but the algae attracts lots of birdlife. What you see will vary with the time of year. Flamingos tend to move in huge flocks around the lakes of East Africa and are a fairly common sight at Momela Lakes. Between October and April the lakes are also home to the migrating waterfowl, which are spending the European winter in these warmer climes.

Climbing Mount Meru

The walk up Mount Meru involves a 3500-m altitude hike, frequently climbed up and down within three days. The last section of the walk to the summit is very steep. It is easy to underestimate what are common problems associated with this walk – altitude sickness and frostbite. Snow is not unknown at the summit. On the ascent you will pass through the changing vegetation. The first change is to lower montane forest at about 2000 m, then to higher montane forest. The road climbs up the mountain up to the heath zone at about 2439 m from where you can climb to the peak. From the road and the park headquarters a track leads up to the Miriakamba Hut, which takes about three hours. The trail continues as a steady climb through montane forest, where there is an abundance of birds and black and white colobus monkeys. The first mountain hut sleeps about 48 people, while the second, Saddle Hut, sleeps about 24. Both huts provide firewood. It is a three-hour walk between the two huts but is a steep climb

and having reached Saddle Hut you can spend the afternoon climbing Little Meru (3820 m), which takes about 1½ hours. From Saddle Hut the climb up to the rim of the mountain and around to the summit usually starts at 0200 in order to see the sunrise from the top. It's a steep climb to Rhino Point (3800 m), before continuing along an undulating ridge of ash and rock to reach Cobra Point (4350 m). The final ascent from Saddle Hut is difficult, cold and can be dangerous, but the views of the cliffs and crater rim are stunning: you can see the ash cone rising from the crater floor and Kilimanjaro floating on the morning clouds. Most of the tour operators in Arusha, and some in Moshi, can arrange climbs. Like the Kilimanjaro climb there are a number of park fees to climb the mountain that are paid to the Tanzania National Parks. Though these are not quite as expensive as for Kili, nevertheless expect to pay in the region of US$400 for a package including park fees, guide, porters, food and accommodation in mountain huts.

The track goes around the lakes reaching the **Small Momela Lake** first. This lake often has a group of hippos wallowing in it. Follow the road anti-clockwise and you will pass **Lake Rishetani**, which is a fantastic emerald green colour. Along this route you will be able to stop off at the various observation sites. The next lake that you will get to is the **Great Momela Lake**, which has a huge variety of birdlife and is a lovely spot. The last two lakes are **Tulusia** and **Lekandiro** where you may see animals grazing.

Mount Meru → *Colour map 1, A4.*

The other major attraction of Arusha National Park is Mount Meru (4565 m), the second highest mountain in Tanzania and also the fifth highest in all Africa. The mountain lies to the west of the Ngare Nanyuki road in the western half of the park. There is a road that leads up the mountain to about 2439 m from the **Momela Gate**, passing through an open space called **Kitoto** from where there are good views of the mountain, but vehicles are no longer allowed to pass this way.

Arusha listings

For Sleeping and Eating price codes and other relevant information, see pages 36-40.

Sleeping

The best hotels in the Arusha area are out of town in the foothills of Mt Meru. They have fine gardens, good standards and charming atmosphere. They are recommended above similar priced hotels in Arusha or its outskirts. If you do not have your own transport most will offer transfers from town and many are used as part of a safari package. At the budget end of the market there are a number of cheap hotels around the stadium and market that cost as little as US$10 and are good value. If using a hotel's 'safe', you are advised to check your money when deposited and on collection, or seal it in a bag with tape. There are reports of false receipts being issued and less money being returned on collection.

Arusha *p258, map p260*

L Arusha Coffee Lodge, a few kilometres from town on the road to the crater on a working coffee estate, T027-250 06309, www.arushacoffeelodge.com, www.elewana .com. One of the most luxurious options in Arusha, with 23 stunning spacious chalets with balconies, fireplaces, facilities to make coffee, enormous beds with mosquito nets, hardwood floors and wooden decks, Zanzibar-style furniture and Persian rugs. Very elegant lounge, and a restaurant for fine dining (see Eating, page 275) with dressed up tables and leather sofas. Swimming pool.

L-A The Arusha Hotel, previously the **New Arusha**, near the clock tower, T027-250 7777, www.thearushahotel.com. Formerly the site of the old German hotel built in 1903, of which the splendid restaurant is the only surviving feature. 86 elegantly decorated rooms, with a/c, phone and internet access. Behind the hotel is a beautiful garden running down to the Themi River. Swimming pool, gym (open to non-residents), snack bar, restaurant serving international food, Italian and Indian dishes, and the bar downstairs leads to the garden. Also a good bookshop, gift/craft shop and a foreign exchange bureau.

A Onsea Country Inn and Guest Cottage, Baraa Rd, about 5 km outside Arusha off Moshi Rd, T0784-833207 (mob), www.on seahouse.com. In a beautiful location overlooking the hills and Mt Meru, this stylish boutique hotel owned by Belgians Dirk and Inneke Janssens has 5 rooms, 3 in the main house and 2 in the guest cottage across the road, which can be used as one huge family suite. All rooms are elegantly furnished and there's a swimming pool in tranquil gardens. Excellent restaurant, on the terrace of the main house with stunning views, see Eating, page 275. Massages are available either in the guest rooms or in the private jacuzzi area. Rates are US$360 for a double room full board, including wines.

B African Tulip, 44/1 Serengeti Rd, T027-254 3004, www.theafricantulip.com. A new boutique hotel, owned by **Roy Safaris**. 29 rooms decorated in smart contemporary style with an African safari theme, all with window seats overlooking the grounds or the roof garden that appropriately is full of African tulips. Rooms have a/c, flat screen TV, Wi-Fi and minibar. There's a chic Zanzibar bar, a Baobab themed restaurant and a pool in lawned gardens. Rates include breakfast.

B-C Naura Springs Hotel, East Africa Community Rd, about 500m from AICC on the opposite side of the road, T027-205 0001/8, www.nauraspringshotel.com. You can't miss the tall, blue-glass building housing Arusha's newest hotel. Beautifully crafted wooden carvings decorate the communal areas but beyond that, the place has little character. The bar and main restaurant are by the main cavernous reception lobby and there's a pool and lawns at the rear, with another bar and restaurant. The salon and gym are still being built. The 124 rooms are spacious but soulless, with flat screen TVs and fridges; some are more attractive than others.

C Karama Lodge & Spa, 3 km from town off the Old Moshi Rd, turn off just past Masai Camp, T027-250 0359, www.karama-lodge. com. 22 thatched stilted log cabins built on the hillside in a pretty tract of forest. Close enough to town but a very peaceful with good views of Meru and Kilimanjaro. Colourful rooms have hanging chairs on the balcony. Rustic bar on a deck, and the restaurant uses ingredients from the garden. A popular choice for a rest after climbing Kilimanjaro or Meru, a spa is currently being built.

C Impala Hotel, 500 m down Old Moshi Rd from the clock tower, T027-254 3082/7, www.impalahotel.com. 160 rooms in an ultra modern block with TV and phone, pleasant garden and patio, and swimming pool. Rates include breakfast, several good restaurants, including an excellent Indian one, and coffee shops, 24-hr room service, gift shop and bureau de change. Arranges tours and safaris through **Classic Tours** (see page 280). Run their own shuttle bus to and from Kilimanjaro airport and Nairobi. A useful hotel with several amenities but somewhat impersonal service.

C-F Ilboru Safari Lodge, 2 km west from town towards Mt Meru off the Nairobi Rd, T0754-270357 (mob), www.ilborusafarilodge. com. Well managed by Aad, a Dutchman and his Tanzanian wife, this popular lodge has 30 en suite rooms in thatched rondavaals with a Masai theme, which were about to be upgraded at the time of our visit. There's an excellent restaurant (see Eating, page 276) with a Dutch pancake place due to open and a German beer garden at weekends. The large swimming pool is open to non-residents. Nearby is the campsite (US$10) with good facilities. Various activities offered, from traditional tingatinga painting to cookery classes. Friendly lodge which is excellent value for money. Highly recommended.

D Arusha Crown Hotel, Makongoro Rd, T027-254 4161, www.arushacrownhotel.com. A modern hotel and very centrally located. 38 rooms on 6 floors, stylish decor throughout (though very much a business travellers' hotel with 24 single rooms), internet access, CCTV

security cameras. Very good restaurant open to non-residents (see Eating, page 275). A single is US$60, a twin or a double US$74, excellent value in this price range. The rooms facing north overlook Meru and directly into the stadium – if there's a match on you can watch the football from bed.

D Arusha Naaz Hotel, near clock tower on Sokoine Rd, T027-250 2087, www.arusha naaz.net. Once you get through the bizarre shopping centre entrance and head up the small staircase, the 21 rooms are centred around a little internal courtyard. Clean, en suite bathrooms, 24 hr hot water, fans and mosquito nets, restaurant with good food (closed in evening), internet access. You can also hire cars from here.

D New Safari, Boma Rd, T027-250 3261, www.thenewsafarihotel.com. Friendly hotel, conveniently located in the New Safari Complex, which also houses businesses such as internet cafés and bureaux de change. Very smart modern building, nice terrace restauranton the 1st floor with good views of Meru, 48 rooms with TV, internet connection for laptops, and minibar with soft drinks.

D Outpost, Serengeti Rd, off the Old Moshi Rd, near **Impala Hotel**, T027-254 8405, www. outposttanzania.com. Run by a Zimbabwe couple, Kathy and Steve Atwell, the staff are superb and very welcoming. Popular with expats. Accommodation either in spacious rooms in the main house or in bandas, the family unit can sleep 6, full English breakfast included. Manicures, pedicures and massages also on offer. A new swimming pool has recently been added together with Café Mambo, a cheerful bakery, café and bar, with chilled music, around the pool area. Highly recommended.

D-E Golden Rose, Colonel Middleton Rd, T027-250 7959, www.hotelgoldenrose.net. Comfortable, good value, self-contained rooms with hot water, telephones, balconies. Bar and restaurant, internet café and bureau de change. Accept Visa and MasterCard but charge 10% more. Reported to have rather noisy generator at back. Can arrange car hire.

D-E Hotel Pepe One, just off Church Rd, T0784-365515 (mob), www.hotelpepeone. co.tz. This popular restaurant now has 5 rooms, all off the main reception area. Rooms are newly decorated with good bathrooms, nets and TV. Tidy and clean but a bit cramped. Lively restaurant serving a varied menu (see Eating, page 276) and is in a quiet location in pretty grounds. Good value at US$45 for a double, breakfast is an extra US$5.

D-E Klub Afriko Hotel and Safaris, Kimandolu, 3 km from town on the Moshi Rd, T027-254 8878, www.klubafriko.com. Set in tropical gardens in a quiet neighbourhood just outside Arusha town. 7 airy en suite bungalows, decorated with local artwork. Excellent food, friendly bar with satellite TV.

D-E L'Oasis Lodge, 2 km out of town, in the quiet residential area of Sekei, T027-250 7089, www.loasislodge.com. 22 rooms, some on stilts and some in the main building, have en suite facilities, and there are 13 smaller twin budget rooms with shared bathrooms. Good food, extensive menu including Thai, Indonesian, Greek, seafood and vegetarian dishes. There's also a more casual lounge bar by the pool which serves burgers and pizzas. Pool with fish and wading birds, a dining area, bar, internet services. Highly recommended.

D-E Le Jacaranda, Vijana Rd, T027-254 4624, www.chez.com/jacaranda. 23 African themed rooms, small but clean with private bathrooms and Masai artwork. Some rooms are in the main building, others are dotted around the gardens. Internet access, comfortable bar area with sofas on terrace overlooking gardens. Crazy golf. Restaurant serves everything from Chinese to Swahili with plenty of vegetarian options (see Eating, page 276).

D-E Pamoja Expeditions, Serengeti Rd, T027-250 6136, www.pamojaexpeditions lodge.com. Rooms are in bungalows in the garden, simply furnished with white-washed walls, nets and TV. There's a small pool in the gardens with plastic chairs and sunbeds. Internet café. Lacking in character compared to its neighbour, the **Outpost**.

D-E Sinka Court, near the market, T027-250 4961, sinkacourthotel@hotmail.com. In a very modern block, 29 rooms with built-for-hotel furniture and excellent bathrooms, a/c, cable TV, mosquito nets, the larger rooms have fridges and floor to ceiling windows, though the view is not up to much as the hotel overlooks an ugly block of flats. Under- ground parking, restaurant and bar.

E Arusha Tourist Centre Inn, Livingstone St, next to **Hotel Fort des Moins**, T027-250 0421, icerestaurant@yahoo.com. The reception area for the hotel is through the **Ice Restaurant and bar** at the front. All 18 rooms are en suite and have TV, phone and mosquito nets. Simple but clean. The owners also run **Arusha Tourist Inn** on Sokoine Rd near Meru House.

E Chinese Everest, Old Moshi Rd, near the **Impala**, T0732-975274 (mob), everesttzus@ yahoo.com. 7 clean and comfortable rooms in the gardens at the back of this popular Chinese restaurant, with friendly and helpful hosts. There are also pleasant gardens at the front of the restaurant, which serves excellent Sechuan food. Internet access. Room rate includes an English or Chinese breakfast. Single, double and triple rooms available. Recommended.

E Hotel Flamingo, Kikuyu St, by the market area, T027-254 8812, flamingoarusha@ yahoo.com A good low budget option. 9 clean, light and airy rooms with mosquito nets and own bathroom. Friendly staff and a pleasant bar area that serves soft drinks only.

E Spices & Herbs, a few metres north of the **Impala Hotel** off Old Moshi Rd, T027-254 2279, axum_spices@hotmail.com. Well appointed, with a garden and veranda leading to the restaurant which specializes in Ethiopian cuisine (see Eating, page 276). The 19 rooms are set around a courtyard to the rear, small but comfortable with hot showers, some are adjoining for families. In the middle of the courtyard are some chairs and a satellite TV.

F Arusha Backpackers, Sokoine Rd, T027- 250 4474, www.arushabackpackers.co.tz. This is a popular low budget option with good facilities, including a lively bar and restaurant on the top floor. Free internet for residents. The 34 rooms are sparsely furnished and some are like windowless cells with nothing but bunk-beds and a chair. But they're still good value at US$16 for a double including breakfast. There are also some dormitories with 2 sets of bunk beds for US$7 per person. Communal toilets and showers.

F Arusha by Night Annexe, on corner of Col Middleton Rd and Stadium Rd, T027-250 6894 . Very basic rooms with bathrooms and hot water, though the plumbing is leaky, and mosquito nets. Small restaurant and courtyard bar, where friendly ladies cook up Tanzania staples plus a stab at something international such as spag bol.

F Palm Court Hotel, 500 m from the bus station off Wachagga St, T0754-975468 (mob). A friendly low-budget option with rooms around the restaurant. Rates include breakfast and are more expensive if you want your own bathroom. Basic but clean, nets, shared hot showers, laundry service, small restaurant, bar, tea and coffee, lounge with satellite TV, exceptionally good value.

Camping

F Arusha View Campsite, next to Equator Hotel, Boma Rd. Very central and very basic camping. Only US$3. It's possible to hire tents but you will need a sleeping bag. Grassy sites next to a small river, mosquitoes love it.
F Masai Camp, 3 km along Old Moshi Rd T027-250 0358, www.masaicamp.tripod.com. Fantastic restaurant, serving Tex Mex, burgers, pizzas and the best nachos in East Africa. Spotless ablutions with steaming hot water, shady camping spots on grassy terraces, some budget rooms in huts, internet, lively bar with frequent party nights and live music, also new cocktail bar. Highly recommended for backpackers. The excellent safari company, **Tropical Trails** (see page 283) is based here.

Around Arusha *p263*
Mountain lodges
B Arusha Mountain Village, 20 km out of town along the Moshi Rd, T027-255 3313

(lodge number), for reservations www.serena hotels.com. Quality lodge in an old colonial homestead. 42 thatched bomas, with hand-carved African animals on the doors, nestled within a coffee plantation. Excellent gardens, splendid location overlooking the Lake Duluti. Very good restaurant, relaxed open bar and impeccable service.

A Dik Dik, 20 km from Arusha off the Moshi Rd near Usa River, T027-255 3499, www.dik dik.ch. Swimming pool, good restaurant, pleasant grounds, set on the slopes of Meru, very proficiently run by Swiss owners, though lacks African atmosphere, concentrates on running upmarket Kilimanjaro climbs. More reasonable rates are available if you are buying accommodation as part of a climb package.

A-B Mount Meru Game Lodge, 20 km from Arusha off Moshi Rd near Usa River, T027-255 3643, www.mountmerugamelodge.com. Small, well run, high-standard establishment in garden setting with charming atmosphere and very good restaurant. 4-poster beds swathed in nets. Impressive animal sanctuary, which includes baboons, vervet monkeys and probably the only Sanje mangabey, *Cercocebus sanjei*, in captivity. A large paddock is home to zebra, waterbuck and eland, as well as saddle-billed and yellow-billed storks, sacred ibis and ostrich. Rates differ by US$100 per room between high and low seasons.

A-B Ngurdoto Mountain Lodge, 27 km from Arusha, 3 km off Moshi Rd, T027-254 2217/26, www.thengurdotomountain lodge.com. Very smart lodge in beautiful grounds with a range of facilities on a 57-ha coffee estate. 60 rooms in double-storey thatched rondavaals, 72 rooms in the main building, and 7 suites, some rooms have disabled access, satellite TV, most with bath-tubs with jacuzzis. Good views of Kilimanjaro and Meru, 3 restaurants, 2 bars, a coffee shop, 18-hole golf course, health club and fully equipped gym, 2 tennis courts, badminton court, swimming pool, toddlers' pool, children's play area and tour desk that can arrange all safaris. An excellent base in the region especially for families.

B Kigongoni Lodge, 10 km east of Arusha, 1 km before Tengeru, 1 km off the Moshi Rd, T027-255 3087, www.kigongoni.net. On a 28-ha coffee farm with good views of Kilimanjaro and Meru, the lodge has 18 cottages, built with local materials, with fireplaces and verandas, 4-poster beds with mosquito nets and en suite bathrooms. Some rooms have internet access, the restaurant serves a set 3-course meal each night and there's a cocktail lounge and a swimming pool on top of a hill with fantastic views. Revenues from the lodge support a local foundation for mentally disabled children and their families. Guided walks available.

B-C Moivaro, 7 km from Arusha off the Moshi Rd, T027-255 3243, www.moivaro. com. 42 lovely double- or triple-bed cottages with verandas and en suite bathrooms. Set in gardens in a coffee plantation, swimming pool, good restaurant and bar, children's playground, massages, jogging or walking trail through the plantation. Internet access.

C Ngare Sero Mountain Lodge, 20 km east of Arusha on the Moshi Rd, T027-255 3638, www.ngare-sero-lodge.com. Just 1.5 km from the main road is a jacaranda avenue leading to a footbridge. You reach the lodge by crossing the lake by the footbridge and climbing steps up through the gardens or by driving around the forest reserve to reach the car park. 10 garden rooms and 2 suites, pool and sauna in the garden, horse riding, yoga classes, trout fishing and trekking on Mt Meru can all be arranged, and you can play croquet on the lawn. Formerly the farm of Haupt-mann Leue, a colonial administrator from the German period, the name means 'sweet waters' and there are magnificent gardens with an estimated 200 species of birds.

C Rivertrees Country Inn, 20 km from Arusha, off the Moshi Rd, near Usa River, T027-255 3894, www.rivertrees.com. Set in natural gardens along the picturesque Usa River, this is a very elegant country lodge with excellent farm cuisine and personal service. There are 8 individually decorated rooms with bathrooms in the farmhouse and 2 garden

cottages with additional decks and fireplaces. Swimming pool, and horse riding village visits and walking trips can be arranged with notice.

D-F Tanzanite, about 22 km along the road to Moshi, near Usa River, T027-257 3038. Popular with locals at the weekend, chalets set in verdant gardens, swimming pool, tennis, restaurant, small animal sanctuary, child friendly, nature trail, lovely surroundings, good value. Camp for US$5.

Camping

F Lake Duluti camping ground, 11 km from town toward Moshi, turn right at the sign and follow the road through a coffee plantation. Secure camping and parking is in a grassy yard around the jetty and bar, though ablutions are basic. There is a basic restaurant with a limited choice of food and you may have to wait. Cold beers and sodas available and you can pay to get your laundry done.

F Meserani Snake Park, 25 km out of town on the road towards the Ngorongoro Crater and Serengeti, T027-253 8282, www.meserani snakepark.com. A hugely popular spot with backpackers, independent overlanders and overland trucks, and just about any safari company on the way to the parks will stop here. Lively atmosphere and friendly, the bar serves very cold beers. The campsite has hot showers and vehicles are guarded by Masai warriors. Meals from simple hamburgers to spit roast impala are on offer (see also page 263).

Arusha National Park *p265, map p266*
Mountain lodges

C Momela Wildlife Lodge, about 50 km from Arusha, just outside Arusha National Park, 3 km to the northeast of the Momela Gate, T027-250 8104, www.lions-safari-intl. com/momella.html. Made famous by the 1960 movie *Hatari* starring John Wayne, which was filmed in the area. The formidable actor stayed here and the hotel was the production base. The lodge will screen the film on request for guests. Beautiful gardens, with a swimming pool, 55 rondavaals with private bathrooms, excellent views of Meru and Kilimanjaro. The lodge is well placed for visits to the Momela Lakes, and nearby are many plains animals and a huge variety of birds.

Camping

E Arusha National Park Campsites, there are 4 sites in the park, 3 are at the base of Tululusia Hill, the other in the forest near Ngurdoto Gate; another is proposed at the edge of Lake Kusare. All have water, toilets and provide firewood. Book through Tanzania National Parks head office, see page 259.

⊘ Eating

Arusha *p258, map p260*
In addition to those listed below, there are also several cafés and restaurants in the new Njiro Cinema Complex, 3 km out of town on the Njiro Rd, including the **Tanzania Coffee Lounge** and the **Oriental Shisha Lounge**, the first Shisha lounge in Arusha.

₸₸₸ Arusha Coffee Lodge, see Sleeping, above. Fabulous setting in a luxurious lodge, lovely wooden building surrounded by decks and overlooking the swimming pool, fine china and crystal, very elegant, big fireplace in the bar area, superb service. At lunch there are set menus with at least 4 main courses to choose from, plus a snack menu. At dinner choose steak, pork, chicken or fish, and then pick a marinade and accompanying sauce, with a wide choice of veg and salad. Wines are from South Africa and Chile. Recommended.

₸₸₸ Arusha Crown Hotel, see Sleeping, above. The downstairs restaurant in this smart hotel is very modern with excellent service and prices are surprisingly cheap for what you get. Dishes include asparagus with crispy bacon and poached egg, pizza, steaks, seafood and fish including red snapper and king fish, lamb chops, curries and schnitzels, and a full Indian menu, good choice of wine and flavoured coffees. Recommended.

₸₸₸ Bayleaf Restaurant, 102 Vijana Rd, T027-254 3055. A stylish new restaurant near **Le Jacarandra**. Excellent quality food, including the quartet starter – a sample of 4 of the starter dishes, *poisson extraordinaire* and fresh ravioli. Expensive and portions are sometimes small. The restaurant is also a boutique hotel with 2 bedrooms. Reports welcome.

₸₸₸ Jambo Makuti Garden, Boma Rd just south of the **New Safari Hotel**, T027-250 3261. Superb breakfasts, baguettes and stuffed chapatis, burgers, juices and shakes during the day, and afternoon tea from 1400-1700 with cakes and muffins. Dinner from 1930, fish, steaks, ribs and vegetarian dishes and a good wine list. The art on the walls is for sale.

₸₸₸ Onsea Country Inn, see Sleeping, above. Stunning views overlooking the Monduli Mountains and Mt Meru. The Belgian chef prepares brasserie dishes which are Belgian/ French with an African influence, accompanied by fine wines. The restaurant has received excellent reports and bookings are essential – this is fast gaining a reputation as the best place to eat in Arusha.

₸₸ Albero, Haile Sellassie Rd, T0762-248779 (mob), air@yahoo.com. A popular Italian restaurant with an Italian chef and a pleasant bar around a huge fig tree. Reasonable prices and generous portions. Pastas range from US$7-9 and pizzas cooked on a wood fired stove from US$6-8.

₸₸ Chopstix, in the shopping centre to the left of Shoprite, T027-254 8366. Quality Chinese takeaway and pizzas. Same chain as **Dragon Pearl**, below.

₸₸ Dragon Pearl, just off the roundabout near Impala, T027-2544107. Mon-Fri 1100-1500, 1800-2230, Sat-Sun 1230-2245. Newer sister restaurant of **Shanghai**, different menu, good food and pleasant outdoor setting in lovely gardens. Wines from South Africa, very good vegetarian dishes, full range of Chinese, some Thai, specialities include fried wonton and sizzling dishes, try the crispy chilli prawns. A Korean chef will grill meat at your table and serve it with sauces, similar to a fondue.

♔♔ **Ilboru Safari Lodge**, see Sleeping, above. This restaurant has become increasingly popular – and deservedly so – since changing ownership recently. It serves a mix of inter-national and Swahili cuisine, along with some Dutch dishes, and a pancake restaurant should be open by the time this book is published. There's a relaxed atmosphere in the Masai-inspired restaurant and if you're lucky, the staff choir will demonstrate their singing talents. Try the Swahili stews, which include a delicious veggie option.

♔♔ **Le Jacaranda**, see Sleeping, above. Restaurant and bar on an attractive upstairs wooden deck, lounge area downstairs, surrounded by pretty gardens. Continental, Indian, Chinese and Swahili meals, grills and steaks, and a wide selection of vegetarian options. BBQs at weekends.

♔♔ **Masai Camp**, 3 km west on Old Moshi Rd, T027-254 8299. Good food and bar, excellent place to meet other travellers, frequent party nights, cocktail bar, serves hamburgers, chips, pizzas and Mexican food on tables in a boma around a roaring fire. Recommended.

♔♔ **Pepe's**, just off Church Rd, T0784-365515 (mob), www.hotelpepeone.co.tz. A lively Italian and Indian restaurant, well known for its pizzas. Tables are set in pretty gardens or in the restaurant with Masai artwork.

♔♔ **Shanghai Chinese Restaurant**, Sokoine Rd near the bridge, beside Meru Post Office, T027-250 3224. Daily 1200-1500, 1830-2230. Extensive menu, fairly authentic, quick, the hot and sour soup is highly recommended.

♔♔ **Spices & Herbs Ethiopian Restaurant**, see Sleeping, above. Open daily 1100-2300. Simple, informal, Ethiopian place with good vegetarian options made from lentils, peas and beans, very good lamb, and continental food (steaks, chops and ribs). Set in a beautifully landscaped garden full of birds. Good service, full bar and live music Thu-Sat. Some accommodation at the back.

♔ **Café Bamboo**, Boma Rd, near the main post office, T027-250 6451. Very pleasant, bright and airy atmosphere, light pine tables and chairs, blue tablecloths, wicker-shaded

lights over each table. Serves good value tasty food, including excellent salads, burgers, juices, fruit salad and ice cream. Fairly busy at lunchtime, closed evenings.

♔ **Cio Gelati**, Shoprite complex, Sokoine Rd. Snacks, samosas, cold orange juice, 14 flavours of ice cream, sundaes, milkshakes, cappuccino, espresso. Uses fresh ingredients and no eggs.

♔ **Dolly's Patisserie**, Sokoine Rd, south of the market. Daily from early morning to 1930. Very smart with modern counters and spotless tiles, fantastic freshly baked French bread, cakes and sweets, excellent biryanis, kormas and masalas, hot and cold drinks.

♔ **Jambo Coffee House**, Boma Rd just south of **New Safari Hotel**. Reasonable snacks and grills, toasted sandwiches, cakes, and excellent coffee (you can also buy coffee beans here).

♔ **McMoody's**, on the corner of Sokoine and Market St, T027-250 3791/2. McDonald's-inspired fast food for those hankering after fries and milkshakes. It has a peculiar circular staircase and mirrored walkway that goes absolutely nowhere. There is an internet café next door and you can take your drinks in.

♔ **Naaz**, Sokoine Rd, 150 m from the clock tower. Snack bar at the end of an arcade serving meat chop, egg chop, samosas, kebabs, tea and coffee, excellent juices, buffet lunches with lots of options for vegetarians. Spotless surroundings.

♔ **Patisserie**, Sokoine Rd, just down the hill from the clock tower. Mon-Fri 0715-1930, Sun 0800-1400. Freshly baked breads, pies, cakes, cookies, croissants, Indian snacks, fresh juices, cappuccino, espresso and hot chocolate. Also internet café.

♔ **Picasso Café**, by Kijenge Supermarket, Simeon Rd, T0756-448585 (mob). Not open in the evenings or on Sun. A great place for an upmarket breakfast or brunch, with a full English for US$7. Popular lunch spot serving sandwiches, crêpes, burgers and delicious cakes. Wine and beer served too.

♔ **PizzArusha**, Levolosi Rd to the north of the market. Superb pizzas, curries and steaks, big cheap portions, one of the best budget places to eat in town. Superb service too.

¶ **Steers**, near the clock tower. South African fast food chain selling ribs and burgers, sodas and shakes, in a/c and spotless environment.

⊕ Bars and clubs

Arusha *p258, map p260*
Bars
There are a number of popular places in town and almost all the hotels and many of the restaurants have bars. There are also several in the new Njiro Cinema Complex, 3 km out of town on the Njiro Rd.
Empire Sports Bar, in the arcade behind the Shoprite, off Sokoine Rd. A large modern bar, with high ceiling and mezzanine floor, pool tables, dart board, long bar, large Tvs for watching sport and some tables outside in the courtyard. Popular with expats.
Greek Club, Old Moshi Rd. Set back from the road in a large white house with Grecian pillars out front. Sports bar with large TVs for football, darts board and pool table. Outdoor tables on a terrace or in the garden.
Matongee, Old Moshi Rd. Outside tables in a spacious garden with *nyama choma* barbecues and plenty of cold beer. Relaxed and good value. Popular with local people.
Via Via, in the gardens of the Natural History Museum on Boma Rd. A popular bar with occasional live bands.

Nightclubs
Chrystal Club & Disco, Seth Benjamin Rd. Open most nights from 2200. Large dance floors with 2 rooms (techno and African/trance) and pool tables. Very lively at weekends, has a wide selection of drinks.
Colobus, Old Moshi Rd just past the Impala Hotel. Popular disco in town, open every night.
Maringu City Centre, just opposite Exim Bank in the town centre. Another popular and quite new nightclub.
Triple A, Nairobi Rd. Open Wed, Fri and Sat, 2100-0500 . Also open on Sun afternoons to allow the kids to get down and boogie. This is easily the largest and most popular nightclub

in Arusha with a big range of music including R&B and hip hop. Enormous dance floor, pool tables, 2 bars, gets completely packed, also runs its own FM radio station.

Around Arusha *p263*
if you are looking for a party with other travellers the best places to go are the Meserani Snake Park and the Masai Camp.

⊙ Shopping

Arusha *p258, map p260*
Bookshops
Arusha Hotel bookshop sells international newspapers and magazines as well as books.
Bookmark, just off Sokoine Rd behind the BP garage. The best bookshop in Arusha. Stocks a wide range of up to date novels, coffee table books on Africa, guide books, maps, intelligent Africana titles, as well as wrapping paper and greeting cards. Prices are steep as everything is imported, but never theless one of the best ranges of books in Tanzania. Small juice bar and internet access.
Kase Stores, Boma Rd. Has a good selection of books, stationery and postcards.

Crafts
There are some craft shops on Goliondoi Rd and near the clock tower with some very good examples of carvings. The curio markets crammed between the clock tower and India Rd are brimming with carvings, masks, beads and some unusual antique Masai crafts including masks, drums, headrests, and beaded jewellery, and similar items are available at the Masai Craft Market on School Rd. Tingatinga paintings (see box, page 78) are for sale at various outlets, including the Il Boru Safari Lodge and at a gallery opposite the Meserani Snake Park.
Cultural Heritage Centre, 3 km out on the road towards Dodoma and the crater. A massive structure show-casing some of the finest of African art, though of course it is very expensive. The items are of very high quality

and there are carvings, musical instruments, cloth, beads, and leatherwork from all over the continent. They can arrange shipping back to your home country and there is a DHL branch office on site. Many of the safari companies stop here en route to the parks.

Markets and shops
The main market is behind the bus station along Market St and Somali Rd. It is very good for fruit, locally made basketware, wooden kitchenware and spices, and is very colourful. The range of fresh produce is very varied and you can buy just about every imaginable fruit and vegetable. If you are shopping, then be prepared to haggle hard and visit a variety of stalls before deciding on the price. Market boys will help carry goods for a fee. In the rainy season watch where you are stepping – it becomes a bit of a quagmire. There are lots of shops along Sokoine Rd. Small supermarkets are found along Sokoine Rd, Moshi Rd and Swahili St. These sell imported food and booze as well as household goods.

Next door to Shoprite is a wholesale food outlet, and outside towards the back on the left is a small arcade of shops, including a jeweller's, a massage place, a Western-style hairdresser and 3 coffee shops.
Kijenge Supermarket, Simeon Rd. Smaller than Shoprite but useful and near the Impala.
Shoprite, at the end of Sokoine Rd, beyond Meru Post Office and opposite the long distance bus station. A South African chain which is beginning to feature in most African cities. An enormous supermarket selling just about anything you might be looking for.

▲ Activities and tours

Arusha *p258, map p260*
Golf
Gymkhana Club, Haile Selassie Rd out towards the High Court. 9-hole golf course. Temporary membership available. Also has facilities for tennis and squash.

Horse and camel riding
Horse safaris are increasingly popular and can be arranged through the tour operators in Arusha. Most of these begin from Usa River, which is 22 km from Arusha on the Moshi road. For camel rides guided by a local Masai, see **Mkuru Camel Sarfari**, page 264.
Equestrian Safaris, based on a farm on the slopes of Mt Meru, www.safaririding.com. Offer day rides, and 3-14 day horse safaris around Kilimanjaro, Meru and Lake Natron. These are for experienced riders as several hours a day are spent in the saddle. A real opportunity to explore terrain where vehicles cannot go. Full board rates inclusive of meals and fly camping are around US$300 per day.
Meserani Snake Park (see page 263). Ride a camel to a nearby Masai village.

Running
Mt Meru Marathon is held yearly and attracts competitors from all around the world.

Swimming
Available at the pool at the **Il Boru Safari Lodge**, open to non-residents.

Tour operators
Note The cost of taking foreign-registered cars into the national parks in Tanzania means that it is usually cheaper to go on a safari in a Tanzania-registered vehicle.

There are over 100 tour operators and safari companies based in Arusha who organize safaris to the different national parks in the northern circuit (see next chapter). Most also offer Mt Kilimanjaro and Meru treks, holidays in Zanzibar, hotel and lodge reservations, vehicle hire, charter flights, cultural tours, and safaris to the other parks. The list below is far from comprehensive. It is just a matter of finding one you like and discussing what you would like to do. See box opposite, for further information. Many have also adopted cultural or environmental policies – supporting local communities, schools or empowerment projects – which

How to organize a safari

→ Figure out how much money you are willing to spend, how many days you would like to go for, which parks you want to visit and when you want to go.

→ If you have the time before arriving in Arusha, check out the websites and contact the safari operators with questions and ideas. Decide which ones you prefer from the quality of the feedback you get.

→ Go to the Tanzania Tourist Board at the clock tower and ask to see the list of licensed tour operators. Also ask to have a copy of the companies that are blacklisted and that are not licensed to operate tours.

→ Pick 3-4 tour operators in your price range.

→ Shop around. Talk to the companies. Notice if they are asking you questions in order to gain an understanding of what you are looking for, or if they are just trying to book you on their next safari (regardless of what would be the best for you). Also, are they open about answering your questions and interested in helping you get the information you need. Avoid the ones that are pressuring you.

→ Make sure you understand what is included in the price, and what is not. Normally, breakfast on the first day and dinner/accommodation on the last day is not included.

→ Listen to the salesperson and guide. They have current news about which parks are best at the moment. If they recommend you a different itinerary than you originally planned, it is probably the best itinerary for game viewing. They know the best areas to visit depending on the time of year and where the animals are in their yearly migrations.

→ Get a contract with all details regarding itinerary, conditions and payment.

→ Ask what kind of meals you can expect. If you are on a special diet, confirm that they can accommodate your needs.

→ Ask how many people will be on the safari. Make sure there is enough room in the vehicle for people and equipment.

→ Talk to the guide. Make sure that he is able to communicate with you, and that he is knowledgeable.

→ If possible, inspect the vehicle you will be using beforehand. If you are going on a camping safari or trek, ask to see the equipment (tents, sleeping bags, etc).

are worth thinking about when choosing a safari operator. On the downside, travellers have reported that rival tour companies sometimes double up, with 2 or 3 groups sharing the same cars and other facilities – all paying different amounts. As a result, itineraries are changed without agreement. It is a good idea to draw up a written contract of exactly what is included in the price agreed before handing over any money. Sometimes touts for rival tour companies are very persistent and this can be very frustrating. To get them off your back, tell

them you have already booked a safari even if you haven't. Once in Arusha, give yourself at least a day or 2 to shop around and organize everything. Likewise, allow for at least 1 night in Arusha on the final day of your safari as you will usually return late.

For details of other safari companies, both within Tanzania and overseas, see page 58. **Aardvark Expeditions**, Old Moshi Rd, Kijenge, T0754-759120 (mob). Good reports about this company, which operates mostly mid-upper range safaris and treks. As well as Meru and Kilimanjaro, they also offer treks to

Ol Donyo Lengai and to Olmeti and Empakai Craters, and safaris across the country.

Abercrombie & Kent, Njiro Hill, T027-250 8347, www.akdmc.com. Quality operator with years of experience, not cheap but they use the best local guides and have a variety of tours in the region, online reservations.

Adventureland Safaris, Sokoine Rd, T0744-886339 (mob), www.adventurelandsafari.com. All safaris, Kili and Meru climbs, cultural tours to the Lake Natron and Lake Eyasi regions, trips to Zanzibar. Budget operator.

Africa Royal Trekking, based at Arusha View Campsite, see Sleeping, page 273, T027-246 3391, www.africa-royal-trekking.com. Safaris, Meru and Kilimanjaro climbs.

Africa Walking Company, awc-richard@habari.co.tz. Specialist Kilimanjaro operator with fixed weekly departures through various tour operators on the quieter routes for Kilimanjaro, the Rongai and Shira routes. Excellent value. Highly recommended.

African Adventures, AICC, Suite 10527, T0744-263147 (mob), www.africanadventures.com. Camping and lodge safaris to the northern circuit, climbing, Zanzibar add-ons.

African Trails Ltd, New Safari Hotel Complex, Boma Rd, 2nd floor, T027-250 4406, www.africantrails.com. Mid-range and budget tours to the major parks.

Angoni Safaris, AICC, www.angoni.com. Safaris throughout Tanzania, cultural tours including trekking and donkey rides. Car hire.

Bobby Tours, Goliondoi Rd, T027-250 3490, www.bobbytours.com. Good value camping

safaris, expect to pay around US$300 for a 3 day/2 night safari to the crater and Serengeti. Established operator but reports of poor camping equipment.

Bush Buck Safaris, Simeon Rd, T027-250 7779, www.bushbuckltd.com. An established operator with 20 years experience, all safaris, hotel reservations, special arrangements for honeymooners, all the vehicles are 4WD landrovers, not minibuses.

Classic Tours and Safaris, Impala Hotel, see Sleeping, page 271, T027-2508448, www.theclassictours.com. Safaris to northern circuit plus mountain climbs, Gombe, Usambara Mountains, all budgets. Recommended.

Duma Safaris, Njiro Rd, T027-250 0115, www.dumasafari.com. Consistently good feedback from readers for this company. Kilimanjaro climb US$850, 6-day northern circuit US$900, some of their profits support a local school, excellent guides and food.

Easy Travel & Tours Ltd, New Safari, see Sleeping, page 271, T027-250 3929. In Dar, see page 93, www.easy travel.co.tz. Budget tours to all the Tanzanian parks, mountain trekking for Kili and Meru, travel agent with representation of Air Zimbabwe and Air Mauritius.

Fly-Catcher Safaris, Serengeti Rd, T027-254 4109, www.flycat.com. Safaris to Rubondo, Serengeti, Kitavi and Mahale. Dutch speaking.

Fortes Safaris, Nairobi Rd, T027-254 4887, www.fortes-safaris.com. Trips to Lake Eyasi, where they have an upmarket tented camp.

Good Earth Tours and Safaris, T027-250 8334, www.goodearthtours.com. Toll free (USA) T877-265 9003. Kili climbs, safaris, beach holidays, standard and luxury lodges.

Green Footprint Adventures, Sekei Village Rd, T0784-330495 (mob), www.greenfoot print.co.tz. Offer more adventurous activities such as canoeing in Manyara and Arusha national parks, night game drives in Manyara, and mid- to high-budget safaris (from US$350 a day) specializing in small camps and lodges.

Hima Tours & Travel, Shule Rd, T0784-211 131 (mob), www.himatours.com. A variety of tours, helpful staff.

Hoopoe Safaris, India St, T027-250 7011, UK address: PO Box 278, Watford WD19 4WH, T+44-(0)1923-255462, www.hoopoe.com. Consistently recommended by travellers. Excellent commitment to local communities and conservation. Range of safaris and climbs, and unusual trekking itineraries including a 5-day trek with donkeys and the Masai. Run exclusive safaris using their **Kirurumu Tented Camps and Lodges**. Some of the permanent camps are listed in the relevant chapters, some move seasonally. Highly recommended.

JMT African Heart, just outside town, not far from **Ilboru Safari Lodge**, T027-250 8414, www.africanheart.com. Luxury and budget safaris. Horseback, motorbike and mountain bike safaris, cultural treks, Kili climbs, Zanzibar.

JM Tours Ltd, Plot 15, Olorien, T027-250 1034, www.jmtours.co.tz. Specializing in travel planning for disabled travellers, school exchange programs and cultural tourism.

Kearsley Travel & Tours, next to Golden Rose Hotel, T027-2508 043/4, www.kearsley. net. Established safari operator with over 50 years experience.

Klub Afriko Safaris, at the Klub Afriko Hotel, see page 272, T027-254 8878, www.klub afriko.com. Various safaris, specializing in Serengeti, Tarangire, Zanzibar and Kilimanjaro.

Laitolya Tours and Safaris, Meru Plaza, Esso Rd, T027-250 9536, www.laitolya.com. Northern circuit, Mikumi, Udzungwa and Bagamoyo. Scheduled and custom-made.

Leopard Tours, Old Moshi Rd, Kijenge, T027-250 3603, www.leopard-tours.com. One of the bigger tour operators offering safaris in the northern circuit, Kilimanjaro climbs, cultural and historical tours, and beach trips.

Lions Safari International, Sakina/Nairobi Rd, T027-250 6423, www.lions-safari-intl.com. Good, professional company operating camping and lodge 3-11 day safaris.

Moon Adventure Tours & Safaris, Seth Benjamin Rd, opposite Meru School, T027-250 4462, www.moon-adventure.com. Low cost camping safaris, Ngorongoro Highlands trekking, birdwatching safaris.

Nature Beauties, Old Moshi Rd, T027-250 4083, www.nature-beauties.com. Alternative routes and trekking safaris. Strong focus on sustainability of environment.

Nature Discovery, Box 10574, T027-254 4063/8406, T0754-400003 (mob), www. naturediscovery.com. Tailor their trips, including Kilimajaro and Oldonyo Lengai climbs, to the traveller and their budget.

Predators Safari Club, Namanga Rd, Sakina, T027-250 6471, www.predators-safaris.com. Wide range of safaris from luxury lodges to camping all over Kenya and Tanzania, good national park combination packages, professionally run. Recommended.

Ranger Safaris, Wachagga St, T027-250 3023, www.rangersafaris.com. Easily one of the biggest safari operators in Tanzania with a wide choice of lodge and camping safaris from 3-10 days and regular departure dates.

Roy Safaris Ltd, 44 Serengeti Rd, T027-250 2115, T027-250 8010, www.roysafaris.com. Good value and experienced operator offering both luxury lodge and camping safaris to the northern circuit game parks and Kili and Meru treks, as well as treks in the Ngorongoro highlands, trips to Zanzibar and cultural tours.

Shidolya Safaris, AICC, T027-254 8506, www.shidolya-safaris.com. Drivers, cooks and guides are excellent, recommended for lodge or camping safaris but not the Kili climb. Birdwatching safaris in Arusha National Park.

Simba Safaris, between Goliondoi Rd and India St, T027-250 1504, www.simbasafaris. com. Kili climbs, reservations for Pemba and Mafia, safari packages, lots of departure dates.

Skylink Travel & Tours, Bushbuck Building, T027-211 5381, www.skylinktanzania.com. Quality travel agent for flights, also has offices in Dar and Mwanza, agent for Avis Rent-a-Car.

Sunny Safaris Ltd, Col Middleton Rd, opposite **Golden Rose Hotel**, T027-250 8184, www.sunnysafaris.com. A very good fleet of game viewing vehicles, lodge and camping safaris, mountain trekking, mountain bike and walking safaris.

Tanganyika Film & Safari Outfitters, T027-250 2713, www.tanzania-safari.com. Top-of-the-range tailor-made safaris for individuals, private groups, professional photographers and filmmakers.

Takims Holidays Tours and Safaris, Uhuru Rd, T027-250 8026, www.takimsholidays.com. An established operator with over 20 years' experience. Photographic safaris to all the

national parks, including Serengeti, Kilimanjaro, Selous and Ruaha. Recommended.

Tanzania Serengeti Adventure, Sokoine Rd, T027-250 8475, T027-250 4069 www.about tanzania.com. Range of tented lodge or budget camping safaris and lodge bookings.

Tanzania Travel Company, AICC, Ngorongoro wing, T027-250 9938, T0754-294365 (mob), www.tanzaniatravelcompany.com. Experienced and reliable, offering a range of classic and budget safaris, Kilimanjaro and Meru climbs, cultural tours, trekking with Masai and trips to Zanzibar. Friendly and helpful, knowledgeable staff. Highly recommended.

Tropical Trails, Masai Camp on Old Moshi Rd, T027-250 0358, www.tropicaltrails.com. Experienced operator offering northern circuit safaris aimed at the budget and mid-range traveller, Lengani, Meru and Kilimanjaro climbs, cultural tours and crater highland trekking. Recommended.

Victoria Expeditions Safaris & Travels, Meru House Inn, Sokoine Rd, T027-250 0444, T0754-288740 (mob), www.victoriatz.com. Professionally run safaris and trekking, northern circuit from 2-7 days camping, Zanzibar beach holidays, Kili climbs. Can accommodate disabled clients.

Wild Frontiers, reservations Johannesburg, T+27-117 022 035, www.wildfrontiers.com. Excellent tour operator offering safaris across Tanzania, particularly northern circuit and southern national parks, and Kilimanjaro treks. They also run lovely mobile camps in the Serengeti and Ngorongoro. One of the few operators approved to undertake walking safaris in the Serengeti (see box page 317). Highly recommended.

Wildersun Safaris and Tours, Joel Maeda Rd, T027-254 8847, www.wildersun.com. Standard safaris and an unusual half-day trip to Lake Manyara National Park for canoeing.

WS Safaris Ltd, Moshono Village, near Baraa Primary School, Box 2288, T027-250 4004, www.wssafari.com. Offering a range of safaris, and tours for US$150 per person per day to the Serengeti and Ngorongoro.

Blacklist At the tourist office there is a blacklist of rogue travel agencies, unlicensed agents and the names of people who have convictions for cheating tourists. It is recommended that you cross-check before paying for a safari. In addition, when going on safari check at the park gate that all the fees have been paid, especially if you plan to stay for more than a day in the park. Also check that the name of the tour company is written on the permit. Sadly there is a lot of cheating at present, and many tourists have fallen victim to well-organized scams. The tourist office also has a list of accredited tour companies.

Babati and Mount Hanang p265
Cultural safaris
Kahembe's Trekking and Cultural Safaris, T0784-397477 (mob), www.kahembecultural safaris.com. A local company whose owner, Joas Kahembe, has been the pioneer for tourism in this rarely visited but rewarding area. Offers a 2-day trek up Mt Hanang along the Katesh route for US$128 per person. The Katesh route can be completed in 1 day

with the ascent and descent taking up to 12 hrs in total. They also have a number of imaginative local tours for US$45 per person per day (US$40 each for 3 or more people). These include 3- to 5-day walking safaris that explore the still largely intact traditional culture of the semi-nomadic pastoralist Barbaig people, and other longer cultural safaris, which have visits to, and stays with, several different local ethnic groups. There is the chance to participate in local brick- and pottery-making and beer brewing, and visit development projects like cattle, dairy farming, or piped water projects. Arranges full board accommodation in local guesthouses and in selected family homes.

☻ Transport

Arusha p258, map p260
Air
Kilimanjaro International Airport, T027-250 2223, is half way between Arusha and Moshi. To get to the airport you can get the Air Tanzania or Precision Air shuttle buses, which leave about 2 hrs before flight departure. **Air Tanzania** fly to **Dar** daily (booking in advance is essential), Mon-Wed, Fri 0800, 1550 and 1930, Thu, Sat-Sun at 1615 (55 mins). Some flights have connections in Dar for **Zanzibar**.

Precision Air fly daily flight to **Dar** at 0915; and to **Nairobi** at 0835, 1615 and 1940. There are flights to **Mombasa** Mon-Wed, Sat-Sun 1440 (1 hr). Also a daily flight to **Shinyanga** (1½ hrs) and **Mwanza** at 1120 (2 hrs).

Closer to town is **Arusha Airport**, 10 km west along the road to Dodoma. This is mostly used for charter flights and scheduled services operated by **Coastal Air**. To **Dar** daily at 1215 via Zanzibar (2 hrs). To **Mwanza** daily 1230 via **Grumeti** (3½ hrs), **Manyara** and the other airstrips in the **Serengeti** (2½ hrs). To **Ruaha** 0800 (3½ hrs) via Manyara (25 mins), Tarangire and Dodoma.

Airline offices Air Tanzania, Boma Rd, T027-250 3201, www.airtanzania.com. Coastal Air, T027-211 7969, T027-211 7960, T0713-530730 (mob), www.coastal.cc. Ethiopian Airlines, New Safari Hotel Complex, Boma Rd, T027-250 6167, www.flyethiopia. com. KLM, New Safari Hote Complexl, Boma Rd, T027-250 8062/3, www.klm.com. Precision Air, New Safari Hotel Complex, Boma Rd T027-250 6903, T027-250 2836, www.precisionairtz.com.

Bus, dala-dala and shared taxi

There are now 2 bus stations in Arusha. The first is on Zaramo St just to the north of the market and buses from here mostly go to places not too far away. Buy your ticket from the driver on the day of travel. There are regular buses and *dala-dala* to **Moshi**, 1½ hrs, US$1.50. You can also get a shared taxi, which will be more expensive.

Long distance buses go from the new bus station opposite the Shoprite Supermarket at the western end of Sokoine Rd. There are reported to be thieves operating around the Arusha bus stations and there are certainly many persistent touts. Go directly to the bus companies' offices and make sure there is the company's stamp on the ticket. There are daily departures to **Tanga** and **Mwanza**: via both the **Serengeti** and **Singida**. There are countless departures each day to **Dar**, 8-9 hrs, around US$30 'luxury', US$20 'semi-luxury' and US$12 'ordinary'. The road has improved considerably and journey times are shortening. **Taqwa** offers a fast, reliable service; **Fresh ya Shamba** and Royale are also very good; **Scandinavia Express Services Ltd**, Kituoni St near the police mess, south of the bus station, T027-250 0153, www.scandinaviagroup.com, are recommended for reliability and safety.

To Kenya *Dala-dala* take 4 or 5 hrs from here, depart regularly through the day, and the border crossing is efficient. There are several through shuttle services to **Nairobi**, including **Riverside Shuttle**, ACU Building, Sokoine Rd, T027-250 2639, www.riverside-shuttle.com, which departs at 0800 and 1400 daily, US$25.

Car hire

Available from most tour companies and **Angoni**, AICC, T027-250 8498, www.angoni. com, which offers car hire and shuttle services; **Avis**, Bushbuck Building, T027-250 9108, www.avis.com.

Cars can also be hired at the Arusha **Naaz Hotel**, **Golden Rose Hotel** and **Meru House Inn**.

🅞 Directory

Arusha *p258*, map *p260*
Banks **Barclays**, Sopa Plaza, Serengeti Rd; **Central Bank of Tanzania**, Makongoro Rd near the roundabout with Goliondoi Rd; **CRDB**, further west along Sokoine Rd, on the corner with Singh St; **Exim**, at the Shoprite Centre; **National Bank of Commerce**, Sokoine Rd down towards the bridge; **Stanbic Bank**, next to the National Bank of Commerce; **Standard Chartered**, Goliondoi Rd. Almost all the town centre banks now have ATMs.
Currency exchange There are many forex offices in town. Some will change both cash and TCs as well as give cash advances in local currency against credit cards. Others will not change TCs – cash only. Most of the bureaux are open Mon-Sun 0900-1700. Good exchange rates at **National Bureau de Change**

opposite the post office at the clock tower. **Impala Hotel** will give cash advances but there is a large fee – approximately 25%. **Immigration** Immigration office, East Africa Rd, T027-250 3569, Mon-Fri 0730-1530 for visa extensions. **Internet** Places to check email are all over town. **The Patisserie**, near the clock tower; an internet café next to Meru House Inn on Sokoine Rd; and **McMoody's**, Sokoine Rd. Typical cost US$0.50 per hr. Worth looking around as there are differences in charges. **Medical services** AICC Hospital, Old Moshi Rd, T027-250 2329; **Mount Meru Hospital**, opposite AICC, East Africa Rd, T027- 250 3352/4; **X-Ray Centre**, near the tourist office, T027-250 2345.

Police Makongoro Rd, T111/112. **Post office** The main post office is by the clock tower opposite the Arusha Hotel, Mon-Fri, 0800-1230, 1400-1630, Sat 0800-1230. Meru Post Office is at the other end of Sokoine Rd beyond the market. There are 3 other post offices around town. **Courier Services** DHL, Sokoine Rd next to the Stanbic Bank, T027-250 6749. **Telephone** The cheapest place to make calls is from the **Telephone House** on Boma Rd, opposite the tourist office. Very efficient service, Mon-Sat 0800-2200, Sun 0900-2000. There are also mobile phone shops all over town if you plan to buy a local SIM card. The main networks are Vodacom, Zain, Tigi and Zantec.

Contents

Footprint features

Northern Circuit game parks

At a glance

⊖ **Getting around** The best option is local tour operators, they cater for every budget. There is some public transport to towns near park borders, then you'll need to book day trips into parks.

◉ **Time required** At least 3 days for the Serengeti and a day for Ngorongoro Crater. If you want to go off the beaten track, a couple of days for Manyara or Tarangire – both are worth exploring.

☼ **Weather** Warm and sunny for most of the year, although evenings can be cool, especially during Jun-Oct. Light rains Nov-Dec and heavy rains end of Mar-May. Hot and sticky before the rains.

✕ **When not to go** Roads in the parks can be challeging and often impassable during the rainy season (Apr-May), with access to the crater floor sometimes restricted.

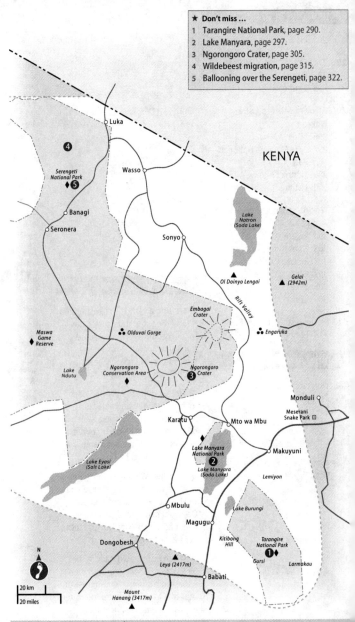

★ **Don't miss ...**
1 Tarangire National Park, page 290.
2 Lake Manyara, page 297.
3 Ngorongoro Crater, page 305.
4 Wildebeest migration, page 315.
5 Ballooning over the Serengeti, page 322.

KENYA

Luka

④

Wasso

Serengeti
National Park
◆⑤

Lake
Natron
(Soda Lake)

Banagi

Seronera

Sonyo

Ol Doinyo Lengai

Gelai
(2942m)

Rift Valley

Embagai
Crater

Maswa
Game
Reserve

Olduvai Gorge

Engaruka

Lake
Ndutu

Ngorongoro
Conservation
Area

Ngorongoro
Crater
③

Monduli

Meserani
Snake Park

Karatu

Mto wa Mbu

Lake Manyara
National Park
②

Makuyuni

Lake Eyasi
(Salt Lake)

Lake Manyara
(Soda Lake)

Lemiyon

Mbulu

Magugu

Lake Burungi

Dongobesh

Kitibong
Hill

Tarangire
National Park
①◆

Gursi

Larmakau

Leya (2417m)

Babati

N

20 km
20 miles

Mount
Hanang (3417m)

Everything you imagine Africa to be is here in the Northern Circuit Game Parks, from the soaring masses of wildebeest galloping across the plains of the Serengeti, to the iconic image of a lone acacia tree at sunset, to exclusive *Out of Africa*-style lodges deep in the bush. By now, the area's extremely experienced in catering for tourists – it's the most visited area of Tanzania – and it's able to provide for most budgets from the uber-luxurious to the camping backpackers.

Despite it's popularity, it's still easy to escape the crowds. Tarangire National Park, famous for its elephants and quirky baobab trees, is overlooked by many travellers wanting to head for the big names in game parks, and yet it has a gentle beauty and varied landscape with tremendous bird life as well as game. Then there's Lake Manyara National Park, where the lake becomes a blanket of pink, as flamingos come here to feed on their migratory route. Also in this region are the little visited Lake Natron and Ol Doinyo Lengai volcano – a challenging climb for robust walkers – which offer a glimpse into the rural lives of the local Masai.

Ngorongoro Crater never disappoints and because of its steep sides down into the crater, it has almost captive wildlife. Even if you see nothing, the stunning landscapes in this 265 sq km caldera plunged 600m from its rim are reward enough. And last but far from least, there's the vast Serengeti. From December to April it's the scene of the world's most famous mass migration, when hundreds of thousands of wildebeest pound the path trodden for centuries to the Masai Mara – definitely a sight not to be missed.

Ins and outs

About 80 km west from Arusha on the road towards Dodoma, there is a T-junction at Makuyuni. The entrance to the Tarangire National Park is 40 km to the south of this junction off the Arusha–Dodoma road, whilst the road that heads due west goes towards Lake Manyara, the Ngorongoro Crater and the Serengeti. This road used to be notoriously bad, with deep ruts and potholes, but it was upgraded a few years ago to smooth tar all the way to the gate of the crater, thanks to overseas funding from Japan. The drive to the gate of the Ngorongoro Crater Reserve takes about four hours and is a splendid journey. On clear days, you'll have a view of Mount Kilimanjaro all the way, arching over the right shoulder of Mount Meru. You will go across the bottom of the Rift Valley and at the small settlement of Mto wa Mbu, pass the entrance to the Lake Manyara National Park at the foot of the Great Rift Escarpment. Just beyond the entrance to the park the road climbs very steeply up the escarpment and there are wonderful views back down onto Lake Manyara. From here the country is hilly and fertile and you will climb up to the Mbulu Plateau which is farmed with wheat, maize and coffee. The extinct volcano of Ol Deani has gentle slopes and is a prominent feature of the landscape.

All the safari operators offer at the very least a three day and two night safari of the crater and Serengeti, most offer extended tours to include Tarangire or Manyara, and some include the less visited Ol Doinyo Lengai and Lake Natron. There is the option of self-drive but as non-Tanzanian vehicles attract much higher entrance fees into the parks, this is not normally cost effective. ▸▸ *For more information on national park fees and safaris, see page 41. For safari tour operators in Arusha, see page 278.*

Tarangire National Park

→ *Colour map 1, A4. 3°50'S, 35°55'E. Altitude: 1110 m.*
Unjustifiably considered the poor relation to its neighbouring parks, Tarangire may have a less spectacular landscape and does make you work harder for your game, but it also retains a real sense of wilderness reminiscent of more remote parks like Ruaha and Katavi. Famous for its enormous herds of elephant that congregate along the river, it is not unusual to see groups of 100 more and there are some impressive old bulls. ▸▸ *For listings, see page 294-295.*

Park fees and information

Tarangire National Park, established in 1970, covers an area of 2600 sq km and is named after the river that flows through it throughout the year. The gate opens at 0630, although an earlier entrance is possible if you have paid the entry fee of US$35 in advance. The best time to visit is in the dry season from July to September when the animals gather in large numbers along the river. Although you may not see as many animals here as in other places, Tarangire is a wonderful park. There are fewer people here than in Ngorongoro and that is very much part of the attraction. One of the most noticeable things on entering the park are the baobab trees that rise up from the grass, instantly recognizable by their massive trunks. As the park includes within its boundaries a number of hills, as well as rivers and swamps, there is a variety of vegetation zones and habitats. The river rises in the Kondoa Highlands to the south, and flows north through the length of the park. It continues to flow during the dry season and so is a vital watering point for the animals of the park as well as those from surrounding areas.

Wildlife

The Tarangire National Park forms a 'dry season retreat' for much of the wildlife of the southern Masailand. The ecosystem in this area involves more than just Tarangire National Park. Also included are the Lake Manyara National Park to the north and a number of 'Game Controlled Areas'. The largest of these are the Lake Natron Game Controlled Area

Tarangire National Park

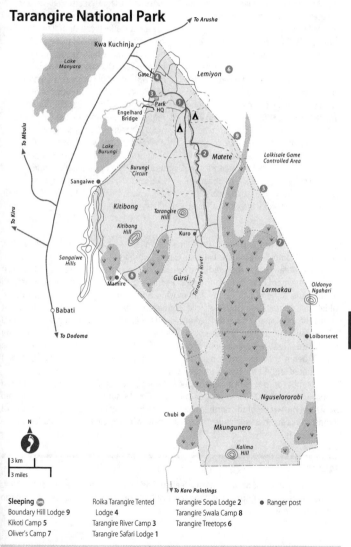

Sleeping 🛌
Boundary Hill Lodge **9**
Kikoti Camp **5**
Oliver's Camp **7**

Roika Tarangire Tented Lodge **4**
Tarangire River Camp **3**
Tarangire Safari Lodge **1**

Tarangire Sopa Lodge **2**
Tarangire Swala Camp **8**
Tarangire Treetops **6**

● Ranger post

Tsetse fly

The tsetse fly is a little larger than the house fly and is found over much of East Africa including Tanzania. It is a carrier of the disease known as 'sleeping sickness' or African trypanosomiasis, known as *nagana* among the people of Tanzania. This disease can be deadly to cattle and is therefore of great economic concern to large rural areas of Africa. The presence of the tsetse fly has meant that large areas of Tanzania are uninhabitable by cattle and consequently human beings, as farmers need to live where their livestock grazes. Instead these regions are left to the wild animals, as interestingly, the tsetse fly does not affect them. Since the colonial era, the areas have been gradually designated as national parks and game reserves. Tanzania is probably the worst affected by tsetse fly of all the countries of East Africa, which goes some way to explain why 23% of the country is in designated parks and reserves. Tsetse flies can also infect humans with sleeping sickness – the disease affects the central nervous system and does indeed make you sleepy during the day – but cases in humans are very rare. Occasionally there have been endemics of sleeping sickness in East Africa, but these usually occur when large groups of people are dispersed, refugees for example, into an infected area. Tsetse flies, however, do administer a wicked bite so try and steer clear of them. They are attracted to large objects and certain smells and dark colours – like cows. If you are riding a horse a tsetse fly is more likely to bite the horse than you.

further north and the Simanjiro Plains Game Controlled Area towards Arusha. The Mto wa Mbu Game Controlled Area, the Lolkisale Game Controlled Area and Mkungunero Game Controlled Area are also included. The key to the ecosystem is the river and the main animal movements begin from the river at the beginning of the short rains around October and November. The animals moving north during the wet season include wildebeest, zebra, Thompson's gazelles, buffalo, eland and hartebeest. The elephant population in this park was estimated at around 6000 in 1987 but numbers are believed to have fallen since then because of poaching. At the height of the rainy season the animals are spread out over an area of over 20,000 sq km. When the wet season ends the animals begin their migration back south and spend the dry season (July-October) concentrated around the River Tarangire until the rains begin again.

The number of species of birds recorded in Tarangire National Park has been estimated at approximately 300. These include migrants that fly south to spend October-April away from the winter of the northern hemisphere. Here you may spot various species of herons, storks and ducks, vultures, buzzards, sparrowhawks, eagles, kites and falcons, as well as ostrich.

Routes

The park is large enough for it not to feel crowded even when there are quite a few visitors. There are a number of routes or circuits that you can follow that take you to the major attractions.

Lake Burungi circuit

Covering about 80 km, this circuit starts at the Engelhard Bridge and goes clockwise, along the river bank. Continue through the acacia trees until about 3 km before the Kuro Range Post where you will see a turning off to the right. Down this track you will pass through a section of Combretum-Dalergia woodland as you head towards the western boundary of the park. The route continues around and the vegetation turns back to parkland with acacia trees and then back to Combretum as the road turns right and reaches a full circle at the Engelhard Bridge. The lake water levels have fallen and Lake Burungi is almost dry. If you are very lucky you may see leopard and rhino in this area, although the numbers of rhino have reportedly decreased.

Lemiyon area

This circuit covers the northern area of the park bound on each side by the eastern and western boundaries park and to the south by the river. This is where you will see the fascinating baobab trees with their large silvery trunks and gourd-like fruits. Their huge trunks enable the trees to survive through a number of rain failures and they are characteristic of this type of landscape. Also found here are acacia trees, which provide food for giraffe. Other animals that you expect to see are wildebeest, zebra, gazelles and elephant.

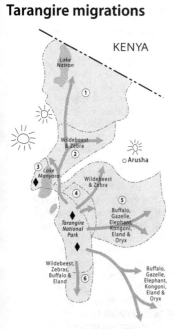

Tarangire migrations

Lake Natron Game Controlled Area **1**
Mto wa Mbu Game Controlled Area **2**
Lake Manyara National Park **3**
Lolkisale Game Controlled Area **4**
Simanjiro Game Controlled Area & Plains **5**
Mkungunero Game Controlled Area **6**

N

Not to scale

Kitibong Hill circuit

This track covers the west section of the park and is centred on Kitibong Hill. It includes acacia parkland in the east and Combretum-Dalbergia woodland in the west, the Gursi floodplains to the south and the foothills of Sangaiwe Hills, which are along the western boundary of the park. This area homes a variety of plains animals including buffalo and elephant.

The Gursi and Lamarkau circuit

The grasslands found in the south of the park are home to many plain-grazing species. You are also likely to see ostrich here. During the wet season a large swamp forms in what is known as Larmakau – a corruption of the Masai word *'o'llakau'*, meaning hippo, which can be seen here.

Without a 4WD you will not be able to see much of the southernmost section of the park and during the wet season it is often impassable to all vehicles. There are two areas in the south – Nguselororobi to the east and Mkungunero in the southwest corner. The former is mainly swamp, with some plains and woodland, and if you are lucky you might see cheetah here. Mkungunero has a number of freshwater pools that serve to attract many different species.

Tarangire Conservation Area

The Tarangire Conservation Area is a 585 sq km area on the eastern boundaries of the park set aside by the local villages. The region comprises four distinct areas, the Lolkisale Conservation Area, the Naitolia Concession Area, the Makuyuni Elephant Dispersal Area, and the Lolkisale Livestock and Wildlife Zone. The Conservation Area was established to protect the main wet-season migration route from the park and provide the animals with a natural sanctuary from the demands of modern farming methods such as extensive deforestation by illegal charcoal collectors and years of indiscriminate poaching. What makes this whole project unique is that revenue goes directly into the local community and members of these same communities are being employed by tourism-based services within the area (see **Boundary Hill Lodge**, below). The local craftsmen have been involved in building the new lodges in the area using local renewable materials from the surrounding regions; the village councils sit on the board of directors; and women empowerment projects and local schools have received funding from the project. For more information visit www.tarangireconservation.com.

⦿ Tarangire National Park listings

For Sleeping and Eating price codes and other relevant information, see pages 36-40.

⦿ Sleeping

Tarangire National Park *p290, map p291*
L Boundary Hill Lodge, located just outside the park within the Lolkisale Conservation Area, T0787-293727 (mob), www.tarangire conservation.com. This lodge – part-owned by the local Masai community and benefiting community projects – has 8 rooms built on the hillside, all affording total privacy with unobstructed views over the savannah and swamps. The rooms are individually designed, some with outdoor baths and toilets with a view. Walking safaris, night drives and fly camping available. Rates from US$240 per person including activities, with special offers on the website.
L Kikoti Camp, in the conservation area adjoining the park, reservations, Arusha, T027-250 8790, www.safarilegacy.com. A small luxury tented lodge built amongst a landscape of ancient boulders, baobab, mopane and fig trees, with 10 spacious tents with grass roofs and wooden decks.

Large eating boma with outside campfire and comfortable deck chairs. Bush breakfast and lunches are served in secluded areas, sundowners on Kikoti Rock. Bush walks as well as game drives on offer and visits to the local Masai village. Rates from US$410 per person.
L Tarangire Sopa Lodge, in the northeast of the park, about 30 km from the main gate, signposted, T027-250 0630/9, www.sopa lodges.com. If you like intimate lodges, then this might disappoint. A large luxury lodge with 75 suites, opulent lounges, bars and restaurant. Excellent food and barbecues, large landscaped swimming pool on the edge of a rocky gorge and a shop. Rooms and the pool area are currently being refurbished. There are less impersonal choices of accommodation in the park. Rates are from US$265 per person full board.
L Tarangire Swala Camp, on the edge of the Gursi swamp, reservations, Arusha, T027-250 9816, www.kusini.com. Camp closed during the rainy season Apr-Jun. A first-class site for birdwatching. Comprises 9 extremely comfortable guest tents raised on a wooden deck above the ground under acacia trees,

with en suite facilities. Silver service dining. The staff and management team at Swala have initiated a conservation project that has recently led to the building of a school for the children of a village that borders Tarangire. Rates US$490 per person full board (not including drives).

L Tarangire Treetops, in the conservation area, T027-250 0630, www.elewana.com. The 20 enormous rooms at this lodge take the form of stilt houses, constructed 3-5 m up in huge baobab and marula trees on a wooded hillside overlooking the Tarangire Sand River. It really is a beautiful and luxurious lodge, but its weakness lies in its location, being a considerable distance on rough roads from the main game-viewing areas in Tarangire. Nevertheless, excellent food and service, a swimming pool, walking safaris and night drives on offer. Rates in the region of US$780 per person full board, including game drives and activities.

A Oliver's Camp, in the eastern part of Tarangire National Park, www.asilialodges.com Intimate small luxury camp with 8 tents, a library and drinks tent, open air dining with the manager and guides who offer walking safaris and game drives during the day. One tent is in a secluded location in the bush for honeymooners, carefully designed to blend into the landscape.

A Roika Tarangire Tented Lodge, on the banks of the river about 5 km from the park gate, T0787-673338 (mob), www.tarangire roikatentedlodge.com Opened in Jan 2008, this tented camp set in 20 ha has 20 rooms themed to individual animals with stunning wood carvings on everything from lamp stands to bedposts. Rather obscure concrete 'animal' baths extend the theme – check out the elephant bath if you can. It's not as scenically striking as its neighbour the **Tarangire River Camp**, and they seem to have gone overboard on the concrete stones in the bar but it does have a quirky charm. Reduced rates during the low season.

B Tarangire River Camp, within a concession area set aside for conservation by the local Masai community of Minjingu, which borders Tarangire in the northwest, 3.5 km from the main gate, T027-254 7007, www.mbalimbali.com. In a beautiful setting overlooking the river and the Masai Steppes, and shaded by a giant baobab tree, the 21 well equipped tents have wooden decks and en suite bathrooms. The main building is an elegant elevated thatch and timber structure comprising a main lounge, wildlife reference library, dining room and cocktail bar.

C Tarangire Safari Lodge, 10 km into the park from the gate, lodge T027-253 1447/8, reservations, Arusha, T027-254 4752, www.tarangiresafarilodge.com. This is a lovely lodge with tents set on an escarpment overlooking the Tarangire River with acacia-studded plains and beautiful sunrises. Sleeps 70, good restaurant and bar with a large swimming pool, children's pool with slide, and considerable discounts for children. This area is relatively free of tsetse flies which are a problem in other areas of the park. Excellent value considering its location within the park. Recommended.

Camping

The **National Park's public campsite** is 10 mins into the park from the gate and set amongst a grove of impressive baobab trees. Toilet and shower facilities are simple but above average. US$30.

There are also 12 special campsites, water and firewood are provided but there are no other facilities. Nor have they been sympathetically located in decent positions with nice views. They are, however, generally pleasant and pretty remote. US$50. These are used by the safari operators on camping tours. Further information is available from Tanzania National Parks, head office, see page 259.

Mto wa Mbu to Lake Natron

From the turn off on the Arusha–Dodoma road, the road heads through the small town of Mto wa Mbu, home to many distinctive red-clad Masai. This used to be a popular stop for safari-goers who wanted to rest and have a break from the bumpy road, but these days the smooth tarmac carries vehicles straight through town. It is, however, the closest town to Lake Manyara National Park gate and from here is another road that goes north to Lake Natron. There are fabulous views over Manyara from the road that climbs up this escarpment from Mto wa Mbu towards the crater. In contrast to Kenya, here there is no eastern wall to the Rift Valley which flattens out as the fault continues south. >> *For listings, see pages 300-302.*

Ins and outs

Getting there There are community initiatives using the local Masai people as guides who can arrange a visit to this region, for example the **Mkuru Camel Safari Cultural Tourism Programme** (see page 264) or the **Engaruka Cultural Tourism Programme** (see below). Several tour operators also offer cultural tours in this region using the local people as guides. These include **Hoopoe, Roy Safaris, Takim's Holidays**, and **Klub Afrifo Safaris** (see Tour operators in Arusha, page 278).

Mto wa Mbu ☺ >> *pp300-302. Colour map 1, A4.*

Mto wa Mbu (meaning Mosquito Creek) is a small, busy market town selling fruit and vegetables grown by the fertile surrounding farms. It is on the route from Arusha to the northern safari circuit of Ngorongoro and Serengeti and only 3 km away from the gate of Lake Manyara National Park. You are likely to be welcomed to the town by people trying to sell the arts and crafts on display in the Masai central market, a cooperative of about 20 curio sellers, behind which is a fresh food market. However, all curios offered here seem to be more expensive than those in Arusha. Mto wa Mbu is a colourful town that's developed over recent years to accommodate its visitors. A new supermarket and bureau de change are due to open, there's a disco (**Safari Park**) near the market, which is popular with backpackers, and bikes are available for hire along the main street. It's worth exploring beyond this main street if you get chance, as you'll find plenty of local bars, a fruit and vegetable market and several local guesthouses for around US$10 a night if you're on a very limited budget.

The area around Mto wa Mbu was dry and sparsely populated until the irrigation programmes began in the 1950s, which transformed the area into an important fruit and vegetable growing region. (Look out for the distinctive red bananas for sale.) The accompanying population growth turned Mto wa Mbu into a melting pot of cultures. There is greater cultural diversity in this area than elsewhere in Tanzania, so in one day you can sample Chagga banana beer, or see a farmer from the Kigoma region make palm oil. The Rangi use papyrus from the lakes to make beautiful baskets and mats, and the Sandawe continue to make bows and arrows, which are used to hunt small game. On the surrounding plains the Masai tend their cattle, and there are occasional Masai cattle markets. Seeing so many red-robed Masai men all together is quite a striking sight.

The **Mto wa Mbu Cultural Tourism programme** ① *further information available from Tanzanian Tourist Information Centre, Arusha, see page 259, or www.infojep.com/culturaltours,* supported by the Tanzanian Tourist Board and SNV, the Dutch Development

Organization, offers an opportunity to support the local inhabitants and learn about their lifestyle. Walking safaris with Masai guides through the farms in the verdant oasis at the foot of the Rift Valley can be arranged. There are walks to Miwaleni Lake and waterfall where papyrus plants grow in abundance, or an opportunity to climb **Balaa Hill**, which overlooks the whole town. The Belgian Development Organization ACT has enabled locals to grow flowers commercially for export and there are colourful flower fields, with the wonderful backdrop of the Rift Valley. Alternatively, you can rent a bicycle and cycle through the banana plantations to see the **papyrus lake**. The landscape is awe inspiring with the escarpment rising vertically up into the sky on the one side and the semi-desert stretching away to the horizon on the other. The guides are all former students of Manyara secondary school and they have a reasonable standard of English. Profits from the tours are invested in development projects and for the promotion of energy-saving stoves.

Lake Manyara National Park ●● ▶ pp300-302. Colour map 1, A4. 3° 40'S, 35° 50'E.

On the way to Ngorongoro Crater and the Serengeti, Lake Manyara is well worth a stop in its own right. Set in the Great Rift Valley, Lake Manyara National Park is beneath the cliffs of the Manyara Escarpment, and was established in 1960. It covers an area of 325 sq km, of which 229 sq km is the lake. The remaining third is a slice of marshes, grassland and acacia woodland tucked between the lake and the escarpment whose reddish brown wall looms 600 m on the eastern horizon. ▶ For more information on national parks, see page 41.

Ins and outs
Getting there There is an airstrip near the park gate, and Coastal Air flies daily from Arusha. By car the park, 130 km west of Arusha, can be reached via the Arusha–Serengeti road. The drive from Arusha takes about 1½ hours.

Getting around The main road through the park is good enough for most vehicles, although some of the tracks may be closed during the wet season.

Park fees and information The best times to visit the park are December-February and May-July. The entrance fee is US$35.

Background
The lake is believed to have been formed 2- to 3-million years ago when, after the formation of the Rift Valley, streams poured over the valley wall. In the depression below, the water accumulated and so the lake was formed. It has shrunk significantly and was probably at its largest about 250,000 years ago. In recent years it has been noted that lake levels are falling in several of the lakes in the region, among them Lake Manyara. This trend often co-exists with the development of salt brines, the rise of which are anticipated.

Wildlife
The park's ground water forests, bush plains, baobob strewn cliffs, and algae-streaked hot springs offer incredible ecological variety in a small area. Lake Manyara's famous tree-climbing lions make the ancient mahogany and elegant acacias their home during the rainy season, and are a well-known but rather rare feature of the northern park. In addition to the lions, the national park is also home to the largest concentration of baboons anywhere in the world. Other animals include elephants, hippo and plains

animals, as well as a huge variety of birdlife, both resident and migratory. At certain times of the year Lake Manyara feeds thousands of flamingos, which form a shimmering pink zone around the lake shore. Other birds found here include ostrich, egrets, herons, pelicans and storks. Also seen are African spoonbills, various species of ibis, ducks and the rare pygmy goose. As with all the other parks, poaching has been a problem in the past and has affected the elephant population in particular. It was a shock when the census of 1987 found that their population had halved to under 200 in just a decade. At the gate of the national park is a small museum displaying some of the park's bird and rodent life.

Routes

A road from the park gate goes through the ground water forest before crossing the Marere River Bridge. This forest, as its name suggests, is fed not by rainfall, but by ground water from the high water table fed by seepage from the volcanic rock of the rift wall. The first animals you will see on entering the park will undoubtedly be baboons. About 500 m after this bridge the road forks. To the left the track leads to a plain known as **Mahali pa Nyati** (Place of the Buffalo), which has a herd of mainly old bulls cast out from their former herds. There are also zebra and impala in this area. This is also a track to the Hippo Pool here, formed by the Simba River on its way to the lake and home to hippos, flamingos and many other water birds.

Back on the main track the forest thins out to bush and the road crosses the Mchanga River (Sand River) and Msasa River. Shortly after this latter bridge there is a turning off to the left that leads down to the lakeshore where there is a peaceful picnic spot. Soon after this bridge, the surroundings change to acacia woodland. This is where the famous tree-climbing lions are found, so drive through very slowly and look for a tail dangling down through the branches.

Continue down the main road crossing the Chemchem River and on to the Ndala River. During the dry season you may see elephants digging in the dry riverbed for water. At the peak of the wet season the river may flood and the road is sometimes impassable as a result. Beyond the Ndala River the track runs closer to the Rift Valley Escarpment wall that rises steeply to the right of the road. On this slope are many different trees to those on the plain and as a result they provide a different habitat for various animals. The most noticeable are the very impressive baobab trees with their huge trunks.

.

.

.

Sleeping
Kiruruma Tented Lodge 2
Lake Manyara 1
Lake Manyara Serena Lodge 3
Lake Manyara Tree Lodge 6
Panorama Safari Camp 4

.

The first of the two sets of hot springs in the park are located where the track runs along the wall of the escarpment. These are the smaller of the two and so are called simply **Maji Moto Ndogo** (Small Hot Water). The temperature is about 40°C, heated to this temperature as it circulates to great depths in fractures that run through the rocks created during the formation of the Rift Valley. The second set of hot springs is further down the track over the Endabash River. These, known as **Maji Moto**, are both larger and hotter, reaching a temperature of 60°C. You are supposed to be able to cook an egg here in about 30 minutes. The main track ends at Maji Moto and you have to turn round and go back the same way. In total the track is between 35 and 40 km long.

North of Mto wa Mbu

Engaruka → *Colour map 1, A4.*

Engaruka, one of Tanzania's most important historical sites, is 63 km north of Mto wa Mbu on the road to Ol Doinyo Lengai and Lake Natron. Access along here is really only feasible by 4WD. The village lies at the foot of the Rift Valley escarpment. Masai cattle graze on the surrounding plains and dust cyclones often arise on the horizon. They are feared as the 'devil fingers' that can bring bad luck when they touch people.

In the 15th and 16th centuries the farming community here developed an ingenious irrigation system made of stone-block canals with terraced retaining walls enclosing parcels of land. The site included seven large villages. Water from the rift escarpment was channelled into the canals that led to the terraces. For some unknown reason the farmers left Engaruka around 1700. Several prominent archaeologists, including Louis Leakey, have investigated these ruins but to date there are many questions left unanswered about the people who built these irrigation channels, and why they abandoned the area. The ruins are deteriorating because, with the eradication of the tsetse fly, Masai cattle now come to graze in this area during the dry season, causing extensive damage.

The **Engaruka Cultural Tourism Programme** ① *further details available from Tanzanian Tourist Information Centre, Arusha, see page 259, or www.infojep.com/cultural_tours,* is supported by the Tanzanian Tourist Board and SNV, the Dutch Development Organization. In half a day you can tour the ruins or visit local farms to see current farming and irrigation methods. A Masai warrior can also guide you up the escarpment – from where there are views over the ruins and surrounding plains – pointing out trees and plants the Masai use as food and medicine along the way. In one day you can climb the peak of **Kerimasi** to the north of the village and there is a two-day hike up Kerimasi and then **Ol Doinyo Lengai** volcano (see below). The sodium-rich ashes from the volcano turn the water caustic, sometimes causing burns to the skin of the local Masai's livestock. Moneys generated are used to exclude cattle from the ruins and start conservation work, and also to improve the village primary school. There is no formal accommodation but it is possible to camp.

Ol Doinyo Lengai → *Altitude: 2886 m.*

① *As the mountain lies outside the conservation area no national park fees are payable.*

Ol Doinyo Lengai, the 'mountain of God', is Tanzania's only active volcano. It is north of and outside the Ngorongoro Conservation area in the heart of Masailand, to the west of the road to Lake Natron. This active volcano is continuously erupting, sometimes explosively but more commonly just subsurface bubbling of lava. It is the only volcano in the world that erupts natrocarbonatite lava, a highly fluid lava that contains almost no silicon, and is also much cooler and less viscous than basaltic lavas.

The white deposits are weathered natrocarbonatite ash and lava and these white-capped rocks near the summit are interpreted by the Masai as symbolizing the white beard of God. The last violent eruption was in 1993 and lava has occasionally flowed out of the crater, indeed there were minor eruptions as recently as 2007 and 2008. Only physically fit people should attempt the climb, note that the summit is frequently wreathed in clouds.

Although it is possible to climb the mountain, the trek up to the crater is an exceptionally demanding one. In parts of the crater that have been inactive for several months the ground is so soft that one sinks into it when walking. In rainy weather the light brown powdery surface turns white again because of chemical reactions that occur when the lava absorbs water. Climbs are frequently done at night as there is no shelter on the mountain and it gets extremely hot. The gradient is very steep towards the crater rim. A guide is required and you are strongly advised to wear sturdy leather hiking boots to protect against burns should you inadvertently step into liquid lava. Boots made of other fibres have been known to melt. Another safety precaution is to wear glasses to avoid lava splatter burns to the eyes.

Lake Natron → *Colour map 1, A4.*
This pink, alkaline lake is at the bottom of the Gregory Rift (part of the Great Rift Valley), touching the Kenyan border and about 250 km from Arusha. It is surrounded by escarpments and volcanic mountains, with a small volcano at the north end of the lake in Kenya, and the much larger volcano, Ol Doinyo Lengai, to the southeast of the lake (see above). The lake is infrequently visited by tourists because of its remoteness but numerous Masai herd cattle around here. The route from Arusha is through an area rich with wildlife, depending on the season, particularly ostriches, zebra and giraffe.

The lake has an exceptionally high concentration of salts and gets its pink colour from the billions of cyano-bacteria that form the flamingo's staple diet. There are hundreds of thousands of lesser flamingos here as this lake is their only regular breeding ground in East Africa. Often more of the birds are found here than at either Lake Magadi in Kenya or Lake Manyara. Lake Natron is also an important site for many other waterbird species, including palearctic migrants. A few kilometres upstream to the Ngare Sero River there are two **waterfalls**. Follow the river from the campsite: with the occasional bit of wading, it is a hike of about an hour.

◉ Mto wa Mbu to Lake Natron listings

For Sleeping and Eating price codes and other relevant information, see pages 36-40.

● Sleeping

Mto wa Mbu *p296*

L-A E Unoto Retreat, 14 km from Mto wa Mbu on the road to Lake Natron, T0787-622 724 (mob), www.maasaivillage.com. A Masai-inspired lodge nestling into the Rift Valley escarpment that resembles an authentic Masai village and blends into the surroundings. The 25 luxurious rooms are in separate bandas

with nice views over Lake Miwaleni which is home to many hippo. 4 of the bandas are designed for wheelchair users, and the honeymoon suite has a personal butler and luxurious heavy wood furniture. A small infinity pool overlooks the lake, bikes can be hired and guests are encouraged to interact with the local Masai on guided walks to the top of the Rift escarpment and to local villages, where the hotel owners recently built a school.

A Lake Manyara View Lodge, signposted on the main road to Ngorongoro about 3 km from Mto wa Mbu, signposted on the left,

T027-250 1329, www.lakemanyaraview.com. Recently opened, with spectacular views. Offer a variety of room styles from makouti-roofed bungalows with terraces overlooking the lake, to rather strange rooms built in the shape of baobab trees. Not all have lake views, so choose carefully. There are 33 rooms, although they plan to increase this to 70. The swimming pool overlooking Lake Manyara is still under construction. At US$340 for a double, prices are on the expensive side and it's difficult to judge at this stage whether they'll be justified. Reports welcome.

B-F Migunga, outside the park, just a couple of kilometres before the gate, T0765-043 676 (mob), www.moivaro.com. This lovely tented camp is set in 14 ha of acacia forest in a secluded part of Migungani Village. Bush-buck and other antelope are sometimes seen on the property. 19 spotless, self-contained tents, dining room and bar under thatch. Less luxurious than the normal tented camps, but much more affordable and rates include meals. There's also a shady campsite with 4 'mobile' tents set up with beds inside for US$20 per person or camping with your own tents for US$10 per person. Mountain biking, bird walks and village tours can be arranged. Reduced rates for low season.

C-F Jambo Lodge and Campsite, in Mto Wa Mbu, just a few doors away from **Twiga Campsite**, T027-253 9311, www.njake.com. Well maintained gardens and spotless en suite rooms in 2-storey houses with TV, fridge, and terrace or balcony. Swimming pool, restaurant and baobab tree bar. Spacious camping ground with good ablutions facilities, US$7 per person or US$20 if hiring a tent.

C-F Kiboko Bushcamp, 2 km before town on the Arusha Rd, 2 km from the main road, T027-253 9152, www.kibokolodge.com. 10 self-contained permanent tents in a lovely tract of acacia forest, set well apart under thatched roofs, though sparsely furnished with small beds and with unattractive concrete showers and toilets. Also has a large campsite but only 2 toilets and showers. Restaurant and bar in a large thatched building which looks rather tired, can organize Masai dancing.

C-F Twiga Campsite and Lodge, left of the main road in Mto wa Mbu going towards the gate of Lake Manyara National Park, T027-253 9101, twigacampsite@hotmail.com. There are some decent tent pitches at the back with plenty of shade, hot showers, a curio shop, and a reasonable bar and restaurant area near the swimming pool. Restaurant serves chicken, beef and rice, etc, and plenty of cold beer. The 34 new rooms are an improvement on the old ones and well worth the extra dollars, with TV, fridge, separate dining area. They're at the far end of the camp and so don't get as much noise from the street as the older rooms, which are fairly basic.

Camping

Sunbright Camp, near Mto wa Mbu, signposted on the right off the main road towards Ngorongoro Crater, T0754-815950 (mob), amiriadamu@yahoo.com. This pretty camp site with lovely gardens is a good option with a spacious bar and restaurant and good facilities. US$7 per person.

Lake Manyara National Park *p297, map p298*

L Kirurumu Tented Lodge, reservations, **Hoopoe Safaris**, Arusha T027-250 7011, T027-250 7541, www.kirurumu.com. Built on the escarpment in a stunning location overlooking the lake, 24 well appointed tents on solid platforms under thatched roofs, with splendid views, excellent service and meals, Relaxing bar with views over Lake Manyara.

L Lake Manyara Serena Lodge, on the edge of the eastern Rift Valley's Mto wa Mbu escarpment direct lodge number, T027-253 9160, reservations www.serenahotels.com. The main attraction here is the lovely infinity pool with views over to the lake. 67 rooms in round bungalows all with lake views, due to be renovated. 2 rooms available for wheelchair users, close to the hotel and main facilities. Wi-Fi available. Offers 'soft adventures' – mountain biking, forest hikes, nature and village walks, night game drives, canoe safaris when the lake isn't too shallow and children's programmes – available to everyone, not just staying guests. Manyara is perhaps the weaker of the 3 Serena lodges in the area, but remains a good and reliable option with fantastic views. Rates from US$550 full board for a double room.

L Lake Manyara Tree Lodge, reservations, Johannesburg, South Africa, T+27-11-809 4300, www.andbeyond.com. Set in the heart of a mahogany forest in the remote south-western region, this is the only lodge within the park and is nicely designed to exert minimal impact on the environment. The 10 luxurious treehouse suites are crafted from local timber and makuti palms, with en suite bathroom and outside shower, deck, fans, mosquito nets and butler service. Dining boma where guests can watch what is going on in the kitchen, breakfast and picnics can be organized on the lake shore. Swimming pool. Around of US$950 per person, but for this you get an impeccable safari experience, full board, wine, transfers, game drives and birdwatching safaris included in the price.

A Lake Manyara Hotel 300 m above the park, reservations, Arusha, T027-254 4595, www.hotelsandlodges-tanzania.com. On the escarpment overlooking the lake and park with wonderful views. Undergoing extensive renovation. There's a beautiful swimming pool in established gardens, a TV room, babysitting service, restaurant and bar (although there have been some negative reports about the food). Village walks and guided mountain bike trails arranged.

E-F Panorama Safari Camp, on escarpment overlooking the lake, 500 m from the main road, T027-253 9286. A very good budget option run by Hungarians. 10 large pre-erected tents with thatched roof, veranda and proper beds, US$40. Small tents with mattress are US$10 or camping with your own equipment is US$5. There's a decent ablutions block with hot water, and a bar and restaurant. Peaceful, away from the noise of the town, this is a good option for independent travellers.

National Park accommodation
There are 10 bandas just before the park entrance in a pretty tract of forest, though mosquitoes are an enormous problem here. Each have an en suite bathroom, sleep 2, and cost US$40 per person. There is also a youth hostel at park headquarters that sleeps 48, with basic facilities. Normally used by large groups only.

Camping There are 2 public campsites at the entrance to the park, with water, toilets and showers that cost US$30. There are 3 special campsites inside the park itself, all of which must be pre-booked as part of a safari and can only be used by one group at a time, US$50. Bookings through Tanzania National Parks head office, Arusha, see page 259.

Lake Natron *p300*

D Lake Natron Tented Camp, southwest of the lake, the only local accommodation near Lake Natron, operated by Moivaro, T027-250 6315, www.moivaro.com. 9 self-contained spacious tents with showers and flush toilets, thatched dining room and bar, swimming pool, solar power in all tents and dining room. You can also camp here if you have your own tent. The camp is an excellent base to explore the surrounding area on hikes and from which to climb Ol Doinyo Lengai. The camp can organize the climb and can offer transfers from and to Arusha if you have no transport.

Camping
Independent overlanders report that it is possible to bush camp reasonably close to the lake, or near the waterfalls on the Ngare Sero River, if fully self-sufficient. Remember that lions may visit the area to drink.

⊖ Transport

Lake Manyara National Park *p297, map p298*
Air
Coastal Air fly to **Arusha** daily at 1155 from the airstrip near the park gate.

Ngorongoro Conservation Area

→ *Colour map 1, A4. 3°11'S 35°32'E.*

*The Conservation area encompasses Ngorongoro Crater, Embagai Crater, Olduvai Gorge –
famous for its palaeontological relics – and Lake Masek. Lake Eyasi marks part of the southern
boundary and the Serengeti National Park lies to the west. The Ngorongoro Crater is often
called 'Africa's Eden' and a visit to the crater is a main draw for tourists coming to Tanzania
and a definite world-class attraction. A World Heritage Site, it's the largest intact caldera in
the world, containing everything necessary for the 30,000 animals that inhabit the crater
floor to exist and thrive. Karatu, the busy town known as 'safari junction', 25 km south of the
conservation area, is often used by budget travellers who want to visit the Ngorongoro Crater
without spending money on a full-on safari from Arusha. You can catch public transport
to Karatu, stay overnight and then take a half day safari to the crater the next morning.*
▶▶ *For listings, see pages 309-312.*

Ins and outs

Getting there and around Ngorongoro is 190 km west of Arusha, 25 km from Karatu and
145 km from Serengeti and is reached via the Arusha–Serengeti road. At Karatu, is the
turning off to Gibb's Farm, 5 km off the main road. From this junction you turn right
towards the park entrance and on the approach to **Lodware Gate**; as the altitude increases
the temperature starts to fall. Your first view of the crater comes at **Heroes' Point** (2286 m).
The road continues to climb through the forest to the crater rim. It is sometimes possible
along this road to spot leopard that inhabit the dense forests at the top of the crater.
During the long rains season (April-May) the roads in the park can be almost impassable,
so access to the crater floor may be restricted. ▶▶ *See also Ins and outs for the crater itself,
page 305.*

Park fees and information On top of the daily fee of US$50 for adults and US$10 for
children (5-16 years) to enter the Ngorongoro Crater Reserve, there is a hefty US$200 fee
per half day excursion to enter the crater itself and a vehicle fee of US$40 per entry. You'll
also need to hire a guide at a daily rate of US$20. For more information, www.ngorongoro-
crater-africa.org. The best times to visit are December-February and June-July.

Background

The Ngorongoro Conservation Area was established in 1959 and covers an area of 8288 sq km.
In 1951 it was included as part of the Serengeti National Park and contained the headquarters of the park. However, in order to accommodate the grazing needs of the Masai
people's livestock it was decided to reclassify it as a conservation area. In 1978 it was
declared a World Heritage Site in recognition of its beauty and importance. Where the road
reaches the rim of the crater you will see memorials to Professor Bernhard Grzimek and his
son Michael. They were the makers of the film *Serengeti Shall Not Die* and published a book
of the same name (1959, Collins). They conducted surveys and censuses of the animals in
the Serengeti and Ngorongoro Parks and were heavily involved in the fight against poachers.
Tragically Michael was killed in an aeroplane accident over the Ngorongoro Crater in 1959
and his father returned to Germany where he set up the Frankfurt Zoological Society. He
died in 1987 requesting in his will that he should be buried beside his son in Tanzania.
Their memorials serve as a reminder of all the work they did to protect this part of Africa.

➜ *Phone code 027.*

The small but burgeoning town of Karatu is 25 km from the gate of the Ngorongoro Crater Reserve, 25 km from Lake Manyara, and 140 km from Arusha. The new road from Arusha to the gates of the Ngorongoro Crater which was completed in 2003 was sponsored by the Japanese government. With completion of this road, Karatu has come into its own and now spreads for several kilometres along the highway. It is locally dubbed 'safari junction' and for good reason. All safaris vehicles en route to the parks in the northern circuit pass through here. Because of its proximity to the crater more and more lodges and campsites are springing up. Some offer very good, and in some cases much cheaper, alternatives to staying within the confines of the Ngorongoro Crater Reserve. However, the disadvantage is not having the views that the lodges on the rim of the crater afford. As well as the accommodation options listed below, those on an organized camping safari

Ngorongoro Conservation Area

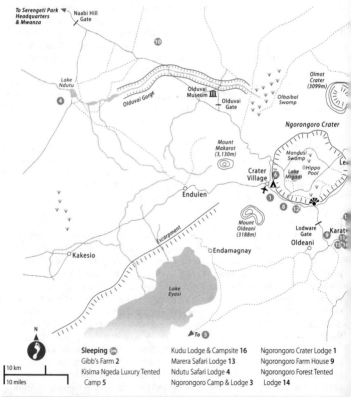

Sleeping 💤	Kudu Lodge & Campsite **16**	Ngorongoro Crater Lodge **1**
Gibb's Farm **2**	Marera Safari Lodge **13**	Ngorongoro Farm House **9**
Kisima Ngeda Luxury Tented	Ndutu Safari Lodge **4**	Ngorongoro Forest Tented
Camp **5**	Ngorongoro Camp & Lodge **3**	Lodge **14**

may find themselves staying at one of the many other campsites around Karatu, as the cheaper companies use these instead of the more expensive campsite at the top of the crater (which, incidentally, is overcrowded, has poor facilities and gets extremely cold). These cater exclusively to the groups who have their own cooks, though there are often also bars to buy beers and soft drinks. There are three banks in town and all have ATMs. For those on self-drive safaris this is the last place to buy provisions and fuel before entering the Ngorongoro Crater Reserve (see Shopping, page 312). Petrol stations spread from one end of town to the other. There are plenty of buses throughout the day between Arusha and Karatu. One option here for budget travellers wanting to visit the Ngorongoro Crater, is to catch public transport as far as Karatu, stay overnight and then take a half day safari to the crater the next morning, and return to Arusha the following afternoon. This is considerably cheaper than booking a safari from Arusha.

Ngorongoro Crater 💿 ▸▸ *pp309-312. Colour map 1, A4.*

The crater has an area of 265 sq km and measures between 16 and 19 km across. The rim reaches 2286 m above sea level and the crater floor is 610 m below it. The crater floor is mainly grassy plain interspersed with a few tracts of sturdy woodland. Scrub heath and remnants of montane forests cloak the steep slopes. There are both freshwater and brackish lakes, and the main water source is Lake Migadi in the centre of the crater; a soda lake that attracts flocks of pink-winged flamingos and plenty of contented hippos who remain partially submerged during the day and graze on grass at night. The views from the rim overlooking Ngorongoro Crater are sensational, and you can pick out the wildlife as dots on the crater floor.

Ins and outs
All the lodges and the public campsite are around the rim of the crater. The descent into it is by way of two steep roads, which are both one-way. You enter by the **Windy Gap** road and leave by the **Lerai** road. The Windy Gap branches off the Serengeti road to the right and descends the northeast wall to the floor of the crater 610 m below. The road is narrow, steep and twists and turns as it enters the crater, which is rather like a huge amphitheatre.

Most people go down into the crater on an organized safari from Arusha (see page 278),

Ngorongoro Serena Lodge **6**
Ngorongoro Sopa Lodge **7**
Ngorongoro Wildlife
    Lodge **8**
Octagon Safari Lodge **15**
Olduvai Camp **10**
Plantation Lodge **11**
Rhino Lodge **12**

or join one in Karatu. Access into it and onto its floor is limited to half a day per visitor, and safaris enter either early in the morning or early in the afternoon. Access is restricted to registered tour operators in Tanzanian-registered vehicles, and for most of the year, only 4WDs are allowed. If you have your own vehicle, you are allowed to take it through the Ngorongoro Crater Reserve (and beyond into the Serengeti) but you are not allowed to take it down into the crater. However, there is the option to leave your own vehicle at the top and Land Rovers and drivers can be hired in Crater Village where you pick up the ranger, which is cheaper than hiring through the lodges.

Background

The name 'Ngorongoro' comes from a Masai word *Ilkorongoro*, which was the name given to the group of Masai warriors who defeated the previous occupants of the area, the Datong, around 1800. The sounds of the bells that the Masai wore during the battle that were said to have terrified their enemies into submission, was '*koh-rohng-roh*' and it is from this that Ngorongoro comes. The Masai refer to the Ngorongoro Southern Highlands as '*O'lhoirobi*', which means the cold highlands; while the Germans also referred to the climate, calling these the 'winter highlands'. Ngorongoro is believed to date from about 2,500,000 years ago – relatively recent for this area. It was once a huge active volcano and was probably as large as Kilimanjaro. After its large major eruption, as the lava subsided its cone collapsed inwards leaving the caldera. Minor volcanic activity continued and the small cones that resulted can be seen in the crater floor. To the northeast of Ngorongoro crater are two smaller craters, Olmot and Embagai. From the crater on a clear day you should be able to see six mountains over 3000 m.

Wildlife

The crater is home to an estimated 30,000 animals and visitors are almost guaranteed to get a good look at some or all of the Big Five. About half of this number are zebra and wildebeest. Unlike those in the neighbouring Serengeti, these populations do not need to migrate thanks to the permanent supply of water and grass through both the wet and the dry seasons. Thanks to the army of pop-up minibuses that go down each day the animals are not afraid of the vehicles and it's not unusual for a pride of lions to amble over and flop down in the shade of a minibus. However, recently introduced regulations limit the number of vehicles around an animal or kill to five, in an effort to reduce the distress and impact of hordes of over-eager safari vehicles when surrounding the wildlife. The crater's elephants are mostly old bulls with giant tusks. The females and calves prefer the forested highlands on the crater rim and only rarely venture down into the grasslands. There are no giraffe. Because of the crater's steep sides they can't climb down, and there is a lack of food at tree level.

In early 2001 huge swarms of *Stomoxys* flies were harmful to many animals and particularly lions, of which six died and 62 were seriously damaged and they apparently left the crater in an attempt to escape. In a previous outbreak of the flies, in 1962, the lion population was decimated, with only eight lions surviving. Numbers have slowly increased since that time, but the Ngorongoro lions, generally bigger and stronger than lions elsewhere, are in danger of extinction, not least because the lack of genetic diversity within the population leaves it vulnerable to events such as *Stomoxys* attacks and disease. There have been reports that since the middle of 2000 many other animals have died of unknown causes, including over 300 buffalo, 200 wildebeest, over 60 zebra and a few hippo and rhino.

Embagai Crater ↠ pp309-312. 2°55'S 35°50'E.

Embagai Crater (also spelt Empakaai) can be visited in a day from any lodge at the Ngorongoro rim. The caldera is approximately 35 sq km. You can walk down to the 80-m deep, alkaline Lake Emakat, which partly occupies the caldera floor. The vegetation is predominantly highland shrubs and grassland but there are small patches of verdant, evergreen forest in the southern part of the caldera. Buffalo, hyenas, leopards and various species of bats may be seen. Birdlife is prolific and includes the lammergeyer, Egyptian vulture, Verreaux's eagle, pelicans, storks, flamingos, duck, sandpiper, doves, kingfishers and ostrich. This is an isolated, beautiful place, accessible by 4WD only. You need to be accompanied by a ranger because of the buffaloes.

Lake Ndutu is a soda lake in the Ndutu woodlands in the western part of the Ngorongoro Conservation Area. Rarely visited, it is home to many flamingo, plains game mammals and their attendant predators.

Olduvai Gorge ● ↠ pp309-312. Colour map 1, A4.

Olduvai Gorge, a water-cut canyon up to 90 m deep, has become famous for being the site of a number of archaeological finds and has been called the 'cradle of mankind'. Lying within the Ngorongoro Conservation Area to the northwest of the crater, the site is about 10-15 minutes off the main road between Serengeti and Ngorongoro. Olduvai comes from the Masai word *oldupai*, which is the name for the type of wild sisal that grows in the gorge.

Archaeological finds

Olduvai Gorge first aroused interest in the archaeological world as early as 1911 when a German, Professor Katurinkle, while looking for butterflies in the gorge, found some fossil bones. These caused great interest in Europe and in 1913 an expedition led by Professor Hans Reck was arranged. They stayed at Olduvai for three months and made a number of fossil finds. At a later expedition in 1933 Professor Reck was accompanied by two archaeologists, Dr Louis Leakey and his future wife Mary.

The Leakeys continued their work and in July 1959, 26 years later, discovered 400 fragments of the skull *Australopithecus-Zinjanthropus boisei* – the 'nutcracker man' – who lived in the lower Pleistocene Age around 1,750,000 BC. A year later the skull and bones of a young *Homo habilis* were found. The Leakeys assert that around 1.8-2 million years ago there existed in Tanzania two types of man, *Australopithecus-Zinjanthropus boisei* and *Homo habilis*. The other two, *Australopithecus africanus* and *arobustus*, had died out. *Homo habilis*, with the larger brain, gave rise to modern man. *Habilis* was a small ape-like creature and, although thought to be the first of modern man's ancestors, is quite distinct from modern man. Tools, such as those used by *Homo erectus* (dating from 1-1½ million years ago), have also been found at Olduvai as well as at Isimila near Iringa. Other exciting finds in the area are the footprints found in 1979 of man, woman and child at Laetoli (a site near Olduvai) made by 'creatures' that walked upright, possibly dating from the same period as *Australopithecus afarensis*, popularly known as 'Lucy', whose remains were discovered near Hadar in Ethiopia in 1974. Dating back 3.6-3.8 million years they pushed back the timing of the beginnings of the human race even further. In 1986 a discovery at Olduvai by a team of American and Tanzanian archaeologists unearthed the remains of an adult female dating back 1,800,000 years. In total the fossil remains of about 35 humans have been found in the area at different levels.

Prehistoric animal remains were also found in the area and about 150 species of mammals have been identified. These include the enormous Polorovis with a horn span of 2 m, the Dinotherium, a huge, elephant-like creature with tusks that curved downwards and the Hipparion, a three-toed, horse-like creature.

At the site there is a small **museum** ① *open until 1500, may be closed during the wet season (Apr-end Jun), entrance US$3*. The building was built in the 1970s by the Leakeys to house their findings. It holds displays of copies of some of the finds, a cast of the footprints and pictures of what life was like for Olduvai's earliest inhabitants. You can go down into the gorge to see the sites and there will usually be an archaeologist to show you around.

Nearby places of interest include **Nasera Rock**, a 100-m monolith on the edge of the Gol Mountain range – it offers stunning views of the southern Serengeti and is a great vantage point from which to watch the annual **wildebeest migration**. This is sometimes called the Striped Mountain, so named for the streaks of blue-green algae that have formed on the granite. **Olkarien Gorge**, a deep fissure in the Gol Mountains, is a major breeding ground of the enormous Ruppell's griffon vulture.

A geological feature of this area are shifting sand-dunes, or *barchan*, crescent-shaped dunes lying at right angles to the prevailing wind. They usually develop from the accumulation of sand around a minor obstruction, for example a piece of vegetation. The windward face has a gentle slope but the leeward side is steep and slightly concave. The *Barchans* move slowly as more sand is deposited; they range in size from a few metres to a great size, as seen in the Sahara or Saudi Arabia.

Lake Eyasi ● ➤➤ pp309-312. Colour map 1, A4.

① *Access to Lake Eyasi is from the Kidatu–Ngorongoro road. The journey takes about 1½-2 hrs, driving southwest of Karatu and the Ngorongoro Crater. There are few tourist facilities here but in recent years it has been included in walking safaris by several companies. There are no set itineraries for the 5 day and 4 night hiking and camping tours but they generally start at Chem Chem Village from where the guides start their search for a Hadzabe camp. Once there, hikers can freely participate in the Hadzabe daily activities, including mending bows, collecting herbal poisons for the arrows, actual hunts, gathering of firewood, plants, water, etc.*

This soda lake, one of several lakes on the floor of the Rift Valley, is sometimes referred to as the 'forgotten lake'. It is larger than Lakes Manyara or Natron and is situated on the remote southern border of the Ngorongoro Conservation Area, at the foot of Mount Oldeani and the base of the western wall of the Rift Valley's Eyasi Escarpment. The Mbula highlands tower to the east. Seasonal water level fluctuations vary greatly and, following the trend in the region, the lake levels are falling and salt brines have developed. It is relatively shallow even during the rainy season. Lake Eyasi mostly fills a *graben*, or elongated depression of the earth's crust, areas that are commonly the sites of volcanic and/or earthquake activity. The Mbari River runs through the swampy area to the northeast of the lake known locally as **Mangola Chini**, which attracts much game.

Two ancient tribes inhabit this area. The **Hadzabe** people (also called the Watindiga) who live near the shore are hunter-gatherers, still live in nomadic groups, hunt with bows and arrows and gather tubers, roots and fruits. These people are believed to have their origins in Botswana, their lifestyle is similar to the San (of the Kalahari) and the Dorobo (of Kenya). It is estimated that they have lived in this region for 10,000 years. Their language resembles the click language associated with the San. Their hunting skills provide all their requirements – mostly eating small antelopes and primates. Their hunting bows are made with giraffe tendon 'strings', and they coat their spears and arrows with the poisonous sap of the desert rose. They live in communal camps that are temporary structures constructed in different locations depending on the season.

Nearby there is a village of **Datoga** pastoral herdsmen, also known as the Barabaig or Il-Man'ati (meaning the 'strong enemy' in the Masai language). The Datoga are a tall, handsome people who tend their cattle in the region between Lake Eyasi and Mount Hanang. The Masai drove them south from Ngorongoro to Lake Eyasi about 150 years ago, and remain their foes. They live in homes constructed of sticks and mud, and their compounds are surrounded by thornbush to deter nocturnal predators. Like the Hadzabe, the Datoga speak a click language and they scarify themselves to form figure of eight patterns around their eyes in a series of raised nodules.

The northeastern region of the lake is a swampy area fringed by acacia and doum palm forests. Nearby are some freshwater springs, and a small reservoir with tilapia fish. These springs are believed to run underground from Oldeani to emerge by the lakeshore. There are several *kopjes* (see page 316) close by the lake. Wildlife includes a profusion of birdlife including flamingos, pelicans and storks as well as leopards, various antelope, hippos and many small primates.

Archaeological excavations of the nearby **Mumba cave shelter** were undertaken in 1934 by Ludwig and Margit Kohl-Larsen, and their discoveries included many fossilized hominoid remains: a complete prehistoric skull, molars and prehistoric tools such as knives and thumbnail scrapers. Animal remains included rhino, antelope, zebra, hippo and catfish. The Mumba cave also contained ochre paintings. It is believed that the Mumba cave shelter was occupied over the years by various people.

⊙ Ngorongoro Conservation Area listings

For Sleeping and Eating price codes and other relevant information, see pages 36-40.

● Sleeping

Karatu *p304, map p304*
L Gibb's Farm, 4 km from Karatu, T027-253 4040, www.gibbsfarm.net. At the edge of a forest facing the Mbulu Hills to the southeast. This charming 80-year old farmhouse set in lush gardens is still a working farm and coffee plantation, originally built by German settlers in 1929. Accommodation is in 22 luxurious farm cottages, recently upgraded and all with private verandas, garden bathrooms and open fireplaces. The restaurant produces excellent meals using organic vegetables grown on the farm. And there's a spa with a difference – a traditional Masai healer provides treatments made from local plants and materials, either in your cottage or in

his thatched house, the Engishon Supat. Recommended.
L Plantation Lodge, 4 km towards the crater, 2 km from the main road, badly signposted so look hard, T027-253 4405 www.plantation-lodge.com. Accommodation in exquisitely stylish rooms on a coffee estate. A huge amount of detail has gone into the safari-style decor. The 16 individual and spacious rooms are in renovated farm buildings throughout the grounds. There are several places to sit and drink coffee or enjoy a sundowner and you can choose to eat at grand dining tables on your veranda, in huge stone halls, in the garden, or in the main house with the other guests. The honeymoon suite has a vast bed, fireplace, jacuzzi and sunken bath, some units are whole houses which are ideal for families. Swimming pool.
L-A Ngorongoro Forest Tented Lodge, along the same road as Marera until you

reach a junction signposted to the right to **Ngorongoro Forest Tented Lodge** and to the left for **Marera Safari Lodge**. T027-250 8089, www.ngorongoroforestlodge.com. Also overlooking the Ngorongoro Forest Reserve, this stylish new lodge has 7 spacious and attractive tented rooms elegantly furnished and with both indoor and outdoor showers. The lounge bar overlooks the forest reserve and the wildlife corridor to Lake Manyara, with vast windows and a telescope for stargazing. US$245 per person full board.

L-C Ngorongoro Farm House, on a 200-ha coffee farm 4 km from the Lolduare Gate of the crater, T0784-207727 (mob), www.tan ganyikawildernesscamps.com. There are 50 rooms spread between 3 separate camps, attractively built in the style of an old colonial farm. In the main thatched building is the bar and a newly renovated restaurant with a wooden terrace overlooking the farmland and flower beds. Swimming pool. Excellent food using fresh vegetables from the farm.

B-C Octagon Safari Lodge and Irish Bar, 1 km outside Karatu signposted on the left off the main road towards Ngorongoro Gate, T0754-650324 (mob), www.octagonlodge. com. Owned by Rory and Pamela, an Irish-man and his Tanzanian wife, this lodge is set in beautiful African gardens. The 12 wood and bamboo chalets all have a Masai theme, are en suite and have balconies looking out onto the gardens. The Irish bar has plenty of whiskies to choose from, along with Guinness, and the food has received good reports. Rates US$125 per person full board.

C Marera Safari Lodge, 4 km off the main Arusha–Ngorongoro Rd, signposted, with **Ngorongoro Forest Tented Lodge** on the right. T027-250 4177, info@mareratours.com. Lovely location on the top of the hill over-looking Ngorongoro Forest Reserve. Each of the 7 en suite tents is on a wooden platform with thatch shelter and a terrace that looks over the forest. There's a restaurant and a bar, and guides are available for walks into the forest and local villages. At US$160 for a double room, a more affordable option than staying on the Crater Rim.

C-F Kudu Lodge and Campsite, signposted to the left if going out of town towards the crater, 600 m off the main road, T027-253 4055, www.kudulodge.com. Established and popular lodge in mature gardens with experienced staff. Accommodation in comfortable rondavaals. There's a variety of options: doubles from US$140, triples US$220, brand new family cottages with kitchen from US$165. A 50% discount is available in low season. The large shady campsite, often used by safari groups, has separate cooking shelters and good ablution blocks with hot water. Camping US$10. Enormous bar with satellite TV, pool table, fireplace and lots of couches, internet café, gift shop and restaurant. Safaris can be organized. Accepts payment in US$, £, € and credit cards.

C-F Ngorongoro Camp and Lodge, on the main road in the middle of Karatu next to a petrol station and bank, T027-253 4287, www.ngorongorocampandlodge.net. This is a good mid-range option, with 32 neat and tidy double rooms with space for extra beds and good showers with plenty of hot water. Full breakfast included, cosy (though expensive) bar with fireplace and satellite TV, restaurant, supermarket. Room rates are overpriced at US$140 for a double but nevertheless, a friendly and comfortable place to stay. Camping is available for US$7 per person. The campsite is 100 m from the main lodge on one of the back roads and there is a bar and kitchen area for the safari cooks. Safaris organized, especially good value are half-day crater tours for US$150 and full day for US$160.

Ngorongoro Crater *p305, map p304*
For other accommodation options within 20 km of the Ngorongoro Crater, outside the conservation area's boundary, see Karatu, page 309.

L Ngorongoro Crater Lodge, central reservations, Johannesburg, South Africa,

T+27-11-809 4300, www.andbeyond.com. A lodge has been on this spot since 1934, but it was completely rebuilt in 1995, and the architecture and style is simply magnificent. It's the most luxurious lodge on the rim of the crater, very romantic and opulent. The individual cottages offer butler service, sumptuous decor, a fireplace and even an ipod station. With unobstructed views down into the crater even from the bathrooms, this is a special place to stay. Very expensive at US$655-1450 per person per night depending on season, but fully inclusive of meals, drinks and game drives The lodge supports local schools, clinics and health initiatives.

L Ngorongoro Serena Lodge, T027-250 4058, www.serenahotels.com. Luxury development built to the highest international standards out of wood and pebbles. Stunningly perched on the rim of the crater and each of the rooms has its own rock enclosed balcony. Telescope provided on main balcony to view the crater. The centre of the public area is warmed by a roaring fire and lit by lanterns. Friendly staff, good food and has its own nursery in the gardens to plant indigenous plant species. Offers hiking and shorter nature walks. Local Masai make up 25% of staff. Rates from US$350 per person.

L Ngorongoro Wildlife Lodge, T027-254 4595, www.hotelsandlodges-tanzania.com. An ugly 1970s concrete block on the rim of the crater with wonderful views, the facilites are fine. 75 rooms with balconies overlooking the crater. Geared to fast throughput of tours. Bar with log fire, TV room with satellite TV, restaurant serving either buffets or à la carte, although there have been poor reports about the quality. Zebra can be seen on the lawns.

L-A Ngorongoro Sopa Lodge, central reservations, T027-250 0630, www.sopa lodges.com. Luxury lodge with 92 suites on the exclusive eastern rim, all enjoying uninterrupted views into the crater. Spectacular African rondavaal design with magnificent lounges, restaurant and entertainment areas, swimming pool and satellite TV. Most of the lodges are on the southern or western crater rim but the Sopa is on the unspoilt eastern rim, way off the beaten track. Unfortunately, this involves an extra 45-50 km journey (one way) over poor quality roads.

B Rhino Lodge, T0762-359055 (mob), www.ngorongoro.cc. Jointly owned by Coastal Aviation and the Pastoralists Council of Ngorongoro, which represents local Masai communities. This former home of the first conservationist to the area was reopened in 2008 after extensive rebuilding and helps to support 6 local Masai villages. It's the only mid-budget option on the crater rim and offers good value with 24 simply furnished, Masai-inspired rooms, all en suite with balconies overlooking the forests. Restaurant and bar area are simple with huge fireplaces. Rates are US$110 per person half board.

National Park campsites

Simba Campsite, about 2 km from Crater Village. A public campsite with showers, toilets and firewood, but facilities have deteriorated and water supplies are irregular – make sure that you have sufficient drinking water to keep you going for the night and the game drive the next day. Given that you are camping at some elevation at the top of the crater, this place gets bitterly cold at night so ensure you have a warm sleeping bag. It gets very busy with tour groups, with up to 200 tents at any one time. The hot water runs out quickly – so don't expect to have a shower here. Many budget safari companies use this site, though **Karatu** is quite frankly a better option. If in your own vehicle, there is no need to book. Just pay for camping (US$30 per person) along with park entry when you enter at the gate.

Elsewhere in the reserve there are 5 special campsites (US$50 per person), usually used by the safari companies going off the beaten track.

Olduvai Gorge p307, map p304

L Olduvai Camp, just south of the Serengeti border, closest lodge to the Olduvai Gorge, reservations through UK T+44-(0)1306 880 770, www.africatravelresource.com. The 3 head guides are all Masai warriors from the villages immediately around the camp and there is the opportunity to go walking with them in the Ngorongoro highlands. Facilities are simple, the 17 tents are of a modest size with thatched roofs and wooden floors, furnished with the basic essentials, en suite bathrooms with flush toilets and bladder showers. The public spaces are limited to 2 small thatched rondavaals and an open fire pit. Has a generator, and lanterns are provided at night. Rates US$455 per person, including all meals, walking guide, park fees and game drive. Compared to the other giant impersonal concrete lodges in the Ngorongoro Conservation Area, this is an intimate, rustic camp that offers the opportunity to sleep on the plains amongst the local Masai.

A Ndutu Safari Lodge, reservations Arusha, T027-250 2829, www.ndutu.com. Established in 1967 by professional hunter George Dove, Ndutu is one of the earliest permanent lodges in the Crater/Serengeti area and has become something of an institution over the years. On the southern shore of Ndutu soda lake, amongst acacia woodland, in a good position for the migration in the calving season, midway between the Ngorongoro Crater and Seronera Lodge in the Serengeti, 90 km to both and near to the Olduvai Gorge. Sleeps 70 in 34 stone cottages. Bar and restaurant, fresh ingredients from Gibb's Farm, restricted use of water as it is trucked in. Rates in the region of US$385 full board for a double room, discounts available in low season. Ndutu was home for over 20 years to the famous wildlife photographer Baron Hugo van Lawick, one of the first filmmakers to bring the Serengeti to the attention of the world. He died in 2002 and was granted the honour of a full state funeral before being buried at Ndutu.

Lake Eyasi *p308, map p304*
L-A Kisima Ngeda Luxury Tented Camp, on the shores of Lake Eyasi, a remote southern corner of Ngorongoro Conservation Area, at the foot of Mount Ol Deani, www. kisimangeda.com. Tents with thatched roofs next to lake, en suite stone baths, wooden furniture, electric lights and plenty of space. Swimming in the lake, all activities on offer including meeting the Hadzabe people.

🍴 Eating

Karatu *p304, map p304*
Bytes, in the middle of town behind a petrol station. Very stylish café-bar with cane furniture, home-made cakes, good coffee, imported alcoholic drinks, delicious daily specials such as Mexican wraps and curries, and internet access. Next door is a shop selling local farm produce and coffee beans.

🛍 Shopping

Karatu *p304, map p304*
For those on self-drive safaris this is the last place to buy food and before entering the Ngorongoro Crater Reserve. There's a market on the left hand side of the road if coming from Arusha which has a good variety of fresh food; meat can be bought from the small butcher at the back and bread from the kiosks.

📋 Directory

Karatu *p304, map p304*
Banks There are 3 banks in town, the **National Bank of Commerce**, on the main road next to the Ngorongoro Safari Lodge and Bytes restaurant; **Exim Bank** on the left as you're driving towards the crater; and the **National Microfinance Bank**, on the right, further up from Exim. All have ATMs.

Serengeti National Park

→ Colour map 1, A4. 2°40'S, 35°0'E. www.serengeti.org.

The Serengeti supports the greatest concentration of plains game in Africa. Frequently dubbed the eighth wonder of the world, it was granted the status of a World Heritage Site in 1978, and became an International Biosphere Reserve in 1981. Its far-reaching plains of endless grass, tinged with the twisted shadows of acacia trees, have made it the quintessential image of a wild and untarnished Africa. Large prides of lions laze easily in the long grasses, numerous families of elephants feed on acacia bark, and giraffes, antelope, monkeys, eland and a whole range of other African wildlife is here in awe-inspiring numbers. The park is the centre of the Serengeti Ecosystem – the combination of the Serengeti, the Ngorongoro Conservation Area, Kenya's Masai Mara and four smaller game reserves. Within this region live an estimated three million large animals. The system protects the largest single movement of wildlife on earth – the annual wildebeest migration. This is a phenomenal sight: thousands upon thousands of animals, particularly wildebeest and zebra, as far as the eye can see. ▶▶ For more information on national parks and safaris, see page 41. For listings, see pages 318-322.

Ins and outs

Getting there There are several airstrips inside the park used by charter planes arranged by the park lodges and by Coastal Air.

By road, the Serengeti is usually approached from the Ngorongoro Crater Reserve. From the top of the crater the spectacularly scenic road with a splendid view of the Serengeti plains winds down the crater walls on to the grasslands below. Along here the Masai tribesmen can be seen herding their cattle in the fresher pastures towards the top of the crater. Shortly before the Serengeti's boundary there is the turning off to Olduvai Gorge where most safari companies stop. Then entry is through the **Naabi Hill Gate** to the southeast of the park where there is a small shop and information centre. From here it is 75 km to **Seronera**, the village in the heart of the Serengeti, which is 335 km from Arusha. Approaching from Mwanza or Musoma on the shore of Lake Victoria, take the road east and you will enter the Serengeti through the **Ndabaka Gate** in the west through what is termed as the Western Corridor to the Grumeti region. This road requires 4WD and may be impassable in the rainy season. There is a third, less frequently used gate in the north, **Ikoma Gate** that lies a few kilometres from Seronera. This also goes to Musoma but again is not a very good road.

Getting around Most tourists use a safari package from either Arusha or Mwanza but it is possible to explore in your own vehicle. However, the roads are quite rough and you can expect hard corrugations, (especially the road from Naabi Hill to Seronera) where there are deep ruts, and in many regions of the park there is a fine top soil known locally as 'black cotton', which can get impossibly sticky and slippery in the wet. This is especially true of the Western Corridor. The dry season should not present too many problems. The Park Headquarters are at Seronera and there are airstrips at Seronera, Lobo and Grumeti, and at many of the small exclusive camps.

Park information and entry fees The entry fee is US$50 for adults and US$10 for children aged between 5 and 16 years.

Climate The dry season runs from June to October, the wet between March and May and in between is a period of short rains, during which time things turn green. At this time of year there are localized rain showers but it's more or less dry. With altitudes ranging from 920 to 1850 m, average temperatures vary from 15 to 25 °C. It is coldest from June to October, particularly in the evenings.

Serengeti National Park

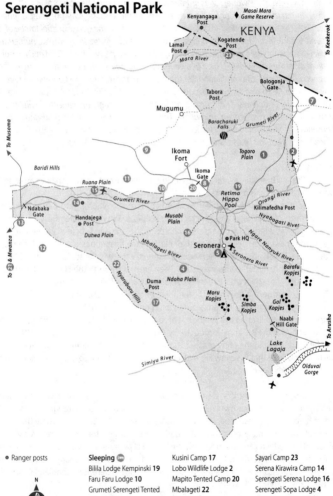

• Ranger posts

Sleeping
Bilila Lodge Kempinski **19**
Faru Faru Lodge **10**
Grumeti Serengeti Tented
  Camp **15**
Ikoma Bush Camp **8**
Kijereshi Lodge **12**
Klein's Camp **7**

Kusini Camp **17**
Lobo Wildlife Lodge **2**
Mapito Tented Camp **20**
Mbalageti **22**
Mbuzi Mawe **18**
Migration Camp **1**
Sabora Lodge **11**
Sasakwa Lodge **9**

Sayari Camp **23**
Serena Kirawira Camp **14**
Serengeti Serena Lodge **16**
Serengeti Sopa Lodge **4**
Serengeti Stopover **13**
Seronera Wildlife Lodge **5**
Speke Bay Lodge **21**

Background

The name is derived from the Masai word *'siringet'* meaning 'extended area' or 'endless plains'. A thick layer of ash blown from volcanoes in the Ngorongoro highlands covered the landscape between 3-4 million years ago, preserved traces of early man, and enriched the soil that supports the southern grass plains. Avoided by the pastoralist Masai because the woodlands had tsetse flies carrying trypanosomiasis (sleeping sickness), the early European explorers found this area uninhabited and teeming with game. Serengeti National Park was established in 1951 and at 14,763 sq km is Tanzania's second largest national park (after Selous). It rises from 920-1850 m above sea level and its landscape varies from the long and short grass plains in the south, the central savannah, the more hilly wooded areas in the north and the extensive woodland in the western corridor. The **Maswa Game Reserve** adjoins its western border.

Wildlife

During the rainy season the wildebeest, whose population has been estimated at around 1,500,000, are found in the eastern section of the Serengeti and also the Masai Mara in Kenya to the north. When the dry season begins at the end of June the annual migration starts as the animals move in search of pasture. Just before this, they concentrate on the remaining green patches, forming huge herds, the rutting season begins and territories are established by the males, who then attempt to attract females into their areas. Once mating has occurred, the herds merge together again and the migration to the

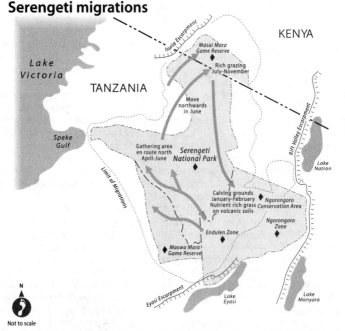

Serengeti migrations

northwest begins. The migrating animals do not all follow the same route. About half go west, often going outside the park boundaries, and then swing northeast. The other half go directly north. The two groups meet up in the Masai Mara in Kenya. To get to the west section of the Serengeti and the Masai Mara, where they will find pasture in the dry season, the wildebeest must cross a number of large rivers and this proves too much for many of them. Many of the weaker and older animals die during the migration. Needless to say predators follow the wildebeest on their great trek and easy pickings are to be had. The animals have to cross the Mara River where massive Nile crocodiles with thickset jaws lick their lips in anticipation of a substantial feed. For any visitor to Tanzania, the herds are a spectacular sight. They return to the southeast at the end of the dry season (October-November) and calving begins at the start of the wet season (March).

🌙 *This migration to the Masai Mara and back again usually lasts seven to eight months and the biggest concentration of wildebeest can be seen in the Serengeti between November and June before they begin to head north again.*

The Serengeti is also famous for cheetah, leopards and lions, some of which migrate with the wildebeest while others remain in the central plain. Prides of lions are commonly seen, leopards are most frequently detected resting in trees during the daytime along the Seronera River, whereas cheetahs are usually spotted near the Simba Kopjes. The elephant population in Serengeti was estimated to have fallen fivefold during the mid 1970-1980s thanks to poaching, though since then the numbers have slowly increased. Birdlife is prolific and includes various species of kingfishers, sunbirds and rollers, ostrich, egrets, herons, storks, ibis, spoonbills and ducks. Birds of prey include Ruppell's vulture and the hooded vulture, several varieties of kestrels, eagles, goshawks and harriers.

Routes

If you are approaching the Serengeti from the southeast (from the Ngorongoro Crater Conservation Area), **Lake Ndutu**, fringed by acacia woodland, lies southeast of the main road. Lake Ndutu is a soda lake, with a substantial quantity of mineral deposits around the shoreline. It is home to many birds, including flamingos. During the rainy season it offers excellent opportunities to see a large variety of animals including predators. Next you will reach the **Short Grass Plains**. The flat landscape is broken by the **Gol Mountains**, to the right, and by kopjes. The grass here remains short during both the wet and dry seasons. There is no permanent water supply in this region as a result of the nature of the soil. However, during the rains water collects in hollows and depressions until it dries up at the end of the wet season. It is then that the animals begin to move on.

The **Southern Plains** provide nutritious grasses for the wildebeest, and when the short rains come in November these mammals move south to feed. In February-March, 90% of female wildebeest give birth and the plains are filled with young calves.

Naabi Hill Gate marks the end of the Short Grass and beginning of the **Long Grass Plains**. Dotted across the plains are **kopjes**. These interesting geological formations are made up of ancient granite that has been left behind as the surrounding soil structures have been broken down by centuries of erosion and weathering. They play an important role in the ecology of the plains, providing habitats for many different animals from rock hyraxes (a small rabbit-like creature whose closest relation is actually the elephant) to cheetahs.

The kopjes that you might visit include the **Moru Kopjes** in the south of the park to the left of the main road heading north. You may be lucky enough to see the Verreaux eagle, which sometimes nests here. The Moru Kopjes have a cave with Masai paintings on the wall and a rock called **Gong Rock** after the sound it makes when struck with a stone.

Take a walk on the wild side

Imagine walking along the iconic plains of the Serenegti, wandering silently past wildlife, taking in all the smells and sights and sounds of the bush on foot, worlds away from the noise and confines of a Land Rover crammed with tourists ...

Until very recently, although an option in game controlled areas and in private concessions on the park borders, walking safaris in the Serengeti National Park itself were prohibited. However, following demand from tour operators and the increasing dual pressure of raising ever more revenue from tourism while minimizing its impact on the environment, TANAPA, the Tanzanian Parks Authority, have finally relented.

Available all year apart from in the rainy season during April and May, the walks themselves are on pre-assigned routes and can last anything from 45 minutes to three days or more. Short walks can be booked through the visitor centre at Seronera (see page 318) and can take you around the Serengeti side of Lake Ndutu in the south of the park or along the Grumeti River near Migration Camp. At the time of writing, other short walks were planned around the Mbalageti River area in the Western Corridor and by the Mara River near Kogatende in the north. The longer, multi-day walks need to be booked well in advance, and allow you to explore the Togoro Plains area between Mbuzi Mawe and Lobo on the northeastern side of the park.

Not surprisingly, the authorities have introduced strict controls and regulations. Walking groups are limited to a maximum of eight people and must be accompanied by a TANAPA armed ranger, who stays at the front of the single-file group, and by a TANAPA guide. The routes are limited to just one group at any one time, so you will effectively have your area of the Serengeti all to yourselves, maintaining its amazing wilderness environment.

Although the walking itself won't be tough – the terrain is mostly gentle and flat – don't underestimate the heat and the potential lack of shade. Take sensible precautions such as plenty of water, a sun hat, a high factor sunscreen and strong shoes, and then relax and enjoy the experience.

Fees and information Park fees range from US$20 for trails up to an hour long, US$50 for trails up to three hours and US$100 per day for multi-day walks and camping. For further information, contact TANAPA, T027-250 3471.

Tour operators On the longer walks, you'll need a tour operator to deal with all the logistics, and it must be one that's been approved by TANAPA to take walking safaris. At present, there are very few of these and a recommended approved operator is **Wild Frontiers**, based in Johannesburg, South Africa, T+27-117 022 035. They will organize food and fly camping (sleeping out in the bush) for overnight stops, have a support vehicle, first aid and communications equipment, and a specially trained guide to accompany you, along with the armed ranger.

There are also the **Simba Kopjes** on the left of the road before reaching Seronera, which, as their name suggests, are often a hideout for lions.

Passing through the Long Grass Plains in the wet season from around December to May is an incredible experience. All around, stretching into the distance, are huge numbers of wildebeest, Thompson's gazelle, zebra, etc.

The village of **Seronera** is in the middle of the park set in the **Seronera Valley**. It forms an important transition zone between the southern grasslands and the northern woodlands. The area is criss-crossed by rivers, and as a result this is where you are most likely to spot game. It is reached by a gravel road, which is in fairly good condition. Seronara is the best area to visit if you can only manage a short safari. It has a visitor centre and the research institute is based here. It also contains a small museum noted for its giant stick insects (near the lodge). In the approach to Seronera the number of trees increases, particularly the thorny acacia trees. You can expect to see buffalo, impala, lion, hippo and elephant. If you are lucky you might see leopard.

About 5 km north of Seronera the track splits. To the right it goes to Banagi and Lobo beyond, and to the left to the Western Corridor, about 20 km north of Banagi Hill, which is home to both browsers and grazers. At its base is the **Retima Hippo Pool** about 6 km off the main track at Banagi. Banagi was the site of the original Game Department Headquarters before it became a national park. North of here the land is mainly rolling plains of both grassland and woodland with a few hilly areas and rocky outcrops.

In the northeast section of the park is the **Lobo Northern Woodland**. Wildlife remains in this area throughout the year including during the dry season. The area is characterized by rocky hills and outcrops, where pythons sunbathe, and woodlands frequented by elephants fringe the rivers. Lobo is the site of the **Lobo Lodge**, 75 km from Seronera. Further north is the Mara River with riverine forest bordering its banks. This is one of the rivers that claims many wildebeest lives every year during the migration. You will see both hippo and crocodile along the river banks.

If you take the left-hand track where the road splits north of Seronera you will follow the **Grumeti Western Corridor**. The best time to follow this track is in the dry season (June-October) when the road is at its best and the migrating animals have reached the area. Part of the road follows, on your right, the Grumeti River, fringed by lush riverine forest, home to the black and white colobus monkey. On the banks of the river you will also see huge crocodiles basking in the sun. The Musabi and Ndoha Plains to the northwest and west of Seronera respectively can be viewed if you have a 4WD. The latter plain is the breeding area of topi and large herds of up to 2000 will often be found here. All but the main routes are poorly marked.

◉ Serengeti National Park listings

For Sleeping and Eating price codes and other relevant information, see pages 36-40.

● Sleeping

Serengeti National Park *p313, map p314*
Inside the park
L **Bilila Lodge Kempinski**, about 20 km north of the Retima Hippo Pool, www.kempinski-bililalodge.com. This lodge is due to open in Jun 2009. It promises to set the benchmark for luxury hotels in the region, with 80 rooms having all the mod cons you'd expect plus a telescope in each room. Suites have their own plunge pools and there's an infinity pool with views over the plains. There will also be a gym, a spa, a library, a business centre, a wine cellar, a boma, a pub and 2 restaurants. Rooms start at US$675.

L **Grumeti Serengeti Tented Camp**, Western Corridor, 93 km west of Seronera and 50 km east of Lake Victoria, central reservations Johannesburg, South Africa, T+27-11-8094300, www.andbeyond.com. Overlooks a tributary of the Grumeti River teeming with hippo and crocodiles. The wildebeest migration also passes through. Real African bush country with an abundance of birdlife including Fisher's lovebird. Central bar/dining area near the river, swimming pool, 10 charming, custom-made tents with stylishly colourful decor, private shower and WC. Solar electricity minimizes noise and pollution. Expensive at US$950 per person in the high season, including all meals and drinks and game drives, but fantastic service and a great location, especially during the migration. Balloon safaris are also available from the lodge.

L Kusini Camp, at the Hambi ya Mwaki-Nyeb Kopjes in the southwest, near the border with the Maswa Game Reserve, reservations Arusha, T027-250 9816/7, www.kusini.com. Closes during the rainy season Apr-May. Well off the usual tourist track, the camp is situated in a conchoidal outcrop of kopjes, offering superb views. 12 stylish tents, 1 of which is a honeymoon suite. Hospitable camp managers arrange sundowners on cushions up on the kopjes and candlelit dinners each evening. There's also a library and lounge. Rates US$650 per person or US$715 for a full game package.

L Lobo Wildlife Lodge, northeast of Seronera in the Lobo area, 45 km from the border with Kenya, reservations, Arusha, T027-254 4595, www.hotelsandlodges-tanzania.com. The 75 rooms built entirely of wood and glass around clusters of large boulders remain almost invisible from distance. The swimming pool and bar, both dug into the rock, afford good views over the savannah.

L Mbuzi Mawe, in the northeast of the park, about 45 km from Seronera, T028-262 2040, www.serenahotels.com. Built around rocky kopjes, Mbuzi Mawe means Klipsringer in Swahili and you'll see several of them skipping up the rocks here, no longer shy of people. It's a charming, understated camp with 16 tents stylishly decorated with private verandas, a relaxing bar and restaurant and friendly staff. US$570 for a double room full board.

L Migration Camp, built within the rocks of a kopje in the Ndassiata Hills near Lobo, over-looking the Grumeti River, T027-250 0630, www.elewana.com. Provides excellent views of the migration. Jacuzzi, swimming pool and restaurant. The 20 richly decorated tents include a secluded honeymoon tent and a family tent sleeping 6, each one is surrounded by a 360º veranda, and there are many secluded vantage points linked by timber walkways, bridges and viewing platforms. Resident game includes lion, leopard, elephant and buffalo. Rates in the region of US$680, or US$780 for a full game package per person.

L Sayari Camp, in the far north of the Serengeti, near the Kenyan border, reservations through Asilia Lodges, Arusha, T027-250 2799, www.asilialodges.com. Formerly a mobile camp that followed the migration, this permanent camp was established in Jun 2006 and is still the only camp in this remote region. 8 luxurious and comfortable tents with en suite bathrooms. The mess tent has a bar, lounge and restaurant centred around a camp fire. Attentive service, rates are all-inclusive. Income from the camp supports education and employment in the nearby villages.

L Serena Kirawira Camp, western Serengeti, T027-250 4058, central reservations www.serenahotels.com. A luxuriously appointed all-inclusive tented camp 90 km from Seronera in the secluded Western Corridor area. A member of Small Luxury Hotels of the World group. All the 25 tents have Edwardian decor and great views across the plains. The central public tent is adorned with exquisite antiques, including an old gramophone, and the swmming pool overlooks the plains. Rates US$890 per person inclusive.

L Serengeti Serena Lodge, 20 km north of Seronera Village, central reservations T027-250 4058, www.serenahotels.com. Another super-luxurious establishment in an idyllic central location with superb views towards the Western Corridor. Set high overlooking the plains, the lodge is constructed to reflect the design of an African village. Each of the 66 rooms are stone-walled and thatched rondavaals, with wooden balcony, natural stone bathrooms, a/c, central heating, carved furniture and are decorated with Makonde carvings. Also has beauty centre and infinity pool with views over the Serengeti. Rates US$320 per person.

L Seronera Wildlife Lodge, in the centre of the Serengeti, near the village of Seronera, T027-254 4595, www.hotelsandlodges-tanzania.com. This large lodge really is at the heart of the Serengeti. Good game viewing year round, but also significant visitor traffic. The public areas are very cleverly built into a rocky kopje, as is the new swimming pool (making it look like an attractive natural pool). The bar is especially nice, but the 75 rooms are in unattractive and old-fashioned accommodation blocks built in the 1970s. Restaurant, shop, bar and viewing platform at the top of the kopje (beware of the monkeys). Campers at the nearby public campsites are allowed into the bar in the evenings (suitably dressed), as driving around the immediate vicinity of Seronera is permitted until 2200.

L-A Mbalageti, in the Western Corridor of the park, T0787-969150 (mob), www.mbalageti.com. In an attractive location on Mwamyeni Hill, with 360° views over the plains and Mbalageti River. The 24 luxury tented chalets are set out in 2 groups – those facing sunrise and those facing sunset, all beautifully furnished and the suites have outdoor baths on private terraces. The lounge is full of African tribal carvings and antiques and the swimming pool, restaurant, bar and outdoor spa with tranquillity pool have fantastic views over the plains. Rates from US$585 for a double room. There are also 14 lodge rooms costing US$395.

L-A Serengeti Sopa Lodge, in the previously protected area of Nyarboro Hills north of Moru Kopjes, central reservations T027-250 0630, www.sopalodges.com. Luxury all-suite lodge with 75 suites . Excellent views of the Serengeti plains through double-storey window walls in all public areas, multi-level restaurant and lounges, and conference facilities, double swimming pool and satellite

TV, way off the beaten track involving an extra 50 km drive over poor roads (one way).

A Serengeti Wilderness Camp, 40 km east of Seronera, overlooking the Tagora Plains, reservations through Wild Frontiers, Johannesberg, South Africa, T+27-117 022 035, www.wildfrontiers.com. You really feel you're in the heart of the bush at this camp, which is semi-permanent and moved every 3 months or so depending on the season to follow the game movement, producing minimal impact on the environment. Unpretentious and friendly, guests here rave about the quality of the food. There's a large dining tent and bar, with a separate lounge area. The 10 comfortable tents are en suite with bucket showers and solar powered lighting. A great option if you want more of a bush experience but one that comes with home comforts. Recommended.

National Park campsites There are several public campsites around Seronera. Be prepared to be totally self-sufficient and if you are self-driving bring food with you as there is little available in Seronera Village. It is not necessary to pre-book the public campsites; you simply pay for camping when you enter the park. Facilities vary but most have nothing more than a long drop and are completely unfenced. The animals do wander through at night so ensure that you stay in your tent. Camps are regularly visited by hyenas each night scavenging for scraps, and lions have also been known to wander through in the middle of the night.

Outside the park
L Klein's Camp, on a private ranch on the north eastern boundary of the park just south of the Kenyan border, central reservations, Johannesburg, South Africa, T+27-118 094 300, www.andbeyond.com. Named after the American big game hunter Al Klein, who in 1926 built his base camp in this valley. The ranch is located on the Kuka Hills between the Serengeti and farmland, which forms a natural buffer zone for the animals and

overlooks the wildlife corridor linking the Serengeti and the Masai Mara. 10 stone and thatch cottages each with en suite facilities. The dining room and bar are in separate rondavaals with commanding views of the Grumeti River Valley, and there's a swimming pool and solar power electricity. Night drives and game walks. US$950 per person per night all inclusive, reductions for low season.

L Sasakwa Lodge, **Sabora Lodge** and **Faru Faru Lodge**, these 3 lodges are located in a 140,000 ha private concession area owned by Singita near the Grumeti River and Ikoma Gate, www.grumetireserves.com. **Sasakwa** has 7 luxury cottages with private pools set on a hill with stunning views over the main migration route. Facilities include a gym and yoga room, an equestrian centre and a helicopter for transfer to the local airstrip. This flagship property costs a hefty US$1600 per person. **Sabora** and **Faru Faru** are both classic tented camps reminiscent of the 1920s safari style, both costing US$995 per person.

A-B Ikoma Bush Camp, 2 km from Ikoma Gate, central reservations T027-255 3242, www.moivaro.com Has the concession for the area to operate game viewing drives and walks, and works in close collaboration with the local villages. This is slightly cheaper than some of the more luxurious tented camps above, and rates are US$180 per person full board in the peak season. The camp is comfortable and secluded, with 39 spacious en suite tents There is hot and cold running water and flush toilets. Electricity is provided by solar power as is the hot water. There is a dining room and bar under thatch.

A-B Mapito Tented Camp, 5 km outside the park, signposted left off the main road, 1 km from Ikoma Gate then about 4 km drive on a dirt-track, T0732-975210 (mob), www.mapito-camp-serengeti.com. More affordable than lodges within the park at around US$200 per person full board, this relaxing camp has 10 large en suite tents with hot water bucket showers and solar powered electricity. They can arrange walking safaris and night game drives as well as cultural visits to villages.

B Speke Bay Lodge, on the shores of Lake Victoria off the main road 15 km from Ndabaka Gate towards Mwanza, T028-262 1236, www.spekebay.com. A lovely, cheaper alternative to staying in the Serengeti if you fancy a break from the bush. Run by a Dutch couple, this lodge has 8 round bungalows (although more are planned) on the shores of Lake Victoria. Rooms are spacious and spotless with a mezzanine floor for triple beds. The bar and restaurant are on a terrace overlooking the beach. With well-established gardens, over 250 bird species and a pod of 10 hippos within its 85 ha, it's a mini nature reserve in its own right. The lodge offers bird walks, canoe trips with local fishermen and boat hire.

D-F Kijereshi Lodge, just outside the far end of the Western Corridor near the Ndabaka Gate, T028-262 1231, www.kijereshiserengeti.com. 23 tents and bungalows, with en suite bathrooms, though not in the same class as some of the other tented camps. Excellent restaurant in an old homestead that sometimes has game meat on the menu, cosy lounge and bar with fire in winter, swimming pool, gift shop, TV room with wildlife videos. This is usually fairly quiet, although it is used by overlander groups at times, but is convenient if you want to enter or exit the park at the Ndabaka Gate from Mwanza or Musoma. The campsite is US$15 and campers can use the other facilities at the lodge. Be warned though – the campsite is 1 km or so from the lodge; exercise extreme caution if walking back in the dark, animals are present. Camping fees are paid directly to the lodge reception here and not on entry to the park.

D-F Serengeti Stopover, along the Mwanza–Musoma Rd on the western edge of Serengeti, 141 km east of Mwanza and 1 km west of Ndabaka Gate, T028-262 2273, www.serengetistopover.com. A good basic restaurant that does the best fish and chips in the area, caught fresh that day from Lake Victoria, which is within walking distance. 10 simple self-contained chalets with TVs, fans and nets, some with verandas and lounge areas, and a campsite. On the border of Kijereshi Game Reserve and the Serengeti, its proximity to the park means that game can be present and you could avoid park entrance fees. Unlike safaris from Arusha, the lodge can arrange day trips into the park that can be very good value. It is run as a community initiative with the local Sukuma people, and tours can be arranged to the local villages. Recommended for budget travellers, you can jump off any of the buses that go between Mwanza and Musoma.

▲ Activities and tours

Serengeti National Park *p313, map p314*
Balloon Safaris
Seronera Lodge and **Grumeti Serengeti Tented Camp**, see Sleeping, above, UK office T+44 (0) 122 587 3756, www.balloon safaris.com. Balloon safaris are available for

US$499 per person; 1-hr balloon flight at sunrise, with a champagne breakfast and transport from your lodge. Especially during the months of the migration, this is often the highlight of visitors' trips to Tanzania. Although expensive, the experience is well worth the treat. Given that there are only 3 balloons, it is essential to pre-book.

🚌 Transport

Serengeti National Park *p313, map p314*
Air
Coastal Air, www.coastal.cc, flies from the Grumeti Serengeti Tented Camp airstrip to **Arusha** daily at 0940 (3 hrs); from the Seronera Wildlife Lodge airstrip to **Arusha** daily at 1105 (3 hrs). From Grumeti Serengeti Tented Camp to **Mwanza** daily at 1355 (3 hrs); from Seronera Wildlife Lodge to **Mwanza** daily at 1540 (3 hrs). These flights stop at the other lodge airstrips on demand.

Contents

Footprint features

Border crossings

Tanzania–Uganda
Bukoba–Kampala, see page 340.

Around Lake Victoria

At a glance

◉ **Getting around** Travel by *dala-dala* and bus is fine in the main towns of Mwanza, Musoma and Bukoba, but local ferries or boats are a far more pleasant option than the rough roads between lakeside towns and villages.

◉ **Time required** 5-7 days, bearing in mind the poor road conditions and time to recover and chill on Rubondo and Lukuba islands.

☀ **Weather** Mostly warm during the day, with cool evenings. Apr-May has the most rainfall, although showers aren't uncommon at any time. Coolest in Jun-Sep.

✖ **When not to go** If using Mwanza as a base for the Serengeti's Western Corridor, avoid the heavy rains Apr-May.

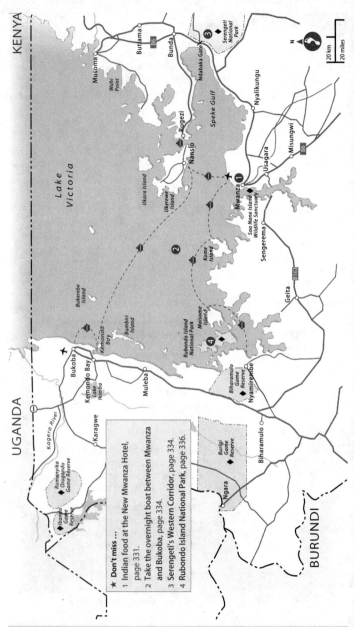

★ Don't miss ...
1 Indian food at the New Mwanza Hotel, page 331.
2 Take the overnight boat between Mwanza and Bukoba, page 334.
3 Serengeti's Western Corridor, page 334.
4 Rubondo Island National Park, page 336.

Lake Victoria, bordered by Kenya, Tanzania and Uganda, is the largest freshwater lake in Africa and the second largest in the world after Lake Superior in North America. Occupying a shallow depression at an altitude of 1135 m, it covers 69,490 sq km, is the source of the White Nile and provides a livelihood for millions of people living around its shores not only in Tanzania but in Kenya and Uganda too. This area is a long way from the coast and transport links leave much to be desired. The road to Mwanza through central Tanzania is in a poor state, and better (albeit slow) access is by train, or by air (though services can be erratic) or by road through Kenya. Mwanza is a busy city, and surprisingly, given its location, the second largest in Tanzania, and there is much activity in exporting fish from Lake Victoria. It is the terminus of a branch of the central railway line from Dar es Salaam, and has trade links with nearby Kenya. Bukoba, on the west side of the lake, is in a very attractive setting. But none of these places feature high on the usual tourist itinerary, though the western section of the Serengeti National Park can be accessed from this region, and the most notable attraction on the lake is the Rubondo Island National Park.

Getting there

Aside from the major tarred road that links Mwanza with the border of Kenya, the roads in the region are very poor, especially after rain. There are frequent buses to the border with Kenya and beyond, and long distance buses to Arusha and Dar es Salaam usually take the route via Kenya. Most people arrive in Mwanza by train on the Central Railway from Dar es Salaam. The railway line, built in the 1920s during the British administration, was completed in 1928. It forms the extension of the Central Line and was considered vital for the development of the northwest area. There are also a number of ferry services operating on Lake Victoria, notably the Mwanza–Bukoba car and passenger ferry which is the only reasonable method of reaching Bukoba. The road to Bukoba around the lake is atrocious and in the past there have been incidents of vehicles being hijacked. This was the region where many refugee camps were located along the Rwanda and Burundi borders. Mwanza has an airport and there are regular flights from both Dar es Salaam and Nairobi. There are also flights to Rubondo Island National Park.

Eastern Lake Victoria

The Tanzania towns of Musoma and Mwanza and the nearby islands offer the opportunity to witness the majesty of Lake Victoria. Mwanza, the second largest town in Tanzania, is the spring board for the ferry across the lake to Bukoba on the western side, easily the best method of getting to the other side, and the terminus for the Central Railway. ➠ *For listings, see pages 330-335.*

Musoma ●❼❶❸❺❻ ➠ *pp330-335. Colour map 1, A3. 1° 50'S, 34° 30'E.*

→ *Phone code: 028. Population: 150,000.*

This small port is set on the east shores of Lake Victoria close to the border with Kenya. It's close to the Western Corridor of Serengeti National Park and so should be one of the centres for safaris to the park. However, because the Kenyan border was closed for several years, and because of its general inaccessibility, it has not developed as such. There is little reason to come here although the views over the lake are very good and it is a bustling and friendly town and capital of Mara Region. Visitors usually pop in on their way to or from Kenya. The weekday market, when women bring their crops of mangoes and green leafy vegetables, ripe avocados and bunches of bright yellow bananas to sell is worth seeing; as are the many varieties of boats on the lake, from large ferries and transport barges to *ngalawa* fishing boats and dugout canoes. Small boats can be taken across the bay and to the little islands nearby for around US$1 per person. They leave from the fish market and harbour on the north shore, not far from the **Afrilux Hotel**.

The town has a climate of hot days and cool nights. Electricity and water supplies can be erratic, and the small hotels will not have generators. None of the hotels currently take credit cards, only the banks will change travellers' cheques, and there are no internet cafés.

Around Musoma

Butiama The home village of Julius Nyerere (see box, page 423) is 48 km from Musoma. The village has a **museum** ① *US$2*, which commemorates Nyerere's life and work.

Exhibits document the rise of nationalism, the independence movement, and the early history of Tanzania, as well as displaying various items of interest that belonged to the late leader, including a copy of Plato's Republic translated into Kiswahili by hand. Tanzania's first president was buried here, not far from the humble dwelling where he was born 77 years before. The bus ride is through pleasant scenery and costs US$1.

Mwanza 🚌🏨🍴🛈🏛🅿🛶🚌🛈 ⟶ pp330-335. Colour map 1, A3. 2° 30'S, 32° 58'E.

→ *Phone code: 028.*

Mwanza is the largest Tanzanian port on Lake Victoria and with a population of roughly 3 million it is Tanzania's second-largest town. It lies on a peninsula that juts into the lake. It is surrounded by rocky hills and the land is dominated by granite outcrops, some of which are very impressive and look as if they are about to topple. The road approach is spectacular, tunnelling through some of the great boulders on the route. As the railway terminus and major lake port, Mwanza is a bustling and lively town. Fishing is a major commercial activity in this area, though tea, cotton and coffee plantations around here produce large volumes of cash crops that pass though Mwanza on their way to market. The produce from the lake region is gathered here and is then transported to the coast by rail. Recently the town has received a major economic boost with the South African takeover of the Mwanza Brewery, and the substantial mining developments in Shinyanga and around Geita. For visitors, the city makes a good base from which to explore nearby Rubondo Island National Park and the western parts of the Serengeti.

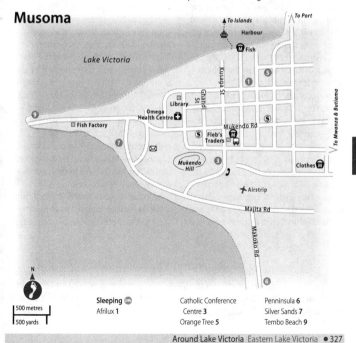

Musoma

Lake Victoria

Sleeping 🛏
Afrilux **1**

Catholic Conference
Centre **3**
Orange Tree **5**

Penninsula **6**
Silver Sands **7**
Tembo Beach **9**

Lake Victoria

Lake Victoria is one of the most important natural water resources in the sub-Saharan region of Africa. It is has a surface area of approximately 69,500 sq km with an adjoining catchment area measuring 184,000 sq km. The Tanzania share of the lake is 49%, Kenya's share is 6% and Uganda has 45%. The surrounding lake communities in all three countries equal approximately 30 million people, a large proportion being totally dependent on the lake for water, food and economic empowerment. Despite its vast size, Lake Victoria remained one of the last physical features in Africa to be discovered by the 19th-century explorers from Europe. Early charts depict a vague patch of water lying to the north and east of the 'Mountains of the Moon' (today's Rwenzori Mountains in Uganda), but it was not until 1858 that explorers Speke and Burton stumbled on to its southern shore near Mwanza in Tanzania. Speke later wrote that he felt no doubt that the lake gave birth to the River Nile, the source of which had been the subject of so much speculation and the object of many explorers' expeditions. He said "the lake at my feet is the most elusive of all explorers' dreams, the source of the legendary Nile".

Lake Victoria is relatively shallow and has a gentle slope to the shores, so any slight change in water level affects a large land area. It's mean depth is 40 m, the deepest part is 82 m. The water balance is dominated by evaporation and rainfall in the lake, with contributions from river inflow and outflow. The outflow of water, into the River Nile through the Owen Falls Dam in Uganda, accounts for only 20% of water loss from the lake. The remaining 80% is taken by evaporation. Similarly, the inflow through the many rivers from the catchment area only contributes 15-20% while rainfall on the lake accounts for 80-85%. Of the inlets, the River Kagera, which flows from Rwanda, contributes about 46%, Kenya's Nzoia and Sondu/Miriu rivers about 15% and 8% respectively and Tanzania's Mara River about 10-15%.

There is a wide variety of fish in the lake. Scientifically, it is puzzling that so many diverse species unique to these waters could evolve in so uniform an environment. Biologists speculate that hundreds of thousands of years ago, the lake may have dried into a series of smaller lakes causing these brilliantly coloured cichlids to evolve differently. These fish are greatly sought after for aquariums. One unique characteristic for which cichlids (tilapia being the best known) are noted for is the female's habit of nursing its fertilized eggs and young in its mouth. To the people of Lake Victoria, the cichlids have been their livelihood – the catch, preparation (sun-drying) and sale of these fish are an important resource for them. Lake Victoria is also a home to a predator fish, the Nile perch, introduced into the lake some 20 years ago as a sport fish.

Warning Lake Victoria is infected with bilharzia (Schistosomiasis) so swimming close to the shore is not recommended.

Ins and outs

Getting around Taxis can be found near the bus and train stations or outside the New Mwanza Hotel. Commuter buses, locally known as 'express', are well distributed throughout the town and are the most popular and cheapest means of transport.
▶ For further details, see Transport, page 333.

Sights

The colonial centre of Mwanza was around the port on the west side of the town. Among the historic buildings in this area are the **Primary Court**, dating from the German period, and the **Mahatma Ghandi Memorial Hall** from the British period. The **clock tower** has a plaque recording that on 3 August 1858, on Isamilo Hill, a mile away, John Hanning Speke first saw the main water of Lake Victoria, which he later proved to be the source of the Nile.

The colonial residences spread over **Capri Point** and social life is centred on the **Mwanza Club** and its golf course, and the **Yacht Club**. One of the celebrated sights is **Bismark Rock**, which appears precariously balanced, just south of the main port.

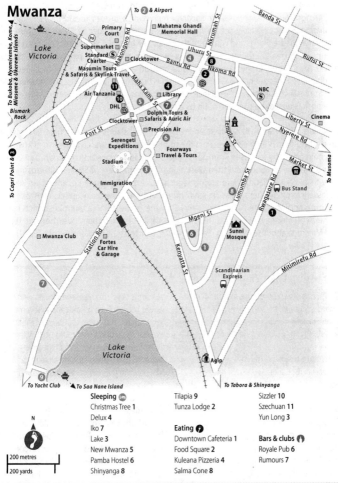

Mwanza

Sleeping
Christmas Tree 1
Delux 4
Iko 7
Lake 3
New Mwanza 5
Pamba Hostel 6
Shinyanga 8

Tilapia 9
Tunza Lodge 2

Eating
Downtown Cafeteria 1
Food Square 2
Kuleana Pizzeria 4
Salma Cone 8

Sizzler 10
Szechuan 11
Yun Long 3

Bars & clubs
Royale Pub 6
Rumours 7

200 metres
200 yards

Around Mwanza

Saa Nane Island ① *Boats from Mwanza depart from the jetty 1 km south of the centre off Station Rd just before the Tilapia Hotel, at 1100, 1300, 1400, 1500 and 1600. Combined boat and entry fee about US$1.50.* This wildlife sanctuary is not far from Mwanza, on the lake. It has hippo, zebra and wildebeest, as well as various caged animals, including some very unhappy-looking hyenas, although it is reported that the number of animals has fallen. It gets very busy at the weekends and despite its location, with rocky outcrops appearing out of a grassy landscape, it is not a particularly pleasant place to visit and is not much more than a glorified zoo with cramped enclosures.

Bujora Sukuma Village Museum ① *18 km from Mwanza on the Musoma road, reached by taking a local bus from the bus station near the market in Mwanza to Kisessa, then walking the remaining 2 km.* Originally set up by missionaries from Quebec in 1952, the museum celebrates the traditions and culture of the Sukuma who make up one of the largest tribal groups in Tanzania. Exhibits include an unusual two-storey royal pavilion in the shape of the royal stool, shrines, and traditional instruments, including a drum collection. Traditional dances are held when the museum is busy, usually on a Saturday, and include the impressive Sukuma snake dance or *Bugobogobo*, which is performed with a live python. It is best to be shown around by a guide, cost US$2.

Ukerewe, Kome and Maisome Islands These three islands on Lake Victoria are very pretty, but there is little else to attract the tourist. Ukerewe Island to the north of Mwanza can be reached by ferry (see Transport, page 333). It is also possible to go by road – east round the lake to Bunda and then west along the north shore of Speke Gulf, crossing by ferry to Ukerewe Island. There are no regular buses on the last leg of this route so it is necessary to hitch. There are some small hotels and a number of cheap restaurants.

Kome and Maisome islands are served by the ferries to Myamirembe, which leave Mwanza on Monday (0800) and Thursday (2100). Kome takes about three hours to reach and Maisome about seven hours. Ferries return from Nyamirembe on Tuesday (0800) and Friday (1900).

◉ Eastern Lake Victoria listings

For Sleeping and Eating price codes and other relevant information, see pages 36-40.

⬤ Sleeping

Musoma *p326, map p326*
For accommodation, see also **Serengeti Stopover**, south of Musoma near the Ndabaka Gate of the Serengeti National Park, page 321.
L Lukuba Island, reservations, Arusha, T027-254 8840, www.lukubaisland.com. This is primarily a fishing lodge on Lukuba Island on Lake Victoria, and guests are transferred from Musoma by boat which takes around 45 mins. 5 grass thatched

buildings nestle in the island's forest with lake views, good cuisine of understandably mostly fish, managed by a friendly couple. Fishing excursions by dhow and motorboat with fish-finding equipment and all the gear from US$25-50 per hr. It is possible to catch Nile perch in these waters and otters and monitor lizards are frequently seen around the island.
E Penninsula, 2 km south from town towards the pleasant suburb of Makoko, south of the airstrip, T028-264 2546. Smart whitewashed building on the beach, rooms have a/c, TV, hot water, and fridges, good value for the standard. Large restaurant

serving Western and Indian dishes, separate beach area with a swimming pool (not always open) and boats.

F Afrilux, central, 500 m from the bus stand, T028-262 0031. Very good value, self-contained rooms with hot water, fans and satellite TV. Restaurant serving filling local and Indian meals and a large garden bar area.

F Catholic Conference Centre, town centre, close to the bus stand, T028-262 0168. Secure and clean. 30 rooms, bathrooms are shared. Good restaurant and bar, with a satellite TV. Recommended for value.

F Orange Tree, in town centre, 1 block back from the **Afrilux**, T028-262 2651. Basic and rundown self-contained double rooms, but fairly friendly with a reasonable bar and restaurant.

F Silver Sands, 1 km west of town centre, T028-262 2740. More than a little rundown, rooms are very basic and not too clean. Shared cold shower, a big garden bar, but no food.

F Tembo Beach, at Old Musoma Pier, 2 km west of town, T028-262 2887. Hotel with private beach on a peninsula. Variety of accommodation from self-contained units with porches and hot water, to camping. Good bar and restaurant facilities, a little dilapidated, but very peaceful, with wonderful views of the lake.

Mwanza *p327, map p329*

B-D New Mwanza, central on Post St, T028-250 1070, www.newmwanzahotel.com. Has recently undergone a major refurbishment, which has introduced plenty of marble and gilt. Well run with attentive and helpful staff and management. The 54 rooms have en suite bathrooms, a/c, satellite TV, and internet access for laptops. Extensive facilities include King's Casino with a number of tables and slots, 24-hr coffee shop and room service, Blue Moon disco, bar and restaurant. The Indian food here is superb and very authentic, cooked by Indian chefs. Eat here even if you are not staying. Also has good buffet breakfasts. Swimming pool, gym, sauna and steam room.

C Tilapia, Station Rd near ferry to Saa Nane Island, 1 km southwest of town, T028-250 0517, www.hoteltilapia.com. Chalet-style accommodation, in 40 self-contained rooms with a/c or fans, TV, fridge, there is also some accommodation on a houseboat moored on the lake by the hotel. Lovely swimming pool, non-guests can swim but have to pay, small gym. Has Indian, Thai and Japanese restaurants and a decking bar overlooking the lake. Fax and internet services, can arrange car hire. A vintage box-body Ford and an old Rolls Royce have been restored and are on display next to reception. The facilities here are superb but some reports from readers say it is a glorified brothel.

D Tunza Lodge, Ilemela Beach, near the village of Hemla, 10 km north of town and 3 km from the airport, T028-256 2215, www.renair.com. A beach resort and the only one of its kind on Lake Victoria. 5 doubles, 5 twins and 3 single rooms, all with en suite bathrooms. Nice gardens leading down to the beach but remember Lake Victoria has bilharzia and swimming close to the shore is not recommended. Can arrange fishing trips, waterskiing and windsurfing. Good bar and restaurant in pleasant thatched building.

F Christmas Tree, Karuta St, just off Mgeni St, T028-250 2001. Modern 3-storey block, simple rooms with hot water in bathrooms. Restaurant good value.

F Hotel Delux, Uhuru St, T028-250 0831. Newly painted, white 5-storey block with shabby rooms, but reasonable for the price. Downstairs restaurant serves huge plates of steaming stews and curries for next to nothing. Rates include basic breakfast.

F Iko Hotel, close to the **Tilapia**, T028-254 0900. 52 a/c rooms, prices vary depending on the size, a little tatty but comfortable and good value. Reasonable restaurant with a bar.

F Lake Hotel, Fourways junction, off Station Rd close to stadium, T028-250 0658. Restaurant, outdoor bar, parking space, noisy and busy. Lots of rooms (but fills up quickly) with fans, mosquito nets, bathrooms.

Good value, rates include a very basic breakfast (pineapple sandwiches?!).

F Pamba Hostel, Station Rd near roundabout, T028-250 2697. Central location, a bit rough and ready, shared facilities, squat toilets, noisy, especially at the weekends when there is a disco. Continental breakfast, restaurant, rooftop bar. Owned by the company that does the catering for all the ferries and trains in Tanzania.

F Shinyanga, Lumumba St. Just off centre, rundown tall blue block with 108 rooms, very basic, mosquito nets, shared bathrooms, no restaurant or bar though there is a fridge in reception selling water and soft drinks.

⦿ Eating

Musoma *p326, map p327*
There are a few basic food canteens around town, and most of Musoma's hotels (see Sleeping, above) provide food, the **Peninsula** and **Afrilux** are particularly recommended.

Mwanza *p327, map p329*
There are a number of cheap restaurants on the corner of Barti St and Nkrumah St, serving up barbecued meat, fried chicken and stews. These include The **Food Square** (♥), which is clean and smart.

♥♥ **Hotel Tilapia**, Station Rd, near ferry to Saa Nane Island, 1 km southwest of town, T028-250 0517. Good standard and popular, restaurants inside in basement and outside on roof serving Chinese, Japanese and Indian food, and a decking bar overlooking the lake. Set courses in the Japanese restaurant are not unreasonable.

♥ **Downtown Cafeteria**, opposite the bus stand. Very busy with market traders and people waiting for buses. Clean and bright with good buffet breakfasts, fresh juices and coffee, and satellite news on the TV.

♥ **Kuleana Pizzeria**, Post St, near the New Mwanza Hotel. Open daily until 1700. Promises cappuccino and the like but doesn't always deliver and some of the menu items are downright strange (avocado gravy?).

The pizzas and home-made bread are very good though and they support street kids.

♥ **Salma Cone**, corner of Barti St and Nkrumah St. Coffee, snacks and ice cream.

♥ **Sizzler**, Kenyatta St, T0741-341118 (mob). Open daily 1100-1500, 1800-2230. Good quality international, Chinese and Indian food, especially the Indian dishes, but perhaps a little pricey. Does not sell booze.

♥ **Szechuan**, Kenyatta St. Better than **Sizzler** above, reasonable quality Chinese food and very authentic Indian food from talented chefs served with roti and naan bread, a wide range of dishes and good for vegetarians.

♥ **Yun Long**, 5-min walk along the lake road, T0744-609790 (mob). Open daily 1200-midnight.Fantastic setting in lovely gardens, with all the tables right on the edge of the lake. There's a large bar under thatch with a full range of imported drinks, 2 pool tables, TV. Try the Chinese-style tilapia fillet with chilli or sweet and sour sauce.

⦿ Bars and clubs

Mwanza *p327, map p329*
Royal Pub, just off Mgeni St. A big outdoor bar under a large canopy, most of the awnings are made from UN tarps, barbecued meals, busy all day, friendly service.

Rumours, Station Rd. Bar with a modern interior and mirrored glass on the exterior, satellite TV and big screen, pool tables, dance floor very popular.

⦿ Entertainment

Mwanza *p327, map p329*
There is a **cinema** on Liberty St – look out for the billboard on the corner of Nyerere/Station road for details of films.
King's Casino is on the 1st floor of the New Mwanza Hotel. Open every evening until very late. Roulette and black jack, slot machines and bar, free drinks to players, no entry fee. The **Blue Moon** disco is also in the hotel.

O Shopping

Musoma *p326, map p327*
Flebs' Traders, Kusaga St. Has a good range of imported items.

Mwanza *p327, map p329*
There is an excellent supermarket on the site of the previous U Turn Restaurant, corner of Nkrumah and Hospital St. This sells frozen meat, toiletries, canned drinks including Diet Coke, English biscuits and chocolate bars, English choc ices, fairly expensive but has an impressive range of products. There is another supermarket at the clock tower roundabout next to Standard Charter Bank.

▲ Activities and tours

Mwanza *p327, map p329*
Tour operators
Dolphin Tours & Safaris, Kenyatta St/ Post St corner, T028-250 0096 (in the same office as **Auric Air**, an air charter company, www.auricair.com). Car hire and tailor-made safaris.
Fourways Travel & Tours, corner of Station and Kenyatta Rds, T028-250 2620, fourways.mza@mwanza-online.com. Very helpful agency, managed by Sharad J Shah. Fishing and wildlife safaris, airport pick ups, and flight tickets.
Masumin Tours & Safaris and Skylink Travel, Kenyatta St, T028-250 0233, www.masuminsafaris.com. Safaris to the parks in the northern circuit from Mwanza, also offers short/long term car hire. Shares an office with Skylink who also have offices in Dar and Arusha, www.skylinktanzania.com. Agents for Avis Car Hire.
Serengeti Expeditions, Kenyatta St, opposite the New Mwanza Hotel, T028-250 0061, www.serengetiexpedition.com. Safaris to the northern circuit, car hire, agents for most of the major airlines including British Airways and KLM.

Yachting
Yacht Club, Station Rd, southern end. Offers sailing on the lake. Well-appointed premises with restaurant, bar and a billiards table. Entrance fee payable for non-members.

⊙ Transport

Musoma *p326, map p327*
Bus
Musoma lies 18 km from the main road that goes from Mwanza to the Kenya border and through buses do not stop here. However there are direct regular buses to **Mwanza** leaving from the bus station, which is behind Kusaga St in the centre. The trip takes 3 hrs, and costs US$4. **Arusha** buses go through the **Serengeti** and the **Ngorongoro Crater Reserve** to **Karatu** and then along the new road to Arusha. This journey takes just about all day and the bus leaves Musoma very early in the morning.

Mwanza *p327, map p329*
Air
Air Tanzania flies twice a day to **Dar** at 0900 and 1800 (90 mins). **Precision Air** operates daily flights to **Dar** at 1100 and 1645 (2 hrs, one way US$150, return US$240); a daily flight to **Nairobi** (Kenya) at 1350 (1 hr 40 mins, one way US$193, return US$285). To **Bukoba** Mon, Wed and Fri at 0800, 1110 and 1755 (55 mins, one way US$65, return US$106). **Coastal Air** flies daily at 0900 to **Arusha** (2 hrs 15 mins) via the camps in the **Serengeti**. There is also a flight from Mwanza to **Rubondo Island National Park** on Tue and Fri at 1620 (40 mins) if there is the demand. **Auricair** run regular charters between Mwanza and **Kampala** (Uganda). The office is at Dolphin Tours (see Activities and tours, above).
    Airline offices Air Tanzania, Kenyatta Rd, T028-250 0368, www.airtanzania.com. **Auricair**, air charter company based at Mwanza Airport, T028-250 0096, www. auricair.com. **Coastal Air**, T022-211 7969/60,

www.coastal.cc. **Precision Air**, Kenyatta Rd, T028-250 0819, and at the airport, www.precisionairtz.com.

Bus

The large bus stand is off Pamba Rd and is fairly organized with kiosks around the edge selling tickets. Locally, there are plenty of buses to **Musoma** costing little more than US$2.50 and taking 3 hrs. Further afield buses go to **Dar** and **Arusha** via **Nairobi**, 30 hrs, US$36. The buses go north across the Kenya border, then to Nairobi via **Kisii**, **Kericho** and **Nakuru**, then south to cross the **Namanga** border into Tanzania again, and onward to Arusha and Dar. These do not run every day.

There is another service to **Dar** via **Singida**, 27 hrs, US$27. Though the roads are not in great condition and the ride is bumpy, the roads in the central region are improving. A couple of times a week there are also buses to **Kigoma** but this is a very poor road and the train is advised for this journey. Buses also go to **Arusha** through the **Serengeti National Park** and **Ngorongoro Crater Conservation Area**, 12-15 hrs, US$25. This service leaves very early in the morning and goes via **Bunda** on the road to the Kenyan border which is tar sealed, then branches off on a horrendously bad dirt road to the Serengeti's Ikoma Gate, or via the Serengeti's Ndabaka Gate 10-15 km south of Bunda on the main road from Musoma towards Mwanza. It then goes through the park via **Seronera** and out again into the Ngorongro Conservation Area at Naabi Hill Gate. It does not stop to look at any animals and takes a little under 2 hrs to cross the Serengeti. The bus continues past the crater (though of course does not go down into it) to **Karatu** and then on to Arusha, arriving there late at night. Although this service is the quickest method of getting between Mwanza and Arusha, foreigners will have to pay the US$30 entrance fee for both the Serengeti and the crater, which means another US$60 is added to the US$25 bus ticket. This makes

it an expensive option with the added disadvantage of speeding past the animals in a crowded bus without being able to stop. An alternative is to arrange a safari of the Serengeti and the crater with one of the tour operators in Mwanza and asked to be dropped off at the end in either Karatu or Arusha. **Scandinavia Express**, Rwegasore St, T028-2503315, www.scandinavia group.com.

To Kenya There is at least 1 bus a day to **Kisumu**, leaving at around 0700.

Car hire

Avis, Kenyatta Rd, opposite Kenya Central Bank, T028-250 0233, www.avis.com, run by Skylink, www.skylinktanzania.com; **Fortes**, just south of the railway station, T028-250 0700, fortes@thenet.co.tz, also has a garage.

Ferry

This is easily the most reliable, enjoyable and comfortable way to travel on to **Bukoba**. The boats, the *MV Serengeti* and the *MV Victoria*, though old, have recently been refitted. There is a ferry on Sun, Tue and Thu from Mwanza to Bukoba, and from Bukoba to Mwanza on Mon, Wed and Fri, both leaving at 1800 taking 10 hrs. Fares are US$15, US$13 and US$9. 1st class provides a berth in a 2-person cabin, 2nd in a 4-person cabin, 3rd is seating or deck space. Earplugs can be a boon. **Nyamirembe** is served by 2 ferries a week, from Mwanza at 0800 on Mon and 2100 on Thu and from Nyamirembe at 0800 on Tue and 1900 on Fri. The journey takes 10 hrs. Ferries call at **Kome** (3 hrs) and **Miasome Islands** (7hrs), leaving Mwanza Mon 0800 and Thu 2100 and cost US$5 (2nd class) and US$3 (3rd). **Ukerewe Island** has a daily ferries (2 hrs 30 mins), leaving Mwanza at 0800 and 1200, and returning at 1600, US$3.

Train

The train from **Dar** to **Mwanza** (1227 km) leaves Dar on Sun, Tue and Fri at 1700. Trains go to **Dar** from Mwanza 5 days a week on Sun, Tue, Thu, Fri, Sat at 1800. Double check departure times. The journey takes roughly 36 hrs. The trip may involve changing trains at **Tabora** (10 hrs from Mwanza). You can also get to **Kigoma** by train from Mwanza (via Tabora). See Tanzania Railways Corporation www.trctz.com for full details of timetables and fares.

❶ Directory

Musoma *p326, map p327*
Medical services Musoma Hospital is next to the market, T028-262 2111; Omega Health Centre, in the town centre, is recommended. **Telephone** Telecoms on Kusaga St have international call facilities and will send faxes.

Mwanza *p327, map p329*
Banks National Bank of Commerce, Liberty Rd; Stanbic Bank is on Nyerere Rd; Standard Chartered Bank, Kenyatta Rd, north of the clock tower; Trust Bank, Station Rd; Victoria Travels, in the arcade of shops in the New Mwanza Hotel is a general travel agent but also offers a bureau de change with competitive exchange rates. Can also buy US$ cash here. All have ATMs. **Courier services** DHL, Kenyatta Rd, T028-250 0910, www.dhl.co.tz; SkyNet has an office in the New Mwanza Hotel. **Immigration** Immigration office, opposite the railway station, T028-250 0585. Mon-Fri 0730-1530. **Internet** Karibu Corner Internet Café, corner of Kenyatta Rd and Post St, US$1 for 1 hr. Several others too. **Medical services** Aga Khan Clinic, Wurzburg Rd; Bugando Hospital, on a hill about 1 km southwest of town, T028-240 6105; Hindu Union Hospital, Belewa Rd; Mwananchi Hospital, Station Rd behind Tanesco. **Police station**, Kenyatta Rd near the ferry terminal. **Post office** Post St.

Western Lake Victoria

The western shores of Lake Victoria are little visited and the principal town of Bukoba, best reached by ferry from Mwanza, is little more than a sleepy backwater in this far north western corner of Tanzania. The roads are so bad in this region that even sodas and beers are delivered to Bukoba by ferry. But the town is relaxed and in a scenic position on the lakeshore, and it provides an unusual access route to Uganda a little way to the north. Further south the highlight of the region is the Rubondo Island National Park where the forests harbour a number of species of game and birds. ▶▶ For listings, see pages 341-344.

Rubondo Island National Park ● ▶▶ *p341-344. Colour map 1, A2. 2° 30'S, 31° 45'E.*

Rubondo National Park is an island northwest of Mwanza and directly south of Bukoba. The park encompasses Rubondo Island as well as several smaller islands nearby. It was gazetted in 1977 with a total area of 460 sq km, about 240 sq km of which is land.

Ins and outs

Getting there Coastal Air has a service that arrives from Mwanza on Tuesday and Friday. The fare is US$70 one way. This flight connects with a service from Mwanza to the camps in the Serengeti, so a visit to Rubondo can be combined with a safari of the parks in the northern circuit. Alternatively, you could catch the ferry to Maisome Island (see page 330) just east of Rubondo, and from Maisome arrange a boat transfer to Rubondo. You can also drive the 10 hours to Nyamirembe (via Gieta) from where the boat journey is about 30 minutes. But this doesn't work out much cheaper than the flight and will take considerably longer. No vehicles are allowed on the island although there is a lorry that can be hired to transport visitors.

Park fees and information Entrance to the park is US$20, or it is US$50 to go sport fishing for the day. The best time to visit Rubondo is November-February.

Wildlife

There are a number of different vegetation types on the island providing differing habitats for a variety of animals. With a high water table the island is able to support dense forest. Other vegetation includes more open woodland, savannah grassland and swamps. There is little 'big game' on the island although some has been introduced, including giraffe, elephant and rhino. Many of the animals were relocated here in the 1970s when the island was identified as a safe haven in the fight

Rubondo Island National Park

Chitebe Island
Chitende Island
Rubiso Island
Miso Island
Kageye & Park HQ
Kalela Island
Ibozya Bay
Mlaga
Iloba Island
Chambuzi Island
Manyila Island
Chitoma Bay
Mamba Island
Lukaga
Lukukuru
Izilamouda Island

Lake Victoria

N

2 km
2 miles

Sleeping ●
Rubondo Island Tented Lodge 1   ● Ranger post

Footprint Mini Atlas
Tanzania

UGANDA

o Bukoba   o Musoma   KENYA

RWANDA

o Mwanza   Arusha o
o Moshi

BURUNDI

Singida o   o Tanga
Tabora o
o Kigoma

RD CONGO   DODOMA □
Morogoro o
o Dar es Salaam

Iringa o

Indian Ocean

N

Mbeya o

ZAMBIA   o Mtwara

200 km
200 miles   Songea o

MALAWI   MOZAMBIQUE

Distance chart

	Arusha	Bukoba	Dar es Salaam	Dodoma	Iringa	Kigoma	Mbeya	Morogoro	Moshi	Mtwara	Musoma	Mwanza	Singida	Songea	Tabora
Bukoba	1103														
Dar es Salaam	649	1479													
Dodoma	438	996	483												
Iringa	695	1253	503	257											
Kigoma	1214	577	1590	1107	1307										
Mbeya	959	1214	893	647	390	917									
Morogoro	624	1286	193	290	310	1397	700								
Moshi	79	1182	570	517	774	1293	1038	545							
Mtwara	1238	2068	589	1072	1092	2109	1192	782	1159						
Musoma	848	626	1422	939	1196	879	1157	1229	927	2011					
Mwanza	826	406	1202	719	976	659	937	1009	905	1791	220				
Singida	352	751	728	245	502	862	607	535	431	1317	4741				
Songea	1225	1726	1033	787	530	1429	512	840	1304	680	1669	449	1032		
Tabora	705	640	1081	598	855	751	574	888	784	1670	583	363	353	1086	
Tanga	435	1538	352	617	637	1724	1027	327	356	941	1221	1261	787	1167	1140

Distances in kilometres   1 kilometre = 0.62 miles

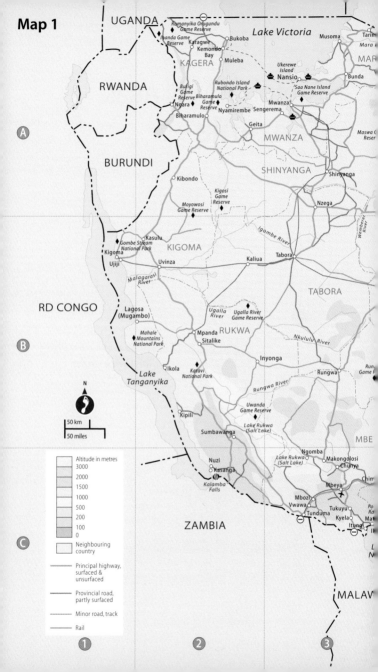

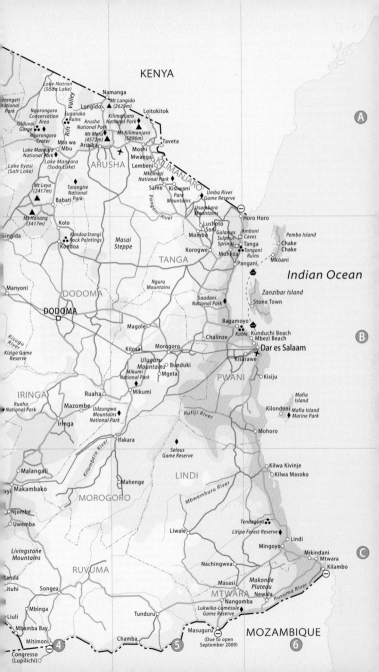

Map 2 National parks & game reserves

❶ Serengeti National Park
Far-reaching plains of endless grass, tinged with the twisted shadows of acacia trees, make this the quintessential image of wild, untarnished Africa. It supports the highest concentration of game in Africa.

❷ Ngorongoro Conservation Area
Often called 'Africa's Eden', Ngorongoro encompasses the volcanic Ngorongoro and Embagai craters, Olduvai Gorge – famous for its palaeontological relics – and Lake Masek. The crater is a world-class visitor attraction.

❸ Arusha National Park
In the shadow of mounts Kilimanjaro and Meru, this is a compact park with three varied habitats: the highland montane forest; a small volcanic crater inhabited by a variety of mammals; and a series of seven alkaline crater lakes.

❹ Kilimanjaro National Park
One of the most impressive sights in Africa, the highest mountain on the continent is visible from as far away as Tsavo National Park in Kenya. Kibo Peak rises to 5895 m.

❺ Gombe Stream National Park
One of Tanzania's most remote parks and famous for its chimpanzee populations.

❻ Mahale Mountains National Park
Another chimpanzee sanctuary with a larger population so there's more chance of sightings here than at Gombe.

❼ Katavi National Park
A very isolated park less frequented by tourists, Katavi is famous for its Roan and Sable antelope and large herds of buffalo.

❽ Ugalla River Game Reserve
Be well prepared to visit this remote park – no accommodation, but it's good for Sable antelope and birdlife.

❾ Ruaha National Park
Although little visited, this is Tanzania's second-largest national park, with vast concentrations of buffalo, elephant, gazelle and over 400 bird species.

❿ Udzungwa Mountains National Park
This forested area plays host to a large number of endangered bird species as well as forest antelope and vervet monkeys.

⓫ Selous Game Reserve
The largest park in Africa and the second largest in the world, Selous covers 5% of Tanzania's total area (although much is off limits to visitors). The area is famous for African wild dogs and some of the last black rhino left in the region.

⓬ Mafia Island Marine Park
The best deep-sea diving in Tanzania in protected coral gardens. The island is the meeting place of large oceanic fish and the vast variety of fish common to the Indian Ocean coral reefs.

Map 3 Dive sites

Njao
Island

Manta Point
Fundu Island

Kokota Island

Chak

Mesali Island

Mkoani

Tanga

Amani

Muheza

Korogwe

TANGA

Pangani

Pemba Channel

Leven
Banks

Kendwa ● Nungwi

Matemwe

Mnemba Island

Zanzibar Isla

Kiwengwa

Uroa

Bokibu
Reef

Bawe
Island

Mwamba

Murogo
Reef

Pange
Island

Stone Town

Zanzibar Channel

Bwejuu

Jambiani

Kizimkazi

Bagamoyo

Fungu
Yasin
Reef

Big T Reef

Bongoyo
Island

Chalinze

Kunduchi Beach

Mbezi Beach

Kisarawe

Dar es Salaam

La
Is

PWANI

Kisiju

Map symbols

□	Capital city	▨	Building
○	Other city, town	▣	Sight
	International border	♦♦	Cathedral, church
	Regional border		Chinese temple
⊖	Customs		Hindu temple
	Contours (approx)	♣	Meru
▲	Mountain, volcano		Mosque
	Mountain pass	⚲	Stupa
	Escarpment	✡	Synagogue
	Glacier	▌	Tourist office
	Salt flat	⏛	Museum
	Rocks	✉	Post office
	Seasonal marshland	ⓟ	Police
	Beach, sandbank	Ⓢ	Bank
⟩⟩⟩	Waterfall	@	Internet
	Reef	♪	Telephone
===	Motorway	⊕	Market
—	Main road	✚	Medical services
—	Minor road	Ⓟ	Parking
= = =	Track		Petrol
∷∷∷	Footpath	♣	Golf
—	Railway	∴	Archaeological site
⊢■	Railway with station	♦	National park,
✈	Airport		wildlife reserve
⛟	Bus station	✲	Viewing point
Ⓜ	Metro station	▲	Campsite
- - - -	Cable car	⌂	Refuge, lodge
++++	Funicular	♜	Castle, fort
⚓	Ferry		Diving
	Pedestrianized street	♔♔♔	Deciduous, coniferous,
⟩ ⟨	Tunnel		palm trees
→	One way-street		Mangrove
⫿⫿⫿⫿	Steps	⌂	Hide
⛉	Bridge	♪	Vineyard, winery
▀▀▀	Fortified wall	⚗	Distillery
	Park, garden, stadium		Shipwreck
◐	Sleeping	✕	Historic battlefield
◐	Eating	⇨	Related map
◐	Bars & clubs		

Index

against poaching and land encroachment. Other animals include crocodile, hippo, bushbuck, sitatunga (a swamp-dwelling antelope only found here and in Selous), vervet monkeys and mongoose. The park is good for hiking and has wonderful birdlife. You are likely to spot fish eagle, martial eagle, sacred ibis, saddle-billed stork, kingfishers, water fowl, cuckoos, bee eaters and sunbirds. There are also animal hides for viewing the wildlife.

Bukoba ⊜❷⊕⌂▲⊖❻ ➤ pp341-344. Colour map 1, A2. 1° 20'S, 31° 59'E.

→ Phone code: 028.

Although it receives few visitors, Bukoba, set in a bay between lush hills, with a population of 81,000 and a university, is now is Tanzania's second largest lake port. But for several centuries, until Bukoba was established at the end of the 19th century, Karagwe, some 100 km inland, was the principal centre. The Bahinda, a cattle-herding people from the interior, operated a feudal system where chiefs took tributes from their subjects and the wealth of the area was based on cattle that were raised successfully despite problems with tsetse flies (see box, page 292). It was founded for the Germans in 1890 by Emin Pasha. It is a lovely part of Tanzania – green and fertile and with a very relaxed way of life.

☐ Bukoba

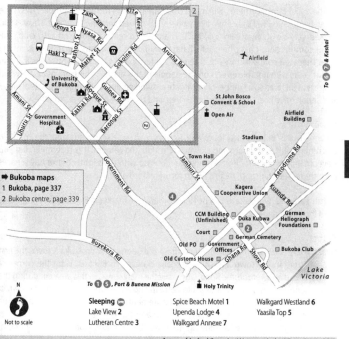

➤ **Bukoba maps**
1 Bukoba, page 337
2 Bukoba centre, page 339

N

Not to scale

To ❶ ❺ , Port & Bunena Mission

Sleeping ⊜
Lake View **2**
Lutheran Centre **3**

Spice Beach Motel **1**
Upenda Lodge **4**
Walkgard Annexe **7**

Walkgard Westland **6**
Yaasila Top **5**

The Hen and the Hawk: a Bukoba Fable

Once upon a time a hen and a hawk who were friends lived together in the same hut. One day, during a great famine the hen went off in search of food. She was successful for she met a man who had some bananas. As she was carrying her load home she met the hawk who asked her how she had got the bananas. The hen, standing on one leg and hiding the other in her feathers, replied that she had paid for them with her foot. The hen told the hawk that he must also buy some food with his foot.

The hawk agreed that this was indeed fair and went off in search of some food. He met a man and offered his leg in return for some food. The man agreed, cut off the hawk's leg and then gave him some food. The hawk had great difficulty walking home with only one leg, trying to balance the load.

When the hawk eventually reached home he saw the hen standing on two legs. He was extremely angry with the hen, saying that although the hen was supposed to be his friend she had cheated him. The hawk told the hen that he could not forgive her and would kill her. The hen replied that he would never succeed in killing her for she would run away. Sure enough the hen ran away and lived with man, while the hawk and all his descendants remain determined to kill the hen and its offspring. This is why the hawk will always try to kill any hen that it sees.

The major food crop here (as in much of the area around the lake) is *matoke*. This is the green banana you will see grown everywhere. It is peeled, wrapped in banana leaves and cooked very slowly by steaming. Vanilla is another recently introduced cash crop. The major commercial crop is coffee, which has contributed significantly to the wealth of the area. There is a coffee factory near the jetty. Unfortunately, the world price has fallen in recent years with notable effects on the people of this district. There are quite a few aid projects in this area so a number of expatriate aid workers live here. Huge deposits of nickel and cobalt have been discovered in the area, and there are plans to exploit these.

Ins and outs

Getting there Bukoba is a long way from anywhere else by bus and the roads in this region, although improving slowly, are rough and remote. It is recommended you travel to Bukoba by ferry from Mwanza and link up with the slightly better bus services from there. See Transport, page 343, for further information.

Getting around Bicycle taxis can be found around the market in Bukoba; they are widely used for short journeys.

Sights

Near the lake shore is a group of buildings from the German period. **Duka Kubwa**, the first general store in the town and the first stone building in Bukoba, is on the corner of Jamhuri Road and Aerodrome Road. Originally the market was in this area but during the British period it was moved about a kilometre inland. When the British took the town in 1914 during the First World War, in their excitement they blew up the German Boma (which was on the site of Holy Trinity Church) and the German Post Office (set under the heliograph – a device for sending messages by mirrors – along the lake shore, or which only the concrete feet still remain). Later the British regretted their impetuosity – they had no administrative centre – and they used the German Hospital (now called the **Old Boma**, and currently housing part of the University of Bukoba). Across the road from the **Lake View Hotel** is a **German cemetery**. Further west is the area with European housing up in the hills. Beyond the aerodrome runway to the east is **Nyamukazi** fishing village. Between Lake View Hotel and the lake shore is the former Gymkhana Club where there was a cricket pitch, a golf course and tennis courts, now called the **Bukoba Club** (see page 343). The centre of town has many Asian-style buildings, now very shabby.

The **Mater Misericordia Cathedral** (Roman Catholic) is an extraordinary building on a huge scale in spectacular style. When it was originally constructed the dome began to subside. All the cladding was removed, new foundations inserted under the building, and the whole shebang raised 3 m on hydraulic jacks. The levitation was done a millimetre at a time and took 10 weeks.

The **Lutheran Cathedral** is an altogether more modest and practical construction in modern style. The Evangelical Lutheran Church of Tanzania (ELCT) has a large presence in Bukoba, including the main office, conference and training centre, Huyawa Orphans Project (all near the **Lake View Hotel**), the Nyumba ya Vijana Youth Centre (near the government hospital) and a bookshop and internet café on Market street.

Coffee has long been the economic mainstay of the region and there is a **coffee factory** on the lake shore by the wharf, south of the administrative centre, and it is usually possible to be shown round. Continuing southwest from the wharf is the **Bunena Roman Catholic Mission** buildings with a spire, gardens and a cemetery.

② Bukoba centre

Sleeping
New Banana 5

Eating
Kopling Café 4
Pizza 1

Rose Café 5
Soft Rock Café 2
West End Café 3

Bukoba–Kampala
Jaguar/Gateway/Dolphin Bus Services, T0744-786364 (mob) runs from Bukoba to Kampala every day at 0700. The journey takes six to eight hours. The bus from Kampala to Bukoba returns at 1100.

The border crossing is fairly efficient and the road from Bukoba is in a reasonable condition. Visas for most nationalities for Uganda cost US$30. Remember, because of the East Africa customs agreement, you are permitted to travel between Tanzania, Kenya and Uganda on single entry visas without getting re-entry visas for each of these countries as long as the visas you have are valid.

Karagwe → *Colour map 1, A2. 2°0s, 31°0'E.*

Located inland, this was an important centre until Bukoba came to prominence with the introduction of access by steamer across Lake Victoria to Mwanza and the rail link to the coast. The surrounding area is rich and fertile and cattle thrive here. The town hosts a sombre reminder of the war with the war with Uganda: a bombed-out and ruined church high atop the hill overlooking the town. In the past few years Karagwe has served as a base for the non-government organizations coping with the exodus of refugees from Rwanda. The refugee camps were to the west of the border, but supplies come through Bukoba and then Karagwe. There are several small hotels charging less than US$5 per night. They are very basic, with shared bathrooms and no running water.

South from Bukoba 🚌🚐 ›› *pp341-344.*

Kemondo Bay port is about 18 km south of Bukoba. On the ferry you don't get a chance to appreciate the attractiveness of the bay entrance to the port as it is usually dark when the boat docks and departs. The quayside is a grand sight when the lake steamers, en route from Bukoba and Mwanza, are in – bags of charcoal and coffee being loaded, great bunches of bananas are piled on deck, joyful reunions at homecomings and tearful partings as relatives and work mates come to bid travellers farewell.

Biharamulo → *Colour map 1, A2. 2°25'S, 31°25'E.*

Continuing south from Muleba, skirting the edge of Biharamulo game reserve (not much wildlife visible from the road), is Biharamulo, a well laid out town that served as an administrative centre during the German period. There are some fine colonial buildings and the entrance to the town is through a tree-lined avenue. The **Old Boma** has been restored and at present the town houses government offices and is a market for the surrounding area; is the nearest town to the game reserve.

Biharamulo, Burigi and other northwest game reserves Adjacent to Rubondo Island National Park on the mainland is the **Biharamulo Game Reserve** (1300 sq km), and adjoining to the west the **Burigi Game Reserve** (2200 sq km). These are to the south of Bukoba on the main Mwanza to Bukoba road but have no facilities and receive very few visitors. Because of the proximity of the large numbers of displaced Rwandan refugees who were put in camps on the edge of the reserves in the Ngara District of northwestern

Tanzania during the 1990s Rwandan crisis, the flora and fauna of the game reserve have been greatly depleted. Many of the animals were poached, trees were cut down for fuel and large tracts of land were cleared for the cultivation of crops. Biharamulo Reserve borders Lake Victoria, at an altitude of between 1250-2000 m, and is contiguous with the Burigi Game Reserve to the west. There are north/south ridges and valleys, and much of it is swampy with a healthy, thriving mosquito population. Most of the larger mammals numbers have been decimated by poaching. Animals that formerly lived in the reserve include hippo, elephant and zebra. A small population of sitatunga antelope also lived here and primates included the red colobus monkey. The birds are believed to have been less adversely affected by human encroachment. They include saddle-billed storks, the rufous-bellied heron, several varieties of starlings, sunbirds and weavers, the grey kestrel and the fish eagle. These days the park is notably good for roan antelope, klipspringer, dik-dik, oribi and impala, but sadly it is mostly used as a hunting concession. There are no visitor facilities and the old guesthouse at Biharamulo has fallen into disrepair.

Other game reserves in northwest Tanzania were also adversely affected including **Moyowosi Game Reserve**, **Ibanda Game Reserve** and **Rumanyika Game Reserve**. The Kagera Kigoma Game Reserve Rehabilitation Project (KKGRRP) is seeking to reverse the extensive damage done to these game reserves, which cover a total area of 14,500 sq km. It is estimated that the mammal population decreased by 90% after the arrival of the refugees. There are plans to rehabilitate the roads and coordinate anti-poaching enforcement strategies.

◉ Western Lake Victoria listings

For Sleeping and Eating price codes and other relevant information, see pages 36-40.

◉ Sleeping

Rubondo Island National Park *p336, map p336*

There are camping facilities and basic banda accommodation (**C-F**) at the National Park's rest camp on the island but they are very basic so you are advised to take all your own equipment. All food supplies must be taken with you. The park headquarters are at Kageye. The rest camp is 1 km from here and about a similar distance to the upmarket tented camp (below). You are permitted to walk from the rest camp to enjoy a meal or a drink at the tented camp, though you need to give some notice for them to prepare food. Further information from the Tanzania National Parks (TANAPA) head office in Arusha, see page 259.

B Rubondo Island Tented Lodge, in a shady tract of forest along the lake shore, Arusha,

T027-254 4109, www.flycat.com. Run by Flycatcher Safaris, there is just 1 luxury camp on Rubondo Island. 20 tents on concrete bases under thatch, set apart from each other with lovely views overlooking the lake and beach. Gardens still need to mature, rustic central area with dining room, bar, lots of lounging space, and small swimming pool set in an outcrop of rock. Walking and fishing safaris can be arranged. Most people visit here as part of a package that includes flights.

Bukoba *p337, maps p337 and p339*

D-E Walkgard Westland Hotel, 3 km from Bukoba on the slopes of the Kashuru Hills, overlooking the lake, T028-222 0935, www.walkgard.com. Comfortable rooms with en suite bathrooms, satellite TV, balconies with great views, but old-fashioned furnishings. Very nice swimming pool with sun loungers. Rates include full English breakfast. Friendly staff can organize boat trips and tours to the local sites. Good restaurant, pool café and bar. Easily the best place to stay in the area.

E Walkgard Annex Hotel, along Uganda Rd, 1.5 km from the airport, T028-222 0626. Offers 13 spacious and comfortable rooms with a/c, TV, phone, fridge. Reasonable food with barbecues, buffets, and bar.

E-F Kamachumu Inn, around 30 km south of Bukoba, the turning for Kamachumu is at Muhutwe, T028-222 2466, www.kamachumu inn.com. A fairly remote, but cosy country inn on the 1800-m plateau of Kamachumu, about 50 mins drive from Bukoba. All rooms have satellite TV and the more expensive have their own bathroom. The gardens are very pleasant with rondavaals. They grow their own vegetables for the restaurant. Beer is available.

E-F Yaasila Top Hotel, next to Spice Beach on the lakeshore. In a nice location, with 15 rooms of which 10 rooms have bathrooms, and 5 budget rooms with shared bathroom. Big difference in price though the better rooms have a balcony facing Lake Victoria together with a king size bed, a fridge, TV and phone.

F Lake View Hotel, on the lake shote, T028-222 0232. Imposing building offering comfortable accommodation, some rooms with bathroom and fans, TV and hot water. Moderate food, good terrace bar, hotel has bureau de change. Good view of the lake. Camping possible.

F Lutheran Centre, off Shore Rd towards the lake, T028-222 0027, elct-nwd@africa online.com. Very comfortable, clean and safe, rooms have TV, a/c and hot water. No alcohol is served, but there is basic and cheap food.

F New Banana, Zam Zam St, east of the market, T028-222 0861. Restaurant, central and well run, outside area with tables, reasonable food and quite popular bar. Simple rooms some with a/c and hot water.

F Spice Beach Motel, on the lake shore, on the lower road to the port, T028-222 0142. Modern bungalow, rooms have TV, hot water and a/c. Very good bar and restaurant. Good place for waiting for the evening ferry to Mwanza even if not staying here.

F Upenda Lodge, Rwaijumba St, off Jamhuri St, T028-222 0620. Courtyard with bar, offers 16 rooms, 3 are larger with extra sitting room, all are s/c with hot water, cable TV and large beds, modern kitchen serving Tanzanian and European dishes.

Biharamulo *p340*

F Sunset Inn, opposite the bus stand. One of the best of the basic guesthouses in town. Spartan rooms with communal bathrooms. Serves food all day, one reader has reported it to be clean and functional but very boring.

🍴 Eating

Bukoba *p337, maps p337 and p339*

🍴 **Kopling Café**, across from the Kahawa Guest House near the cathedral. Inexpensive fish, meat, rice and *matoke*, TV.

🍴 **Lake View Hotel**, see Sleeping, above. Good variety of moderate food, including many Western dishes and excellent barbecued kebabs. Overpriced and slow service. Nice atmosphere in the outside terrace beer garden with a view of the lake, gets busy especially at the weekends.

🍴 **Pizza Restaurant**, just off Jamhuri St in commercial centre. Open mornings only, and not every morning at that. Small restaurant with very good pizzas, sausage and chips, samosas and juices.

🍴 **Rose Cafe**, Jamhuri St. Serves local food, including *matoke*, beans, *sambusas*, *mchicha*, and fruit juice.

🍴 **Soft Rock Café**, off Karume St on Kashai Rd. A sports bar with an outside patio bar with satellite TV. Serves tasty grilled chicken and fish with chips.

🍴 **Spice Beach**, Lower Port Rd on the beach. Good grills and kebabs; if you order the day before they will lay on an Indian meal. Pool table and TV. Particularly charming at night when ferry boats are docked at the port.

🍴 **West End Café**, on roundabout at north-west end of town. Serves mostly simple grills, and is quite popular, with TV and music.

♫ Bars and clubs

Bukoba *p337, maps p337 and p339*
Garden View Bar, in Hamugembe, on the road to Uganda, about 1 km. Disco on Fri and Sat.
NBC Club, just to west of Jamhuri St. Owned and run the employees of the National Bank of Commerce, sometimes has a disco on Fri and Sat, and also serves cold beer.

O Shopping

Bukoba *p337, maps p337 and p339*
Cosmopolitan Provision Store, also known as **Mama Cosmo**. Sells many imported Western items, including cheese and wine. A good place to stock up on snacks or the ferry, open daily, though closes for lunch.

▲ Activities and tours

Bukoba *p337, maps p337 and p339*
Bukoba Club has tennis, snooker, table tennis and darts. Indians sometimes play cricket on the open grassy area near the club. The **Kaitaba Stadium** hosts soccer matches of the home Kagera Sugar team, and **Walkgard Hotel** has a swimming pool which non-guests can use for a small fee.

⊖ Transport

Bukoba *p337, maps p337 and p339*
Transport to and from Bukoba is fitful. Buses, ferries and flights are all rescheduled on a regular basis, depending on demand, and you must check before you travel.

Air
Precision Air, flies to **Mwanza**, Mon, Wed and Fri 0700, 0915 and 1240 (55 mins). **Coastal Air** has a service to Mwanza on Wed and Sat.

Airline offices Coastal Air, T022-211 7969/60, www.coastal.cc; **Precision Air**, near the bus stand, T028-222 0545, Dar office T022-213 0800, www.precisionairtz.com.

Bus
The bus stand is in the centre of Bukoba town near the clock tower. To **Karagwe**, buses Mon-Sat (4 hrs to cover 100 km, US$2.50). Local buses west to **Bugene** and **Kaisho** US$4 and south to **Biharamulo** US$9.

Tashrif, T028-222 0427, kiosk at the bus stand, have a bus that does the central line route to **Dar** on Tue, Thu and Sat via **Nzega**, **Singida**, **Dodoma**, and **Morogoro** (up to 24 hrs). Services go to **Kigoma** though these are rough rides on poor roads and each journey can take days rather than hours. These depart very early in the morning at about 0500, generally only go twice a week and in wet season less so.

To Uganda Bukoba offers a useful service between Tanzania and Uganda, see border box, page 340, for further information.

Ferry
Easily the most reliable and comfortable way to travel to **Mwanza**. The boats, the *MV Serengeti* and the *MV Victoria*, though old, have been refitted. There is a ferry on Mon, Wed and Fri to Mwanza at 1800 (10 hrs). Fares are US$15, US$13 and US$9. 1st class provides a berth in a 2-person cabin, 2nd in a 4-person cabin, 3rd is seating or deck space. The ferry makes a stop in **Kemondo Bay** an hour after departure from Bukoba Port.

Biharamulo *p340*
Bus
Buses to **Bukoba**, leave when full (6 hrs to cover 200 km). The road is unsealed and in poor shape. Also buses to **Mwanza**, (3 hrs).

① Directory

Bukoba *p337, maps p337 and p339*
Banks CRDB, near the market, Kashozi Rd.
National Bank of Commerce, near the
Catholic Cathedral on Jamhuri Rd, has ATM.
Internet Bukoba Cyber Centre, opposite
the CRDB bank, US$0.50 per hr; **Post office**,
internet café open Mon-Fri 0800-2000, Sat
0800-1800, Sun 1030-1600, US$0.50 per hr.
Medical services Bukoba Medical
Centre, Zam-zam St off Kashozi Rd.T028-222
0510, **Post office** Near the NBC bank.

Contents

Footprint features

Central Region

At a glance

⊖ **Getting around** *Dala-dala* and buses are plentiful in the main towns, but you're better off travelling by train rather than road between villages and towns, and you can only access Gombe and Mahale by boat.

◉ **Time required** At least 2 days to see the chimps at Gombe and another 2 if you want to add Mahale to your itinerary. Allow yourself plenty of time and flexibility to get to your destination.

☀ **Weather** Dry and dusty, but relatively cool in the towns during Jun-Oct. Light rains Nov-Mar and then heavy rains until Jun.

✖ **When not to go** Gombe, Mahale and Katavi can theoretically be visited all year but can be hard-going and slippery during the rainy season (Apr-May).

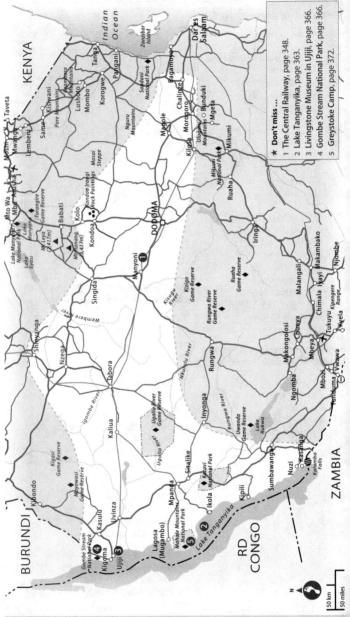

★ **Don't miss...**
1 The Central Railway, page 348.
2 Lake Tanganyika, page 363.
3 Livingstone Museum in Ujiji, page 366.
4 Gombe Stream National Park, page 366.
5 Greystoke Camp, page 372.

The central route from Dar es Salaam to Kigoma in the far west passes through a number of different landscapes and vegetational zones. The distance between the towns is large and much of this route is sparsely populated. The major towns that you pass through are Morogoro, Dodoma and finally Tabora before reaching Kigoma. The Central Railway line is the focus of this route, and it follows the old slave and caravan trail from the coast to Lake Tanganyika. The road is good only as far as Dodoma, just over a third of the distance to Kigoma, though there are currently major road building projects going on in the central region. On the shores of Lake Tanganyika are Mahale and Gombe Stream national parks, both famous for their substantial chimpanzee populations. Also to the west of the region is the Katavi National Park which is so remote it only receives a handful of visitors each year. These parks are not easy to get to but nevertheless offer safari experiences away from the hordes of pop-up minibuses of the northern circuit in landscapes that are more wild and untouched.

Ins and outs

For access to the destinations in the central area and for budget travellers not wanting to take the expensive flights to Kigoma, the only real option is the train. The **Central Line** goes from Dar to Morogoro, then heads northwest through Dodoma to Tabora, where it splits and the two lines go either to Mwanza on Lake Victoria or Kigoma on Lake Tanganyika. To either destination this is a lengthy journey, but the train is an interesting experience and relatively comfortable, especially if you travel first class. It stops at dozens of stations en route through the central area (hence the 36-hour journey time from Dar to Kigoma) and at each the villagers meet the train to sell their wares – anything from live chickens to wooden spoons. Although there are some buses that link the towns, they are infrequent, uncomfortable and slow, and the roads are very poor, especially after the rains when many become impassable. However, things are changing and there have been some major road-building operations in recent years. The Nzega–Shinyanga– Mwanza road is now tarred and the Singida–Dodoma road has been improved. The Chinese are working on the Nzega–Singida road, and the South Africans on the Tabora–Shinyanga road. The only feasible option for getting to Katavi National Park is by flying, and safaris here are usually arranged with an additional trip by air to Mahale National Park.

Dar es Salaam to Dodoma

From Dar the road heads inland to Morogoro where another road and the railway veer off to cross the largely empty expanses of rural central Tanzania. The towns in the region have little to offer the visitor, but Morogoro is a lively centre surrounded by attractive mountains and Dodoma holds the inauspicious title of being the capital of the country. ▸▸ *For listings, see pages 352-355.*

Chalinze ▸▸ *Colour map 1, B5.*

Chalinze lies 100 km to the west of Dar es Salaam, a small town, essentially a truckstop, and the main fuelling centre for travellers to north and south Tanzania (it's also a big HIV/AIDS centre). There are six petrol stations and hundreds of little bars – everyone's accommodated for. This makes Chalinze a buzzing place in the evenings, and a good place to break a journey for 30 minutes. Look out for the young men who sell little home-made toy trucks and buses on the roadside – replicas of the passing vehicles painted in the same colour and complete with company logos. About 200 m along the Dar road from the junction is a petrol station with a good restaurant, just look for the thatched roof. Most of the buses stop here for a quick break.

Morogoro ⬤⬤⬤⬤⬤ ▸▸ *pp 352-355. Colour map 1, B5. 6° 50'S, 37° 40'E.*

→ *Phone code: 023. Population: 250,000. Altitude: 500 m.*

Morogoro lies in the agricultural heartland of Tanzania, and is a centre of farming in the southern highlands. Tobacco is grown in the region and accumulated here before going on to market, and fruit and vegetables from here are transported the 195 km to Dar es Salaam. In addition to its agricultural importance, Morogoro is also the centre for missionary work that goes on in the country, and the various missions and their schools and hospitals are a central feature of the town. Morogoro is based at the foot of the Uluguru Mountains, which reach a height of 2138 m and provide a spectacular backdrop to the town; the peaks are often obscured by dramatic, swirling mists. It was here that Smuts was confident he would confront and destroy the forces of von Lettow in the First World War – only to be bitterly disappointed (see page 418).

Morogoro has been particularly unlucky in that the two main enterprises that were expected to provide substantial employment in the area, the Groundnut Plantation at Kongwa on the road to Dodoma (see page 421) and the state-owned Morogoro shoe factory, have been failures. However, the countryside is green and fertile, large sisal plantations predominate, and the market is probably the largest in the country and worth visiting to soak up the atmosphere. Just about anything that grows and can be eaten can be bought here. It's a good place to stock up on fresh produce if heading south to Malawi and Zambia.

Morogoro is also the largest town near the **Selous Game Reserve** (see page 378), which lies to the south of Mikumi National Park (100 km further down the road), along the most frequently used road route. It was en route to Morogoro that Edward Sokoine, the Prime Minister, widely expected to be Nyerere's successor, was killed in a road accident in October 1984. The Agricultural University in Morogoro has been named after him.

Morogoro

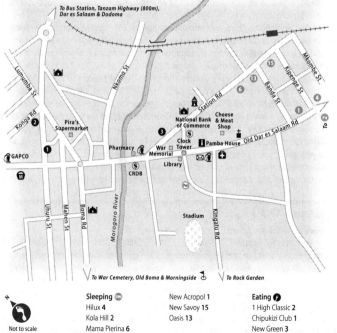

Not to scale

Sleeping		Eating
Hilux **4**	New Acropol **1**	1 High Classic **2**
Kola Hill **2**	New Savoy **15**	Chipukizi Club **1**
Mama Pierina **6**	Oasis **13**	New Green **3**

Sights

The old German **Boma** is to the south of the town in the foothills of the **Uluguru Mountains**, along Boma Road. The mountains dominate Morogoro, with a range of impressive summits, and the lower slopes are densely cultivated and terraced. Higher up they are forested and there are some splintered rock bastions. Further back they rise to over 2438 m. There are three birds endemic to the Ulugurus, the Loveridge sunbird, the black cap shrike and Mrs Moreau's warbler.

At the top of Kingalu Road there is a pretty **rock garden**, laid out around a mountain stream with a café.

The **War Cemetery** ① *locked although it is reasonably easy to obtain a key from Dimitri at Mama Pierina's (see Sleeping, page 353)*, south on Boma Road and then turn west, is interesting in that it records the deaths in both the German and the British and Empire Forces. There are two graves of Germans from before 1914, a postal officer and a train driver. Also here is the grave of Kannanpara John, born in Kerala, India, and the first Asian priest of the Diocese of Central Tanganyika. The involvement of the British Empire in the First World War is apparent with 49 graves for troops and support service personnel of regiments from South Africa, Gold Coast, West Africa and the British West Indies, as well as East Africa. There is a special plinth to the 'Hindus, Mohammedans and Sikhs' who died in Imperial Service. These troops were accompanied by 'followers', including their families, traders and craftsmen, and three of these – 'Jim', 'Aaron' and 'Harr' – are recorded as having died in the fighting around Morogoro. The plinth for the Germans records about 180 dead, a mixture of German officers and African soldiers of the Schuztruppe (see box, page 419).

Further along Boma Road, well into the Ulugurus, is **Morningside**, one of the summits above Morogoro and a relatively popular climb. The area, with its pretty valleys and good fishing in the mountain streams, is reminiscent of Switzerland. Morningside is almost 10 km from the centre of Morogoro, and whilst you could walk alone it is advisable to take a local guide as there may be opportunist thieves on the road. Morningside is a 15-minute walk from the village of Ruvuma which can be reached by car or bicycle by following the Boma road out of Morogoro. However, before you go you are likely to spend a number of hours traipsing around various offices in Morogoro to obtain the necessary 'thumbs up' and obligatory yellow receipt of permission which must be obtained prior to climbing the summit. Go to the Uluguru Information Office in Pamba House, opposite the post office, who will direct you to the Catchment Forest Officer, who in turn will help you get an official receipt which should cost no more than US$5 per day per person. Alternatively, enlist the help of a local or guesthouse owner and the process may become much simpler.

Dodoma ●❶❷❸❹ ➤ *pp352-355. Colour map 1, B4. 6° 8'S, 35° 45'E.*

→ *Phone code: 026. Population: 150,000. Altitude: 1113 m.*

In the very heart of Tanzania, 453 km west of Dar es Salaam, Dodoma is the nation's official political capital and the seat of government in the country. The government legislature divide their time between here and Dar es Salaam. Much smaller and less developed than the country's commercial centre, Dar, Dodoma is on the eastern edge of the southern highlands; a dry, windy and some say desolate place to choose for a capital, lying at an altitude that gives it warm days and cool nights.

Dodoma was formerly a small settlement of the semi-pastoral Gogo people. Caravan traders passed through the plateau and it developed into a small trading centre. It owes its growth to the Central Railway and the Germans' plan to take advantage of Dodoma as a trading and commercial centre. During the First World War the town was important as a supply base and transit point. In the years after the war, however, two famines struck the area and an outbreak of rinderpest followed. The British administration was less keen than the Germans to develop Dodoma as the administrative centre, its only real advantages being its central position and location on the railway line. But from 1932, Cape to London flights touched down here and Dodoma received all Dar es Salaam's mail, which was then transferred by rail.

As it is in the very centre of the country, Dodoma was designated the new capital by the former president Nyerere. However the process of transfer has never fully taken off and today only one government ministry has its permanent base in Dodoma. The area's water shortage and poor road network are important contributing factors, and thus the city functions as a capital only when parliamentary sessions are held. On the approach road from Dar is a sprawling housing estate of unfinished and empty houses – a one-time, unsuccessful, effort to move civil servants here. Besides this, and being the CCM party political headquarters, the most notable thing about Dodoma is probably that it is the only wine-producing area in the country and the Tanganyika Vineyards Company is active in promoting its products. It is also an important beef producing area and delicious roasted meat can be found in the many open bars scattered around town.

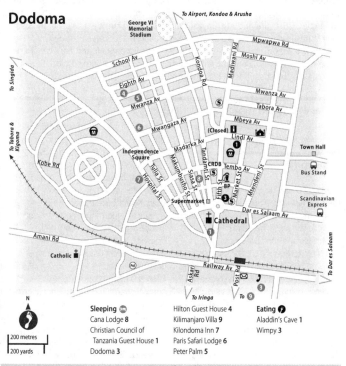

Dodoma

Sleeping
Cana Lodge 8
Christian Council of
  Tanzania Guest House 1
Dodoma 3

Hilton Guest House 4
Kilimanjaro Villa 9
Kilondoma Inn 7
Paris Safari Lodge 6
Peter Palm 5

Eating
Aladdin's Cave 1
Wimpy 3

A cattle **market** (*mnada*) takes place each Saturday on Kondoa Road, 5 km from the centre. It is an important event for many locals and is an interesting spectacle. All in all, Dodoma is a peaceful town surrounded by a large number of missions. Few tourists stay long here, although as the designated administrative centre the city is becoming fairly important for foreign businesses. Opposite the **Aladdin's Cave** shop in town a tourist information centre has been built and a sign put up. It is, however, completely empty.

Around Dodoma → *Colour map 1, B4.*

Kondoa Irangi Rock Paintings About 180 km down the Great North Road to Arusha in the Great Rift Valley, these are the nearest attraction to Dodoma and are among the finest rock paintings in the world. They are a fine example of ancient art and a further reminder of the existence of ancient humanity in this part of Africa (the rock shelters were used in the later Stone Age by the Bushmanoid tribes who were mainly hunters). The paintings vary in quality, size, style and colour. The most important are from the pre-agriculturalist period, red pigment outlines in streaky and silhouette styles more than 3000 years old. There are patterned designs, human and animal figures, mainly giraffe, eland and elephant, and hunting scenes. 'Late whites' from a later period are mostly abstract finger paintings. More than 100 sites were described by Mary Leakey in the 1950s but only recently have efforts been made to preserve and promote them, and they are currently nominated for designation on the World Heritage List. At **Kolo** where interesting paintings are most accessible, guides must be hired from the visitors' centre office run by the Department of Antiquities. Other sites include **Kinyasi**, **Pahl**, **Swera** and **Tumbelo**. Many of the shelters have fantastic views over the plains for miles around. ▸▸ *See Sleeping, below.*

Mount Hanang, sometimes called the forgotten mountain and East Africa's ninth highest, rises some 1828 m above the Mangati Plain and is accessed off the road from Dodoma to Arusha, southwest of Babati, northwest of Singida, see page 265.

◉ Dar es Salaam to Dodoma listings

For Sleeping and Eating price codes and other relevant information, see pages 36-40.

● Sleeping

Morogoro *p348, map p349*
There is a dense crop of cheap guesthouses on the streets around the market where you will get a bed and a mosquito net, and not much else, for around US$5.

C-D New Acropol, Old Dar es Salaam Rd, T023-260 3403, newacropolhotel@morogoro. net. Canadian-run hotel set in very pretty gardens. Verandas, lovely furnishings, efficient and professional staff, excellent food and comfortable surroundings. Double rooms with a/c, TV, hot water and mosquito nets, single and family rooms also available. Varied menu with bar snacks, burgers and

pizzas, and a selection of puddings, cakes and ice cream.

E Hilux Hotel, Old Dar es Salaam Rd, T023-260 3946, hiluxhotel@yahoo.com. Smart, functional hotel with good facilities aimed at businessmen and conference-goers. Rooms have a/c, satellite TV and en suite bathrooms with hot water, and include a full breakfast. A busy lively covered outdoor bar and restaurant offers good value food, including pasta, meat grills and seafood.

E Hotel Oasis, Station Rd, T023-260 4178, hoteloasistz@morogoro.net. Efficient and well run, clean rooms, outdoor swimming pool with mountain views. The large restaurant offers a wide range of Indian, Chinese and European dishes, as well as a buffet at the weekends, and this is probably the best food in Morogoro. There is also a fantastically stocked bar.

E-F Kola Hill Hotel, 3 km from town on the Old Dar es Salaam Rd, T0744-388013 (mob). Efficient and very clean in a peaceful out of town location with excellent views of the mountains. Single storey chalet-style accommodation laid out in attractive gardens, each with en suite bathroom, a/c and TV, (rooms with fans are cheaper). Rates include breakfast. Bar in thatched banda with pool table. Restaurant has meat dishes and bar snacks. A taxi here costs very little or you can get a *dala-dala*.

F Mama Pierina, Station Rd next to Hotel Oasis, T0741-786913 (mob). Family-run guesthouse with comfortably furnished veranda, run by Dimitri a friendly Italian/Greek. Worn but comfortable rooms with fan, mosquito net and hot water, breakfast included. Probably best known for its good food, Greek, Indian and Italian dishes including pizzas.

F New Savoy Hotel, just opposite the railway station, T023-260 3041. This was the former **Banhof Hotel** built in the German period by the Greeks and the scene of an elaborate prank by von Lettow in the First World War (see page 418). It is now rather run down and shabby, but the buildings are impressive and set in attractive gardens. Rooms are spacious and provide functional accommodation for those on a budget who enjoy 'character' (such as the original Armitage Shanks sinks and plastic flowers). Food is available and there's a lively bar offering a disco at the weekends.

Dodoma *p350, map p351*

The town can be very busy when parliament is in session or there is a CCM meeting, so try to book ahead. There has been a recent mushrooming of new hotels though, rather oddly, many are hidden away on back streets. These are modern, featureless and mostly aimed at visiting civil servants. They usually offer single or very small double rooms. You will find all of them empty at the weekends when the town is exceptionally quiet.

C-D Dodoma Hotel, close to the railway station, T026-232 1641, dodomahotel@ kicheko.com. Old German Hotel, now extended and completely refurbished. Easily the best place to stay and it is deservedly popular. The 91 rooms are on the small side but are of a good standard with new furniture, café, shop, hair salon, internet café, small swimming pool, restaurant and bar. Everything is centred around an attractive courtyard, a good place to come for a drink even if you are not staying. Food here includes steak, chicken, Indian and Chinese.

D-E Kilondoma Inn, Hospital St, south of Independence Sq. Tiny, tiny rooms really only suitable for 1 person though they do have double beds, with fans and mosquito nets, spotless bathrooms with long drop loos. Breakfast included.

D-F Cana Lodge, 9th St, T026-232 1199. Offers 17 rooms of various size which is reflected in the price, with fans, cable TV, hot water and mosquito nets. Small restaurant serving soups, snacks, a stab at Western pasta dishes. Modern block but old fashioned chunky furniture.

E-F Hilton Guest House, off Tulia St, to the northeast of the market, T026-232 1831. Ornate pillars outside and mirrored windows. Smart but small rooms, hot water in new shiny tiled bathrooms. Breakfast included.

E-F Paris Safari Lodge, Tulia St, T026-235 2990. Rooms with reliable hot water, clean but not as modern as some of the other places.

E-F Peter Palm, Mjimpya St, T026-232 0154, T0744-265224 (mob). Block with miniscule rooms and only just enough room for the bed and bathroom. Cool white tiles throughout. Basic breakfast included.

F Christian Council of Tanzania Guest House, 5th St, next to the cathedral, T026-232 1682. Extremely basic with canteen, cold showers, water supply from petrol barrels, refilled every 3-4 days, off-putting toilets and mosquito nets. Food not recommended. No booze but there's a bar across the road.

F Kilimanjaro Villa, 500 m from the railway station. Basic but affordable and clean though a little way out in a residential area, run by a friendly group of women though English is a problem here. Rooms without bathrooms (cold water) are a little cheaper. Sells beer and you can get tea in the morning.

Around Dodoma *p352*
Kondoa Irangi Rock Paintings
You can camp near the visitors' centre but there is no other accommodation near the paintings. The closest guesthouses are in Kondoa, a small town 20 km south of Kolo on the Arusha-Dodoma road, 5 hrs by bus from Dodoma or 9 hrs from Arusha.

F New Planet, near the bus stand, Kondoa. The best guesthouse in Kondoa has clean single and double rooms with basic private bathrooms and a reasonable restaurant.

Eating

Morogoro *p348, map p349*
There are few restaurants in Morogoro and the best eating is to be found at the hotels. Food stalls on the street offer chips and meat, the market has an excellent variety of fresh fruit, and some of the shops offer soft drinks and tinned food.

1 High Classic, Konga Rd. Fairly central, bright and well maintained, has satellite TV, grills, chips, omelettes, pilau and local dishes. Good value.

Chipukizi Club, central location. A typical local bar with a pool table, satellite TV and barbecued food.

New Green Restaurant, Station Rd. Open daily 1100-1600, 1900-2230. Excellent Indian dishes, a favourite haunt amongst expats in town, bar.

Dodoma *p350, map p351*
It might have been expected that the transfer of the seat of government would have seen the emergence of some reasonable restaurants but this doesn't appear to have been the

case at all. The best place to eat by far is the **Dodoma Hotel**. There are several places in the back streets north of Mwangaza Av where you can get a whole chicken, chips and salad on a large plate to share. There is a supermarket a few metres to the northwest of the roundabout near the cathedral that sells imported items such as Pringles and Weetabix, and booze.

Aladdin's Cave, on Market St near the corner with Lindi Av. An Indian-run shop selling lots of sweets and chocolate, ice cream and juice, foreign magazines and there is an internet café. Closes for a few hours in the afternoon.

Wimpy, on the corner of the roundabout opposite the Anglican Church, though is nothing like any Wimpy in the Western world. There are tables outside, stools around a bar, and food includes small snacks such as greasy donughts but not much else.

Shopping

Morogoro *p348, map p349*
Although at one time there was a shop run by the German Mission which used to sell pastries, cheesecake and ice cream, these days it has closed. However, you can still order meats and cheeses and other specialized food items from the same building. Turn right after passing the cathedral on your right off the Dar es Salaam Rd and the building is easily identified as it is an all-white multi-storeyed building on the left. To the left of the building are 2 large wrought-iron gates, enter here and you will see a doorway on your right in a basement – ring the bell at the top of the steps and ask for Papa Joe. If in doubt chat to the *askaris* outside who will be very helpful. Conflicting information suggests you may or may not need to order a day in advance.

GAPCO petrol station, near the market. Also sells wide range of goods but no alcohol.

Pira's Supermarket, Lumumba St, T023-260 4594. A wide range of items including wines, cheeses, and meat including pork.

⊖ Transport

Morogoro *p348, map p349*
Air
Morogoro has an airstrip, but there are no regular flights.

Road
The 196-km road to Morogoro from **Dar** is tarmac. At Morogoro the road divides northwest to **Dodoma** and southwest which passes through the **Mikumi National Park**, and then on to **Iringa** and **Mbeya** and, ultimately, the **Zambian border**. Buses leave from the Ipogoro Stand a couple of kilometres out of town on the main road. This enormous bus stand has space for over 85 buses. There is a good choice of buses, and it is safest (the road is busy and notorious for accidents) and most comfortable to opt for a large coach rather than a minibus. There are numerous buses making the trip to **Dar** (2 hrs). Buses from Dar to **Mbeya** pass through Morogoro until midday arriving in Mbeya about 2000-2100 (US$13, depending on how pushy you're feeling – because of competition amongst the bus companies there is room for negotiation here) and to **Iringa** (US$6). Buses also go to **Dodoma** (3 hrs).

Note At the bus stand be very careful with your luggage and don't be fooled by young men posing as ticket collectors. Don't part with your ticket at any time and only show it to a conductor once your journey has started. You should not pay for a normal or average amount of luggage, so ignore anyone who tries to charge you extra for luggage.

Train
It's not really worth getting the train to **Dar** from Morogoro (or vice versa), you are better off taking the bus, but if you really want to, see **Tanzania Railways Corporation** www.trctz.com, for full details of timetables and fares and for other routes west from here.

Dodoma *p350, map p351*
Air
Despite it being the capital, there are very few flights from Dodoma. **Coastal Air**, T022-211 7969-60, www.coastal.cc, flies to **Arusha** on Mon, Thu and Sat at 1300 (2 hrs). This flight only runs if there are enough takers.

Bus
The main bus stand is opposite the town hall 2 blocks up from Dar es Salaam Av. The **Scandinavia Express** terminal is on Dar es Salaam Av, T026-232 2170, www.scandinaviagroup.com. Buses go to **Arusha** via **Chalinze** daily (12-15 hrs). They can fill up so it's advisable to book a seat a day in advance. A journey to Arusha via Konoa takes 2 days on a largely unsurfaced road. The road to **Dar** is surfaced all the way. Buses go daily and take about 4-6 hrs.

Train
Overnight trains to **Dar** leave at 1840 on Sun, Tue, Thu, Fri, Sat. See **Tanzania Railways Corporation** www.trctz.com, for full details of timetables and fares, see also Kigoma Transport, page 374.

⊕ Directory

Morogoro *p348, map p349*
Banks CRDB is just past the war memorial on the left hand side of the Dar es Salaam Rd before crossing the river into the centre of town; **National Bank of Commerce**, just off Machupa Rd opposite the post office. Both have ATMs. **Internet** There are a number of internet cafés in the town centre. The regional library just past the post office offers reliable internet connection at US$0.50 per hour. **Medical services** The Aga Khan Hospital and dispensary are suitable for minor ailments. Pharmacy opposite the CRDB bank on the Dar es Salaam Rd.

Dodoma *p350, map p351*
Banks CRDB, Bank St has ATM.

Tabora and around

The region around Tabora was once frequently crossed by Livingstone on his quest to explore central Africa but few people visit today and there is little of interest for the visitor to Tanzania. However, the Central Railway splits at Tabora and anyone riding the train will spend either a few hours or a whole day here depending on what direction they are travelling, to Mwanza via Shinyanga, Kigoma or Dar. ▸▸ *For listings, see pages 360-362.*

Tabora ⬤🅿🅽🅷🅲🅾 ▸▸ *pp 360-362. Colour map 1, B3. 5° 25'S, 32° 50'E.*

→ Phone code: 026. Population: 100,000.

The railway continues along the old caravan trading route to Tabora, founded in 1820 by Arab slave traders and of enormous historical interest. During the German occupation, Tabora was one of the most populated and prosperous towns in the whole of East Africa. From 1852 Tabora was the Arab's slaving capital (*Kazeh*) in Unyanyembe, the kingdom of Nyamwezi (Tanzania's second-largest tribe) with famous chieftains Mirambo and Isike. Ivory and humans were bartered in exchange for guns, beads and cloth. Its heyday was in the 1860s when 500,000 caravans annually passed through the town and many trade routes converged here. The Germans realized this and constructed a fort. (Isike later fought the Germans here in 1892, and the Germans captured the town in 1893.)

The building of Mittelland Bahn (the Central Railway) in 1912 increased the town's importance. It fell to Belgian forces from the Congo after 10 days' fighting on

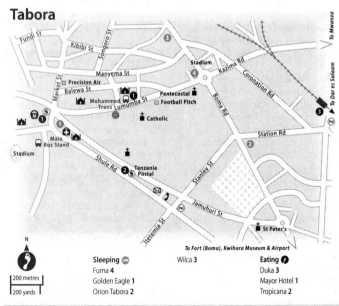

Tabora

Sleeping 🛏
Fuma 4
Golden Eagle 1
Orion Tabora 2
Wilca 3

Eating 🍴
Duka 3
Mayor Hotel 1
Tropicana 2

The miombo woodland of Tanzania

A type of woodland called miombo is found in large parts of south, central and western Tanzania. At a glance these areas appear to be ideally suited for agricultural and other development. However, this area is infected with the tsetse fly (see page 292), which is a serious hindrance to settlement and so parts of it are very thinly populated.

If you are visiting miombo country around the rains it is a very colourful sight – all reds, pinks and browns – and plenty of shade. However, in the dry season all the leaves fall and bush fires are common. There is little shade and the slate grey bark of the trees seems to shimmer in the heat. One of the most successful economic activities in areas of miombo is the cultivation of tobacco. This has been introduced in the Urambo area and is ideal as tsetse fly make the area unsuitable for livestock.

11 September 1916. Tabora was a 'railway town' by the time the British took over. The explorers Burton, Speke, Livingstone and Stanley all used the town as an important base for their journeys into more remote areas. Tabora School (1925) was important for nurturing future leaders including Nyerere. However, these days not much happens here and it's little more than a collection of dusty streets. But it is here that the railway divides, one line going on to Kigoma, the other north to Mwanza and for this reason people often stay a night here in order to change trains.

Sights

Tabora is dominated by the **Fort** (or boma) on a hill overlooking the town built by the Germans at the turn of the century. This is southeast of the town centre along Boma Road at the junction of Boma Road and School Street. Do not take pictures as it is a military building. The **central market** is worth a wander around and has an excellent second-hand clothing section, which is cheaper than in some of the other cities.

Kwihara Museum ① *to get there follow the road out of town past the fort, after the roundabout take the right-hand fork, a taxi there and back will cost in around US$9*, about 10 km outside the town, this is probably one of the major attractions of Tabora. It is dedicated to Dr Livingstone. The museum is in the house that he occupied for about 10 months before setting off on the final leg of the journey in 1872 that was to be his last. He died less than a year later at Chitambo, Zambia. The museum, although rundown, is interesting and contains various letters, maps, pictures, etc associated with the man, as well as with other early missionaries and explorers.

Ugalla River Game Reserve ›› *Colour map 1, B2. 6° 30' S, 32° E.*

① *There is no formal entrance into the park but the Ugalla River is around 40 km south of the central railway. From Tabora follow the road along the railway to Usoke from where there is a track heading south to the village of Sire, but you will need to ask locally which this is.*

The Ugalla River Game Reserve, to the west of Tabora, is approximately 5000 sq km. Its inaccessibility and lack of facilities mean that is rarely visited by tourists. It is between Tabora and Lake Rukwa, approximately 100 km north east of Mpanda, well off the beaten track. It consists of miomba woodlands, and is home to the rare sable antelope, lion, leopard and cheetah, elephant, buffalo and waterbuck. West of the Ugalla River there are chimpanzees living in the riverine forests. There is abundant birdlife with over 300 different species recorded, including the pygmy goose, various herons and the glossy ibis. If you do manage to get there be aware that there are no tourist facilities and you must bring all your own supplies. Be prepared to be totally self-sufficient.

Shinyanga ➤➤ ⊜❶⊜⦿ ➤➤ pp 360-362. Colour map 1, A3.

→ Phone code: 028.

Shinyanga is a large, sprawling town with buildings and roads in poor condition, mostly built in the 1940s and 1950s when the area was thriving on gold, diamonds and cotton. During that time a large number of Europeans lived here and many vets from the UK were employed at a research station involved in eradicating *rinderpest*.

The region is known for its cattle production and African dew-lapped cows can be seen everywhere. Some gold is still found in the area and mined in open-cast pits with the ore broken with large mortars and pestles. There's still a lot of cotton here too and it's brought to the area's ginneries for processing. Rice is also grown and just outside town are several large, circular, covered stores where the surplus is kept to be distributed in the event of crop failure. The area has been deforested, the timber being used for firewood and now the region is hot, dry and dusty.

The inhabitants are very friendly and there is no problem walking around, especially in the day time. Education has always been very important in Shinyanga and now there is a big college on the road to Kamborage Stadium. There is a sizeable Indian community and also many Africans of Arab descent, hence the large number of Muslims.

There are no large shops, but a great number of stores selling only a few items – many with a dressmaker and sewing machine outside. Every day there is a busy market selling just about everything.

Electricity and water supply is unreliable and when there is water (not every day) it is so muddy it has to be filtered as well as boiled. The water treatment works built by the Germans in the mid-1980s is no longer in use.

 Mosquitoes are a major problem here – the region is known for having drug-resistant malaria strains. Report unusual symptoms to a doctor immediately.

Sights

About 15-20 minutes along the road to the southeast of Shinyanga, on the right you come to a turning for **Mwadui Mine**, where there is a tree-lined road leading up to the compound. In the 1960s it was a flourishing diamond mine with its own hospital, churches, supermarket and schools. A Dakota flew weekly to Nairobi from the on-site airstrip for shopping trips. (The same Dakota still flies to Dar es Salaam and onward to South Africa, with diamonds.) The Mwadui diamondiferous kimberlite pipe was one of the largest in the world but a combination of flooding and exhaustion of the ore reserves have led to a reduction in the output. The most famous stone mined here was the 'Williamson pink' diamond found in October 1947, given to Princess Elizabeth as a wedding gift. It weighed 23.6 carats after cutting and polishing, and was a beautiful rose colour.

This Williamson diamond mine is part-owned by the Tanzanian Government (30%) and De Beers (70%), who are refurbishing the mine, but only industrial diamonds are now found. It covers a huge area and sometimes it is possible to get a permit to look around. Many people dig up their own land in areas close to the Mwadui Mine in the hope of discovering the precious stones. The Sukuma people of this region have always strongly

Shinyanga witches

Shinyanga has attracted an unenviable reputation for its appalling treatment of elderly women. Years of cooking over open cow dung fires have caused many of the women to develop red, inflamed eyes. This feature has been interpreted as a sign that the elderly person is a witch and therefore responsible for all manner of ills from crop failures, to ill health or other misfortunes. In recent years, many elderly women have been killed, usually by machete blows to their heads, but their possessions left untouched. In the two-year period up to October 1999 it was reported that 168 women and 17 men had been killed after being accused of witchcraft.

Some of the killings have been attributed to polygamous males moving on to younger wives and using accusations of witchcraft to incite vigilantes to kill their elderly spouses. Sometimes the motive is acquisition of property owned by the elderly. Another theory is that the reason these poor women are killed is as human sacrifices, offered up to bring good luck to people prospecting for diamonds and gold. Finally, there are the irresponsible activities of soothsayers. Soothsayers are asked to identify enemies, who are accused of perpetrating evil spells against the client. Over half the population of Shinyanga follow traditional religions that recognize witchcraft and condone the killings.

The situation is complicated by the activities of a local enforcement group known as SunguSungu. Their founder decreed that they should go about their work bare-chested, and this rules out the participation of women. SunguSungu claim to apprehend the perpetrators of witchcraft killings, extracting confessions by beatings. When SunguSungu thugs are handed over to the police, it has been difficult to secure prosecutions because people are unwilling to testify as they fear reprisals from the witch-killers and their families.

The police say that more secure dwellings need to be provided for the elderly and that they should live with their families and not alone, as has been the custom in Shinyanga region.

believed in the power of witchcraft. Offerings of grain and domestic animals are made on the advice of the witch doctors to enhance their chances of successful prospecting.

Within a few kilometres of leaving Shinyanga going south to Nzega, houses give way to plains and baobab trees. To the left is a vast open area and the smoke of the engine at **Manonga Ginnery** in Chomachankula Village can be seen way off in the distance with large blue hazy hills behind. Further along the main road is a strange sight – an **oasis** with a group of palms providing Shinyanga with a good supply of dates. The baobabs have a crop of heavy seed pods, which the children harvest to sell in the market. They are popular and taste similar to sherbet.

Further on is a large area used as paddy fields during the rains and you can often see oxen working. Away to the left on the plains is the main **gold region** where settlements have sprung up.

Dr Livingstone

David Livingstone was born on 19 March 1813 in Blantyre in Scotland. He had a strict Scottish upbringing, and his first job was in a factory. He studied during the evenings and at the age of 27 finally qualified as a doctor. In 1840 he joined the London Missionary Society, was ordained in the same year and set off for Africa. On the voyage out he learnt to use quadrants and other navigational and mapping instruments, which were to prove vital skills during his exploring of uncharted parts of Africa. In 1841 he arrived in South Africa and journeyed north in search of converts.

In his first few years as a missionary Livingstone gained a reputation as a surveyor and scientist. His first major expedition into the African interior came in 1853, lasted three years, and included in 1855 the discovery of the Victoria Falls. When he returned to England in 1856 he was greeted as a national hero, was awarded a gold medal by the Royal Geographical Society, and made a Freeman of the City of London.

He returned to Africa in 1858 and began his quest for the source of the Nile in 1866. This trip was funded by a grant from the British government, which enabled Livingstone to be better equipped than during his previous expedition. During this journey little was heard of him and rumours reached Britain of his apparent death. Henry Morton Stanley, a newspaper reporter for the New York Herald, was sent by James Gordon Bennett, his publisher, to find Livingstone. On 1871 Stanley found Livingstone's camp at Ujiji, a small town on the shores of Lake Tanganyika, greeting him with the now legendary, 'Dr Livingstone, I presume?' At the time of the meeting Livingstone had run short of supplies, in particular quinine, which was vital in protecting him and his companions from malaria.

Livingstone set out on his last trip from near Tabora and continued his explorations until his death at Chitambo in what is now Zambia. His heart was buried at the spot where he died, his body embalmed and taken by Susi and Chumah, his two servants, to Bagamoyo (see page 106) from where it was shipped back to England. He was buried at Westminster Abbey and a memorial was erected at Chitambo.

◉ Tabora and around listings

For Sleeping and Eating price codes and other relevant information, see pages 36-40.

● Sleeping

Tabora *p356, map p356*
D-E Orion Tabora, formerly **Railway Hotel**, T026-260 4369, oriontbrhotel@spidersat.net. This is an historic old German Hotel (there once used to be a sign here warning that the hotel did not permit black people or dogs), close to the station, with sweeping steps up to the outside terrace. The more modern rooms are around the back of the main building. There's a bar and restaurant serving good food, and an extensive buffet breakfast is included in the price. Easily the best option.
E-F Golden Eagle, Songeya Rd, T026-260 4623. Reasonable value rooms with or without bathrooms, fans, mosquito nets and spotless white sheets, are upstairs around a bright, freshly painted, courtyard. A good location for early morning buses. Simple food and beer in the restaurant.
E-F Wilca, Boma Rd, T026-2604105. Comfortable and well run, friendly staff,

very nice bar, *nyama choma* grill and good restaurant, the rooms have satellite TV and hot water in the bathrooms. There are only 10 rooms so you may need to get here early to get one. This is by far the best of a whole bunch of guesthouses in this area, most of which are very basic. Avoid the **Wild Roses** nearby, it's not nice at all.

F Fuma Hotel, off Lumumba Rd. 12 spotless rooms around a small courtyard, each one is named after a month of the year, mosquito nets, some with bathrooms for not much more. Good value and secure parking behind a locked gate. Small restaurant and bar near the entrance.

Shinyanga *p358*
D-E Mwoleka, T028-276 2249. En suite, mosquito nets and fans, it is clean, has quite good food and a locked compound for cars.
D-E Shinyanga Motel, T028-276 2458. Has been refurbished with en suite bathrooms, but close to railway, so noisy. African and some Indian dishes can be made on request.

🍴 Eating

Tabora *p356, map p356*
🍽 **Orion Tabora**, T026-260 4369. The best food in town is to be found at the Tabora Hotel, there's a formal dining room or you can eat in the comfy bar in front of the enormous satellite TV. Snacks such as fish fingers, chicken bites or sandwiches, or main meals of curries and grilled fish or chicken. If you arrive early in the morning off the train, you can come and eat breakfast here.
🍴 **Mayor Hotel**, behind Market St near the National Bank of Commerce. Excellent breakfasts available, buffet-style canteen, surprising variety of food including lots of vegetables, plastic seats overlooking the bicycle-mending stalls, clean kitchen. There is another branch on Lumumba St.
🍴 **Tropicana Restaurant**, next to the Tanzania Postal Bank on Shule Rd. High ceilings with fans, lots of fake flowers, good for breakfast,

snacks and grills, a big urn is on the go all day for tea and coffee.
🍴 **Wilca**, simple menu but food is well prepared and served in a nice outdoor bar area with pool table.

Shinyanga *p358*
🍴 **Green View Bar**, on road to Mwanza. Serves chargrilled chicken in the evening. An attractive place under thatched rondavaals. Masoi, the owner, makes you welcome. To one side of the road leading to the bar there is a soccer pitch used by the locals and most evenings the teams of shirts versus no-shirts can be seen playing.
🍴 **Mama Shitta's Café**, in the centre of town. Serves excellent local dishes cooked over charcoal – beef, roast potatoes with crispy onions, rice, and many vegetables. Cold sodas are available and the staff will bring back cold beer from the nearby bar.

🍸 Bars and clubs

Tabora *p356, map p356*
Duka Bar, opposite the station. Garden bar with pool table and TV, good place to wait for the train; watch the mosquitoes though.

🚌 Transport

Tabora *p356, map p356*
Air
There is an airport at Tabora and there are flights by **Precision Air** Fri-Wed. A taxi to the airport costs US$5-6 and taxis go out there to meet the incoming flight.

Flight to **Dar** leaves at 1550 (one way US$155, return US$245), arrives in **Kigoma** at 1645 (one way US$85), departs Kigoma at 1710 and arrives in **Dar** at 1950.

Airline offices Precision Air, Market St to the north of the National Bank of Commerce, TT023-260 4818, Dar T022-213 0800, T022-212 1718, www.precision airtz.com.

Bus

The Tabora bus stand is off Market St with a huge soccer stadium behind. It is fairly well organized with the bus company kiosks around the perimeter. Buses go daily to **Mwanza** (8 hrs), **Dar** (16 hrs), **Dodoma** (11 hrs), and **Arusha** (15 hrs). Most of these services leave very early in the morning. Buses also serve closer destinations such as **Shinyanga**, **Ngeza** and **Singida**. Another bus depot away from the station is **Mohammed Trans Ltd**, Lumumba Rd next to the Mayor Hotel, T0748-566505 (mob), www.mtlid.com. The road from Tabora west to **Kigoma** is impassable in places during the rainy seasons. There is, however, talk about upgrading it.

Train

Both the **Kigoma** and **Mwanza** services stop at Tabora. The railway station is 3 km outside the town. A taxi there costs US$1-2. If it is on time the train from Dar arrives about 2100. The train from Mwanza usually arrives earlier in the day. Then the trains are split and the carriages shunted around, which takes around 2 hrs during which you may have to swap trains depending in what direction you are going. Both trains then depart again to Kigoma and back to Mwanza respectively and arrive at each of these destinations the following morning. See **Tanzania Railways Corporation** www.trctz.com for full details of timetables and fares and see Kigoma Transport, page 374.

Shinyanga *p358*
Air

There is a grass airstrip a few kilometres out of town toward Mwanza. When the cows are shooed off, a joint **Air Tanzania/Precision Air** flight flies to **Dar** via **Mwanza** on Mon, Wed, Thu, Fri, and Sun 1550.

Bus

Shinyanga is 162 km from **Mwanza**, and the road between the 2 has recently been tarred and the journey takes a little over 2 hrs. There are a great number of buses in every direction.

Train

Shinyanga is on the Central Line railway on the branch line between **Mwanza** and **Tabora**. See Tabora Transport, above.

❻ Directory

Tabora *p356, map p356*
Banks The National Bank of Commerce on Market St has an ATM. **Internet** There is an internet café on Lumumba Rd near the Catholic Cathedral. However Tabora does not have its own server and is expensive.

Shinyanga *p358*
Medical services Kalandoto Hospital, on the main Shinyanga–Mwanza road, 20 mins out of town, run by the African Inland Church, T028-228627. Several American doctors and nurses work here, some for over 30 years. It is the best place to go if taken ill in the region. The state-run **Shinyanga Hospital** is in the centre of town, T028-22235/6.

Lake Tanganyika

Despite its remote location in the extreme north west of Tanzania, Lake Tanganyika has a number of attractions. Here are the attractive lakeside national parks of Mahale and Gombe famous for their chimpanzee populations, and further south is the wild and scenic Katavi National Park. A safari here gives you the feeling of having the park to yourself. The region is an adventurous destination to get to and explore for the budget traveller by train or ferry, though reasonably accessible for those who can afford to visit by plane. ▸▸ *For listings, see pages 371-374.*

Kigoma ⊕⬤⬤⬤ ▸▸ *pp371-374. Colour map 1, B1. 4° 55'S, 29° 36'E.*

→ *Phone code: 028. Population: 80,000. Altitude: 800 m.*

Capital of the Western Region of Tanzania, Kigoma is a small, sleepy town 1254 km west of Dar es Salaam with one tree-lined main road. It overlooks the picturesque Lake Tanganyika on its western side and has scenic rolling hills to the east. It is the main railway terminus

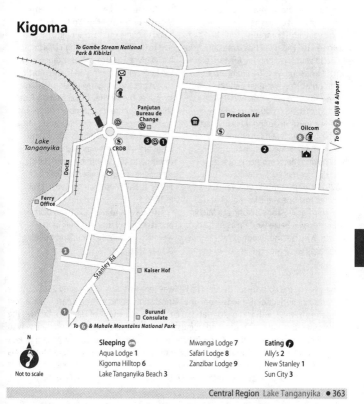

Kigoma

Not to scale

Sleeping 🛏
Aqua Lodge **1**
Kigoma Hilltop **6**
Lake Tanganyika Beach **3**

Mwanga Lodge **7**
Safari Lodge **8**
Zanzibar Lodge **9**

Eating 🍴
Ally's **2**
New Stanley **1**
Sun City **3**

The graveyard at Kigoma

At the graveyard at the top of the hill in Kigoma there are three gravestones dating back to the late 19th century. Two of them belong to members of the London Missionary Society (LMS) – Rev J B Thompson and Rev A W Dodgshun.

The LMS had sent an expedition of four ministers and two laymen to establish a mission on the shores of Lake Tanganyika under the leadership of Rev Roger Price. Following the death of the bullocks used to carry their equipment inland – they were struck down by tsetse fly – Price returned to the coast to try to persuade the missionary authorities to establish a string of mission stations along the road heading into the interior. The expedition that continued on to the Lake divided into two, with Thompson – who had had seven years' experience as a missionary in Matabeleland – taking the forward party with Dodgshun, who had only recently left training, following on behind.

The advance party reached Ujiji on 23 August 1878. Thompson, who had been seriously ill during the early part of the journey, again fell ill and died on 22 September. Meanwhile Dodgshun was having many problems of his own and did not reach Ujiji until 27 March 1879, by which time he was very unwell. He died just one week later on 3 April.

A third gravestone belongs to Michel Alexandre de Baize (known as Abbé de Baize), who had gone out to Africa under the auspices of the French government.

He was a young man, with no experience of Africa or of exploration. He had been generously equipped with a large sum of money by the French government and had a huge array of supplies and equipment, including such things as rockets, fireworks, coats of armour and a barrel organ. He planned to travel across Africa from east to west and set off from Bagamoyo with a small army of about 800 men. However, he was beset by troubles. He was attacked at night, many of his porters deserted and so much of his equipment had to be abandoned, and many of his supplies were stolen.

When he reached Ujiji he apparently became upset that the White Fathers failed to come out to greet him. He is said to have paraded through Ujiji firing his revolver. He received assistance from the LMS before setting off for the north shores of Lake Tanganyika. During that stretch of the journey he offended a local chief and set fire to a number of huts and had to be rescued by the LMS at Ugaha. He then fell ill and the LMS again came to his aid. When he was well enough he returned to Ujiji where he again fell ill. He died on 12 December 1879. The LMS finally abandoned their station at Ujiji in 1884.

The graveyard has fallen into disrepair and it is difficult to find. Walk in the direction of Ujiji, after the CCM building turn to the right.

in the west of the country for the Central Railway that was built in the early 20th century to transport agricultural goods from the African hinterland to the coast. Just a few kilometres to the south is the old Arab slave trading settlement of Ujiji (see below), the famous meeting place of Stanley and Livingstone. Most people come here on their way to Burundi or Zambia across the lake on the steamer *MV Liemba* (see box, opposite) or else on their way to **Gombe Stream National Park** (see page 366) or the **Mahale Mountains National Park**, also famous for chimpanzees, lies to the south of Kigoma but is very remote and is accessed most easily by plane from Kigoma (see page 368).

MV Liemba

The steamer *Liemba*, originally named Gotzen, was built in Germany in 1913 and transported at great expense to Kigoma where it was reconstructed. Its first trial runs took place in June 1915 and average speeds of around 8 knots were reached. It was the flagship of the German flotilla on Lake Tanganyika and was used during the First World War as armed transport, particularly to carry troops down the lake from Kigoma to Kasanga. The *Gotzen* was the largest ship on the lake at this time and could carry about 900 men in a quarter of the time that it took the dhows to do the same journey.

In June 1916 the *Gotzen* was attacked by Belgian planes but was not too seriously damaged. In July of the same year, when the railway to Kigoma was captured, the Germans scuttled her.

After the war, the *Gotzen* was raised from the deeps and refitted. On 16 May 1927 the ship was rechristened *Liemba*, the name by which Lake Tanganyika had originally been known by local people, and in trials that month managed an average speed of 8.5 knots – not bad for a ship that had spent from 26 July 1916 to 16 March 1924 at the bottom of the lake. It is still in operation today.

Since then the *Liemba* has steamed the lake from end to end almost continuously, for a period of over 80 years (however, see page 373). She has probably completed the nearly 1000 km, week-long round trip between Kigoma and Mpulungu in Zambia over 4000 times, perhaps steaming over 4 million kilometres. She is generally believed to be the oldest operational passenger vessel in the world.

The **Mahale Mountains Wildlife Research Centre** ① *on the road to the Hilltop Hotel, T028-280 2072*, has an office in Kigoma but the staff here are not terribly informative and can only show you a dusty old brochure.

The **railway station** is a very imposing building built before the First World War by the Germans. The nearby **Kaiser Hof**, another German building, was built for the Kaiser and today is used as the State House (do not take photographs). Intriguingly there is a tunnel between this house and the railway station which was a secret escape route for the Kaiser. The major industry in Kigoma is fishing and this is mostly done in the afternoon when hundreds of dhows set sail across the lake from **Kibirizi** Village, 3 km north of Kigoma. In this village you can see the fishermen building dhows or stringing fishing nets together. There is also a large depot here for the petrol companies that transport fuel across the lake.

Fossilized fish remains in the extensive sedimentary deposits of Lake Tanganyika are currently being examined as part of the **Nyanza Project** in Kigoma. Lake Tanganyika is considered to be an evolutionary 'hot spot' due to its lengthy, complex geological history. Over 1500 species of animals and plants have been identified in this biologically diverse lake. Cichlid fish, gastropods and crustaceans account for most of the endemic species.

Ujiji ▸▸ *Colour map 1, B1.*

① *There are regular dala-dala to/from Kigoma, ask to be dropped off at Livingstone St and the museum is a few mins' walk towards the lake.*

This small market village 10 km south of Kigoma has a thriving boat-building industry. It used to be the terminus for the old caravan route from the coast and the resulting Arab influence is clear to see. The houses are typical of the coastal Swahili architecture and the population is mainly Muslim. The **post office** on Kigoma Road is a substantial structure dating from the German period. It is, however, most famous for being the place where the words 'Dr Livingstone, I presume' were spoken by Henry Morton Stanley (see page 360). The two men met on the 10th November 1871. The site where this is thought to have occurred is marked by a plaque, between the town and what used to be the shore, on Livingstone Street. The original mango tree under which the two gentlemen met died in the 1920s, but there are two very large mango trees that are supposed to have been grafted from the original one. After the meeting Livingstone left Uijiji and went to Tabora with Stanley. The site is now the **Livingstone Museum** and the museum curator will show you around for a small tip and tell you the story. He will also proudly tell you about the day he met Michael Palin when he visited here during the making of *Pole to Pole*. In the main building of the museum are some faded drawings and books and rather comical brightly painted, full size papier mâché figures of the two men shaking hands. There is also a small plaque in the grounds to Speke and Burton, the first Europeans to set eyes on Lake Tanganikya on 14 February 1858.

Gombe Stream National Park ● ₩ *pp371-374. Colour map 1, B1. 4° 38'S, 31° 40'E.*

In the extreme northwestern corner of Tanzania on the shore of Lake Tanganyika and sharing a border with Burundi, Gombe Stream National Park is one of Tanzania's most remote. The park is most famous for the work of Jane Goodall, the resident primatologist who spent many years in its forests studying the behaviour of the endangered chimpanzees. Guided walks deep into the forest to observe and sit with the extraordinary primates for an entire morning are possible and an incredible experience. Aside from chimpanzee viewing, many other species of primates and mammals live in Gombe Stream's tropical forests, as well as a wide variety of tropical birdlife.

Gombe Stream National Park

Ins and outs

Getting there You can get a boat fairly easily from Kigoma (16 km south of the park). They normally leave around 1400-1500, the trip takes about three hours. Arrange with the boatman what time you want to return the next day. As the boats only leave in the afternoon it is essential to spend at least one night in the park. You can also organize a transfer by motorboat from the **Lake Tanganyika Beach Hotel** or **Aqua Lodge** in Kigoma (see Sleeping, page 371).

Motorboats cost around US$150 per return trip, can carry up to 20 people and take two to three hours each way. Hotels will organize for a cook to go with you if you are staying in the park's bandas. You can also arrange a tour through **Chimpanzee Safaris** at the Kigoma Hilltop Hotel, see page 371.

Park fees and information The main purpose of the park is research rather than tourism and the facilities there are minimal. The park headquarters is at Kasekela. The entrance fee is US$100 per person per 24-hour period. An obligatory guide is US$10 per trip for up to five people. Note that children under seven cannot go chimp-tracking in either Gombe or Mahale. The park can be visited all year.

Background
In 1960 Jane Goodall set up the area as a chimpanzee research station. She wrote a book on the findings of her research called *In the Shadow of Man*. Her work was later filmed by Hugo van Lawick, the wildlife photographer. This attracted much publicity to the reserve and in 1968 the Gombe Stream National Park was established. It covers an area of 40 sq km, making it the smallest park in Tanzania. It is made up of a narrow, mountainous strip of land about 16 km long and 2.5 km wide that borders Lake Tanganyika. The mountains, which rise steeply from the lake to 681-1500 m, are intersected by steep valleys, which have streams running in them and are covered in thick gallery forest (that is, the river banks are wooded, but beyond is open country).

Wildlife
There are approximately 90 chimpanzees in the park divided into two family troops. They each guard their territory fiercely. One of the groups often goes down to the valley so you can see them from there. Alternatively, there are a number of observation points around the park and the wardens usually know where to go to see them. However, there is no guarantee that you will see the chimpanzees during your visit. They are less visible here than at Kibale Forest in western Uganda. Other primates include red-tailed and blue colobus monkeys. Birdlife is also prolific and includes various barbets, starlings, sunbirds, kingfishers, the palm-nut vulture, crowned eagle and the rufous-bellied heron. Recently, problems have been reported at Gombe. It is thought that the chimps have got far too used to humans and in 2002 an adult male called Frodo actually ripped a human baby off the back of its mother (a park ranger's wife) and ate it. Gombe has also lost at least four chimps since 2002 to disease suspected to be human-borne. As chimpanzees can catch many of our diseases, you will not be allowed to visit Gombe if you have a cold or any other infectious illness.

Routes
It is compulsory to take a guide with you to the forest. From the guesthouse there is a trail leading to a lovely waterfall just over 2 km away in a valley. If there are no chimps in this valley, one of the guides will take you further into the forest to try and track them down. It can be hard, slippery walking up and down the valleys through the forest. Another route you can take (which does not require a guide) is along the lake shore.

Mahale Mountains National Park ⬤ ➤➤ pp371-374. Colour map 1, B1.

This is another chimpanzee sanctuary established in 1985 as a national park covering an area of 1577 sq km, and lying at an altitude of over 1800 m. The park is about half way down the eastern shore of Lake Tanganyika, 120 km south of Kigoma. Although Gombe is more famous, the primate population in Mahale Mountains is more numerous and sightings more regular and prolonged (reputedly, the only person who stayed in Mahale and didn't see chimps, was Bill Gates). Hikes to their habitation areas are accessible and not strenuous. As well as being the premium location in all Africa for viewing chimpanzees in the wild, Mahale Mountains is also in a stunningly beautiful lakeshore setting, with superb white sand beaches and clear water for swimming (though check with the lodge staff before swimming as some parts of Lake Tanganyika are affected by bilharzia).

Ins and outs

Getting there There are no roads running into the park and the only access is by boat or plane. The most practical, though most expensive, way of getting there is by charter flight direct to the park's landing strip. Return flights from Kigoma cost in the region of US$300 per person and return flights from Arusha around US$600 per person. These can be organized as part of a package through the operators who run the luxury lodges or from the Hilltop Hotel in Kigoma (see Sleeping page 371). Many of the packages also include stays in Katavi National Park (see below) and flights go via Katavi en route between Mahale and Arusha. A cheaper though more difficult alternative is organizing a boat transfer from the Tanganikya Beach Hotel or Aqua Lodge in Kigoma (see Sleeping, page 371). Motorboats cost in the region of US$800 per return trip, can carry up to 20 people and take six to eight hours each way. The hotels will organize for a cook to go with you if staying in the park's rest house. In theory it is also possible to take the lake ferry (*MV Liemba* or *MV Mwongozo*) to the park from Kigoma, though this is an adventurous option, see page 373. You get to Lagosa (also known as Mugambo) after about six hours at about 0300 and will have to get a small boat to take you to the shore. From Lagosa you will have to hire another boat to take you the three-hour journey to the park office at Bilenge. As you are relying on the lake ferry you will have to stay until the next ferry comes through on the way back to Kigoma, which is usually about a week later although it is not very reliable.

Park fees and information The park office is at Bilenge where all fees are paid. From here there is a boat transfer to Kasiha Village 10 km south of Bilenge, where the chimp walks go from, which is also the location of

Mahale Mountains National Park

Sitete
Park HQ
Kasoge
Masala
Mount Muhensabantu
Mount Humo
Mount Nkungwe
Igabulilo
Montane Forest
Lubugwe
Masaba
Mugewe
Lumbye
Lake Tanganyika

N
Not to scale

Sleeping 🛏
Greystoke Camp **1**
National Park Rest
Camp **2**

Nkungwe Camp **3**

Ranger Post ●

the national park rest camp. Entrance fee is US$80 per person per 24-hour period. An obligatory guide is US$10 per forest walk. The best time to visit is May-September, during the drier months.

Wildlife

The park is largely made up of montane forests and grasslands and some alpine bamboo. The eastern side of the mountains is drier, being in the rain shadow, and the vegetation there is the drier miombo woodland (see box, page 357), which is found over much of west Tanzania and east DR Congo. The highest peak reaches 2460 m and the prevailing winds from over the lake, when forced up to this level, condense and ensure a high rainfall. The wildlife found here is more similar to that found in western Africa than eastern. Other than the chimpanzees, it includes porcupine, colobus monkeys (both red and the Angolan black and white), and elephant, although there are also giraffe, zebra, buffalo and roan antelope. The range and numbers of animals has increased since the *Ujaama* villagization programme of the 1970s. Indeed animals such as the leopard and lion have reappeared in the area. Birdlife includes the fish eagle, kestrel, kingfisher, barbet and starling, similar to those found at Gombe Stream. The chimpanzee population has been the focus of much research by scientists from around the world. According to a recent census there are now more than 700 individuals in about 15 communities. Some of these groups are accessible to visitors, others are the subject of research studies, but most live undisturbed deep inside the forest.

Katavi National Park ● ▶▶ pp371-374. Colour map 1, B2. 7° S, 31° E.

① *The best time to visit is Jul-Oct. The park entry fee is US$20.*

Katavi National Park is 40 km southeast of Mpanda town astride the main Mpanda–Sumbawanga road. It was upgraded to a national park in 1974 and now covers an area of 4471 sq km. Travelling south from Mpanda or north from Tunduma (the border town of Tanzania and Zambia), the road passes through the park. However, like the Ugalla River Game Reserve, its isolation and lack of facilities has meant that it receives few tourists (about 200 a year). It offers unspoilt wildlife viewing in what is the country's third largest national park, in a remote location far off the beaten track.

Katavi National Park

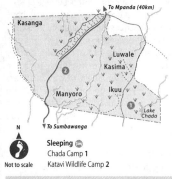

Sleeping
Chada Camp **1**
Katavi Wildlife Camp **2**

Not to scale

The scenery is as varied as it is pristine. Flood plains of thick reeds and dense waterways are home to a huge population of hippo, and in the woodlands to the west, forest canopies shelter herds of buffalo and elephant. Seasonal lakes fill with dirt-coloured water after the rains and animals from all corners of the park descend on them to drink. The park is characterized by miombo woodland (see box, page 357), and acacia parkland as well as some water-logged grassland plains. There is a large swampy area around the Katuma River, which joins the two lakes in the park – Lake Katavi and Lake Chada. The park is famous for its sable and roan antelope, rarely found in other Tanzanian parks, and also for its large amounts of buffalo which can be seen in herds 1500 strong. It also has a high density of crocodiles, Defassa water buck, topi, eland, hartebeest and greater kudu. Other large mammals seen here include hippo, crocodile, zebra, elephant, various antelope as well as lion and, if you are lucky, leopard. Over 400 species of birds have been identified. The park has many waterbirds and birds of prey including the black heron, Dickinson's kestrel, bee-eaters, strikes, weavers, nightjars and the Go-away bird.

South to Mbeya ⊜❼❸❻ ▶▶ pp371-374.

Kipili and Kirando → Colour map 1, B2.
On the shores of Lake Tanganyika, Kipili is one of the MV Liemba's ports of call. Just a few kilometres north is a very pretty town called Kirando. The **Bahama Guest House** on the main road in Kipili is near the bus stop and offers very basic but cheap accommodation (no mosquito nets). Tasty food is available next door. To link to the road to Mbeya take a bus to Sumbawanga. The buses (cost about US$8) leave at 0700 and just after arrival of the ferry. The roads are poor and it is a very slow journey taking about 24 hours.

Sumbawanga → Colour map 1, B2. Phone code: 025.
This is a lovely large town with some impressive buildings, in particular the Roman Catholic church. There is a large market selling second-hand clothes, and a separate one selling a wide range of fruit, vegetables and fish. The town is very clean, with a newly laid tarmac road and its name is said to mean 'witch people'.

The **Rukwa Rift Valley** is currently being investigated in several sites by archaeologists. Near Sumbawanga is the **Milanzi Rockshelter** dating from the Upper Palaeolithic period. It is still used today as an ancestor shrine. **Chamoto Hill**, north of the village of Igurusi, was discovered by E Haldemann during the 1950s and many artefacts were identified. Northeast of Sumbawanga on the shores of Lake Rukwa is the village of **Mkamba**, identified as an **Early Iron Age site** where a virtually complete pot was found in the sediment in 1989 by researchers from the University of Alberta.

In October 2000 an earthquake destroyed several houses in Nkasi District, part of the Kipili–Sumbawanga area. One person was killed and several injured.

Nuzi and Kasanga → Colour map 1, C2.
Southwest of Sumbawanga on Lake Tanganyika is the charming, unspoilt village of Nuzi, surrounded by palm trees. There's no electricity or piped water and only one very basic hotel – bucket shower, no mosquito nets (but lots of mosquitoes). Transport by truck from Sumbawanga will cost US$5 and take eight hours on a very poor road.

Nuzi is a short walk (5 km) away from the next, larger village of Kasanga Bismarck. It is possible to arrange for a local fisherman to take you by boat from Nuzi to Kasanga. The trip takes about 30 minutes and costs about US$1 per person. The MV Liemba also calls here. Shopping is very expensive and it is difficult to buy mineral water, toilet paper, fresh fruit and snacks. There are two or three restaurants serving local food – the fish is cheap and very good. Kasanga has one guesthouse. If waiting to board the lake ferry one can visit the nearby ruins of the German Fort Bismarckburg.

Kalamba waterfalls Close by, near the border with Zambia, are the Kalamba waterfalls, which merit a visit despite the poor road. They are said to be the second highest in Africa and there are many crocodiles there. They are 211 m high and the width varies between 3-15 m seasonally. If you don't fancy riding in the back of a truck for several hours it is possible to organize a trip from **Upendo Hotel** in Sumbawanga (see Sleeping, below). A car and driver will cost just under US$100 but it will still take five hours each way. It is not clear whether the falls lie in Tanzania or Zambia in this border region so it is best to go with a guide who has been arranged in Kasanga.

◉ Lake Tanganyika listings

For Sleeping and Eating price codes and other relevant information, see pages 36-40.

◓ Sleeping

Kigoma *p363, map p363*
B-C Kigoma Hilltop Hotel, on headland overlooking the lake, T028-280 4435/7, or through Dar, T022-233 7181. Luxurious resort with 30 a/c cottages with colonial-style furnishings, TV, fridge and balcony, suites also available. Restaurant, swimming pool, gym, tennis courts. The facilities are there but when it comes to service, food and style the Hilltop falls short. No alchohol is served though you can bring your own and drink in your room. It is still the best place to stay in Kigoma. **Chimpanzee Safaris**, www.chimpanzeesafaris.com, has an office here and can arrange tours to their luxury camps at Gombe and Mahale by motorboat and private plane. Transfer rates start from US$300 per person for the return flight to Mahale and US$300 for the return boat ride to Gombe (this takes several people).
D-E Lake Tanganyika Beach Hotel, overlooking the lake, T028-280 2694. With beautiful views, very clean, 24-hr water, toilet and shower in room. Price includes breakfast. Bar and restaurant, lake-shore walks south (past the power station and local prison that resembles a medieval fort), disco on Sat. Like the **Hilltop**, can arrange private boat trips to Gombe Stream or Mahale Mountains national parks.
E-F Aqua Lodge, on lake shore (no phone). 9 comfortable rooms with bathroom. The only trouble is that TANESCO have built their diesel generator (which supplies electricity to

the whole of Kigoma) right across the road and the thundering noise is constant. Despite this, the beach is lovely here with palm trees and umbrellas, food is available but you need to pre-order it, no alcohol, can arrange boat trips to Gombe.
F Mwanga Lodge, close to the Zanzibar Lodge, Mwanga. Very similar, though not as smart. Rooms with shared bathroom.
F Safari Lodge, next to Oilcom petrol station on the main street. Very basic, plain and bare rooms, mosquito netting on the windows, shared toilet and sink.
F Zanzibar Lodge, Mwanga, on the Ujijij road about 2 km from Kigoma, T028-280 3306. Nowhere near the lake, but handy if catching buses (which depart from Mwanga). Good smart option with a restaurant and bar. Rooms with or without bathrooms are neat and surround a courtyard.

Gombe Stream National Park
p366, map p366
B-C Gombe Luxury Tented Camp, T028-280 4435/7, www.chimpanzeesafaris.com. Near the Mitumba Stream at the northern end of the park on the lakeshore, on a spacious beach. All the tents are under big shady trees. There is a small reception area made out of local wood with a thatched roof and wooden deck, where there is a library, a curio shop, a bar and lounge. Power from a generator (lights off at 2245). The tents face the lake on raised wooden platforms. Meals either in the main mess tent or on the beach.

National park accommodation
There is a hostel that sleeps 12 people but this can only be used for organized groups.

Beds and mattresses are provided but all cooking equipment and food should be brought with you. The Tanzania National Parks Authority (TANAPA) operates simple bandas with 4 beds in each, bookings can be made through the Tanzania National Parks head office in Arusha, see page 259. The park bandas here are rather grim blocks, the verandas of which are caged in to protect you from baboons and chimpanzees. Facilities are basic. You can stay in the bandas in one of two ways: either be completely self-sufficient and bring everything with you, or come on a package trip from Kigoma, bringing a cook, food and bedding. Camping is allowed with permission. The prrice for camping and banda accommodation is US$20, hostel accommodation is US$10.

Mahale Mountains National Park
p368, map p368
L Greystoke Camp, info@nomad.co.tz, www.greystoke-mahale.com. Operated by Nomad Safaris who do not take direct bookings, email them and they'll send a list of their agents. In a stunning spot, on a white sand beach where the forest-clad Mahale Mountains plunge into Lake Tanganyika. Established in 1992, Greystoke, which also goes under the name of Zoe's Camp, was the first accommodation in Mahale and remains the best place to stay by some considerable margin. The 6 suites are open-fronted, with adjoining bathrooms and upstairs decks. Apart from trekking to see the chimps, kayaking and snorkelling is on offer, they have their own dhow for fishing trips, the staff will arrange intimate dinners on the beach for couples, there's a fantastic bar on a rocky headland very good food and service. One of the finest safari camps in Tanzania with a price tag to match.
A Nkungwe Camp, on a sandy beach near the ranger post, T028-280 4435/7, www.chimpanzeesafaris.net. This simple camp is of a reasonable standard but not significantly cheaper than **Greystoke Camp**. The 8 tents are raised on wooden platforms

overlooking the lake, with toilet and hot shower and a veranda; there's a communal lounge, dining area, curio shop, library and beach hut complete with chunky cushioned lounge beds.
E National Park Rest Camp, Kasiha Village 10 km south of the park office at Bilenge. Further information from Tanzania National Parks (TANAPA) head office in Arusha, see page 259. Facilities are minimal, bring all food, drinking water and cooking equipment from Kigoma. There are 4 rooms with shared bathrooms and 6 newer rooms with bathroom, though there is no running water or electricity so bucket showers and paraffin lamps are provided.

Katavi National Park *p369, map p369*
The nearest hotels and other facilities are at Mpanda, which is 40 km away.
L Chada Camp, operated by Nomad Safaris, info@nomad.co.tz, www.chada-katavi.com. They do not take direct bookings, email them and they will send a list of their agents. Accessed by private plane, this is a superb bush camp in the heart of the park offering unsterilized safaris for people who really want to get out in the wilds. 6 luxury tents, excellent food, game drives, guided walks, fly camping safaris, elegantly hosted but still refreshingly simple and earthy.
C Katavi Wildlife Camp, Foxes of Africa, Dar, T022-244 0194, www.tanzaniasafaris.info. Luxury tented camp camouflaged from the animals in a clump of trees, hosted by a zoologist who takes guests on game drives and walks. Accessed by private plane, usually from Ruaha.

Sumbawanga *p370*
Of the number of very basic guesthouses around the bus stand, the better ones are: **Zanzibar Guest House** (**F**), clean, communal bath facilities, mosquito nets; and **Upendo Hotel** (**F**), double rooms with bathroom, and reasonable bar and restaurant attached.
E-F Moravian Centre, Nyerere Rd, central, T025-280 2853. Rooms with or without

bathrooms, breakfast included, nothing remarkable but fairly new and very clean. Canteen serving basic local dishes.

🍴 Eating

Kigoma *p363, map p363*

🍴 **Ally's**, along Ujiji Rd going east. Quite reasonable, closed during Ramadan, serves stews and kebabs and is consistently busy.

🍴 **Lake Tanganyika Beach Hotel**, by the lake. Probably the best place to eat and drink in town with tables right next to the lake, very good views, bar in main building and another on the lakeshore. The staff are very friendly and there is a lot on the menu such as curries, fish and steak.

🍴 **New Stanley Restaurant**, town along the main street, opposite the *dala-dala* stand. The best of the cheap options. Several outside terraces including one with a pool table. Fish or chicken and chips, or a daily set meal of soup, curry and fruit.

🍴 **Sun City**, on the main road. Has a pool table and slot machines and also sells popcorn and ice cream. There are also a number of food stalls around the station.

🚌 Transport

Kigoma *p363, map p363*
Air
Precision Air, flies to **Dar** at 1710 Fri-Wed and arrives at 1950.

Airline offices Precision Air, just off the main street opposite the market, T028-280 4720, closed in the afternoon when the man in the office goes to the airport to meet the flight.

Bus
Long-distance bus services go from **Mwanga**, 2 km from Kigoma on the Ujiji road, where there are several bus company kiosks. Services go to **Mwanza** and **Bukoba** though these are rough rides on poor roads

and each journey can take days rather than hours. These depart very early in the morning (about 0500) and generally only go once a week and in wet season less so. If running, the bus to Bukoba goes on Fri and to Mwanza on Sat.

Ferry
The famous ferry on Lake Tanganyika is the *MV Liemba*. The ferry leaves Kigoma at 1600 on Wed for **Mpulungu** (Zambia), arriving there at 0800 on Fri morning, a 40-hr journey. It stops at lots of small ports on the way. If travelling to **Mbeya**, and wanting to remain in Tanzania, it may be worth disembarking at **Kasanga**, or **Kipili** (journey time 24 hrs) or at the town of **Kirando** just north of Kipili. Kirando may be preferable to Kipili because you arrrive while it is still daylight, there is no port but small boats take passengers to the shore for approximately US$0.60. Buses to **Sumbawanga** will be waiting. On the return leg it departs Mpulungu at 1600 on Fri and reaches Kigoma at 1100 on Sun. Kigoma–Kipili and Kigoma–Kirando 1st class US$37, 2nd class US$32, 3rd class US$26; Kigoma–Kasanga 1st class US$52, 2nd class US$43, 3rd class US$32; Kigoma–Mpulungu (Zambia) 1st class US$55, 2nd class US$45, 3rd class US$40; Kigoma–Bujumbura (Burundi) 1st class US$30, 2nd class US$25, 3rd class US$20 (though boats are not presently running to Burundi). Plus US$5 port tax. The journey can be very crowded and rowdy at times. 3rd class are benches or deck space, 2nd class cabins are small, hot and stuffy with 4 or 6 bunks. 1st class cabins have 2 bunks, a window, fan, and meals and drinks are available. Book and pay for your ferry at least 1-3 days in advance. For information phone the booking office in Kigoma, T028-280 2811.

The port in Kigoma is fairly organized and there is a large seating area under a tin roof for waiting ferry passengers. There is also an immigration and customs post for passengers arriving from Zambia. These are also found on arrival at Mpulungu in Zambia, and at Kasanga the Tanzania immigration and customs officials come on board the boat.

At **Kibirizi**, Village 3 km north of Kigoma, down at the boat yard, local motorboats depart for **Burundi** about twice a week when there is a demand. There is an immigration, customs and police post just to the back of the boats.

Gombe Stream National Park can be reached by lake taxis (small boats with an outboard motor), which are hired at Kigoma (ask around for the best price). The journey takes about 3 hrs. A passenger boat heads north from Kibirizi at around 1500 and a trip to Gombe will cost approximately US$3. The boat returns the next day, passing Gombe at about 0730. You can get to Kibirizi by walking north along the railway track from Kigoma; any hotel should be able to provide further details.

Train

The journey from Kigoma to **Dar** is 1254 km and it takes about 36 hrs although it may be worth getting on or off at **Morogoro** or **Dodoma** and doing the last stretch to or from Dar by road, saving a few hours. In 1st class there are only 2 beds in the compartment, in 2nd class there are 6. It is easy to buy fruit and small meals at the stations along the way. There is also a reasonable restaurant car, which offers beef or chicken with rice or chips for US$3, and warm drinks including beer; book ahead if at all possible. Local people fear theft on the train, especially at stations. The women frequently lock themselves inside their compartment and don't go out at night. Police ride on the train. Kigoma–Dar costs

US$40 (1st class), US$30 (2nd class sittting), US$13 (3rd class). See **Tanzania Railways Corporation** www.trctz.com for full details of timetables and fares.

Sumbawanga p370

Regular bus service to **Mbeya** via **Tunduma**. Be warned of serious competition from ticket sellers – there is room to bargain. Expect to pay around US$7. Buses leave at 0600-0700 and take around 8 hrs. In the morning several 4WDs leave from the petrol stations for the Zambian border or to **Kasanga** on Lake Tanganyika. The journey takes the best part of the day.

⊙ Directory

Kigoma p363, map p363

Banks CRDB, on the roundabout next to the police station; **National Bank of Commerce**, next to the market; **Panjutan Bureau de Change**, on the main road up from the station, has erratic opening hours but changes a surprisingly wide range of currencies. All have ATMs. **Embassies and consulates** Burundi Consulate, in a house just out of town on the road to the Hilltop Hotel, T028-280 2865. **Internet** There are a couple of internet places in town on the main road up from the railway station, they are expensive at US$3 an hr. **Medical services** Maweni Hospital, T028-280 2671, 1 km or so down the road towards Ujiji. **Post office** About 500 m to the north of the main round-about past the Caltex station.

Contents

Footprint features

Border crossings

Southwest Tanzania

At a glance

○ **Getting around** For the Selous and Ruaha, unless you have your own vehicle, it's best to use a tour operator because public transport is very limited. Local buses and *dala-dala* travel between the main towns in the region, where there are plenty of taxis.

◎ **Time required** 5-7 days for a safari, another 5 days to take in the towns and hike in the highlands.

☼ **Weather** The highlands can be quite cool and have higher rainfall. The best time to visit the parks is during the dry season from Jun-Nov, when the temperatures are warm but not too overbearing.

✖ **When not to go** Avoid the rainy season from the end of Mar-May, when many of the more remote roads are impassable.

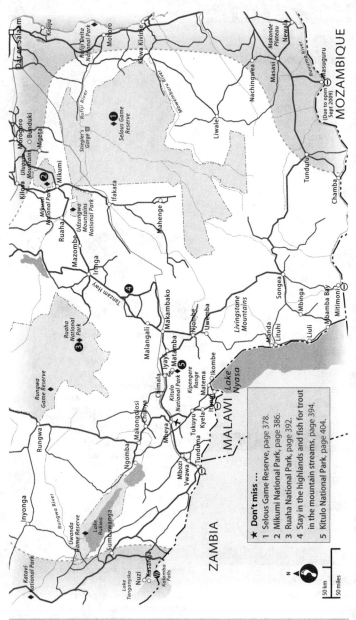

★ **Don't miss ...**
1 Selous Game Reserve, page 378.
2 Mikumi National Park, page 386.
3 Ruaha National Park, page 392.
4 Stay in the highlands and fish for trout
  in the mountain streams, page 394.
5 Kitulo National Park, page 404.

MOZAMBIQUE

ZAMBIA

MALAWI

Dar es Salaam

Kisiju

Rufiji Delta National Park

Mohoro

Kilwa Kivinje

Makonde Plateau

Newala

Nachingwea

Masasi

Ruvuma River

Masuguru

Due to open Sept 2009

Kilosa

Uluguru Mountains

Morogoro

Bunduki

Mgeta

Mikumi

Stiegler's Gorge

Selous Game Reserve

Rufiji River

Mbemkuru River

Liwale

Tunduru

Chamba

Mikumi National Park

Mazombe

Udzungwa Mountains National Park

Ruaha

Ifakada

Mahenge

Livingstone Mountains

Songea

Mbinga

Liuli

Mbamba Bay

Mitimoni

Iringa

Tanzam Hwy

Makambako

Njombe

Uwemba

Manda

Lituhi

Ruaha National Park

Rungwa Game Reserve

Malangali

Chimala

Matamba

Iyayi

Matema

Ikombe

Lake Nyasa

Mbeya

Tukuyu

Kyela

Ityai

Kitulo National Park

Kipengere Range

Makongolosi

Rungwa

Rungwa River

Ngomba

Inyonga

Uwanda Game Reserve

Lake Rukwa

Sumbawanga

Mbozi

Vwawa

Tundima

Katavi National Park

Lake Tanganyika

Nuzi

Kalambo Falls

Nsanga

N

50 km
50 miles

The little-visited southwest of Tanzania has lots to offer, from the country's largest wilderness area in the Selous, to the pretty Kitulo National Park, tiny in comparison to its vast neighbour yet bursting with rare flowers. Wildlife lovers who want to escape the safari convoys should come to this region – although you may work harder to see your game, you'll rarely see the crowds of the northern circuit. Frequently dubbed the 'southern circuit', the parks here, particularly Ruaha National Park and the Selous, a UNESCO World Heritage Site, have some fabulous lodges and are teeming with birdlife as well as animals. There's a real sense of the wild in the Selous too, especially in the southern region beyond the Rufiji River, which is just opening up to photographic safaris.

The major towns in the southwest are Iringa and Mbeya. Mbeya is on the railway that links Tanzania with Zambia. Road communications are good, and the main road that cuts through southwest Tanzania is the extension of Zambia's Great North Road and the continuation of the road that runs down the length of Lake Malawi in Malawi to the south. Take time to chill at Matema, on Lake Nyasa's northernmost shore (the Tanzanian name for the lake), and stroll along its beach or explore the lush highlands with high peaks and crater lakes around Tukuyu and Mbeya.

The southwest looks set to welcome more visitors soon as it opens the gates to its new Songwe International Airport (Tanzania's fourth) at the end of 2009. About 20 km south of Mbeya, it will undoubtedly bring changes as well as tourists to the area.

Ins and outs

Getting there and around
From Dar es Salaam the Tanzam Highway through the southwest heads out to Chalinze and Morogoro (see page 348). To the south of it are the limited road access points to the Selous Game Reserve whilst 70 km to the southwest of Morogoro the road runs through a 50-km stretch of the Mikumi National Park. Beyond the Mikumi National Park the road climbs into the Kitonga Hills, which are part of the Udzungwa Mountains. It is quite a journey, with sharp bends, and dense forest all around. Part of the road runs alongside the Ruaha River gorge, often dubbed 'Baobab Valley' by veteran overlanders. Eventually the road levels out to the plateau and Iringa. To the northwest of Iringa is the Ruaha National Park. Mbeya lies 390 km to the southwest along the road which passes though vast pine plantations and rural farms. About midway between the two towns is the junction with the road that heads due south to the little-visited extreme southwest of Tanzania around Songea and the eastern shore of Lake Nyasa. Except for the steep climb up to Iringa through Baobab Valley where the tar has melted, the Tanzam Highway is in fairly good condition. From Dar es Salaam there are regular buses linking the towns on this route. The TAZARA railway runs from Dar to Mbeya and on to Zambia.

Climate
The southern highlands of Tanzania form one of the largest blocks of highland in East Africa. They mostly have a high rainfall and because of their altitude are cool. Like the rest of south Tanzania (and unlike the highlands to the north) they have one long wet season and one long dry one. High rainfall and rich soil mean that this area is agriculturally productive in both food and cash crops (tea and coffee). As with most highland areas in East Africa they are associated with the Rift Valley system and there has been much volcanic activity in the area over the years.

Selous Game Reserve

→ Colour map 1, B5. 9° S, 38° E.
This enormous reserve in south Tanzania, first established in 1922, is the largest park in Africa and the second largest in the world, covering an area of 45,000 sq km, or 5% of Tanzania's total area, roughly the size of Switzerland. Until recently, from the visitor's point of view, all these facts and figures were a bit misleading given that the majority of visitors were restricted to the area north of the Rufiji River. South of here has hitherto been the sole domain of trophy hunters, who for a hefty fee, are allowed to shoot a restricted quota of wildlife in private concession areas only, the proceeds ostensibly going towards further conservation. However, all this may well change – one former hunting concession has recently opened their 120,000 ha of land as an exclusive photographic safari location and hopes to set a trend (see box, page 382, and Lukula Camp, page 384). The landscape in the north is largely open grassland and acacia woodland, cut across by slivers of riverine forest and patches of miombo woodland. Its rivers, hills and plains are home to roaming elephant populations, the area's famous wild dogs and some of the last black rhino left in the region, though the density of animals in the park is lower than that of other parks. During a game drive you are unlikely to see any other vehicles and the Selous offers you a chance to see a wild and expansive Africa far from paved roads and curio shops. ▸▸ *For listings, see pages 384-385.*

Ins and outs

Getting there There are a number of approaches to the park. The most convenient is certainly by air and there are airstrips at all the camps. The flight takes about 35 minutes from Dar es Salaam to the northern airstrips and costs about US$150. Coastal Air flies daily from Dar at 0830 and 1430 and Zan Air operates daily flights from Zanzibar at 0800 and Dar at 0840.

If going overland, take the Dar es Salaam–Kibiti–Mkongo road. The road to Kibiti (145 km from Dar) is tarmac for about one third of the distance, but after that is very poor. Kibiti is the last place you will be able to get petrol. It is then 30 km from Kibiti to Mkongo, where a west turning will take you on to the final 75 km to Mtemere Gate. It will take about seven to eight hours by road from Dar. The other road you can take is the Dar es Salaam–Morogoro–Matombo–Kisaki road, which will take you into the north section of the park. From Kisaki it is 20 km to Matambwe Gate. This route is a total of 350 km and will take eight to nine hours. The road from Morogoro is rough, should only be attempted in the dry season and will require a 4WD. You will have to bring plenty of fuel from Dar es Salaam,

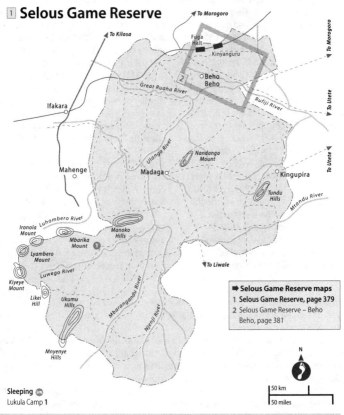

1 Selous Game Reserve

To Morogoro

To Kilosa

Fuga Halt

Kinyanguru

2 ○ Beho Beho

Great Ruaha River

Rufiji River

To Morogoro

To Utete

To Utete

Ifakara

Ulanga River

Nandanga Mount

Mahenge ○

Madaga ○

○ Kingupira

Tundu Hills

Mtandu River

Ironola Mount

Luhombero River

Manoko Hills

Mbarika Mount 1

Lyambero Mount

Luwego River

Mborangandu River

To Liwale

Kiyeye Mount

Likei Hill

Ukumu Hills

Njenji River

➡ Selous Game Reserve maps
1 Selous Game Reserve, page 379
2 Selous Game Reserve – Beho Beho, page 381

Mnyenye Hills

N

Sleeping
Lukula Camp 1

50 km
50 miles

Frederick C Selous: Greatest of the White Hunters

Born in 1852 in London, the young Selous went to Rugby school. An early expedition saw him trek to a lake 25 km from Rugby, strip off, swim through the icy water to a small island and shin up a tree to collect eight blue heron's eggs. On returning to school he was rewarded by being made to copy out 63 lines of Virgil for each egg. Undeterred, and inspired by the writings of Livingstone, Selous wanted to visit Africa. After toying with the idea of becoming a doctor, he travelled to South Africa in 1871, and rapidly established himself as a supreme tracker and hunter.

Hunting was tough. The rifles were heavy muzzle-loaders, and powder was carried loose in one pocket, ignition caps in another and a supply of four ounces of lead bullets in a pouch. It was not uncommon for a hunter to be knocked out of the saddle by the gun's recoil and accidents were common.

Selous killed much game in his early years, partly for trophies in the case of lion and rhinoceros, for ivory in the case of elephants, and anything else as meat for his party. His skills were based on absorbing the skills of African hunters and trackers, and in 1881 he published the first of a series of highly successful books on his methods and exploits, *A Hunter's Wanderings in Africa*. In 1887 he began a career of paid work leading safaris for wealthy clients, which culminated in a huge expedition organized for President Roosevelt in 1909. (A young British diplomat in South Africa, H Rider Haggard, based Allan Quatermain on Selous and his adventures in his novel *King Solomon's Mines*, published in 1895.)

During one visit to England, Selous took delivery of a new .450 rifle at his hotel an hour before he was due to catch the boat train from Waterloo to return to Africa. There was no time to test the sights and alignment on a rifle range, so Selous ordered a cab to stand by, flung open his bedroom window, squeezed off five shots at a chimney stack, checked that the grouping was satisfactory with his binoculars, swiftly packed the rifle and skipped down to the cab, pausing only to remark that he had heard shots on his floor and that the manager had better look into it.

By 1914, Selous, now married, had retired to Surrey and busied himself with running his own natural history museum. At the outbreak of war, despite being 63, he was determined to serve in East Africa, where he felt his skills would be useful. He joined the Legion of Frontiersmen, a colourful outfit that included French Legionnaires, a Honduran general, Texan cowboys, Russian émigrés, some music hall acrobats and a lighthouse keeper.

In January 1917, scouting in the campaign against General von Lettow Vorbeck (see page 418), he was killed by a German sniper at Beho Beho on the Rufiji River (now part of Selous Game Reserve).

Morogoro or Kibiti for your whole stay in the reserve. There are no car repair facilities here and drivers are advised to carry essential items such as tools, spare tyre, tyre repair kit, shovel and drinking water.

Getting the train is another option. Take the **TAZARA** ① *www.tazara.co.tz*, railway as far as Fuga. From here, by prior arrangement, the lodges will collect you. This may be expensive unless you get a group together to share the cost. The train to the Selous from Dar es Salaam is fairly reliable.

There are no buses to the Selous and hitching is almost impossible. Because of its inaccessibility, most people go to the Selous on organized safaris from Dar, see page 93.

Park fees and information Park fees are US$30 per adult per day, and US$5 per child between 5 and 16. If you stay at camps within the reserve's boundaries, there's an additional fee of US$25 per person, and vehicle fees are US$30. Part of the reason for the lack of human habitation in this area is that it is infested with the tsetse fly (see page 292). Use insect repellent on exposed areas of your body.

Climate The best time to visit is July-October. The camps and lodges are closed at the peak of the wet season from Easter-June, when the rains render many of the roads impassable, but check as they have been known to stay open in drier years.

Background

The park is named after Captain Frederick Selous, a British explorer and hunter who wrote a book about the region and his travels, and was killed in action in January 1917 while scouting in the area (see box, page 382). His grave is near Beho Beho.

The game reserve has an interesting history. In the days of the slave trade the caravan routes passed through the park. It is said that the occasional mango groves that can be

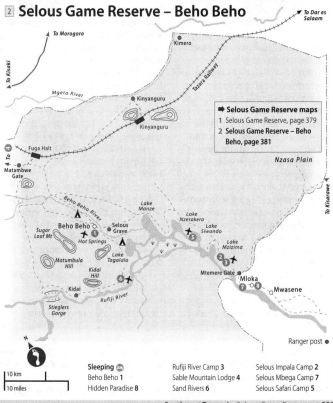

② Selous Game Reserve – Beho Beho

➡ **Selous Game Reserve maps**
1 Selous Game Reserve, page 379
2 Selous Game Reserve – Beho Beho, page 381

To Dar es Salaam
To Morogoro
To Kisaki
Kimero
Mgeta River
Tazara Railway
Kinyanguru
Kinyanguru
Fuga Halt
Matambwe Gate
Nzasa Plain
To Kisarawe
Beho Beho River
Lake Manze
Lake Nzerakera
Beho Beho
Selous Grave
Lake Siwando
Sugar Loaf Mt
Hot Springs
Lake Mzizima
Matambula Hill
Lake Tagalala
Kidai Hill
Mtemere Gate
Mloka
Kidai
Rufiji River
Mwasene
Stieglers Gorge
Ranger post ●

N

10 km
10 miles

Sleeping
Beho Beho **1**
Hidden Paradise **8**

Rufiji River Camp **3**
Sable Mountain Lodge **4**
Sand Rivers **6**

Selous Impala Camp **2**
Selous Mbega Camp **7**
Selous Safari Camp **5**

The Selous Project

Although the Selous Game Reserve is the size of Switzerland, only a fraction of it in the north has been accessible to most tourists, with the vast wilderness south of the Rufiji River reserved as private concessions for trophy hunting.

The debate about whether hunting is good for conservation has rumbled on for years. Those in favour support the view that it's OK for trophy hunters to pay big bucks to kill a limited quota of big game – lions, elephants, leopards and other wild animals that collectively represent the spirit of the African bush – because the proceeds help the economy and aid conservation. Those against it argue that quotas aren't adhered to or policed, that the practice simply isn't financially or environmentally sustainable and that the local communities most in need of the benefits of this strange kind of tourism never actually benefit from it, and so increase poaching as a means to survive.

In late 2008, a new camp opened in southern Selous which hopes to change this uneasy dichotomy between north and south, and to change the mindset in political circles about the value of trophy hunting and conservation. Surprisingly, the two men behind it were professional hunters who've decided that hunting as a conservation tool doesn't work. Anton Turner and Ryan Wienand have teamed up with Great Plains Conservation, a conservation eco-tourism organization, to create The Selous Project.

It will still bring in the big bucks, offering exclusive use of a 120,500-ha private concession called Lukula for a group of up to eight people, staying in a luxurious appointed camp on the banks of the Luwego River (see Sleeping, page 384). But crucially, the focus is on shooting with cameras rather than guns. The Selous Project offers guests a photographic safari with the chance to track wild animals on foot – elephant or buffalo – or to observe lions from a hide, canoe in the river to see hippos up close, or hike and fly-camp under the stars. All exciting stuff, but just as exciting is the whole ethos behind it.

Through the Selous Project, they aim to protect and monitor wildlife in the area, reduce poaching, increase the number of key species like lion, leopard, elephant and the increasingly vulnerable African wild dog, and teach local children about wildlife and conservation. Beyond this, there's the social side of living in a wilderness – the local communities will appreciate conservation efforts only if they lead to a better life for them too and in this vein, in consultation and collaboration with the villages concerned, the project plans over time to offer local training and employment, a guide training school, micro-financing projects like beekeeping, fish farming and sustainable forestry, and better medical care.

It's early days of course, and the project is still in its infancy. The wildlife in the area is good but still wary – the legacy of its hunting past – so it's not a Ngorongoro Crater type experience, where it's teeming with animals used to humans. But it does offer you a chance to experience the real wilderness and to connect with the bush in a way most parks don't – and at the same time, help conservation and local communities.

seen grew from the mango stones discarded from the caravans on their way from the coast. In the early 20th century during German colonial rule some of this area was designated as game reserves but in those days big game hunting was the most significant activity. In 1910 Kaiser Wilhelm gave part of the reserve to his Kaiserin as an anniversary gift.

This is how the nickname 'Shamba la Bibi', meaning 'The Woman's Field' and referring to the section of the present Selous north of the Rufiji River, came to be. In 1922, the land area was increased and named after Frederick Selous. From then until 1975, when the current boundaries were delineated, the reserve's size increased steadily to today's 45,000 sq km.

Wildlife
There are supposed to be over a million animals in the park, which is probably best known for its large numbers of elephant. However, poaching has been an enormous problem in the past and the numbers have been reduced substantially in recent years. A very disturbing report that came out in 1988 estimated that the elephant population had fallen by 80% in the Selous in just 10 years, from 1977 (census estimated population at 22,852) to 1987 (population estimated at 3673). However, more recent estimates of the numbers of elephant show an increase. Rhino have also been seriously affected and their population in the Selous is estimated to have fallen from 2500 in 1976 to fewer than 50 in 1986. Numbers are still low but thought to be increasing slowly. Other animals you may see include lions, buffalo, hippo, African wild dogs and crocodile, while over 400 species of birds have been recorded (including herons, fish eagles, kingfishers, and other various waterfowl and birds of prey). The overall population of African wild dogs is greatly depleted in East Africa. The canines living in the Selous Game Reserve and Mikumi National Park are one of the largest remaining viable wild dog populations in Africa. The proximity of areas for trophy hunters exacerbates the difficulty of viewing the animals here.

Routes

Great Rufiji River
Central to the park is the Great Rufiji River. This river and its associated water system has the largest catchment area of any river in East Africa and is probably the most significant feature of the park. It rises from the south and becomes the Rufiji where the Luwegu and Mbarangandu join. Other rivers join it and further north it swings east before it is forced through Stiegler's Gorge. At its delta, opposite Mafia Island, millions of tonnes of silt are deposited every year during the wet season and it swells to such an extent that it renders much of the park inaccessible. During dry season it subsides and sand banks are revealed.

Stiegler's Gorge
Named after a German explorer who was killed here by an elephant in 1907 and in the north of the reserve at the junction of the Rufiji and Ruaha rivers, Stiegler's Gorge is a 40-km, two-hour drive from Matambwe. It is a bottleneck as the water from this huge catchment area is forced through the narrow gorge. The gorge is about 7 km long, 100 m wide and deep. If you have a head for heights there is a cable car that spans it.

Beyond the gorge the river widens again and splits to form a number of lakes – Tagalala, Manze, Nzerakera, Siwando and Mzizima. The swampy area is home to many animals that congregate here especially when water is scarce during the dry season, in particular elephant, buffalo and, of course, hippo, sometimes in large numbers.

Other attractions in the park include the hot springs known simply as **Maji Moto** (hot water in Kiswahili). These are on the eastern slopes of Kipalala Hill and the water flows down into Lake Tagalala. You get to them by walking (with a ranger at all times) up the ravine. The water emits a strong smell of sulphur. The highest springs are the hottest, while further down they are sufficiently cool for you to be able to swim in them.

Walking and boating safaris

Apart from seeing the Selous by road, other popular ways are by foot or by boat. Because the Selous is a game reserve, rather than a national park, its visitors are subject to less restrictions, making it one of the few protected wildlife areas where you are allowed to walk and all camps can arrange walking safaris. You will normally set off early in order to avoid the worst of the midday sun and you must be accompanied by an armed ranger. Animal sightings tend to be rarer on walking safaris as the animals frequently shy away from humans. However, it is very pleasant to be able to stretch your legs and get a different perspective of the country. Trekking safaris of several days are also a possibility as is fly camping away from the main lodges. Some lodges arrange boat trips up the Rufiji River.

◉ Selous Game Reserve listings

For Sleeping and Eating price codes and other relevant information, see pages 36-40.

◉ Sleeping

Selous Game Reserve *p378, maps p379 and p381*

L Beho Beho, perched on the lower slopes of Namikwera Hill overlooking Kipalala Hill, reservations UK, T+44 (0)193 226 0618, www.behobeho.com. Expensive resort and one of the first camps to open in the northern sector. Panoramic views over the Rufiji River flood plain from spacious verandas. 8 a/c stone cottages with flush toilets and open-air showers. Lounge and dining area, billiards room and swimming pool. One of the most luxurious lodges in the area. Rates include full board and all activities – game drives and boat and walking safaris.

L Lukula Camp, see box page 382, southern Selous, reservations Dar, T0767-224 0331 (mob), www.selousproject.com. The only camp in remote southern Selous, it has its own airstrip. This new camp on the Luwego River has 4 huge luxury tents in classic safari style with furniture made from recycled hardwoods. The lovely adjoining *bustani* (garden) bathrooms use local materials like river stone and bamboo but still manage flushing toilets. There's a dining area, lounge and library, and a camp fire and boma overlooking the river. The camp can be booked on an exclusive use basis for up to 8 people at a rate of US$6270 per night (plus park fees) during the main dry season. It's open year round, with heavily reduced rates in their Adventure seasons bordering the dry season, and particularly in their Patrolling and Monitoring season from Feb-Apr, for more intrepid people who want to get involved in conservation operations.

L Sand Rivers, www.sand-rivers-selous.com. A Nomad Safaris property, email them (info@nomad.co.tz) and they will send a list of their agents. 5 cottages, 2 suites with their own plunge pools and 1 new house, the Rhino House, which is perfect for honeymooners. The most luxurious and isolated of the lodges, with superb food and service. Walking safaris and fly camping. Swimming pool set in rocks next to the river. US$900 per person.

L Selous Impala Camp, on the banks of the Rufiji River, T022-245 2005, www.adventure camps.co.tz. A popular camp with 8 fairly small but comfortable and nicely furnished en suite tents raised on wooden platforms. Offer all the usual activities as well as fishing and fly camping, and there's a relaxing pool that overlooks the river. Owned by Coastal Aviation, deals are available if you fly to Selous with them. Rates vary from US$500-600 per person.

L Selous Safari Camp, bookings through Selous Safari Co, Dar, T022-211 1728, www.selous.com. May remain closed longer than other camps because its on the floodplain. A luxury tented lodge overlooking the lakes. 13 individual tents, divided between the north and south camps, with toilets, showers, solar powered electricity and a swimming pool. Impeccable and attentive service.

Animals wander freely around the camp at night, including elephant and hippo. Boats and fishing equipment are available, and morning and evening game drives included. Rates are US$630-875 per person full board, depending on the season. The tents in the north camp can be booked in their entirety (either 4 or 6 tents sleeping 8-12 people) as an exclusive section with its own pool, kitchen, living area and jetty.

A Rufiji River Camp, overlooking the Rufiji River, reservations Dar, T0784-237422 (mob) or UK, T+44(0) 145 2862288. This is the oldest camp in the reserve. 20 tents with bathrooms, electricity and mosquito nets, spaced out along the river in an attractive tract of woodland. Restaurant, bar and swimming pool. Rates around US$400 per person, inclusive of park fees, full board and 2 excursions per day, from a choice of fishing, boat safaris, game drives or walking safaris.

A Sable Mountain Lodge, just outside the reserve, 10 km along the road from Kisaki, a 20-min drive from the airstrip at Matembwe, bookings through A Tent With a View Safaris, Dar, T022-211 0507, www.selouslodge.com. 8 comfortable stone cottages, the honey-moon cottage overlooks a small waterhole, plus 4 new luxury bandas, 2 of which have private plunge pools. Swimming pool over a natural spring and treehouse overlooking a waterhole. Rates US$295-345 per person full board and inclusive of 2 activities a day and park fees. Luxury mobile camping is US$695 per person per night. Useful for people who don't want inclusive game drives, as they will also take bookings on a simple full board basis.

B Selous Mbega Camp, bookings through Baobab Village Co Ltd, Dar, T022-265 0250, www.selous-mbega-camp.com, www.baoba bvillage.com. Originally a tented camp just outside Mtemere Gate, a new camp has been developed here, due to open in summer 2009, with a swimming pool, 8 en suite cottages and 4 apartments. The Original Camp will still function as a satellite camp and has 8 tents on raised platforms overlooking the river and a simple central bar and restaurant with a good varied menu and excellent service. Game drives, fishing, half-day boat safaris, village tours and walks at additional cost. Not as luxurious as the other camps but at US$95 per person sharing, full board, it's not bad value.

D Hidden Paradise, Mloka Village, about 7 km from Mtemere Gate, T022-277 2215, ftts@raha.com. Basic tents with mattresses. Has a restaurant (no beer) and can organize game drives and boat safaris, US$30 each. No running water.

Camping

You can camp beside the bridge over the Beho Beho River a few kilometres northwest of Beho Beho itself, and at a site beside Lake Tagalala. There are no facilities apart from a pit latrine, so bring everything with you. Small fires made with dead wood are permissible and rainwater can be collected nearby. Camping fees must be paid in advance at one of the gates, US$30 per person. No camping is permitted outside the official camping sites, but arrangements can be made for special campsites in the Mtemere-Manze zone for US$40. Further information from Chief Warden, Wildlife Division of the Ministry of Natural Resources and Tourism, Selous Game Reserve Office, Dar, T022-286 6064, scp@africaonline.co.tz.

⊖ Transport

Selous Game Reserve *p378, maps p379 and p381*
Air
There are airstrips at all the camps. **Coastal Air** flies daily to **Dar** at 0945, 1315 and 1525 (35 mins, US$150). These flights continue on to **Zanzibar**. On Mon, Thu and Sat there is also a flight between the Selous and **Ruaha** at 0930 (2 hrs). **Zan Air** flies daily to **Dar** and **Zanzibar** at 1015.

Train
The train to **Dar** is not that reliable, as it comes from Zambia and is often delayed.

Mikumi National Park

→ *Colour map 1, B5. 7° 26'S, 37° 0'E. Altitude: 549 m.*
Between the Uluguru Mountains and the Lumango range, Mikumi is the fourth largest park in Tanzania and has a wide variety of wildlife that is easy to spot and well used to game viewing (the park is popular with weekend visitors as it only takes about four hours on a good road to drive the 300 km from Dar es Salaam). It borders the Selous Game Reserve and Udzungwa National Park, and the three locations make a varied and pleasant safari circuit. Mikumi has a pretty, undulating landscape with good resident game, but it is not as spectacular as the other parks. ▸▸ *For listings, see page 388.*

Ins and outs

Getting there From Morogoro the main Tanzania–Zambia road travels through cultivated land for about 100 km before reaching the boundary of the park. The national park is on both sides of the road, so drive with care. The speed limit along this stretch is 50 kph and the road now has speed bumps – animals had been killed before by speeding vehicles. There is an airstrip near the park headquarters suitable for light aircraft; a flight from Dar es Salaam will take approximately 45 minutes.

Park fees and information Park entry fee is US$20 for adults and US$5 for children aged 5-16 years, per 24 hours. The best time to visit is September-December. Take a guide for a short time when you first arrive, it isn't expensive (about US$10) and can greatly improve chances of seeing the rarer types of game. ▸▸ *For more information on national park fees and safaris, see page 41.*

Background

The park was gazetted in 1964 during the construction of the Morogoro–Iringa highway, and is set in a horseshoe of the towering Uluguru mountain range, which rises to 2750 m and covers an area of 3230 sq km. It lies between the villages of Doma and Mikumi from which it takes its name. Mikumi is the Kiswahili name for the borassus palm found in the area.

Wildlife

The landscape is typically woodland and grassy plains, which are fed by the Mkata River flood plain, an area of lush vegetation that attracts a number of animals throughout the year. These include lion, eland, hartebeest, buffalo, wildebeest, giraffe, zebra, hippo and elephant. Up to 300 species of birds stop over on migratory routes over Tanzania. Birdlife is particularly abundant here with many species present which are seen infrequently in other game parks of northern Tanzania. They include the violet turaco and the pale-billed hornbill, along with various species of storks, pelicans, herons, ibis, kestrels, kites and eagles. The Mikumi forest elephants are much smaller than their big game park counterparts and are mainly grazers so they do not cause as much damage to the trees. It's not unusual to see them, and sometimes lion, from the main road, especially in the evening or night. They seem quite accustomed to the traffic that rumbles past.

Routes

From the park gate the road leads to the floodplain of the Mkata River, which is particularly important for the wildlife. To the north the floodplain remains swampy throughout the year, while in the south water channels drain to the Mkata River. Here you will see, among other animals, elephant, buffalo and hippo. About 15 km northwest of the park gate there are hippo pools where there are almost always a number of hippos wallowing in the mud.

Other areas worth visiting are the Choga Wale area and Mwanambogo area – the latter can only be reached in the dry season. The track is to the east of the flood plain and heads north towards the Mwanambogo Dam. The Kisingura circuit is another popular drive, as is the Kikoboga area where you are likely to see elephant, particularly December and January.

The road that goes along the river is a good one to take for viewing. It passes through a patch of woodland and some swampy areas before coming on to the grasslands of the Chamgore. Chamgore means 'place of the python' and here there are two waterholes that are always ideal for spotting game. Hill Drive leads up the foothills of the Uluguru Mountains and from here you will get wonderful views all around. The vegetation is miombo woodland and the ebony tree grows here.

To get to the south part of the park take the track that branches off opposite the park entrance, which heads towards an area called Ikoya. Here you will see sausage trees, *Kigelia africana*, with their distinctive pods hanging down. This is also where you may see leopard.

Mikumi National Park

Sleeping
Mikumi Wildlife Camp 1
Foxes Safari Camp 2
Genesis 3

Mikumi Medical Centre
Guest Cottages 4
Vuma Hills 6

Waterholes

3 km
3 miles

⊙ Mikumi National Park listings

*For Sleeping and Eating price codes and other
relevant information, see pages 36-40.*

⊖ Sleeping

Mikumi National Park *p386, map p387*
The small village of Mikumi has a number
of cheap hotels and guesthouses.
L Foxes Safari Camp, reservations Foxes
of Africa, T0784-237422 (mob), UK T+44(0)
145 286 2288, www.tanzaniasafaris.info.
Luxury tented camp raised on wooden
decks overlooking the Mkata River floodplain.
8 large thatched tents with bathrooms and
2 double beds, scattered around a granite
kopje. The central boma area for eating is
perched on top of a hill.
L Vuma Hills, reservations, Foxes of Africa,
T0784-237422 (mob), UK T+44 (0)145 286
2288, www.tanzaniasafaris.info. 16 luxury
tents with bathrooms, private verandas
and colonial decor. The dining area and bar
overlook the swimming pool. Slightly more
luxurious than the **Foxes Safari Camp**.
A Mikumi Wildlife Camp, also known as
Kikoboga, about 300 m off the main road
to the right, near the park headquarters,
reservations Dar, T022-260 0352, obh@bol.
co.tz. 12 very comfortable stone bandas,
some with 3 or 4 beds in 1 or 2 rooms – good
value for families or groups. Bar and lounge

under a huge fig tree, dining room in a
rondavaal. Small stone swimming pool,
good views from the sun deck and there
is an observation tower for game viewing.
E-F Genesis Hotel, Mikumi Village on the
Iringa side, T023-262 0466. Very comfortable
banda accommodation with satellite TV and
bathroom. Breakfast included. Camping costs
US$5 per person. Restaurant with reasonable
menu, nice bar, secure. There is also a snake
park attached.
**E-F Mikumi Medical Centre Guest
Cottages**, if driving from the park entrance
to Mikumi, keep going until you cross the
railway, the centre is on the left a few hundred
metres on. Excellent place to stay, run by a
Dutch organization who have funded the
building of the guest cottages as a continuing
source of income for the medical centre.
Facilities include fully equipped kitchen (take
own food), shower room with hot water,
lounge/dining room and a number of rooms
with fans and nets. Camping is also possible
for US$5 per person.

Camping
National Park Campsite, about 4 km into
the park from park entrance gate. Water
and firewood usually available, otherwise
it's very basic.

Udzungwa Mountains National Park

→ *Colour map 1, B5. 7° 50'S, 37°E. www.udzungwa.org.*
The Udzungwa Mountains rise up from the western edge of the Selous Game Reserve. Botanical diversity is exceptional, and the park is host to a large number of endangered bird species as well as forest antelope and vervet monkeys. This is a forest area and covers approximately 1990 sq km lying between 250-2576 m (on the highest peak, Luhomero). Views from the peaks of the mountains, towards the Selous Game Reserve and the distant Indian Ocean coast are incredible and well worth the effort. Recently classified as a national park, where previously it was a national forest reserve, the conservation programme is designed to benefit the local people and improve their social amenities of health and education, water supplies and transport and to encourage them to cooperate fully in the conservation programme with the National Park Management. ▸▸ *For listings, see page 390.*

Ins and outs

Getting there By car the park is about six hours' drive from Dar es Salaam and 75 km from the Mikumi National Park. To reach the park headquarters, turn south off the main Dar–Mbeya highway at Mikumi and follow the signs to Ifakara. The tarmac road continues to Kidatu where you cross the Ruaha River. Follow the gravel road another 24 km and you will reach Manug'ula, the signposted turning for the park headquarters is on the right. Buses to Ifakara can drop off here. Charter flights can be arranged from Dar to nearby airstrips at Msolwa and the Kilombero Sugar Company. By train, the TAZARA train stops in Manug'ula. ▸▸ *For further details, see Transport, page 390.*

Park fees and information Permits are valid for 24 hours and are available at the park headquarters; adults US$20, children aged 5-16 years US$5. A guide/ranger costs US$10 per group. To contact the park warden in charge, T023-262 0224, udzungwa@gmail.com. The best time to visit is September-December.

Wildlife

The Udzungwa Mountains are part of the Eastern Arc Range of mountains which stretch from southern Kenya to southern Tanzania. The Eastern Arc are small and fragmented mountains, each block having a patchwork of dense tropical forests with high rainfall. River catchments protected within the park boundary are important for hydroelectricity production, local communities' water supply and agriculture. The national park protects more than 2500 plant species of which 160 are used locally as medicinal plants. Over 300 animal species have been recorded, including 18 vertebrate species found only in the Eastern Arc Mountains. The recently discovered Sanje mangabey and the Iringa red colobus are thought to be endemic to the region, and there are also elephant, buffalo, lion and leopard present. Birds found here include sunbirds, shrikes and the Iringa akalat. To the south lies the green Kilombero Valley, with the jagged slopes of the Mbarika Mountains, 100 km away, clearly visible rising out of the lowlands. There are no roads or tracks through the park but guided walks are available, so hikers have the park to themselves. A variety of trails are available to suit different abilities, including short half-day trails, mountain climbing trails with overnight camping and long-range wilderness trails taking several days.

Ifakara → *Colour map 1, B5.*

ⓘ *Take the ordinary TAZARA train (not the international train) from Dar and booking in advance is essential, T022-286 5187, www.tazara.co.tz. The station is 11 km north of the town centre. Buses go from Kariakoo to Ifakara daily.*

For those with a penchant for getting off the beaten track, a visit to this isolated central Tanzanian town southeast of Iringa and 100 km from Mikumi is recommended. Ifakara is a verdant, tree-dotted old trading station close to the Kilombero River in a highly fertile area. The most important crop of the local Pogoro people is rice and there is thriving trade in this commodity between Ifakara and Dar es Salaam. Tropical hardwoods (from the rainforests north of Ifakara) are also being sent from here to the coast for export.

The countryside surrounding Ifakara is very attractive and is ideal for cycling (bikes can be hired from the town centre); it is also rich in birdlife. The Kilombero River flows past about 10 km to the south of the town and supports a large seasonal wetland in the Kilombero Valley. The area has several species of endemic birds, including the Kilombero weaver; the only sustainable population in Tanzania of the very rare puku antelope; and a fair amount of lion and elephant. At Kivukoni there is a ferry crossing for the road to Mahenge. There are hippos in the river here and it is possible to arrange a trip in a dug-out canoe to see them.

◉ Udzungwa Mountains National Park listings

For Sleeping and Eating price codes and other relevant information, see pages 36-40.

Rates are US$25 per person full board. Student discounts can be negotiated.

● Sleeping

Udzungwa Mountains National Park *p389*
E Goa Guest House, 100 m from the market on Uhuru Rd. The best of the local lodges. Clean, simple doubles with fan and bathroom.

Camping
There are designated campsites (US$30) with basic facilities. Bring your own equipment.

Ifakara *p390*
E St Francis' Hospital Guest House, on the edge of the hospital compound, www.ifakara.org. Single and double rooms, simply furnished and with mosquito nets.

● Transport

Ifakara *p390*
Bus
Several companies run buses from Ifakara. By far the best of these is **Zanil's**, which has daily buses leaving at 1000 for **Morogoro** and **Dar**. Book a seat on the left-hand side for good views of the Udzungwa Mountains. For the more adventurous there are also daily bus services to **Mahenge** and **Malinyi** (towns to the south and west of Ifakara).

Train
TAZARA trains leave for **Dar** at inconvenient times: Thu 0500 and Sun 0600 (9 hrs). Note that the timetables change frequently, so check www.tazara.co.tz before travelling.

Iringa and around

→ *Colour map 1, B4. 7° 48'S, 35° 43'E. Phone code: 026. Population: 90,000. Altitude: 1635 m.*
Up in the chilly highlands, Iringa, set on a plateau 502 km from Dar es Salaam on the main Tanzania–Zambia road beyond Mikumi National Park, commands a panoramic view over the surrounding boulder-strewn countryside. Maize, vegetables, fruits and tobacco are grown in the fertile soil around here and consequently the safe and welcoming town has an excellent market, where you can barter for almost every vegetable under the sun. About four hours' drive and 130 km west of Iringa, Ruaha National Park is a huge undeveloped wilderness, whose ecology is more like that of southern Africa. ▸▸ *For listings, see pages 394-397.*

Ins and outs

Getting there If travelling on a bus which is not terminating in Iringa you may find yourself getting off at the bus stand on the main road at the bottom of the hill a few kilometres outside Iringa town. Taxis into town cost US$2 or there are regular *dala-dala*.

Sights

On the drive to Iringa you are likely to see giraffe, elephant, zebra and baboons close by. If travelling by bus avoid sitting at the rear as there are a number of speed bumps on this stretch of road. From Mikumi the road steadily climbs upwards to the chilly highlands of Iringa. On arrival you will notice the distinct drop in temperature and vendors on the roadside arranging rows of welly-boots and jackets to sell. Be sure to take some warm clothes. During German occupation, the German military constructed the town as a fortified defence against marauding Hehe tribal warriors intent on driving them out of the region. **Gangilonga Rock**, a site just outside the town, is a legendary spot where the Hehe chief at that time, Chief Mkwawa, met with his people and decided how to fight the

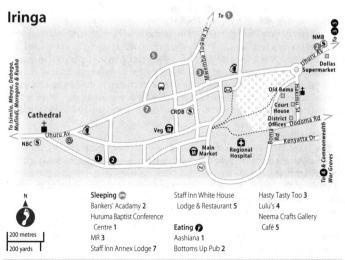

Iringa

Sleeping 🛏
Bankers' Acadamy 2
Huruma Baptist Conference
  Centre 1
MR 3
Staff Inn Annex Lodge 7

Staff Inn White House
  Lodge & Restaurant 5

Eating 🍴
Aashiana 1
Bottoms Up Pub 2

Hasty Tasty Too 3
Lulu's 4
Neema Crafts Gallery
  Café 5

Germans in an uprising of 1894. He was finally defeated in 1898 but, refusing to be captured by the Germans, he committed suicide.

The pleasant albeit slightly chilly climate attracted settlers and there is an impressive legacy of German colonial architecture, including the old **Boma**, the **Town Hall**, the **Hospital** and **Post Office**. Iringa was also the site of several battles during the First and Second World Wars, and **Commonwealth War Graves** are just outside town.

Isimila Stone Age site ① *About 20 km from town. Can be reached by buses going to Mbeya, then a walk to the site of about 2 km. A taxi from Iringa will cost around US$25. Entry to museum US$3.* This is considered to be one of the finest stone age sites in East Africa. Once a shallow lake, now dried up, the site was discovered in 1951 by a South African, D Maclennan, and excavated in 1957-1958 by Dr Clark Howell and G Cole, sponsored by the University of Chicago. Soil erosion in a *korongo* (a watercourse, which is dry for most of the year) exposed a great number of Acheulian stone tools, including pear-shaped axes, cleavers and spherical stones, which had been artificially shaped. They are believed to date from 60,000 years ago. Also among the finds were fossilized animal bones, including a now extinct form of hippopotamus (*H Gorgops*), whose eyes protruded like periscopes and a short-necked giraffe (*Sivatherium*). It is believed that early hominoids used this area as both a watering place and to hunt the animals that came to drink there. A small museum was built on the site in 1969 and displays some of the tools, fossils and bones found during excavations.

Isimila Gully is upstream from the site and is a spectacular natural phenomenon. Erosion over the millennia has left standing several pillars that tower above you.

Ruaha National Park and Rungwa Game Reserve ●● ▸▸ *pp394-397.*

Ruaha National Park is one of the most remote parks in Tanzania, and visitor numbers reflect that: 2500 per annum to Ruaha, compared to 250,000 to the Serengeti. Yet it is Tanzania's second largest national park, with vast concentrations of buffalo, elephant, gazelle, and over 400 bird species. Elephants are found here in some of the highest concentrations in the country, travelling in matriarch-led herds through ancient grazing lands and seasonal supplies of water. The Ruaha River is the main feature of the park, and meanders through its borders. Most of the national park is on the top of a 900-m plateau whose ripples of hills, valleys, and plains makes the game viewing topography uniquely beautiful. Small mountains run along the southwest borders of the park and their tree-covered slopes are visible in the distance. During the rainy seasons, dry river beds swell with the biannual deluge and within days, a thin coat of green covers all the land in sight.

Ins and outs

Getting there From Iringa the road passes through densely populated countryside until the development gradually thins out. The vegetation becomes miombo woodland and about 60 km from Iringa the turning off to the right to the park is indicated. It is another 50 km down this road to the park boundary and from there about 10 km to Ibuguziwa where you pay the park entrance fees and cross the Ruaha River. About 1 km beyond the river there is a junction. To the right the track goes to Msembe and the park headquarters and to the left to Ruaha River camp. There is an airstrip at the park headquarters for light aircraft, and Coastal Air flights from Dar and Zanzibar (via Selous) land here on Mondays, Thursdays and Saturdays. ▸▸ *See Transport, page 397.*

Park fees and information Entry fees are US$20 per 24 hours for adults, US$5 for children aged between 5-16 years. A two-hour foot safari with an armed ranger can be arranged at park headquarters. ▸▸ *For more information on national park fees and safaris, see page 41.*

Climate Visiting is possible during both the dry 'yellow' season and the wet 'green' season, even in January when the rain is heaviest because the rains are short and most of the roads are all-weather. However, in the wet season the grass is long and game viewing is almost impossible, so it's best to visit from July-December.

Background
Ruaha National Park was classified a national park in 1964. The area was a part of Sabia River Game Reserve, established by the German colonial government in 1911, and later renamed the Rungwa Game Reserve. It covers an area of 12,950 sq km which is the size of Belgium and ranges from 750 m to 1900 m above sea level. The park gets its name from the river that forms part of its boundary. The name *Ruaha* is from the word *Luvaha*, which means 'great' in the Hehe language and the river certainly is that. It is vital to the economy of the country for it supplies much of Tanzania with electricity through hydroelectric power from the dam at Kidatu. Further downstream the Ruaha joins the Ulanga to form the Rufiji River.

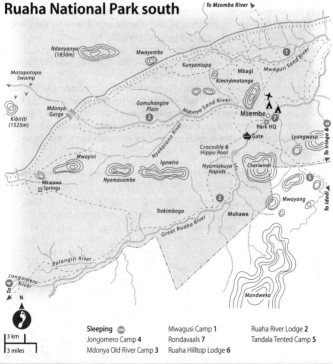

Ruaha National Park south

Sleeping
Jongomero Camp **4**
Mdonya Old River Camp **3**

Mwagusi Camp **1**
Rondavaals **7**
Ruaha Hilltop Lodge **6**

Ruaha River Lodge **2**
Tandala Tented Camp **5**

Wildlife

There is a wide variety of wildlife in this park, largely due to the different vegetation types found here. There are four major vegetation zones: the river valleys, the open grassland, the miombo woodland (see box, page 357), and undulating countryside where baobabs dominate. Animals include elephant, lion, zebra, giraffe, Cape hunting dogs, ostrich, greater and lesser kudu, gazelle (and other antelope) and, in the river, hippo and crocodile. There are over 480 recorded species of bird in the park. The rare Eleonora's falcon may be sighted here, as well as the pale-billed hornbill and violet-crested turaco. Pel's fishing owls are also seen, as well as several species of bat. Unfortunately, poaching here is a serious problem and the animal population has suffered enormously from this. In particular rhinos, which were once found here, are probably now extinct. The elephant population also fell tremendously from over 22,000 in 1977 to under 4000 in 1987. In 1988 the government instigated the Selous Conservation Programme with support form WWF which, with new manpower resources, considerably helped guard the reserve from poaching. This coincided with the international ban on ivory in the early 1990s and since then elephant numbers have climbed quickly and there are now thought to be about 70,000.

Routes

Around Msembe is bush country, with acacia and baobab trees, and elephants are often found here. Along the river, particularly during the dry season, many animals congregate and you may see confrontations between lion and buffalo. You can expect to see elephant, giraffe, baboon, warthog, buffalo, zebra, all sorts of antelope and if you are lucky leopard and cheetah. In the river itself are both hippo and crocodile.

The Mwagusi Sand River joins the Ruaha about 10 km from Msembe. If you cross this river and follow the track you will get to Mwayembe Hill and the escarpment where there is a salt lick often frequented by elephant and buffalo.

The Mdonya Sand River joins the Ruaha between the ferry and the park headquarters. From the ferry a drive southwest will take you past the Nyamakuyu Rapids and Trekimboga to where the Jongomero joins the Ruaha, about 40 km upriver. This is a good place to see hippo and crocodile. Roan and sable antelopes, which are difficult to see elsewhere, can also been seen here. There are supposed to be rhino in the western part of the park, but the location is kept secret.

◉ Iringa and around listings

For Sleeping and Eating price codes and other relevant information, see pages 36-40.

◍ Sleeping

Iringa and around *p391, map p391*
A Highland Fishing Lodge, Mufindi, go past Kisolanza Farm and turn off at Mafinga, the junction just past a Total petrol station (about 45 mins from Iringa), head towards Sawala along this unsurfaced road for 30 km until a signposted turning to the left, follow signs for a further 11 km, reservations Foxes of Africa,

Dar, T0784-237422 (mob), UK T+44-(0)145 286 2288, www.tanzaniasafaris.info. Above the Great Rift Valley, south of Iringa, in the scenic southern highlands and set among the tea plantations. 9 well appointed log cabins command fine views across the valley and have bathrooms and private verandas. There is a TV room with pool table, living room with large log fires and dining room serving meals cooked using fresh produce from the farm. Full board and activities include mountain biking, horse riding, birdwatching, walking, canoeing and swimming in dammed pools.

Trout fishing available at extra cost (this is thought to be the only place where naturally bred rainbow trout are found in Tanzania). Buses run to Sawala from Mafinga, pre-arrange for someone to meet you at the lodge sign.

C-F The Old Farm House, Kisolanza Farm, from Iringa (travelling towards Mbeya) pass by Ifunda (on your right), and when you reach Ulete Mission (again on your right) Kisolanza Farm is shortly after on the left, T0754-306144 (mob), www.kisolanza.com. Charming old house with thatched guest cottages, 50 km southwest of Iringa adjacent to the Dar–Mbeya Rd. The home of the Ghaui family for over 70 years. Pleasant climate at an altitude of over 1600 m, large freshwater dam offers excellent swimming and fishing, nearby golf at Mufindi. A separate site for campers and overlanders is available in a secluded area away from the main house. Site has showers, WC, stone-built BBQ and plenty of shade. Fresh food, including bread, meat and eggs available to buy from the farm, and all meals. Very friendly management.

E MR Hotel, off Uhuru Av, near bus station, T026-270 2779, www.mrhotel.co.tz. Popular with expats and Japanese. This is the best hotel in town, but there's little competition. Big rooms have hot showers and satellite TV. Excellent restaurant with American diner-style interior, which unusually offers a separate vegetarian menu, but slow service. Many staff speak good English. Price includes breakfast.

E-F Huruma Baptist Conference Centre, Mkwawa St, 1 km north of centre, T026-270 1532, reservations@baptist-conference hotel.com. In pleasant, walled grounds with a pool, very good value, very clean, good food. The garden and main driveway have benches and bandas from where you can enjoy the views of the surrounding countryside. Rates around US$30, including breakfast. Camping is also available for US$5. Can arrange transport to Ruaha and Mikumi National Parks.

F Bankers' Academy, Uhuru Av, T026-270 2431.The previous Bankers' Academy is still used for educational and training purposes although involves less students than in the past, and college rooms are available for visitors. Simple accommodation with dated decor though very clean and well maintained, about US$18 for a double en suite room. There are cheaper rooms for US$4 at the back, just past the main gates (take the left turn and follow the drive up to the back gates and security desk). Double rooms with communal bathroom in a hall of residence. The guards at the gate will find the appropriate lady to administer keys, etc. No hot water, fans or mosquito ets but very cheap.

F Staff Inn Annex Lodge, off the main Uhuru Rd, T026-270 0165. Sister lodge to the **White House**. Double rooms with bathrooms, TV, clean, comfortable and modern if a little small. A bustling friendly environment with welcoming staff but often full. Great value for money. Restaurant and bar serves local and Indian dishes in a modern diner-style restaurant with veranda.

F Staff Inn White House Lodge & Restaurant, behind the bus stand, T026-270 0161. Double or single rooms with mosquito nets and hot water. The restaurant at the front serves local, Chinese and Western dishes from US$3. Convenient for those who are late arriving or starting early, however, it's rather run down and grubby.

Camping

Riverside Campsite, at an attractive site on the Little Ruaha River, 15 km southeast of Iringa, 2 km off the road to Dar (the Tanzam Highway), T026-272 5280, www.riverside campsite-tanzania.com. Although mainly a campsite (US$6 per person), this place also has lovely chalets and tented bandas near the river, including a family banda with self-catering facilities. En suite bandas are US$25 per person, tented bandas with shared showers and toilets are US$20 per person and tents with beds are US$15 per person. Friendly, hot showers, toilets, cold drinks, barbecue under a large tree, fresh farm produce and other food supplies if requested in advance, separate area for overlanders. Horse riding can be arranged at the nearby farm, mountain bikes for hire, birdwatching, refreshing swimming in the river. They also have their own Swahili language school and offer both intensive and longer courses. There are regular *dala-dala* along the Tanzam Highway to Iringa, a taxi from town may cost up to US$15.

Ruaha National Park *p392, map p393*
L Jongomero Camp, in the remote south-western sector of Ruaha, reservations Selous Safari Co, T022-211 1728, www.selous.com. A luxury tented lodge set under shady acacia trees on the banks of the Jongomero Sand River. 8 large and well appointed en suite tents under enormous thatched roofs with spacious private verandas, comfortable dining and living areas, natural rock pool for swimming, excellent food and good service, airstrip for direct access, full board rates and game drives included. Walking safaris can also be organized with prior notice.
L Mdonya Old River Camp, near Mdonya Falls, a 2-hr drive from the airstrip, T022-245 2005, www.adventurecamps.co.tz. A rustic tented camp with 11 twin-bedded tents with verandas, open air showers and toilets in reed walls, centred around a large lounge/dining/bar tent overlooking a sand river which is a natural wildlife corridor. All game drives and meals included. Attentive staff. Owned by Coastal Airlines, special packages are available if you book your flights through them.
L Mwagusi Camp, owned and run by Chris Fox and managed separately from the other Foxes' lodges, reservations TropicAfrica in the UK, T+44-(0)752 517 0940 www.ruaha.org. Without doubt the best safari camp in the park. It is in a better position than other lodges, is more stylish and luxurious and more professional and competent about its game-viewing. The site overlooks the Mwagusi Sands River, which does not dry up and so attracts all kinds of wildlife to drink there. It's a tented camp with en suite showers, hot water in the morning, evening and on request. The site has 10 luxury thatched tented rooms, and is 30 mins away from the airstrip. As soon as you disembark from the

plane you are among the wildlife. The owner will take you on game drives and is very experienced, alternatively short guided walking tours are available, giving you an opportunity to 'touch the wild'. Animals wander freely through the camps. All-inclusive rate, US$600 per person per night.
L Ruaha River Lodge, 18 km south of Msembe, reservations through Foxes of Africa, Dar, T0784-237422 (mob), www.tanzaniasafaris.info. Banda accommodation in 1 of 3 sites, on and around a kopje overlooking the Ruaha River. In wonderful settings, each camp has a restaurant and bar. Peter and Sarah Fox, who have lived in Ruaha for decades, are your hosts. During the dry season (Oct) the animals remain around here. Vehicle hire available.
L Tandala Tented Camp, just outside the park before the park gate, T026-270 3425, www.tandalatentedcamp.com. Walking safaris are permitted here as it is outside the park. Tents are built on elevated platforms, bathrooms in thatch and stone, solar power, leather sofas in the lounge area, nice bar with pool table crafted out of old railway sleepers, French and Greek cuisine, lovely swimming pool surrounded by wooden deck.
C Ruaha Hilltop Lodge, outside park, 5 km from the entrance, T026-270 1806, www.ruaha hilltoplodge.com. A beautifully designed, outstandingly run safari lodge overlooking miombo woodland and views of Ruaha. A family business set up by 2 brothers from Iringa. Accommodation in comfortable cottages each with own balcony and bathroom. The spacious bar and restaurant offer amazing views at sunset and superb food. This is the cheapest option around Ruaha and the management are very accommodating, flexible and keen for business. Transport from Iringa can be arranged through the owner.

Camping
Rondavaals and campsite, at the park headquarters. Hot showers, pit latrines, very basic banda accommodation and camping. US$40 for the huts and US$30 camping.

There are also 2 campsites inside the park, bring everything you need with you (firewood is supplied). Further information from Tanzania National Parks head office, Arusha, see page 259.

🍴 Eating

Iringa and around *p391, map p391*

🍴🍴 **Bottoms Up Pub**, also called **Shooters**, Majumba St. Tue-Sun. Pub serving Chinese, Indian and local dishes, including seafood and pizzas. Good value and friendly service. A favourite with expats at weekends, has a pool table and TV for football games.

🍴🍴 **Neema Crafts Gallery Café**, off Uhuru Av. A community initiative employing deaf and disabled people, this is a great place to eat. Serves Italian paninis, home-made cakes and ice cream, and there's a good book exchange.

🍴 **Aashiana**, central, between Uhuru Av and the market. A huge variety of predominantly Indian foods, snacks and beverages. Great food and fantastic value for money.

🍴 **Hasty Tasty Too**, Uhuru Av, opposite Hoteli ya Kati. Indian run café serving a good variety of meals and snacks, including wraps, burgers, cakes, hot chocolate, milkshakes and toasted sandwiches. A relaxed yet busy café with outdoor seating. Popular with expats.

🍴 **Lulu's**, Dodoma Rd. Mon-Sat 0830-1500, 1830-2100. Pleasant, with garden seating and picnic umbrellas. Meals and light snacks, including toasted cheese sandwiches. Clean and friendly.

🍴 **White House Restaurant**, behind the bus station. Good range of local and Chinese meals and snacks, outside seating, good place to wait for buses.

🛍 Shopping

Iringa and around *p391, map p391*
The **market** offers a variety of fresh foods and a number of grocery shops around the side of the market sell packaged European foods.

Dollas supermarket, opposite the Banker's Academy, Uhuru St. Sells a wide range of imported goods although at foreign prices.
Neema Crafts, just off Uhuru Av, near NMB Bank, T0786-431274 (mob), www.neema crafts.com. The best place for local souvenirs, this is a community craft workshop training and employing local deaf and disabled people, selling beautiful beadwork, paper products, clothes, jewellery and crafts. There's a great café here too, see Eating, opposite.

🚌 Transport

Iringa and around *p391, map p391*
Bus
Buses leave from the main bus stand in the centre of town. The bus offices all have kiosks here. **Scandinavia Express**, T026-270 2308, www.scandinaviagroup.com, buses to **Dar**, 7 hrs, US$15; **Morogoro**, 5 hrs, US$10; **Mbeya**, 5 hrs, US$10; **Songea**, 10 hrs, US$14. Kings Cross buses to **Dodoma** leave daily at 0800 (10 hrs, US$12).

Ruaha National Park *p392, map p393*
Air
Coastal Air fly to **Dar** and **Zanzibar** (via **Selous**) Mon, Thu and Sat at 1145 (US$300).

🗂 Directory

Iringa *p391, map p391*
Banks CRDB Bank, Uhuru Av; National Bank of Commerce, Uhuru Av near the cathedral, NMB Bank, Uhuru Av, past Banker's Academy. All have ATMs. A Barclays Bank is due to open shortly. **Internet and telephone** Try at the side of the MR Hotel, US$1 per hr, or at the post office (often busy). Iringanet Internet Café opposite GAPCO petrol station offers great service and plenty of terminals, US$1 per hr. You can also make international telephone calls from here. A new Wi-Fi internet café is planned at **Neema Crafts**.

Tanzam Highway to Lake Nyasa

On its way to Mbeya, the Tanzam Highway from Iringa cuts through mixed woodland and savannah as well as cultivated land. Towards the end of the rainy season the scenery looks almost Mediterranean with its cultivated rolling hillsides flecked with the yellow of sunflower crops and wild flowers. Gradually it opens up to more savannah and various roads off the main road will lead you into the Usangu Plains. Roughly midway between Iringa and Mbeya is the junction town of Makambako. Heading south from here through fertile, rolling hills leads down to the eastern side of Lake Nyasa and Mbamba Bay via the towns of Njombe and Songea. The road is in good condition as far as Songea but then it deteriorates considerably for the 170 km from Songea to Mbamba Bay on the eastern shore of Lake Nyasa.
▸▸ *For listings, see pages 400-401.*

Makambako ▸▸ *Colour map 1, C4.*

About halfway between Iringa and Mbeya, Makambako developed because of its station on the Tanzania–Zambia Railway and because it is a stop for road traffic passing through from Zambia. It is also at the intersection with the road to Njombe and Songea. It is not a pleasant place to stay, however, and the much more friendly and amenable Njombe is only 60 km to the south on a good surfaced road. If you do stay, there are several cheap hotels and a Lutheran church hostel, but only the comfortable **Uplands Hotel** offers a good degree of safety and food. The railway canteen also offers good food during the day and there are other cheap local restaurants.

Njombe ●❷❸❹ ▸▸ *pp400-401. Colour map 1, C4. 9°20'S 34°50'E.*

→ *Phone code: 026.*
Set among attractive green rolling highlands, Njombe is an undistinguished Tanzanian town in a wonderful location. The surrounding hills are excellent walking country and are easily accessible from the town. Being 1859 m above sea level the climate here is cool all year round. There are several wattle and tea plantations in Njombe district, some of which can be seen on the road between Iringa and Mbeya. The town was set up in rich farming country of the Southern Highlands, possibly because of the aerodrome, an early refuelling point en route to South Africa. Nearby is a spectacular **waterfall**, within an easy walking distance north on the road to Makambako, and wattle estates and a tanning factory on the hill opposite (Kibena). The Anglican Universities' Mission to Central Africa (UMCA) Diocesan HQ, Bishop's House and cathedral are worth a visit – Njombe is very much the centre of missionary activity and the old town hotel was bought by the mission. There is a single high street with a few shops and not much else.

Songea ●❷❸❹ ▸▸ *pp400-401. Colour map 1, C4. 10°40'S 35°40'E.*

→ *Phone code: 025. Altitude: 4000 ft.*
The provincial headquarters of Southern Province, Songea, northeast of Mbamba Bay on Lake Nyasa and 540 km south of the Makambako junction, was comparatively isolated until the construction of the sealed road. Tobacco is the main cash crop in the area, although Mbinga, to the south, is an important centre for coffee growing. It was named

after the Ngoni chief of the same name. It's a pleasant enough place, although there is little to keep you in the town itself, but it is surrounded by attractive rolling countryside and hills, which are good for walking in. Matogoro peak, in part of the **Matogoro forest reserve**, is within easy reach to the southeast of the town – take one of the tracks leading off the road to Tunduru. There are fine views from the top.

Songea and the surrounding area is home to the Ngoni, a group descended from an offshoot of the Zulus who came from South Africa in the mid-19th century fleeing the rule of King Chaka in about 1840. The Ngoni had to fight several tribes in the area to establish a foothold. They were hunters and farmers and later on strongly resisted the German colonial settlement. From 1905-1907, there was an extensive two-year insurgence against the Germans, triggered by the harsh working conditions in the cotton plantations. It was known as the Maji Maji Rebellion and was led by a witch-doctor named Kinjekitile, who told his followers that with the help of his magic potion, which could transform bullets into water, they would be invincible. Warriers shouted '*maji maji*' (meaning 'water water'), while going into battle armed only with swords, pangas and clubs, convinced that in doing so they would disable the German arms. The rebellion was finally suppressed locally when the Ngoni chiefs were all hanged in Songea by the Germans in 1907. The tree used to execute the local chieftains survives.

Mbamba Bay ⬤🅿🅕🅖 ⤐ *pp400-401. Colour map 1, C4. 11°13′S 34°49′E.*

The route from Songea to Mbamba Bay is very scenic, passing up, down and around the green hills and mountains surrounding Mbinga before descending to Lake Nyasa. The road is bad, however, and the journey is pretty awful in the rainy season. In the dry season there are sometimes buses from Songea that leave very early in the morning, but mostly

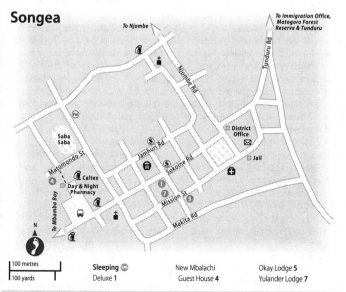

Songea

To Njombe

To Immigration Office, Matogoro Forest Reserve & Tunduru

Njombe Rd

Tunduru Rd

Saba Saba

Matomondo St

Jamhuri Rd

District Office

Jail

Sokoine Rd

Caltex

Day & Night Pharmacy

To Mbamba Bay

Mission St

Makita Rd

N

100 metres
100 yards

Sleeping 🛏	New Mbalachi	Okay Lodge **5**
Deluxe **1**	Guest House **4**	Yulander Lodge **7**

local landrovers make the journey, and then only sporadically so. The only option is to get as far as Songea and wait for transport.

Mbamba Bay (known in the German colonial period as Sphinxhaven) is a modest village on a glorious bay surrounded by hills on the eastern shore of Lake Nyasa (to Malawians, Lake Malawi). Most people coming to Mbamba Bay will be here to connect with (or arriving on) the ferries (*ëmeli*) going north to Itungi or across the lake to Nkhata Bay in Malawi and will probably only stay overnight. The scenic surroundings of Mbamba Bay, however, may well entice you into waiting for a later ferry. Many of the houses here are made in the traditional style with sun-dried, baked bricks, topped with thatch made from a long grass called *nyasi*. There's nothing much to do, but what a setting for doing nothing. If Mbamba Bay was in Malawi the place would be heaving with tourists, as it is you're likely to have the place to yourself. The magnificent **Mohalo Beach**, reportedly over 20 km in length, lies 4-5 km south of Mbamba Bay. It can be reached by walking along the road to Mbinga and taking a right at the junction after 1.5 km or so, or alternatively by hiring a dug-out canoe to take you around the headland (this takes about 45 minutes). It is an ideal place for camping. There is another long beach to the north of the village.

◉ Tanzam Highway to Lake Nyasa listings

For Sleeping and Eating price codes and other relevant information, see pages 36-40.

● Sleeping

Njombe *p398*

A number of basic guesthouses can be found around the bus stand.

F Chani, 10 mins walk north of the centre, T026-278 2357. Offers 8 double and 4 single rooms with en suite showers and toilets, some rooms are carpeted, regularly used by Peace Corps volunteers. Bar and good restaurant, but there is often a long wait for food, an hour or more, even if you pre-order.

F Milimani Hotel, near the post office, T026-278 2408. Offers 20 spacious double rooms, some a little larger than others, each with a bathroom and hot shower. Seating in the bar is arranged like a cinema, facing a satellite TV screen, popular with locals especially when football is showing. The restaurant serves tasty, generously portioned meals but you should pre-order. Excellent value.

Songea *p398, map p399*

There are few accommodation options in Songea and these are limited to half a dozen nondescript basic local guesthouses. The best of the bunch are listed below.

F The Deluxe Hotel, Sokoine Rd, opposite the market. Cheap and not so cheerful rooms on 2 storeys with mosquito nets.

F New Mbalachi Guest House, very close to the bus stand, go to the back of the bus stand and walk down the passageway between the Caltex pumps and Day & Night dispensary. Very clean rooms with nets.

F Okay Lodge, 1 block south of the market, T025-260 2640. Good doubles with bathrooms. Food and beer is available.

F Yulander Lodge, opposite Okay Lodge. Spotless, spacious rooms with bathroom.

Mbamba Bay *p399*

Accommodation is very limited. There are a few basic lodging houses offering very ordinary rooms for under US$10, including the Satellite and the Mabuyu guesthouses.

F Nema Beach Guest House, on its own beach about 1.5 km from the centre of the village. The best place for longer stays but inconvenient for overnights. Very good clean rooms with bathrooms. There is also a bar restaurant and pharmacy here.

🍴 Eating

Njombe p398

For a town of its size Njombe is particularly poorly served for restaurants – but then you won't have come here for the cuisine. Good simple meals are available from the restaurants at the hotels (see Sleeping, above).

Songea p398, map p399

Most guesthouses have small restaurants but the best is probably the restaurant at the Okay Lodge (see Sleeping, above), which does decent simple meals such as fish and chips or *ugali* and stew.

Mbamba Bay p399

Food is very limited, there is one restaurant at the Nema Beach Guesthouse House (see Sleeping, above), which isn't bad, but it's inconvenient if you're not staying there.

🚌 Transport

Njombe p398
Bus

To Dar, 2 direct buses daily leaving 0500-0600 (9-10 hrs, US$18). To Songea, Iringa and Mbeya: there are numerous buses daily, they all take around 3-4 hrs and cost around US$7. The bus stand is very busy, watch out for theft.

Songea p398, map p399
Car

To Mozambique Vehicles can cross a new bridge (yet to be officially opened) from Kivikoni to Congresso (Lupilichi). Visas are not available at the border and must be obtained in Dar beforehand. There are immigration facilities in Songea (see opposite). For up-to-date information, see www.mozguide.com. For further information on travelling to Mozambique, see border box, page 153.

Bus

There are several buses daily to Dar all leaving early. The journey takes around 12 hrs and costs US$30.There are 3 buses daily to Mbeya, 6-7 hrs, US$14. Buses to Njombe are numerous, 3-4 hrs, US$8. On both of these routes buses go when full. To Mbamba Bay (outside the rainy season) there are 2 daily buses leaving between 0600-0700 (8-10 hrs, US$10). Book a seat the day before. There is at least 1 bus leaving Songea for Tunduru early every other morning, US$14. Try to book a seat in front of the back axle in view of the appalling state of the roads.

Mbamba Bay p399
Bus

The 170 km road to Songea is very rough in parts and the bridges are occasionally severely damaged. It is very slow and becomes treacherous in the wet.

Ferry

The ferry journey up the lake to Itungi, cruises along the eastern shore of Lake Nyasa with the impressive Livingstone Mountains looming in the background. For details of ferries on Lake Nyasa see box page 411.

📁 Directory

Songea p398, map p399
Customs and immigration Customs office within the post office. **Immigration Office**, in the Ministry of Finance Building on Tunduru Rd, if you arrive from or are heading to Mozambique and need your passport stamped. **Post office** Mission St.

Mbeya and around

→ *Colour map 1, C3. 8° 54'S, 33° 29'E. Phone code: 025. Population: 160,000. Altitude: 1737 m.*
Near the Zambian border deep in the southern highlands, the city of Mbeya is the major agricultural capital in the country's southwest region. The Mbeya mountain range lies to the north, and the Poroto mountain range lies to the southeast. Large coffee and tea plantations, banana farms, and fields of cocoa are all grown around the region and come to Mbeya for packaging and transport. Mbeya's location also makes it an ideal transit point for good travelling by road and rail between Tanzania and neighbouring Zambia and Malawi. Other towns in the Mbeya region worth heading for are Tukuyu, on the road to the border with Malawi, which offers good trekking in the surrounding hills, and Matema, on the shores of Lake Nyasa, a remote and traditional settlement with spectacular lakeside scenery.
▶▶ *For listings, see pages 407-412.*

Mbeya ●🔒🅿️🏔️🏤🅲 ▶▶ *pp407-412.*

The town was founded in the late 1920s when the gold mines at Lupa became active, and continued to grow after they closed in 1956. However, recent international exploration of five licensed sites of an 150-sq km area near the town of Makongolosi, to the north of the old **Lupa Goldfields**, have indicated that there are still significant deposits of gold, silver, copper and diamonds, which it may prove economically viable to extract.

Mbeya has developed into a bustling, if a little rundown, town and is an ideal base from which to explore the Southern Highlands. Being only 114 km from the Zambian border and the last main station on the TAZARA railway line makes it a popular overnight stop and important trading centre. However, remember that it's still 875 km from Dar es Salaam and was rather isolated until the construction of the railway and the sealed road.

Excursions and walking

Although there is little of interest in Mbeya itself, it is an excellent point from which to make excursions into the outstandingly beautiful surrounding countryside. There are endless options, particularly for hikers and cyclists. Tourism is still a micro industry in this region which may explain the laid-back and unobtrusive approach of the available tour guides. ▶▶ *To organize a guide, see Activities and tours, page 409.*

Between Mbeya and Lake Rukwa is the small town of **Galula**, at the northern end of the Songwe River Valley. Galula has an imposing Catholic church built by the French White Fathers. Nearby are lake deposits indicative of a previously much larger lake and evidence of Iron Age and Late Stone Age sites have been found on the river terraces. At **Mapogoro**, northeast of the Lupa Goldfields, close to the village of Njelenje, volcanic **rock shelters** were identified in 1990 by researchers from the University of Alberta. Many artefacts of the Late Stone Age were found.

The **Mbozi Meteorite** is a 12-tonne mass, believed to be the eighth largest in the world and to have landed over 1000 years ago. The meteor is roughly rectangular in shape and approximately 5 m in diameter. There is evidence that many small samples have been removed for analysis judging from what appear to be saw indentations in several places. It is 40 km southwest of Mbeya, along the road to Zambia; take the turning off just after Mbowa, it's a good 10-15 km from the highway.

The **Ngozi Crater Lake**, 38 km south of Mbeya, is worth a visit but you will need a guide to get there, see page 405.

Walking This is walking country and you will be able to get some tremendous views of the surrounding countryside. The mountain to the north of the town and part of the Mbeya Range is **Kaluwe** (known as Loleza Peak) and rises to 2656 m. It can be reached in about two hours and is well worth it if you have a spare afternoon. The view from the summit is breathtaking and if you enjoy a good romp the pathway is quite rugged and steep. The hillsides are dotted with wild flowers and the peace is only disturbed by the bells of cattle and birdsong. From Mbeya turn right just after the Catholic cathedral and mission and head straight – find the path that leads up a slope and follow it (it passes a number of Christian monuments and crosses along the way). This leads to the summit.

Mbeya Peak, rising to 2826 m, is the highest peak in the range and looms to the north above the town. There are two possible routes, one harder than the other. The first is down a track about 13 km down the Chunya Road. From the end of this track the climb will take about one hour, including a walk through eucalyptus forest and high grass.

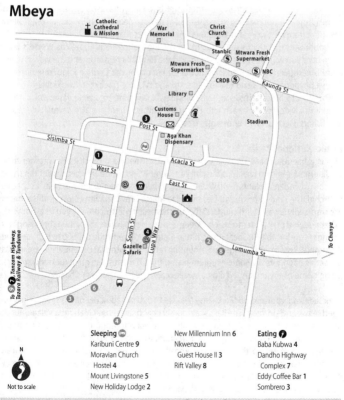

Mbeya

Catholic Cathedral & Mission
War Memorial
Christ Church
Stanbic
Mtwara Fresh Supermarket
Mtwara Fresh Supermarket
NBC
CRDB
Kaunda St
Library
Customs House
Stadium
Post St
Aga Khan Dispensary
Sisimba St
Pol
Acacia St
West St
East St
South St
Lupa Way
Gazelle Safaris
Lumumba St
To Tanzam Highway, Tazara Railway & Tunduma
To Chunya

N
Not to scale

Sleeping
Karibuni Centre **9**
Moravian Church
  Hostel **4**
Mount Livingstone **5**
New Holiday Lodge **2**

New Millennium Inn **6**
Nkwenzulu
  Guest House II **3**
Rift Valley **8**

Eating
Baba Kubwa **4**
Dandho Highway
  Complex **7**
Eddy Coffee Bar **1**
Sombrero **3**

Border essentials: Tanzania–Zambia

Mbeya–Tunduma

There are frequent small buses from Mybeya to the Zambian border at Tunduma, these take two hours and cost US$2.50. Through buses for Zambia pass through Mbeya at around 1500, having come from Dar, and head on through to Lusaka (Zambia) arriving there at 0600 the following morning. However, the large buses can get stuck at the border for a considerable time and there are often delays.

Note It is possible to cross into Zambia by train, see page 412 for further information.

The second, and more difficult route, is only recommended for those prepared for a steep climb and, in parts, a real scramble. This begins from the coffee farm at Luiji. There is very good accommodation here at the **Utengele Coffee Lodge** (see Sleeping, page 407). At the top you can catch your breath and admire the view for miles around.

Another worthwhile, but also energetic trek is to **Pungulume** (2230 m) at the west end of the range. It is approached from the road at its base near Njerenji. Alternatively, follow the ridge from Mbeya Peak. (Avoid this trek in the wet season.)

Probably one of the best viewpoints in the Mbeya Range is known as **World's End**. From here you will see the Usangu Flats and the Rift Valley Escarpment; the view is really quite breathtaking. To get to it go about 20 km down the Chunya Road, due north of Mbeya beyond World's End to a forest camp and take the track off to the right.

The **Poroto Mountains**, southeast of Mbeya, are home to a wide variety of birdlife, including Livingstone's turaco and the green barbet. There are also several species of kingfishers, woodpeckers and eagles (see below).

Kitulo National Park

This is a beautiful park, unusually primarily established to protect its flora rather than wildlife, and is known locally as Bustani ya Mungu – God's Garden – because of the sheer number of endemic plants here. With over 350 species of plants, among them 45 species of orchid, the landscape during December to March is awash with colour, but the paths are also sadly awash with mud. It's by far the best time to come if you're a botanist, otherwise you may prefer to visit between September to November when the hiking will be more comfortable. Its location on Kitulo Plateau at an altitude of 2600 m between the Kipengere, Poroto and Livingstone mountain ranges ensure that distant views are just as attractive and there are some excellent hiking trails here. It's also great for birdwatchers, being home to the endangered blue swallow and the rare Denham's bustard.

Park fees and information Park entry fees are US$20 per adult per day, US$5 for children aged between 5-16 years. The Park's temporary headquarters is at Matamba Village, about an hour's drive from the plateau, and is reached via a twisting dirt road from Chimala, off the main Mbeya–Dar es Salaam road. (Matamba is about 100 km from Mbeya.) TANAPA are planning to set up three special campsites in the park, but at present the nearest accommodation is fairly basic, at the adjacent Kitulo Farm. Otherwise, it's a long journey back to Mbeya or Matema. For further information on the park, contact TANAPA on T027-250 3471, or look at www.tanzaniaparks.com.

TAZARA railway

The TAZARA (Tanzania and Zambia Railway Authority) railway runs from Dar es Salaam to Kapiri Moshi in Zambia. It was built by the Chinese between 1970-1975 and is an impressive feat of engineering. The track covers 1870 km, and it passes over 300 bridges, through 23 tunnels and past 147 stations. At a cost of US$230 million, this was the largest railway project at the time since the Second World War. The railway was Zambia's answer to the closure of its routes to Southern African ports as a result of Rhodesia's Unilateral Declaration of Independence in 1965. Initially, it was meant to handle all of landlocked Zambia's freight, and it did. But since the reopening of the southern routes following independence in Mozambique in 1975 and the coming of majority rule in Zimbabwe in 1980, Zambia's dependency on the Dar es Salaam port has lessened. As a result, the volume of cargo along the railway has been considerably reduced. However, its passenger trains, built to carry 600-plus people, are almost always full to capacity, and for people living along the route, the train is the cheapest and most convenient link to the rest of Zambia or Tanzania. The railway is also a lifeline to villagers living along its route. When they hear the train coming, people bearing baskets full of red onions, potatoes, rice, bananas, tomatoes, plantains and oranges rush to meet it.

Tukuyu ◎▲◉◐ ⟫ pp407-412. 9° 17'S, 33° 35'E. Colour map 1, C3.

→ Altitude: 1615 m.

This is a small town about 40 km south of Mbeya, on the road to Lake Nyasa. It was an administrative centre for the Germans and there is a group of colonial buildings to the southeast of the town, but all in all it's a pretty dreary place and appears quite bleak when hidden under swirling mists. On the other hand, it has a glorious location in the scenic **Poroto Mountains**. There's nothing to keep you in the town itself but a great deal to see in the surrounding countryside. The dark volcanic soils provide a fertile productive region swathed in banana trees and fresh mountain air. Tukuyu is an important tea-growing area and the road to Kyela is lined with the picturesque fields of plantations.

Trekking

Tukuyu is a good centre for trekking but it is necessary to engage a guide (see Activities and tours, page 409). Among the local attractions are **Mount Rungwe**, the most important mountain in this area, and at 2961 m the highest mountain in southern Tanzania. Its slopes are vast and wild with over 100 sq km of uninhabited forest, upland scrub and rock terrain. It is accessed from Isangole, 10 km north of Tukuyu, and will take at least a full day to climb. Other attractions are the **Masoko Crater Lake**, 15 km to the southwest, and the **Kaporogwe Falls**, south of Tukuyu, which are around 40 m high and in an attractive lush setting. Halfway down there is a cave behind the falls, which it is possible to enter. There's good swimming at the bottom in the pool the falls cascade into. To reach them go about 6 km down the main road towards Kyela to the Ushirika Village bus stop. From there it's about 2½ hours to walk or you can hire a bicycle at the main road (with or without rider).

Ngozi Crater Lake, about 20 km north of Tukuyu in the Poroto Mountains, is a beautiful lake lying in the collapsed crater of an extinct volcano the sides of which plunge down steeply from a rainforest-covered rim. The forest is home to colonies of colobus monkeys. Witch-doctors are said to call upon ancestral powers here and local legend claims that there is an underwater snake-like monster hidden deep in the waters of the lake, causing the surface waters to change colour from time to time. To get there catch a *dala-dala* going to Mbeya up to Mchangani Village (this takes 1-1½ hours). It's advisable to arrange for a guide at Mchangani to take you up to the lake as the route is by no means obvious. It's a two-hour walk from the main road to Ngozi. The second half of the walk entails a steep climb through rainforest before you emerge at the crater rim. From here the views across the lake are spectacular. You could camp at the top, in which case you would be there for sunset and dawn.

Daraja la Mungu (Bridge of God), also known as Kiwira Natural Bridge, is an unusual rock formation spanning a small river close to Tukuyu. To get there take a *dala-dala* going to Mbeya and get off at Kibwe (12 km north of Tukuyu). Here change to one of the Land Rovers waiting at the beginning of the road branching off to the left (ask for Daraja la Mungu). It's a further 12 km down this rough road. There are apparently also hot springs (*maji ya moto*) a little further on and nearby is Kijunga waterfall.

Kyela ⬤🕐🕑 ▸▸ *pp407-412. Colour map 1, C3.*

Kyela is a small commercial centre northwest of Lake Nyasa and the nearest town to the Malawi border. The surrounding countryside is fertile, abounding with banana plants, mango trees, maize, bamboo and also rice, particularly prized throughout Tanzania and much of it being transported to Dar es Salaam after harvest. Unfortunately, the town itself doesn't match its attractive surroundings; it is dusty and characterless and on arrival you'll probably be keen to get out as soon as possible. However, if you're hoping to catch the ferry to Mbamba Bay or Nkhata Bay (in Malawi) at least one night in Kyela is necessary, as this is the access town for the ferries that leave from Itungi.

Matema ⬤🕐 ▸▸ *pp407-412. Colour map 1, C3.*

Matema is the secret paradise of the southwest of Tanzania and a walk along the lakeshore here will simply take your breath away. The slopes of the Livingstone Mountains – vertiginous rock, meadows and plunging waterfalls – provide a backdrop for the blue waters and sandy beaches of the lakeshore. Although not the easiest place to reach (largely because of the difficulty in getting there by public transport, vehicles to Matema are painfully slow, uncomfortable and extraordinarily over-crowded) don't be put off by tales of woe – it is well worth the trip. To get there, turn off to the left just before the Malawi border where a gravel road takes you to Matema. The village itself is very friendly, with banana trees and flowers and pigs, dogs and chickens milling around. In the market bamboo wine is drunk literally by the bucket load, and grilled meat (especially pork) is offered by the vendors.

A walk along the mountainside to the village of **Ikombe**, the site of a former mission, is a highly recommended excursion. The mountainside comprises steep slopes and deep valleys which are home to fresh mountain streams, butterflies and wild flowers. Alternatively, it is possible to hire a dugout canoe which takes 30 minutes each way between Matema and Ikombe depending on the wind. Enquire locally about excursions and you will be sure to find a willing and helpful guide who will ensure that the relevant permission is sought. The beach is safe for swimming, and reportedly clear of bilharzia,

Border essentials: Tanzania–Malawi

Kyela (Tanzania)–Karonga (Malawi)

Warning Touts are a real problem around the bus station in **Mbeya**, don't fall for the scam of buying a ticket all the way to Malawi – at the time of writing, no buses from Mbeya actually cross the border and you end up paying for the whole trip but only going as far as Kyela – the touts promise that a bus will meet you at the Malawian side of the border, but of course, it never materializes.

There are frequent buses to **Kyela** (close to Lake Nyasa) from Mbeya, these take three hours and cost US$3. Ask to be dropped off at the turn-off to the border before you reach the town of Kyela. From there it is about 5 km to the border and you should be able to get a lift or a bicycle taxi. Locals will be clamouring to carry your luggage, change your money and show you the way although there is often a price to pay. Some of the minibuses to **Mbeya** go via the border (30 minutes, US$1) but it is far more convenient to take a taxi, which only takes 5-10 minutes. Private taxis cost US$5, or there are shared taxis which squeeze six passengers and associated luggage into a five-seater vehicle for US$1 per person. Shared taxis leave from the corner opposite the Pattaya Guest House on the right hand side (as if you're heading for the TAZARA office).

After Tanzanian immigration formalities you cross the bridge over the Songwe River to the Malawi immigration on the other side. It's a friendly border. Your yellow fever card may be checked. A few minutes' walk from the immigration office is a bus stand where you can pick up a bus to **Karonga** (approximately two hours, US$1, paid in Malawi Kwacha). From Karonga public transport continues on to Mzuzu, Lilongwe and Blantyre.

Note Malawi is one hour behind Tanzanian time.

---

but check locally. There are supposed to be hippos and crocodiles in the river that flows into the lake about 3 km or so west of the village. It is a pleasant walk along the beach.

The **Wakisi**, one of the peoples who make up the population of the surrounding area, are well known throughout Tanzania for their pottery skills. The role of the Wakisi women is not only to raise and rear children, farm, and look after the home but also to make the pots – a woman's skill affects her ability to marry. In the market in Matema large piles of Wakisi pots can be seen bound up awaiting transportation to Mbeya, Iringa and even as far away as Dar es Salaam. The Saturday market in Lyulilo attracts buyers from all over the region.

⊚ Mbeya and around listings

For Sleeping and Eating price codes and other relevant information, see pages 36-40.

⊜ Sleeping

Mbeya *p402, map p403*
C-E Utengule Coffee Lodge, 20 km north-west of Mbeya on a coffee estate beneath

Mbeya Peak and 90 km from the Zambian border, T0753-020901 (mob), www.riftvalley-zanzibar.com. The signposted turning is roughly 12 km from Mbeya on the main road, it is then about another 8 km to the hotel. A charming country lodge, with restaurant, bar, 16 comfortable rooms and very good food. It has a swimming pool, squash and tennis court, and hires out mountain bikes. Camping is also available at US$10. A good base for excursions into the mountains, for which the lodge can arrange guides.

D Mount Livingstone Hotel, opposite mosque on Lumumba St, T0713-323906 (mob), www.twiga.ch/TZ/mtlivingstone.htm Possibly Mbeya's most established hotel, centrally located, private drive and pleasant gardens. All rooms have bathrooms with hot water and TV. Clean, comfortable, professionally run and recently renovated. The bar has an extensive wine and cocktail list, good food in the restaurant. Double rooms from US$65. Camping is also available. Accepts payment in €, £ and US$.

E Nkwenzulu Guest House II, set back from the main road close to the bus stand, T025-250 2225. A little more secure than the other nearby guesthouses, with high walls and iron gates. Garden with seating and umbrellas. All rooms have bathrooms, hot water and nets. Breakfast included in the price.

E Rift Valley, town centre, T025-250 4351, www.twiga.ch/TZ/riftvalley.htm. Multi-storey hotel with 75 en suite rooms. Doubles from US$20. Restaurant and bar with reasonably priced main courses. Rates include breakfast.

E-F Karibuni Centre, 500 m off the Tanzam highway at the Mbalizi Evangelical Church, T025-250 3035, www.twiga.ch/TZ/karibuni center.htm. Run by a Swiss missionary in a forest area. In a clean and peaceful setting, good simple food in the restaurant (Mon-Sat), safe car parking. Also has a small guesthouse with rooms for less than US$10 and camping facilities (US$3 per tent). The church runs a school for mechanics, so this is a good place for vehicle repairs.

F Moravian Church Hostel, from the bus station, head up the hill directly opposite and follow the path round, T025-250 3263. Very clean and friendly, twin rooms only, good security with safe parking for vehicles. If you are catching an early bus you can pay an *askari* to accompany you.

F New Holiday Lodge, central, near Rift Valley Hotel, T025-250 2821. Doubles only,

with or without bathrooms, TVs available for extra. Clean, a little old-fashioned but pleasant with friendly staff and restaurant and veranda at the front.

F New Millennium Inn, opposite the main bus stand, T025-250 0599. A Greek-style villa with secure private parking. Very convenient for early starts or late arrivals. Rooms have hot water and mosquito nets. Friendly staff and beautifully tended garden, no bar or restaurant.

Tukuyu *p405*

E-F Landmark Hotel, in the centre of town at the main crossroads, T025-255 2450. This impressively smart modern hotel is an unexpected find, with a large manicured garden, mirrored windows and shining granite-topped reception desk. Friendly and professional staff who speak a wide range of European languages. Modern rooms with satellite TV, phones and hot water. Camping available for under US$10. Bar, large restaurant with a reasonable menu, and private car park. Breakfast included.

F Langiboss Hotel, about 1 km from the town centre on the road to Masoko, T025-255 2080. Basic accommodation but in a stunning location. Rooms with or without bathrooms, clean and simple, food can be arranged with notice, well stocked bar not to mention the year round Christmas decorations. Staff also arrange tours in the local area.

Kyela *p406*

There are several basic guesthouses in the centre offering a bed in a bare room and shared bathroom for around U$5. These include: Bikutuka Guest House, Kilimanjaro Guest House, and Livingstone Cottage.

F Gwakisa Guest House, on the same road near the market, T025-254 0029. Clean and efficiently family-run guesthouse which offers secure, pleasant rooms with mosquito nets and fans. Double US$5, single US$3.

F Pattaya Central, opposite the bus stand, T025-254 0015. The best of all. Has spotless rooms, all with fans and hot water but no mosquito nets. The only drawback may be the noise resulting from its central location.

Matema *p406*
E-F Matema Lake Shore Resort, signposted from the village, on the beach, T025-250 4178, www.twiga.ch/TZ/matemaresort.htm. Popular with expats, spotlessly clean and well run, offers a variety of accommodation, from beachfront chalets sleeping up to 5 with private verandas (US$28), to double rooms with shared bathrooms (US$10). The beach is raked and cleaned daily with palms planted to create some privacy for sunbathing. Good restaurant. No alcohol available.
E-F Matema Lutheran Guest House, centre of the village, T0787-275164 (mob). Guesthouse in superb location with 8 good rooms, some have up to 5 beds and are ideal for families. Also has good value accommodation in bandas. Simple and spotlessly clean. It's possible to camp. US$10 per person and up to US$30 for a double, breakfast included.

♦ Eating

Mbeya *p402, map p403*
♦♦ **Dandho Highway Complex**, outside town on the highway to the east of the turn off to Mbeya, T025-250 0838. Large-scale project started by a local businessman, although far from completion. A variety of buildings built around a central thatched banda with restaurant and bar, swimming pool (US$1.50) and in the future accommodation. Food includes meat and fish dishes, and bar snacks. Also live music and disco.
♦♦ **Mount Livingstone Hotel**, see Sleeping, above. The best place to eat in town with a great choice of seafood, meat grills and Mediterranean dishes from US$5. Extensive wine and cocktail menu suggest that there's potential for a fun night out.
♦ **Baba Kubwa**, just off Lupa Way. Indian-run café with a wide variety of Indian and African dishes and snacks, also cold beers. The outside area is popular in the evenings.

♦ **Eddy Coffee Bar**, Sisimba St, near the market. Reasonably priced local dishes, licensed restaurant, satellite TV, some outdoor seating.
♦ **Sombrero**, just off Post St, near customs house and library. Diner-style restaurant with fixed seats. Whilst waiting for food you can admire the peculiar tardis-like glass locked bar. A variety of Indian and African dishes.

Kyela *p406*
♦ **New Steak Inn**, near the market. Surprisingly plush restaurant for a Tanzanian town of this size. It does good basic dishes like chicken and chips and a variety of snacks. Very popular with locals and has a healthy buzz.

○ Shopping

Mbeya *p402, map p403*
Mtwara Fresh, is a locally run supermarket with outlets in the centre of town. Packed and fresh produce, including brown bread and cheese, friendly staff and open until late. Worth a visit if planning a picnic.

For souvenirs there are a variety of craft stalls on the walk from the main bus stand to the town and on Kaunda St near the banks.

▲ Activities and tours

Mbeya *p402, map p403*
Gazelle Safaris, Lupa Way, south from the market, T025-250 2482, www.gazellesafaris. com. A British/Tanzanian operation that organizes everything from local day trips and hikes to safaris across Tanzania. They also arrange flights and car hire.
Peter's Walking Adventure Tours, South St, T0755-075552 (mob), peterwalkingtours@ hotmail.com. Peter Nsopela is a highly enterprising and enthusiastic local guide who has set up business on his own. Occasionally Peter takes on work for **Sisi Kwa Sisi** and has been recommended by Sisi Kwa Sisi, amongst many others, as a reputable and fun guide.

Offers guided trips to all sites of local interest. A 1-day trip costs between US$15-25.

Sisi Kwa Sisi Society, near the Memorial of Friendship with Japan, on the walk from the bus station towards town, T0744-463471 (mob), www.twiga.ch/TZ/tourguideeg.htm. Theoretically open daily from 0800-1800, although during the 'low season' the hours may be revised. Literally meaning 'Us for Us', it is an affiliated partner of the Cultural Tourism Programmes of the north of Tanzania. Like those programmes, Sisi Kwa Sisi offers tours of the area and uses profits to help the local community, in this case through agricultural projects. Tours offered include visits to all attractions in the Mbeya, Tukuyu and Matema areas, with the chance to experience the traditional local cultures. The guides speak good English, and some speak French and German. The office provides a variety of information with maps, and a book-swap library. The staff are a wealth of local information. Depending on transport an average day trip costs US$15-20 per person. Further details from the Tanzanian tourist information centre in Arusha, see page 259 or www.infojep.com/culturaltours.

Tukuyu *p405*
Langiboss Hotel, see Sleeping, above. Staff here can arrange tours in the local area and organize guides for trekking.
Rungwe Tea & Tours, near the post office, T025-255 2489, www.rungweteatours.com. A community based tour operation with profits benefiting local villages. Tours include visits to local tea farms and attractions, including Mt Rungwe, Ngozi Crater Lake and Kaporogwe Falls. Good reports, friendly staff and knowledgeable guides.

⊙ Transport

Mbeya *p402, map p403*
Air
Work on building Songwe International Airport had halted for some time but is now expected to be completed by the end of 2009. It is 20 km south of Mbeya. There is also a small airfield about 5 km south of Mbeya which operates infrequent charter flights.

Bus
Touts are a real problem around the bus station here and will do their utmost to sell you tickets. Only buy tickets from the bus company offices and in particular, don't fall for the scam of buying a ticket all the way to **Malawi**, see border box, page 407.

Scandinavia Express, T025-250 4305, www.scandinaviagroup.com, buses are very regular to **Dar** via **Morogoro** (10-12 hrs, around US$26 luxury, US$20 semi-luxury and US$15 ordinary). Fixed departure times are 0630 and 0700. The road goes through the **Mikumi National Park** (see page 386). There are 2 buses a week to **Tabora** on a poor road, (24 hrs, US$10).

There are 3 buses daily to **Songea** (6-7 hrs, US$12). To **Njombe** buses leave several times a day (3-4 hrs, US$7). To **Iringa** (4-5 hrs, US$8) several times a day. To **Tunduma** buses leave frequently (1-2 hrs, US$3).

To Zambia For more information on getting to the Zambian border, see border box, page 404.

Train
The TAZARA railway station is outside the town on the Tanzam highway. The ticket office at the rather impressive glass station is open until 1700 Mon-Fri and 1300 Sat. Trains are often full and booking in advance is advised through the Tanzanian-Zambia Railway Authority in Dar, T022-286 5187, or www.tazara.co.tz for online reservations. In Mbeya, try and purchase tickets the day before travel as although it is possible on the day, the queues are long and chaotic. Currently the ordinary train to **Dar** departs on Tue at 1000 and arrives 24 hrs later. The express train departs on Wed and Sat at 1300 and arrives in Dar the following morning at 1000. 1st class US$21/25, 2nd Class US$15/18,

Ferries on Lake Nyasa

There is a ferry service of sorts between Itungi and Mbamba Bay and Nkhata Bay in Malawi on Lake Nyasa. The boats are run by **Marine Services Company**, based in Mwanza, Customer Information Centre T028-250 3079, www.marineservices tz.com, branch office in Kyela T0713-736681. However, the best source of information regarding sailing times are the local businessmen and traders who use the ferries regularly. If you can afford the time, take a trip to the port at Itungi itself, 10 km from Kyela on the lakeshore where the ferries go from, and ask there.

MV Songea

In theory, the *MV Songea* runs weekly, leaving Itungi port on Thursday at 1300. It travels around the lake, stopping frequently, as far as **Mbamba Bay** arriving on Friday at 0900, where it then crosses to **Nkhata Bay** in Malawi, arriving there on Saturday at 0800 and begins the return journey on Saturday at midday arriving in Itungi on Sunday at 1400.

Ticket information and facilities

Tickets can be bought on the day of travel, although the office advises booking in advance for first class tickets. However, the unreliable nature of services would suggest that you don't part with any money until the day of travel is a dead cert. Tickets can be bought at the port and arriving several hours before the estimated time of departure will ensure that you have time to buy tickets and read several novels before there's even a hint of movement. A first class ticket to Mbamba Bay will

cost about US$20. First class cabins are for two people and are small but comfortable. Try to get a cabin facing the lake-shore. In third class you get a wooden bench if you're lucky and plenty of company. Many passengers end up sleeping on the floor so be prepared (second class seems to have disappeared) Food and drink is theoretically available on board, but don't count on it.

Note As ever, these timetables can be a work of fiction – there are frequent delays and on occasions, the boat simply won't run at all. In its absence crossing the lake is not easy (private boats cross very infrequently), so it is not advisable to rely on boat travel between Tanzania and Malawi. If you do get across the lake then there is an immigration office in Mbamba Bay where you can get an exit stamp from Tanzania or buy an entry visa.

MV Iringa

MV Iringa, run by the same company as *MV Songea*, skirts the Tanzanian side of the lake only, stopping at various villages between **Itungi** and **Manda**, leaving Itungi Monday 1000 to reach Manda at 1200, departing again Tuesday 0300 and returning to Itungi Tuesday 1600. Again, the same words of caution about reliability and conditions apply.

If you can cope with these uncertainties, however, travelling on the lake is a great way to get a slice of local life and at the same time take in some of the beautiful shoreline scenery.

Becky Stickland and Sue Watt

3rd Class US$12/15 for ordinary/express trains respectively. The route between Mbeya and Dar passes through lovely countryside. However, the frequent stops

and jerky motions involved in braking and acceleration, mean that the journey is quite a tiring experience.

To Zambia There are 2 express trains per week which terminate in **New Kapiri Moshi**, departing on Wed and Sat at 1200 arriving the following day at 0900. Passports and immigration matters are dealt with on the train. Fares vary from US$17-29 depending on which class you choose to travel in. At least 2nd class is advisable. Although the above are official departure times, after the multitude of children, boxes, chickens and associated needs of train travel are boarded, departure is usually delayed by a few hours. In 1st and 2nd class, bunks are provided, and there is a buffet carriage which provides reasonable food and beers etc, though it is advisable to take along some basic provisions.

Tukuyu *p405*
Bus
From **Mbeya** buses run regularly to **Kyela** and the Malawi border passing through Tukuyu. The 1½ hr journey from Mbeya costs US$1. Both **Scandinavia Express** and **Kilimanjaro Express** services run buses to **Dar** daily, reporting time is 0600, journey time around 11 hrs, and the fare is US$20. Ticket offices are found at the bus stand just off the main Mbeya-border road.

Kyela *p406*
Bus and pickup trucks
You have to be an early riser to catch a bus going to **Dar** (US$22-26, 13 hrs). They leave between 0440-0500 and pick up passengers at **Tukuyu** and sometimes **Mbeya** too. There are numerous minibuses going to **Mbeya**, which if you're very lucky will take 3 hrs, but normally more like 4 hrs, and can take up to 6 hrs or more. Most buses pass by the border and wait to fill up which can be a time-consuming process. Be prepared! It costs US$3. For **Tukuyu**, catch a bus going to Mbeya (US$1.50, 2-3 hrs). The bus to **Itungi** for the Nyasa ferry 30 mins, US$1.

To **Matema**, pickups leave at 0600, and the later you leave it the less chance you have of arriving on the same day due to

scant transport for the last leg of the journey between **Ipinda** and Matema. Pickup trucks run from the stand opposite the Gwambuzi Guest House and can be quite an adventure because of the bumpy roads (clinging to fellow passengers is necessary to avoid falling out). The pickups drop off in the small town of **Ipinda** and cost US$1. From here buses leave for Matema, 1-2 hrs, US$1.50 but are irregular and tend not to run after midday – aim to arrive early morning to ensure a link to Matema.

To Malawi For information on getting to the Malawi border, see box, page 407.

Matema *p406*
Bus and pickup trucks
From Matema to **Kyela**, transport is scarce and there is just 1 bus leaving the stand for **Ipinda** each day at 0600, which occasionally continues to Kyela. Once in Ipinda there are plenty of pickups to Kyela.

❶ Directory

Mbeya *p402, map p403*
Banks CRDB, Kaunda St; National Bank of Commerce, on the corner of Kaunda St, opposite the stadium, has reasonable rates and is the best place to cash TCs (they will change most major currencies, taking about 10 mins); Stanbic Bank, on the corner with Lupa Way. All have ATMs, CRDB's tend to offer a slightly better rate of exchange.
Internet Gazelle Safari Café, Lupa Way, US$1 per hr. **Medical services** Aga Khan Dispensary, Post St opposite the post office, T025-250 2043, for malaria testing and other minor ailments, provides an efficient service; Mbeya Medical Centre, the main state hospital in the region, T025-250 3571/3351.
Post office Near the library at the end of Post St.

Tukuyu *p405*
Banks National Bank of Commerce, Main St.

Contents

Footprint features

Background

History

Earliest times

From oral history, archaeology, linguistic analysis and anthropology (although no written records), a certain amount can be deduced about the early history of Tanzania. The Olduvai Gorge (see page 307) has become known as the cradle of mankind and the era of Australopithecine man probably lasted several million years. The bones of two types of hominids from the Australopithecine era found there have provided evidence of human evolution. These are *Zinjanthropus*, the 'Nutcracker Man' and *Homo habilis*, the 'Handy Man'. They lived together about 2 million years ago and until recently it was thought that *Homo habilis*, capable of using tools, evolved into *Homo erectus*, and then into modern man – *Homo sapiens*. But this is now under some debate as in 2001, in the Lake Turkana region of Kenya, a *Homo erectus* complete skull (1.4 million years old) was found within walking distance of an upper jaw of a *Homo habilis* (1.5 million years old). This proved that they must have lived in the region at the same time, and one theory now is that they have evolved from another, older common ancestor; a missing link that has not yet been found.

By about 500,000 years ago *Homo erectus* was on the scene (somewhere between the Australopithecine and *Homo sapiens* eras). The brain was larger and the hands more nimble and therefore better at making tools. The development of tool-making is clearly seen at Olduvai Gorge. The different layers of rock contain tools of different ages, which show the development from crude tools to more efficient and sharper implements. Another collection of such tools can be found at Isimila near Iringa (see page 392).

The Middle Stone Age saw the further development of hunter-gatherers who used tools, and were advanced in human ingenuity and craftsmanship and the use of fire. Progress accelerated in the Late Stone Age, which began about 100,000 years ago, and there are a number of sites from this era in Tanzania, particularly well known because they are the locations of rock painting.

The virtual disappearance of these people was a result of the migration and expansion of other people who were more numerous and more advanced. The most significant factor about these migrating people was that instead of being hunter-gatherers they were food producers – either by agriculture or by keeping livestock. They spoke the language of the Cushitic group (legendary biblical descendants of the Cush in Ethiopia, Somalia and north Sudan) and came from the north from around 1000 BC onwards. They did not have iron-working skills and this meant that the efficiency of their agriculture was limited.

Bantu migration

Later still, during the past 1000-2000 years, two other groups migrated into the area. These were both Negroid but were of different linguistic groups – the Bantu from the west and the Nilo-Hamite pastoralists from the north. A process of ethnic assimilation followed and the Cushitic intermarried with the newcomers and adopted their languages. The Bantu possessed important iron-processing skills, which greatly improved agricultural efficiency and this enabled population growth. There was not one single migration but a series of waves of various groups, expanding and contracting, assimilating and adapting. The present ethnic mix is as a result of this process over many centuries.

The most recent of the Nilotic migrations was by the Masai. By about the year 1800 they had reached the area around Dodoma where their advance was stopped by the Gogo and the Hehe (see page 428). Their reputation as a warrior tribe meant that the north part of Tanzania was largely avoided by slave traders and caravan routes.

As a result of these migrations north and central Tanzania has great ethnic diversity. In this part of the country there are Khoisan, Cushitic, Nilotic and Bantu-speaking peoples. The rest of the country is entirely Bantu speaking; indeed about 95% of Tanzanians born today are born into a family speaking one of the Bantu dialects. Swahili itself is a Bantu tongue and this has developed into the national language and as such is a significant unifying force.

Arab traders

Initially Swahili was a coastal language and developed as the language of trade. The earliest visitors to Tanzania were Arab traders who arrived on the coast, and their influence can be seen in the coastal settlements such as Kilwa (see page 135). By the 13th century there was a bustling trade on the coast. Initially the trade was dominated by the Persians, Arabs, Egyptians, Indians and Chinese but the Arab influence began to dominate and with it the spread of Islam. The major trading objects were gold, ivory and rhino horns, exchanged for guns, textiles and beads. These coastal towns were very much orientated towards the sea and away from the interior until the beginning of the 16th century when the development of long-distance trade led to more integration. Caravan routes began to extend from the coast to the Congo and Buganda.

Portuguese seafarers

By the mid-15th century the Portuguese had arrived on the scene. Vasco da Gama noted the beauty of Kilwa, and attempted to take control of the gold trade. The Portuguese were later expelled by the Arabs and the influence of the Arabs increased again. A period of reduced trading activity followed until the latter half of the 18th century when it flourished again, this time the commodity being slaves. Around 1776 the only trading route inland went southwest from Kilwa to the area around Lake Nyasa and this became increasingly important through the slave trade. During the 18th century Kilwa became East Africa's major slave-trading port, drawing first on the peoples of southeast Tanganyika and then on the Lake Nyasa area.

During the 19th century the trade pattern shifted as a result of the changes in the supply of ivory. During the first half of the century, most of the ivory had come from within what was to become Tanganyika. However, as Tanganyika's elephants were destroyed, so the price of ivory rose. Prices at Tabora are reported to have increased tenfold between 1846 and 1858 and the hunters began to look further afield, eventually leaving Tanganyika altogether. As the hunters moved away the chiefs in these areas lost their major source of revenue and it was this that led some of them to look to the new trade in slaves.

The slave trade

Caravan routes into the interior developed in the 19th century and trade centres developed at places such as Ujiji and Tabora. Humans and ivory were exchanged for guns, beads and cloth. The slaves were largely obtained by bartering with the local chiefs rather than by force. Some of the more militarized tribes raided their neighbours and 'prisoners of war' were then sold on to the Arabs as slaves. Convicted criminals were often sold as slaves and this penalty was sometimes extended to include their families.

The size of the slave trade remains a matter of speculation. However, it has been estimated that approximately 1,500,000 slaves from the interior reached the coast and 10 times that number died en route. Bagamoyo was a terminus of the trade and from there they were taken to Zanzibar, which developed into an important trading centre. The slaves were either put to work in the plantations of Pemba and Zanzibar or were shipped to the Middle East.

By the 1830s Zanzibar had become sufficiently prosperous from the sale of slaves and spices for the Omani Sultan Seyyid Said to move his capital from Muscat to Zanzibar. For some time Britain tried to suppress the slave trade by signing various agreements with the Omani Sultans but it was not until 1873 that the trade was officially abolished when an agreement was signed with Sultan Barghash (Seyyid Said's successor). However, this prohibition was implemented only slowly and the practice continued on the mainland for some years. By the 1880s the internal market for slaves had become more important than the external.

The first Europeans

The first Europeans in this part of Africa (since Vasco da Gama) were missionaries and explorers. In 1844 John Krapf, a German working for the Church Missionary Society of London, arrived in Zanzibar. He was joined by John Rebmann who was to become the first European to set eyes on Mount Kilimanjaro in 1848. The two British explorers Burton and Speke, sent by the Royal Geographical Society, arrived in Zanzibar in 1856 and journeyed along the caravan routes into the interior. In 1858 Speke came across the huge expanse of water, which he named Lake Victoria. Dr Livingstone was perhaps the most celebrated of all the missionaries, being found, after no news of him for several years, by HM Stanley, a newspaper reporter (see box, page 360).

By the 1880s considerable numbers of Europeans were arriving in East Africa as missionaries, big game hunters, traders and adventurers. Some had political ambitions, including two Germans, Carl Peters and HH Johnson, who wanted to see this part of Africa under the control of Germany. They formed the Society for German Colonization from which emerged the German East Africa Society. Emissaries of the Society signed 'protective treaties' with unsuspecting and often illiterate chiefs from the interior. These so-called treaties of friendship were then used by the German East Africa Company to exploit the areas that they covered with the apparent agreement of local authorities.

Both Germany and Britain made claims over East Africa, which were resolved by a series of agreements. The Berlin Conference of November 1884 to February 1885 was convened by Bismarck and was important in demarcating European spheres of influence in Africa. This saw the recognition of the German 'protective treaties' and by early 1885 several chiefdoms were formally placed under the control of the German East Africa Company. Three years later the Germans were shaken by an uprising of both Arabs and Africans and the German government took control in 1891. The Anglo-German Agreement of November 1886 defined the north boundary from the coast inland to Lake Victoria. A month later another agreement saw the defining of the boundary with Mozambique. These and various other treaties saw Zanzibar, Pemba and a 16-km coastal strip go to the Sultan under British Protectorate rule in 1890, while what is now mainland Tanzania, Rwanda and Burundi became German East Africa. But it was not until 1898 that German rule was secured and consolidated with the death of Mkwawa, chief of the Hehe who had resisted German domination.

Central and northern railways

The first railway to be constructed in Tanganyika was the Tanga (Northern) line which began when the German authorities decided in 1891 that a metre-gauge line should be built from Tanga to Muheza, and then on to Korogwe. Eventually this line would be continued on to Moshi and Arusha. A small port was built at Tanga to land equipment and material and the construction of the line began in 1893. Labour was scarce and at times had to be imported from Mozambique making progress slow. It took two years for the laying of just 40 km as far as Muheza. Financial difficulties caused construction to be halted periodically and the line finally reached Korogwe in 1902 and Moshi in 1911. Unfortunately much of this line, built at great expense over a long period of time, was destroyed by the Germans as they retreated in 1914.

Meanwhile the central route of the old slave trail to Lake Tanganyika was receiving attention. Dar es Salaam had been made the capital of the German protectorate in 1891 and talk of the construction of a railway began soon after. However, delays again ensued and it was not until 1905 that construction began on a line from Dar es Salaam to Morogoro. This was to be built by a private company with a grant from the Imperial German Government. The Maji Maji rebellion created problems with the supply of labour, but the line reached Morogoro in December 1907. By 1914 the line had been extended as far as Kigoma although it was clear that it

had little commercial value and traffic was extremely light.

Planning continued for other lines but the First World War intervened and much of the work already carried out was destroyed. Most of the bridges between Dar es Salaam and Kigoma were blown up, and the rolling stock destroyed. A line was built during the war, linking the Tanga line to the Kenya railway system which facilitated the advance and occupation of Tanga by the British.

Following the war many repairs were carried out so that the goods traffic on the railways increased. However, the problems returned with the depression of the 1930s which severely affected revenues. The non-metre gauge lines were closed and about 40% of the staff were laid off. The Second World War saw an increase in the activities of the railways, and following the war the 'Groundnut Scheme' (see box, page 421), involved the hasty construction of a branch line from Lindi on the coast to Nachingwea, one of the areas where groundnuts were to be grown. The scheme was a monumental failure, the expected traffic never materialized, and the line was abandoned.

In 1948 the railway and port services in Tanganyika were amalgamated with the Kenya and Uganda railways under the East Africa High Commission. A regional authority, East African Railways & Harbours (EAR&H), ran the railways until 1977 when the East African Community collapsed, severing the rail link through Taveta to Kenya, with Tanzania assuming responsibility for its own network.

Mount Kilimanjaro

While Germany and Britain were deciding the north boundary, Kaiser William I insisted that Mount Kilimanjaro should be German because it had been discovered by a German, John Rebmann. Queen Victoria generously 'gave' the mountain to her grandson, the future Kaiser William II, on his birthday in 1886, reportedly explaining, by way of justification, that 'William likes everything that is high and big'. The boundary was thus moved so that Kilimanjaro is now found within Tanzania. Instead of marking the boundary by pencilling it in with a ruler from the coast to Lake Victoria in one go, a freehand detour was made when the ruler hit the mountain, before carrying on again with the ruler and pencil on the far side.

The German colonial period

There were a number of phases of German colonial rule. The first, around the turn of the century, saw attempts at establishing a settler economy. This was to be based in the north highlands and agriculture was to be the mainstay of the economy. It was initially not a great success. Revolts occurred in Bagamoyo, Pangani and Tanga, which were all crushed. The best-known uprising was the Maji Maji rebellion, which occurred in the south of the country from 1905 to 1906 (see page 399). Discontent was initially aroused over a cotton scheme that benefited the Africans little although they were obliged to provide all the manual labour. The uprising was unique in eastern Africa for it was cross-tribal and included a large area – almost the whole of the country south of Dar es Salaam.

The uprising led to a major reappraisal of German colonial policy. The administrators realized that development would be almost impossible without a contented local population. This period saw the building of the railway to Tabora to open up the area to commerce, and crops such as coffee and groundnuts were encouraged. Economic activity increased and a world boom led to the re-emergence of a settler cash crop economy as the most significant part of colonial policy. In particular the boom saw prices of sisal and rubber soar. Most farming took place along the coast and on the slopes of Mount Kilimanjaro and Mount Meru. Inland the threat of the tsetse fly hindered development as domestic animals could not be raised in affected areas. Missionary activity led to the growth of clinics and schools.

First World War

With the outbreak of hostilities in Europe, the German commander General Paul von Lettow Vorbeck realized that his meagre forces could not defeat the British but he resolved to aid Germany's efforts in the European theatre of war by tying up as many British military resources as possible. Von Lettow, his German officers and African troops conducted an astonishing rearguard campaign, retreating from Kenya through what is now Tanzania and Mozambique, and was undefeated when Germany surrendered in Europe.

Von Lettow arrived in Dar es Salaam at the start of 1914 to take command of the German forces. He was 44 years old, son of a general, a professional soldier and experienced in bush warfare from service in German South West Africa (now Namibia). His forces consisted of around 2500 *Schutztruppe* (see box, opposite) *askaris* in 14 field companies, and he promptly signalled his intentions by capturing Taveta across the border in Kenya. The British assembled a force of 5000 mainly British, South African and Indian troops and von Lettow withdrew to begin his epic, 4000-km, four-year campaign. When faced by overwhelming odds von Lettow fell back, but at defendable positions, although always hopelessly out-numbered, he inflicted fearful losses on his adversaries, most notably at Tanga and Kibata.

The British fared better when commanded by the South African, Jan Christian Smuts, for 11 months in 1916. A rare combination of intellectual, politician and soldier, he later became Prime Minister of South Africa. During the war, however, found himself pursuing an infuriatingly elusive, and surprisingly humorous, foe. He was convinced that he would trap and destroy von Lettow's troops in Morogoro, where retreat to the south was blocked by the Ulunguru Mountains. But as his forces marched into the town they heard a

Schutztruppe – an African fighting elite

It was recognized by the Germans from the start that white troops in East Africa would be nothing more than a 'walking hospital'. So, under German officers, an African fighting force of *askaris* was recruited, thoroughly drilled, trained, disciplined and well paid – 30 rupees a month for privates (about US$80 in present-day values) and 150 rupees for non-commissioned officers.

The *Shutztruppe* became an elite. The uniform was a khaki jacket, trousers and puttees and a black leather belt with ammunition pouches. Head gear was a *kepi* – rather like a khaki fez with a chin-strap and a gold Imperial eagle on the front. The non-commissioned officers decorated their *kepis* with feathers. Each soldier had his own servant (an *askari*-boy). When travelling, a *Schutztruppe* private would send his *askari*-boy ahead to a village with a cartridge. This was an order to the local headman to have ready four beds (one for the *askari*, one for his rifle, one for his ammunition pouch and one for his uniform) – and some 'blankets' – a selection of the village girls.

Tough, resilient, and brave, around 150 *askaris* made up a field company that included two machine-gun teams. With several hundred porters carrying food and ammunition, it was highly mobile. During the First World War, the British were contemptuous of these African troops, thinking they would collapse when faced with European and Indian forces. In the event, the *Schutztruppe* was never defeated, and inflicted fearful losses on the British and their allies.

mechanical piano playing *Deutschland Uber Alles* in the Bahnhof Hotel and, in the empty *Schutztruppe* barracks, on every item of furniture, was a piece of human excrement.

Never defeated, at the end of the campaign von Lettow and his force numbered 155 Germans 1156 *Schutztruppe askaris* and about 3000 camp-followers made up of porters and *askari* wives and children, many of the latter born during the campaign. Over 250,000 Allied troops had been thrown against them at one time or another during the four years. But with their ultimate defeat in the First World War, the Germans lost control of German East Africa. The northwest, now Rwanda and Burundi, went to the Belgians. The rest was renamed Tanganyika, and the British were allocated a League of Nations mandate.

Von Lettow returned to Germany, in 1920 entered politics and for 10 years was a Deputy in the Reichstag. In 1930 he resigned and in 1935 Hitler suggested he become Ambassador to Britain. Von Lettow declined. It is said he told Hitler to 'go fuck himself', but von Lettow subsequently denied he had ever been that polite. In 1958, at the age of 88, von Lettow returned to Dar es Salaam. He was met at the dockside by a crowd of elderly *Schutztruppe askaris* who carried him shoulder-high to an official reception at Government House. In 1964 the German Bundestag finally voted the funds to settle the back-pay owing to the *Schutztruppe* at the surrender in 1918. Over 300 veterans, some in faded and patched uniforms presented themselves at Mwanza. Only a handful had their discharge papers. Those who didn't were handed a broom and taken through arms drill, with the orders given in German. Not one man failed the test. The same year, at the age of 94, von Lettow died.

The British period

From 1921 Britain introduced the policy of Indirect Rule, which had proved effective in other parts of colonial Africa. This involved giving a degree of political responsibility to local chiefs and ruling through them. Economic development between the wars was negligible. Tanganyika had few exportable products – unlike Uganda, there was no major cash crop such as cotton suited to production by small African farmers. The most significant export was sisal, a spiky plant that yields fibres that can be made into ropes and twine, but this required long-term, large-scale, capital-intensive investment and was not suitable for small-scale African production. It was produced almost entirely by British and Asian companies with a local workforce. The most successful African cash crop was coffee grown by the Chagga on the slopes of Mount Kilimanjaro, and by the Haya west of Lake Victoria. Coffee growing was extended to Africans by the British in 1922. Previously only settlers were allowed to grow coffee on estates established by the Germans from 1910.

Most British settlers went to Kenya where there was already a sizeable settler community and the highlands provided an attractive climate. Moreover the British presence seemed more secure in Kenya, which was a colony. The League of Nations mandate required Britain to prepare Tanganyika for eventual self-government, and the British kept expenditure on administration, infrastructure and education to a minimum.

The 1920s saw the emergence of the first African political groups. In 1922 the African Civil Servants Association of Tanganyika Territory was formed in Tanga, and in 1929 the Tanganyika African Association (TAA). Throughout the 1930s and 1940s, unions and agricultural cooperatives developed. These were not primarily political associations although their formation obviously led to increased political awareness. The major issues were land-use policies, aimed in particular at soil conservation, and the eviction of Africans to make way for white settlers. The African population in 1950 was about 8 million, compared to an Asian population of 55,000 and European population of 17,000. However, Europeans and Asians dominated local government councils even in areas that were almost exclusively African. These were issues upon which the TAA focused. In 1953 Julius Nyerere became the leader of the TAA and the movement towards independence developed momentum. In July 1954, at a meeting of all political elements, the Tanganyika African National Union (TANU) was created with the slogan *Uhuru na Umoja* (Freedom and Unity).

There were two major strengths to this movement in comparison to other similar movements in other parts of Africa. Firstly, there was no dominating tribal group, and secondly, Swahili had developed into the major language, encouraged by German colonial policy, and this served as an important unifying force. A further point of relevance in the run-up to independence was that after the Second World War Tanganyika was given UN Trustee status in place of the mandate. Both the mandatory system and the trusteeship system were very important because they meant that controversial issues could be referred to the UN Council, unlike in other colonial territories. In December 1956 Nyerere addressed the UN General Assembly's Fourth (Trusteeship) Committee, which gave him a platform to present the views of Tanganyikans to the outside world.

The first elections were held in two phases, in September 1958 and February 1959, and TANU won a sweeping majority. These were multiracial elections but even the European and Asian candidates owed their success to TANU. Tanganyika attained Independence on 9 December 1961 with Nyerere as the first Prime Minister. The constitution was subsequently changed and Tanzania became a republic with Nyerere as President.

Post-Independence Tanzania

In 1964 Zanzibar and Tanganyika merged to form Tanzania (see page 169). An awkward union has resulted in which Zanzibar has retained its own President, Parliament, a full range of Ministries and handles most of its own finances. The President of Zanzibar was,

The Groundnut Scheme

Immediately after the Second World War there was an attempt by the British Labour government to grow groundnuts on an enormous scale. Three sites were chosen in the south, near Lindi at Nachingwea; just north of Morogoro at Kongwa; and at Urambo west of Tabora on the Central Railway line. The scheme aimed to alleviate the worldwide shortage of edible oils following the war. The operation was to be capital-intensive, with a military-style approach to planning, and there was immense enthusiasm among the British who went out to run the programme (and who became known as 'groundnutters'). It was thought that with modern methods and enough machinery it would be impossible for the scheme to fail. It was a complete disaster. When finally abandoned a total of £36.5 m was written off. This huge sum was equal to a little less than the entire Tanganyikan government expenditure from 1946-1950.

The reasons for failure were numerous and included inadequate planning, which meant the environmental and climatic problems were not properly considered; unsuitable machinery (which meant that it was actually more efficient to clear the land by hand); and failure to test the scheme by way of a pilot project. Other difficulties included insufficient rain and inadequate capacity in the transport system to keep the tractors supplied with fuel.

The project is held up as an example of everything that was wrong with attempting to impose European agricultural techniques without adequate consideration of local African conditions.

Kongwa is now a ranch, Urambo has been given over to tobacco, and at Nachingwea oilseeds and cereals are grown.

---

ex officio, one of the two Vice-Presidents of Tanzania until the multiparty elections in 1995. Despite having a population that is less than 5% of the total, Zanzibar has almost a third of the seats in the Tanzanian Assembly.

After Independence there was pressure to replace Europeans with Africans in the administration and the business sector. There was also considerable demand for basic education and health services. Although economic progress was significant in these early years, there was an impatience at the slow pace of development, and Nyerere made plans for a bold, radical change.

This culminated in the 1967 Arusha Declaration, a programme of socialist development accepted by TANU and which was then amplified in a number of pamphlets by Nyerere. Its two main themes were egalitarianism and self-reliance and it was broadly based on the Chinese communist model. (It has been said that Tanzania took the Chinese model, mistakes and all and then added a few mistakes of its own.) Politicians were subject to a leadership code, which required that they had no private sources of income, and no more than one house or car. Banks, plantations and all major industries were nationalized. The cornerstone of the programme was the villagization and agricultural collectivization programme known as *Ujamaa*. This, and efforts in the rest of the economy, would, it was hoped, lead to the development of a just and prosperous society. Education was considered to be one of the most important aims of the programme and as a result Tanzania achieved some of the highest literacy rates in Africa. In the initial years there was success, too, in extending basic health care in the rural areas.

Ujamaa

Ujamaa, a programme for advancement in the rural areas, was an important element in post-independence Tanzanian philosophy. Intended to involve the voluntary movement of people into villages, its major objective was to raise output through collectivization and large-scale agricultural production. Emphasis was also on the social benefits – the provision of services such as piped water, electricity, schools and clinics. Self-reliance was the key and the villages were meant to be set up and run by the villagers themselves.

There were three phases of villagization in the decade from 1967. The first was voluntary movement on a locally selective basis combined with compulsory movement in Rufiji and Handeni, which were areas worst affected by drought and flood. From 1970 to 1973 this was replaced by a 'frontal approach' whereby incentives were given for people to move to villages, which included financial and technical assistance. The reluctance of people to move of their own accord meant the targets were not reached and after 1973 these methods were replaced by the use of force in support of rapid villagization. The results were dramatic. In 1970 the villagized population stood at about 500,000, or less than 5% of the population. After the first year of compulsory movement Nyerere claimed that there were over 9 million people – or about 60% of the mainland population, living in villages. Force was justified on the grounds that people could not always see what was best for them and had to be shown the way. As it is easier to provide amenities such as piped water and electricity to people grouped in villages, the *Ujamaa* did provide some benefits.

However, attempts to farm collectively were disastrous and agricultural output fell. The programme was vigorously resisted in the major coffee-growing areas of Kagera (west of Lake Victoria) and in Kilimanjaro region. By 1977 the *Ujamaa* programme was effectively abandoned, although considerable villagization remains.

Late 20th century to the present

In 1973 it was decided to move the capital city from Dar es Salaam on the coast to Dodoma in the centre. The position of this city is suitable in so far as it is on communication networks and is in the centre of the country about 320 km inland. However, it is also a dry and desolate area and the major problem with the plan has been the cost of moving. A Presidential official residence, the Prime Minister's office, and a National Assembly building have all been established there but the cost of relocation and the unwillingness of government employees have forced the rest of central government to remain in Dar.

In 1975 a law was passed that gave legal supremacy to TANU as the national political party, and in 1977 TANU and the Afro-Shirazi party (which had taken control in Zanzibar after the revolution) merged to form *Chama Cha Mapinduzi* (CCM) the 'party of the Nation'. The 1970s saw the gradual disintegration of the East Africa Community (EAC), which involved Kenya, Tanzania and Uganda in a customs union and provision of common services. Tanzania and Kenya had different ideological perspectives, and the three countries could not agree on the distribution of the costs and services of the EAC. Things came to a head over East African Airways. The failure of Tanzania and Uganda to remit funds to Kenya caused Kenya to 'ground' the airline (conveniently when all the planes were sitting on the tarmac in Kenya) and Tanzania reacted by closing the border with Kenya in February 1977. The border was only reopened in 1983 after the ownership of the EAC's assets was finally agreed.

In 1978 Tanzania's relations with neighbouring Uganda worsened and skirmishes on the border were followed by an announcement by Idi Amin that Uganda had annexed the Kagera salient. This is an area of about 1800 sq km of Tanzanian territory west of Lake Victoria. The Organization of African Unity (OAU) applied pressure, which caused

Julius Nyerere

Julius Kambarage Nyerere was born in 1922 in Butiama, east of Lake Victoria. He was the Roman Catholic son of a Zanaki chief. His father died having had 26 children by 18 wives. The name Nyerere means 'caterpillar' in the Zanaki language and was supposed to have been given to Nyerere's father because at the time of his birth (around 1860) the countryside was infested with them. Nyerere attended a boarding school in Musoma and, from 1937, the Tabora Government Secondary School. He was baptized in 1943 and the same year he entered Makerere College, Uganda. After Makerere he returned to Tabora where he taught history and biology at St Mary's Catholic Boys' School operated by the White Fathers. In 1949 he went to Edinburgh University and in 1952 obtained his Master of Arts in Economics and History (he was the first Tanzanian to be educated in Britain). In 1953 he married Maria Gabriel Magigo who was also a Catholic of the Msinditi tribe and was to become its first woman teacher. He paid the traditional bride-price of six head of cattle for her and they had seven children.

Nyerere subsequently took a teaching post at the Catholic Secondary School of St Francis at Pugu a few kilometres west of Dar es Salaam and it was from here that he became involved in politics. In 1954 he became president of the Tanzania

African Association and was instrumental in converting this into the political organization TANU. He was appointed a temporary member of the Tanganyika Legislative Council in 1954, and a full member of the Legislative Assembly in 1958 where he remained until his assumption of the Presidency in 1962. In his acceptance speech, he said "We will light a candle on the top of Kilimanjaro which will shine beyond our borders, giving hope where there is despair, love where there is hate, and dignity where before there was only humiliation." While some of his policies were criticized, throughout his term he placed a great faith on rural African people and their traditional ways of life. He resigned as President in 1985 and became known as 'Mwalimu', which means teacher. He moved back to his childhood home of Butima, and continued to be an advocate for poor African countries around the world. He was undoubtedly one of Africa's greatest statesmen, admired for his integrity, modest lifestyle and devotion to equality and human rights. On his death in October 1999, the ANC released a statement: "The organization weeps in memory of this giant amongst men ... an outstanding leader, a brilliant philosopher and a people's hero – a champion for the entire African continent."

Uganda to withdraw, but fighting continued. In January 1979 a Tanzanian force of over 20,000 invaded Uganda, Amin's army capitulated and the Tanzanians rapidly took control of the southern part of the country. The invading force had withdrawn by 1981 having spent the interim period in Uganda overseeing the election of Milton Obote for the second time. A remarkable feature of this episode is that, despite being the only African country ever to win a war in the 20th century, this event is not celebrated in Tanzania. The only monument is a small pyramid on columns, located on the road from Bukoba to Masaka, just south of the border. It is dedicated to the 16 Tanzanian soldiers who died in the war.

In 1985 Nyerere decided to step down as President of Tanzania (the first President in post-independence Africa to retire voluntarily). He remained as Chairman of the party (CCM) before formally retiring from politics in 1990. Vice-President Sokoine, who had been widely thought of as Nyerere's successor, had been killed in a car crash in October 1984. Ali Hassan Mwinyi, who was then President of Zanzibar, was nominated to be the sole candidate for President and was elected in October 1985.

Throughout the early 1980s Tanzania had been put under pressure to accept economic reforms suggested by the World Bank and International Monetary Fund. These financial institutions, as well as Western governments, aid donors and foreign investors argued that the socialist development strategy had led to a crisis involving falling incomes, decaying infrastructure, deteriorating health and educational provision and a climate of petty corruption. For many years Tanzania resisted changes, but eventually the climate of opinion changed in 1986, under Mwinyi, a market economy strategy was adopted, and Tanzania began an economic recovery.

In 1993, Tanzania allowed political parties other than CCM to form. In October 1995 there were elections in which CCM won a substantial majority of seats in the Union Assembly. The Presidency was won by the CCM candidate, Benjamin Mkapa, Mwinyi having retired after two terms in office. Mkapa won comfortably with 62% of the vote, and the practice of having two Vice-Presidents (with one being the President of Zanzibar) was discontinued.

In 1995, the main opposition in Zanzibar, the Civic United Front (CUF) ran CCM very close in both the Zanzibar Assembly and in the race for the Zanzibar Presidency. There were allegations of election fraud, supported by evidence from international observers. Nonetheless, CCM formed the administration in Zanzibar, and Salim Amour was installed as Zanzibar's President. It was around this time that various Zanzibari separatist groups formed in exile, some wishing merely for independence, others pressing for an independent Islamic state, but splits within the separatist movement have enabled the government to contain the problem so far.

The 2000 election was fought by fewer parties, but the opposition was still divided, and CCM and Mkapa had comfortable victories. In Zanzibar the incumbent President, Salim Amour, having completed two terms, was prevented from running again. His successor as CCM candidate for the Presidency was Amani Karume, son of the former President. On election day there was chaos at the polls, and elections in 16 constituencies had to be re-run. Despite opposition claims of electoral fraud, the outcome was a victory for CCM and Karume. Seif Shariff Hamad, the CUF leader, got the remaining 33%. His party won 16 assembly seats on the island of Pemba. Both parties signed a reconciliation agreement in 2001 and Zanzibar is set to remain part of Tanzania. But the CUF, which enjoys strong support on Pemba, has called for greater autonomy and some CUF members have called for independence. In 2005, Zanzibar presented its new flag, the first time for over 40 years that the archipelago has flown its own flag since uniting with Tanganyika to form Tanzania in 1964, though Zanzibar's government has stressed the adoption of a flag does not mean that this is a move towards independence.

In April 2004 Tanzania celebrated its 40th birthday as an independent country and in 2005 went to the polls again. Mpaka had already served for two terms and the constitution didn't allow him to stand for a third. There were 10 party candidates for presidency but Jakaya Mrisho Kikwete from the CCM and the former Minister of Foreign Affairs under Mpaka won a land-sliding 80% of the vote. Karume kept his position on Zanzibar with 53% of the vote, though this time round it was much closer with Shariff Hamad getting 46%. Nevertheless the election was largely without incident.

Overall, since 1995 Tanzania's political stability has remained excellent. The government has stayed secure in a period that has seen the advent of multiparty democracy and economic policies that have changed from socialism to capitalism. There is still significant room for improvement on poverty reduction, public services and infrastructure but on the whole Tanzania is fairly stable and has good prospects for the future. Fairly young (he was only 55 when he became president) Kikwete is well respected, and during his 10 year term as Minister of Foreign Affairs was involved in conflict resolution for troubled neighbours Burundi and the Democratic of Congo and is currently the Chairperson of the African Union. He was close to Nyerere, and to some regard his governing philosophies of investing in people have been influenced by Nyerere. Education is one of his priorities and since 2005, 1500 new secondary schools have been built across Tanzania and a new university is currently being built in Dodoma. Other successes include progressive anti-corruption initiatives and the launch of nationwide voluntary HIV/AIDS testing programme, for which Kikwete and his wife were the first to take the test.

Economy

Economic strategy underwent a profound change in 1967 when financial and business enterprises were taken into public ownership and a major reorganization of the agricultural sector was introduced, involving collective production and relocating the population into villages. By 1977, the collectivization of agriculture had virtually been abandoned. In 1986 Tanzania signed an agreement with the IMF, which heralded the beginnings of a reversal of economic strategy to more encouragement for the private sector and reliance on market forces, rather than on planning and central control.

Economic structure
Despite still being a third world country, there has been a steady growth rate of GDP of about 7% per annum and GDP was US$56.22 billion in 2008, or per head, US$1400. For many years Tanzania was among the 50 poorest countries in the world, but it currently ranks at about 150. Agriculture is the most important sector, and cash crops such as coffee, sisal, cashews, cotton and cloves are important foreign exports and produce 27% of GDP and, more importantly, provide the livelihood of 80% of the population. The industry sector is small and is mainly limited to processing agricultural products and light consumer goods and provides 10% of GDP and the services sector provides 50% of GDP, of which 17% is in Tanzania's tourist industry. Industry and services combined generate 20% of employment. The main commodity source of export income which stands at about US$2.5 billion per year is agriculture, which accounts for 85% of all exports. The remaining 15% includes minerals and manufactures.

Tanzania's economy has benefited from mining and mineral resource projects over recent years, including the opening of gold mines in the interior and gas extraction plants along the coast. Mining has been an important factor in the industrial sector, and eight new gold mines have opened since 1998: almost exclusively in the Lake Victoria region. Tanzania is now Africa's third largest producer of gold after South Africa and Ghana, and presently 50 tonnes worth about US$700 million is mined annually with these figures increasing all the time. The World Bank offers insurance for foreign investment in Tanzania, and these measures have assisted in attracting exploration capital to the country. Since the outset of the foreign companies establishing the mines, there has been an agreement with the government that they pay royalties to the government but not taxes (expected to be about 20%) until their initial investment in the mines and equipment has been recouped, which is likely to be in the next few years. In the near future the export of gold will contribute greatly to the county's GDP. Other resources that have been tapped into recently include gas, and a gas field is now operational on the offshore island of Songo Songo. Construction of the pipeline network was completed in May 2004, and it now transports natural gas to Dar where it is used as the principal fuel for turbine generators at Songa's Ubungo power plant, which generates about 190MW of electricity – or 45% of the country's capacity – for the national grid. A proportion of the gas also supplies a number of other industries and power plants in Dar es Salaam.

In recent years inflation has followed global trends and has risen from about 5-6% during 2000-2005, to about 9% in 2009, due mainly to the increase of costs of imports including oil and petroleum products. The International Monetary Fund (IMF) gave Tanzania some foreign debt relief by reducing it from US\$7.8 billion to US\$1.8 billion at the end of 2006 as part of the Multilateral Debt Relief Initiative (MDRI) agreed at the G8 Summit in 2005. However the government is continuing to borrow to finance poverty-reduction strategies.

People

In terms of both population and geographical area, Tanzania is a large country in the African context. The population has been growing rapidly at 2.07% a year, and in 2005 the population was estimated at 40.2 million people, 1 million of which live on Zanzibar and Pemba, and 2.5 million in Dar es Salaam. This gives a population density of 4.5 persons per sq km, rather higher than the African average. However, the distribution is very uneven, with the areas around Mount Kilimanjaro and west of Lake Victoria heavily populated, while in the south and southwest there is much uncultivated fertile land. Urbanization is not as advanced as elsewhere in the continent, and about 80% of the population is rural.

The population is largely made up of mixed Bantu groups but there are 129 recognized ethnic groups, of which the Sukuma, Haya, Nyakyusa, Nyamwezi, and Chagga have more than 1 million members.

The largest ethnic groups are the Sukuma and the Nyamwezi, and although no group makes up more than 15% of the population, about a dozen of the largest groups make up about 50% of the population. Most of these are of Bantu origin (see page 414), although there are some Nilotic groups as well, and about 95% of the population is Bantu-speaking. The most important Bantu language is Swahili (Kiswahili in the language), a language which is the mother tongue of the people of Zanzibar and Pemba as well as some coastal people. Swahili became a *lingua franca* before the colonial period in some areas and this was encouraged by both the Germans and the British. In 1963 it became the national language.

Sukuma
This is Tanzania's largest ethnic group and makes up between 10 and 13% of the population. The name means 'people of the north' and the group lives just to the south of Lake Victoria around Mwanza. In the pre-colonial period they were organized into a large number of small chiefdoms. They practise mixed agriculture, with both cattle-herding and cultivation. This is also an important cotton growing area.

Nyamwezi
The Nyamwezi people are found to the south of the Sukuma people in north Tanzania and in many ways are similar to them. Like the Sukuma they were formerly made up of a large

number of very small chiefdoms. Some of these chiefs tried later to dominate wider areas. Their identity is fairly recent and rather fragile. They are primarily a cultivating people and have established a reputation as traders. The name means 'people of the moon'.

Makonde
These people are located in the southeast part of the country and are fairly isolated on the Makonde Plateau. Although they are one of the five largest groups the Makonde have been little affected by colonial and post-colonial developments. They are renowned for being a conservative people who are determined to defend their way of life. This is facilitated by the difficulty in reaching this part of Tanzania. Even today communications with the southeast are poor, particularly during the wet season. The Makonde are perhaps most famous for their beautifully crafted woodcarvings. They are also found in Mozambique.

Chagga
The Chagga (or Chaga) are found around the south slopes of Mount Kilimanjaro and around Moshi and constitute the third largest group in Tanzania. They are greatly advantaged by living in a fertile and well-watered region, which is ideally suited to the production of coffee. They were also one of the first groups to be affected by the Christian missionaries, in particular the Roman Catholics and Lutherans, and this meant that the initial provision of education in the area was ahead of many other areas. The high level of education and opportunity of cash-cropping have resulted in a comparatively high level of income, and also a relatively high level of involvement in community activity. One example of the form that this has taken is through cooperative action in the production and marketing of coffee.

The Chagga believed that the god they called Ruwa was greater than all the other gods that they worshipped. They believed all men had their origin in him and that, as he did not trouble them with petty demands, unlike some other gods, he must love men. He lived in a place in the skies that they called *nginenyi*, which means blue skies. Sacrifices would be made to Ruwa when someone was ill or when there was a famine or epidemic. Usually prayers would be said and then a goat would be slaughtered. The goat should be a male of uniform colour without any spots, and it should not have had its tail docked. Sacrifices would also be offered to the spirits of the dead. When a person dies it is believed that they live in the new world but in a different form. The spirits of the dead are able to return to the world to demand what is due to them from their relatives. It is said that their physical presence is not noticed but they appear in dreams or through the noises made by animals.

Haya
The Haya people are different from most other ethnic groups in Tanzania. They live in the far northwest of Tanzania, to the west of the shores of Lake Victoria. Although they have common traditions, social system, culture and language as well as territorial identity, they are divided into several chiefdoms, which suggests that in this case political unity is not an essential part of tribal identity. The Haya are cultivators, growing coffee and plantains, and live in densely populated villages. Exactly similar to the situation in Kilimanjaro region, the high altitude of west of Lake Victoria provided a pleasant climate for missionaries and the Catholics and Protestants competed for converts by providing education here, and this, combined with the production of coffee, had a beneficial effect on the economy.

Hehe

The Hehe people live in the central south region of Tanzania around Iringa. They have a strong sense of being Hehe, and have their own more or less distinctive social system and culture with a unifying political system. However, within this group there are differences in the way of life and social systems between those who live in the drier eastern parts of the region and those in the wetter uplands to the west. These are caused by environmental factors as well as the effects of distance. Despite this, one observer has suggested that there is a greater unity and identity among the Hehe than there is with any other group of people.

Masai

The Masai inhabit the north border area with Kenya, but are found as far south as Morogoro and Tabora. They are a spectacular group of tall, slender cattle-herders, living off milk, blood and meat. All life is centred on cattle and the number of cows and children a man has is a measure of his wealth. Young men leave to become *moran* before returning to begin family life. As *moran* they carry spears, wear distinctive red garments and have elaborately decorated faces, bodies and hair. The women have shaven heads and often wear many coils of beads on their necks and shoulders. Clans are governed by elders or discuss matters and make decisions. Houses are built within *manyattas* – a sort of kraal that protects the cattle from wild animals at night.

Shirazi

The Shirazi is the name given to people who are a mixture of Africans and people who are said to have come at a very early time from the Shiraz area of Iran. They are divided into three 'tribes' called the Hadimu, Tumbatu and Pemba. The Africans are descendants of mainlanders who came to the islands of Zanzibar and Pemba, often as slaves although later of their own accord. Descendants of the Shirazis have intermixed with other Swahili people and have become more African in race, speech and culture.

Swahili

This is the general term given to the coastal people who have a Muslim-orientated culture. They are the descendants of generations of mixing of slaves, migrant labourers and Afro-Arabs. Archaeological evidence suggests the Swahili have inhabited the East African Coast since the 1st century AD. Arabic and Chinese medieval documents record the presence of a people involved in the long distance trade of ivory, slaves, gold, and grain in exchange for textiles, beads, weapons, and porcelain. The Swahili were, and are, an urban people living in 'stone towns' up and down the coast and on Zanzibar island.

Other African groups

The **Hi** people are a small group of click-speakers. They are hunter-gatherers and live on the southwest shores of Lake Eyasi, in the central north part of Tanzania. Other click speakers found in Tanzania include the **Hadzabe** and the **Sandawe**. The Hadzabe live in the same area as the Hi and the groups are believed to be closely related. The Sandawe live in the interior central region of Tanzania to the north of Dodoma. The **Dorobo** are a small group of hunter-gatherers who are found throughout Masailand and in Kenya.

Non-Africans

This group makes up under 1% of the population of Tanzania and comprises Europeans, Asians and Arabs.

Social development

In 2008 adult literacy was estimated at around 78%. In 2001, 500 more primary schools were built and primary school fees were abolished to encourage enrolment, which has risen from 58% in 2000 to 96% in 2008. Secondary education in Tanzania has recently significantly improved since 2005 as 1500 new secondary schools have been built (there were only 595 in 2000) and the government has recruited 6000 more teachers, including bringing many out of retirement. This has been part of the five-year Secondary Education Development Programme (SEDP), and the government has placed a high priority on education as a means to reduce poverty. As a result, enrolment to secondary schools has risen from just 7% in 2005 to 49% in 2009. Tertiary education enrolment rates are 1.8%, slightly lower than Kenya, though again reforms in 2000 increased the number of accredited universities and places of higher education from four to 19, and there's presently a new government university being built in Dodoma.

Life expectancy, at 52 years, is about the African average, and provision of medical care, indicated by numbers of doctors per head, is slightly better than the average elsewhere on the continent. The fertility rate of about 4.7 children per woman is about average for Africa, but the infant mortality rates of 70 deaths per 1000 births are high, and are a reflection of the concentration of medical services in the urban areas and comparative neglect of the majority of the population in the countryside. Food availability in some arid areas, that are also prone to droughts, means that about 38% of the population is considered to be malnourished, which gives cause for concern.

Land and environment

Geography

Tanzania is a large coastal country (approximately 945,000 sq km) which lies just below the Equator and includes the islands of Pemba and Zanzibar between 1° S and 11° S latitude and 30° to 40° E longitude. It is bounded by Kenya and Uganda to the north, Rwanda, Burundi and DR Congo to the west, Zambia, Malawi and Mozambique to the south. Temperatures range from tropical to temperate moderated by altitude. Most of the country consists of high plateaux but there is a wide variety of terrain including mangrove swamps, coral reefs, plains, low hill ranges, uplands, volcanic peaks and high mountains, as well as depressions such as the Rift Valley and lakes. Dar es Salaam is the main port and there are hydro-electric schemes on the Rufiji and Pangani rivers. Mineral deposits include diamonds, gold, gemstones (tanzanite, ruby, emerald, green garnet, sapphire), graphite, gypsum, kaolin and tin.

Climate

Because Tanzania lies below the equator, the coolest months occur during the northern hemisphere's summer, and all-year round the weather remains pleasant and comfortable. There is a long dry season between June to October, when temperatures range from around 10°C in the northern highlands to about 23°C on the coast. On the plains and the lower-altitude game reserves, the temperatures from June to October are warm and mild. On the coast, these months are some of the most pleasant to visit, with balmy, sunny weather much of the day and cooling ocean breezes at night. This is followed by short rains in November and December. January to March can be very hot with temperatures of

25-35°C across the country (with the exception of Kilimanjaro and Meru), and are followed by heavy rains in April and May. The timing of the rains has been less regular in recent years and the volume also varies from year to year, and from region to region. Short rains have tended to spread from November to May with a drier spell in January and February. In northeast Tanzania, the long rains are in March to June. A quarter of the country receives an annual average of 750 mm of rain, but in some areas it can be as high as 1250 mm. The central area of the country is dry with less than 500 mm per annum. In many areas two harvests can be grown each year. ▶▶ *For more information on when to visit, see page 18. For climate charts, see page 19.*

Vegetation

Kenya is justifiably famous for its flora and fauna. In areas of abundant rainfall, the country is lush, supporting a huge range of plants, and the wide variety of geographical zones house a corresponding diversity of flora. The majority of the country is covered in savannah-type vegetation characterized by the acacia. The slopes of Kilimanjaro are covered in thick evergreen temperate forest from about 1000 m to 2000 m; then to 3000 m the mountains are bamboo forest; above this level the mountains are covered with groundsel trees and giant lobelias. Mangroves are prolific in the coastal regions.

Wildlife

Mammals

Practically everyone travelling around East Africa will come into contact with animals during their stay. Of course there is much more than the big game to see and you will undoubtedly travel through different habitats from the coast to the tropical rain forests but the mammals are on the top of most people's 'to see' lists. ▶▶ *See African Wildlife colour section in the middle of the guide.*

Big Nine The 'big five' **Elephant** (*Loxodonta africana*), **Lion** (*Panthera leo*), **Black Rhino** (*Diceros bicornis*), **Buffalo** (*Syncerus caffer*) and **Leopard** (*Panthera pardus*), was the term originally coined by hunters who wanted trophies from their safaris, but nowadays the **Hippopotamus** (*Hippopotamus amphibius*) is usually considered one of the Big Five for those who shoot with their cameras, whereas the Buffalo is far less of a "trophy". Equally photogenic and worthy to be included are: **Zebra**, **Giraffe** and **Cheetah** (*Acinonyx jubatus*). Whether they are the Big Five or the Big Nine these are the animals that most people come to Africa to see, and, with the possible exception of the **Leopard**, you have an excellent chance of seeing all of them.

   They are all unmistakable and when seeing them for the first time in the wild you will find that they are amazingly familiar and recognizable. The only two that could possibly be confused are the Leopard and the Cheetah. The **Leopard** is less likely to be seen as it is more nocturnal and more secretive in its habits than the Cheetah. It frequently rests during the heat of the day on the lower branches of trees, and, as you drive round the parks, your best bet is to look for the animal's tail, which hangs down below the branches, and can be quite easily spotted while the rest of the animal remains well concealed. If you are lucky you will see one with its kill, which it may have hauled up into the lower branches (see African Wildlife colour section, page ii).

   Cheetahs are often seen in family groups walking across the plains or resting in the shade. They are slimmer and longer legged than Leopards, with a characteristic sway back.

The black "tear" mark on the face is usually obvious through binoculars. (If all else fails you can identify Cheetahs by the accompanying minibuses.)

Lions (*Panthera leo*), usually found in open savannah in Africa, are, after tigers, the second largest carnivorous members of the cat family. They live in prides or permanent family groups, numbering up to around 30 animals, and are the only felid to do so. The prides are usually composed of a group of inter-related females and their cubs, led by a dominant male, or occasionally, a group of males. There is no dominant lioness. They communicate with one another with a range of sounds that vary from roaring, grunting and growling to meowing. Roars, more common at night, can reach sound levels of over 110 decibels and be heard from distances of up to 8 km. The females do most of the hunting (usually ungulates like zebra and antelopes), while the males are mostly involved in protecting their pride from other lions and predators. Lions are very sociable except when eating, when aggressive fighting can break out. Although the females kill most of the prey the males are first to feed, followed by the lionesses, the cubs just getting the leftovers. (The main cause of cub death is starvation.) Lions augment their diet by scavenging prey killed by other predators.

Elephants are awe-inspiring and it is wonderful to watch a herd at a waterhole. Although they have suffered terribly from the activities of poachers in recent decades they are still readily seen in many of the game areas.

The other animals which have suffered badly in recent times are the two Rhinos. The **White Rhino** (*Diceros simus*) is now probably extinct in much of its former range in eastern Africa though it flourishes in the southern part of the continent. The **Black Rhino** has also diminished in number in recent years and there are very few in Tanzania, though there's a good chance of seeing the few elderly black rhino in the Ngorongoro Crater, and a couple have recently been transferred from southern Africa and released in the Grumeti region of the Serengeti. The two rhinos may be distinguished by the shape of their mouth. The White Rhino has a square muzzle, whereas the Black has a long upper lip (the difference is in fact quite easy to see). Their names have no bearing on the colour of the animals as they are both a rather nondescript dark grey. In some guide books the White Rhino is described as being paler in colour than the Black Rhino, but this by no means obvious in the field. The name White Rhino is derived from the Dutch word "weit" which means wide and refers to the shape of the animal's mouth. The Black Rhino on the other hand is a browser, that is to say it feeds usually on shrubs and bushes. It achieves this by using its long, prehensile upper lip which is well adapted to the purpose. If you see rhino with their young you will notice that the White Rhino tends to herd its young in front of it, whereas the Black Rhino usually leads its young from the front.

The **Buffalo**, considered by hunters to be the most dangerous of the big game, can be seen everywhere, sometimes in substantial herds in many areas. Beware: these animals, cut off from the herd, can become bad-tempered and easily provoked.

The **Hippo** is another animal which appears harmless, even comic (from a safe vantage point). During the day it rests in the water and you can get excellent views and interesting photographs, particularly if there are displaying males active in the area. These Hippos will "yawn" at each other and two animals will sometimes spar. At night the Hippo leaves the water and ranges very far afield to graze (a single adult animal needs up to 60 kg of grass every day). Should you meet a Hippo on land by day or night keep well away. If you get between it and its escape route to the water, it may well attack and there have been fatalities in Africa by people getting trampled. (These animals are now considered as dangerous as buffalos, once thought to be the most dangerous of all the big mammals.)

In many ways the most stunning of the Big Nine is the **Giraffe**. It may not be as magnificent as a full-grown Lion, nor as awe-inspiring as an Elephant, but its elegance is unsurpassed. To see a small party of Giraffe galloping across the plains is seeing Africa as it has been for hundreds of years. The **Common Giraffe** (*Giraffa camelopardalis*) which has two forms, or races: one is the **Masai Giraffe** which occurs in southwest Kenya and Tanzania. This has a yellowish-buff coat with the characteristic patchwork of brownish markings with very jagged edges. In most animals there are only two horns, though occasionally animals are seen with three horns. The other form of the Common Giraffe is known as **Rothschild's Giraffe** and occurs west and north of the Masai Giraffe and into Uganda as far west as the Nile. It is usually rather paler and heavier looking than the Masai Giraffe and can have as many as five horns, though more commonly three. Both male and female animals have horns, though in the female they may be smaller. The lolloping gait is very distinctive and it produces this effect b the way it moves its legs at the gallop. A horse will move its fore and hind legs diagonally when galloping, but the giraffe moves both hind legs together and both fore legs together. It achieves this by swinging both hind legs forward and outside the fore legs. It is not a dumb and voiceless animal as many believe but can produce a low groaning noise and a variety of snorts.

The **Zebra** forms herds, often large ones, sometimes with antelope. The **Common** or **Burchell's Zebra** (*Equus burchelli*) has broad stripes which cross the top of the hind leg in unbroken oblique lines. Although they all look identical, each individual has a different pattern of stripes. A zebra defends itself by kicking its hind legs, which is far more effective then it sounds and even large predators like lion find it difficult to bring down an adult.

Larger antelope The first animals that you will see on safari will almost certainly be antelope. These are by far the most numerous group to be seen on the plains. Although there are many different species, it is not difficult to distinguish between them. For identification purposes they can be divided into the larger ones which stand at 48 in (about 120 cm) or more at the shoulder, and the smaller ones at 36 in (about 90 cm) or less.

For the record, it is worth pointing out here that antelope are not 'deer', which do not occur in Africa, except in parts of the very north, but you will undoubtedly hear many people refer to them as such. There are many differences between the two groups. For example, deer have antlers, which are solid, boney, branching outgrowths from the skull and which are shed annually. Antelope, on the other hand, have horns, which are hollow, unbranched sheaths made of modified skin, rather like finger and toe nails. They are not shed seasonally and if a horn is lost it is not replaced.

The largest of all is the **Eland** (*Taurotragus oryx*) which stands 175-183 cm (69-72 in) at the shoulder. It is very cattle-like in appearance, with a noticeable dewlap and shortish spiral horns, present in both sexes. The general colour varies from greyish to fawn, sometimes with a rufous tinge, with narrow white stripes on the sides of the body. It occurs, usually in small herds, in a wide variety of grassy habitats.

Not quite as big, but still reaching 140-153 cm (55-60 in) at the shoulder, is the **Greater Kudu** (*Tragelaphus strepsiceros*) which prefers fairly thick bush, sometimes in quite dry areas. Although nearly as tall as the Eland it is a much more slender and elegant animal altogether. Its general colour also varies from greyish to fawn and it has several white stripes running down the sides of the body. Only the male carries horns, which are very long and spreading, with only two or three twists along the length of the horn. A noticeable and distinctive feature is a thick fringe of hair which runs from the chin down the neck. Greater Kudu usually live in family groups of not more than half a dozen individuals, but occasionally larger herds of up to about 30 can be seen. Its smaller relative, the **Lesser Kudu** (*Strepsiceros imberis*), looks quite similar, with similar horns, but stands only 99-102 cm (39-40 in) high. It lacks the throat fringe of the bigger animal, but has two conspicuous white patches on the underside of the neck. It inhabits dense scrub and acacia thickets in semi-arid country, usually in pairs, sometimes with their young.

The **Roan Antelope** (*Hippoptragus equinus*) and **Sable Antelope** (*Hippotragus niger*) are similar in general shape, though the Roan is somewhat bigger, being 140-145 cm (55-57 in) at the shoulder, compared to the 127-137 cm (50-54 in) of the Sable. In both species, both sexes carry ringed horns which curve backwards, and these are particularly long in the Sable. There is a horse-like mane present in both animals. The Sable is usually glossy black with white markings on the face and a white belly (the female is often a reddish brown in colour). The Roan can vary from dark rufous to a reddish fawn and also has white markings on the face. The black males of the Sable are easily identified, but the brownish individuals can be mistaken for the Roan. Look for the tufts of hair at the tips of the rather long ears of the Roan (absent in the Sable). The Sable is found in well wooded areas. The Roan generally is more widespread and is found in open grassland. Both the Roan and the Sable live in herds.

Another large antelope with a black and white face is the **Oryx** (*Oryx beisa*). This occurs in two distinct races, the **Beisa Oryx** which is found north and west of the Tana River in Kenya, and the **Fringe-eared Oryx** which occurs south and east of this river. Both these animals stand 122 cm (48 in) at the shoulder and vary in colour from greyish (most Beisa Oryx) to sandy (most Fringe-eared Oryx), with a black line down the spine and a black stripe between the coloured body and the white underparts, rather like that on found on the much smaller Thomson's Gazelle. They both also have very long straight (not curving) horns, present in both sexes, and which make identification of this animal quite easy. The two races may be distinguished by the long dark fringe of hair on the tips of the ears in the Fringe-eared Oryx, absent in the Beisa Oryx. The Beisa Oryx is found in herds in arid and semi desert country and the Fringe-eared Oryx, also in herds, in similar habitat, but also sometimes in less dry habitats.

The two **Waterbuck** are very similar, both being about 122-137 cm (48-54 in) at the shoulder, with shaggy grey-brown coats which are very distinctive. The males have long gently curving horns which are heavily ringed. The two species can be distinguished by the white mark on the buttocks. In the **Common Waterbuck** (*Kobus ellipsiprymnus*) this forms a clear half ring on the rump and round the tail, whereas in the **Defassa Waterbuck** (*Kobus defassa*) this ring is filled in, forming a white patch. Both animals occur in small herds, in grassy areas, often near water. Solitary animals are also often seen. They are fairly common.

The **Wildebeest** or **Gnu** (*Connochaetes taurinus*) is well-known to many people from published photographs of the spectacular annual migration through the Serengeti National Park. It is a big animal about 132 cm (52 in) high at the shoulder, looking rather like an American bison from a distance, especially when you see the huge herds straggling across the plains. The impression is strengthened by its buffalo-like horns (in both sexes) and humped appearance. The general colour is greyish with a few darker stripes down the side. It has a noticeable beard and long mane.

The four remaining large antelope are fairly similar, but, as there is not a lot of overlap in their ranges, it is not too difficult to identify them. Three of these four are **Hartebeest** of various sorts and the fourth is called the **Topi**. All four antelope have long, narrow horse-like faces and rather comical expressions. The shoulders are much higher than the rump giving them a very sloped back appearance, especially in the three hartebeest.

Again all four have short, curved horns, carried by both sexes. In the three hartebeest the horns arise from a boney protuberance on the top of the head and curve outwards as well as backwards. One of the hartebeests, **Jackson's Hartebeest** (*Alcelaphus buselaphus*) (about 132 cm, 52 in) is similar in colour to the **Topi** (*Damaliscus korrigum*) (about 122-127 cm, 48-50 in) being a very rich dark rufous in colour. But the Topi has dark patches on the tops of the legs, a coat with a rich satiny sheen to it, and more ordinary looking lyre-shaped horns. Of the other two hartebeest, **Coke's Hartebeest** (*Alcephalus buselaphus*) (about 122 cm, 48 in), also called the **Kongoni**, is usually considered to be a race of Jackson's Hartebeest, but is a very different colour being a more drab pale brown with a paler rump. Finally **Lichtenstein's Hartebeest** (*Alcephalus lichtensteinii*) (about 127-132 cm, 50-52 in) is also fawn in general colouration, but usually has a rufous wash over the back. Also look out for dark marks on the front of the legs, and often, a dark patch on the side near the shoulder. All four of these antelope are found in herds, in the case of Topi quite large herds. Sometimes they mix with other plain dwellers such as zebra. The hartebeest has the habit of posting sentinels, solitary animals who stand on the top of anthills keeping a watch out for predators.

Smaller antelope The remaining common antelopes are a good deal smaller than those described above. The largest is the **Impala** (*Aepyceros melampus*) which is 92-107 cm (36-42 in) at the shoulder and a bright rufous in colour with a white abdomen. From behind, the white rump, with black lines on each side, is characteristic. Only the male carries the long, lyre shaped horns. Just above the heels of the hind legs is a tuft of thick black bristles, unique to the Impala, which are surprisingly easy to see as the animal runs. Also easy to see is the black mark on the side of abdomen, just infront of the back leg.

Two slightly smaller antelope are **Grant's Gazelle** (*Gazella granti*), about 81-99 cm (32-35 in) at the shoulder, and **Thomson's Gazelle** (*Gazella thomsonii*), about 64-69 cm (25-27 in) at the shoulder. They are superficially similar. Grant's, the larger of the two and has longer horns, but this is only a good means of identification when the two animals are seen together. The general colour of both varies from a bright rufous to a sandy rufous. In both species the curved horns are carried by both sexes. Thomson's Gazelle can usually be distinguished from Grant's by the broad black band along the side between the rufous upper parts and white abdomen, but not invariably, as some forms of Grant's also have this dark lateral stripe. If in doubt, look for the white area on the buttocks which extends above the tail on to the rump in Grant's, but does not extend above the tail in Thomson's. This is the surest way to distinguish them. The underparts are white. Thomson's Gazelle or "Tommies", are among the most numerous animals that inhabit the plains of Kenya and Tanzania. You will see large herds of them often in association with other game. Grant's Gazelle, occurs on rather dry grass plains.

The **Bohor Reedbuck** (*Redunca redunca*) and the **Oribi** (*Ourebia ourebi*) are not really very similar, but they do both have a curious and conspicuous patch of bare skin just below each ear. The horns (carried only by males) are quite different being sharply hooked forwards at the tip in the Bohor Reedbuck, but straight in the Oribi and this is enough to distinguish them. There is a slight difference in size, the Bohor Reedbuck being about 71-76 cm (28-30 in) at the shoulder and the Oribi only about 61 cm (24 in). The Oribi is more slender and delicate looking than the Bohor Reedbuck, with a proportionally longer neck. Both animals are a reddish fawn, but the Oribi tends to be duller or more sandy in appearance. Both Oribi and Bohor Reedbuck are usually seen in pairs in bushed grassland, never far from water.

The last two of the common smaller antelopes are the **Bushbuck** (*Tragelaphus scriptus*) which is about 76-92 cm (30-36 in) at the shoulder, and the tiny **Kirk's Dikdik** (*Rhynchotragus kirkii*) only 36-41 cm (14-16 in). Both are easily identified. The Bushbuck's colour varies from chestnut (probably the most common) to a darkish brown. The coat has a shaggy appearance and a variable pattern of white spots and stripes on the side and back. There are, in addition, two white crescent shaped marks on the front of the neck. The horns, present in the male only, are short, almost straight and slightly spiralled. The animal has a curious high rump which gives it a characteristic crouching appearance. The white underside of the tail is noticeable when it is running. The Bushbuck tends to occur in areas of thick bush especially near water. They lie up during the day in thickets, but are often seen bounding away when disturbed. They are usually seen either in pairs or singly. Kirk's Dikdik is so small it can hardly be mistaken for any other antelope. In colour it is a greyish brown, often washed with rufous. The legs are noticeably thin and stick-like, giving the animal a very fragile appearance. The snout is slightly elongated, and there is a conspicuous tuft of hair on the top of the head. The male carries the very small straight horns.

Other mammals Although the antelope are undoubtedly the most numerous animals to be seen on the plains, there are others worth keeping an eye open for. Some of these are scavengers which thrive on the kills of other animals. They include the dog-like Jackals, of which there are three main species, all similar in size, (about 86-96 cm, 34-38 in, in length and 41-46 cm, 16-18 in at the shoulder). The **Black-backed Jackal** (*Canis mesomelas*), which is the most common and ranges throughout the area, is a rather foxy reddish fawn in colour with a noticeable black area on its back. This black part is sprinkled with a silvery white which can make the back look silver in some lights. In general colour the **Side-striped Jackal** (*Canis adustus*) is greyish fawn and it has a variable and sometimes ill-defined stripe along the side. It is most likely to be seen around Lake Victoria and in Tanzania.

The other well known plains scavenger is the **Spotted Hyaena** (*Crocuta crocuta*). It is a fairly large animal, being about 69-91 cm (32-36 in) at the shoulder. Its high shoulders and low back give it a characteristic appearance. It is brownish with dark spots and has a large head. It usually occurs singly or in pairs, but occasionally in small packs.

A favourite and common plains animal is the comical **Warthog** (*Phacochoerus aethiopicus*). This is unmistakeable being almost hairless and grey in general colour with a very large head with tusks and wart-like growths on the face. They are often seen in family parties. The adults will run at speed with their tails held straight up in the air, followed by the young.

In suitable rocky areas, such as *kopjes*, look out for an animal that looks a bit like a large grey-brown guinea pig. This is the **Rock Hyrax** (*Heterohyrax brucei*), an engaging and fairly common animal that lives in communities in rocky places.

The most common and frequently seen of the monkey group are the Baboons. The most widespread species is the **Olive Baboon** (*Papio anubis*), which occurs almost throughout the area. This is a large (127-142 cm, 50-56 in), heavily built animal olive brown or greyish in colour. Adult males have a well-developed mane. In the eastern part of Kenya and Tanzania, including the coast, the Olive Baboon is replaced by the **Yellow Baboon** (*Papio cynocephalus*) 116-137 cm (46-54 in), which is a smaller and lighter animal than the Olive Baboon, with longer legs and almost no mane in the adult males. The tail in both species looks as if it is broken and hangs down in a loop. Baboons are basically terrestrial animals, although they can climb very well. In the wild they are often found in acacia grassland, often associated with rocks, and are sociable animals living in groups called troops. Females are very often seen with young clinging to them. In parts of East Africa they have become very used to the presence of man and can be a nuisance to campers. They will readily climb all over your vehicle hoping for a handout. Be careful, they have a very nasty bite and can carry rabies.

The smaller monkey that makes a nuisance of itself is the **Vervet or Green Monkey** (*Cercopithicus mitis*), which is the one that abounds at campsites and often lodges. This has various forms, the commonest and most widespread having a black face framed with white across the forehead and cheeks. Its general colour is greyish tinged with a varying amount of yellow. The feet, hands and tip of the tail are black.

Chimpanzees (*Pan troglodytes*) are not animals you will see casually in passing, you have to go and look for them. They occur only in the forests in the west of Tanzania.

At dusk in Africa you'll notice many bats appearing. The most spectacular of them is the **Straw-coloured Fruit Bat** (*Eidolon helvum*) which has a wing span of 76 cm (30 in).

Birds

East Africa is one of the richest areas of birdlife in the world. The total number of species is in excess of 1300, and it is possible, and not too difficult to see 100 different species in a day. You will find that a pair of binoculars is really essential, and even a simple pair will make a lot of difference. The birds described here are the common ones and, with a little careful observation, you will soon find that you can identify them. They have been grouped according to the habitat in which you are most likely to see them. Remember that birds, on the whole, are creatures of habit, with likes and dislikes about habitat. You will not see a Jacana far from water, nor will the Red-cheeked Cordon-bleu venture into the forest.

Urban birds The first birds that you will notice on arrival in any big city will almost certainly be the large numbers soaring overhead. Early in the morning the numbers are few, but as the temperature warms up, more and more are seen circling high above the buildings. Many of these will be **Hooded Vultures** (*Neophron monachus*) 66 cm (26 in) and **Black Kites** (*Milvus migrans*) 55 cm (22 in). They are both rather nondescript brownish birds which are superficially similar. They are, however, easily distinguished by the shape and length of the tail. The tail of the Hooded Vulture is short and slightly rounded at the end, whereas the Black Kite (which incidentally is not black, but brown) has a long, narrow tail which looks either forked when the tail is closed or slightly concave at the end when spread. The end of the tail never looks rounded. In flight the Kite looks very buoyant and uses its tail a lot, twisting it from side to side. Also soaring overhead in some cities you will see the **Marabou Stork** (*Leptoptilos crumeniferus*) 152 cm (60 in). Although this bird is a stork it behaves like a vulture, in that it lives by scavenging. Overhead its large size, long and noticeable bill and trailing legs make it easily identified. The commonest crow in towns and cities is the **Pied Crow** (*Corvus albus*) 46 cm (18 in). This is a very handsome black bird with a white lower breast which joins up with a white collar round the back of the neck. In towns along the coast you will see another member of the crow family the **Indian House Crow** (*Corvus splendens*) 38 cm (15 in). This is not indigenous to Africa, but was introduced and is spreading along the coast. It is a slender, shiny black bird with a grey neck. In gardens and parks there are a number of smaller birds to look out for. The **Dark-capped or Common Bulbul** (*Pycnonotus barbatus*) 18 cm (7 in), can be heard all day with its cheerful call of "Come quick, doctor, quick". It is a brownish bird with a darker brown head and a slight crest. Below, the brown is paler fading to white on the belly, and under the tail it is bright yellow.

There are a large number of Weaver birds to be seen, but identifying them is not always easy. Most of them are yellow and black in colour, and many of them live in large noisy colonies. Have a close look at their intricately woven nests if you get the chance. The commonest one is probably the **Black-headed Weaver** (*Ploceus cucullatus*) 18 cm (7 in), which often builds its colonies in bamboo clumps. The male has a mainly black head and throat, but the back of the head is chestnut. The underparts are bright yellow, and the back and wings mottled black and greenish yellow. When the bird is perched, and seen from behind, the markings on the back form a V-shape.

Also in parks and gardens, and especially among flowers, you will see members of another large and confusing bird family: the Sunbirds. The thickset and sturdy looking **Scarlet-chested Sunbird** (*Nectarinia senegalensis*) 15 cm (6 in) often perches on over-head wires allowing you to get a good look at it. The male is a dark velvety brown colour with a scarlet chest. The top of the head and the throat are an iridescent green. The tail is short. There are two common thrushes often seen in parks and gardens. They look rather similar, but do not occur in the same areas. The **Olive Thrush** (*Turdus olivaceous*) 23 cm (9 in) is the common thrush of the highlands, where it is often seen in gardens. The very similar garden thrush of lower areas, is the **African Thrush** (*Turdus pelios*) 23 cm (9 in). Both birds are brown, but the Olive Thrush is a much richer looking bird with a rufous belly and a bright orange bill. The African Thrush has a wash of rufous on the side and is duller looking.

Birds of open plains Along with the spectacular game, it is here that you will see many of the magnificent African birds. In particular, there are two large birds which you will see stalking across the grasslands. These are the **Ostrich** (*Struthio camelus*) 2 m (7 ft) and the **Secretary Bird** (*Sagittarius serpentarius*) 101 cm (40 in). The Secretary Bird is so called because the long plumes of its crest are supposed to resemble the old time secretaries who carried their quill pens tucked behind their ears. The bird is often seen in pairs as it hunts for snakes, its main food source. The Ostrich is sometimes seen singly, but also in family groups. There are other large terrestrial birds to look out for, and one of them, the **Kori Bustard** (*Otis kori*) 80cm (35 in), like the Secretary Bird quarters the plains looking for snakes. It is quite a different shape, however, and can be distinguished by the thick looking grey neck (caused by loose feathers). It is particularly common in the Serengeti National Park and in the Masai Mara. The other large bird that you are likely to see on the open plains is the **Ground Hornbill** (*Bucorvus cafer*) 107 cm (42 in). When seen from afar, this looks for all the world like a turkey but close up it is very distinctive and cannot really be mistaken for anything else. They are very often in pairs and the male has bare red skin around the eye and on the throat. In the female this skin is red and blue.

Soaring overhead on the plains you will see vultures and birds of prey. The commonest vulture in game areas is the **African White-backed Vulture** (*Gyps africanus*) 81 cm (32 in). This is a largish, brown bird with a white lower back, and it has, of course, the characteristic bare head of its family. Because they are commonly seen circling overhead, the white rump is sometimes difficult to see. So look out for the other diagnostic characteristic – the broad white band on the leading edge of the undersurface of the wing. The **Bateleur** (*Terathopius ecaudatus*) 61 cm (24 in) is a magnificent and strange looking eagle. It is rarely seen perched, but is quite commonly seen soaring very high overhead. Its tail is so short that it sometimes appears tailless. This, its buoyant flight and the black and white pattern of its underparts make it easy to identify.

Where there is game look out for the Oxpeckers. The commonest one is the **Red-billed Oxpecker** (*Buphagus erythrorhynchus*) 18 cm (7 in). These birds are actually members of the starling family although their behaviour is not like that of other starlings. They associate with game animals and cattle and spend their time clinging to, and climbing all over the animals while they hunt for ticks, which form their main food. There are other birds which associate with animals in a different way. For example the **Cattle Egret** (*Bubulcus ibis*) 51 cm (20 in), follows herds and feeds on the grasshoppers and other insects disturbed by the passing of the animals. Occasionally too, the Cattle Egret will perch on the back of a large animal, but this is quite different from the behaviour of Oxpeckers. Cattle Egrets are long legged and long billed white birds which are most often seen in small flocks. In the breeding season they develop long buff feathers on the head, chest and back.

Birds of dry, open woodland The two habitats of open plain and dry open woodland form a vast area of Africa and most of the game parks come into these categories. As well as being quintessentially African, this dry open woodland with acacia thorn trees is an extremely rewarding area for birdwatching. It supports an enormous variety of species and it is relatively easy to see them.

The Guinea Fowls live in flocks and if you surprise a group on the road they will disappear into the bush in a panic, running at great speed. There is more than one sort of Guinea Fowl, but they are rather similar, being a slate grey with white spots. The **Vulturine Guinea Fowl** (*Acryllium vulturinum*) 59 cm (22 in), is a most handsome bird with long blue, white and black feathers covering its neck and upper body. The rather small head itself is bare, hence the bird's name. The **Helmeted Guinea Fowl** (*Numida meleagris*) 55 cm (21 in), is rather less handsome, but with its dark slate and white spotted plumage and the boney "helmet" on its head, it is nonetheless a striking bird.

The tops of the thorn trees are used as observation perches by a number of different species. Especially noticeable is the **Red-billed Hornbill** (*Tockus erythrorhynchus*) 45 cm (17 in), which has blackish-brown back, with a white stripe down between the wings. The wings themselves are spotted with white. The underparts are white and the bill is long, curved and mainly red. As the bird flies into a tree the impression is of a black and white bird with a long red bill and a long tail. Another striking bird which perches on tree tops is the **White-bellied Go-away Bird** (*Corythaixoides leucogaster*) 51 cm (20 in). This gets its strange name from its call "Go-away, go-away". It is a basically grey bird with a very upright stance. The top of the head carries a long and conspicuous crest. The belly is white and the long tail has a black tip. It is usually seen in small family parties.

The strange looking, brightly coloured bird **d'Arnaud's Barbet** (*Trachyphonus darnaudii*) 15 cm (6 in) is quite common in the dry bush country. The impression you get is of a very spotted bird, dark with pale spots above, and pale with dark spots below. It has a long dark tail which again is heavily spotted. Its call and behaviour is very distinctive. A pair will sit facing each other with their tails raised over their backs wagging them from side to side, and bob at each other in a duet. All the while they utter a four note call over and over. "Do-do dee-dok". They look just like a pair of clockwork toys. Another brightly coloured bird is the **Lilac-breasted Roller** (*Coracias caudata*) 41 cm (16 in), which is very easy to see as it perches on telegraph poles or wires, or on bare branches. The brilliant blue on its wings, head and underparts is very eye catching. Its throat and breast are a deep lilac and its tail has two elongated streamers. It is quite common in open bush country. Also often seen sitting on bare branches is the **Drongo** (*Dicrurus adsimilis*) 24 cm (9 in), but this is an all black bird. It is easily identified by its forked tail, which is "fish-tailed" at the end. It is usually solitary.

There are two common birds which in the field look rather similar, although they are not related at all. These are the **White-crowned Shrike** (*Eurocephalus rueppelli*) 23 cm (9 in), and the **White-headed Buffalo Weaver** (*Dinemellia dinemelli*) 23 cm (9 in). They both occur in small flocks in dry acacia country and are both thickset, rather chunky birds, which appear basically dark brown and white. To distinguish between them look at the rump which is red in the White-headed Buffalo Weaver, but white in the White-crowned Shrike. This is usually easy to see as they fly away from you.

There are many different species of starling to be seen in eastern Africa, and most are beautifully coloured. Two of the most spectacular are the **Ashy Starling** (*Cosmopsarus unicolor*) 32cm (13in), and the **Superb Starling** (*Spreo superbus*) 18 cm (7 in). The Superb Starling is the more widespread and is seen near habitation as well as in thorn bush country. The car park between the Serengeti National Park and the Ngorongoro Crater Conservation Area is probably the best place to see the Superb Starling, so called because its vibrant glossy colours. The Ashy Starling is endemic to Tanzania and can only be found in the baobab trees in Tarangire National Park. They can also be seen around the Tarangire Safari Lodge and have been known to fly into the lodge itself. Both are fairly tame and are usually seen hopping about on the ground. Another long-tailed bird quite commonly seen in bush country is the **Long-tailed Fiscal** (*Lanius cabanisi*) 30 cm (12 in). It is black and white, and usually seen perched on wires or bare branches. It can be identified by its very long all-black tail and mainly black upperparts, which are grey on the lower back and rump.

Finally look out for three birds which though small are very noticeable. The **Red-cheeked Cordon-bleu** (*Uraeginthus bengalus*) 13 cm (5 in), is a lovely little blue bird with a brown back and bright red cheek patches. They are seen in pairs or family parties, and the females and young are somewhat duller in colour than the males. They are quite tame and you often see them round the game lodges. In the less dry grasslands you can see the beautiful red and black Bishop birds. There are two species both of which are quite brilliant in their colouring. The brightest is the **Red Bishop** (*Euplectes orix*) 13 cm (5 in), which has brown wings and tail, and noticeable scarlet feathers on its rump. The almost equally brilliant **Black-winged Bishop** (*Euplectes hordeaceus*) 14 cm (5.5 in), may be distinguished from the Red Bishop by its black wings and tail and rather less obvious red rump. Both species occur in long grass and cultivation, often, but not invariably, near water.

Birds of more moist areas Although so much of eastern Africa consists of grass plains, to the west of the area there are moist wooded grass lands which support a very different variety of bird species. The tall and elegant **Crowned Crane** (*Balearica pavonina*) 1 m (40 in), is quite common near Lake Victoria, though it also occurs in much of the rest of the area as well. It cannot really be mistaken for anything else when seen on the ground. In flight the legs trail behind and the neck is extended, but the head droops down from the vertical. Overhead flocks fly in loose V-shaped formation. The curious **Hamerkop** (*Scopus umbretta*) 58 cm (23 in), is another unmistakable bird. It is a rather dull brown in colour and has a stout, moderately long bill. Its most distinctive feature is the large crest which projects straight backwards and is, rather fancifully, said to look like a hammer. It is a solitary bird usually seen on the ground near water, sometimes even roadside puddles. It nests in trees, and builds an enormous nest, which is so large and strong that it can easily support the weight of a man. Another rather dull looking ground bird which is common is the **Hadada Ibis** (*Hagedashia hagedash*) 76 cm (30 in). This is a greyish olive bird with a long down curved bill and a green wash on the wings. It is almost invariably seen in pairs and flies off with its characteristic loud call "Ha-da-da, Ha-da-da". It is one of Africa's most familiar birds, and walks about on lawns and open spaces. The **Black-and-white Casqued Hornbill** (*Bycanistes subcylindricus*) 70 cm (28 in), is yet another loud and conspicuous bird, but it is always seen in trees, and is particularly common in moist woodland in the west. The siilar **Silvery-cheeked Hornbill** (*Bycanistes brevis*) 70 cm (28 in), replaces it to the east, though their habitat requirements are broadly similar. Both are basically black and white birds, but the wings of the Silvery-cheeked Hornbill are wholly black, whereas the Black-and-white Casqued Hornbill has a large white patch on the black wings. Look also at the casque on top of the bill, which is carried by both species. This casque is all pale in the Silvery-cheeked, but, as its name would suggest, black and white in the other bird. The moist forests and woodlands around Lake Victoria which are the home of the Black-and-white Casqued Hornbill, are also home to the **Grey Parrot** (*Psitticus erithacus*) 30 cm (12 in). This bird is usually seen in flocks and is best distinguished both in flight and at rest, by its bright red tail. The **Paradise Flycatcher** (*Terpsiphone viridis*) male 33 cm (13 in), female 20 cm (8 in), is very easily identified by its very long tail and bright chestnut plumage. The head is black and bears a crest. The tail of the female is much shorter, but otherwise the sexes are similar. It is seen in wooded areas, including gardens and is usually in pairs. (In certain parts, notably eastern Kenya its plumage is often white, but it still has the black head. Sometimes birds are seen with partly white and partly chestnut plumage.) Another long-tailed bird is the **Speckled Mousebird** (*Colius striatus*) 36 cm (14 in). They are usually seen in small flocks and follow each other from bush to bush. The mainly brown plumage has a speckled appearance and the tail is long and graduated. It has a red rather parrot-shaped bill and a crest.

Water and waterside birds The inland waters of Africa form a very important habitat for both resident and migratory species. A lot can be seen from the shore, but it is especially fruitful to go out in a boat, when you will get quite close to, among others, the large and magnificent herons which occur here. The king of them all is the aptly named **Goliath Heron** (*Ardea goliath*) 144 cm (58 in), which is usually seen singly on mud banks and shores, both inland and on the coast. Its very large size is enough to distinguish it, but the smaller **Purple Heron** (*Ardea purpurea*) 80 cm (34 in), which frequents similar habitat and is also widespread, may be mistaken for it at a distance. If in doubt, the colour on the top of the head (rufous in the Goliath and black in the Purple) will clinch it, also the Purple is much more slender with a slender bill.

The Flamingos are known to most people and will be readily identified. However, there are two different species which very often occur together. The **Greater Flamingo** (*Phoenicopterus ruber*) 142 cm (56 in), is the larger and paler bird and has a pink bill with a black tip. The **Lesser Flamingo** (*Phoenicopterus minor*) 101 cm (40 in), is deeper pink all over and has a deep carmine bill with a black tip. They both occur in large numbers in the soda lakes of western Kenya, but are also seen in several lakes in Tanzania. The magnificent **Fish Eagle** (*Haliaeetus vocifer*) 76 cm (30 in), has a very distinctive colour pattern. It often perches on the tops of trees, where its dazzling white head and chest are easily seen. In flight this white and the white tail contrast with the black wings. It has a wild yelping call which is usually uttered in flight. Try and watch the bird as it calls: it throws back its head over its back in a most unusual way.

There are several different kingfishers to be seen, but the most numerous is the black and white **Pied Kingfisher** (*Ceryle rudis*) 25 cm (10 in). This is easily recognized as it is the only black and white kingfisher. It is common all round the large lakes and also turns up at quite small bodies of water. It hovers over the water before plunging in to capture its prey.

In quiet backwaters with lily pads and other floating vegetation you will see the **African Jacana** (*Actophilornis africana*) 25 cm (10 in). This is a mainly chestnut bird almost invariably seen walking on floating leaves. Its toes are greatly elongated to allow it to do this. When flying away from you the legs dangle right down distinctively. Do not confuse this with the **Black Crake** (*Limnocorax flavirostra*) 20 cm (8 in), which also frequents the quieter backwaters. This is an all slatey black bird with bright pink legs. It is rather shy and disappears into the vegetation at your approach. But if you wait quietly it will reappear.

Marine wildlife

To most visitors the East African beaches mean the reef. The fish and coral here are indeed wonderful, and can be observed without having to dive to see them. Many of the fish do not have universally recognized English names, but one that does is the very common **scorpion** or **lion fish** (*Pterois*), which is probably the most spectacular fish you can see without going out in a boat. It is likely to be wherever there is live coral, and sometimes it gets trapped in the deeper pools of the dead reef by the retreating tide. It can be up to 26 cm long and is easily recognized by its peculiar fins and zebra-like stripes. Although it has poisonous dorsal spines it will not attack if left alone.

While most visitors naturally want to spend time diving and snorkelling on the live reef and watching the brilliant fish and many coloured living corals, do not bypass the smaller, humbler creatures which frequent dead as well as living coral. **Sea urchins** (*Echinoidea*) are usually found further out towards the edge of the reef, but can be found anywhere. There are two forms, the more common **short-needled sea urchin** and the much less common **long-needled** variety. Their spines are very sharp and treading on them is extremely painful. Look out also for the common **brittle stars** (*Ophiuroidea*) which frequent sandy hollows. They vary considerably in size, but are usually 10 cm across. They are so called because the arms break off very readily, but they will grow again. These are not sea urchins, though they are related, and can be picked up for a closer look, but handle them carefully.

Other living creatures which can be seen crawling along in the shallows include the **sea slug** (*Nudibranchia*) and the **snake eel** (*Ophichthidae*). Both are quite common in sandy places. The unlovely sea slug is blackish brown and shaped a bit like the familiar garden slug, though much bigger. It often has grains of sand sticking to it. Don't be put off by the name of the snake eel, it is quite harmless. It looks a bit like a snake and has alternating light and dark bands on its body. What are beautiful, without doubt, are the **starfish** (*Asteroidea*) which are best seen by going out in a boat, but some can be seen nearer shore.

The commonest shells are without doubt the **cowries**. Many dead ones can be found on the beach. The two most common are the **ringed cowrie** (*Cypraea annulus*) and the **money cowrie** (*Cypraea moneta*). Of these the ringed is especially plentiful and is a pretty grey and white shell with a golden ring. The money cowrie, once used as currency in Africa, varies in colour from greenish grey to pink according to its age. The big and beautiful **tiger cowrie** (*Cypraea tigris*) is also seen occasionally. This can be up to 8 cm in length. There is quite a lot of variation in colouring, but it is basically a very shiny shell with many dark round spots on, much more like a leopard than a tiger.

Freshwater fish

The king of the freshwater fish is without doubt the massive **Nile perch** (*Lates albertianus*). This huge predator lives on other fish, and originally came from the Nile below Murchison Falls, but was introduced into Lake Kyoga and the Nile above the Falls in 1955 and 1956. It has now spread to Lake Victoria itself, which has proved to be very much a mixed blessing as while it's an important food source for local people it eats many smaller species of fish. Weights of 20 to 40 kg are common and there are several records of over 100 kg. Also caught commonly in fresh waters is the **tilapia** (*Tilapia nilotica*), a much smaller, rather bony fish which makes good eating. Unlike the Nile perch this much smaller fish is herbivorous, and is now being farmed in fish ponds and fed largely on the green leaves of the cassava plant.

Books

History

Millar, C *Battle for the Bundu*. Account of the First World War in German East Africa.
Hibbert, C *Africa Explored: Europeans in the Dark Continent; 1769-1889*. Fascinating detail on the early explorers and their motivations, including the search for the source of the Nile.
Packenham, T *The Scramble for Africa*. First published in 1974, this classic book documents the European colonization of Africa.

Natural history

Grzimek, B *Serengeti Shall Not Die*. Classic account of this world-famous park and one of the earliest publications to highlight the need for conservation of African animals.
Goodall, J *In the Shadow of Man*. Gives a flavour of what is involved in making a life's work of studying a particular species, chimps.

Field guides

Stuart, C *Field Guide to the Larger Mammals of Africa*. Covers the more easily identified large and some smaller mammals.
Briggs, P *East African Wildlife*. Covers the wildlife in East Africa, including birds and butterflies. Has many striking photographs.
Stevenson, T and Fanshawe, J *The Birds of East Africa*. Comprehensive bird field guide with detailed illustrations.

Travellers' tales

Hemmingway, E *Green Hills of Africa*. An account of safaris in East Africa from 1933.
Dahl, R *Going Solo*. Impressions of a young man sent out to work in the colonies before the First World War.

Fiction

Boyd, W *An Ice-cream War*. Neatly observed, humorous and sensitive tale set against the First World War campaign in East Africa.
Boyd, W *Brazzaville Beach*. Although written as a West African story, it's clearly based on Jane Goodall and the chimps of Gombe.

Other guides

Jafferji, J and Rees, B *Images of Zanzibar*, superb photographs, and a good introduction to, and souvenir of, Zanzibar. Javed Jafferi (www.javedjafferji.com) owns Gallery Publications (www.gallery-publications.net) in Stone Town, and over the last decade has been a prolific book and magazine publisher, and among his many other titles are: *A Taste of Zanzibar*, a Zanzibar recipe book; *Historical Zanzibar – Romance of the Ages*, an illustrated account of Zanzibar's turbulent past with archive photographs of the slave and ivory trade; and *Swahili Style*, which examines the unique blend of architectural styles that make up Zanzibar's historic quarter, illustrated with sketches and colour photographs. In total Javed has published 40 souvenir books on Tanzania including some of the parks and reserves, and they can be bought in his own Zanzibar Gallery (page 162), and other shops in Stone Town, A Novel Idea bookshop in Dar es Salaam (page 91) and the duty free shops at the airport.

Magazines

Travel Africa Magazine, www.travelafrica mag.com. Inspiring and up-to-date reading if planning a trip to Tanzania or any other African country.

Contents

Footprint features

Footnotes

Swahili words and phrases

Swahili (or more correctly Kiswahili meaning the language of the Swahili) is spoken over much of East Africa and is not a difficult language but in *Shadows on the Grass* (1960) Karen Blixen called it "a primitive ungrammatical lingua franca", an observation that will infuriate Swahili scholars, particularly in Zanzibar where they take pride in the beautiful and pure form of the language spoken there. It is the main language of instruction in primary schools, everyone speaks it, and it is continually absorbing new words and concepts (see box). Swahili was successful as one of the unifying factors that Julius Nyerere employed after independence to promote Tanzania as a nation and as the collective identity of its people. Those new to Swahili often have difficulty with the use of prefixes for plurals, adjectives and demonstratives. Thus *mzungu* is a European, *wazungu* is Europeans and, for example, the word for 'big' (*kubwa*) alters if you were to say a 'big book' (*kitabu kikubwa*) as opposed to a 'big person' (*mtu mkubwa*). However, to get by in Tanzania, rather than reach fluency, such details are not necessary.

For those wanting to go further the *Swahili Dictionary* compiled by DV Perrot (Teach Yourself Books, New York: Hodder and Stoughton) contains a concise grammar and a guide to pronunciation as does *Teach Yourself Swahili* by Joan Russell (McGraw Hill). The *Swahili Phrasebook* by Martin Benjamin (Lonely Planet) has some useful phrases.

Basics

Please	*Tafadhali*	Four	*Nne*
Thank you	*Asante*	Five	*Tano*
Good morning	*Habari za asubuhi*	Six	*Sita*
Good afternoon	*Habari za mchana*	Seven	*Saba*
Good evening	*Habari za jioni*	Eight	*Nane*
Good night	*Usiku mwema*	Nine	*Tisa*
Sorry	*Pole*	10	*Kumi*
Hello	*Hujambo*	11	*Kumi na moja*
Goodbye	*Kwa heri*	12	*Kumi na mbili*
Yes	*Ndiyo*	20	*Ishirini*
No	*Hapana*	21	*Ishirini na moja*
OK	*Sawa/Haya*	22	*Ishirini na mbili*
Good	*Nzuri*	30	*Thelathini*
Bad	*Mbaya*	40	*Arobaini*
How much?	*Bei gani/Ni shilingi ngapi*	50	*Hamsini*
Where is?	*Wapi*	60	*Sitini*
Why?	*Kwa nini*	70	*Sabini*
Food	*Chakula*	80	*Themanini*
Water	*Maji*	90	*Tisini*
Room	*Chumba*	100	*Mia*
Bed	*Kitanda*	1000	*Elfu*
Toilet	*Choo*	10,000	*Elfu kumi*
One	*Moja*	100,000	*Laki mmoja*
Two	*Mbili*	1,000,000	*Milioni mmoja*
Three	*Tatu*		

Useful phrases

A respectful greeting to elders, actually meaning "I hold your feet"	Shikamoo
Their reply: "I am delighted"	Marahaba
How are you?	Habari yako?
I am fine	Nzuri/Sijambo
I am not feeling good today	Sijiziki vizuri leo
How are things?	Mambo?
Good/cool/cool and crazy	Safi/poa/poa kichizi
See you later	Tutaonana baadaye
Welcome!	Karibu!
Welcome again!	Karibu tena!
Where can I get a taxi?	Teksi iko wapi?
Where is the bus station?	Stendi ya basi iko wapi?
Straight on	Moja kwa moja
Turn left	Pinda kushoto
Turn right	Pinda kulia
When will we arrive?	Tutafika lini?
Can you show me the bus?	Unaweza ukanioyesha basi?
How much is the ticket?	Tiketi ni bei gani?
Is it safe walking here at night?	Ni salama kutembea hapa usiku?
I don't want to buy anything	Sitaki kununua chochote
I have already booked a safari	Nimeshalipia safari
I have already been on safari	Nimekwenda safari tayari
I don't have money	Sina hela
I'm not single	Nina mchumba/siko peke yangu
Could you please leave me alone?	Tafadhali, achana na mimi
Stop bothering me	Acha kunisambua
It is none of your business!	Hayakuhusu!
Chill out/relax/be cool	Poa/Safi
Excuse me	Samahani
Let's go	Twende
Can I come in?	Hodi (to which the reply should be **Karibu!**)
Is there hot water?	Je kuna maji moto?
I have bought things like these already	Nimenunua vitu kama hivyo tayari
Reduce the price	Punguza bei
I am not a rich person	Mimi si tajiri
Do you speak English?	Unazungumza Kiingereza?
Is there space (in the bus/dala-dala)	Ipo nafasi (katika basi/dala-dala)?
Is someone sitting here?	Mtu anakaa hapa?
When will we arrive?	Tutafika lini?
I would like ...	Naomba ...
I would like a cold beer	Naomba bia moja baridi
I cannot help you	Siwezi kukusaidia

Language section compiled with the help of Jono Jackson

Swahili slang

Swahili, by origin a Bantu language, has been greatly influenced by Arabic and more recently further enriched by borrowing from other languages including English. There are several examples where are two Swahili words, each with the same meaning but with different origins. The origins of some words that have been adopted are very obvious. Modern transport has yielded, for example, *basi* (bus), *treni* (train), *stesheni* (station), *teksi* (taxi), *petroli*, *tanki*, *breki*. A rich man is *mbenzi* because he would be expected to drive a Mercedes. A traffic bollard is a *kiplefti*.

Other adoptions may not seem immediately obvious – for example, 'electricity' is sometimes called *elekrii* but more commonly stimu because the electricity generating stations used to be run by steam engines. In the same way the word for steamship, *meli*, derives from the fact that when the word was first used most of the ships would have carried mail. The dockyards are *kuli* because the dockyard workers were known as 'coolies'.

The Second World War also produced a number of words that were adopted into the Swahili language, many of them relating to animals: a submarine is *papa*, the word for shark, a tank was *faru*, for rhino, an aeroplane is *ndege ulaya*, which means white-man's bird.

Swahili, like all other languages, also has a large collection of slang. For example the period shortly before pay day when all the previous month's money has been spent is known as *mwambo*, which is derived from the word *wamba*, to stretch tight.

Coins have also been given a variety of nicknames. Examples include *ng'aru*, which derives from the word to shine, *ku-ngaa*. During the colonial era the shilling, which had a picture of the king's head on it, was known as *Usi wa Kinga* meaning the king's face. Five and 10 cent pieces, which used to have a hole in the centre, were nicknamed *sikio la Mkwavi* meaning 'the ear of the Mkwavi', after the Kwavi people who pierce their ear lobes and often used to hang coins from them as decoration. A slang phrase for bribery is *kuzunguka mbuyu*, which literally translated means to go behind a baobab tree, the implication being that behind such a wide tree as the baobab no one will see the transaction that takes place. The slang term for liquor is *mtindi*, which actually means skimmed milk – it was probably used to conceal what was really being drunk. A frequently used term for drunk is *kupiga mtindi*, which translates as 'to beat up the liquor' and is used in the same way that we would use 'to go on a binge'. Someone who is drunk may be described as *amevaa miwani*, or 'wearing spectacles', suggesting that he can't see well as a result of the alcohol! A similar phrase is *yuko topu*, which translates to 'he is full right up to the top'.

Clothes have also attracted various nicknames. *Americani* was the name given to the cheap cloth imported from America during the colonial era. Drainpipe trousers were known as *suruwali ya uchinjo*, which means cut-off trousers – because being so narrow they look as if part of them is missing. Many of the names are derived from English words, such as *tai* (tie), *kala* (collar), and *soksi* (socks). The phrase used by off-duty policemen to describe their clothes also needs little explanation: *kuvaa kisivilyan*, which means 'to wear civilian clothes', while a fashionable haircut is known as *fashun*.

Many of the examples here were collected by R H Gower, a colonial administrator in Tanganyika.

Index → *Entries in bold refer to maps.*

Advertisers' index

Acknowledgments

Lizzie Williams

Firstly, grateful thanks must go to Michael Hodd for his work in compiling the original Footprint East Africa, which still forms the core of the *Tanzania Handbook*. For this edition many thanks go to Jono Jackson for his detailed research in Tanzania and help with the language section. Thanks to long term friends in East Africa Bulawayo Bruce, Dutch Pete and Sparky for their snippets of information and to readers who wrote in with their suggestions, which include Meliza Barel, Suzanne Heuts, Gabriel Gloeckler, Charlotta and Heribert Heck, Anna Bryant, Ted Loman, Peter Garrison, Stefano Magnani and Robert Helwick. As always, also thanks for the staff at Footprint for putting everything together. Finally, a huge thanks goes to Sue Watt for coming on board at the last moment and for all her hard work in updating this edition.

Sue Watt

I could probably fill another chapter just thanking all the people who've helped me with the marathon task of updating this edition at short notice and for pulling out all the stops – apologies if some names have been left out. I'm hugely indebted to Deb Adderson and her excellent team, especially George Mambo, at Wild Frontiers, for putting together the Northern Circuit trip; to Richard Marsden of AWC for sorting out flights and with Natasha, Henry and Elijah providing a home from home in Arusha; and to Adam Fuller and his team at the lovely Southern Sun Hotel for doing the same in Dar. Thanks to Francis and the 'and beyonders' at Ngorongoro Crater Lodge for the most beautiful view on Valentine's Day morning overlooking the crater; to Stuart and Nick at the Old Boma, Mikindani for all their help with travelling around the southern coast (maybe Wales will get the Grand Slam next year, Stuart ...); to Sam Diah of Tanzania Travel Company (who first took me up Kili nine years ago – bumping into you again was fate!) and his partner Mr Muhidin of Marzouk Tours for organizing my tour around Zanzibar; to Hussein of Furaha Tours for his local knowledge on Stone Town; to Jamilla at Kilwa Seaview Resort, Annette at Tarangire Safari Lodge, Mr Yassir at Tembo House, Gabriel at Mafia Island Lodge (next time, I will swim with the whale sharks), and to Matt and team at Fundu Lagoon on Pemba for a truly relaxing final evening after a hectic few weeks. Thanks too to the helpful staff at Dar es Salaam and Arusha Tourist Offices and Sarah Finlayson and Taoufik Hedfi for their invaluable holiday homework. To Sara Chare, Sarah Sorensen, Kassia Gawronski and Alan Murphy at Footprint, to my co-author Lizzie Williams and to Claire Boobbyer for her long distance support. And finally, but most importantly, huge thanks to my partner Will Whitford, for sharing the journey in every sense of the word – here's to the next one ...

About the authors

Lizzie Williams

Originally from London, Lizzie worked and lived in Africa for 14 years. Starting out on trips across the continent as a tour leader on overland trucks, she has sat with a gorilla, slept amongst elephants, fed a giraffe and swum with a hippo and is now something of an expert on border crossings and African beer. For Footprint she is a author of the *South Africa*, *Namibia*, *Kenya* and *Tanzania* handbooks; she has written the only country guide to Nigeria and the first city guide to Johannesburg for Bradt; is author of the *AA Key Guide to South Africa*, *AA Spiral Guide to South Africa* and *Africa Overland*, a glossy look at the overland route from Nairobi to Cape Town, is co-author of the DK Eyewitness to Kenya, and has contributed to Turkey and Egypt for Rough Guides. She had written various online African destination guides for leading websites in the UK and US, including Frommers, British Airways and www.worldtravel guide.net. When not on the road, Lizzie lives in Cape Town.

Sue Watt

Sue Watt is a freelance travel writer based in London. Before contracting the travel bug, she led a life of crime, professionally at least, working for the Crown Prosecution Service and then as a business manager for a barristers' chambers specializing in criminal law. She packed it all in to take a gap year with her partner Will, travelling around Nepal for four months and then across Africa for eight, in the process trekking to the summits of the five highest mountains on the continent. Inspired by her travels and an overwhelming desire never to work in an office again, Sue turned to writing and has since been published in *Travel Africa Magazine*, *The Independent*, *Guardian Unlimited*, *Italy Magazine* and is a contributor to *1001 Escapes to Make Before You Die*.

Credits

Footprint credits

Editor: Sara Chare
Map editor: Sarah Sorensen
Colour section: Kassia Gawronski

Managing Director: Andy Riddle
Commercial Director: Patrick Dawson
Publisher: Alan Murphy
Editorial: Felicity Laughton, Nicola Gibbs,
Ria Gane, Jen Haddington, Alice Jell

Cartography: Robert Lunn, Kevin Feeney,
Emma Bryers
Cover design: Robert Lunn
Design: Mytton Williams
Marketing: Liz Harper, Hannah Bonnell
Sales: Jeremy Parr
Advertising: Renu Sibal
Business development: Zoë Jackson
Finance and administration:
Elizabeth Taylor

Photography credits

Front cover: Kitch Bain/Shutterstock
Back cover: Zanzibar city, Stone Town,
Prisma/Superstock
Wildlife colour section: NATUREPL

Manufactured in Italy by LegoPrint
Pulp from sustainable forests

Footprint feedback

We try as hard as we can to make each
Footprint guide as up to date as possible
but, of course, things always change. If you
want to let us know about your experiences –
good, bad or ugly – then don't delay, go to
www.footprintbooks.com and send in
your comments.

Publishing information

Footprint Tanzania
2nd edition
© Footprint Handbooks Ltd
June 2009

ISBN: 978 1 906098 483
CIP DATA: A catalogue record for this book
is available from the British Library

® Footprint Handbooks and the Footprint
mark are a registered trademark of Footprint
Handbooks Ltd

Published by Footprint
6 Riverside Court
Lower Bristol Road
Bath BA2 3DZ, UK
T +44 (0)1225 469141
F +44 (0)1225 469461
www.footprintbooks.com

Distributed in the USA by Globe Pequot Press,
Guilford, Connecticut